June 20-22, 2016
Vigo, Galicia, Spain

Association for Computing Machinery

Advancing Computing as a Science & Profession

IH&MMSec'16

Proceedings of the 2016 ACM

Information Hiding and Multimedia Security Workshop

Sponsored by:

ACM SIGMM

Supported by:

Gradiant, AtlantTIC, CNRS, CRIStAL, WITDOM, Atos, Amped Software, Intel, Universidade de Vigo, FEUGA, GPSC, Xunta de Galicia, IGAPE, Concello de Vigo, and Turismo de Vigo

Association for Computing Machinery

Advancing Computing as a Science & Profession

The Association for Computing Machinery
2 Penn Plaza, Suite 701
New York, New York 10121-0701

Notice to Past Authors of ACM-Published Articles
ACM intends to create a complete electronic archive of all articles and/or other material previously published by ACM. If you have written a work that has been previously published by ACM in any journal or conference proceedings prior to 1978, or any SIG Newsletter at any time, and you do NOT want this work to appear in the ACM Digital Library, please inform permissions@acm.org, stating the title of the work, the author(s), and where and when published.

ISBN: 978-1-4503-4290-2 (Digital)

ISBN: 978-1-4503-4602-3 (Print)

Additional copies may be ordered prepaid from:

ACM Order Department
PO Box 30777
New York, NY 10087-0777, USA

Phone: 1-800-342-6626 (USA and Canada)
+1-212-626-0500 (Global)
Fax: +1-212-944-1318
E-mail: acmhelp@acm.org
Hours of Operation: 8:30 am – 4:30 pm ET

Printed in the USA

Preface

Welcome to the *4th ACM Information Hiding and Multimedia Security Workshop – IH&MMSec'16* in Vigo, Spain. Vigo and its University are home to one of the pioneering research groups in Information Hiding and Multimedia Security that has been active in this area for the past 20 years. Over those years, the field has grown into maturity thanks to the efforts of many researchers, scientists and practitioners all over the world.

In response to our call for papers, we received in total 61 submissions. The 5 countries with the highest numbers of submissions were China, USA, France, India and Germany. Except for 3 papers which were withdrawn before the double-blind review process ended, the remaining 58 submissions received at least 3 independent reviews each. These reviews were provided by the Program Committee members, assisted in some cases by external reviewers. Based on these timely and high-quality reviews, the Technical Program Chairs selected the 21 best submissions. The low acceptance rate of 36.2% (21/58) reflects our intention to maintain IH&MMSec as a premier scientific venue in the field of Information Hiding and Multimedia Security. The accepted papers cover the fields of steganography and steganalysis, forensics, fingerprinting, reversible watermarking, privacy, information hiding and cryptography.

We sincerely thank all the submitting authors for their contributions, and the reviewers for their invaluable help. We expect the selected papers to be of wide interest to researchers working in the field and to participants from industry and from government institutions.

The technical program also includes two invited keynote speakers. The first presentation is given by Dr. Battista Biggio, from University of Cagliari, on the exciting topic of adversarial machine learning. The second presentation is about the fascinating work that Mr. Martino Jerian, CEO and founder of Amped Software, is doing in transplanting the results in media forensics from academia to the market.

As usual, the workshop is structured into three days with the afternoon of the second day devoted to a social event. The social event is designed to promote discussions and to help establish relationships for future collaboration among participants, and, of course, enjoy the paradisiac Cíes Islands. This year IH&MMSec also features an "ongoing" session, where authors have been invited to present their latest, unfinished work to receive feedback from their peers. The summaries of these presentations have been also included in these proceedings.

We also thank our supporters Gradiant, AtlantTIC, Amped Software, Cristal/CNRS, Atos, the WITDOM project, Intel, and the supporting institutions Xunta de Galicia, Concello de Vigo, FEUGA, Turismo de Vigo, IGAPE, University of Vigo and GPSC. Heartfelt thanks are due to Dr. Juan Ramón Troncoso-Pastoriza for his invaluable help with the local organization of the workshop, to Drs. Kai Wang and Daniel González for their hard work with the publicity and the liaison with our supporters, and to Dr. Pedro Comesaña-Alfaro for his assistance with the publication of these proceedings.

Finally, we hope that you will find this program very interesting and that you will enjoy your stay in Vigo, the Olive City.

IH&MMSec'16 General Chairs

Fernando Pérez-González
University of Vigo, Spain

Patrick Bas
CNRS, University of Lille, France

IH&MMSec'16 Program Chairs

Tanya Ignatenko
Eindhoven University of Technology, the Netherlands

François Cayre
University of Grenoble Alpes, France

Table of Contents

IH&MMSec 2016 Workshop Organization

General Chairs: Fernando Pérez-González *(University of Vigo, Spain)*
Patrick Bas *(CNRS, University of Lille, France)*

Technical Program Chairs: Tanya Ignatenko *(Eindhoven University of Technology, The Netherlands)*
François Cayre *(Grenoble INP, University of Grenoble Alpes, France)*

ACM Liaison: Jana Dittmann *(University of Magdeburg, Germany)*

Industrial Liaison: Daniel González-Jiménez *(Gradiant, Spain)*

Steering Committee: Patrizio Campisi *(University of Roma TRE, Italy)*
George Danezis *(University College London, UK)*
Jana Dittmann *(University of Magdeburg, Germany)*
Jessica Fridrich *(SUNY Binghamton, USA)*
Stefan Katzenbeisser *(TU Darmstadt, Germany)*
Balakrishnan Prabhakaran *(University of Texas at Dallas, USA)*

Publication Chair: Pedro Comesaña-Alfaro *(University of Vigo, Spain)*

Publicity Chair: Kai Wang *(CNRS, University of Grenoble Alpes, France)*

Local Arrangements Chair: Juan-Ramón Troncoso-Pastoriza *(University of Vigo, Spain)*

Program Committee: Mauro Barni *(Università di Siena, Italy)*
Patrick Bas *(CNRS, University of Lille, France)*
Patrizio Campisi *(University of Roma TRE, Italy)*
François Cayre *(Grenoble INP, University of Grenoble Alpes, France)*
Ee-Chien Chang *(National University of Singapore, Singapore)*
Marc Chaumont *(Université de Nîmes, France)*
Rémi Cogranne *(Université de Technologie de Troyes, France)*
Pedro Comesaña-Alfaro *(University of Vigo, Spain)*
Jana Dittmann *(University of Magdeburg, Germany)*
Jean-Luc Dugelay *(EURÉCOM, France)*
Dominik Engel *(Fachhochschule Salzburg, Austria)*
Zekeriya Erkin *(TU Delft, The Netherlands)*
Caroline Fontaine *(CNRS, France)*
Jessica Fridrich *(SUNY Binghamton, USA)*
Tanya Ignatenko *(Eindhoven University of Technology, The Netherlands)*
Neil F. Johnson *(Booz Allen Hamilton, USA)*
Stefan Katzenbeisser *(TU Darmstadt, Germany)*
Andrew D. Ker *(Oxford University, UK)*
Matthias Kirchner *(SUNY Binghamton, USA)*
Christian Kraetzer *(University of Magdeburg, Germany)*
Chang-Tsun Li *(University of Warwick, UK)*

Program Committee
(Continued): Chih-Yang Lin *(Asia University, Taiwan)*
Qingzhong Liu *(Sam Houston State University, USA)*
Paulo Lobato Correia *(Universidade de Lisboa, Portugal)*
Chun-Shien Lu *(Academia Sinica, Taiwan)*
Wojciech Mazurczyk *(Warsaw University of Technology, Poland)*
Fernando Pérez-González *(University of Vigo, Spain)*
Tomáš Pevný *(Czech Technical University in Prague, Czech Republic)*
Alessandro Piva *(Università degli Studi Firenze, Italy)*
William Puech *(Université de Montpellier, France)*
Thomas Schneider *(TU Darmstadt, Germany)*
Pascal Schöttle *(University of Innsbrück, Austria)*
Yun-Qing Shi *(New Jersey Institute of Technology, USA)*
Ned Smith *(INTEL, USA)*
Thomas Stütz *(Fachhochschule Salzburg, Austria)*
Nicolas Tsapatsoulis *(Cyprus University of Technology, Cyprus)*
Andreas Uhl *(Universität Salzburg, Austria)*
Claus Vielhauer *(Fachhochschule Brandenburg, Germany)*
Sviatoslav Voloshynovskiy *(Université de Genève, Switzerland)*
Kai Wang *(CNRS University of Grenoble Alpes, France)*

IH&MMSec 2016 Sponsors & Supporters

Sponsors:

Corporate Supporters:

Institutional Supporters:

ix

Machine Learning under Attack:
Vulnerability Exploitation and Security Measures

Invited Keynote

Battista Biggio
Department of Electrical and Electronic Engineering
University of Cagliari, Piazza d'Armi, 09123 Cagliari, Italy
battista.biggio@diee.unica.it

ABSTRACT

Learning to discriminate between secure and hostile patterns is a crucial problem for species to survive in nature. Mimetism and camouflage are well-known examples of evolving weapons and defenses in the arms race between predators and preys. It is thus clear that all of the information acquired by our senses should not be considered necessarily secure or reliable. In machine learning and pattern recognition systems, however, we have started investigating these issues only recently. This phenomenon has been especially observed in the context of adversarial settings like malware detection and spam filtering, in which data can be purposely manipulated by humans to undermine the outcome of an automatic analysis. As current pattern recognition methods are not natively designed to deal with the intrinsic, adversarial nature of these problems, they exhibit specific vulnerabilities that an attacker may exploit either to mislead learning or to evade detection. Identifying these vulnerabilities and analyzing the impact of the corresponding attacks on learning algorithms has thus been one of the main open issues in the novel research field of adversarial machine learning, along with the design of more secure learning algorithms.

In the first part of this talk, I introduce a general framework that encompasses and unifies previous work in the field, allowing one to systematically evaluate classifier security against different, potential attacks. As an example of application of this framework, in the second part of the talk, I discuss evasion attacks, where malicious samples are manipulated at test time to evade detection. I then show how carefully-designed poisoning attacks can mislead some learning algorithms by manipulating only a small fraction of their training data. In addition, I discuss some defense mechanisms against both attacks in the context of real-world applications, including biometric identity recognition and computer security. Finally, I briefly discuss our ongoing work on attacks against clustering algorithms, and sketch some promising future research directions.

IH&MMSec 2016 June 20-23, 2016, Vigo, Spain

© 2016 Copyright held by the owner/author(s).

ACM ISBN 978-1-4503-4290-2/16/06.

DOI: http://dx.doi.org/10.1145/2909827.2930784

CCS Concepts

•**Security and privacy** → *Malware and its mitigation; Denial-of-service attacks;* Biometrics; •**Computing methodologies** → **Machine learning; Adversarial learning;**

Keywords

Secure Pattern Recognition; Adversarial Machine Learning; Evasion Attacks; Poisoning Attacks

Short Biography

Battista Biggio received the M.Sc. degree (with honors) in Electronic Engineering (2006) and the Ph.D. degree in Electronic Engineering and Computer Science (2010) from the University of Cagliari (Italy). Since 2007, he has been with the Department of Electrical and Electronic Engineering of the University of Cagliari, where he is currently a post-doctoral researcher. In 2011, he visited the University of Tübingen (Germany), and worked on the security of learning algorithms to training data contamination. His research interests include secure machine learning, multiple classifier systems, kernel methods, computer security and biometrics. On these topics, he has published more than 50 papers on international conferences and journals, collaborating with several research groups from academia and companies throughout the world. Dr. Biggio has also recently co-founded a company named Pluribus One, where he is responsible of leveraging machine-learning algorithms to drive product innovation. He regularly serves as a reviewer and program committee member for several international conferences and journals on the aforementioned research topics. Dr. Biggio is a member of the IEEE and of the IAPR.

1. REFERENCES

[1] M. Barreno, B. Nelson, A. Joseph, and J. Tygar. The security of machine learning. *Machine Learning*, 81:121–148, 2010.

[2] M. Barreno, B. Nelson, R. Sears, A. D. Joseph, and J. D. Tygar. Can machine learning be secure? In *ACM Symp. Information, Computer and Comm. Sec.*, ASIACCS '06, pages 16–25, New York, NY, USA, 2006. ACM.

[3] B. Biggio, S. R. Bulò, I. Pillai, M. Mura, E. Z. Mequanint, M. Pelillo, and F. Roli. Poisoning complete-linkage hierarchical clustering. In P. Franti, G. Brown, M. Loog, F. Escolano, and M. Pelillo,

editors, *Joint IAPR Int'l Workshop on Structural, Syntactic, and Statistical Pattern Recognition*, volume 8621 of *LNCS*, pages 42–52, Joensuu, Finland, 2014. Springer Berlin Heidelberg.

[4] B. Biggio, I. Corona, Z.-M. He, P. P. K. Chan, G. Giacinto, D. S. Yeung, and F. Roli. One-and-a-half-class multiple classifier systems for secure learning against evasion attacks at test time. In F. Schwenker, F. Roli, and J. Kittler, editors, *Multiple Classifier Systems*, volume 9132 of *LNCS*, pages 168–180. Springer International Publishing, 2015.

[5] B. Biggio, I. Corona, D. Maiorca, B. Nelson, N. Šrndić, P. Laskov, G. Giacinto, and F. Roli. Evasion attacks against machine learning at test time. In H. Blockeel, K. Kersting, S. Nijssen, and F. Železný, editors, *European Conf. on Machine Learning and Principles and Practice of Knowledge Discovery in Databases (ECML PKDD), Part III*, volume 8190 of *LNCS*, pages 387–402. Springer Berlin Heidelberg, 2013.

[6] B. Biggio, I. Corona, B. Nelson, B. Rubinstein, D. Maiorca, G. Fumera, G. Giacinto, and F. Roli. Security evaluation of support vector machines in adversarial environments. In Y. Ma and G. Guo, editors, *Support Vector Machines Applications*, pages 105–153. Springer International Publishing, 2014.

[7] B. Biggio, L. Didaci, G. Fumera, and F. Roli. Poisoning attacks to compromise face templates. In *6th IAPR Int'l Conf. on Biometrics (ICB 2013)*, pages 1–7, Madrid, Spain, 2013.

[8] B. Biggio, G. Fumera, and F. Roli. Multiple classifier systems for robust classifier design in adversarial environments. *Int'l J. Mach. Learn. and Cybernetics*, 1(1):27–41, 2010.

[9] B. Biggio, G. Fumera, and F. Roli. Pattern recognition systems under attack: Design issues and research challenges. *Int'l J. Patt. Recogn. Artif. Intell.*, 28(7):1460002, 2014.

[10] B. Biggio, G. Fumera, and F. Roli. Security evaluation of pattern classifiers under attack. *IEEE Trans. on Knowledge and Data Engineering*, 26(4):984–996, April 2014.

[11] B. Biggio, G. Fumera, F. Roli, and L. Didaci. Poisoning adaptive biometric systems. In G. Gimel'farb, E. Hancock, A. Imiya, A. Kuijper, M. Kudo, S. Omachi, T. Windeatt, and K. Yamada, editors, *Structural, Syntactic, and Statistical Pattern Recognition*, volume 7626 of *LNCS*, pages 417–425. Springer Berlin Heidelberg, 2012.

[12] B. Biggio, G. Fumera, P. Russu, L. Didaci, and F. Roli. Adversarial biometric recognition : A review on biometric system security from the adversarial machine-learning perspective. *Signal Processing Magazine, IEEE*, 32(5):31–41, Sept 2015.

[13] B. Biggio, B. Nelson, and P. Laskov. Poisoning attacks against support vector machines. In J. Langford and J. Pineau, editors, *29th Int'l Conf. on Machine Learning*, pages 1807–1814. Omnipress, 2012.

[14] B. Biggio, I. Pillai, S. R. Bulò, D. Ariu, M. Pelillo, and F. Roli. Is data clustering in adversarial settings secure? In *Proceedings of the 2013 ACM Workshop on Artificial Intelligence and Security*, AISec '13, pages 87–98, New York, NY, USA, 2013. ACM.

[15] M. Brückner, C. Kanzow, and T. Scheffer. Static prediction games for adversarial learning problems. *J. Mach. Learn. Res.*, 13:2617–2654, September 2012.

[16] D. M. Freeman, S. Jain, M. Dürmuth, B. Biggio, and G. Giacinto. Who are you? a statistical approach to measuring user authenticity. In *23rd Annual Network & Distributed System Security Symposium (NDSS)*. The Internet Society, 2016.

[17] L. Huang, A. D. Joseph, B. Nelson, B. Rubinstein, and J. D. Tygar. Adversarial machine learning. In *4th ACM Workshop on Artificial Intelligence and Security (AISec 2011)*, pages 43–57, Chicago, IL, USA, 2011.

[18] M. Kloft and P. Laskov. Online anomaly detection under adversarial impact. In *Proceedings of the 13th Int'l Conf. on Artificial Intelligence and Statistics (AISTATS)*, pages 405–412, 2010.

[19] M. Kloft and P. Laskov. Security analysis of online centroid anomaly detection. *Journal of Machine Learning Research*, 13:3647–3690, 2012.

[20] D. Maiorca, I. Corona, and G. Giacinto. Looking at the bag is not enough to find the bomb: an evasion of structural methods for malicious pdf files detection. In *8th ACM SIGSAC Symp. on Information, Computer and Comm. Sec.*, ASIA CCS '13, pages 119–130, New York, NY, USA, 2013. ACM.

[21] F. Roli, B. Biggio, and G. Fumera. Pattern recognition systems under attack. In J. Ruiz-Shulcloper and G. S. di Baja, editors, *Progress in Pattern Recognition, Image Analysis, Computer Vision, and Applications*, volume 8258 of *LNCS*, pages 1–8. Springer, 2013.

[22] B. I. Rubinstein, B. Nelson, L. Huang, A. D. Joseph, S.-h. Lau, S. Rao, N. Taft, and J. D. Tygar. Antidote: understanding and defending against poisoning of anomaly detectors. In *9th ACM SIGCOMM Internet Measurement Conf.*, IMC '09, pages 1–14, New York, NY, USA, 2009. ACM.

[23] N. Šrndić and P. Laskov. Detection of malicious pdf files based on hierarchical document structure. In *20th Annual Network & Distributed System Security Symposium (NDSS)*. The Internet Society, 2013.

[24] H. Xiao, B. Biggio, G. Brown, G. Fumera, C. Eckert, and F. Roli. Is feature selection secure against training data poisoning? In F. Bach and D. Blei, editors, *JMLR W&CP - Proc. 32nd Int'l Conf. Mach. Learning (ICML)*, volume 37, pages 1689–1698, 2015.

[25] F. Zhang, P. Chan, B. Biggio, D. Yeung, and F. Roli. Adversarial feature selection against evasion attacks. *IEEE Trans. on Cybernetics*, 46(3):766–777, 2016.

Bringing Multimedia Security from the Research Lab to the Forensic Lab

Martino Jerian
CEO and Founder,
Amped Software, Italy

Abstract

The work done by researchers in the field, on multimedia security, is laying the foundations for increasing the capabilities of the community of forensic practitioners. However, very often there is a big gap between what is studied at the research level and what is available to the law enforcement labs in their everyday work. Often researchers achieve a very high level of expertise in their specific fields, but miss out on the context in which the technologies must be used, while the end users are often not aware of such technologies or don't have the skills or the time to work with them. Having worked on both sides of the fence, Martino Jerian, CEO and founder of Amped Software, will tell the story of how a project initially started as a master thesis at university, became one of the standard tools for image and video forensics, used by law enforcement and intelligence agencies in more than 50 countries worldwide.

Martino Jerian will show how some technological partnerships with universities managed to yield very good practical results both on the business and research level. It will show how expert researchers are actually amazed and excited when they are directed and pushed to face real problems out of the lab and see the result of their research in a finished product which helps to solve cases and, sometimes, saves lives.

Martino Jerian will then showcase the software Amped Authenticate, which is the world leading tool for image forgery detection, as an example of a success story of building a bridge between the researchers and the forensic community.

Bio

Martino Jerian founded Amped Software in 2008, with the mission to create revolutionary products that could become the standard tools for working with images and videos during investigations and for forensic applications. Amped Software products are used by the world's leading top forensic labs, law enforcement, government, military, and security organizations. Martino Jerian also works as a forensic video and image analyst, evaluating hundreds of different cases every year and has published several scientific papers on the topic of image and video forensics.

IH&MMSec'16, June 20-23, 2016, Vigo, Spain.
ACM ISBN 978-1-4503-4290-2/16/06.
DOI: http://dx.doi.org/10.1145/2909827.2930785

A Deep Learning Approach To Universal Image Manipulation Detection Using A New Convolutional Layer

Belhassen Bayar
Drexel University
Dept. of ECE
Philadelphia, PA, USA
bb632@drexel.edu

Matthew C. Stamm
Drexel University
Dept. of ECE
Philadelphia, PA, USA
mstamm@coe.drexel.edu

ABSTRACT

When creating a forgery, a forger can modify an image using many different image editing operations. Since a forensic examiner must test for each of these, significant interest has arisen in the development of universal forensic algorithms capable of detecting many different image editing operations and manipulations. In this paper, we propose a universal forensic approach to performing manipulation detection using deep learning. Specifically, we propose a new convolutional network architecture capable of automatically learning manipulation detection features directly from training data. In their current form, convolutional neural networks will learn features that capture an image's content as opposed to manipulation detection features. To overcome this issue, we develop a new form of convolutional layer that is specifically designed to suppress an image's content and adaptively learn manipulation detection features. Through a series of experiments, we demonstrate that our proposed approach can automatically learn how to detect multiple image manipulations without relying on pre-selected features or any preprocessing. The results of these experiments show that our proposed approach can automatically detect several different manipulations with an average accuracy of 99.10%.

CCS Concepts

•Computing methodologies → Image processing;

Keywords

Image forensics; Universal forgery detection; Convolutional neural networks

1. INTRODUCTION

Over the past several years, researchers have developed a variety of information forensic techniques to determine the authenticity and processing history of digital images [20]. Much of this research has focused on identifying traces left in an image by specific editing operations, then developing algorithms designed to detect these traces. This approach has been used to develop algorithms targeted at detecting image manipulations such as resizing and resampling [17, 8], median filtering [9, 7], contrast enhancement [19], etc.

While the development of targeted editing detectors has led to many important advances in information forensics, this approach to image authentication suffers an important drawback: Since a forger has many editing operations at their disposal, a forensic investigator must apply a large number of forensic tests to determine if and how an image has been edited. If multiple forensic tests are run on an image, the investigator must address several new problems such as controlling the overall false alarm rate between multiple tests and dealing with conflicting results. Furthermore, as new image editing operations are developed, researchers must identify traces left by these new operations and design associated detection algorithms.

In response to these issues, there has been significant interest in the development of universal forensic algorithms designed to detect many, if not all, editing operations. Recent experimental evidence has shown that tools initially developed to perform steganalysis are capable of detecting a wide variety of image editing operations [18]. These tools from steganalysis operate by building local models of pixel dependencies by analyzing the joint distribution of pixel value prediction errors, then extracting detection features from these joint distributions [16, 4]. Another recent effort towards developing universal forensic detectors operates by building Gaussian mixture models (GMMs) of image patches in unaltered and manipulated images [3]. A series of binary manipulation detectors for several editing operations are used then by comparing the log-likelihood of an image patch under the GMM for different possible manipulations. While these techniques show great promise, they each learn detection features from pre-selected models. As a result, a natural question remains: Can strong universal detection features be discovered without requiring human analysis or imposing a predetermined model on the data?

In this work, we propose a new universal approach for performing image editing detection that is capable of *automatically learning* traces left by editing. To accomplish this, we make use of tools from deep learning known as convolutional neural networks (CNNs). CNNs have recently fueled dramatic advances in image recognition due to their ability to adaptively learn classification features rather than rely on human-selected features [12]. These features are extracted from an image via a set of convolutional filters whose coefficients are learned using a technique known as back-

IH&MMSec 2016, June 20-23, 2016, Vigo, Spain

© 2016 ACM. ISBN 978-1-4503-4290-2/16/06. . . $15.00

DOI: http://dx.doi.org/10.1145/2909827.2930786

propagation, then aggregated using an operation known as pooling. Though CNNs are able to adaptively learn good features for object recognition, they are not well suited for performing image manipulation detection in their existing form. Instead of learning filters that identify traces left by editing and manipulation, the convolutional layers will extract features that capture an image's content.

In this paper, we propose a new form of convolutional layer designed to suppress an image's content and adaptively learn manipulation detection features. Using this new convolutional layer, we propose a CNN architecture capable of automatically learning how to detect multiple image manipulations without relying on pre-selected features or models. Through a series of experiments, we evaluate our CNN's ability to act as a universal image manipulation detector. The results of these experiments show that our proposed approach can automatically detect several different manipulations with an average accuracy of 99.10%.

2. BACKGROUND

In this section, we give a brief overview of CNNs. A CNN is a special type of multi-layer neural network used in deep learning that has recently gained significant attention in the computer vision and machine learning communities [10, 21]. Convolutional neural networks first appeared in the late 1980's with the handwritten zip code recognition [13] as an extended version of artificial neural networks (ANN). They have been also applied to handwritten digit recognition[11], images, speech and time series data [12]. Instead of relying on hand-designed features, CNNs are able to adaptively learn classification features. A deep learning to constructing CNNs, i.e., stacking many hidden layers on top of one another, has recently proved very effective for problems such as object recognition [10]. These recent advances have been fueled by the use of GPUs to overcome the computational expense of estimating the large number of hyper-parameters that a deep network involves.

While the particular design or "architecture" of CNNs may vary, they are built using a common set of basic elements and share a similar overall structure. The first layer is a convolutional layer, comprising several convolutional filters applied to the image in parallel. These filters act as a set of feature extractors—their outputs are known as feature maps.

In this paper, matrices are denoted by bold letters, e.g., $\boldsymbol{h}$, $\boldsymbol{w}$; and scalars by regular letters. More specifically, $\boldsymbol{w}(i,j)$ denotes the $(i,j)^{th}$ entry in the matrix $\boldsymbol{w}$ and $\boldsymbol{w}_{ij}$ denotes the $(i,j)^{th}$ matrix in a set of matrices. The superscript $\cdot^{(n)}$ denotes the layer order in the network.

More specifically, the analytical expression of the convolution within the CNN architecture is given in Eq. (1):

$$h_j^{(n)} = \sum_{k=1}^{K} h_k^{(n-1)} * w_{kj}^{(n)} + bj^{(n)}, \qquad (1)$$

where $\boldsymbol{h}_j^{(n)}$ is the jth feature map output in the hidden layer $h^{(n)}$, $\boldsymbol{h}_k^{(n-1)}$ is the kth channel in the hidden layer $h^{(n-1)}$, $\boldsymbol{w}_{kj}^{(n)}$ is the kth channel in the jth filter in $h^{(n)}$ and $b_j^{(n)}$ is its corresponding bias term. The convolutions and associations of these feature maps throughout layers strengthen the learning ability of a CNN model to predict classes.

Though initially seeded with random values, the filter coefficients are learned via a process known as back-propagation

algorithm which we explain in details later. A convolutional layer is typically followed by a pooling layer whose purpose is to reduce the dimensionality of the feature maps. This reduces the computational cost associated with training the network and decreases the chances of over-fitting. Pooling layers operate by dividing feature maps into small, possibly overlapping windows, then retaining only single value per window. Two of the most popular forms of pooling are max-pooling and mean-pooling which retain the maximum and mean value of each window respectively.

Most CNN architectures are built by stacking several convolutional layers and pooling layers on top of one another. This enables the CNN to learn a set of low-level features in early layers, then hierarchically group them into high-level features in later layers. After this, the final set of feature maps are passed to a set of fully connected layers that perform the classification. As in a traditional neural network, every neuron in a fully connected layer is connected to each of the outputs of the previous layer. Multiple fully connected layers can be stacked on top of one another to form deep architectures. The final (visible) fully connected layer of neurons is trained to produce class scores for each class. If sigmoids are used as activation functions for each neuron in this layer, the class scores can be interpreted as class probabilities.

During training the coefficients of the convolutional filters $\boldsymbol{w}_{ij}$ are automatically learned using an iterative algorithm which alternates between feedforward and backpropagation passes of the data. The ultimate goal of this algorithm is to minimize the average loss between the actual labels and the network outputs, i.e.,

$$E = \frac{1}{m} \sum_{i=1}^{m} \sum_{k=1}^{c} y_i^{*(k)} \log\left(y_i^{(k)}\right), \qquad (2)$$

where $y_i^{*(k)}$ and $y_i^{(k)}$ are respectively the true label and the network output of the ith image at the kth class with m training images and c neurons in the output layer.

To this aim, a variety of solvers could be used to solve the underlying optimization problem. In this paper we consider the stochastic gradient descent (SGD) to train our model. The iterative update rule for the kernel coefficients $\boldsymbol{w}_{ij}^{(n)}$ in CNN during the backpropagation pass is given below:

$$\boldsymbol{w}_{ij}^{(n)} = \boldsymbol{w}_{ij}^{(n)} + \Delta \boldsymbol{w}_{ij}^{(n)} \qquad (3)$$
$$\Delta \boldsymbol{w}_{ij}^{(n)} = m \cdot \Delta \boldsymbol{w}_{ij}^{(n)} - d \cdot \epsilon \cdot \boldsymbol{w}_{ij}^{(n)} - \epsilon \cdot \frac{\partial E}{\partial \boldsymbol{w}_{ij}^{(n)}},$$

where $\boldsymbol{w}_{ij}^{(n)}$ represents the ith channel from the jth kernel matrix in the hidden layer $h^{(n)}$ that convolves with the ith channel in the previous feature maps denoted by $h_i^{(n-1)}$, $\Delta \boldsymbol{w}_{ij}^{(n)}$ denotes the gradient of $\boldsymbol{w}_{ij}^{(n)}$ and ϵ is the learning rate. The letters m and d are respectively the momentum and the decay. The bias term $b_j^{(n)}$ in (1) is updated using the same equations presented in (3). The use of the *decay* and *momentum* strategy is mainly for fast convergence as explained by LeCun *et al.* in [14].

3. NEW CONVOLUTIONAL LAYER

Though CNNs are able to adaptively learn strong classification features for object recognition, they are ill suited for

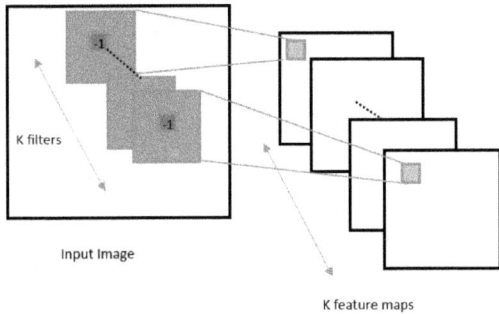

Figure 1: Our proposed convolutional layer. The red coefficient is -1 and the coefficients in the green region sum to 1.

performing manipulation detection in their standard form. This is because in their existing form, CNNs will tend to learn features that represent an image's content rather than manipulation detection features. This effect has recently been observed by Chen et al. during their efforts train a CNN to perform median filtering detection [2]. In their experiments, Chen et al. found that the CNN was not able to learn median filtering detection features if images are directly fed to the input layer. Instead, they first extracted a high dimensional feature set from the image known as the median filter residual, then provided this to the input layer of the CNN.

To overcome this problem, we propose a new form of convolutional layer that will force the CNN to learn manipulation detection features from images without requiring any preliminary feature extraction or pre-processing. The key idea behind developing this layer is that certain local structural relationships exist between pixels independent of an image's content. Manipulations will alter these local relationships in a detectable way. As a result, manipulation detection feature extractors must learn the relationship between a pixel and its local neighborhood while simultaneously suppressing the content of the image so that content dependent features are not learned. For this to occur, the first convolutional layer must not be allowed freely evolve into any set of filters. Instead, it must be constrained to evolve filters with the desired properties described above.

To accomplish this, we propose creating the first layer of our CNN using convolutional filters that are constrained to learn only a set of prediction error filters. Prediction error filters are filters that predict the pixel value at the center of the filter window, then subtract this central value to produce the prediction error. More explicitly, each of the K filters $\boldsymbol{w}_k^{(1)}$ in the first layer of the CNN have the following constraints placed on them:

$$\begin{cases} \boldsymbol{w}_k^{(1)}(0,0) = -1 \\ \sum_{\ell,m \neq 0} \boldsymbol{w}_k^{(1)}(\ell,m) = 1 \end{cases} \quad (4)$$

where $\boldsymbol{w}_k^{(1)}(\ell,m)$ is the filter weight at the (ℓ,m) position and $\boldsymbol{w}_k^{(1)}(0,0)$ is the filter weight at the center of the filter window. Each filter in this layer is initialized by randomly choosing each filter weight, then enforcing the constraints in (4). During training, the constraints in (4) are again enforced during each iteration after the filter weights have undergone their stochastic gradient descent updates. This

allows the CNN to adaptively learn a strong set of manipulation detection feature extractors, rather than having the chosen a priori.

Pseudocode summarizing the training algorithm for our new layer is shown below:

Algorithm 1 Training algorithm for our new convolutional layer

---

1: *Initilize $\boldsymbol{w}_k$'s using randomly drawn weights*
2: i=1
3: **while** $i \leq max\_iter$ **do**
4:     *Set $\boldsymbol{w}_k(0,0)^{(1)} = 0$ for all K filters*
5:     *Normalize $\boldsymbol{w}_k^{(1)}$'s such that $\sum_{\ell,m \neq 0} \boldsymbol{w}_k^{(1)}(\ell,m) = 1$*
6:     *Set $\boldsymbol{w}_k(0,0)^{(1)} = -1$ for all K filters*
7:     *Do feedforward pass*
8:     *Update filter weights through stochastic gradient descent and backpropagate errors*
9:     i = i+1
10:     **if** training accuracy converges **then**
11:         exit
12: **end**
13: *Enforce constraints on $\boldsymbol{w}_k$'s given in Steps 4 through 6*

We note that our proposed constrained convolutional layer takes inspiration from a wide array of previous information forensic and steganographic research. Many forensic and steganalysis algorithms can be viewed as specific forms of the following detection approach: Predict each pixel value on the basis of its neighbors according to a fixed rule, calculate the prediction error, create a lower dimensional feature vector or test statistic from these prediction errors, then make a decision on the basis of this feature vector or test statistic. This approach has also been recently applied to camera model identification [1]. It is quite easy to see that steganalysis algorithms such as rich models [4] and SPAM [16] are very successful instances of this approach. Furthermore, forensic algorithms for detecting several manipulations such as resizing (using linear predictor residues [8]) and median filtering (using streaking artifacts [9] or median filter residuals [7]) can also be viewed as specific forms of this approach.

While each of these algorithms discussed above rely on a fixed predictor or set of predictors chosen a priori, our proposed constrained convolutional layer enables a set of predictors to be *learned directly from the training data*. Furthermore, the higher layers of our CNN (described in Section 4) are able to *learn* the appropriate method for extracting low dimensional detection features from the high dimensional prediction errors. As a result, our proposed universal forensic approach does not require analysis by a human expert to create a detector for a new manipulation. This is particularly important because the design of detection features and an appropriate detection rule by a human expert is both time consuming and difficult.

4. NETWORK ARCHITECTURE

In this section, we present our proposed CNN architecture for performing manipulation detection. Fig. 2 shows our proposed CNN architecture as well as detailed information about the size of each layer. As depicted in Fig. 2, our network contains 8 layers, namely our proposed new convolutional layer, 2 convolutional layers, 2 max-pooling layers and 3 fully-connected layers. Images are fed into the CNN

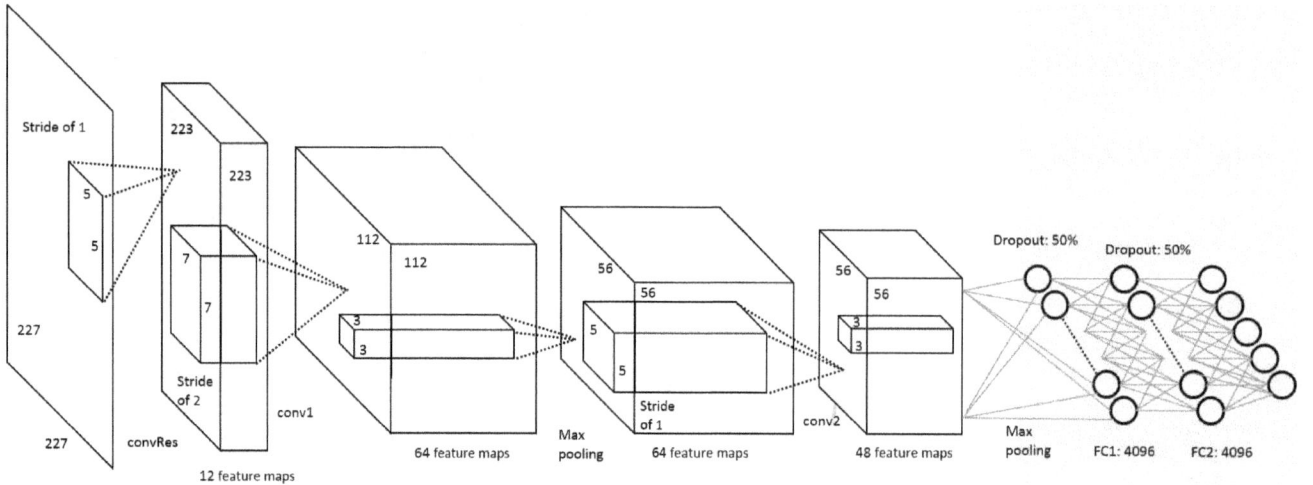

Figure 2: An illustration of the proposed CNN Architecture. The network's input dimension is 51529 neurons and the remaining 8 layers have 596748, 802816, 200704, 150528, 37632, 4096, 4096 and 5 neurons respectively

through an input layer, also known as the data layer. The first layer of our network is 227×227 grayscale image.

4.1 Convolutional Layer

In our architecture, we use two types of convolutional layers, i.e., regular and our proposed type of convolution. Throughout the regular convolutional layers, inputs are called images. Specifically, an input image of dimension $w \times l \times c$ from a hidden layer $h^{(n-1)}$ is convolved with k different kernels of dimension $s \times s \times c$ where w and l are respectively, the width and the height of the input image, c is the number of feature maps in the hidden layer $h^{(n-1)}$ and s is the filter size. The number of feature maps in the input image of the hidden layer $h^{(n)}$ is k. The convolution is applied to all the $s \times s$ local regions of the image, also called receptive fields, with an overlapping distance called stride.

In our model, we have 2 non-constrained convolutional layers respectively called conv1 and conv2. As can be seen in Fig. 2, conv1 has 64 kernels that we depict only one of size $7 \times 7 \times 12$ with stride of 2 which yields $112 \times 112 \times 64$ feature maps. conv2 has 48 kernels of size $5 \times 5 \times 64$ with stride of 1 which yields $56 \times 56 \times 48$ feature maps

A convolutional layer is commonly followed by a nonlinear mapping applied in an activation layer. An activation layer is simply a nonlinear function applied to each pixel value. In our work we use the Rectified Linear Unit (ReLU), i.e., $f(x) = \max(0, x)$ [15]. Krizhevsky *et al.* showed that in practice, CNNs with ReLU neural activations train several times faster than other activation functions [10].

The first layer in our CNN is our proposed constrained layer discussed in Section 3. We refer to this layer as conv-Res (see Figs. 1 and 2). Specifically, we have a set of 5×5 constrained prediction error filters with stride of 1. From Fig. 2, we use 12 kernels whose outputs are 12 223×223 feature maps. These latter convolutional outputs are considered as a new image with 12 channels. Therefore, the next convolutional kernel in conv1 has 12 channels. This type of convolution is not followed by a ReLU mapping mainly because the output feature maps carry the fingerprints left by a tampering operation which can be destroyed by the nonlinear operator.

4.2 Max-Pooling

We use the overlapping max-pooling layer similarly to [10] which is a subsampling approach. The goal of pooling layer is to reduce the resolution of the feature map and make it robust to variations for previous learned features. Explicitly, this method consists of computing the maximum value in each neighborhood at different positions. We use a kernel size of 3 and a stride of 2. We can see from Fig. 2 that the size of the feature map in conv1 is reduced from $112 \times 112 \times 64$ to $56 \times 56 \times 64$ after the first max-pooling layer. The output of the second max-pooling layer is a set of $37,632$ neurons, i.e. feature maps of size $28 \times 28 \times 48$, reduced from the previous feature maps of size $56 \times 56 \times 48$.

Furthermore, the max-pooling layers are followed by a Local Response Normalization (LRN) similarly applied in [10] where the central value in each neighborhood is normalized by the surrounding pixel values. This type of operation is also called "brightness normalization".

4.3 Dropout & Fully-Connected Layers

The dropout technique [5] applied in the fully-connected layers fc1 and fc2 consists of setting to zero the neurons of the hidden layer with probability 0.5. It reduces the complex co-adaptations of neurons and forces them to learn more robust features. From Fig. 2 we have 4096 neurons in fc1 and fc2. Therefore, only 2048 neurons contribute in the forward pass and the backpropagation.

Finally, the output layer has one neuron corresponding to each possible class, i.e. one neuron for unaltered images as well as a neuron for each possible manipulation. In the experiments conducted in this paper, we considered 4 different manipulations, therefore out output layer has 5 neurons. A softmax operator is applied in fc3 to scale the output values as the probabilities of an example to belong to each class.

5. EXPERIMENTAL RESULTS

5.1 Experimental Setup

To evaluate the performance of our proposed CNN model for image editing detection, we first built an experimental

Table 1: CNN detection accuracy rate for binary detectors

	Median Filtering	Gaussian Blurring	AWGN, $\sigma = 2$	Re-sampling
Accuracy	99.31%	99.32%	99.68%	99.40%

Table 2: Confusion matrix showing the detection accuracy of our multiclass CNN

	Original	Median Filtering	Gaussian Blurring	AWGN, $\sigma = 2$	Re-sampling
Original	**98.40%**	0.52%	0.29%	0.34%	0.44%
Median Filtering	0.23%	**98.27%**	1.24%	0.12%	0.12%
Gaussian Blurring	0.00%	0.18%	**99.75%**	0.00%	0.06%
AWGN, $\sigma = 2$	0.03%	0.04%	0.14%	**99.77%**	0.00%
Resampling	0.27%	0.20%	0.15%	0.00%	**99.35%**

database of unaltered and edited images. Our experimental image datasets have been collected from 12 different camera models and devices with no previous tampering or pre-processing. We created a set of grayscale images by retaining only the green color layer from each image. We cropped each original image in the center, then subdivided it into 256×256 blocks. More explicitly, every block corresponds to a new image that has its corresponding different tampered images. In total we created a set of $261,800$ unaltered blocks. Next, we generated a set of altered images. We did this by applying the following operations to a set of unaltered image:

- Median Filtering with a 5×5 kernel.

- Gaussian Blurring with a 5×5 kernel and a standard deviation $\sigma = 1.1$.

- Additive White Gaussian Noise (AWGN) with standard deviation 2.

- Resampling (resizing) using bilinear interpolation and a scaling factor 1.5.

We then cropped these images into 256 by 256 blocks to create a total of $333,200$ manipulated blocks. During training and testing all the blocks are further cropped to 227 by 227 blocks.

We implemented all of our CNNs using the Caffe deep learning framework [6]. We ran our experiments using one Nvidia GeForce GTX 980 GPU with 4GB RAM. To facilitate this, we converted our datasets to the lmdb format. We set the training parameters of the stochastic gradient descent as follows: $momentum = 0.9$, $decay = 0.0005$, and a fixed learning rate $\epsilon = 10^{-6}$ over all iterations. The choice of the learning rate ϵ is very crucial for both accuracy and the stability of the weights gradient. A larger learning rate would yield numerically unstable filters weights. We set the batch size for training and testing to 32 images.

5.2 Results

In what follows, we use our suggested CNN model as a binary and multi-class classifier and we present our simulation results.

5.2.1 Binary Classification Approach

In our first set of experiments, we trained different CNNs to detect each of the four manipulations discussed in Section 5.1. Each CNN corresponds to a binary classifier that detects one type of possible image operation with the same architecture outlined in Section 4. The output layer corresponds to two neurons, i.e., original v.s. tampered image. Decision made by picking the class corresponding to the neuron with the highest activation. We chose $43,500$ unaltered blocks and their corresponding tampered blocks to build our training data for each type of forgery. Similarly we picked $16,000$ unaltered blocks and their corresponding tampered blocks to build our testing data for each type of forgery. That is, for every binary classifier we have a total number of $87,000$ blocks for training and $32,000$ blocks for testing.

Table 1 summarizes the performance of our proposed model for binary classification to detect the underlying image operations. We can see from this table that our CNNs are able to distinguish between unaltered and manipulated images with at least 99.31% accuracy. We also note that we chose to stop the training process after achieving an accuracy higher than 99% since it increases slowly above that rate. Therefore, these results represent a lower-bound accuracy of what our model can achieve.

Our model converges to a very high accuracy after few thousands of iterations. Furthermore, we note that on our machines this typically takes less than one hour.

5.2.2 Multi-class Classification Approach

In our second experiment we trained a multiclass CNN to detect multiple types of image forgery, i.e., median filtering, guassian blurring, additive white gaussian noise and re-sampling v.s. authentic image. Following the first set of experiments, a decision is made by picking the class corresponding to the neuron with the highest activation. Given the memory constraints of our machines, we picked $17,400$ unaltered blocks and their four corresponding tampered blocks to build our training data. Similarly we picked $6,400$ unaltered blocks and their four corresponding tampered blocks to build our testing data. That is, we have a total number of $87,000$ blocks for training and $32,000$ blocks for testing.

The CNN was trained over $56,000$ iterations and then fine-tuned for $9,000$ iterations with fixed filters in all the convolutional layers. Since CNNs have many hyper-parameters that must be learned throughout all layers, this constraint during fine-tuning helps to direct the neurons in the fully connected layers toward more optimal weights. That is, we need to direct the gradient direction to a better minima by fine-tuning only the fully-connected layers. This procedure has increased the accuracy of our model by $\approx 1\%$. The entire training typically converges in less than 6 hours.

Our simulation results are summarized in Table 2. Our proposed model achieves an accuracy of 99.10% of detecting the different four types of forgery. From this confusion matrix, we can see that our CNN can detect each manipulation with very high accuracy.

These results are significant for several reasons. First, they show that our CNN represents a universal manipulations detection approach since it can be trained to detect multiple manipulations without altering its architecture. Second, and perhaps most surprisingly, our CNN can be trained to automatically learn detection features for each manipulation without requiring human intervention. This suggests that as new manipulations are considered or developed, our CNN can potentially learn to detect them without needing a human expert to identify detection features.

6. CONCLUSION

In this paper, we proposed a novel CNN-based universal forgery detection technique that can automatically learn how to detect different image manipulations. To prevent the CNN from learning features that represent an image's content, we proposed a new form of convolutional specifically designed to suppress an image's content and learn manipulation detection features. We accomplished this by specifically constraining this new convolutional layer to learn prediction error filters. Through a series of experiments, we demonstrated that our CNN-based universal forensic approach can automatically learn how to detect multiple image manipulations without relying on pre-selected features or any pre-processing. The results of these experiments demonstrated that our proposed approach can automatically detect several different manipulations with an average accuracy of 99.10%.

7. REFERENCES

[1] C. Chen and M. C. Stamm. Camera model identification framework using an ensemble of demosaicing features. In *Information Forensics and Security (WIFS), 2015 IEEE International Workshop on*, pages 1–6. IEEE, 2015.

[2] J. Chen, X. Kang, Y. Liu, and Z. J. Wang. Median filtering forensics based on convolutional neural networks. *IEEE Signal Processing Letters*, 22(11):1849–1853, Nov. 2015.

[3] W. Fan, K. Wang, and F. Cayre. General-purpose image forensics using patch likelihood under image statistical models. In *IEEE International Workshop on Information Forensics and Security (WIFS)*, pages 1–6, Nov. 2015.

[4] J. Fridrich and J. Kodovskỳ. Rich models for steganalysis of digital images. *IEEE Transactions on Information Forensics and Security*, 7(3):868–882, 2012.

[5] G. E. Hinton, N. Srivastava, A. Krizhevsky, I. Sutskever, and R. R. Salakhutdinov. Improving neural networks by preventing co-adaptation of feature detectors. *arXiv preprint arXiv:1207.0580*, 2012.

[6] Y. Jia, E. Shelhamer, J. Donahue, S. Karayev, J. Long, R. Girshick, S. Guadarrama, and T. Darrell. Caffe: Convolutional architecture for fast feature embedding. *arXiv preprint arXiv:1408.5093*, 2014.

[7] X. Kang, M. C. Stamm, A. Peng, and K. J. R. Liu. Robust median filtering forensics using an autoregressive model. *IEEE Transactions on Information Forensics and Security,*, 8(9):1456–1468, Sept. 2013.

[8] M. Kirchner. Fast and reliable resampling detection by spectral analysis of fixed linear predictor residue. In *Proceedings of the 10th ACM Workshop on Multimedia and Security*, MM&Sec '08, pages 11–20, New York, NY, USA, 2008. ACM.

[9] M. Kirchner and J. Fridrich. On detection of median filtering in digital images. In *IS&T/SPIE Electronic Imaging*, pages 754110–754110. International Society for Optics and Photonics, 2010.

[10] A. Krizhevsky, I. Sutskever, and G. E. Hinton. Imagenet classification with deep convolutional neural networks. In *Advances in neural information processing systems*, pages 1097–1105, 2012.

[11] B. B. Le Cun, J. S. Denker, D. Henderson, R. E. Howard, W. Hubbard, and L. D. Jackel. Handwritten digit recognition with a back-propagation network. In *Advances in neural information processing systems*. Citeseer, 1990.

[12] Y. LeCun and Y. Bengio. Convolutional networks for images, speech, and time series. *The handbook of brain theory and neural networks*, 3361(10):1995, 1995.

[13] Y. LeCun, B. Boser, J. S. Denker, D. Henderson, R. E. Howard, W. Hubbard, and L. D. Jackel. Backpropagation applied to handwritten zip code recognition. *Neural computation*, 1(4):541–551, 1989.

[14] Y. A. LeCun, L. Bottou, G. B. Orr, and K.-R. Müller. Efficient backprop. In *Neural networks: Tricks of the trade*, pages 9–48. Springer, 2012.

[15] V. Nair and G. E. Hinton. Rectified linear units improve restricted boltzmann machines. In *International Conference on Machine Learning*, pages 807–814, 2010.

[16] T. Pevny, P. Bas, and J. Fridrich. Steganalysis by subtractive pixel adjacency matrix. *IEEE Transactions on Information Forensics and Security*, 5(2):215–224, June 2010.

[17] A. C. Popescu and H. Farid. Exposing digital forgeries by detecting traces of resampling. *IEEE Transactions on Signal Processing*, 53(2):758–767, Feb. 2005.

[18] X. Qiu, H. Li, W. Luo, and J. Huang. A universal image forensic strategy based on steganalytic model. In *Proceedings of the 2nd ACM workshop on Information hiding and multimedia security*, pages 165–170. ACM, 2014.

[19] M. C. Stamm and K. J. R. Liu. Forensic detection of image manipulation using statistical intrinsic fingerprints. *IEEE Trans. on Information Forensics and Security*, 5(3):492 –506, 2010.

[20] M. C. Stamm, M. Wu, and K. J. R. Liu. Information forensics: An overview of the first decade. *IEEE Access*, 1:167–200, 2013.

[21] C. Szegedy, W. Liu, Y. Jia, P. Sermanet, S. Reed, D. Anguelov, D. Erhan, V. Vanhoucke, and A. Rabinovich. Going deeper with convolutions. In *Proceedings of the IEEE Conference on Computer Vision and Pattern Recognition*, pages 1–9, 2015.

Forensics of High Quality and Nearly Identical JPEG Image Recompression

Cecilia Pasquini
University of Trento, Italy
cecilia.pasquini@unitn.it

Pascal Schöttle
Universität Innsbruck, Austria
pascal.schoettle@uibk.ac.at

Rainer Böhme
Universität Innsbruck, Austria
rainer.boehme@uibk.ac.at

Giulia Boato
University of Trento, Italy
boato@disi.unitn.it

Fernando Pèrez-Gonzàlez
University of Vigo, Spain
fperez@gts.uvigo.es

ABSTRACT

We address the known problem of detecting a previous compression in JPEG images, focusing on the challenging case of high and very high quality factors (≥ 90) as well as repeated compression with identical or nearly identical quality factors. We first revisit the approaches based on Benford–Fourier analysis in the DCT domain and block convergence analysis in the spatial domain. Both were originally conceived for specific scenarios. Leveraging decision tree theory, we design a combined approach complementing the discriminatory capabilities. We obtain a set of novel detectors targeted to high quality grayscale JPEG images.

Keywords

JPEG forensics; High quality images; Double compression.

1. INTRODUCTION

Reconstructing the compression history of JPEG images is relevant in multimedia forensics. Traces of prior compression may indicate multiple processing steps, potentially including forgeries. In recent years the problem of detecting traces of multiple compressions has been extensively studied. This has resulted in a number of forensic approaches targeted to detect double or multiple compression.

The known approaches face some important limitations. First, multiple compression detectors are generally evaluated by considering quite strong quantization. Typically, the tested JPEG quality factors (QF) are lower than 90. However, high and very high quality JPEG compression is relevant as memory and bandwidth are cheap. One may also speculate that counterfeiters store intermediate versions at high quality to avoid visible artifacts and detectable traces. Second, cases where the second compression has a lower quality than the prior compression remain hard to detect with the known methods. Third, the majority of techniques is based on DCT coefficients. These techniques typically fail in detecting previous compressions performed with the same quantization matrix. While some progress has been made in this direction [6, 16, 7, 3], a combination of these techniques with the ones based on DCT coefficients remains unexplored.

In this paper, we close this gap. We focus on the specific scenario where both the primary and secondary quality factors are larger or equal to 90. We aim at detecting a previous compression also in those cases where the quantization matrix used in the secondary compression is identical or nearly identical to the primary one. In order to achieve this goal, we consider two different and recently proposed approaches: the one based on block convergence in the spatial domain [7, 3] and the one based on Benford–Fourier analysis [10]. After assessing the strengths and limitations on each of them in the considered scenario, we proposed to combine them. Decision tree theory offers a general framework to do this systematically. This results in a set of double compression detectors for high quality JPEG images, parameterized by the observable quality factor of the image under investigation. We show that the combined classification tests lead to considerable benefits in terms of classification accuracy compared to the state of the art.

This work introduces several contributions: we improve both state of the art detectors individually and adapt them to high and very high JPEG qualities. For Benford–Fourier we propose to adaptively choose the DCT frequencies used in the test in order to accommodate for the fact that quantization matrices for nearly identical quality factors do not differ in every coefficient. We simplify the depth of the block convergence analysis to the relevant number of iterations. We build and evaluate a joint detector that outperforms each of the improved methods individually.

The paper is structured as follows: Section 2 discusses the decision problems studied in the literature and proposes terminology to precisely define the tests in this paper. Section 3 describes the two forensic techniques we consider for our joint detector. In Section 4, we measure the performance of both techniques in the considered scenario and improve them. Section 5 presents the combination approach and reports the performance of the combined detectors. Finally, Section 6 concludes with an outlook on future work.

IH&MMSec 2016, June 20-23, 2016, Vigo, Spain

© 2016 ACM. ISBN 978-1-4503-4290-2/16/06. . . $15.00

DOI: http://dx.doi.org/10.1145/2909827.2930787

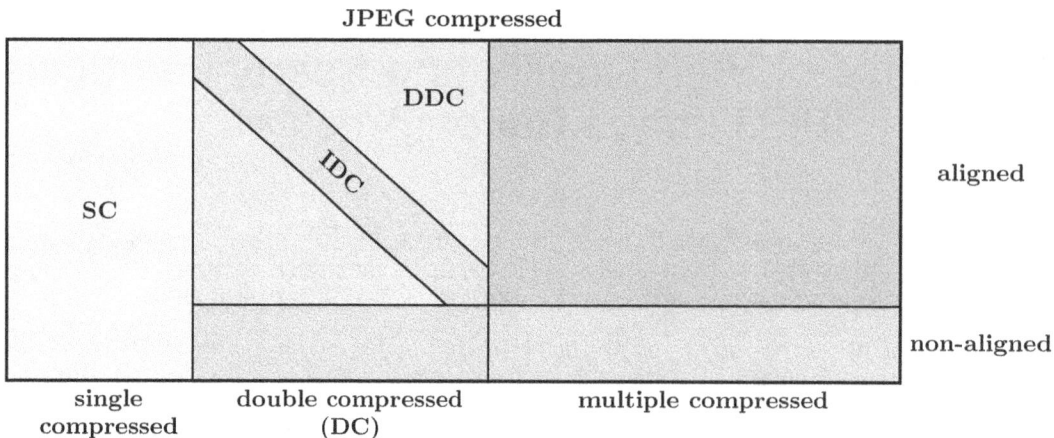

Figure 1: Representation of the multiple JPEG compression detection problem

2. PROBLEM STATEMENT

Figure 1 depicts the possible status of a JPEG image. Either the image was compressed only once and belongs to the strict subset of single compressed JPEG images (**SC**), or it was compressed multiple times. In the latter case, (some of) the compressions could be non-aligned (light gray subset) or all of them can be aligned (dark gray subset). In this paper we focus on aligned compressions, thus we do not depict the non-aligned set in full detail. Both subsets, aligned and non-aligned, can be further distinguished into the subset of images that were compressed exactly twice (**DC**) and the subset of images with more than two compressions. Again, we concentrate on the relevant case for this paper. Aligned and double compressed JPEG images can be further divided into those that were compressed twice with the same quantization matrix (**IDC**) and those that were the quantization matrices differ between the two compressions (**DDC**). It is known that different quantization tables are generated as function of the quality factor (QF), a natural number between 1 and 100. The lower the quality factor, the higher are the values in the quantization table. Then, further distinctions are possible. For instance, **DDC** could be splitted into the set where the QF of the first compression was strictly higher or strictly lower than the QF of the second compression.

Ideally, a general framework for detecting multiple JPEG compressions should differentiate between all of the depicted subsets, although most of the approaches in the literature restrict themselves to the distinction of some of the subsets. One of the most studied problem is certainly the distinction between **SC** and **DC** images in the aligned case, which is addressed in [13, 1, 4, 8], while some approaches target also a multiple recompression [9, 10]. However, most of them fail when dealing with images in **IDC**, thus specific approaches have been designed for this case, targeting also the detection of multiple recompression with the same quantization matrix [7, 3, 6, 16].

Given the diversity of statistical traces in **DDC** and **IDC** images, in the proposed approach we reformulate the **SC** vs **DC** discrimination problem as the distinction of the three different sets **SC**, **DDC** and **IDC**. Moreover, we focus on the case of QF≥ 90 both for the primary and secondary com-

pression and indicate such scenario as *HQ-DC* (high quality double compression) for the sake of clarity.

3. CURRENT APPROACHES

In this section, we will briefly recall the main rationale and procedures of the two state-of-the-art approaches that are leveraged in this work, stressing the different forensic scenarios for which they were originally designed.

3.1 Benford–Fourier analysis

The Benford–Fourier (BF) coefficients have been introduced in [12] and they proved to be particularly suitable for the analysis of DCT coefficients, thus providing an effective tool for different tasks in image forensics. In particular, given a continuous random variable Z with pdf $f_Z(z)$, its *Benford–Fourier coefficient* at $\omega \in \mathbb{R}$ is defined as

$$a_\omega = \int\limits_{-\infty}^{+\infty} f_Z(z) e^{-j\omega \log_{10} z} dz.$$

In [11] and [10], BF coefficients have been used to study the distribution of 8×8 DCT coefficients for the detection of previous compressions in uncompressed format and JPEG format images, respectively. In particular, given the analyzed image the BF coefficients are estimated by the formula

$$\hat{a}_\omega = \frac{\sum_{m=1}^{M} e^{-j\omega \log_{10} z^m}}{M} \qquad m = 1, \dots, M \qquad (1)$$

where z^m is the realization of the random variable representing the absolute value of DCT coefficients at a certain frequency in the m-th block of the image, M is the total number of 8×8 blocks.

In particular, in [10] such estimates are computed for a number of DCT frequencies in a subset $F \subset \{1, \dots, 64\}$. Specifically, there is a BF coefficient at certain ω^f for each $f \in F$, thus obtaining a vector

$$\hat{\mathbf{a}} = [\hat{a}_{\omega^1}, \dots, \hat{a}_{\omega^F}].$$

After an estimation of their pdf in the different quantization chains, the elements in $\hat{\mathbf{a}}$ are combined to compute the likelihood function $\mathcal{L}(H|\hat{\mathbf{a}})$ for a certain hypothesis of compression history H. The null hypothesis H_N is given by the fact that the last JPEG compression (whose parameters are known from the image under investigation) is the only one that occurred in the digital history of the image, while the alternative hypotheses depend on the forensic scenario considered (in [10], single and triple compression are analized). For instance, in a double compression detection framework each alternative hypothesis H_A is represented by the fact that the image was previously compressed with a primary quality factor among a predefined set. For each H_A, the logarithmic likelihood ratio (LLR) is computed as follows

$$\text{LLR} = -2 \cdot \ln\left[\frac{\mathcal{L}(H_N|\hat{\mathbf{a}})}{\mathcal{L}(H_A|\hat{\mathbf{a}})}\right], \qquad (2)$$

and the maximum value of the LLR over all the alternative hypotheses, indicated as LLR_m, is considered. If $\text{LLR}_m > 0$ then the null hypothesis is rejected, otherwise it is accepted.

In [10], the method has been tested on single and double compressed images created by combining the quality factors in $\{50, 60, 70, 80, 90\}$, i.e., the difference between the primary and secondary quality factor is in any case at least 10. It provided good accuracies, which are generally maintained in the cases of stronger secondary compression but dramatically drops in the case of identical recompression.

3.2 Block convergence

In [7], the authors propose a technique to identify the number of JPEG compressions with quality factor 100 in grayscale images. In this case the quantization table is composed only of the value 1 and we will indicate such setting as JPEG-100. It is observed that for JPEG-100 the 8×8 blocks are transformed in the DCT domain, rounded to the nearest integer and transformed back to the pixel domain, where they are again rounded to the nearest positive integer and truncated to the value range. The authors show that for some of the blocks none of the pixel values change during a JPEG-100 compression. They call these blocks stable and conjecture that after repeated JPEG-100 compression, all blocks of a grayscale image will converge, i.e., become stable. Furthermore, the percentage of blocks that becomes stable after a certain number of recompressions is largely independent of the image content. In particular, given a subject JPEG-100 image, the authors propose to discard the flat blocks (i.e., the ones which contain a single value and are stable from the beginning) and, among the remaining ones, count the ones that become stable after each JPEG-100 re-

compression. Hence, the ratio of stable blocks (for different numbers of JPEG compressions) is computed by:

$$r = \frac{b_{\text{stable}} - b_{\text{flat}}}{b_{\text{total}} - b_{\text{flat}}}, \qquad (3)$$

where b_{total} is the total number of blocks in the image, b_{flat} is the number of flat ones and b_{stable} is the number of stable ones. The value of r is then used to identify the number of previous JPEG-100 compressions.

This approach has been extended in [3] to color images, for which all the three color channels need to be analyzed and the block convergence path is studied with respect to a number of additional aspects, such as the kind of color space conversion and the subsampling/upsampling methods. Moreover, in this work the authors propose to fit a theoretical distribution (specifically, the beta distribution) to the ratios of stable blocks observed after different numbers of recompressions.

The technique has been tested on images that were recompressed multiple times with the very same quality factor and provided accurate results in case of very high quality images (QF$\in \{100, 99\}$). It also has been noted that the accuracy decreases together with the quality factor.

4. INDIVIDUAL APPROACHES

As already mentioned in Section 1, we focus on the detection of high quality double compression in JPEG images, i.e. with quality factors higher or equal to 90. In this section we first describe our set-up and then show the performance of the techniques mentioned in the last section in our scenario. Furthermore, we improve both methods.

4.1 HQ-DC scenario

In our forensic scenario, each grayscale test image has a *current quality factor* QF$_c \in \{90, 91, \ldots, 100\}$ which is known from the given JPEG file and a *previous quality factor* QF$_p \in \{90, 91, \ldots, 100, \text{NC}\}$, where we will use the notation QF$_p =$NC if the image is single compressed and has no primary quality factor. We will represent a JPEG compression history as square brackets containing the ordered sequence of quality factors applied. Thus, in our tests the compression history of the image under investigation can be either [NC, QF$_c$] (only the last JPEG compression occurred) or [QF, QF$_c$] (a previous compression occurred), where QF is searched within set $\mathcal{QF}_{range} = \{90, 91, \ldots, 100\}$.

This kind of setting implies a limited difference between the quantization tables used in the primary and secondary

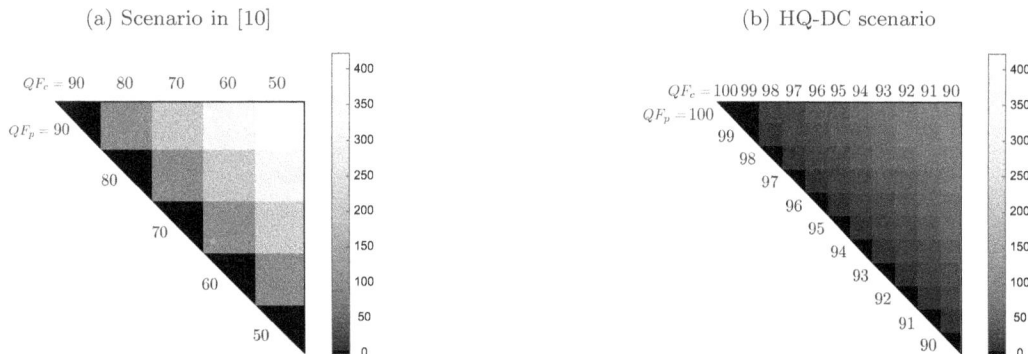

(a) Scenario in [10]

(b) HQ-DC scenario

Figure 2: Euclidean norm of the quantization table difference in the different double compression chains

NC	100	99	98	97	96	95	94	93	92	91	90
100											
99											
98											
97											
96											
95											
94											
93											
92											
91											
90											

Table 1: Example of result representation. Each cell refers to a compression chain specified by the quality factors at the corresponding row and column. Current quality factors QF_c are reported row-wise and primary ones are reported column-wise. Colors match the ones used in Figure 1.

JPEG compression, as well as generally small primary quantization steps which makes the detection of a previous quantization more difficult. Figure 2 shows the Euclidean norm of the differences between the quantization tables (luminance channel) of the quality factors considered for the experimental setting in [10], compared with the ones of the HQ-DC scenario. We refer to the standard quantization tables used by the `libjpeg` library released by the IJG (Independent JPEG Group), as they are often used in common software.

With respect to the scenario described in Section 2, our goal is to design a test that analyzes a JPEG image with $QF_c \geq 90$ either belonging to **SC**, **DDC**, or **IDC** and assign it to the correct set[1]. Table 1 serves an example of the result representation for our experimental setting: green cells refer to compression chains of the form [NC,QF_c] (class **SC**), blue cells to compression chains of the form [QF_c,QF_c] (class **IDC**), and red cells to compression chains of the form [QF,QF_c], QF$\neq QF_c$ (class **DDC**). In the following, the numbers in each cell will indicate the classification accuracy (i.e., the percentage of images that are assigned to the correct class) with respect to the specific test considered.

For our experiments, we consider two datasets composed of images in TIFF format and widely used in the literature: the UCID database [15] (1338 images, 384×512) and a subset of the DRESDEN database [5] (1488 images, 3872×2592 and 3008×2000). For each image we create single and double compressed versions by combining all the quality factors in $\mathcal{QF}_{range}$. Thus, each image is processed according to 132 different compression chains, 11 with single compression and 121 with double compression. We limit our analysis to grayscale images and consequently apply the approaches to the luminance channel only. We employ the state-of-the-art libraries `libtiff 3.6.1` and `libjpeg 8d` to read TIFF and write grayscale JPEG images, respectively.

In this section, for the sake of brevity, we report the results for the UCID database only, as those for the DRESDEN database are very similar. We reproduced the experimental setting used in [10], where a set of 600 UCID images was used for estimating the prediction error parameters (which are employed also for other datasets). Such images are then excluded from the Benford–Fourier analysis, while the remaining ones are used for testing.

---

[1]With a slight abuse of notation, we will indicate as **SC**, **DDC** and **IDC** the sets introduced in Section 2, although they only refer to the case of high quality JPEG compression (QF$\geq$ 90).

4.2 Benford–Fourier analysis

We first consider the method proposed in [10], that we indicate as `BF_baseline`. Here, a predefined set of 9 DCT frequencies (specifically $F = \{4, 6, 11, 13, 15, 22, 24, 26, 28\}$ in zigzag order) is used to compute (2). Moreover, the potential primary quality factor is searched within the whole set $\mathcal{QF}_{range} = \{90, 91, \ldots, 100\}$, thus each image is classified either as belonging to **SC** (if the maximum value of LLR is below 0), **DDC** (if the estimated compression chain [QF,QF_c] is such that QF$\neq QF_c$) or **IDC** (if the estimated

NC	100	99	98	97	96	95	94	93	92	91	90
100	0.05	0.98	0.00	0.98	1.00	1.00	1.00	1.00	1.00	1.00	1.00
99	0.01	0.99	0.00	1.00	1.00	1.00	1.00	1.00	1.00	1.00	1.00
98	0.08	0.04	0.03	0.91	0.99	1.00	1.00	1.00	1.00	1.00	1.00
97	0.21	0.07	0.07	0.65	0.81	1.00	1.00	1.00	1.00	1.00	1.00
96	0.20	0.03	0.02	0.26	0.90	0.81	0.99	1.00	1.00	1.00	1.00
95	0.24	0.04	0.08	0.21	0.69	0.71	0.76	0.95	1.00	1.00	1.00
94	0.27	0.02	0.03	0.41	0.62	0.97	0.78	0.74	0.91	1.00	1.00
93	0.43	0.06	0.07	0.25	0.71	0.88	0.98	0.83	0.57	0.99	0.99
92	0.57	0.01	0.04	0.03	0.49	0.17	0.90	0.94	0.77	0.41	0.81
91	0.54	0.12	0.14	0.75	0.80	0.89	0.98	1.00	0.95	0.76	0.37
90	0.69	0.05	0.06	0.11	0.26	0.72	0.78	1.00	1.00	0.98	0.71

Table 2: Accuracy of the `BF_baseline` test.

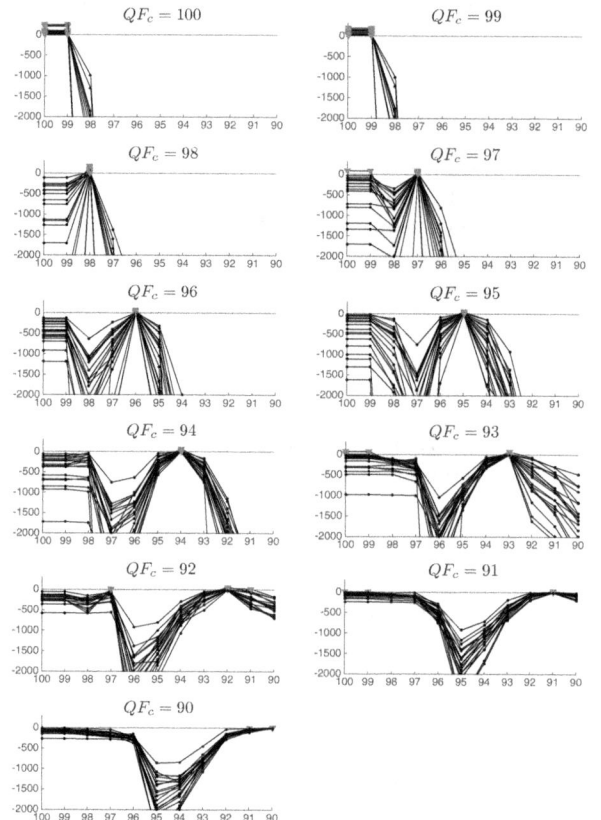

Figure 3: Values of the LLRs among different QF_c for 20 randomly selected UCID images. In each plot the horizontal axis contains the quality factors in $\mathcal{QF}_{range}$. The vertical axis represents the value of LLR, that we report in the interval $[-2000, 200]$ in order to compare its behavior across the different QF_c. Each black line corresponds to an image and each value of the LLR that lies above 0 is marked in red.

compression chain is such that $QF = QF_c$). However, the performance of `BF_baseline` degrades when moving from the scenario in Fig. 2a to the HQ-DC one, as reported in Table 2.

We notice that, although the accuracy for **DDC** is generally high when $QF_p < QF_c$ (the upper triangle of the table), we have a substantial misclassification for **SC**. By exploring the results more closely, we obtain that the Benford–Fourier analysis for images in **SC** generally leads to values of LLR higher than 0 when the alternative hypothesis is given by $[QF_c, QF_c]$. This can be observed in Fig. 3, where we report the values of the different LLRs yielded by the quality factors in $\mathcal{QF}_{range}$ for single compressed images.

Moreover, we have high values of the LLR when the primary quality factor tested is high or close to QF_c, even for lower current quality factors. The former phenomenon is due to the small steps used in the primary quantization. The latter one is caused by the fact that the quantization tables of QF_c and the one tested might share the very same quantization steps for all or some of the DCT frequencies used in the computation of the LLR, thus decreasing the distinguishability of the two hypotheses. For instance, the quantization table of 99 is equal to 1 up to the 37-th frequency and it fully coincides with the one of 100 at the DCT frequencies used for the computation of the LLR. Thus, when analyzing a JPEG image with $QF_c = 100$, the hypothesis $[99, 100]$ will yield the very same LLR as $[100, 100]$. This likely causes misclassification.

In order to cope with this issue, we propose to adaptively select the set F according to the binary hypothesis test, i.e., choosing the first 9 DCT frequencies in zigzag order among the ones that actually have different primary quantization steps. In the case of $[NC, 100]$ vs $[99, 100]$, the algorithm will choose the frequencies $\{37, 38, 41, 45, 46, 47, 48, 49\}$, where quantization steps for 99 are equal to 2. This implicitly forces to exclude the hypothesis $[QF_c, QF_c]$ from the pool of alternative ones (as no suitable DCT frequencies would be identified) and to set $\mathcal{QF}_{range} = \{90, 91, \ldots, 100\} \setminus QF_c$. By this, we reduce the misclassification for single compressed images while being aware that the possibility of identical double compression needs to be assessed. In other words, we can design a new BF test, that we will denote as `BF_adaptive`, that has two possible outcomes: the image belongs either to the union **SC** $\cup$ **IDC** (LLR is below 0 for every hypothesis) or to **DDC** (at least one hypothesis has a LLR higher than 0).

We report in Fig. 4 an example of the different values of LLR obtained with the two different tests, where we can notice the benefit of the frequency selection. Moreover, the accuracy results of this approach are reported in Table 3. They show that the accuracy for **DDC** is unaltered with respect to the baseline approach. Misclassification for **SC** is now reduced, although it is no longer distinguished from **IDC** (for this reason the accuracy on **IDC** is also very high). On the other hand, the lower triangle of the table (especially when $QF_p > 95$) remains an issue.

Thus, we can conclude that the Benford–Fourier analysis with adaptive selection of the DCT frequencies is suitable to detect non-identical double compression and is particularly accurate when $QF_p < QF_c$ or $QF_p \leq 95$. This suggests that other techniques can be used to extend the analysis to the detection of identical recompression.

$$QF_c = 95, QF_p = 94$$

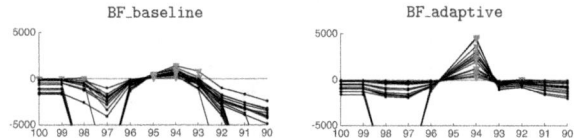

Figure 4: Effect of the adaptive DCT selection on the computation of LLR in case of a double compressed image with $QF_p = 94$ (for the `BF_adaptive` test the LLR for $[QF_c, QF_c]$ is not available).

NC	100	99	98	97	96	95	94	93	92	91	90
100	1.00	1.00	0.99	1.00	1.00	1.00	1.00	1.00	1.00	1.00	1.00
99	0.95	0.13	0.96	1.00	1.00	1.00	1.00	1.00	1.00	1.00	1.00
98	0.94	0.14	0.18	0.94	1.00	1.00	1.00	1.00	1.00	1.00	1.00
97	0.91	0.17	0.22	0.79	0.91	1.00	1.00	1.00	1.00	1.00	1.00
96	0.94	0.11	0.12	0.47	0.88	0.95	1.00	1.00	1.00	1.00	1.00
95	0.92	0.13	0.16	0.36	0.85	0.95	0.93	0.99	1.00	1.00	1.00
94	0.95	0.15	0.18	0.20	0.20	0.98	0.99	0.94	0.99	1.00	1.00
93	0.93	0.16	0.19	0.35	0.32	0.96	0.99	0.99	0.93	0.99	1.00
92	0.94	0.15	0.20	0.24	0.23	0.53	0.96	0.99	0.99	0.94	0.99
91	0.91	0.16	0.18	0.69	0.79	0.83	0.99	1.00	1.00	0.99	0.90	1.00
90	0.93	0.14	0.19	0.20	0.38	0.44	0.94	1.00	1.00	1.00	0.99	0.93

Table 3: Accuracy of the `BF_adaptive` test

4.3 Block convergence

We compute for each UCID image the ratio r as in Equation (3), by recompressing the image with the current quality factor QF_c. Then, we used the 600 UCID images discarded in the Benford–Fourier analysis for fitting theoretical models, while the remaining ones are used for evaluating the different tests designed (i.e., the results in the tables refer to the very same images for both methods).

As a first approach, we adopt a maximum likelihood test as proposed in [3], which searches among the pool of potential primary quality factors $\mathcal{QF}_{range} = \{90, 91, \ldots, 100\}$ and is based on a theoretical approximation of the empirical data distribution. In particular, we fit a beta distribution for each of the 132 different compression chains and design a first discrimination test, that we will indicate as `BC_ML`, consisting of the following steps:

- Given an image with a certain QF_c, the value of r is computed.

- We consider all the beta distribution pdfs $p_{[QF, QF_c]}(\cdot)$ that were previously estimated from every compression chain $[QF, QF_c]$, where QF varies in $\mathcal{QF}_{range} \cup \{NC\}$.

- We evaluate each pdf for r and pick the one that yields the maximum value: if it corresponds to a QF $\in \mathcal{QF}_{range}$ then the image is classified as double compressed, while if it corresponds to the case of NC it is classified as single compressed.

It has to be pointed out that the `BC_ML` is in principle able to distinguish between the three different sets **SC**, **DDC** and **IDC**, as is the `BF_baseline`. However, it also has problems in accurately classifying **SC**, as shown in Table 4.

On the other hand the double compressed images are usually correctly identified, in both the **DDC** and **IDC** set (for $QF_c \geq 94$). We can identify the reason of the misclassification for **SC** by looking at the estimated beta pdfs reported in Fig. 5. Notice that they are strongly overlapping

	NC	100	99	98	97	96	95	94	93	92	91	90
100	0.99	1.00	1.00	1.00	1.00	1.00	1.00	1.00	0.99	0.99	0.99	0.99
99	0.78	0.53	1.00	1.00	1.00	1.00	1.00	0.99	0.99	0.98	0.98	0.98
98	0.75	0.27	0.28	0.99	0.76	0.98	0.96	0.97	0.98	0.98	0.99	0.98
97	0.26	0.75	0.76	0.81	0.99	0.95	0.96	0.99	0.98	0.98	0.99	0.99
96	0.38	0.64	0.63	0.69	0.76	0.98	0.91	0.88	0.88	0.97	0.95	0.94
95	0.01	0.99	0.99	0.99	0.99	0.99	0.98	1.00	0.99	0.99	0.99	1.00
94	0.12	0.90	0.89	0.89	0.89	0.88	0.91	0.97	0.95	0.93	0.92	0.89
93	0.10	0.90	0.90	0.90	0.90	0.89	0.90	0.92	0.89	0.96	0.94	0.94
92	0.17	0.82	0.81	0.82	0.82	0.82	0.83	0.83	0.83	0.33	0.89	0.88
91	0.19	0.80	0.80	0.80	0.80	0.80	0.79	0.81	0.80	0.81	0.16	0.88
90	0.07	0.88	0.89	0.89	0.91	0.90	0.90	0.91	0.89	0.89	0.91	0.18

Table 4: Accuracy of the BC_ML test

	NC	100	99	98	97	96	95	94	93	92	91	90
100	1.00	1.00	1.00	1.00	1.00	1.00	1.00	1.00	1.00	1.00	1.00	1.00
99	1.00	1.00	1.00	1.00	1.00	1.00	1.00	0.99	0.99	0.99	0.98	0.98
98	1.00	1.00	1.00	0.99	1.00	1.00	1.00	0.99	0.99	0.99	1.00	0.99
97	1.00	1.00	1.00	1.00	0.98	1.00	1.00	1.00	1.00	1.00	1.00	1.00
96	1.00	1.00	1.00	1.00	1.00	0.97	1.00	1.00	1.00	1.00	1.00	1.00
95	1.00	1.00	1.00	1.00	1.00	1.00	0.96	1.00	1.00	1.00	1.00	1.00
94	1.00	1.00	1.00	1.00	1.00	1.00	1.00	0.96	1.00	1.00	1.00	1.00
93	0.75	0.72	0.72	0.71	0.69	0.77	0.70	0.67	0.96	0.51	0.59	0.61
92	0.03	0.03	0.03	0.02	0.03	0.02	0.03	0.02	0.01	0.99	0.01	0.01
91	0.02	0.02	0.02	0.02	0.02	0.02	0.02	0.02	0.02	0.01	0.99	0.00
90	0.02	0.02	0.02	0.02	0.02	0.02	0.02	0.02	0.02	0.01	0.01	0.99

Table 5: Accuracy of the BC_threshold test with $t = t_1$

	NC	100	99	98	97	96	95	94	93	92	91	90
100	0.99	1.00	0.00	0.00	0.00	0.00	0.00	0.00	0.00	0.00	0.00	0.00
99	0.98	0.96	1.00	0.00	0.00	0.00	0.00	0.00	0.00	0.00	0.00	0.00
98	0.98	0.98	0.98	1.00	0.72	0.16	0.17	0.16	0.11	0.10	0.05	0.09
97	0.99	0.99	0.99	0.97	1.00	0.78	0.57	0.29	0.35	0.27	0.23	0.22
96	1.00	1.00	1.00	0.99	0.98	1.00	0.83	0.90	0.75	0.26	0.50	0.53
95	1.00	1.00	1.00	1.00	1.00	1.00	1.00	0.88	0.95	0.96	0.95	0.77
94	1.00	1.00	1.00	1.00	1.00	1.00	1.00	0.99	0.97	1.00	1.00	1.00
93	1.00	1.00	1.00	1.00	1.00	1.00	1.00	1.00	0.85	1.00	1.00	1.00
92	1.00	1.00	1.00	1.00	1.00	1.00	1.00	1.00	1.00	0.20	1.00	1.00
91	1.00	1.00	1.00	1.00	1.00	1.00	1.00	1.00	1.00	1.00	0.16	1.00
90	1.00	1.00	1.00	1.00	1.00	1.00	1.00	1.00	1.00	1.00	1.00	0.11

Table 6: Accuracy of the BC_threshold test with $t = t_2$

in the cases of single compression and double compression with $QF_p > QF_c$.

Also in light of the results obtained in Section 4.2, this suggests to reformulate the test with the goal of correctly distinguishing **SC** and **IDC**. In this case, the fitted distribution is clearly separated from the other ones (at least for $QF_c \geq 94$) and represents a relevant open issue for the Benford–Fourier analysis. Moreover, Figure 5 also indicates that for $QF_c \leq 93$ almost all of the blocks are already stable. Thus, we would not gain any information by recompressing the image multiple times and get the whole convergence path, as suggested in [3].

Then, we can design a simple threshold-based test (indicated as BC_threshold) on r such that an image is classified as belonging to **SC** $\cup$ **DDC** if $r \leq t$, or to **IDC** otherwise. The choice of the threshold t can be performed according to different criteria related to the application scenario. As an example, we report in Table 5 and 6 the results obtained by fixing the threshold for each QF_c in two different ways:

- t_1 is such that $\int_0^{t_1} p_{[QF_c, QF_c]}(r)dr = 0.01$ (we target 99% accuracy on **IDC**),

- t_2 is such that $\int_{t_2}^1 p_{[NC, QF_c]}(r)dr = 0.01$ (we target 99% accuracy on **SC**.

In practice, we have that both thresholds yield good accu-

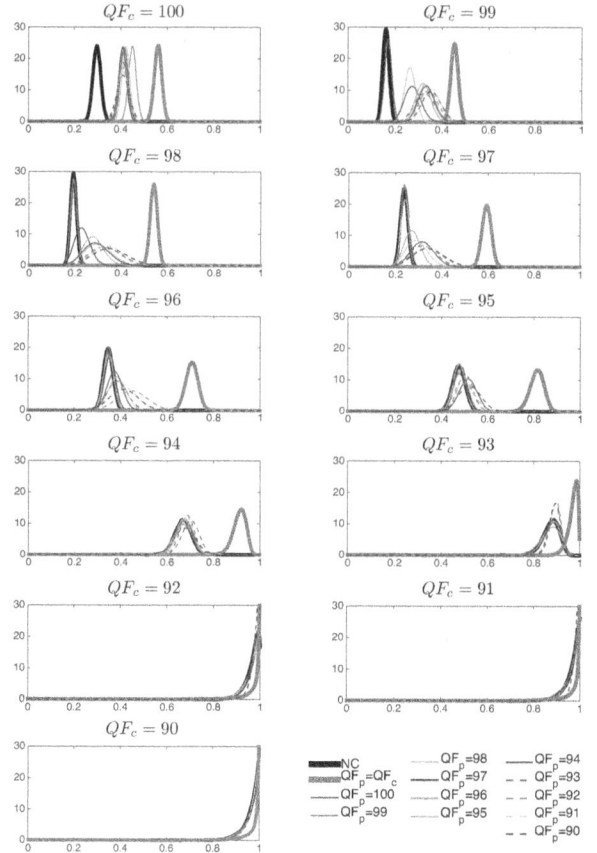

Figure 5: Beta distributions of r fitted for different QF_c and QF_p. In each plot the black bold line represents the single compression case with the corresponding QF_c, while the red bold line represents the identical double compression $[QF_c, QF_c]$; other previous quality factors are reported in the legend.

racies for **IDC** when $QF_c \geq 94$ (as it can be expected from Fig. 5), while if $QF_c \leq 93$ we have misclassification either for **SC** and **DDC** (with $t = t_1$) or **IDC** (with $t = t_2$). Then, we can consider the threshold-based approach on block convergence ratio as accurate for the discrimination of single compressed and identically recompressed images when quality factors are ≥ 94.

5. COMBINED APPROACH

In light of the results from Section 4, we can notice that the pros and cons of the two techniques are mostly complementary, thus suggesting the development of a combined approach for coping with the HQ-DC scenario. In particular, results from the previous section show that the BF_adaptive test distinguishes with good accuracy images in **SC** $\cup$ **IDC** from images in **DDC** (with misclassification cases for $QF_p > QF_c$); on the other hand, the BC_threshold correctly distinguishes images in **SC** $\cup$ **DDC** from images in **IDC** (with misclassification cases for $QF_c \leq 93$).

The goal is to design a classification test for high quality JPEG images that is able to correctly assign an image to one of the three classes (**SC**, **DDC** or **IDC**) by relying on the knowledge of LLR_m (the maximum LLR value obtained from the Benford–Fourier analysis by excluding QF_c) and r,

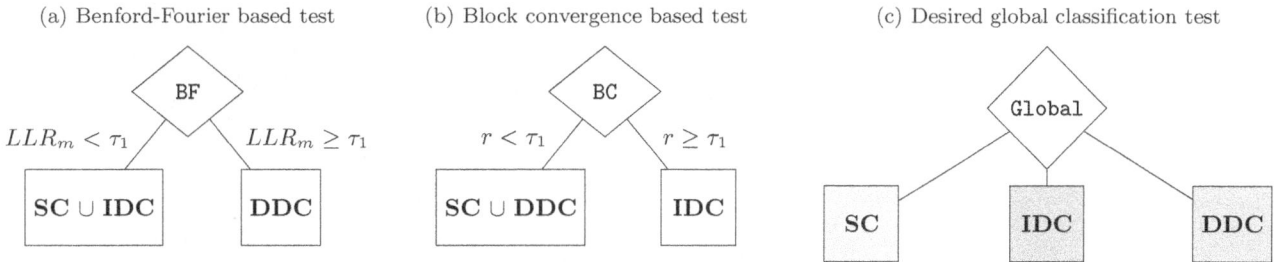

| (a) Benford-Fourier based test | (b) Block convergence based test | (c) Desired global classification test |

Figure 6: Decision trees for different tests.

the ratio of stable blocks after recompressing with QF_c.

This task can be accomplished by means of decision tree induction theory [2, 14], which allows us to determine decision rules on the pair $(LLR_m, r) \in \mathbb{R} \times [0, 1]$ obtained from the analyzed image.

5.1 Decision tree induction

The decision tree (DT) is one of the most used ways to represent a classification test, which is expressed as a recursive partitioning of the instance space (in our case $\mathbb{R} \times [0, 1]$). The problem of building (or *inducing*) a tree starting from a set of labeled cases (i.e., a set of attribute tuples and corresponding classes) has been extensively studied in the literature [2], providing a number of effective and efficient solutions. A tree is composed by a number of nodes, each of them related to a specific attribute thresholding operation. Nodes that are followed by a subtree are called internal nodes. Otherwise, they are called leaves and they represent the fact that a decision has been reached (i.e, the analyzed attribute tuple has been assigned to a class and no further thresholding is performed). In our case every attribute tuple is a pair (LLR_m, r), while the possible classes are **SC**, **DDC** or **IDC**.

In our visual representations of the trees, we will indicate internal nodes as diamonds containing the name of the test used (i.e., BF for Benford–Fourier and BC for block convergence analysis), while leaves are denoted with squares. We number each internal node in top-bottom/left-right order and we denoted as τ_i the threshold used in the i-th internal node. As an example, in Fig. 6 we represent the classification tests used in Section 4, and the one that we want to design. Please, note that the global test in Fig. 6c discriminates between the three different classes and the accuracy values in the following tables will be computed accordingly, i.e., reporting in each cell the percentage of images that have been correctly assigned to **SC**, **IDC** or **DDC**.

The induction process generally consists of a *growing* phase, where the tree is developed according to greedy algorithms, and a *pruning* phase, where the tree is further reduced by replacing a subtree with a decision leaf [14]. All these operations pursue the goal of maximizing accuracy on a given training set (a set of samples for which both the attributes and the corresponding classes are known) while minimizing the complexity of the tree, and are performed according to certain criteria and metrics. The result is a list of sequential decision rules that indicates how to optimally threshold the values LLR_m and r, and in which order. In the following, DT induction is used to derive accurate classification tests starting from a number of labeled training images.

It is worth pointing out that, differently from other kind of classifiers, decision trees are easy to interpret and represent. Moreover, their complexity can be controlled in several ways, like fixing a maximum number of nodes or a minimum number of leaves. This results in a classification test combining multiple attributes that can be easily conveyed and explained.

5.2 Experimental set-up

In our test, we consider the 738 UCID images used in the previous section and, additionally, 500 DRESDEN images. For both datasets a number of images has been randomly chosen for the training set of the DT (200 and 100 images, respectively), while the remaining ones are used for testing.

Among the existing toolboxes available for the DT induction, we used the `fitctree` MatLab function contained in the Statistics and Machine Learning Toolbox. We used the default options, with the exception of the prior probability of each class, that we explicitly set uniform. In other words, we consider as equally probable images in **SC**, **DDC** and **IDC**.

Moreover, in each experiment we both determine a *full* DT (i.e., the one that is built in the growing phase) and a *pruned* one, obtained by forcing the algorithm to reduce the tree until it contains less than 8 nodes, in order to have a simplified version.

5.3 Overall decision tree

We first try to build a DT that can be applied to a high quality image regardless of its current quality factor. In this case, the training set is composed of each training image processed according to the 132 different quantization chains, i.e., by using all the quality factors.

The full DTs obtained are quite complex for both datasets, presenting 3137 and 1395 nodes for UCID and DRESDEN datasets, respectively. They are quite accurate on the training set, while the performance strongly degrades when moving to the testing set (see Tables 11, 12, 13 and 14 in Appendix A.1). This suggests that the algorithm is forced to create a high number of nodes to cope with the specificity of the training set, but it is sensitive to the images it contains. In other words, it suffers from overfitting.

On the other hand, it is worth noticing that the pruned DTs obtained (reported in Fig. 7) have the same structure for both datasets (i.e., using BF analysis first to identify **DDC** images and then employ block convergence to distinguish between **SC** and **IDC**), thus differing only in the thresholds used.

Moreover, by observing the accuracies (reported in Tables 7 and 8) we can notice that the pruned versions achieve good results both in the training and testing set when QF_c is high,

(a) Training set

Table 7 (a) Training set — UCID

NC	100	99	98	97	96	95	94	93	92	91	90
100	1.00	1.00	0.99	1.00	1.00	1.00	1.00	1.00	1.00	1.00	1.00	1.00
99	0.97	0.10	0.97	1.00	1.00	1.00	1.00	1.00	1.00	1.00	1.00	1.00
98	0.96	0.11	0.15	0.95	1.00	1.00	1.00	1.00	1.00	1.00	1.00	1.00
97	0.95	0.12	0.17	0.69	0.95	1.00	1.00	1.00	1.00	1.00	1.00	1.00
96	0.99	0.04	0.03	0.39	0.79	0.99	0.98	1.00	1.00	1.00	1.00	1.00
95	0.10	0.06	0.06	0.15	0.76	0.91	0.98	0.98	0.99	1.00	1.00	1.00
94	0.01	0.02	0.03	0.04	0.04	0.95	0.99	0.99	0.98	0.99	1.00	0.99
93	0.01	0.01	0.01	0.07	0.12	0.91	0.98	0.98	1.00	0.96	0.98	0.99
92	0.00	0.01	0.01	0.02	0.01	0.35	0.91	0.96	0.97	1.00	0.95	0.99
91	0.00	0.01	0.03	0.43	0.56	0.69	0.97	1.00	1.00	0.96	0.99	0.98
90	0.01	0.00	0.01	0.01	0.06	0.21	0.81	1.00	0.99	0.98	0.93	1.00

Table 7 (b) Testing set — UCID

NC	100	99	98	97	96	95	94	93	92	91	90
100	1.00	1.00	0.99	1.00	1.00	1.00	1.00	1.00	1.00	1.00	1.00	1.00
99	0.95	0.13	0.95	1.00	1.00	1.00	1.00	1.00	1.00	1.00	1.00	1.00
98	0.95	0.13	0.16	0.96	1.00	1.00	1.00	1.00	1.00	1.00	1.00	1.00
97	0.94	0.11	0.16	0.83	0.94	1.00	1.00	1.00	1.00	1.00	1.00	1.00
96	0.98	0.04	0.07	0.41	0.90	0.98	1.00	1.00	1.00	1.00	1.00	1.00
95	0.01	0.03	0.04	0.17	0.87	0.95	0.99	0.99	1.00	1.00	1.00	1.00
94	0.00	0.00	0.02	0.04	0.03	0.98	0.98	1.00	0.97	1.00	1.00	1.00
93	0.00	0.01	0.01	0.15	0.16	0.96	0.99	0.96	0.99	0.96	0.98	1.00
92	0.00	0.01	0.01	0.02	0.03	0.45	0.95	0.97	0.95	1.00	0.96	1.00
91	0.00	0.00	0.01	0.48	0.68	0.83	1.00	1.00	0.99	0.92	1.00	0.95
90	0.00	0.00	0.00	0.01	0.09	0.28	0.85	1.00	1.00	0.97	0.90	1.00

Table 7: Accuracies of overall pruned DT for UCID dataset

Table 8 (a) Training set — DRESDEN

NC	100	99	98	97	96	95	94	93	92	91	90
100	1.00	1.00	0.92	1.00	1.00	1.00	1.00	1.00	1.00	1.00	1.00	1.00
99	1.00	0.00	1.00	1.00	1.00	1.00	1.00	1.00	1.00	1.00	1.00	1.00
98	0.99	0.00	0.00	1.00	1.00	1.00	1.00	1.00	1.00	1.00	1.00	1.00
97	1.00	0.00	0.00	0.20	1.00	1.00	1.00	1.00	1.00	1.00	1.00	1.00
96	1.00	0.00	0.00	0.03	0.36	1.00	1.00	1.00	1.00	1.00	1.00	1.00
95	0.00	0.00	0.00	0.03	0.24	0.86	1.00	1.00	1.00	1.00	1.00	1.00
94	0.00	0.00	0.00	0.00	0.00	0.87	1.00	1.00	1.00	1.00	1.00	1.00
93	0.00	0.01	0.01	0.01	0.01	0.66	0.96	1.00	1.00	1.00	1.00	1.00
92	0.00	0.01	0.01	0.01	0.01	0.03	0.83	0.99	1.00	1.00	1.00	1.00
91	0.00	0.01	0.01	0.11	0.14	0.18	0.88	1.00	1.00	1.00	1.00	1.00
90	0.00	0.01	0.01	0.02	0.02	0.02	0.89	0.99	1.00	1.00	1.00	1.00

Table 8 (b) Testing set — DRESDEN

NC	100	99	98	97	96	95	94	93	92	91	90
100	1.00	1.00	0.91	1.00	1.00	1.00	1.00	1.00	1.00	1.00	1.00	1.00
99	1.00	0.00	1.00	1.00	1.00	1.00	1.00	1.00	1.00	1.00	1.00	1.00
98	1.00	0.00	0.00	1.00	1.00	1.00	1.00	1.00	1.00	1.00	1.00	1.00
97	1.00	0.00	0.00	0.23	1.00	1.00	1.00	1.00	1.00	1.00	1.00	1.00
96	0.97	0.00	0.00	0.02	0.34	1.00	1.00	1.00	1.00	1.00	1.00	1.00
95	0.00	0.00	0.00	0.03	0.20	0.85	1.00	1.00	1.00	1.00	1.00	1.00
94	0.00	0.00	0.01	0.01	0.01	0.89	1.00	1.00	1.00	1.00	1.00	1.00
93	0.00	0.01	0.02	0.02	0.02	0.62	0.96	1.00	0.99	1.00	1.00	1.00
92	0.00	0.02	0.02	0.02	0.02	0.03	0.84	0.99	1.00	0.99	1.00	1.00
91	0.00	0.02	0.02	0.12	0.18	0.16	0.90	0.99	1.00	1.00	1.00	1.00
90	0.00	0.02	0.03	0.04	0.05	0.05	0.91	0.98	1.00	1.00	1.00	1.00

Table 8: Accuracies of overall pruned DT for DRESDEN dataset

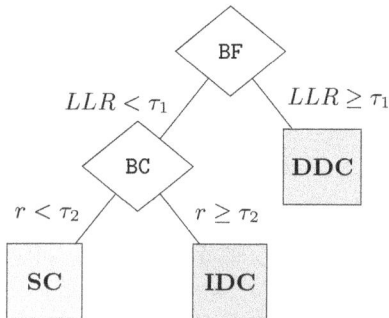

Figure 7: Overall best pruned decision tree

whereas the misclassification for **SC** is noticeably higher for lower values of QF_c in both datasets.

In line with what we observed in Section 4, these results confirm that the thresholds to be used differ when varying QF_c due to the non-homogeneous behavior of the attributes, especially for r.

5.4 QF_c-specific decision trees

Given the results obtained when using the same thresholds for every image, a reasonable solution would be to differentiate the classification test according to the current quality factor, i.e., performing the tree induction process separately for different QF_c. Indeed, it is worth observing that the current quality factor is known, thus such approach is feasible in a realistic forensic scenario.

We repeat the DT building for the 11 different values of QF_c, where the training set is now composed only of images compressed once or twice with QF_c as last quality factor. On the one hand, we have that the full trees have very good

accuracies on the training sets but the performance degrades when applied to the testing sets, as shown in Tables 15, 16, 17 and 18 in Appendix A.2.

On the other hand, pruned trees lead to stable results for training and testing set for both datasets (Tables 9 and 10). For the sake of brevity, we only report the pruned trees obtained from the UCID dataset (Fig. 8), together with the different thresholds determined in each case. It is interesting to observe how the structure of tree varies among the quality factors, allowing either two or three levels of depth and splitting the nodes in different ways. For instance, we can observe that the first attribute chosen by the algorithm is LLR_m for $QF_c \leq 92$, while it switches to r for higher QF_c for which the block convergence is more accurate.

The results in Tables 9 and 10 indicate that the pruned DTs determined separately for different values of QF_c yield accurate results. Note that in Tables 3, 5 and 6 the accuracies are computed with respect to the classes discriminated in the two single tests (**SC** ∪ **IDC** vs **DDC** for BF and **SC** ∪ **DDC** vs **IDC** for BC), while the QF_c-specific DTs achieve good accuracy for all the three possible classes. Thus, we can conclude that the capability of BF and BC of correctly identifying **DDC** and **IDC**, respectively, is generally maintained, while the global misclassification on the three classes is highly reduced.

In light of these results, we consider the QF_c-specific decision trees as a possible effective solution for the distinction of images in **SC**, **DDC** and **IDC** in the HQ-DC scenario.

6. CONCLUSIONS

We have addressed the single vs double compression discrimination problem for grayscale JPEG images compressed with high nearly-identical quality factors (≥ 90). After analyzing the performance of the Benford–Fourier analysis in the DCT domain and the block convergence analysis in the

(a) Decision tree for $QF_c \in \{100, 98\}$

(b) Decision tree for $QF_c \in \{99, 97, 96\}$

(c) Decision tree for $QF_c \in \{95, 93\}$

(d) Decision tree for $QF_c = 94$

(e) Decision tree for $QF_c \in \{92, 91, 90\}$

(f) Values of τ_1, τ_2, τ_3 for all DTs

QF	τ_1	τ_2	τ_3
100	0.52	324.13	0.34
99	0.41	749.80	5369.97
98	0.47	316.85	0.24
97	0.47	192.85	5088.69
96	0.54	27.56	5033.25
95	0.61	38.13	–
94	0.74	38.46	0.71
93	0.92	19.93	–
92	19.35	0.99	–
91	33.66	0.99	–
90	22.79	0.99	–

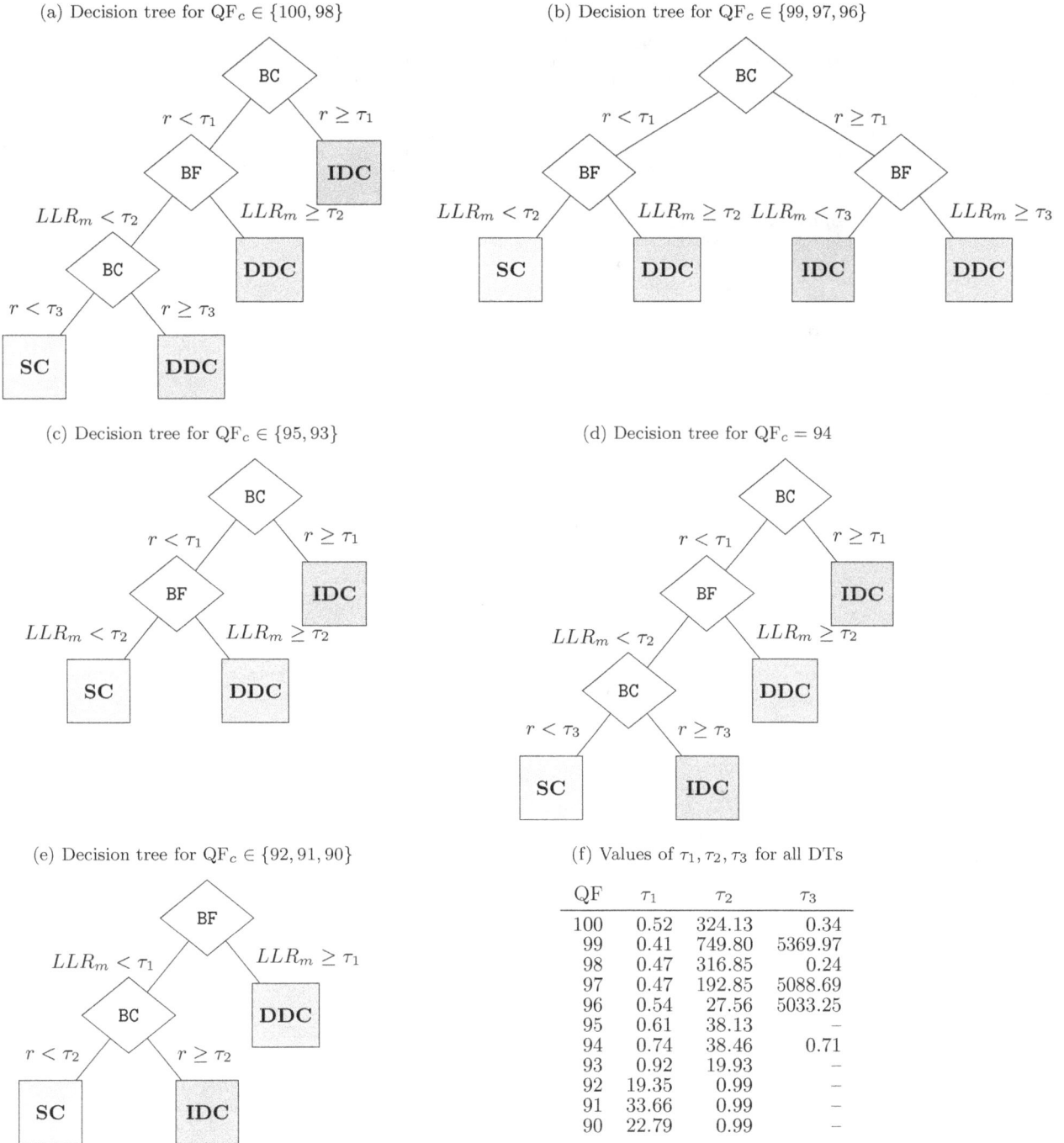

Figure 8: Pruned decision trees and thresholds for different quality factors for the UCID dataset

pixel domain, we have studied the problem of combining the two techniques to obtain an accurate discrimination between single compressed images (**SC**), double compressed images with a different quality factor (**DDC**) and images recompressed with the same quality factor (**IDC**).

The final set of detectors on both the datasets considered proves to be very accurate for **SC** images (accuracy $\geq$ 97.5%), **DDC** images with $QF_p < QF_c$ (accuracy $\geq$ 99.0%) and **IDC** with $QF_c \geq 93$ (accuracy $\geq$ 99.5%).

The results obtained suggest a number of open issues and directions for future work. The first evident space of im-

provement is represented by the low detection rate of certain compression chains. For instance, the **DDC** cases where $QF_p > QF_c$ are often misclassified when $QF_p \geq 96$. The same happens for the **IDC** images when $QF_c \leq 92$. Indeed, none of the methods considered is able to correctly identify them and the combined global test does not achieve good performance in those cases, although it leads to improvements with respect to the two separate techniques. As a future perspective, additional methods could be used to cope with these specific issues and incorporated in the final decision tree. For instance, the approaches in [6] or [16] could

(a) Training set.

NC	100	99	98	97	96	95	94	93	92	91	90
100	1.00	1.00	1.00	1.00	1.00	1.00	1.00	1.00	1.00	1.00	1.00
99	1.00	0.04	1.00	0.99	1.00	1.00	1.00	1.00	1.00	1.00	1.00
98	1.00	0.04	0.09	1.00	1.00	1.00	1.00	1.00	1.00	1.00	0.99
97	1.00	0.01	0.03	0.68	0.99	0.98	1.00	1.00	1.00	1.00	1.00
96	0.99	0.04	0.04	0.40	0.80	0.99	0.98	1.00	1.00	1.00	1.00
95	0.99	0.05	0.05	0.15	0.76	0.91	0.99	0.97	0.98	0.99	1.00	0.99
94	1.00	0.02	0.02	0.02	0.04	0.95	0.99	0.98	0.91	0.98	0.99	0.99
93	1.00	0.02	0.06	0.14	0.17	0.93	0.98	0.99	0.86	0.97	0.98	1.00
92	0.99	0.03	0.06	0.07	0.06	0.39	0.92	0.97	0.98	0.36	0.97	1.00
91	0.98	0.01	0.03	0.44	0.56	0.69	0.97	1.00	1.00	0.96	0.28	0.98
90	1.00	0.01	0.02	0.03	0.10	0.24	0.85	1.00	0.99	1.00	0.95	0.23

(b) Testing set.

NC	100	99	98	97	96	95	94	93	92	91	90
100	1.00	1.00	1.00	1.00	1.00	1.00	1.00	1.00	0.99	1.00	1.00	1.00
99	0.99	0.08	1.00	1.00	1.00	1.00	1.00	1.00	1.00	1.00	1.00
98	0.99	0.02	0.06	1.00	1.00	1.00	1.00	1.00	0.99	0.99	0.99	0.98
97	1.00	0.01	0.01	0.79	1.00	1.00	1.00	1.00	1.00	1.00	0.99	1.00
96	0.98	0.06	0.08	0.42	0.91	1.00	0.99	1.00	1.00	1.00	1.00	1.00
95	0.99	0.03	0.04	0.15	0.86	0.95	1.00	0.98	1.00	1.00	1.00	1.00
94	1.00	0.00	0.01	0.02	0.03	0.98	0.98	1.00	0.92	1.00	1.00	1.00
93	0.99	0.03	0.04	0.20	0.20	0.95	0.99	0.98	0.96	0.98	0.99	1.00
92	0.99	0.02	0.04	0.05	0.07	0.49	0.95	0.99	0.97	0.40	0.97	1.00
91	0.99	0.00	0.01	0.48	0.68	0.83	1.00	1.00	0.99	0.92	0.28	0.96
90	0.99	0.01	0.01	0.01	0.14	0.32	0.88	1.00	1.00	0.99	0.94	0.26

Table 9: Accuracies of QF_c-specific pruned DT for UCID dataset.

(a) Training set.

NC	100	99	98	97	96	95	94	93	92	91	90
100	1.00	1.00	1.00	1.00	1.00	1.00	1.00	1.00	1.00	1.00	1.00
99	1.00	0.03	1.00	1.00	1.00	1.00	1.00	1.00	1.00	1.00	1.00
98	1.00	0.00	0.01	1.00	0.99	1.00	1.00	1.00	1.00	1.00	1.00
97	0.96	0.01	0.04	0.79	1.00	1.00	1.00	1.00	1.00	0.99	0.99	0.98
96	1.00	0.02	0.01	0.07	0.88	1.00	1.00	1.00	1.00	1.00	1.00
95	0.98	0.06	0.10	0.30	0.47	0.93	1.00	1.00	1.00	1.00	1.00
94	1.00	0.01	0.01	0.01	0.01	0.87	1.00	1.00	1.00	1.00	1.00
93	0.97	0.10	0.11	0.16	0.13	0.78	0.97	1.00	1.00	1.00	1.00
92	0.99	0.04	0.07	0.07	0.07	0.08	0.89	0.99	1.00	0.87	0.73	0.99
91	1.00	0.01	0.01	0.11	0.14	0.18	0.88	1.00	1.00	1.00	0.78	0.88
90	0.99	0.04	0.08	0.08	0.10	0.11	0.90	0.99	1.00	1.00	1.00	0.76

(b) Testing set.

NC	100	99	98	97	96	95	94	93	92	91	90
100	1.00	0.99	1.00	1.00	1.00	1.00	1.00	1.00	1.00	1.00	1.00
99	0.99	0.02	0.99	1.00	1.00	1.00	1.00	1.00	1.00	1.00	1.00
98	1.00	0.00	0.01	1.00	0.98	1.00	1.00	1.00	1.00	1.00	1.00
97	0.94	0.04	0.05	0.77	1.00	1.00	1.00	1.00	1.00	1.00	1.00	0.99
96	0.97	0.04	0.04	0.06	0.85	1.00	0.99	0.99	0.99	1.00	0.99	0.99
95	0.97	0.06	0.07	0.28	0.36	0.95	1.00	1.00	1.00	1.00	1.00
94	0.99	0.01	0.02	0.02	0.02	0.89	1.00	0.99	1.00	1.00	1.00	1.00
93	0.94	0.11	0.12	0.14	0.13	0.71	0.97	1.00	0.99	1.00	1.00	1.00
92	0.96	0.07	0.07	0.09	0.08	0.09	0.86	0.99	1.00	0.89	0.68	0.98
91	1.00	0.02	0.02	0.12	0.18	0.16	0.90	0.99	1.00	1.00	0.78	0.85
90	0.97	0.07	0.09	0.10	0.11	0.11	0.92	0.98	1.00	0.99	0.99	0.75

Table 10: Accuracies of QF_c-specific pruned DT for DRESDEN dataset.

be employed for identifying **IDC** with $QF_c \leq 92$. Moreover, a limitation of the proposed approach is that it does not explicitly incorporate the knowledge of the size of the image under investigation.

Finally, the process of decision tree induction is currently performed by means of standard tools. A potential improvement would be to design induction tools specifically tailored to the forensic scenario considered, by customizing the criteria that rule the construction of the tree.

7. ACKNOWLEDGMENTS

The first author would like to thank the BIT PhD School (Bolzano-Innsbruck-Trento Joint School for Information Technology) for supporting this joint research.

8. REFERENCES

[1] T. Bianchi, A. Piva, and F. Pérez-González. Near optimal detection of quantized signals and application to JPEG forensics. In *IEEE Workshop on Informations Forensics and Security (WIFS)*, 2013.

[2] L. Breslow and D. Aha. Simplifying decision trees: A survey. *The Knowledge Engineering Review*, 12(1):1–40, 1997.

[3] M. Carnein, P. Schöttle, and R. Böhme. Forensics of high-quality JPEG images with color subsampling. In *IEEE Workshop on Informations Forensics and Security (WIFS)*, 2015.

[4] Y. Chen and C. Hsu. Detecting recompression of JPEG images via periodicity analysis of compression artifacts for tampering detection. *IEEE Transactions on Information Forensics and Security*, 6, n. 2:396–406, 2011.

[5] T. Gloe and R. Boehme. The Dresden image database for benchmarking digital image forensics. In *ACM Symposium on Applied Computing*, volume 2, pages 1585–1591, 2010.

[6] F. Huang, J. Huang, and Y. Shi. Detecting double JPEG compression with the same quantization matrix. *IEEE Transactions on Information Forensics and Security*, 5(4):848–856, 2010.

[7] S.-Y. Lai and R. Böhme. Block convergence in repeated transform coding: JPEG-100 forensics, carbon dating, and tamper detection. In *IEEE International Conference on Acoustics, Speech, and Signal Processing (ICASSP)*, pages 3028–3032, 2013.

[8] B. Li, Y. Shi, and J. Huang. Detecting doubly compressed JPEG images by using mode based first digit features. In *IEEE Workshop on Multimedia Signal Processing (MMSP)*, pages 730–735, 2008.

[9] S. Milani, M. Tagliasacchi, and S. Tubaro. Discriminating multiple JPEG compression using first digit features. In *IEEE International Conference on Acoustics, Speech, and Signal Processing (ICASSP)*, pages 25–30, 2012.

[10] C. Pasquini, G. Boato, and F. Pérez-González. Multiple JPEG compression detection by means of Benford-Fourier coefficients. In *IEEE Workshop on Informations Forensics and Security (WIFS)*, pages 113–118, 2014.

[11] C. Pasquini, F. Pérez-González, and G. Boato. A Benford-Fourier JPEG compression detector. In *IEEE International Conference on Image Processing (ICIP)*, pages 5322–5326, 2014.

[12] F. Pérez-González, T. Quach, S. J. Miller, C. Abdallah, and G. Heileman. Application of Benford's law to images. *S. J. Miller, A. Berger and T. Hill (Eds), The Theory and Applications of Benford's law, Princeton University Press*, 2015.

[13] T. Pevný and J. Fridrich. Detection of double-compression in JPEG images for applications in steganography. *IEEE Transactions on Information Forensics and Security*, 3(2):247–258, 2008.

[14] L. Rokach and O. Maimon. Top-down induction of decision trees classifiers - a survey. *IEEE Transactions on Systems, Man, and Cybernetics*, 35(4):476–487, 2005.

[15] G. Schaefer and M. Stich. UCID - An uncompressed colour image database. In *SPIE Storage and Retrieval Methods and Applications to Multimedia*, volume 5307, 2004.

[16] J. Yang, J. Xie, G. Zhu, S. Kwong, and Y. Shi. An effective method for detecting double JPEG compression with the same quantization matrix. *IEEE Transactions on Information Forensics and Security*, 9(11), 2014.

APPENDIX

A. RESULTS FOR FULL DECISION TREES

A.1 Overall full decision tree

NC	100	99	98	97	96	95	94	93	92	91	90
100	1.00	1.00	0.99	1.00	1.00	1.00	1.00	1.00	1.00	1.00	1.00
99	1.00	0.62	0.96	1.00	1.00	1.00	1.00	1.00	1.00	1.00	1.00
98	1.00	0.67	0.69	0.99	1.00	1.00	1.00	1.00	1.00	1.00	1.00
97	1.00	0.64	0.64	0.85	0.99	1.00	1.00	1.00	1.00	1.00	1.00
96	1.00	0.70	0.72	0.79	0.93	0.96	0.99	1.00	1.00	0.99	1.00
95	0.98	0.64	0.63	0.70	0.91	0.96	0.99	0.99	1.00	1.00	1.00
94	0.96	0.59	0.60	0.61	0.64	0.95	0.98	0.94	0.98	0.99	1.00
93	0.95	0.49	0.53	0.59	0.60	0.94	0.98	0.99	0.92	0.98	0.99
92	0.95	0.50	0.53	0.54	0.54	0.69	0.95	0.99	0.99	0.93	0.99
91	0.97	0.49	0.55	0.76	0.83	0.85	0.99	1.00	1.00	1.00	0.95
90	0.94	0.50	0.56	0.55	0.58	0.65	0.92	0.99	0.99	0.99	0.97

Table 11: Training set UCID

NC	100	99	98	97	96	95	94	93	92	91	90
100	0.91	0.95	0.99	1.00	1.00	1.00	1.00	1.00	1.00	1.00	1.00
99	0.70	0.44	0.63	1.00	1.00	1.00	1.00	1.00	1.00	1.00	1.00
98	0.54	0.45	0.46	0.93	1.00	1.00	1.00	1.00	1.00	1.00	1.00
97	0.54	0.49	0.47	0.89	0.86	1.00	1.00	1.00	1.00	1.00	1.00
96	0.45	0.61	0.60	0.75	0.96	0.67	1.00	1.00	1.00	1.00	1.00
95	0.35	0.56	0.58	0.66	0.93	0.94	0.77	0.98	0.99	1.00	1.00
94	0.36	0.48	0.48	0.51	0.49	0.98	0.98	0.57	0.98	1.00	1.00
93	0.39	0.36	0.32	0.46	0.47	0.97	0.99	0.98	0.45	0.99	0.99
92	0.32	0.34	0.40	0.37	0.40	0.64	0.97	0.99	0.98	0.58	0.99
91	0.32	0.34	0.42	0.72	0.84	0.89	1.00	1.00	1.00	0.96	0.56
90	0.33	0.36	0.39	0.43	0.52	0.58	0.94	1.00	1.00	0.99	0.96

Table 12: Testing set UCID

NC	100	99	98	97	96	95	94	93	92	91	90
100	1.00	1.00	0.96	1.00	1.00	1.00	1.00	1.00	1.00	1.00	1.00
99	1.00	0.68	1.00	1.00	1.00	1.00	1.00	1.00	1.00	1.00	1.00
98	0.99	0.68	0.66	1.00	1.00	1.00	1.00	1.00	1.00	1.00	1.00
97	1.00	0.68	0.63	0.82	1.00	1.00	1.00	1.00	1.00	1.00	1.00
96	1.00	0.74	0.78	0.75	0.99	0.99	1.00	1.00	1.00	1.00	1.00
95	0.96	0.71	0.67	0.80	0.79	0.98	1.00	1.00	1.00	1.00	1.00
94	0.99	0.81	0.78	0.81	0.86	0.99	1.00	0.99	1.00	1.00	1.00
93	1.00	0.71	0.75	0.79	0.85	0.94	1.00	1.00	0.94	1.00	1.00
92	0.94	0.66	0.71	0.71	0.70	0.64	0.96	1.00	1.00	1.00	1.00
91	1.00	0.58	0.59	0.69	0.73	0.73	0.93	1.00	1.00	1.00	0.99
90	0.99	0.76	0.77	0.82	0.74	0.75	0.96	0.99	1.00	1.00	1.00

Table 13: Training set DRESDEN

NC	100	99	98	97	96	95	94	93	92	91	90
100	0.93	0.98	0.93	1.00	1.00	1.00	1.00	1.00	1.00	1.00	1.00
99	0.74	0.47	0.93	1.00	1.00	1.00	1.00	1.00	1.00	1.00	1.00
98	0.54	0.54	0.45	0.96	1.00	1.00	1.00	1.00	1.00	1.00	1.00
97	0.56	0.42	0.43	0.68	0.98	1.00	1.00	1.00	1.00	1.00	1.00
96	0.54	0.62	0.64	0.66	0.97	0.97	1.00	1.00	1.00	1.00	1.00
95	0.53	0.49	0.51	0.71	0.76	0.96	0.99	1.00	1.00	1.00	1.00
94	0.43	0.66	0.69	0.67	0.63	0.97	1.00	0.96	1.00	1.00	1.00
93	0.43	0.63	0.67	0.63	0.66	0.91	0.98	1.00	0.51	1.00	1.00
92	0.40	0.45	0.49	0.48	0.49	0.46	0.93	1.00	1.00	0.88	1.00
91	0.42	0.49	0.51	0.55	0.59	0.60	0.93	1.00	1.00	1.00	0.87
90	0.34	0.52	0.54	0.60	0.58	0.58	0.95	0.99	1.00	1.00	1.00

Table 14: Testing set DRESDEN

A.2 QF$_c$-specific full decision trees

NC	100	99	98	97	96	95	94	93	92	91	90
100	1.00	1.00	1.00	1.00	1.00	1.00	1.00	1.00	1.00	1.00	1.00
99	1.00	0.61	1.00	1.00	1.00	1.00	1.00	1.00	1.00	1.00	1.00
98	1.00	0.65	0.66	1.00	1.00	1.00	1.00	1.00	1.00	1.00	1.00
97	1.00	0.63	0.67	0.86	1.00	0.98	1.00	1.00	1.00	1.00	1.00
96	1.00	0.78	0.69	0.82	0.94	1.00	0.99	1.00	1.00	1.00	1.00
95	1.00	0.73	0.73	0.81	0.95	0.98	0.99	1.00	1.00	1.00	1.00
94	1.00	0.77	0.80	0.74	0.79	0.98	1.00	0.99	0.99	0.99	1.00
93	0.98	0.66	0.73	0.74	0.73	0.98	1.00	1.00	0.98	0.98	0.99
92	0.97	0.48	0.61	0.60	0.58	0.75	0.96	0.99	0.98	0.97	0.99
91	0.95	0.47	0.53	0.76	0.79	0.88	0.99	1.00	1.00	0.99	0.94
90	0.95	0.52	0.51	0.68	0.73	0.71	0.96	1.00	1.00	1.00	0.99

Table 15: Training set UCID

NC	100	99	98	97	96	95	94	93	92	91	90
100	1.00	1.00	1.00	1.00	1.00	1.00	1.00	1.00	0.99	1.00	1.00
99	0.77	0.43	1.00	1.00	1.00	1.00	1.00	1.00	1.00	1.00	1.00
98	0.58	0.43	0.47	1.00	1.00	1.00	1.00	1.00	1.00	1.00	1.00
97	0.52	0.49	0.54	0.91	1.00	1.00	1.00	1.00	1.00	1.00	1.00
96	0.41	0.61	0.63	0.74	0.95	1.00	1.00	1.00	1.00	1.00	1.00
95	0.43	0.62	0.64	0.71	0.95	0.98	1.00	0.99	1.00	1.00	1.00
94	0.38	0.64	0.63	0.68	0.64	0.99	0.99	1.00	0.99	1.00	1.00
93	0.42	0.57	0.58	0.65	0.67	0.98	1.00	0.99	0.97	0.99	0.99
92	0.40	0.38	0.44	0.45	0.45	0.69	0.97	1.00	0.98	0.55	0.99
91	0.38	0.32	0.33	0.73	0.80	0.89	1.00	1.00	1.00	0.95	0.56
90	0.30	0.44	0.51	0.50	0.66	0.66	0.96	1.00	1.00	1.00	0.99

Table 16: Testing set UCID

NC	100	99	98	97	96	95	94	93	92	91	90
100	1.00	1.00	1.00	1.00	1.00	1.00	1.00	1.00	1.00	1.00	1.00
99	1.00	0.61	1.00	1.00	1.00	1.00	1.00	1.00	1.00	1.00	1.00
98	1.00	0.51	0.54	1.00	1.00	1.00	1.00	1.00	1.00	1.00	1.00
97	1.00	0.57	0.65	0.88	1.00	1.00	1.00	1.00	1.00	1.00	1.00
96	1.00	0.71	0.76	0.77	0.99	1.00	1.00	1.00	1.00	1.00	1.00
95	1.00	0.78	0.74	0.82	0.91	1.00	1.00	1.00	1.00	1.00	1.00
94	1.00	0.79	0.72	0.83	0.82	0.99	1.00	1.00	1.00	1.00	1.00
93	1.00	0.77	0.78	0.86	0.77	0.96	0.99	1.00	1.00	1.00	1.00
92	1.00	0.75	0.79	0.79	0.79	0.76	0.98	0.99	1.00	0.96	1.00
91	1.00	0.69	0.78	0.79	0.76	0.76	0.97	1.00	1.00	1.00	0.97
90	0.99	0.62	0.71	0.73	0.75	0.73	0.93	0.99	1.00	1.00	1.00

Table 17: Training set DRESDEN

NC	100	99	98	97	96	95	94	93	92	91	90
100	1.00	0.99	1.00	1.00	1.00	1.00	1.00	1.00	1.00	1.00	1.00
99	0.79	0.40	0.99	1.00	1.00	1.00	1.00	1.00	1.00	1.00	1.00
98	0.59	0.43	0.41	1.00	1.00	1.00	1.00	1.00	1.00	1.00	1.00
97	0.57	0.40	0.41	0.84	1.00	1.00	1.00	1.00	1.00	1.00	1.00
96	0.55	0.62	0.63	0.65	0.97	1.00	1.00	1.00	1.00	1.00	1.00
95	0.54	0.55	0.57	0.75	0.81	1.00	1.00	1.00	1.00	1.00	1.00
94	0.51	0.61	0.69	0.72	0.64	0.99	1.00	0.99	1.00	1.00	1.00
93	0.44	0.60	0.65	0.70	0.65	0.89	0.99	1.00	0.99	1.00	1.00
92	0.47	0.56	0.60	0.60	0.62	0.65	0.96	1.00	1.00	0.90	1.00
91	0.41	0.56	0.56	0.57	0.61	0.62	0.94	1.00	1.00	1.00	0.86
90	0.47	0.49	0.52	0.52	0.56	0.54	0.97	0.99	1.00	1.00	1.00

Table 18: Testing set DRESDEN

A Higher Order Analysis of the Joint Capacity of Digital Fingerprinting Codes against the Interleaving Attack

[Extended Abstract]

Hiroki Koga
University of Tsukuba
1-1-1 Tennoudai, Tsukuba, Ibaraki, Japan
koga@iit.tsukuba.ac.jp

Kaoru Itabashi
University of Tsukuba
1-1-1 Tennoudai, Tsukuba, Ibaraki, Japan

ABSTRACT

Digital fingerprinting codes are embedded to licenced digital contents for preventing illegal distribution by colluders. Digital fingerprinting codes are usually required to have the ability to specify a part (or all) of the colluders with high probability who generate a pirated copy. In this paper we evaluate the joint capacity $C(\boldsymbol{p}_{\mathsf{INT}})$ of the digital fingerprinting code against the interleaving attack by c colluders. Quite recently, Laarhoven [14] shows that $C(\boldsymbol{p}_{\mathsf{INT}}) \approx \frac{1.1604}{2c^2 \ln 2}$ for sufficiently large c. However, this formula includes numerical optimization and is not a good approximation of $C(\boldsymbol{p}_{\mathsf{INT}})$ for small values of c. In this paper we obtain two series that yield various upper and lower bounds of $C(\boldsymbol{p}_{\mathsf{INT}})$, respectively, which give fairly well approximation of $C(\boldsymbol{p}_{\mathsf{INT}})$ for a wide range of c. The upper and the lower bounds are obtained by using the Taylor expansion indicated by Furon and Pérez-Freire [8] together with the analysis of the l-th moments of a binomial distribution around its mean for $l \geq 2$. In particular, the lower bounds give approximation of $c^2 C(\boldsymbol{p}_{\mathsf{INT}})$ for various ranges of c.

CCS Concepts

•Security and privacy → Information-theoretic techniques;

Keywords

Digital fingerprinting code, anti-collusion code, interleaving attack, joint capacity.

1. INTRODUCTION

Digital fingerprinting codes are used to prevent illegal distribution of pirated copies of licenced digital contents. When a user purchases a licenced digital content, a content supplier distributes a digital content to the user to which a codeword of a digital fingerprinting code corresponding to the user is embedded. In the framework of digital fingerprinting codes

The 4-th IH & MMSEC June 20–22, 2016, Vigo, Spain

© 2016 ACM. ISBN 978-1-4503-4290-2/16/06. . . $15.00

DOI: http://dx.doi.org/10.1145/2909827.2930788

we consider the existence of malicious colluders who collude to generate a pirated copy. Digital fingerprinting codes are often designed so that all or a part of such colluders can be specified from a pirated copy.

After Boneh and Shaw published a seminal paper [1], digital fingerprinting codes have been studied by various authors. Information-theoretic analyses on the performance of digital fingerprinting codes are given by [2–14]. In particular, [7–9,11–14] treat the digital fingerprinting codes that enable to specify all the colluders with negligible probability. One of the main interests is evaluation of the joint capacity. Here, the joint capacity is defined as the maximum of the mutual information with respect to the distribution that is used for generation of a code. The joint capacity actually means the maximum exponent of the number of users such that all the $c \geq 2$ colluders can be specified with negligible probability. It is known that the joint capacity of binary digital fingerprinting codes is equal to $1/c$ against deterministic attacks such as the AND and the OR attacks [14].

This paper is concerned with the joint capacity $C(\boldsymbol{p}_{\mathsf{INT}})$ of binary digital fingerprinting codes against the interleaving attack of c colluders . For the case where c is sufficiently large, while [8,11,12] show that $C(\boldsymbol{p}_{\mathsf{INT}}) \approx \frac{1}{2c^2 \ln 2}$, [14] shows that $C(\boldsymbol{p}_{\mathsf{INT}}) \approx \frac{1.1604}{2c^2 \ln 2}$. Since numerical evaluation shows that $c^2 C(\boldsymbol{p}_{\mathsf{INT}})$ is very close to $\frac{1.1604}{2 \ln 2} = 0.837$ for all $c \geq 40$, the latter formula seems to be valid. However, the formula in [14] contains the following three problems: (a) the formula does not give a good approximation of $C(\boldsymbol{p}_{\mathsf{INT}})$ for small c, (b) the deviation is based on the unproved result that the argument attaining $C(\boldsymbol{p}_{\mathsf{INT}})$ is $O(\frac{1}{c})$, and (c) numerical optimization is needed to obtain the coefficient 1.1604.

In this paper we obtain a series which gives various lower bounds of $C(\boldsymbol{p}_{\mathsf{INT}})$ which are close to $C(\boldsymbol{p}_{\mathsf{INT}})$ for certain ranges of c. We use the Taylor expansion of the binary entropy that originates from [8] and compute the l-th moments of a binary distribution around its mean for $l \geq 2$. Such l-th moments are obtained from a property of the Bernstein polynomials [15]. Although [11] uses an asymptotic property of the Bernstein polynomials, in this paper we use a certain property of the Bernstein polynomials for finite c more directly. This enables us to analyze higher order terms of $C(\boldsymbol{p}_{\mathsf{INT}})$ with respect to c.

We can also obtain a series that yields upper bounds of $C(\boldsymbol{p}_{\mathsf{INT}})$ from the Taylor expansion. Although this series is similar to the series for the lower bound, the former has the second and the third terms that are of higher orders with respect to c than the latter. As a byproduct, we can characterize the argument that attains $C(\boldsymbol{p}_{\mathsf{INT}})$ with increasing c, though giving a complete proof on the above (b) remains open.

The rest of this paper is organized as follows. In Section 2 we explain a framework of a digital fingerprinting code. Sections 3 and 4 are devoted to development of the lower and the upper bounds of $C(\boldsymbol{p}_{\mathsf{INT}})$. respectively.

2. PROBLEM FORMULATION

In this section we formulate the problem of digital fingerprinting code with introducing notations.

2.1 Generation of a Code

Letting $n \geq 1$ be an arbitrary integer, denote by $\mathcal{U}_n = \{1, 2, \ldots, M_n\}$ a set of users, where M_n means the number of users and is dependent on n. Each user purchases a licence of a digital content from a contents supplier. The contents supplier distributes the digital content to user j to which a codeword $\boldsymbol{X}^{(j)} = X_1^{(j)} X_2^{(j)} \cdots X_n^{(j)}$ is embedded by some digital watermarking scheme, where $X_l^{(j)} \in \mathcal{X}$ for all $1 \leq j \leq M_n$, $1 \leq l \leq n$ and $\mathcal{X} = \{0, 1\}$. In this paper, we assume that for each $1 \leq l \leq n$ and $1 \leq j \leq M_n$ $X_l^{(j)}$ is randomly and independently generated according to the probability distribution satisfying

$$\Pr\{X_l^{(j)} = 1\} = w,$$

where $w \in (0, 1)$ is a positive constant. We call $\mathcal{C}_n = \{\boldsymbol{X}^{(1)}, \boldsymbol{X}^{(2)}, \ldots, \boldsymbol{X}^{(M_n)}\}$ a code.

2.2 Attack by Colluders

We assume the existence of a set of c colluders $\mathcal{K} = \{k_1, k_2, \ldots, k_c\} \subset \mathcal{U}_n$ who forges a pirated digital content. Denote by $\boldsymbol{Y} = Y_1 Y_2 \cdots Y_n \in \mathcal{Y}^n$ a binary sequence that is generated by $\mathcal{K}$, where $\mathcal{Y} = \{0, 1\}$. We consider the situation where $\mathcal{K}$ chooses a conditional probability distribution $P_{Y|X_1 \cdots X_c}$ and generates $\boldsymbol{Y}$ satisfying

$$Y_l \sim P_{Y|X_1 \cdots X_c}(\cdot | X_l^{(k_1)}, X_l^{(k_2)}, \ldots, X_l^{(k_c)})$$

randomly and independently for all $l = 1, 2, \ldots, n$. The conditional probability distribution $P_{Y|X_1 \cdots X_c}$ that $\mathcal{K}$ chooses must satisfy the following two conditions:

- **Condition 1 (Marking Assumption [1]):**

$$P_{Y|X_1 \cdots X_c}(0|0, \cdots, 0) = P_{Y|X_1 \cdots X_c}(1|1, \cdots, 1) = 1.$$

- **Condition 2 (Fairness [7]):**
  For all permutations $\pi : \{1, 2, \ldots, c\} \to \{1, 2, \ldots, c\}$ and $x_1, x_2, \ldots, x_c \in \mathcal{X}$ $P_{Y|X_1 \cdots X_c}$ satisfies

$$P_{Y|X_1 \cdots X_c}(1|x_1, x_2, \ldots, x_c)$$
$$= P_{Y|X_1 \cdots X_c}(1|\pi(x_1), \pi(x_2), \ldots, \pi(x_c)).$$

Various authors use this attack model [7, 8, 11, 13, 14]. Under Condition 2 each member of $\mathcal{K}$ becomes fair in the sense that contributions to $\boldsymbol{Y}$ of each $\boldsymbol{X}^{(k_1)}, \boldsymbol{X}^{(k_2)}, \ldots, \boldsymbol{X}^{(k_c)}$ are indistinguishable.

The conditional probability distributions $P_{Y|X_1 \cdots X_c}$ corresponding to well-known attacks such as the AND (all zero) attack, the OR (all one) attack, the majority attack and the minority attack satisfy Conditions 1 and 2. For example, in the AND attack $P_{Y|X_1 \cdots X_c}(1|x_1, \ldots, x_c) = 1$ if $(x_1, \ldots, x_c) = (1, \ldots, 1)$ and $P_{Y|X_1 \cdots X_c}(1|x_1, \ldots, x_c) = 0$

otherwise. In this paper we focus on the interleaving attack with the conditional probability distribution defined by

$$P_{Y|X_1 \cdots X_c}(1|x_1, \ldots, x_c) = \frac{z}{c}, \quad (1)$$

where $z = x_1 + x_2 + \cdots + x_c$.

It is important to notice that $P_{Y|X_1 \cdots X_c}$ satisfying condition 2 is specified by a $(c + 1)$-dimensional vector $\boldsymbol{p} = (P_{Y|Z}(1|0), P_{Y|Z}(1|1), \ldots, P_{Y|Z}(1|c))$, where $Z = X_1 + X_2 + \cdots + X_c$ and $P_{Y|Z}(y|z)$ denotes the conditional probability of $Y = y$ given $Z = z$. For example, we have $\boldsymbol{p}_{\mathsf{AND}} = (0, 0, \ldots, 0, 1)$ in the AND attack and $\boldsymbol{p}_{\mathsf{INT}} = (0, 1/c, 2/c, \ldots, (c-1)/c, 1)$ in the interleaving attack. Hereinafter, we use the notation $\boldsymbol{p} = (p_0, p_1, \ldots, p_c)$ to denote an attack by c colluders. Due to Condition 1, $p_0 = 0$ and $p_c = 1$ always hold.

2.3 Joint Capacity

The contents supplier tries to identify all the members of $\mathcal{K}$ when he/she finds a pirated copy. We assume that the content supplier can extract $\boldsymbol{Y}$ from the pirated copy without any error. An identifier $\psi_n : \mathcal{Y}^n \to \binom{\mathcal{U}_n}{c}$ is defined as a mapping that outputs an estimate $\hat{\mathcal{K}}$ of the colluders given $\boldsymbol{Y}$ as an input, where $\binom{\mathcal{U}_n}{c}$ denotes all the subset of $\mathcal{U}_n$ of size c. Here, we assume that the identifier knows not only $\boldsymbol{X}^{(j)}$, $1 \leq j \leq M_n$, but also the number of colluders c and an attack $\boldsymbol{p}$. Given an attack $\boldsymbol{p}$, the probability of error of the identification is given by

$$P_n = \Pr\{\psi_n(\boldsymbol{Y}) \neq \mathcal{K}\}, \quad (2)$$

where $\Pr\{\cdot\}$ means the probability with respect to the joint distribution of the random variables $\boldsymbol{X}^{(1)}, \boldsymbol{X}^{(2)}, \ldots, \boldsymbol{X}^{(M_n)}$ and $\boldsymbol{Y}$.

We are interested in the the number of users for which a digital fingerprinting code can reliably identify all the colluders. To this end, we define the joint capacity as follows:

DEFINITION 1. *Fix the number c and an attack $\boldsymbol{p}$ of c colluders. A rate R is called achievable if there exists a probability distribution P_X over $\mathcal{X}$ and a sequence of identifiers $\{\psi_n\}_{n=1}^{\infty}$ such that*

$$\liminf_{n \to \infty} \frac{1}{n} \log M_n \geq R \quad (3)$$

and

$$\lim_{n \to \infty} P_n = 0, \quad (4)$$

where $\log(\cdot) = \log_2(\cdot)$ throughout this paper. The supremum of the achievable rate R is called the joint capacity and is denoted by $C(\boldsymbol{p})$.

It is known that $C(\boldsymbol{p})$ can be written as

$$C(\boldsymbol{p}) = \max_{0 < w < 1} \frac{1}{c} I(X_1 \cdots X_c; Y), \quad (5)$$

[7, 11], where $I(X_1 \cdots X_c; Y)$ denotes the mutual information between $(X_1, \ldots, X_c)$ and Y. It is known that $C(\boldsymbol{p}_{\mathsf{AND}}) = C(\boldsymbol{p}_{\mathsf{OR}}) = 1/c$ [14]. In addition, while [8] claims that $C(\boldsymbol{p}_{\mathsf{INT}}) = \frac{1}{2c^2 \ln 2}$ for sufficiently large c, [14] points out that $C(\boldsymbol{p}_{\mathsf{INT}}) \approx \frac{1.1604}{2c^2 \ln 2}$ for all sufficiently large c, where $\ln(\cdot)$ denotes the natural logarithm.

3. ASYMPTOTIC LOWER BOUNDS

In this section we consider the joint capacity $C(\boldsymbol{p}_{\mathsf{INT}})$ against the interleaving attack $\boldsymbol{p}_{\mathsf{INT}}$ and develop its lower bounds. Although [14] gives the formula $C(\boldsymbol{p}_{\mathsf{INT}}) \approx \frac{1.1604}{2c^2 \ln 2}$ for sufficiently large c and numerical computation shows validity of this formula (see Figs.1–3 appearing afterward), the formula contains a numerical optimization (i.e., the coefficient 1.1604 is not completely theoretical). In addition, [14] assumes that the maximum in (5) is attained at $w = O(1/c)$. Although this choice is crucial in the analysis, no fair reason for this choice is clearly explained.

In this section we take an approach similar to [8, 14] but characterize $C(\boldsymbol{p}_{\mathsf{INT}})$ in a different way.

We have the following theorem.

THEOREM 1. *The joint capacity $C(\boldsymbol{p}_{\mathsf{INT}})$ is lower bounded by*

$$C(\boldsymbol{p}_{\mathsf{INT}}) \geq \frac{1}{2\ln 2}\frac{1}{c^2} + \frac{1}{12\ln 2}\frac{1}{c^2 \ln c} + \frac{1}{12\ln 2}\frac{1}{c^2 \ln^2 c} + o\left(\frac{1}{c^2 \ln^2 c}\right). \quad (6)$$

In order to prove Theorem 1, recall that under an attack $\boldsymbol{p} = (p_0, p_1, \ldots, p_c)$ satisfying Conditions 1 and 2, the mutual information $I(X_1 \cdots X_c; Y)$ can be expressed as follows:

$$I(X_1 \cdots X_c; Y) = h\left(\sum_{z=0}^{c} \alpha_z(w)p_z\right) - \sum_{z=0}^{c} \alpha_z(w)h(p_z), \quad (7)$$

where $h(w) = -w\log w - (1-w)\log(1-w)$ denotes the binary entropy and

$$\alpha_z(w) = \binom{c}{z}w^z(1-w)^{c-z}, \quad z = 0, 1, \ldots, c.$$

(e.g., [11]). Since $p_z = z/c$ for $z = 0, 1, \ldots, c$ in the interleaving attack, it is easily verified that

$$\sum_{z=0}^{c} \alpha_z(w)\frac{z}{c} = \frac{1}{c}\sum_{z=0}^{c} z\binom{c}{z}w^z(1-w)^{c-z} = w$$

because the above sum means the expectation of z/c with respect to the binomial distribution $B(c; w)$. Then, (7) yields the following formula of $C(\boldsymbol{p}_{\mathsf{INT}})$:

$$C(\boldsymbol{p}_{\mathsf{INT}}) = \max_{0<w<1} \frac{1}{c}\left[h(w) - \sum_{z=0}^{c} \alpha_z(w)h\left(\frac{z}{c}\right)\right]. \quad (8)$$

We use the following lemma that is obtained from the Taylor expansion of $h\left(\frac{z}{c}\right)$ around an arbitrarily fixed w.

LEMMA 1. *It holds that*

$$C(\boldsymbol{p}_{\mathsf{INT}}) = \max_{0<w<1}\left[\frac{1}{2\ln 2}\frac{1}{c^2} - \sum_{l=3}^{\infty} \frac{h^{(l)}(w)}{l!}T_{c,l}(w)\frac{1}{c^{l+1}}\right], \quad (9)$$

where $h^{(l)}(w)$ denotes the l-th derivative of $h(w)$ and $T_{c,l}(w)$ is defined as

$$T_{c,l}(w) = \sum_{z=0}^{c} \alpha_z(w)(z-cw)^l, \quad l = 0, 1, 2, \cdots.$$

PROOF. Fix $w \in (0, 1)$ arbitrarily. From the Taylor expansion of $h\left(\frac{z}{c}\right)$ around w, we have

$$\sum_{z=0}^{c} \alpha_z(w)h\left(\frac{z}{c}\right) = \sum_{z=0}^{c} \alpha_z(w)\sum_{l=0}^{\infty} \frac{h^{(l)}(w)}{l!}\left(\frac{z}{c}-w\right)^l$$

$$= \sum_{l=0}^{\infty} \frac{h^{(l)}(w)}{l!}\sum_{z=0}^{c} \alpha_z(w)(z-cw)^l\frac{1}{c^l}$$

$$= \sum_{l=0}^{\infty} \frac{h^{(l)}(w)}{l!}T_{c,l}(w)\frac{1}{c^l}, \quad (10)$$

where $h^{(0)}(w) = h(w)$. By taking $T_{c,0}(w) = 1, T_{c,1}(w) = 0, T_{c,2}(w) = cw(1-w)$ [15] and $h^{(2)}(w) = -\frac{1}{\ln 2}\frac{1}{w(1-w)}$ into consideration, the right side of (10) can be written as follows:

$$\sum_{l=0}^{\infty} \frac{h^{(l)}(w)}{l!}T_{c,l}(w)\frac{1}{c^l}$$

$$= h(w) - \frac{1}{2\ln 2}\frac{1}{c} + \sum_{l=3}^{\infty} \frac{h^{(l)}(w)}{l!}T_{c,l}(w)\frac{1}{c^l}. \quad (11)$$

Then, the claim of this lemma immediately follows from the combination of (8), (10) and (11). $\square$

The following lemma describes properties of $T_{c,l}(w)$. Letting f be a polynomial with variables x and y, let $\deg_x f$ and $\deg_y f$ denote the degrees with respect to x and y, respectively.

LEMMA 2 ([15]). *Letting $l \geq 1$ be an arbitrary integer, it holds that $T_{c,2l}(w) = f_{2l}(W)$ and $T_{c,2l+1}(w) = (1-2w)g_{2l+1}(W)$, where $W = w(1-w)$ and f_{2l} and g_{2l+1} are polynomials of c and W satisfying $\deg_c f_{2l} = \deg_c g_{2l+1} = l$ and $\deg_W f_{2l} = \deg_W g_{2l+1} = l$, respectively. In addition, both f_{2l} and g_{2l+1} have terms of order $c^l W^l$.*

The polynomials $T_{c,l}(w)$, $l = 2, 3, 4, 5, 6$, are expressed as follows: [15]:

$$T_{c,2}(w) = cW,$$
$$T_{c,3}(w) = (1-2w)cW,$$
$$T_{c,4}(w) = 3c^2W^2 + c(W - 6W^2),$$
$$T_{c,5}(w) = (1-2w)[10c^2W^2 + c(W - 12W^2)],$$
$$T_{c,6}(w) = 15c^3W^3 + 5c^2W^2(5 - 26W),$$
$$+ cW(120W^2 - 30W + 1).$$

Actually, $T_{c,l}(w)$ means the l-th moment around the mean of the binomial distribution $B(c; w)$. In particular, $T_{c,2}(w) = cw(1-w)$ implies its variance.

PROOF OF THEOREM 1: We fix a sufficiently large c and substitute $w = \frac{\ln c}{c} \in (0, 1)$ to the right side of (9). We also use

$$h^{(l)}(w) = \frac{(l-2)!}{\ln 2}\left[(-1)^{l-1}w^{-(l-1)} - (1-w)^{-(l-1)}\right]$$

for all $l \geq 2$. Notice that this formula actually implies that

$$h^{(l)}\left(\frac{\ln c}{c}\right) = \frac{(l-2)!}{\ln 2}\left[(-1)^{l-1}\left(\frac{c}{\ln c}\right)^{l-1} + O(1)\right]$$

for all $l \geq 2$.

25

We evaluate the terms in the sum in (9) separately. For $l = 3$, it holds that

$$\frac{h^{(3)}(\frac{\ln c}{c})}{3!} T_{c,3}\left(\frac{\ln c}{c}\right)\frac{1}{c^4}$$
$$= \frac{1}{6\ln 2}\left(\frac{1}{c^2 \ln c} - \frac{3}{c^3}\right) + o\left(\frac{1}{c^3}\right),$$

and, similarly, for $l = 4$ we have

$$\frac{h^{(4)}(\frac{\ln c}{c})}{4!} T_{c,4}\left(\frac{\ln c}{c}\right)\frac{1}{c^5}$$
$$= -\frac{1}{4\ln 2}\frac{1}{c^2 \ln c} - \frac{1}{12\ln 2}\frac{1}{c^2 \ln^2 c} + o\left(\frac{1}{c^2 \ln^2 c}\right).$$

Furthermore, for $l = 5$ and $l = 6$ it holds that

$$\frac{h^{(5)}(\frac{\ln c}{c})}{5!} T_{c,5}\left(\frac{\ln c}{c}\right)\frac{1}{c^6} = \frac{1}{2\ln 2}\frac{1}{c^2 \ln^2 c} + o\left(\frac{1}{c^2 \ln^2 c}\right)$$

and

$$\frac{h^{(6)}(\frac{\ln c}{c})}{6!} T_{c,6}\left(\frac{\ln c}{c}\right)\frac{1}{c^7} = -\frac{1}{2\ln 2}\frac{1}{c^2 \ln^2 c} + o\left(\frac{1}{c^2 \ln^2 c}\right).$$

It is important to notice that due to Lemma 2 $T_{c,l}(w)$ has a term $Dc^{\lfloor l/2 \rfloor}W^{\lfloor l/2 \rfloor}$ for every $l \geq 2$, where D is a constant, which has the greatest degree with respect to both c and W. Therefore, we have

$$\frac{h^{(l)}(\frac{\ln c}{c})}{l!} T_{c,l}\left(\frac{\ln c}{c}\right)\frac{1}{c^{l+1}} = o\left(\frac{1}{c^2 \ln^2 c}\right) \quad \text{for all } l \geq 7.$$

The claim of Theorem 1 follows as a consequence of the above evaluations. $\square$

Theorem 1 has the following corollary. Actually, the proof of Theorem1 is valid if we substitute $w = \frac{s(c)}{c}$ instead of $w = \frac{\ln c}{c}$ into the right side of (9), where $s(c)$ is required to satisfy

$$\frac{s(c)}{c} \in (0,1), \quad \lim_{c \to \infty}\frac{s(c)}{c} = 0, \quad \lim_{c\to\infty} s(c) = \infty. \quad (12)$$

An example of such $s(c)$ is $(\ln c)^\alpha$ for an arbitrarily fixed $\alpha > 0$.

COROLLARY 1. *Fix $s(c)$ satisfying (12) arbitrarily. Then,*

$$C(\boldsymbol{p}_{\mathsf{INT}}) \geq \frac{1}{2\ln 2}\frac{1}{c^2} + \frac{1}{12\ln 2}\frac{1}{c^2 s(c)} + \frac{1}{12\ln 2}\frac{1}{c^2 s^2(c)}$$
$$+ o\left(\frac{1}{c^2 s^2(c)}\right). \quad (13)$$

We can continue computation of higher order terms of the Taylor expansion by using the recurrence relation

$$T_{c,l+1}(w) = W\left[T'_{c,l-1}(w) + c\,l\,T_{c,l-1}(w)\right]$$

[15], where $T'_{c,l-1}(w)$ denotes the derivative of $T'_{c,l-1}$ with respect to w. By using Mathematica 10.4, we can obtain

$$C(\boldsymbol{p}_{\mathsf{INT}}) \geq \frac{1}{2\ln 2}\frac{1}{c^2} + \frac{1}{12\ln 2}\frac{1}{c^2 s(c)} + \frac{1}{12\ln 2}\frac{1}{c^2 s(c)^2}$$
$$+ \frac{19}{120\ln 2}\frac{1}{c^2 s(c)^3} + \frac{9}{20\ln 2}\frac{1}{c^2 s(c)^4}$$
$$+ \frac{863}{504\ln 2}\frac{1}{c^2 s(c)^5} + o\left(\frac{1}{c^2 s(c)^5}\right), \quad (14)$$

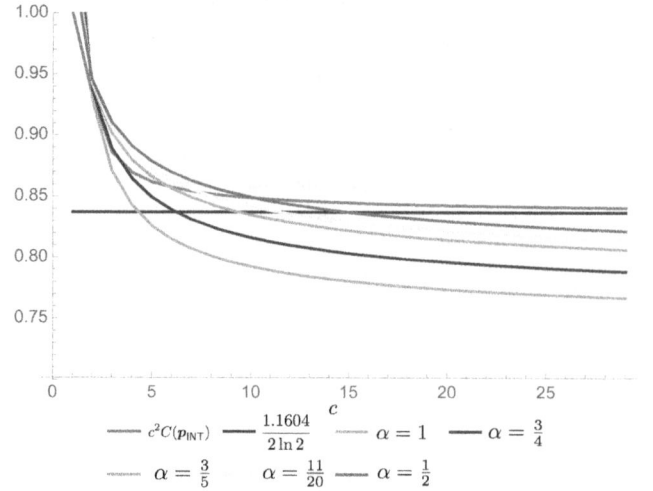

Figure 1 Behaviors of lower bounds for $2 \leq c \leq 30$ and $s(c) = (\ln c)^\alpha$.

where $s(c)$ satisfies (12).

Hereinafter, we give numerical results obtained by using Mathematica 10.4. In Fig. 1 we compare $c^2 C(\boldsymbol{p}_{\mathsf{INT}})$ with its lower bound $\frac{1}{2\ln 2} + \frac{1}{12\ln 2}\frac{1}{s(c)} + \frac{1}{12\ln 2}\frac{1}{s^2(c)}$ for $2 \leq c \leq 30$ under the choices of $s(c) = (\ln c)^\alpha$, $\alpha = 1, \frac{3}{4}, \frac{3}{5}, \frac{11}{20}, \frac{1}{2}$. The values of $c^2 C(\boldsymbol{p}_{\mathsf{INT}})$ are computed numerically. Figure 1 tells us that the gap between $c^2 C(\boldsymbol{p}_{\mathsf{INT}})$ and $\frac{1.1604}{2\ln 2}$ becomes smaller as c becomes large. Figure 1 also indicates that the lower bound with $s(c) = (\ln c)^{\frac{3}{4}}$ gives a well approximation of $c^2 C(\boldsymbol{p}_{\mathsf{INT}})$ for $2 \leq c \leq 4$. In addition, the lower bounds with $s(c) = (\ln c)^{\frac{3}{5}}$, $s(c) = (\ln c)^{\frac{11}{20}}$, and $s(c) = (\ln c)^{\frac{1}{2}}$ are close to $c^2 C(\boldsymbol{p}_{\mathsf{INT}})$ around $c = 6$, $c = 8$ and $c = 10$, respectively.

Figure 2 shows that $c^2 C(\boldsymbol{p}_{\mathsf{INT}})$ (red line), $\frac{1.1604}{2\ln 2}$ (blue line) and five asymptotic lower bounds obtained by summing the first two terms (green line), the first three terms (purple line), the first four terms (orange line), the first five terms (yellow line) and the first six terms (brown line) of (14) multiplied by c^2, where $s(c) = (\ln c)^{\frac{3}{4}}$ and c varies between 2 and 100. For $c \geq 40$ there is almost no gap between $c^2 C(\boldsymbol{p}_{\mathsf{INT}})$ and $\frac{1.1604}{2\ln 2}$. All of the above sum become smaller than $c^2 C(\boldsymbol{p}_{\mathsf{INT}})$ as c becomes large.

On the other hand, Fig. 3 gives the asymptotic behavior of the five lower bounds with $s(c) = (\ln c)^{\frac{1}{2}}$ for $2 \leq c \leq 1000$. All of the five curves are below $c^2 C(\boldsymbol{p}_{\mathsf{INT}})$ if $c \geq 750$. However, the curves in Fig. 3 are more slowly recreasing than the corresponding curve in Fig. 2, respectively.

4. ASYMPTOTIC UPPER BOUNDS

In the preceding section we have established various lower bounds of $C(\boldsymbol{p}_{\mathsf{INT}})$ by using the Taylor expansion of $h(z/c)$. In this subsection we discuss an upper bound of $C(\boldsymbol{p}_{\mathsf{INT}})$.

We have the following theorem.

THEOREM 2. *Let $\varepsilon > 0$ and $\eta > 0$ be an arbitrarily small constants. If c is sufficiently large, it holds that*

$$C(\boldsymbol{p}_{\mathsf{INT}}) \leq \frac{1}{2\ln 2}\frac{1}{c^2} + \frac{1+\eta}{12\ln 2}\frac{(\ln c)^{\frac{1+\varepsilon}{2}}}{c^2} + \frac{(1+\eta)^2}{12\ln 2}\frac{(\ln c)^{1+\varepsilon}}{c^2}$$
$$+ \cdots. \quad (15)$$

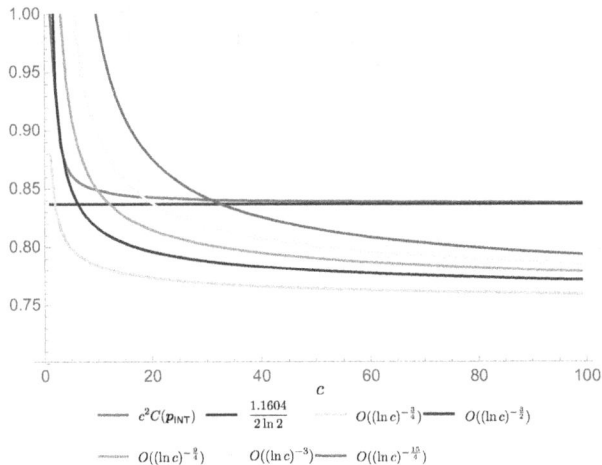

Figure 2 Asymptotic behaviors of lower bounds for $2 \le c \le 100$ and $s(c) = (\ln c)^{\frac{3}{4}}$.

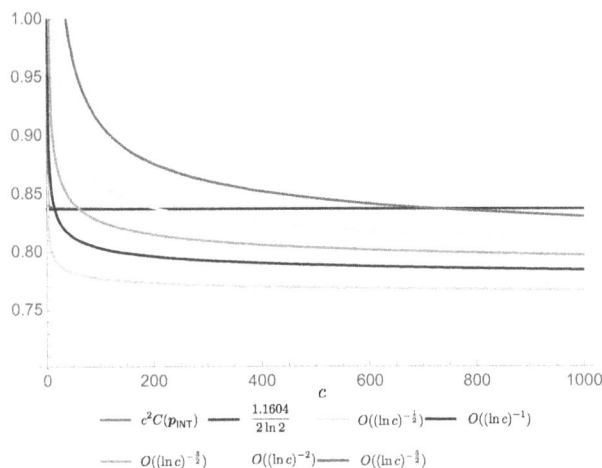

Figure 3 Asymptotic behaviors of lower bounds for $2 \le c \le 1000$ and $s(c) = (\ln c)^{\frac{1}{2}}$.

In order to prove Theorem 2, we evaluate the value of $w = w_c^*$ that achieves the maximum in the right side of (8). Since the binary entropy satisfies $h(w) = h(1-w)$ for all $w \in (0,1)$, the right side of (8) is symmetric with respect to $w = 1/2$. This means that we can assume that $w_c^* \le \frac{1}{2}$.

The following lemma guarantees that $w_c^* = \Omega(1/(c(\ln c)^{\frac{1+\varepsilon}{2}}))$, where $\varepsilon > 0$ is an arbitrarily small constant.

LEMMA 3. *Let $\varepsilon > 0$ be an arbitrarily fixed constant. Then, we have $w_c^* \ge 1/(c(\ln c)^{\frac{1+\varepsilon}{2}})$ if c is sufficiently large.*

PROOF. We prove the claim by using a contradiction argument. Assume that $w_c^* < 1/(c(\ln c)^{\frac{1+\varepsilon}{2}})$. Then, from the definition of w_c^* it holds that

$$C(\boldsymbol{p}_{\mathsf{INT}}) = \frac{1}{c}\left[h(w_c^*) - \sum_{z=0}^{c} \alpha_z(w_c^*)h\left(\frac{z}{c}\right)\right].$$

Notice that, since $w_c^* < \frac{z}{c}$ for $z = 1, 2, \ldots, \lfloor\frac{c}{2}\rfloor$, we have

$h(\frac{z}{c}) > h(w_c^*)$. Similarly, we also have $h(\frac{z}{c}) = h(1-\frac{z}{c}) > h(w_c^*)$ because $w_c^* < 1 - \frac{z}{c}$ for $z = \lceil\frac{c}{2}\rceil, \lceil\frac{c}{2}\rceil+1, \ldots, c-1$. Hence, in view of $h(0) = h(1) = 0$ and $\sum_{z=0}^{c} \alpha_z(w_c^*) = 1$ it holds that

$$\begin{aligned} C(\boldsymbol{p}_{\mathsf{INT}}) &< \frac{1}{c}\left[1 - (w_c^*)^c - (1-w_c^*)^c\right]h(w_c^*) \\ &< \frac{1}{c}\left[1 - (1-w_c^*)^c\right]h(w_c^*) \\ &< \frac{1}{c}\left[1 - \left(1 - \frac{1}{c(\ln c)^{\frac{1+\varepsilon}{2}}}\right)^c\right]h\left(\frac{1}{c(\ln c)^{\frac{1+\varepsilon}{2}}}\right). \end{aligned}$$

Then, it follows from the inequality $(1-t)^m \ge \exp[-\frac{mt}{1-t}]$ for $t \in (0,1)$ and $m > 0$ that

$$\begin{aligned} \left(1 - \frac{1}{c(\ln c)^{\frac{1+\varepsilon}{2}}}\right)^c &\ge \exp\left[-\frac{\frac{1}{(\ln c)^{\frac{1+\varepsilon}{2}}}}{1 - \frac{1}{c(\ln c)^{\frac{1+\varepsilon}{2}}}}\right] \\ &\ge \exp\left[-\frac{1}{(\ln c)^{\frac{1+\varepsilon}{2}} - \frac{1}{c}}\right] \\ &\ge \exp\left[-\frac{2}{(\ln c)^{\frac{1+\varepsilon}{2}}}\right] \\ &\ge 1 - \frac{2}{(\ln c)^{\frac{1+\varepsilon}{2}}}, \end{aligned} \tag{16}$$

where the third inequality follows from $\frac{1}{c} \le \frac{1}{2}(\ln c)^{\frac{1+\varepsilon}{2}}$ and the last inequality follows from the inequality $e^{-t} \ge 1 - t$ for $t \ge 0$. Therefore, we have

$$1 - \left(1 - \frac{1}{c(\ln c)^{\frac{1+\varepsilon}{2}}}\right)^c \le \frac{2}{(\ln c)^{\frac{1+\varepsilon}{2}}}. \tag{17}$$

On the other hand, since the definition of $h(w)$ implies that

$$h\left(\frac{1}{c(\ln c)^{\frac{1+\varepsilon}{2}}}\right) \le \frac{1}{\ln 2}\frac{(\ln c)^{\frac{1-\varepsilon}{2}}}{c} + o\left(\frac{(\ln c)^{\frac{1-\varepsilon}{2}}}{c}\right), \tag{18}$$

the combination of (17) and (18) yields

$$C(\boldsymbol{p}_{\mathsf{INT}}) \le \frac{2}{\ln 2}\frac{1}{c^2(\ln c)^{\varepsilon}} + o\left(\frac{1}{c^2(\ln c)^{\varepsilon}}\right), \tag{19}$$

which contradicts Theorem 1 because ε is a positive constant. $\square$

The following lemma is obtained from the Taylor expansion of $h(\frac{z}{c})$ in (8) around $w = w_c^*$. The proof is similar to the proof of Theorem 1 and therefore is omitted.

LEMMA 4. *It holds that*

$$\begin{aligned} C(\boldsymbol{p}_{\mathsf{INT}}) &= \frac{1}{2\ln 2}\frac{1}{c^2} + \frac{1}{12\ln 2}\left[\frac{1}{W_c^*} - 1\right]\frac{1}{c^3} \\ &\quad + \frac{1}{12\ln 2}\left[\frac{1}{(W_c^*)^2} - \frac{3}{W_c^*}\right]\frac{1}{c^4} + \cdots, \end{aligned} \tag{20}$$

where $W_c^* = w_c^*(1 - w_c^*)$.

Note that Lemma 4 tells us that

$$\begin{aligned} C(\boldsymbol{p}_{\mathsf{INT}}) &\le \frac{1}{2\ln 2}\frac{1}{c^2} + \frac{1}{12\ln 2}\frac{1}{W_c^*}\frac{1}{c^3} \\ &\quad + \frac{1}{12\ln 2}\frac{1}{(W_c^*)^2}\frac{1}{c^4} + \cdots. \end{aligned} \tag{21}$$

Then, the claim of Theorem 2 follows from $1/W_c^* = \frac{1}{w_c^*(1-w_c^*)} \leq (1+\eta)c(\ln c)^{\frac{1+\varepsilon}{2}}$ by virtue of Lemma 3 if c is sufficiently large.

The upper bound (21) indicates the order of W_c^* with respect to c. Assume that $W_c^* \doteq \frac{\ln c}{c}$ for example, where for two sequences $\{a_c\}_{c=1}^{\infty}$ and $\{b_c\}_{c=1}^{\infty}$ $a_c \doteq b_c$ means that $\frac{a_c}{b_c}$ tends to a constant as $c \to \infty$. Then, (21) tells us that

$$C(\boldsymbol{p}_{\mathsf{INT}}) - \frac{1}{2\ln 2}\frac{1}{c^2} \leq \frac{A}{12\ln 2}\frac{1}{c\ln c} + o\left(\frac{1}{c\ln c}\right), \quad (22)$$

where A is a positive constant. On the other hand, Corollary 1 with $s(c) = \sqrt{\ln c}$ yields

$$C(\boldsymbol{p}_{\mathsf{INT}}) - \frac{1}{2\ln 2}\frac{1}{c^2} \geq \frac{1}{12\ln 2}\frac{1}{c\sqrt{\ln c}} + o\left(\frac{1}{c\sqrt{\ln c}}\right),$$

which contradicts (22) if c is sufficiently large. This kind of contradiction always occurs if we set $W_c^* \doteq \frac{\tilde{s}(c)}{c}$ for $\tilde{s}(c)$ satisfying $\frac{\tilde{s}(c)}{c} \to 0$ and $\tilde{s}(c) \to \infty$ as $c \to \infty$ because we can choose $s(c) = \sqrt{\tilde{s}(c)}$ in Corollary 1. This argument, together with $W_c^* = w_c^*(1-w_c^*)$ and $w_c^* < 1/2$, leads to the following corollary.

COROLLARY 2. *For any $s(c)$ satisfying (12), $\frac{cw_c^*}{s(c)} \to 0$ as $c \to \infty$.*

By setting $s(c) = c^{1-\alpha}$ in Corollary 2, where $\alpha \in (0,1)$ be any fixed constant, we have $c^{\alpha}w_c^* \to 0$ as $c \to \infty$. This equation holds if $w_c^* = O(\frac{1}{c})$. However, "only if" part is not true. This is because the same equation holds if $w_c^* = O(\frac{\ln c}{c})$. Similarly, even if we set $s(c) = (\ln c)^{\alpha}$ for an arbitrarily fixed $\alpha > 0$, w_c^* can be $O(\frac{\ln(\ln c)}{c})$. Hence, a small theoretic gap remains between the claim of Corollary 2 and $w_c^* = O(\frac{1}{c})$.

5. CONCLUSION

In this paper we have discussed the joint capacity $C(\boldsymbol{p}_{\mathsf{INT}})$ of digital fingerprinting codes against the interleaving attack of c colluders. We have obtained lower bounds and upper bounds of $C(\boldsymbol{p}_{\mathsf{INT}})$ which are dependent on c. In particular, the lower bounds give a fairly well approximation of $c^2 C(\boldsymbol{p}_{\mathsf{INT}})$ for appropriate ranges of c respectively. In addition, the upper and the lower bounds enable us to characterize the argument that attains the maximum that is involved in the definition of the joint capacity.

6. REFERENCES

[1] D. Boneh and J. Shaw, "Collusion-secure fingerprinting for digital data," *IEEE Trans. Inf. Theory*, vol. 44, no. 5, pp. 1897–1905, 1998.

[2] A. Barg, G. R. Blakley and G. Kabatiansky, "Collusion-secure fingerprinting for digital data," *IEEE Trans. Inf. Theory*, vol 49, no. 4, pp. 852–865, 2003.

[3] G. R. Blakly and G. Kabatiansky, "Random coding technique for digital fingerprinting codes: fighting two pirates revisited," *Proc. 2004 IEEE ISIT*, Chicago, p. 202, 2004.

[4] A. Somekh-Baruch and N. Merhav, "On the capacity game of private fingerprinting systems under collusion attacks," *IEEE Trans. Inf. Theory*, vol. 51, no. 3, pp. 884–899, 2005.

[5] G. Tardos, "Optimal probabilistic fingerprint code," *J. ACM*, vol. 55, no. 2, Article 10, 2008.

[6] N. P. Anthapadmanabhan, A. Barg and I. Dumer, "On the fingerprinting under the marking assumption," *IEEE Trans. Inf. Theory*, vol. 54, no. 6, pp. 2678–2689, 2008.

[7] P. Moulin, "Universal fingerprinting: capacity and random-coding exponents," *Proc. 2008 IEEE ISIT*, Tronto, Canada, pp. 220–224, 2008. (Full version is available as arXiv:0801.3837v3 [cs.IT])

[8] T. Furon and L. Pérez-Freire, "Worst case attacks against binary probabilistic traitor tracing codes," *IEEE Int. Workshop on Information Forensics and Security*, Dec. 2009. (Full version is available as arXiv:0903.3480v2 [cs.IT])

[9] H. Koga, "On the capacity of the AND anti-collusion fingerprinting codes," *IEICE Technical Report*, IT2009-140, 2010.

[10] D. Boesten and B. Škorić, "Asymptotic fingerprinting capacity for non-binary alphabets," *Proc. 13th Information Hiding Conference (IH2011)*, LNCS 6958, pp. 1–13, Springer, 2011.

[11] Y. W. Huang and P. Moulin, "On the saddle-point solution and the large-collusion asymptotics of fingerprinting games," *IEEE Trans. Information Forensics and Security*, vol. 7, no. 1, pp. 160–175, 2012.

[12] Y. W. Huang and P. Moulin, "n the fingerprinting capacity games for arbitrary alphabets and their asymptotics," *IEEE Trans. Information Forensics and Security*, vol. 9, no. 9, pp. 1477–1490, 2014.

[13] T. Laarhoven,"Capacities and capacity-achieving decoders for various fingerprinting games," *Proc. 2nd ACM Workshop on IH & MMSec*, pp. 123–134, 2014.

[14] T. Laarhoven, "Asymptotics of fingerprinting and group testing: tight bounds from channel capacities," *IEEE Trans. Information Forensics and Security*, vol. 10, no. 9, pp. 1967–1970, 2015.

[15] G. G. Lorentz, *Bernstein Polynomials (Second Edition)*, Chelsea Publishing Company, 1986.

7. ACKNOWLEDGMENTS

This research is supported in part by JSPS Grant-in-Aid for scientific research (C) 26330003.

Efficient HS based Reversible Data Hiding Using Multi-feature Complexity Measure and Optimized Histogram

Junxiang Wang
Jingdezhen Ceramic Institute
School of Mechanical and Electronic Engineering
Jingdezhen Ceramic Institute,
Jiangxi 333403, China
+86-13879898917
wjx851113851113@163.com

Jiangqun Ni
Sun Yat-sen University
School of Information Science and Technology
Sun Yat-sen University,
Guangdong 510006, China
+86-13822251698
(corresponding author)
issjqni@mail.sysu.edu.cn

Xing Zhang
Sun Yat-sen University
School of Information Science and Technology
Sun Yat-sen University,
Guangdong 510006, China
+86-15626145335
zhangxingkof@hotmail.com

ABSTRACT

Histogram-shifting (HS) embedding as a most successful reversible data hiding (RDH) scheme is widely investigated. How to take advantage of covers' redundancy is one of the key issues for performance improvement of RDH. Among them, sorting technique is of practically importance, which uses in priority smooth areas with high correlation to hide message. For conventional schemes, usually a single empirical feature in the context of local cover object, such as local variance, is utilized as complexity measure for sorting, which may not effectively exploit the covers' correlations and thus lead to limited performance improvement. In this paper, a general framework for optimal construction of complexity measure with multi-feature is developed, which includes optimal feature selection and weight parameters determination based on an optimization model. In addition, the optimal truncation point for the top $\chi(\%)$ of the sorted cover is determined based on the payload constraint to construct the optimal histogram for further performance improvement of HS embedding. Compared with previous approaches, experimental results demonstrate the superiority of the proposed scheme.

CCS Concepts

• **Security and privacy→Authentication •Information systems→Information extraction • Computing methodologies→Image processing**

Keywords

Reversible data hiding, histogram shifting (HS), multi-feature selection, complexity measure, optimized histogram.

1. INTRODUCTION

As a special data embedding scheme, reversible data hiding (RDH) [1]can not only precisely extract the secret data as traditional schemes, but also perfectly reconstruct the original cover image without any distortion. It is this fact that makes RDH widely used in

IH&MMSec 2016, June 20-23, 2016, Vigo, Spain
© 2016 ACM. ISBN 978-1-4503-4290-2/16/06...$15.00
DOI: http://dx.doi.org/10.1145/2909827.2930789

some specific scenarios, such as military, medical and legal applications, where even the slight distortion in recovered images is not tolerated.

In recent years, many RDH schemes have been reported and can be mainly classified into three categories: i.e.,lossless compression (LC)[2-3], difference expansion (DE) [4-12] and histogram shifting (HS) [13-16]. Actually, these three categories all tended to exploit as much cover's redundancy as possible to acquire a larger space for secret message embedding and meanwhile reduce the distortion caused by embedding operation. LC algorithms usually employed the medium to lower bit planes of the spatial pixels or transform coefficients to seek redundancy. Due to weak and instable correlation in one bit-plane, LC based scheme usually cannot achieve desired performance. Later, Tian et al.[4] proposed the first DE scheme, which calculates one difference between two adjacent pixels and then doubles (expand) the value to vacate its LSB to hide 1-bit secret data. To further exploit image correlation, DE is extended on prediction errors, and known as prediction-error expansion (PEE)[5-10]. On the other hand, histogram shifting (HS)based scheme was initially proposed by Ni *et al.* [13] in 2006, which selected a pair of peak and zero bins in histogram and then shifted the bins between the two bins by 1 towards zero bin for reversible data embedding. The rate and distortion performance of HS based reversible data hiding depends heavily on the sharpness of histogram and the way to determine the peak and zero bin pairs. Recently, Li et al. [17] proposed a general framework for HS based reversible embedding and demonstrated that DE could be considered as a special case of HS. Therefore, we focus on the HS based embedding throughout the paper.

During HS, how to generate a sharp histogram is of vital importance. Currently, the mainstream HS schemes are based on prediction and interpolation, e.g., the gradient adjusted predictor (GAP) for half enclosed prediction [8,9],rhombus prediction [6,7] and some interpolation schemes [15] for fully enclosed prediction. It is clear that the more pixels in context are involved, i.e. fully enclosed prediction, the more accurate prediction is achieved, which means local correlation is better exploited. However, for a nature image with rich content, its statistical characteristic varies from place to place. Therefore, even the best predictor could not lead to the expected sharp histogram in a global sense. A feasible way to tackle the issue is sort the cover elements according to some complexity measure (CM) and then take the top $\chi(\%)$ of the sorted ones for histogram generation based on the given payload [7,8], i.e., to embed the data in priority to the smooth areas of image with high correlation. In this way, a sharper histogram is generated than the one in global sense, which leads to better rate and distortion performance, especially for the low to medium payload applications [11,12].

In general, the sorting technique for HS embedding consists of the following steps. Firstly, for each cover element, its CM is calculated according to its neighborhood region to characterize its smoothness level or correlation. Then, all the cover elements are sorted according to their CMs' ascend order. Finally, an optimal truncation point is determined to take the top $\chi(\%)$ of the sorted ones based on the given payload to generate the optimized histogram. Among them, CMs' construction can make a significant difference in rate and distortion performance of HS based embedding. In previous sorting methods [6,7], one simple feature was utilized to compute the CM value of cover elements, which may not fully characterize the correlation of a cover element with its neighboring ones, especially for images with rich texture contents. In addition, a generalized criteria should be given to make the CM with multiple features to be optimized.

In this paper, we propose a general framework for construction of optimized CM with multiple features, which could not only characterize the correlation of a cover element with its neighboring ones, but also achieve feature's selection by using optimized weighting parameters. Firstly, for each cover element, several candidate features are calculated according to its neighboring ones to build a candidate feature set. Then, its CM is obtained through the linear combination of the multiple features, where the corresponding feature parameter weight is optimized based on a given criteria. Finally, to further improve its performance, the optimal truncation point for the top $\chi(\%)$ of the sorted cover element is determined according to the given payload to generate the optimized histogram.

The rest of the paper is organized as follows. Some preliminaries related to our scheme are briefly given in Section II. A general framework for construction of multi-feature based complexity measure is presented in Section III. The generation of optimized histogram and the embedding/ extraction schemes are described in Section IV, which are followed by the experimental results and analysis in Section V. Finally, the conclusions are summarized in Section VI.

2. PRELIMINARY

2.1 PEE based RDH embedding framework

1) Prediction

The first step of HS based RDH is to generate a PE based histogram. The precise rhombus prediction and double-layered embedding proposed in Sachnev et al.'s work [6] is employed in our method for prediction (see Fig. 1 for an illustration), in which the cover image is divided into two sets denoted as "Cross" and "Round". One half of the secret message is embedded into Cross set and the rest is embedded into the Round set. In this case, double-layer embedding needs to be implemented to hide the data in the whole image, and the prediction of Round pixels is processed only after the embedding in Cross set is completed. In the decoding phase, the embedded message and pixels in Round set is extracted and recovered first, which is then used to reconstruct the marked Cross set and extract the corresponding hidden message. Since the embedding in Cross and Round sets is implemented similarly, we only take the Cross layer for illustration.

As shown in Fig. 1(b), each x_i in Cross set is predicted using its four neighbors in Round set to obtain $\hat{x}_i$ as

$$\hat{x}_i = \left\lceil \frac{v_1 + v_2 + v_3 + v_4}{4} \right\rceil \tag{1}$$

where $\lceil g \rceil$ is ceiling function returning the nearest integer no less than the input.

Then the prediction error is computed by

$$e_i = x_i - \hat{x}_i \tag{2}$$

Thus, all the e_i will be arranged in the raster scan order to generate an array as cover, denoted as $\mathbf{PE} = \{e_i \mid i \in [1, size]\}$, where $size$ is the number of e_i.

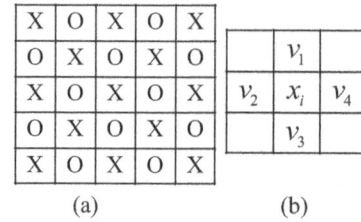

X	O	X	O	X				
O	X	O	X	O			v_1	
X	O	X	O	X		v_2	x_i	v_4
O	X	O	X	O			v_3	
X	O	X	O	X				

(a)   (b)

Figure 1 The sketch of rhombus prediction

2) HS based RDH embedding

After $\mathbf{PE}$ generation, the HS embedding procedure is performed to obtain marked prediction error $\overset{\circ}{e}_i$. First, for a histogram of $\mathbf{PE}$ (PEH), a peak bin with highest frequency and a zero bin with zero frequency in the histogram should be determined and denoted as (P_1, Z_1). HS then shifts the histogram bins between P_1 and Z_1 towards Z_1 direction by one unit to create a vacant position near P_1. Finally, each predictive error e_i is scanned to embed 1-bit message w when P_1 is encountered. When $P_1 < Z_1$, HS is performed by

$$\overset{\circ}{e}_i = \begin{cases} e_i + 1, & e_i \in [P_1 + 1, Z_1 - 1] \\ e_i + w, & e_i = P_1 \\ e_i, & otherwise \end{cases} \tag{3}$$

If $P_1 > Z_1$, HS embedding is similarly implemented. Note that the embedding capacity is $h(P_1)$, where $h(i)$ denotes the frequency of occurrence for value i in histogram.

When relative large payload is required, however, multiple embedding strategy should be employed, which uses multiple pairs of different peak and zero bins from the histogram at a time, and performs multiple HS based embedding consecutively based on the resulting histogram. Generally, with given data payload and cover image, the design of HS based multiple reversible embedding can be formulated as the optimization problem to find a set of optimal peak and zero bins while minimizing its distortion. One can follow Wang et al. work in [18] for HS based optimized multiple embedding.

Finally, the marked pixel $\overset{\circ}{x}_i$ is generated by $\overset{\circ}{x}_i = \hat{x}_i + \overset{\circ}{e}_i$ to generate the stego-image.

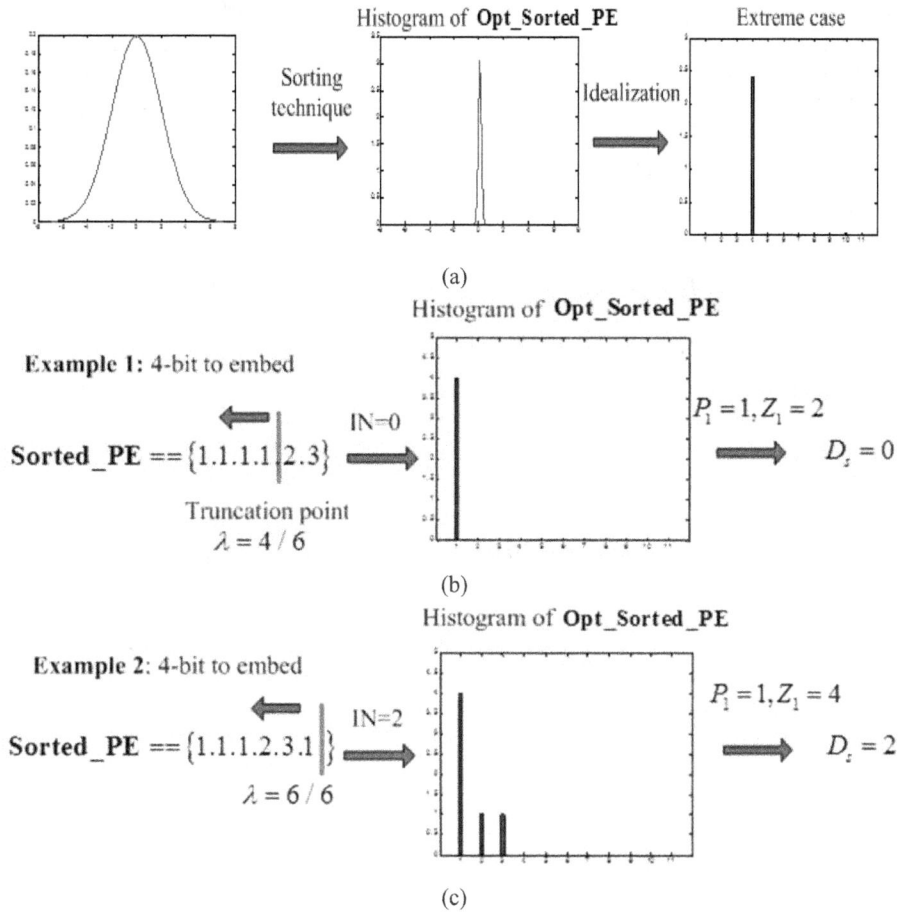

Figure 2 The sketch map forbasic idea and extreme case

2.2 Sorting technique

To improve the rate and distortion performance of HS based embedding, sorting technique[6,7]could be incorporated in the above embedding framework. For low to medium payload, sorting technique could lead to embedding hidden message in priority into smooth region with high correlation. For each cover element x_i, its neighboring region in image will be utilized to compute a complexity measure (CM), which used to characterize its smoothness level and indicate the sorting process. In general, more smooth region in image with less CMs may lead to less prediction error and more preferable for data hiding. With this concept in mind, sorting technique is employed to sort all e_i in **PE** in the ascending order according to their CMs and generated a sorted **PE**, denoted as **Sorted_PE**. Then, based on the given payload, the optimal truncation point, denoted as $\chi(\%)$, is determined to select the top of the **Sorted_PE** to build a sharper histogram, denoted as **Opt_Sorted_PE**. Notice that, to achieve the perfect reconstruction, the same structure for CM calculation should remain unchanged for both embedding and extraction process.

3. CONSTRUCTION of MULTI-FEATURE BASED COMPLEXITY MEASURE

3.1 Basic idea

As mentioned in Section 2.1, assume the '0' and '1' in the secret message of length C are equally distributed, the distortion D between original and stego pixels can computed by

$$D = \sum_{i \in [P_1+1, Z_1-1]} h(i) \times (\Delta i)^2 + \sum_{'i = P_1' \text{ 'and' } w=1'} (\Delta i)^2$$
$$= \sum_{i \in U(Pb, Zb)} h(i) + \frac{1}{2}C, \quad (\Delta i = 1) \qquad (4)$$

where the former term is shifting distortion, denoted as D_s, caused by bins' shifting in the range $[P_1+1; Z_1-1]$. The other one is the embedding distortion, denoted as D_e, at peak bin P_1, which means only half of the peak bins P_1 are shifted by 1.

It is easy to follow that, when the secret data is given, D_e are determined, and D_s is considered as the cost for the data embedding. Thus, how to effectively minimize D_s is critical, which corresponds to decrease the bins and their frequencies between $[P_1+1, Z_1-1]$.

Now, we consider an extreme case as shown in Fig. 2(a). If we could generate an idealized histogram with required P_1 (for payload constraint)next to Z_1, namely no other bins besides P_1

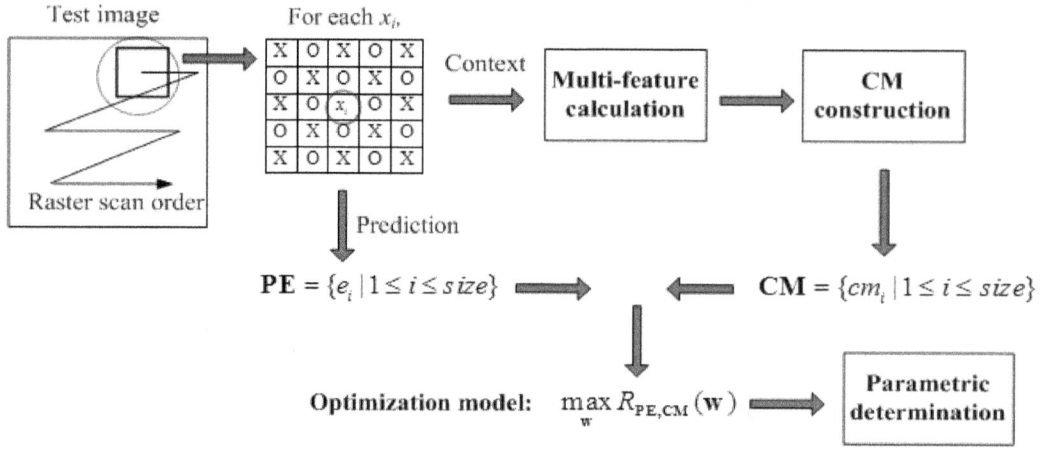

Figure 3 the general framework for construction of complexity measure

involved in the HS based embedding process, i.e., $D_s = 0$,and minimum D is obtained. Let **Sorted_PE_I** be the idealized sorted errors in absolute **PE** value ascending order, the dissimilarity between **Sorted_PE** and **Sorted_PE_I** can be evaluated with Inverse Number (IN). As illustrated in Fig.2(b), to duplicate the extreme case, **Sorted_PE** with CM should be exactly generated as **Sorted_PE_I** , namely the IN should be zero. Then by means of appropriate truncation point, the resulting **Opt_Sorted_PE** can be used to generate the ideal histogram as shown in Fig. 2(b). Otherwise, when the IN is larger as shown in Fig. 2(c), the **Sorted_PE** tends to be more disordered, which results in a flatter histogram and the corresponding performance is degraded. In fact, to guarantee the reversibility, instead of **PE** , which is unavailable in the decoder side, the sorting is implemented according to CMs, which could be computed based on the same structure and are available in both encoder and decoder sides. Note that CMs is only an approximate measure for **PE** ,utilization of CM based sorting to generate the perfect **Sorted_PE_I** with IN = 0 is not feasible in practice, especially for images with rich texture.

To generate the best possible **Sorted_PE** with smaller IN value, it is better to properly employ the structure on cover element's neighboring region or multi-features to construct CMs with stronger correlation with **PE** . In addition, for given payload, the truncation point $\chi(\%)$ needs to be determined to generate a sharper **Opt_Sorted_PE** . The general framework based on the basic idea is illustrated in the next sub-Section.

3.2 General framework

As shown in Fig.3, a general framework for construction of complexity measure is proposed, which includes (1) Multi-features calculation; (2) CM construction; (3) Optimization model development; and (4) Weighting parameters' determination.

(1) Multi-features calculation.

For each pixel x_i , its neighboring region is determined and then the initial multiple features are computed to form a candidate set. To fully exploit the cover's correlation among neighboring region, multi-features could be designed from a variety of sources, i.e. empirical features employed in existing schemes[6,7], features from Rich model set for steganalysis, some geometry moments and etc. In this paper, for each x_i , 12 features are computed, denoted as $\mathbf{F}_i = \{f_i^k \mid k \in [1,12]\}$. To highlight the general framework, the

details on multi-features' calculation and their descriptions are included in Appendix A.

(2) CM construction.

Based on the multi-feature $\mathbf{F}_i$, one can calculate CM value for pixel x_i , denoted as cm_i ,through linear combination of the 12 features, which is described in (5):

$$cm_i = \sum_{k=1}^{12} w_k \cdot f_i^k \qquad (5)$$

where w_k is the weighting parameter for f_i^k and the parameter set is denoted as $\mathbf{w} = \{w_k \mid 1 \le k \le 12\}$ .A larger w_k indicates that the corresponding feature f_i^k is more important for the construction of complexity measure. When w_k is much less, the feature f_i^k could be ignored. Therefore, a threshold could be predefined for feature selection. When all the e_i in $\mathbf{PE} = \{e_i \mid i \in [1,\text{size}]\}$ are processed, the corresponding CM array is generated and denoted as $\mathbf{CM} = \{cm_i \mid i \in [1,\text{size}]\}$.

(3) Optimization model development.

Based on the basic idea, our aim is to construct the appropriate **CM** with high correlation with **PE** and use to implement the sorting of **PE** .Thus, for all the pixels in each set (Cross or Round), we could firstly compute the **PE** , multiple features and **CM** , respectively. And then, the correlation coefficient between **PE** and **CM** is utilized as an objective for optimization, which is denoted as $R_{\text{PE,CM}}$ and calculated by

$$R_{\text{PE,CM}}(\mathbf{w}) = \frac{\text{cov}(\mathbf{PE},\mathbf{CM})}{\sigma_{\text{PE}} \cdot \sigma_{\text{CM}}}$$

$$= \frac{\sum_{i=1}^{\text{size}} (e_i - \bar{e})(cm_i - \overline{cm})}{\sqrt{\sum_{i=1}^{\text{size}} (e_i - \bar{e})^2} \cdot \sqrt{\sum_{i=1}^{\text{size}} (cm_i - \overline{cm})^2}} \qquad (6)$$

where $\text{cov}(\mathbf{PE},\mathbf{CM})$ is the covariance between **PE** and **CM** , σ_{PE} and σ_{CM} are their standard deviations, $\bar{e}$ and $\overline{cm}$ are the means of **PE** and **CM** , respectively.

Finally, the optimization model is developed as

$$\underset{\mathbf{w}=\{w_k \mid 1 \le k \le 12\}}{\text{Max}} R_{\text{PE,CM}}(\mathbf{w}) \qquad (7)$$

The optimization model in (7) is then solved to obtain the optimal weighting parameters $\mathbf{w}$.

(4) Determination of optimal weighting parameters

Note that candidate features $f_i^k, (1 \le i \le \text{size})$ described in Appendix A could be multifarious, thus each feature should be rescaled to the same range, say $[1,1000]$, to reach a feasible optimization solution.

In addition, for a given image, $\mathbf{PE}$ is determined and all related terms except cm_i and $\overline{cm}$ in $R_{\mathbf{PE,CM}}(\mathbf{w})$ are constants. Thus, the objective function is simplified to be

$$R_{\mathbf{PE,CM}}(\mathbf{w}) = A \cdot \frac{\sum_{i=1}^{\text{size}} B_i \cdot (cm_i - \overline{cm})}{\sqrt{\sum_{i=1}^{\text{size}} (cm_i - \overline{cm})^2}} \qquad (8)$$

where A and B are constants.

The optimization model in (7) is a nonlinear optimization problem, and can be effectively solved with Sequential Quadratic Programming (SQP) by using Matlab function "fmincon()". SQP is one of the state-of-the-art algorithms for nonlinear programming (NLP). The basic idea of SQP is to model NL Pat a given approximate solution by a quadratic programming (QP) sub-problem and then use the solution to this sub-problem to construct a better approximation. This process is iterated to create a sequence of approximations that will converge to a final solution [19]. At each iteration, the QP problem can be solved using active set method described in [20].

By solving the optimization problem in (7), the optimal weighting parameters $\mathbf{w}$ are obtained, which is then used to compute $\mathbf{CM}$ for sorting of $\mathbf{PE}$. It is noted that optimal parameters $\mathbf{w}$ should be shared by both encoder and decoder for reversible embedding.

4. OPTIMIZED HISTOGRAM AND IMPLEMENTATION DETAILS

4.1 Optimized truncation point

With the obtained CM for given image, the **Sorted_PE** is generated. Then the optimal truncation point $\chi(\%)$ could be determined to build an optimized histogram for given payload, i.e. **Opt_Sorted_PE**.

For HS based reversible embedding, the optimal $\chi(\%)$ is searched between a predefined interval, denoted as $[\chi_{\min}, \chi_{\max}]$, where $\chi_{\min}$ and $\chi_{\max}$ are positive integer in the range $[1,100]$. Then, one can follow the procedure adopted in Wang et al. work in [18] to fast evaluate each χ's distortion. As a by-product, the optimal side information (peak and zero bins) can be determined in the same procedure.

In the paper, the lower bound $\chi_{\min}$ is the small enough value corresponding to the given payload. Note the factor that the proposed CM construction framework usually generate a sharper **Opt_Sorted_PE** than the ones with some traditional schemes, e.g., Sachnev et al.'s method [6], thus the truncation point χ for our scheme should be less than the one with conventional methods, denoted as χ_{trad}. Therefore, we can set $\chi_{\max}$ to be χ_{trad} in our scheme. And the optimal χ is searched in a much reduced interval $[\chi_{\min}, \chi_{\max}]$. To speed up the search for optimal χ, some empirical

search strategies are adopted in our scheme, which will be discussed later in Section 5.

4.2 Location map generation

HS based embedding in prediction errors may cause some marked pixels be not in the range $[0,255]$, which is known as overflow or underflow. The Luo's method [15] is employed to avoid the possible overflow/underflow. In HS based embedding, due to at most one unit shift occurs in each level embedding. When multiple embedding is utilized with several pairs of peak and zero bins as described in [18], the maximum accumulative modification of one pixel can be evaluated by the number of selected peak and zero bin pairs. Assume that L is the maximum modification, we only perform HS based multiple embedding on the prediction errors of pixels in range $[L, 255-L]$ to avoid overflow or underflow and then utilize a location map (LM) to distinguish the source of the overlapped range (OR) $[0,L] \cup [255-L+1]$. If original pixel is located in OR, then indicator '0' is recorded in LM. Otherwise, if the marked pixel after embedding or shifting is in OR, '1' is recorded in LM. Finally, the compressed LM (CLM) is hidden in the cover image for auxiliary information. In general, the size of CLM is tiny for most natural images.

During the extraction, LM is first extracted in decoder. Then the stego image is scanned to extract secret message. When those pixels located in $[0,L] \cup [255-L+1]$, the LM is consulted to determine the source, when bit in LM is '0', then keep current pixel unchanged, otherwise, recover the original pixel, and extract the secret data if there is secret data hidden in it.

4.3 Auxiliary information

In RDH, some auxiliary information (AI) should be embedded into the cover image as a part of payload for blind data extraction and image restoration, which includes:

(1) the number of selected peak and zero bin pairs;

(2) the set of selected peak and zero bins;

(3) the maximum modification L to avoid overflow or underflow;

(4) the truncation point $\chi(\%)$;

(5) the optimal weighting parameters $\mathbf{w}$ for multiple features;

(6) the compressed LM and its size.

It is noted that the auxiliary information only occupies a very small portion of the payload, especially for those cover images without overflow and underflow.

4.4 Data Embedding

Assume that C is the length of binary secret message, the embedding process is similarly performed as Section 2.1 and briefly described as follows:

1) With the cover image divided into Cross and Round sets as shown in Fig. 1(a), assign half of the secret message of length $\frac{1}{2}C$ for each set, respectively.

2) Evaluate the maximum modification L and reserve enough room in the beginning of the Cross set to hide auxiliary information(AI).

3) For each pixel x_i located in $[L, 255-L]$ in Cross set, compute its prediction value $\hat{x}_i$, prediction error e_i, multi-feature $\mathbf{F}_i = \{f_i^k \mid k \in [1,12]\}$, respectively. When all the pixels are processed, $\mathbf{PE} = \{e_i \mid 1 \le i \le \text{size}\}$ is generated.

Table I. The comparison of different CM construction methods under different payloads for test image Lena

bpp	Schemes	Image Set	Optimal percentage ($\chi(\%)$)	Distortion D for each Set	R for truncated array	R for whole array	IN for truncated array	IN for whole array	PSNR (dB)	Improved
0.05	Varsiliy	X-Set	48	11124	0.0835	0.4368	468013	1058982	58.624	
		O-Set	50	12201	0.1024	0.4367	493023	1058875		
	Hwang	X-Set	39	10769	0.0949	0.4445	367550	1058096	58.804	0.474
		O-Set	39	11610	0.1231	0.4406	368730	1058608		
	Our	X-Set	23	9630	0.1703	0.6565	204873	1054847	59.278	
		O-Set	39	10408	0.1587	0.6529	366911	1054046		
0.3	Varsiliy	X-Set	78	138616	0.2067	0.4368	792120	1058982	47.4182	
		O-Set	83	170198	0.1742	0.4225	850119	1061801		
	Hwang	X-Set	78	138957	0.2404	0.4445	791033	1058096	47.4102	0.2261
		O-Set	79	170432	0.1874	0.4258	804592	1061013		
	Our	X-Set	76	130300	0.2709	0.6565	768916	1054847	47.6443	
		O-Set	75	162837	0.2207	0.6239	758535	1057578		

4) Solve the optimization problem in (7) to obtain optimal parameters **w** for a given image, and then calculate the $\mathbf{CM} = \{cm_i, \ 1 \le i \le size\}$.

5) Sort each e_i according to its cm_i in **CM** and then generate **Sorted_PE**.

6) Determine the optimal truncation point $\chi(\%)$ according to the given payload, and generate the **Opt_Sorted_PE** as cover. As described in Section 4.1, in the process of determination truncation point $\chi(\%)$, the optimal side information (peak and zero bins) is obtained at the same time.

7) Scan the pixels in **Opt_Sorted_PE** to embed secret message with given side information, and generate LM. For each x_i, if it is located in $[0,L] \cup [255-L+1]$, append bit `0' to LM. Otherwise, perform embedding process on it and generate stego version $x_i'$. If $x_i'$ is located in $[0,L] \cup [255-L+1]$, append bit `1' to LM.

8) Collect AI of Cross set and record LSBs of the remained area in Cross set as parts of payload. Then assemble them and the rest $\frac{1}{2}C$ secret to hide in Round set.

9) Follow the Step 3-7 to perform data embedding in Round set.

10) By using LSB replacement, embed the AI of Round set into the reserved area of Cross set to generate the stego image.

4.5 Data extraction

Data extracting is the reverse process.

1) Divide the pixels of stego image into Cross and Round sets.

2) Extract AI of Round set from the LSBs of the reserved pixels of stego-image.

3) Recover the Round set. Locate each potential marked pixel x_i' in $[L, 255-L]$ or located in $[0,L] \cup [255-L+1]$ with corresponding bit `1' in LM in Round set. Then, compute its prediction value $\hat{x}_i^\mu$, prediction error e_i', and multi-feature as embedding process.

4) Perform the same sorting process to acquire the identical **Sorted_PE** as the embedding process.

5) Extract the parameter $\chi(\%)$ from AI to obtain **Opt_Sorted_PE**, and then perform the reverse extraction to recover it original version e_i and extract 1-bit secret data.

6) Recover each pixel in Round set. Scan all the pixels as the embedding order, Round set and its payload could be acquired.

7) Extract AI of Cross set from the extract payload from Round set, and recover reserved pixels in Cross set with LSB replacement.

8) Follow the Step 3-7 to recover Cross set.

5. EXPEIMENTAL RESULTS

In this section, simulation results are given to demonstrate the performance of the proposed method. Four standard 512×512 sized gray-scale images, including Lena, Baboon, F16 and Boat, are used in our experiments. All these images are downloaded from the USC-SIPI database[21].

5.1 Comparison of various CM construction methods

We firstly compare multi-feature based CM construction method with other two typical ones (Sachnev et al. [6] and Hwang et al. [7]) with single feature as CM. In the interest of fair comparison, all the schemes are implemented on the same prediction as described in Section 2.1. Since the double-layered embedding is performed in both sets (Cross and Round sets, denoted as X-set and O-set respectively), the comparison is individually implemented.

Table I summarizes the corresponding results under various payloads for test image Lena. It is observed that our method achieves the highest correlation R for whole array among those schemes, which means a better **CM** with highest correlation with **PE** is achieved by our method due to the optimization model. Since the actual cover is the truncated into **Opt_Sorted_PE**, R between **CM** and **Opt_Sorted_PE** is given and denoted as "R for truncated array" in Table I, which also achieves the desired values. Having the high correlation with **PE**, multi-feature based CM construction method leads to a better **Sorted_PE** with less IN as shown in "IN for truncated array" and "IN for whole array" in Table I, which verifies our conclusion in Section 3. Consequently, for given payload, smaller truncation point $\chi(\%)$ is needed to generate a much sharper histogram, which results in a better rate and distortion performance as shown in "D for each set" and "PSNR" in Table I. Table II shows the performance comparison for all the test images at different payloads, which further demonstrates the superiority of proposed multi-feature based CM construction method.

Table II. The comparison of different CM construction methods for various test images

Test image	bpp	0.05	0.1	0.3	0.5	0.7
Lena (dB)	Varsiliy	58.624	55.119	47.418	47.418	39.598
	Hwang	58.804	55.203	47.410	47.410	39.605
	Our	59.278	55.523	47.644	47.644	39.742
	Improved	0.474	0.320	0.226	0.226	0.137
Baboon (dB)	Varsiliy	53.143	47.352	37.486	32.247	——
	Hwang	53.417	47.632	37.634	32.256	——
	Our	53.740	47.977	37.945	32.645	——
	Improved	0.322	0.344	0.310	0.389	——
F16 (dB)	Varsiliy	61.126	57.837	51.346	46.750	42.994
	Hwang	61.638	58.121	51.430	46.843	43.053
	Our	62.206	58.438	51.526	46.908	43.080
	Improved	0.567	0.317	0.095	0.065	0.027
Boat (dB)	Varsiliy	55.8308	51.8912	42.9439	37.8108	34.6248
	Hwang	55.9561	51.8848	42.9185	37.8604	34.4558
	Our	56.3569	52.0865	43.1596	38.1897	34.7753
	Improved	0.4008	0.1952	0.2157	0.3293	0.1505

5.2 Determination of optimized truncation point

The search interval for truncation point is initialized as $[\chi_{\min}, \chi_{\max}]$ as discussed in Section 4.1. Table III gives the experimental results under different payloads for test image Lena and Table IV shows the results for various teat images at 0.3 bpp. The experiment results suggest that the PSNR vs χ is approximately piecewise monotonous and has a minima. Therefore, we develop an empirical search strategy, which is summarized as follows.

(1) When payload >0.1bpp, the optimal χ is near to $\chi_{\max}$. Thus the search is performed downwards one by one from $\chi_{\max}$ to $\chi_{\min}$. In this way, the iteration number " num " as shown in Table III and IV, is significantly reduced.

(2) When payload <0.1bpp, a two-step coarse-to-fine search strategy is adopted to find the optimal χ.

1. Coarse Search

(a) Initialize the search interval $[\chi_1, \chi_2]$, where $\chi_1 = \chi_{\min}$ and $\chi_2 = \chi_{\max}$.

(b)Set search step t as half of the interval size, i.e, $t = \lceil (\chi_1 + \chi_2)/2 \rceil$. If $D(t) < D(\chi_2)$, where $D(x)$ represents the distortion corresponding to the truncation point x, let $\chi_2 = t$ and then go back to (b). Otherwise, it goes to fine search.

2. Fine Search

(a) Set $\chi_1 = t$, and search downwards one by one from χ_2 to χ_1. If $D(\chi_2 - 1) < D(\chi_2)$, let $\chi_2 = \chi_2 - 1$, then go to (a). Otherwise, go to (b).

(b) Let $\chi = \chi_2$, and output χ as the optimal truncation point. As shown in Table III at 0.05 bpp, the initial interval is $[6, 42]$. Then we implement the binary search until $D(t) \geq D(\chi_2)$, and have the interval $[15, 24]$ for fine search. Implement the fine search from

24 to 15, we find $D(22) > D(23)$. Therefore, $\chi = 23$ is determined as the optimal truncation point, and the correspondingiteration number num is 5, i.e. ,

Table III.The optimal truncation point χ for test image Lena

bpp	Interval $[\chi_{\min}, \chi_{\max}]$	Truncation point χ	Iteration number num
0.05	[6,42]	23	5
0.1	[11,49]	46	5
0.3	[31,78]	76	4
0.5	[51,81]	75	8
0.7	[72,84]	80	6

Table IV.Determination of the optimal truncationpoint χ for various test images at 0.3 bpp

Test image	Interval $[\chi_{\min}, \chi_{\max}]$	Truncation point χ	Iteration number num
Lena	[31,78]	76	4
Baboon	[31,45]	43	4
F16	[31,64]	59	7
Boat	[31,79]	78	3

$42 \rightarrow 24 \rightarrow 15 \rightarrow 23 \rightarrow 22$. According to our simulation results, less than 10 iteration number is required for most cases, indicating that the proposed search strategy is quite affordable for practical applications.

5.3 Comprehensive performance comparison and analysis

We then proceed to compare the comprehensive performance between our scheme and some state-of-the-art reversible data hiding methods, which include Schnev et al. [6], Luo et al. [15], Wu et al. [14], Li et al. [11], Xuan et al. [16] and Ou et al. [12]. The performance comparison is shown in Fig.4. For most cases, our scheme achieves the best rate and distortion performance among all the methods, except F16. Firstly, compared with some schemes, e.g., Xuan et al. [16] and Wu et al. [14], fully enclosed rhombus prediction has certain advantage and thus make our scheme outperform them with clear margin. Moreover, for the scheme based on the same rhombus prediction, i.e. Schnev et al.[6], our scheme also achieves significant performance improvement, which mainly attributes to the effectiveness of the proposed multi-feature CM construction method. Thus, the superiority of our scheme is verified. Moreover, it is observed that, for small to medium data payload (Payload<0.4 bpp), our scheme achieves significant performance improvement over other involved schemes. However, for large data payload (Payload>0.4 bpp), although our scheme outperforms consistently other methods in most cases, its performance tends to be similar to some schemes. This is because the key objective of our scheme is to improve existing sorting technique by using multi-feature based CM construction method and thus generate a better **Sorted_PE**. In other words, the smooth regions in cover image are chosen in priority to build **Opt_Sorted_PE** for data hiding. However, at high payload, almost all the pixels should be involved for data hiding. Under the circumstances, our scheme could not show its advantage at large payload.

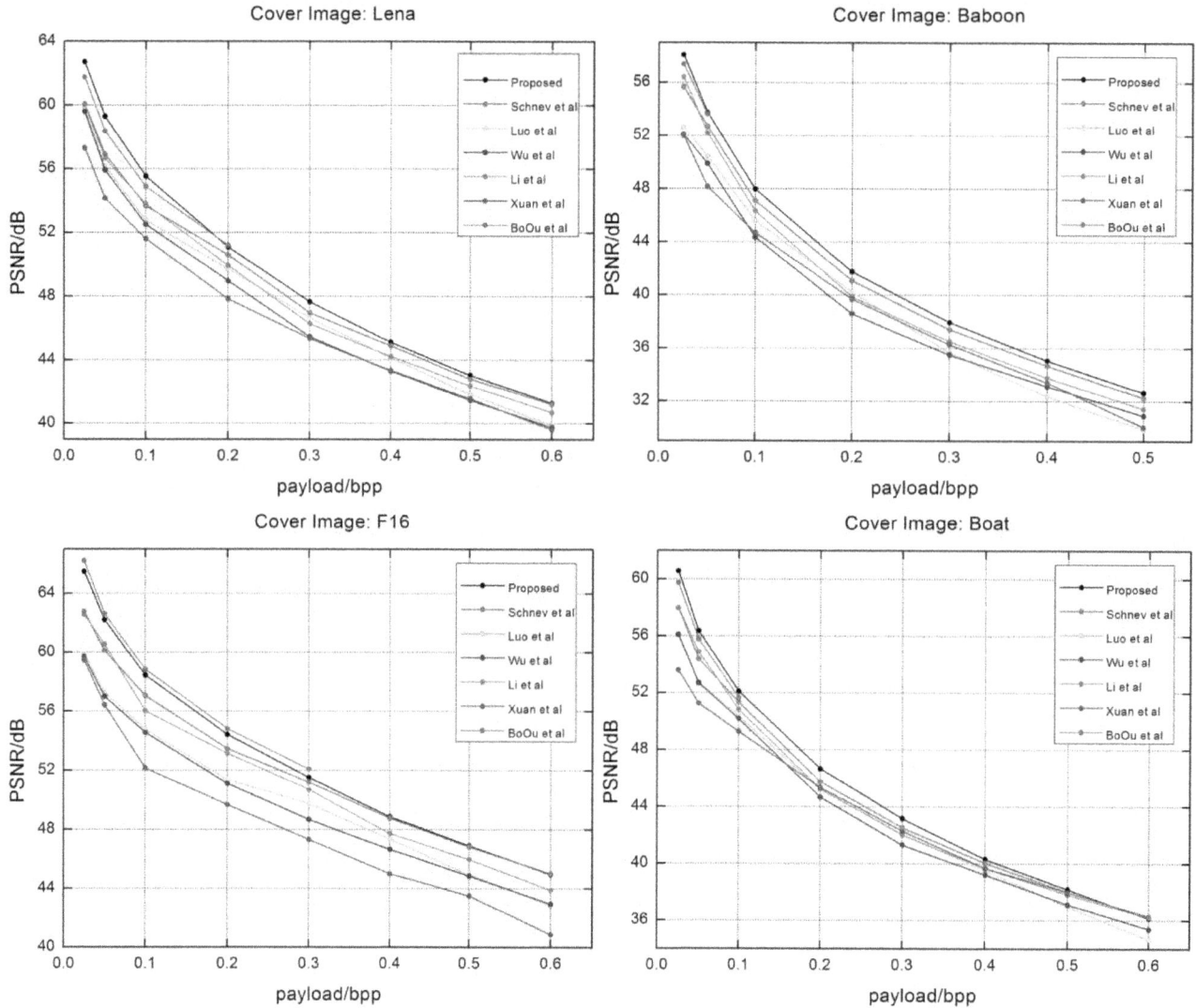

Fig. 4 Performance comparison between the proposed method and other ones

As a special case, it is also observed that the proposed scheme cannot compete with Ou et al's method [12] for F16 at small data payload, which is the state of the art for small payload embedding. This is because Ou et al's method utilized 2-D prediction-error histogram (PEH) to exploit image correlation and could hide $\log_2 3$ bit secret data for smooth region with much less distortion compared with conventional 1-D PEH based schemes. Thus its superiority is mainly manifested in smooth images with less texture contents, e.g., F16. In contrast, our scheme could not exemplify its advantage in smooth region of images. Nevertheless, our scheme has some advantage on embedding capacity for images with rich texture contents. Since Ou et al's method [12] generally utilized adjacent two prediction-errors, which consists of 4 pixels in all, as one unit to hide no more than $\log_2 3$ bit secret data in non-smooth region. Therefore, taken as a whole, the proposed scheme could achieve a much larger payload than Ou et al's method.

5.4 Practical evaluation of computational complexity

In this subsection, we further evaluate the practical computation cost in terms of computation time (CmpTime) for our proposed scheme. Since any HS based embedding process needs to undergo three similar steps, i.e., generation of cover images, peak and zero bin selection and reversible embedding, we only test computation cost of the distinct parts compared with others, i.e. multi-feature based complexity measure construction and the determination of optimized truncation point χ.

In our simulation, we test the CmpTime of the proposed scheme for various images at 0.3bpp. The simulation is implemented with Matlab on a 3.2 GHz Intel Pentium(R) Dual Core CPU with 4GB memory. The results are summarized in Table V. Although it may take relatively more time in multiple features' calculation and iterative search of optimal χ, it is still quite affordable for practical applications.

6. Conclusion

In this paper, a general framework for construction of multi-feature based complexity measure (CM) is proposed, which helps to fully exploit the image correlation for efficient HS based reversible embedding. Firstly, for each pixel, its multiple features are computed on its neighboring region, and then corresponding CM is calculated through linear combination of these features. An optimization model is developed to ensure the **CM** array for all the cover elements has high correlation with corresponding prediction errors array (**PE**). By solving the optimization model, the optimal weighting parameters for CM are determined. To further improve the rate and distortion performance, the optimal truncation point $\chi(\%)$ is determined during a predefined interval to generate optimal histogram. Compared with previous approaches, experimental results demonstrate the superiority of the proposed scheme.

Table V. Computation time (CmpTime) of the proposed scheme for various images at 0.3 bpp (Unit: second)

Test image	Cmptime for CM construction	Cmptime for χ determination
Lena	5.932	5.832
Baboon	5.901	5.645
F16	7.194	11.069
Boat	5.745	3.691

ACKNOWLEDGMENTS

This work was supported in part by the National Natural Science Foundation of China under Grant61379156 and Grant 61402209, in part by the National Research Foundation for the Doctoral Program of Higher Education of China under Grant20120171110037, in part by the Key Program of Natural Science Foundation of Guangdong under Grant S2012020011114, and in part by Invention Patent and Industrialization Technology Demonstration Project of Jiangxi Province under Grant 20143BBM26113.

REFERENCES

[1] J. M. Barton, "Method and apparatus for embedding authentication information within digital data," U.S. Patent 5646997, 1997.

[2] J. Fridrich, M. Goljan and R. Du, "Invertible authentication," *In Proc. SPIE Security and Watermarking of Multimedia Contents III,* San Jose, CA, pp. 197-208, 2001.

[3] M.U. Celik, G. Sharma, A. M. Tekalp and E. Saber, "Lossless generalized-LSB data embedding," *IEEE Trans. Image Process,* vol.14, no.2, pp.253–266, 2005.

[4] J. Tian, "Reversible watermarking using a difference expansion," *IEEE Trans. Circuits Syst. Video Technol.,* vol.13, no.8, pp.890–896, 2003.

[5] D. M. Thodi and J. J. Rodriguez, "Expansion embedding techniques for reversible watermarking," *IEEE Trans. Image Process.,* vol. 16, no. 3,pp. 721–730, Mar. 2007.

[6] V. Sachnev, H. J. Kim, J. Nam, S. Suresh and Y. Q. Shi, "Reversible watermarking algorithm using sorting and prediction," *IEEE Trans. Circuits Syst. Video Technol.,* vol.19, no.7, pp. 989-999, 2009.

[7] H. J. Hwang, H. J. Kim, V. Sachnev, and S. H. Joo, "Reversible watermarking method using optimal histogram pair shifting based on prediction and sorting," *KSII Transactions on Internet and Information Systems,* vol. 4, no. 4, pp. 655-670, 2010.

[8] M. Fallahpour, "Reversible image data hiding based on gradient adjusted prediction," *IEICE Electron. Exp.,* vol. 5, no. 20, pp. 870–876, 2008.

[9] D. Coltuc, "Improved embedding for prediction-based reversible watermarking," *IEEE Trans. Inf. Forensics Security,* vol. 6, no. 3, pp. 873–882, Sep. 2011.

[10] I. C. Dragoi, and D. Coltuc, "Local-prediction-based difference expansion reversible watermarking," *IEEE Trans. Image Process.,* vol. 23, no. 4, pp. 1779–1790, Apr. 2014.

[11] X. L. Li, B. Yang, and T. Y. Zeng, "Efficient reversible watermarking based on adaptive prediction-error expansion and pixel selection," *IEEE Trans. Image Process.,* vol.20, no.12, pp.3524–3533, 2011.

[12] B. Ou, X. L. Li, Y. Zhao, R. R. Ni, Y. Q. Shi "Pair-wise prediction-error expansion for efficient reversible data hiding," *IEEE Trans. Image Process.,* vol. 22, no. 12, pp. 5010-5021, 2013.

[13] Z. Ni, Y. Q. Shi, N. Ansari and W. Su, "Reversible data hiding," *IEEE Trans. Circuits Syst. Video Technol.,* vol.16, no.3, pp.354-362, 2006.

[14] H. T. Wu and J. Huang, "Reversible image watermarking on prediction errors by efficient histogram modification," *Signal Process.,* vol.92, no.12, pp.3000–3009, 2012.

[15] L. Luo, Z. Chen, M. Chen, X. Zeng and Z. Xiong, "Reversible image watermarking using interpolation technique," *IEEE Trans. Inf. Forensics Security,* vol.5, no.1, pp.187–193, 2010.

[16] G. R. Xuan, Y. Q. Shi, P. Chai, X. Cui, Z. Ni, X. Tong, "Optimum histogram pair based image lossless data embedding," *In Proc. International Workshop on Digital Watermarking,* vol.5510, pp.84-102, 2008.

[17] X. Li, B. Li, B. Yang, and T. Zeng. "General framework to histogram shifting-based reversible data hiding". *IEEE Trans. Image Process.,*22(6):2181–2191, Jun. 2013.

[18] J. Wang, J. Ni, X. Zhang and Y. Shi. Rate and Distortion Optimization for Reversible Data Hiding Using Multiple Histogram Shifting. *IEEE Trans.on Cybernetics,* 99(1):1–12, Jan. 2016.

[19] P. T. Boggs and J. W. Tolle, \Sequential quadratic programming," *Acta numerica,* vol. 4, pp. 1-51, 1995.

[20] R. Fletcher, Practical methods of optimization. John Wiley & Sons, 2013.

[21] http://sipi.usc.edu/database/

APPENDIX A

During the framework for multi-feature based complexity measurement construction, 12 initial features are constructed to better exploit the correlation among the cover image. For each x_i, its neighboring pixels in the 5×5 sized block belongs to different set are chosen as context and denoted as $\{v_i \mid i \in [1,12]\}$ as follows.

		v_5		v_{12}	
X	O	X	O	X
	v_6		v_1		v_{11}
O	X	O	X	O
	X	v_2 O	X x_i	v_4 O	X
	v_7		v_3		v_{10}
O	X	O	X	O
		v_8		v_9	
X	O	X	O	X

Firstly, left gradient and right gradient are introduced and denoted as lg_i and rg_i, respectively, which could be computed by

$$\begin{cases} lg_1 = (v_5 - v_1, v_2 - v_1) \\ lg_2 = (v_1 - v_4, v_3 - v_4) \\ lg_3 = (v_2 - v_3, v_8 - v_3) \\ lg_4 = (v_6 - v_2, v_1 - v_2) \end{cases} \text{ and } \begin{cases} rg_1 = (v_{12} - v_1, v_4 - v_1) \\ rg_2 = (v_{11} - v_4, v_{10} - v_4) \\ rg_3 = (v_4 - v_3, v_9 - v_3) \\ rg_4 = (v_1 - v_2, v_3 - v_2) \end{cases}. \quad (A.1)$$

Both gradients can reflect the maximum change of pixel value and the most rapid changing direction.

For each x_i, those typical features are calculated to build a features set $\mathbf{F} = \{f_i^k \mid k \in [1,12]\}$, which represents its local texture.

(1) Maximum pixel value of four neighboring pixels. namely f_i^1 is computed as

$$f_i^1 = \max\{\mathbf{v}\} \tag{A.2}$$

where $\mathbf{v} = \{v_1, v_2, v_3, v_4\}$.

(2) Minimum pixel value of four neighboring pixels.

$$f_i^2 = \min\{\mathbf{v}\} \tag{A.3}$$

(3) Larger one between the horizontal and vertical second-order differences, denoted as $hsod$ and $vsod$, respectively. The feature value f_i^3 is computed as

$$f_i^3 = \max\{hsod, vsod\} \tag{A.4}$$

where $hsod = |v_1 + v_3 - 2\hat{x}_i|$ and $vsod = |v_2 + v_4 - 2\hat{x}_i|$ .In addition, $\hat{x}_i$ is computed by (1)

(4) Smaller one between above-mentioned both differences and computed as

$$f_i^4 = \min\{hsod, vsod\} \tag{A.5}$$

(5) Sum of absolute values of four neighboring pixels' second-order differences. The second-order difference is computed by using Diagonal Laplacian Filter, i.e. $sod_1 = v_2 + v_4 + v_5 + v_{12} - 4v_1$, $sod_2 = v_1 + v_3 + v_6 + v_7 - 4v_2$, $sod_3 = v_2 + v_4 + v_8 + v_9 - 4v_3$, $sod_4 = v_1 + v_3 + v_{10} + v_{11} - 4v_4$. Then the feature value f_i^5 is defined as

$$f_i^5 = \sum_{k=1}^{4} |sod_k| \tag{A.6}$$

(6) Sum of the differences between four neighboring pixel values. The feature value f_i^6 is defined as

$$f_i^6 = \sum_{k=1}^{4} \Delta v_k \tag{A.7}$$

where $\Delta v_1 = |v_1 - v_2|$, $\Delta v_2 = |v_2 - v_3|$, $\Delta v_3 = |v_3 - v_4|$, $\Delta v_4 = |v_4 - v_1|$

(7) Variance of the differences between four neighboring pixel values. This feature is previously used in [7] for sorting, and the feature value f_i^7 is defined as

$$f_i^7 = \frac{1}{4} \sum_{k=1}^{4} (\Delta v_k - \Delta \bar{v})^2 \tag{A.8}$$

where $\Delta \bar{v} = (\Delta v_1 + \Delta v_2 + \Delta v_3 + \Delta v_4)/4$ is the mean of those differences.

(8) Local variance of current pixel. This feature is adopted in [6] for sorting and calculated by using four neighboring pixels' value and current pixel's prediction value $\hat{x}_i$, i.e.,

$$f_i^8 = \frac{1}{4} \sum_{k=1}^{4} (v_k - \hat{x}_i)^2 \tag{A.9}$$

.(9) Sum of the magnitudes of its neighboring pixels' left gradient. The feature value f_i^9 is computed as

$$f_i^9 = \sum_{k=1}^{4} |lg_k| \tag{A.10}$$

where $| \ |$ is the function that returns a vector's magnitude.

(10) Sum of the magnitudes of those right gradient. The feature value f_i^{10} is computed as

$$f_i^{10} = \sum_{k=1}^{4} |rg_k| \tag{A.11}$$

(11) Sum of the magnitudes of the differences between four neighboring pixels' left gradient. The feature value f_i^{11} is computed as

$$f_i^{11} = \sum_{k=1}^{3} \sum_{l=k+1}^{4} |lg_k - lg_l| \tag{A.12}$$

(12) Sum of those right gradient. The feature value f_i^{12} is computed as

$$f_i^{12} = \sum_{k=1}^{3} \sum_{l=k+1}^{4} |rg_k - rg_l| \tag{A.13}$$

A Novel CDMA Based High Performance Reversible Data Hiding Scheme

Bin Ma
School of Information Science
Qilu University of Technology
3501 Daxue Road, Jinan,
China,250353
sddxmb@126.com

Jian Xu
School of Computer and Information
Shandong Univ. of Fina. and Econ.
7366 Bicyclic East Road, Jinan,
China, 250014
sdfixj@126.com

Yun Q. Shi
Dept. of Elec. and Comp. Engineering
New Jersey Institute of Technology
University Heights, Newark,
New Jersey 07102, USA
shi@njit.edu

ABSTRACT

In this paper, based on the principle of Code Division Multiple Access (CDMA), a novel reversible data hiding scheme is presented. The to-be-embedded data are represented by different orthogonal spreading sequences and embedded into a cover image while degrading the image quality slightly. According to the feature of orthogonality, different spreading sequences are repeatedly embedded into the image without disturbing each other, and most elements of different spreading sequences are mutually cancelled in the process of multilevel data embedding. Thus, it keeps the distortion of the embedded image at a relatively low level even with a high embedding capacity. Moreover, the location-map of the proposed scheme can be highly compressed and thus the size is quite small; it further helps to obtain high net embedding capacity. Experimental results have demonstrated that the CDMA based reversible data hiding scheme can achieve higher image quality at the moderate-to-high embedding capacity than other state-of-the-art reversible data hiding works.

Keywords

Code division multiple access (CDMA); reversible data hiding; prediction-error; embedding capacity; location-map.

1. INTRODUCTION

Reversible data hiding is a kind of distortion-free data embedding technique, which allows one to hide the secret data into an image in such a way that the original image can be recovered completely from the marked image after the embedded data having been extracted exactly. This makes it an ideal solution for some critical applications where the cover image is so important that even the slight changes in pixels' values is unacceptable, such as military and medical imagery. In such a scenario, any changes would affect the intelligence of the image, and the access to the original data is always desired.

IH&MMSec 2016, June 20-23, 2016, Vigo, Spain
© 2016 ACM. ISBN 978-1-4503-4290-2/16/06...$15.00.
DOI: http://dx.doi.org/10.1145/2909827.2930790

A lot of reversible data hiding schemes have been proposed in recent years. Early reversible data hiding schemes are mainly based on lossless compression techniques, in which certain bits of the image pixels are losslessly compressed to create vacancies for data embedding. Fredrich et al. [1] developed a reversible data hiding method through compressing the least significant bit planes of the host image and embedded secret data into the saved space. Celik et al. [2] enhanced Fredrich et al.'s method and presented a higher performance scheme by compressing the quantization residues with a kind of more efficient compression method. However, these schemes usually suffer from undesirable distortion at low embedding capacity and lack of security control algorithm. Later on, more efficient algorithms which emphasize on increasing the embedding capacity and retaining the image high quality have been presented.

One of the most popular RDH schemes is histogram modification scheme proposed by Ni et al. [3], in which a gap is created near the highest histogram bins by shifting it right-hand/left-hand bins with one position, and the pixels associate with the highest bins are used to encode the embedding bits. Lee et al. [4] exploited the histogram features of difference image, and have embedded more data into the image than Ni et al.'s scheme. Yang et al. [5] proposed a kind of interleaving prediction method, by which the number of prediction-errors is as many as the pixels, and thus the embedding capacity is improved significantly. Later on, Xuan et al. [6] embedded data into image prediction-errors by using histogram pairs, four thresholds are employed for optimal embedding and thus high performance is achieved at the low-to-moderate embedding capacity. Li et al. [7] have proposed using the two-dimensional difference-histogram to improve the embedding performance at low payload, and the embedding capacity is increased at the cost of very small image distortion.

Difference expansion is another fruitful RDH approach introduced by Tian [8], in which the difference of the two adjacent pixels is expanded and one bit is then embedded into the space created by expansion. Thodi and Rodriguez [9] proposed an improved difference expansion method, namely prediction-error expansion method, to exploit the correlation between a pixel and its neighborhood, which introduce smaller image distortion than Tian's method at same embedding capacity. Sachnev et al. [10] presented a high performance prediction-error expansion scheme based on the rhombus-error-prediction method, which allows embedding more data into the image with less distortion, and the location map is not needed in most cases. In [11], Li et al. proposed adaptively embedded 1 or 2 bits into expandable pixels according to the local complexity with prediction-error expansion method, and thus the image distortion is restrained in the process data embedding.

Although most schemes have tried to exploit more efficient error prediction methods to keep the image in good quality after the data having been embedded, a lot of big-value prediction-errors would still be involved for data hiding when the payload is high; the image quality drops rapidly with the increase of the embedding capacity in most cases. In this paper, we first present a CDMA based high performance reversible data hiding scheme. The to-be-embedded data are represented by different orthogonal spreading sequences and repeatedly embedded into the cover image, hence the embedding capacity is enlarged; in the meantime, most elements of different spreading sequences are mutually cancelled in the process of multilevel data embedding, that keeps the image in good quality even with high embedding capacity. Moreover, in a CDMA based reversible data hiding system, only the receiver who knows the same spreading sequence as the sender can decode and obtain the embedded data, and the security of the system is then improved.

The rest of the paper is organized as follows. Section II introduces the CDMA based data hiding method in detail. In Section III, the performance of the CDMA based reversible data hiding scheme is discussed. The experimental results are demonstrated and analyzed in Section IV. The conclusions are drawn in Section V.The proceedings are the records of the conference.

2. CDMA BASED REVERSIBLE DATA HIDING SCHEME

CDMA is a kind of spectrum spreading technique for data communication, in which the secret message are represented by different orthogonal spreading sequences and transmitted together in the same channel so that the frequency resource is saved. The principle of CDMA based data communication system can be described as follows:

Suppose $S = (s_\sigma)_{1 \times m}$ is a zero-mean spreading sequence with size of $1 \times m$ and satisfies:

$$s_\sigma \in \{-1,1\} \ , \quad \sum_{\sigma=1}^{m} s_\sigma = 0 \tag{1}$$

The cross correlation of any two different spreading sequences is:

$$\langle S_i, S_j \rangle = S_i \cdot S_j^T = 0 \quad (i \neq j) \tag{2}$$

Eq.(2) shows that the spreading sequences are orthogonal to each other. In a CDMA based data communication system, each sender is assigned with an antipodal spreading sequence for signal transmitting. The secret message is modified according to the rule: the secret bit "1" is denoted by itself and the secret bit "0" is denoted by "-1". Thus the modified secret message is only composed of elements "1" and "-1". The compound signal in the encoding side is

$$I = b_1 S_1 + b_2 S_2 + \cdots + b_j S_j + \cdots + b_n S_n \tag{3}$$

where, I is the compound signal to be transmitted, $b_1, b_2 ... b_j ... b_n$ are the bits of the modified secret message, n is the number of spreading sequence (the same as the bits to be embedded), $S_1, S_2 ... S_j ... S_n$ are the orthogonal spreading sequences. At the decoding side, the embedded bit can be extracted as

$$\frac{I \cdot S_j}{|S_j|^2} = \frac{(b_1 S_1 + b_2 S_2 + \cdots + b_j S_j + \cdots + b_n S_n) \cdot S_j}{|S_j|^2} = \frac{b_j S_j \cdot S_j}{|S_j|^2} = b_j \tag{4}$$

where, $| \ |^2$ is the module-square of the spreading sequence. S_j is the specified spreading sequence. The result b_j is the bit of the modified secret message, and by which the original message can be obtained simply. According to the orthogonality of different spreading sequences, only the decoder who has the same spreading sequence as the encoder can obtain the secret message correctly. Therefore, different signals can be transmitted simultaneously in the same channel and the channel capacity is enlarged. For example, suppose two orthogonal sequences are $S_1 = (1,-1,1,-1)$ and $S_2 = (1,-1,-1,1)$. Apparently, S_1 and S_2 are zero-mean and orthogonal to each other. The two secret bits are "1" and "0", and they are changed to "1" and "-1" as the modified secret message. Thus, the two bits are represented by the spreading sequences and are transmitted together in a CDMA based data communication system, and the compound signal is $S = S_1 + (-S_2) = S_1 - S_2 = (0,0,2,-2)$. At the receiver side, for the decoder with the spreading sequence S_1, the decoding result is $\frac{S \cdot S_1^T}{|S_1|^2} = \frac{(S_1 - S_2) \cdot S_1^T}{|S_1|^2} = \frac{S_1 \cdot S_1^T}{|S_1|^2} = 1$, which represents the bit 1; for the decoder with the spreading sequence S_2, the decoding result is $\frac{S \cdot S_2^T}{|S_2|^2} = \frac{(S_1 - S_2) \cdot S_2^T}{|S_2|^2} = \frac{-S_2 \cdot S_2^T}{|S_2|^2} = -1$, which represents the bit 0 apparently. The result would be neither "1" nor "-1" if other sequences are utilized to decode the compound signal. Since the orthogonal spreading sequences can be generated in different ways and it is impossible for eavesdroppers to guess them exactly, the CDMA based signal transmitting system can provide high capacity and security.

Actually, the CDMA based data communication system can be viewed as a data hiding system, the secret massage is as the to-be-embedded data and the transmission channel is as the cover image. Inspired by the principle of CDMA based data communication system, a CDMA based reversible data hiding scheme is proposed and described carefully in the following paragraphs.

2.1 CDMA Based Data Embedding

Suppose $W_{in} = [\omega_1, \omega_2, \cdots, \omega_n] (\omega_i \in \{1,0\}, i \in \{1,2,...,n\})$ is the initial binary secret sequence to be embedded. The elements are changed to a series of antipodal bits according to

$$b_i = \begin{cases} 1 & if \ \omega_i = 1; \\ -1 & if \ \omega_i = 0; \end{cases} \tag{5}$$

where $b_i \in \{-1,1\}$, $i \in \{1,2,...,n\}$, the initial to-be-embedded data are changed to $W_c = [b_1, b_2, \cdots, b_n]$ according to Eq.(5). Choose the row or the column of a specific Hadmard matrix to form the spreading sequence as $S_i = \{s_1, s_2 \cdots, s_l\} (i \in \{1,2,...,k\})$. According to the feature of the Hadmard matrix, these spreading sequences are zero-mean and orthogonal to each other. The length "l" of each sequence is an even number, and the number of "1"and "-1" in each spreading sequence is equivalent.

Let I be the original image with the size of $N \times N$, Choose pixels of the image in a given order to form the vector $V_j = [p_1, p_2, \cdots, p_l] (j \in \{1,2,...,N \times N / l\})$, "l" is the length of the vector, which is the same as the length of S_i. Then, the data can be embedded into the image as:

$$\hat{V}_j = V_j + \alpha[b_1 S_1 + b_2 S_2 + \cdots + b_i S_i + \cdots + b_k S_k] \quad (6)$$

The Eq. (6) shows that k bits have been embedded into the vector V_j. Here, k is the number of to-be-embedded bits, which is the same as the number of the orthogonal spreading sequences. α is a positive integer denote the gain factor, which control the embedding intensity. The bigger the α value is, the noisier the image would be. The marked image is obtained by replacing all V_j vectors with $\hat{V}_j$ simply.

2.2 CDMA Based Data Extraction

Let $\hat{I}$ be the received marked image. The vector $\hat{V}_j$ is constructed in the same method as that in the embedding stage. Each embedded bit can be extracted by calculating the cross correlation between $\hat{V}_j$ and spreading sequence S_i.

$$\left\langle \hat{V}_j, S_i \right\rangle = \hat{V}_j \cdot S_i^T = V_j \cdot S_i^T + \alpha \left[b_1 S_1 \cdot S_i^T + b_2 S_2 \cdot S_i^T + \cdots + b_k S_k \cdot S_i^T \right] \quad (7)$$

Since the spreading sequences are orthogonal to each other. The Eq. (7) can be simplified as:

$$\left\langle \hat{V}_j, S_i \right\rangle = V_j \cdot S_i^T + \alpha b_i S_i \cdot S_i^T \quad (8)$$

Eq.(8) shows that the spreading sequences are mutually independent in the process of data embedding. Since the spreading sequences are orthogonal to each other, the prior data embedding has no impact on the followings.

In Eq. (8), as $b_e \in \{-1,1\}$, α is a positive integer and $S_i \cdot S_i^T$ is always positive, the sign of expression $\alpha b_e S_i \cdot S_i^T$ is determined by b_e. Thus, when $\left|V_j \cdot S_i^T\right| < \left|\alpha b_e S_i \cdot S_i^T\right|$ is satisfied, the sign of $\left\langle \hat{V}_j, S_i \right\rangle$ would be determined by the sign of $\alpha b_e S_i \cdot S_i^T$. In such conditions, we can extract the embedded bit b_e by the function of $sign(\left\langle \hat{V}_j, S_i \right\rangle)$ as

$$b_e = sign\left\langle \hat{V}_j, S_i \right\rangle \quad if \left|V_j \cdot S_i^T\right| < \left|\alpha S_i \cdot S_i^T\right| \quad (9)$$

Eq. (9) shows that when the value of expression $\left|\alpha S_i \cdot S_i^T\right|$ is greater than $\left|V_j \cdot S_i^T\right|$, the secret data bit can be embedded and extracted correctly. Moreover, in the case of $\left|V_j \cdot S_i^T\right| < \left|\alpha S_i \cdot S_i^T\right|$, the max value of $\left\langle \hat{V}_j, S_i \right\rangle$ would be less than $2\left|\alpha S_i \cdot S_i^T\right|$. Therefore, at the decoding side, if $\left|\hat{V}_j \cdot S_i^T\right| \geq 2\left|\alpha S_i \cdot S_i^T\right|$ is satisfied, it is obvious that the vector must not has been embedded with a bit. As all of the vectors satisfied the condition of $\left|\hat{V}_j \cdot S_i^T\right| < \left|\alpha S_i \cdot S_i^T\right|$ are employed for data embedding clearly. Hence, only the vectors satisfy $\left|\alpha S_i \cdot S_i^T\right| \leq \left|\hat{V}_j \cdot S_i^T\right| < 2\left|\alpha S_i \cdot S_i^T\right|$ need to be recorded to determine whether the vector has been embedded with a bit (as shown in Figure 1). Thus, the location-map would be highly compressed and would be very small in our proposed scheme; it helps to embed more data into the cover image.

In addition, since S_i is a zero-mean spreading sequence and the V_j is consisted by neighboring pixels, the value of $V_j \cdot S_i^T$ equals the sum of the difference of pixel-pairs in the vector V_j. Therefore, the result of $V_j \cdot S_i^T$ would be very small if the elements of V_j are similar. Fortunately, according to the redundancy of the natural image

content, the neighboring pixels are very similar, especially in the smooth regions of an image. Hence, the value of $V_j \cdot S_i^T$ is usually very small and the data can be embedded with low image distortion. On the other hand, the choice of the gain factor also influences the performance the proposed scheme. The bigger the value of α is, the larger the value of $\alpha S_i \cdot S_i^T$ is, the more pixels can be involved for data embedding, and thus the embedding capacity is enlarged. However, the distortion of the image would grow rapidly with the increase of the gain factor α. Eq. (9) also shows that only the decoder who knows the spreading sequence and the gain factor the same as the encoder can extract the embedded data correctly, it would improve the security of the proposed scheme.

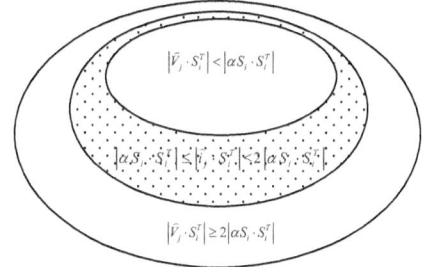

Figure 1. Distribution of pixels with different value of $\left\langle \hat{V}_j, S_i \right\rangle$.

2.3 CDMA Based Original Image Recover

After the correct extraction of the embedded data from the marked image, the original cover image can be completely recovered with

$$V_j = \hat{V}_j - \alpha \left[b_1 S_1 + b_2 S_2 + \cdots + b_k S_k \right] \quad (10)$$

3. PERFORMANCE ANALYSIS OF THE PROPOSED SCHEME

The proposed method makes the use of the correlations among the neighboring pixels for data hiding. Thus, the more the elements are similar in a vector, the more the vector suitable for data embedding. Here, to improve the performance of the proposed scheme, we employ the prediction-error matrix of the cover image generate from the rhombus-error-prediction method for data embedding. (inspired by reference [10]). Generally, the prediction-errors derived from this method are very small and follow the Laplacian distribution, the histogram of the prediction-errors distributes sharply around zero (as shown in Figure 2). Thus, the vectors with small and similar elements can be achieved and the embedding capacity is enlarged. The main idea of the rhombus-error-prediction method is as follows: denotes the image pixel value as $u_{x,y}$, where x and y are subscripts of the row and column. Its four neighbors $(u_{x,y-1}, u_{x+1,y}, u_{x,y+1}, u_{x-1,y})$ are used to predict the value of $u_{x,y}$ as

$$u'_{x,y} = \left\lfloor (u_{x,y-1}, u_{x+1,y}, u_{x,y+1}, u_{x-1,y})/4 \right\rfloor \quad (11)$$

where, $u'_{x,y}$ is the predicted value of the pixel $u_{x,y}$. The prediction-error is marked as $d_{x,y} = u_{x,y} - u'_{x,y}$. Then, the bit is embedded by modifying $d_{x,y}$ to $D_{x,y}$, and the original pixel value $u_{x,y}$ is changed to $U_{x,y} = D_{x,y} + u'_{x,y}$, Then, the $U_{x,y}$ would be utilized to construct the marked image. The decoding process of the rhombic error-prediction method is the converse of the encoding stage. The trivial description is omitted.

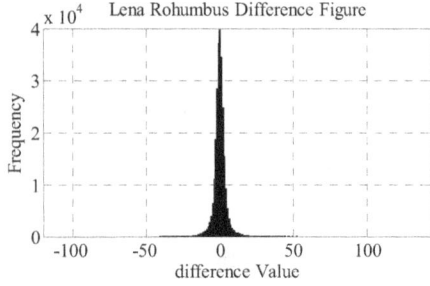

Figure 2. The prediction-errors distribution of image Lena

Different from most CDMA based data communication system using long orthogonal spreading sequences, we make the use of short spreading sequence with only 2 elements for reversible data hiding. Assume the two orthogonal spreading sequences derived from Hadmard matrix are (1, -1) and (1, 1), the gain factor $\alpha = 1$, it can be obtained from Eq. (9) that all of the vectors with elements' difference (or sum) belong to {-1, 0, 1} are suitable for data embedding, and the maximum change of the elements' (or pixels') value is 1 at most for each time data embedding. Hence, the embedding capacity is enlarged and the image quality is well maintained for every time data embedding.

Furthermore, according to the orthogonality of the spreading sequences, data can be embedded independently. The first time data embedding has no influence on the second time data embedding. Thus, multilevel embedding can be employed to improve image embedding capacity, different orthogonal spreading sequences can be repeatedly embedded into the cover image. The embedding capacity would be further enlarged with the multilevel data embedding.

On the other hand, the maximum change of the elements' (pixels') value in a marked vector is "1" after the first time data embedding in the case of $\alpha = 1$. Moreover, most elements' value would be changed back and remain unchanged after the second time data embedding. As the spreading sequences employed for data embedding are orthogonal to each other and most elements of different spreading sequences would be mutually cancelled in the process of multilevel data embedding. The image distortion is well restrained in the process of multilevel data embedding.

Here, we evaluate the performance of our proposed scheme by comparing with the reversible data hiding methods of Prediction-error (difference) Expansion and of Histogram Modification. As to the scheme of Prediction-error (difference) Expansion method, when the pixels with prediction-errors of "0" or "-1" are employed for data embedding, the change of the value of the marked pixels is 0 or 1. But, it would be 2 or 3 if the pixels with prediction-error of "1" are employed for data embedding. The image quality degrades quickly with the increases of the embedding capacity. Similarly, as far as the method of histogram modification is concerned, when two histogram bins (such as -1 and 0) are employed for data embedding, the change of marked pixels is 0 or 1, but all of the histogram bins uninvolved for data embedding must be shifted 1 position to create space for data embedding (by modifying the value of the pixels corresponding to the shifted histogram bins with one grayscale level). Furthermore, as the payload increases, more histogram bins (such as 1,-1) would be involved for data embedding, the histogram bins on the right-hand/left-hand side of the selected histogram bins would be shifted at least 2 positions to create space for data

embedding, the image distortion grows rapidly with the increase of the payload. As our proposed scheme only changes the value of the embedded pixels by 1 for each time data embedding, and most elements of different spreading sequence would be mutually cancelled in the process of multilevel data embedding, comparing with the schemes we have discussed above, our proposed scheme achieves high performance at the moderate-to-high embedding capacity.

To make things clear, we provide an example to demonstrate the performance of our proposed scheme. Supposing the two to-be-embedded data bits are "0" and "1", which would be changed to "-1" and "1" according to Eq.(5). The original vector V_1 from the prediction-error matrix is (1, 0) and two orthogonal spreading sequences are (1, -1) and (1, 1), respectively. The first bit "-1" is denoted by the spreading sequence (-1, 1) and added to the vector V_1 in the first time data embedding, the marked vector $\hat{V}_1$ thus becomes (0, 1); the second bit '1' is denoted by the spreading sequence (1, 1), and the marked vector is then changed to (1, 2) after two times embedding. At the decoding side, the embedded bits "0" and "1" can be extracted exactly and the original vector can be recovered according to the proposed scheme. As shown in Table 1.

Table 1. The process of multilevel data extraction

First time of data extraction	Second time of data extraction
$\langle \bar{V}_1, S_2 \rangle = (1,2)(1,1)^T = 3;$	$\langle \hat{V}_1, S_1 \rangle = (0,1)(1,-1)^T = -1;$
$2\lvert \alpha S_2 \cdot S_2^T \rvert = 4;$	$2\lvert \alpha S_1 \cdot S_1^T \rvert = 4;$
$\therefore \lvert \bar{V}_1 \cdot S_2^T \rvert = \lvert \langle \bar{V}_1, S_2 \rangle \rvert < 2\lvert \alpha S_2 \cdot S_2^T \rvert$	$\therefore \lvert \hat{V}_1 \cdot S_1^T \rvert = \lvert \langle \hat{V}_1, S_1 \rangle \rvert < 2\lvert \alpha S_1 \cdot S_1^T \rvert$
thus,	*thus,*
$b_2 = sign(\langle \bar{V}_1, S_2 \rangle) = sign(4) = 1;$	$b_1 = sign(\langle \hat{V}_1, S_1 \rangle) = sign(-1) = -1;$
$\omega_2 = 1;$	$\omega_1 = 0;$
$\hat{V}_1 = \bar{V}_1 - \alpha b_2 S_2 = (0,1)$	$V_1 = \hat{V}_1 - \alpha b_1 S_1 = (1,0)$

Note: the order of bit extraction is reverse to that of the embedding.

Then, after two times data embedding, if we still have data remains to be embedded, the data can be embedded in the same method with different vectors from the prediction-error matrix or with different spreading sequences from the Hadmard matrix, the embedding capacity thus increases continuously.

In addition, it should be noticed that the PSNR (peak signal to noise ratio) of the marked image after the first time data embedding is 48.13dB at least, even if all of the pixels are involved for data embedding. As most elements of spreading sequences are mutually canceled in the process of multilevel data embedding, only the value of second element changes 2, the first element stays the same after the second time data embedding. Thus, the worst PSNR value after two times data embedding is still no less than 45.12dB in the case of all the pixels have been involved for the two times data embedding. Therefore, the distortion caused to the cover image is limited in the process of multilevel data embedding. The proposed scheme may achieve high embedding capacity while introducing limited distortion to the cover image.

4. EXPERIMENTS AND DISCUSSIONS

In this section, three images include Airplane, Lena and Baboon from USC_SIPI database is employed to evaluate the performance the proposed data hiding scheme. All of these images have been popularly used in the RDH research community. The three selected images have different features, image Airplane has large amount of low-frequency (smooth areas) components, image Baboon contains much high-frequency components (noisy areas), and image Lena is rich in moderate-frequency components. Thus, the performance of the proposed scheme can be comprehensively testified with these three images. To facilitate the comparison, the size of all images is set to 512×512 and the grayscale level is 8 bits. All experiments are conducted by embedding and decoding a random binary sequence generated by Matlab function randint(). The location-map is employed to identify the data embedding positions, which is compressed with JBIG2 technique and saved through the LSB replacement method. That is, the least significant bits (LSB) of some specified pixels are collected and set aside to create space for the saving of the location-map, and thus these LSBs are embedded as auxiliary message along with the to-be-embedded data. As the number of the vectors unsuitable for data embedding in our proposed scheme is small, the location-map is highly compressed and the size is quite small. The capacity-distortion behavior is employed to evaluate the performance of our proposed scheme.

Figure3-5 have demonstrated the PSNR-BPP (bit per pixel) curves of our proposed scheme compared with other state-of-the-art reversible data hiding schemes, including the histogram modification based scheme adopted by Xuan *et al.* [6] and Li *et al.* [7], the prediction-error (difference) expansion based schemes adopted by Sachnev *et al.* [10] and Li *et al.* [11]. The results have demonstrated that the performance of our proposed scheme could achieve higher PSNR values than other advanced schemes at the moderate-to-high embedding capacity. In Figure 3, the results in the test image Lena have shown that the PSNR values of the proposed scheme exceeds Xuan *et al.*'s results [6] at 0.20 bpp, Li *et al.*'s results [11] at about 0. 13 bpp, Sachnev *et al.*'s results [10] at 0.16 bpp and Li *et al.*'s results [11] at 0.21 bpp, respectively. At the same time, Figure4-5 have illustrated that the PSNR of the proposed scheme exceeds other best performance schemes at 0.08 bpp and 0.36 bpp, respectively, in image Baboon and Airplane.

The explanation for these test results is as follows. When the payload is small, for the proposed method, two pixel values will be changed for one bit embedding when the length of spreading sequence is 2. Hence, the image distortion is larger than other schemes at the low payload. However, with the payload increases, multilevel data embedding would be employed to accommodate more data into to the cover image. Different orthogonal spreading sequences are repeatedly embedded into the marked image, and most elements (at least half of them) of different spreading sequences are mutually cancelled in the process of multilevel data embedding. The distortion caused by the proposed scheme thus decreases gradually and the PSNR-BPP curve declines slowly. This leads to that the proposed scheme achieves higher PSNR value than others at the moderate-to-high embedding capacity.

Note that the prediction-error expansion based schemes, reported in Sachnev *et al.* [10] and Li *et al.* [11], has the distortion caused to the cover image, which can be expressed as 2p+0 or 2p+1 (p is the absolute value of prediction-errors employed for data embedding). The value of pixel changes 0 or 1 when the prediction-error "0" or "-1" is used for data embedding; the change of pixel's value is 1 or 2 if the prediction-error "1" is employed, and the change of pixel's value would be 4 or 5 if the prediction-error "2" is employed, and so on. The distortion of the cover image grows fast with the increases of the payload.

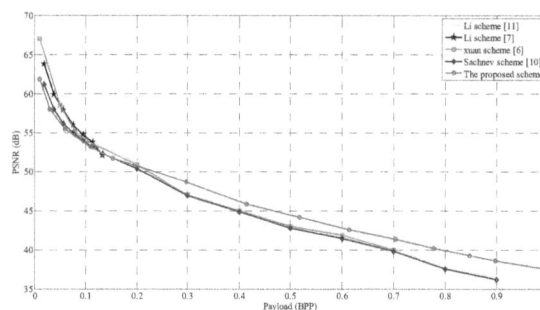

Figure 3 Performance of proposed scheme on Lena compared with other schemes.

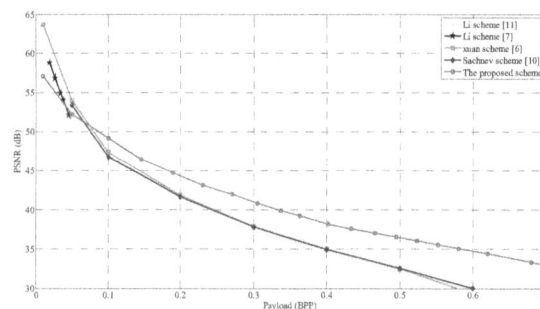

Figure 4 Performance of proposed scheme on Baboon compared with other schemes.

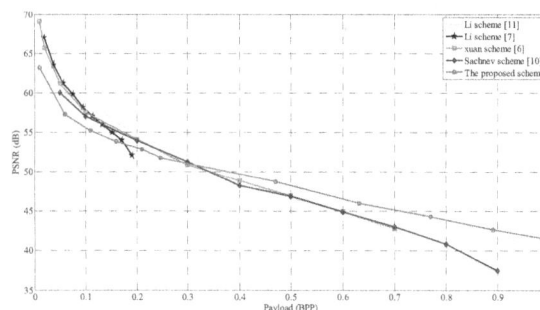

Figure 5 Performance of proposed scheme on Airplane compared with other schemes.

As for the histogram modification scheme adopted by Xuan *et al.* [6] and Li *et al.* [7]. Its performance relies on the magnitude of the highest histogram bins (generally they are histogram bins "0" and "-1"), when the amount of embedding bits less than the number of pixels associated with the highest histogram bins, the distortion caused to the cover image is 0 or 1, and the value of the pixels not associate with the highest histogram bins (i.e., the absolute values of the pixel's prediction-errors are larger than those of the selected histogram bins) would be changed by 1 at least to ensure the reversibility. But when the size of payload is large than the magnitude of the highest histogram bins, multilevel data embedding should be employed and the histogram bins (such as "1" or "-2") would be utilized for data embedding, the distortion introduced to the cover image becomes 1 or 2, and all the non-involved pixels need to shift 2 grayscale positions at least. The image quality would degrade rapidly with the payload increases.

However, in the proposed scheme, the spreading sequences are directly added to the vectors generated from prediction-error matrix and no histogram bins need to be shifted. The value of the marked pixels is only changed by 1 for first time data embedding, and all of the prediction-errors belongs to {-1, 0, 1} would be involved for data embedding (in the case of the length of spreading sequence is 2 and the gain factor is 1). Moreover, as the payload increases, the data can be embedded repeatedly into the cover image upon the orthogonality of the spreading sequences, and most elements of different spreading sequences are mutually cancelled in the process of multilevel data embedding. Thus, the proposed scheme achieves higher performance than other works at the moderate-to-high embedding capacity.

In addition, Figure3-5 also have shown that the performance of the proposed scheme exceeds other schemes at different embedding rate. The value of PSNR achieved by the proposed scheme surpasses other schemes at low embedding rate on image with much high-frequency components such as image Baboon; however, it oversteps other schemes at moderate embedding rate on image having much low-frequency components such as images of Airplane and Lena. This is due to the fact that the prediction-errors of image having much low-frequency components usually are very small (actually the value of most of the prediction-errors is 0) and distribute very closely to the zero, the image distortion caused by data embedding is less than those with much high-frequency components at the same embedding capacity. Thus, only after quite a lot data bits have been embedded (generally after the prediction-errors of "0" and "-1" having been utilized), the proposed scheme can achieve high PSNR values than conventional works for images having much low-frequency components.

5. CONCLUSIONS

In this paper, a CDMA based reversible data hiding scheme is presented for the first time to the best of our knowledge. Different from the conventional CDMA based communication or watermarking system using very long spreading sequences, short spreading sequences are adopted in this scheme. The to-be-embedded data bits are represented by different orthogonal spreading sequences and embedded into the image. Due to the orthogonality of spreading sequences, the data can be embedded repeatedly into the cover image and most elements of different spreading sequences are mutually cancelled in the process of multilevel data embedding. Therefore, the cover image is kept in good quality even at high embedding payload. Moreover, in a CDMA based reversible data hiding system, only the decoder who knows the spreading sequence and the gain factor the same as the encoder can extract the secret data correctly, which would increase the security of the proposed scheme. Experimental results have demonstrated that the performance of the proposed scheme is superior to other state-of-the-art reversible data hiding schemes at the moderate-to-high embedding capacity.

6. ACKNOWLEDGMENTS

This paper is supposed by Shandong Provincial Natural Science Foundation, China (No. ZR2012F014), Natural Science Foundation of China (No. 41202206) and Jinan University & Institutes Innovation Program (No. JN201402005).

7. REFERENCES

[1] J. Fridrich, M. Goljan and R. Du. "Invertible authentication", *Proc. SPIE Photonics west,* vol. 3971, Califonia, Jan. 2001, pp. 197-208.

[2] M.U. Celik, G. Sharma, A.M. Tekalp and E.Saber. "Reversible data hiding", *Proc. Int. Conf. Image Processing,* vol. II, Sep. 2002, pp. 157-160.

[3] Z. Ni, Y. Q. Shi, N. Ansari and W. Su. "Reversible data hiding", *IEEE Trans. Circuits syst. Video technol.,* vol. 16, no. 3, Mar. 2006, pp.354-362,

[4] S. K. Lee, Y.H. Suh and Y. S. Ho. "Reversible image authotication based on watermarking," *in Proc. IEEE Int. Conf. Multimedia Expo,* Jul. 2006, pp.1321-1324.

[5] C. H. Yang and M. H. Tsai. "Improving histogram-based reversible data hiding by interleaving predictions" , *IET image processing,* vol.4, Apr. 2010, pp. 322-326,

[6] G. R. Xuan, X. Tong, J. Teng, X. Zhang and Y.Q. Shi. "Optimal histogram-pair and prediction error based reversible data hiding," *Proc. of inter. workshop of digital watermarking,* Shanghai, 2012.pp 368-383.

[7] X. Li, W. Zhang, X. Gui and B. Yang. "A novel reversible data hiding scheme based on two-dimensional difference-histogram modification," *IEEE Trans. Inf. Forensic and Security,* vol.8, no.7, 2013, pp. 1091-1100.

[8] J. Tian, "Reversible data embedding using a difference expansion", *IEEE Trans. Circuits and Syst. Video Technol.,* vol. 13,no.8, Aug.2003, pp.890-896.

[9] D. M. Thodi and J. J. Rodriguez, "Expansion embedding techniques for reversible watermarking", *IEEE Trans. Image Process.,* vol. 16, no. 3, Mar. 2007, pp. 721-730.

[10] V. Sachnev, H. J. Kim, J. Nam, S. Suresh, and Y. Q. Shi, "Reversible watermarking algorithm using sorting and prediction," *IEEE Trans on Cir. and Syst.,* vol. 19, no. 7, 2009, pp. 989-999.

[11] X. Li, B. Yang and T. Zeng. "Efficient reversible watermarking based on adaptive prediction-error expansion and pixel selection," *IEEE Trans. on Image Proc.,* vol.20, no.12, 2011, pp. 3524-353.

Dynamic Privacy-Preserving Genomic Susceptibility Testing

Mina Namazi
Signal Theory and
Communications Department
University of Vigo
36310 Vigo, Spain
mnamazi@gts.uvigo.es

Juan Ramón
Troncoso-Pastoriza
Signal Theory and
Communications Department
University of Vigo
36310 Vigo, Spain
troncoso@gts.uvigo.es

Fernando
Pérez-González
Signal Theory and
Communications Department
University of Vigo
36310 Vigo, Spain
fperez@gts.uvigo.es

ABSTRACT

The field of genomic research has considerably grown in the recent years due to the unprecedented advances brought about by Next Generation Sequencing (NGS) and the need and increasing widespread use of outsourced processing. But this rapid increase also poses severe privacy risks due to the inherently sensitive nature of genomic information. In this work, we address privacy-preserving genetic susceptibility tests outsourced to an untrustworthy party, enhancing previous approaches in terms of computation and communication efficiency by leveraging the use of somewhat homomorphic lattice encryption and relinearization operations to achieve more efficient constructions. Additionally, we also propose a more general construction which deals with several different medical units (such as pharmaceutical companies or hospitals), managing patients' consent to the disclosure of test results for each of these units, which may dynamically join the system. Our scheme features an attribute-based homomorphic cryptosystem which enables enforcing the patient's access policy referred to the different medical units.

Keywords

Privacy Preserving Techniques; Genomic Privacy; Lattice-Based Cryptography; Attribute Based Encryption

1. INTRODUCTION

The advent of Next Generation Sequencing enables an increasing use of genomic data in various domains such as health care, biomedical research, disease susceptibility tests, and forensics criminal investigations [10]. Nowadays, genomic data can be inexpensively sequenced and stored in a digital format, becoming widely available for the aforementioned applications, and rapidly surpassing the computation capacity of in-house infrastructures in medical centers and laboratories. Hence, outsourcing genomic processing arises as a necessity to cope with the volume of sequenced data.

IH&MMSec 2016, June 20–23, 2016, Vigo, Spain.

© 2016 ACM. ISBN 978-1-4503-4290-2/16/06. . . $15.00

DOI: http://dx.doi.org/10.1145/2909827.2930791

The benefits of a widespread use and study of genomic data in advancing medicine research are unquestionable, but the inherently sensitive and identifiable nature of the genome entails severe privacy risks. Whenever a patient reveals her sequenced genomic data to a genomic center for running some tests, she loses control over these data and over the amount of leaked personal information: the lab has access to more information than just the test results, therefore harming the patient's privacy. Moreover, the genomic information can be linked to ancestors and relatives of an individual, so its leakage also affects their privacy. These issues are aggravated when the sequences are outsourced to an untrustworthy environment, like a Cloud service, for their processing. Outsourcing genomic data exposes them to the service and infrastructure providers and makes them vulnerable to attacks and accesses violating patients' privacy.

Consequently, the rapidly decreasing cost of DNA sequencing which pushes forward the availability of genomic test services also evidences the need of technological means for protecting these sequences from unauthorized access and processing. These privacy issues have motivated recent proposals of mechanisms for performing outsourced calculations on genomic sequences in a privacy-preserving way. In this work we focus on one of the most recent privacy-preserving mechanisms for disease susceptibility outsourced processing by Ayday *et al.* [2], and enhance it with two main contributions: a) Our proposed scheme features lattice-based somewhat homomorphic encryption in order to enable fully outsourced processing in the service provider, with no intermediate interaction needed by the medical center or the patient for running the susceptibility tests, and moves the bulk of data processing to the outsourced environment, which has enough computational power to operate on big data without having access to the original DNA of the patient; b) we generalize our construction to allow for different medical centers with variable access structures to the data, controlled and defined by the patient, in static and dynamic configurations.

1.1 Notation and Structure

We use calligraphic $\mathcal{L}$ letters when referring to the participants in the protocols. Uppercase letters denote matrices and lowercase letters denote elements from a polynomial ring; boldface letters denote vectors of polynomials; $a \cdot b$ denotes a polynomial product, and $\boldsymbol{a} \cdot \boldsymbol{b}$ an scalar product between vectors of polynomials. The subindex $\boldsymbol{x}_{E_P}$ denotes the result of the encryption of x with the key belonging to $\mathcal{P}$. The key owner will be omitted when there is no ambiguity.

The rest of the paper is organized as follows: Section 2 introduces some recent related work. Section 3 revises some concepts used for our proposed constructions. In Section 4 we revise Ayday et al.'s scheme and present our enhancements based on somewhat homomorphic lattice encryption. Section 5 sketches our proposed extended scheme, with static and dynamic management of several medical units. Finally, Section 6 draws some conclusions and hints for future work.

2. RELATED WORK

The recent privacy-preserving genomic works can be classified into three main categories: The first category deals with *private string searching and comparing*, initiated by Troncoso-Pastoriza et al. [13]; within this category, Chen et al. [6] recently proposed a private read mapping protocol, aligning short DNA sequences to human DNA with a secure and efficient algorithm.

The second category tackles *private release of aggregated data*; Wang et al. [14] have recently proposed a secure and privacy-preserving method to find homologous genes.

The third category, to which this work belongs, deals with *private clinical gemomics*, the field that most directly impacts citizens and their need for immediate privacy. Within this category, Baldi et al. [3] proposed a medical tool for supporting privacy preserving string comparison methods for individual medical tests over genomic data, and Canim et al. [5] applied hardware encryption for efficiently processing biomedical data; finally, one of the most representative and recent works has been proposed by Ayday et al. [2], which addresses secure medical tests of certain disease susceptibility on patients' genomic data.

For this purpose, they claim that existing secure searching methods do not provide a proper framework for various types of genomic tests to develop proper personalized medical methods, and they propose to use a trusted party, who helps in sequencing, generating and distributing secrets required for the system among the other parties. Additionally, their solution is outsourced, featuring a storing and processing unit ($\mathcal{SPU}$) between the patient and the medical center, in such a way that the calculations are shared between the medical center and the $\mathcal{SPU}$ through an additive homomorphic encryption and a partial decryption process, relieving the patient from most of the computations.

We advance and enhance this proposal with two main contributions: we enable that the $\mathcal{SPU}$ can execute all the heavy computations needed for operating on encrypted data, without the need to interact with the medical center, which only has to decrypt the results; for this purpose, we introduce a lattice-based somewhat homomorphic encryption which enables our fully secure outsourced protocol.

Furthermore, Ayday's scheme allows neither that different medical units can join the protocol, nor that the patient updates her consent on the tests that can be performed on her data, therefore obliging her to re-upload the whole sequenced data if any change occurs. Our second contribution enables more than one medical unit through different patient-defined access rights coded as attributes; to this aim, we apply attribute-based encryption (ABE) over lattices with homomorphic properties, and we also sketch a

dynamic scheme which supports new medical centers to join the system and a dynamic modification of the access policies.

3. PRELIMINARIES AND CRYPTOSYSTEM

For the sake of completeness, we present some concepts and background needed for later describing our proposed schemes. We briefly revise the background on genomic sequences needed to implement a susceptibility test, and also the structure of Bloom filters; finally, we present a somewhat homomorphic cryptosystem based on the Ring Learning with Errors hardness problem, and the primitives we use for building our privacy-preserving susceptibility protocol.

3.1 Genomic Background

Every human being's aligned genomic sequence has over 3 billion base pairs of short reads [1] sampled randomly, comprising between 100 and 400 nucleotoides each.

After being sequenced, the position of the first aligned nucleotide in a short read content is denoted as the short read's position with respect to the reference genome, in the form $L_{i,j} = \langle x_i | y_j \rangle$, where $x_i \in [1, 23]$ represents the chromosome and $y_j \in [1, 2.4 \cdot 10^8]$ represents the position of the short read within chromosome x_i. Due to mutations, sequencing errors and inheritance, a patient's sequence differs from the reference genome. A *Cigar String* represents these variants as pairs of nucleotide lengths and the associated operations (see Fig. 1). The most common and relevant variants are called SNPs (Single Nucleotide Polymorphisms); they represent positions in the genome holding a nucleotide that varies between individuals. SNPs are particularly suitable for running susceptibility tests of certain diseases. Weighted averaging [8] or Likelihood Ratio (LR) tests [12] are commonly used to measure the susceptibility to a given disease; we give the formula for these tests in Section 4.

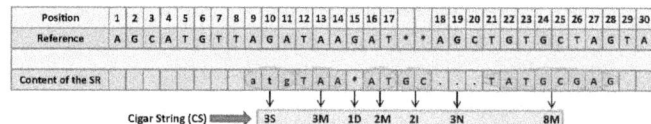

Figure 1: Short read aligned to the reference [1].

There are over 100 million different SNPs recognized in the human population (and growing), with every individual carrying around 4 million of them. The positions of these 4 million SNPs are different in each individual. Following a similar notation as in [2], we refer to these set of SNPs as "real SNPs" and the remaining ones as "potential SNPs"; the i-th SNP for patient $\mathcal{P}$ is represented as $\mathrm{SNP}^{P,i}$, where $\mathrm{SNP}^{P,i} = 1$ if $\mathcal{P}$ has a real SNP at this location, and $\mathrm{SNP}^{P,i} = 0$ otherwise[1]; Γ^P denotes the set of positions for real SNPs of patient $\mathcal{P}$ (at which $\mathrm{SNP}^{P,i} = 1$), and γ^P the set of positions of potential SNPs, at which $\mathrm{SNP}^{P,i} = 0$.

3.2 Bloom Filters

The problem of calculating a susceptibility function mainly deals with appropriately weighting the SNPs which have some contribution in the corresponding disease, depending

---

[1]Besides the presence or absence of a SNP, the formulation can be extended to consider the type of SNP (homozygous or heterozygous), encoded as $\{0, 1, 2\}$ instead of just $\{0, 1\}$. We refer the interested reader to [2] for further details.

on whether they are present (or absent) in the patient. Determining whether they are present or not can be reduced to a membership problem in the sets Γ^P and γ^P.

Ayday *et al.* [2] propose to use Bloom Filters as efficient data structures to support set membership queries in a set L^P of ordered elements represented as an array of n bits, where a small probability of false positives is allowed. The Bloom filter is built as follows: all the n bits are initially set to 0; the generator can then define κ independent hash functions ($\kappa \ll n$), $H_1, H_2, ..., H_\kappa$ with range $\{0, n-1\}$. For each element of the set Γ^P, the κ hash functions will output κ (possibly repeated) bit positions in $\{0, n-1\}$, which are set to one in the Bloom Filter bit string; the filter is eventually composed of the final n-bit string and the κ hash functions. In order to check for membership of an element i in L^P, anyone with the filter can run the hash functions on i; if any of them hashes to a position where the filter bit string has a 0, i does not belong to Γ^P.

3.3 RLWE-based Homomorphic Encryption

RLWE (*Ring Learning with Errors*) is the hardness problem in which the most recent lattice-based cryptosystems are based; it is an efficient algebraic variation of Learning With Errors (LWE) introduced by Lyubaskevsky *et al.* [9] as an indistinguishability problem between two pairs of values: for a security parameter λ, let $f(x) = x^d + 1$ where $d = d(\lambda)$ is a power of 2. Let $q = q(\lambda) \geq 2$ be an integer, $R = \mathbb{Z}[x]/(f(x))$ and $R_q = R/qR$ two polynomial quotient rings. Let $\chi = \chi(\lambda)$ be an error distribution over R. For the secret $s \in R_q$, the RLWE distribution produces (a_i, b_i) such that a_i is sampled uniformly from R_q, and $b_i = a_i \cdot s + e_i$ with $e_i \leftarrow \chi$. RLWE assumes that this distribution is indistinguishable from sampling (a_i, b_i) uniformly in R_q^2.

Some of the most recent and efficient homomorphic cryptosystems are based on RLWE. We will focus here only on leveled Somewhat Homomorphic Encryption (SHE), which holds the necessary properties to achieve our purposes. An SHE cryptosystem comprises four functions SHSetup, SHGen, SHEnc, SHDec; we exemplify them with the scheme by Brakersky *et al.* [4] adapted to non-binary plaintexts:

SHSetup$(1^\lambda) \to pp_{SW}$: This function outputs the public parameters $pp_{SW} = (d, q, \chi)$, where q is a module, $d = d(\lambda)$ is the lattice dimension, and $\chi = \chi(\lambda)$ is an error distribution such that RLWE is secure against attacks with at least 2^λ as security parameter.

SHGen$(pp_{SW}) \to (\boldsymbol{sk}_u, \boldsymbol{pk}_u)$: It generates a public-secret key pair for user u. For this purpose, it samples randomly $s' \leftarrow \chi$, and outputs $\boldsymbol{sk}_u = \boldsymbol{s} = (1, s') \in R_q^2$. In order to generate the public key, two polynomials $a \leftarrow R_q$ and $e \leftarrow \chi$ are sampled randomly, such that $\boldsymbol{pk}_u = (b = a \cdot s' + te, -a)$ with $t \in \mathbb{Z}$ being the allowed plaintext cardinality. It must be noted that the public key is just an encryption of zero.

SHEnc$(pp_{SW}, \boldsymbol{pk}_u, m) \to \boldsymbol{m}_E$: To encrypt a message $m \in R_t$, randomly sample $r \leftarrow \chi$ and $e \leftarrow \chi^2$. The encryption of m is $\boldsymbol{m}_E = (m, 0) + t \cdot \boldsymbol{e} + \boldsymbol{pk}_u \cdot r \in R_q^2$.

SHDec$(pp_{SW}, \boldsymbol{s}, \boldsymbol{m}_E) \to m$: It outputs the decrypted $m = [[\boldsymbol{m}_E \cdot \boldsymbol{s}]_q]_t$, where $[.]_t$ is the modular reduction modulo t.

For the sake of clarity, we will omit the pp_{SW} argument in the encryption/decryption functions from now on. This somewhat homomorphic cryptosystem can homomorphically evaluate bounded polynomials of (sublinear) degree N (only logarithmic depth), at the cost of an increase of the ciphertext noise after each homomorphic operation, there-

fore increasing the decryption error rate of the ciphertex as the polynomial factor grows per operation. Addition of plaintexts is equivalent to adding two ciphertext pairs $(\boldsymbol{m}'_E = \boldsymbol{m}_E^{(1)} + \boldsymbol{m}_E^{(2)})$, and multiplication of two plaintexts is homomorphic to the tensor product between the two ciphertexts $(\boldsymbol{m}'_E = \boldsymbol{m}_E^{(1)} \otimes \boldsymbol{m}_E^{(2)})$, which becomes a three-dimensional ciphertext that can be decrypted with the secret key $\boldsymbol{s}'' = (1, s', s' \cdot s')$ (for further details, we refer the reader to [4]).

A homomorphic multiplication increases the dimension of the ciphertext, so Brakerski *et al.* introduced modulus switching and key switching techniques working in a leveled chain of keys $\{\boldsymbol{s}_0, \boldsymbol{s}_1, ..., \boldsymbol{s}_N\}$ to tackle the problem. Without going into details which are out of the scope of this paper, the combined techniques allow for a reduction of an expanded three-dimensional ciphertext back into a regular two-dimensional ciphertext, with the help of a relinearization matrix $\boldsymbol{B}$ which holds encryptions of pieces of $\boldsymbol{s}''$ under the destination key $\boldsymbol{s}_2$.

While this process is originally intended as a dimension reduction to allow for the homomorphic evaluation of higher degree polynomials, the relinearization step can be used in a more general way, as a proxy re-encryption, in order to change a ciphertext between a key $\boldsymbol{s}_{u_1}$ to another ciphertext under key $\boldsymbol{s}_{u_2}$ by using a relinearization matrix $\boldsymbol{B}_{u_1, u_2}$.

KSwitch$(\boldsymbol{m}_{E_{u_1}}, \boldsymbol{pk}_{E_{u_1}}, \boldsymbol{B}_{u_1, u_2}) \to \boldsymbol{m}_{E_{u_2}}$: outputs an encryption of m under the key $\boldsymbol{s}_{u_2}$; $\boldsymbol{B}_{u_1, u_2}$ is the relinearization matrix between keys $\boldsymbol{s}_{u_1}$ and $\boldsymbol{s}_{u_2}$ produced by user u_1.

As the degree of the evaluated polynomials defining the susceptibility functions is known beforehand, we do not need a Fully Homomorphic Encryption (FHE), and we can get a much more efficient solution by running an SHE adjusted to the needed polynomial degree. Furthermore, we leverage the relinearization function as a proxy re-encryption primitive to enable the proposed dynamic system.

4. PRIVACY-PRESERVING GENOMIC SUSCEPTIBILITY TESTING

This section revises the recently proposed privacy preserving protocol by Ayday *et al.* [2] and presents our enhanced version. Table 1 summarizes the notation for this section.

Γ^P	Set of positions of real SNPs of patient $\mathcal{P}$
γ^P	Set of positions of potential SNPs of patient $\mathcal{P}$
$SNP^{P,i}$	i-th SNP for patient $\mathcal{P}$. $SNP^{P,i}$ equals 0 when it belongs to γ^P, and 1 when the patient presents a variant (it belongs to Γ^P)
Ω_x	Set of positions of SNPs which are related to disease x.
$\text{pr}_b^{x,i}$	$\Pr(x \mid SNP^{P,i} = b)$, with $b \in 0, 1$. Probability of developing disease x conditioned on the value of the i-th SNP
$c^{x,i}$	Contribution (likelihood) of the i-th SNP $SNP^{P,i}$ to the susceptibility to disease x
$S^{P,x}$	Predicted susceptibility of patient $\mathcal{P}$ to disease x

Table 1: Used Notation

There are several ways to calculate the genetic susceptibility to a given disease, but we exemplify here the weighted average method, generalizing the descriptions given in [1, 2]. Due to prior studies on a given population, a medical center $\mathcal{MC}$ knows that disease x is related to SNPs in a set Ω_x, in such a way that their presence or absence contributes by increasing or decreasing the susceptibility by a determined value (see Table 1). For this set of SNPs, the susceptibility of a patient for developing a disease x can be calculated as:

$$S^{P,x} = \frac{1}{\sum_{i \in \Omega_x} c^{x,i}} \times \left\{ \Sigma_{i \in \Omega_x} c^{x,i} \{ \frac{pr_0^{x,i}}{0-1} [\text{SNP}^{P,i} - 1] + \frac{pr_1^{x,i}}{1-0} [\text{SNP}^{P,i} - 0] \} \right\}. \quad (1)$$

It is possible to calculate the susceptibility by computing the Likelihood Ratio, which we omit here due to lack of space, but it is analogous to the case of Eq. (1).

4.1 Overview of Ayday *et al.*'s Scheme

Ayday *et al.* [2] propose several mechanisms with different levels of privacy to compute Eq (1) in an untrustworthy Storage and Processing Unit ($\mathcal{SPU}$), being the highest level the one using Paillier encryptions [11] to conceal the values and positions of the patient's SNPs, and a partial decryption step (which they denote proxy encryption) to interactively perform part of the process between the medical center $\mathcal{MC}$ and the $\mathcal{SPU}$. All parties are assumed semi-honest and follow the established protocols.

Patient $\mathcal{P}$ owns a biological sample and a pair of Paillier keys. The $\mathcal{MC}$ has the knowledge of the parameters for calculating the susceptibility to disease x. Additionally, [2] introduces a trusted certificate institute $\mathcal{CI}$, which performs the sequencing and encryption of the patient's DNA from her sample; it also generates the Paillier keys and shares a (regular non-homomorphic) symmetric encryption key with patient $\mathcal{P}$. The target of a privacy-preserving protocol in this scenario is to securely calculate Eq. (1) while concealing the patient DNA from both the $\mathcal{MC}$ and $\mathcal{SPU}$, outsourcing most of the processing load to the $\mathcal{SPU}$.

Prior to the protocol execution, the $\mathcal{CI}$ obtains the Paillier and symmetric encryption parameters $pp = (pp_{SE}, pp_{Pa})$ and generates and distributes the corresponding key pairs (sk_P, pk_P) for the patients. It also distributes the symmetric keys for the patient $k = (sk_{P,CI})$.

Sequencing and generation of input encryptions After $\mathcal{P}$ sends her biological sample to $\mathcal{CI}$ for sequencing, $\mathcal{CI}$ obtains the positions of SNPs in sets Γ^P and γ^P, encoded as $\text{SNP}^{P,i}$. With the values of these positions, $\mathcal{CI}$ builds the Bloom Filter BF representing the positions included in Γ^P, encrypts these positions l_i and an arbitrary value l_0 (different from all the real or potential SNP indices) representing the 0 location with the patient's symmetric key, obtaining $\{l_{i,E_{P,CI}}\}$ and $l_{0,E_{P,CI}}$; it also encrypts the values of $\text{SNP}^{P,i}$ using the patient's Paillier key pk_P. Then, $\mathcal{CI}$ sends the BF and $l_{0,E_{P,CI}}$ to the patient, and the pairs of encrypted positions and encrypted SNPs to the $\mathcal{SPU}$; the $\mathcal{SPU}$ can therefore index the encrypted SNPs with the encrypted position, without knowing neither the value of the SNP nor its actual position.

Susceptibility test

Step 1: In order to run the analysis, $\mathcal{MC}$ marks the location of those SNPs in Ω_x it needs to run the test and sends these positions to patient $\mathcal{P}$.

Step 2: $\mathcal{P}$ runs the BF for these positions; for those in the BF (present variants), $\mathcal{P}$ encrypts the corresponding location $l_{i,E_{P,CI}}$ and sends it to $\mathcal{SPU}$. For those not in BF, $\mathcal{P}$ sends the encryption $l_{0,E_{P,CI}}$. Additionally, she sends one half of her secret key, $sk_{P(1)}$ to the $\mathcal{SPU}$ and the other half $sk_{P(2)}$ to $\mathcal{MC}$ to perform a partial (proxy) decryption.

Step 3: The $\mathcal{SPU}$ re-randomizes the corresponding SNP

encryptions $\text{SNP}_{E_P}^{P,i}$ for the indices $l_{i,E_{P,CI}}$ and sends the results to $\mathcal{MC}$.

Step 4: The $\mathcal{MC}$ computes the susceptibility test Eq. (1) on the patient's encrypted SNPs by using the homomorphic properties of Paillier encryption scheme, knowing the values of $pr^{x,i}$ and $c^{x,i}$, and sends the encrypted results to the $\mathcal{SPU}$.

Step 5: The $\mathcal{SPU}$, by using its half of $\mathcal{P}$ secret key $sk_{P(1)}$, partially decrypts the result and sends it back to the $\mathcal{MC}$.

Step 6: The $\mathcal{MC}$ uses $sk_{p(2)}$ to decrypt the message and recover the required test result, $S^{P,x}$.

The security of this scheme is based on the one wayness and semantic security of the underlying Paillier encryption scheme.

4.2 Proposed Scheme

Ayday's scheme presents a series of limitations and drawbacks: firstly, it employs Paillier, an additively homomorphic scheme which translates clear-text additions into multiplications of ciphertexts and clear-text products by known values into exponentiations under encryption. Therefore, in order to keep the susceptibility parameters hidden from the $\mathcal{SPU}$, the protocol must incur in two additional communication rounds between the $\mathcal{MC}$ and the $\mathcal{SPU}$ (steps 2, 3 and 4), and it must move the bulk of the computation to the $\mathcal{MC}$ instead of the $\mathcal{SPU}$. These two facts go against the initial targets of a privacy-preserving outsourced scheme; we overcome them by relying on a somewhat homomorphic lattice-based encryption (see Section 3.3) instead of Paillier. Secondly, they use a partial decryption in order to transfer the values between the $\mathcal{MC}$ and the $\mathcal{SPU}$, in such a way that the patient is required to send part of her key to these two parties; instead, we leverage the relinearization (key switching) process of leveled cryptosystems to provide proxy re-encryption functionalities and produce the test results encrypted under the key of the $\mathcal{MC}$.

We develop our modified protocol in the same scenario, with the same parties $\mathcal{P}$, a $\mathcal{CI}$, one $\mathcal{MC}$ and one $\mathcal{SPU}$. The setup step in the $\mathcal{CI}$ is essentially unaffected: it runs the set up and key generation algorithms (in our case, for a lattice-based SHE scheme, see Section 3.3) and distributes them among the parties. It also sequences the DNA sample of the patient, builds a Bloom Filter and sends the corresponding encryptions of the real and potential SNPs to the $\mathcal{SPU}$. The main difference lies in the encrypted execution of Eq. (1) for which our protocol is able to run the whole function homomorphically with both patient data and susceptibility parameters encrypted, sending the results directly to the $\mathcal{MC}$ under its own key. Regarding the attained privacy, we achieve that the $\mathcal{SPU}$ does not get to know any data about the patient or about the susceptibility parameters.

The complete instantiation of our proposed privacy-preserving susceptibility test based on SHE is depicted in Fig. 2, and described as follows:

Step s1: $\text{Setup}(1^\lambda) \to pp$: The $\mathcal{CI}$ runs the setup algorithms for the SHE $\text{SHESetup}(1^\lambda) \to pp_{SW} = (n, q, \chi)$, and the symmetric encryptions $\text{SESetup}(1^k) \to pp_{SE}$, obtaining $pp = (pp_{SE}, pp_{SW})$.

Step s2: $\text{Gen}(pp) \to k$: $\mathcal{CI}$ runs $\text{SHGen} \to (\boldsymbol{sk}_u, \boldsymbol{pk}_u)$ to obtain the keys of the SHE scheme for the patients, medical center and $\mathcal{SPU}$. It also runs $\text{SEGen} \to sk_{P,CI}$ to generate symmetric keys between $\mathcal{P}$ and $\mathcal{MC}$.

Sequencing and generation of input encryptions

Step e1: $\mathcal{P}$ sends her biological sample to the $\mathcal{CI}$.

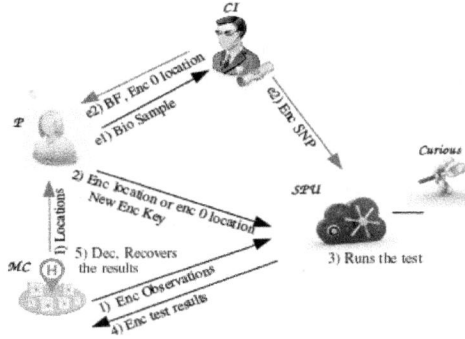

Figure 2: Proposed Privacy Preserving Scheme

Step e2: The $\mathcal{CI}$ sequences the sample, builds the patient's Bloom filter BF and symmetrically encrypts the positions $\{l_{i,E_{P,CI}}\}$ and $l_{0,E_{P,CI}}$ as in the previous scheme. Moreover, it encrypts the values of $\text{SNP}^{P,i}$ using the patient's SHE public key $\boldsymbol{pk}_P$. Then, the $\mathcal{CI}$ sends the BF and $l_{0,E_{P,CI}}$ to $\mathcal{P}$, and the pairs of encrypted positions and SNPs to the $\mathcal{SPU}$. Finally, either $\mathcal{MC}$ or $\mathcal{P}$ generates the relinearization matrix $\boldsymbol{B}_{P,MC}$ which enables the proxy re-encryption between the patient's SHE key $\boldsymbol{sk}_P$ and the $\mathcal{MC}$ key through a KSwitch operation, and sends it to the $\mathcal{SPU}$.

Encrypted susceptibility test

Step 1: The $\mathcal{MC}$ marks the location of SNPs in Ω_x and sends them to $\mathcal{P}$. Additionally, it sends the contributions of these SNPs to the disease x encrypted under $\mathcal{P}$'s SHE key to $\mathcal{SPU}$: $\{\boldsymbol{pr}_{E_P}^{x,i}, \boldsymbol{c}_{E_P}^{x,i}\}_{i \in \Omega_x}$.

Step 2: $\mathcal{P}$ runs the BF for these positions; for those in the BF (present variants), $\mathcal{P}$ encrypts the corresponding location $l_{i,E_{P,CI}}$ and sends it to $\mathcal{SPU}$, for those not in BF, $\mathcal{P}$ sends the encryption $l_{0,E_{P,CI}}$.

Step 3: The $\mathcal{SPU}$ computes the susceptibility test Eq. (1) on patient's encrypted SNPs and $\mathcal{MC}$'s encrypted susceptibility parameters for x by using the homomorphic properties of the SHE scheme, obtaining the encrypted value of $\boldsymbol{S}_{E_P}^{P,x}$ under $\mathcal{P}$'s key.

Step 4: The $\mathcal{SPU}$ runs $\text{KSwitch}(\boldsymbol{S}_{E_P}^{P,x}, \boldsymbol{pk}_P, \boldsymbol{B}_{P,MC}) \rightarrow \boldsymbol{S}_{E_{MC}}^{P,x}$ as a proxy re-encryption to get the result encrypted under the medical center's key, and sends it to $\mathcal{MC}$.

Step 5: The $\mathcal{MC}$ decrypts the clear-text test result $S^{P,x}$ of patient $\mathcal{P}$ for the disease x using its own SHE secret key.

4.3 Discussion and implementation details

The first enhancement of our modified scheme resides in replacing additively homomorphic Paillier encryptions by a lattice-based somewhat homomorphic encryption based on RLWE; this allows to perform the whole computation of the encrypted susceptibility function at the $\mathcal{SPU}$, removing step 3 in the original protocol and moving the computation in the original step 4 to the $\mathcal{SPU}$ instead of the $\mathcal{MC}$.

We achieve this goal by taking advantage of working with both SNPs and susceptibility parameters encrypted at the same time by means of the proposed SHE scheme, hence preserving both the privacy of $\mathcal{P}$'s genomic data and the confidentiality of the $\mathcal{MC}$'s test from the $\mathcal{SPU}$. Therefore, we are complying with the requirement of a truly outsourced secure computation, and the $\mathcal{SPU}$ is not only a helper party as in [2], but it can be instantiated by an untrustworthy computing infrastructure like a Cloud service, while minimizing

the computation requirements on the side of the $\mathcal{MC}$ and patient $\mathcal{P}$, whose involvement in our protocol are reduced to only encrypting inputs and decrypting outputs.

Secondly, we use key switching as a proxy re-encryption, so that the patient does not need to intervene in the last step of the protocol, therefore substituting steps 5 and 6 of the original scheme, and removing the need for partial decryption keys to allow the $\mathcal{MC}$ to decrypt the final result.

Another consideration has to do with the efficiency of the computation outsourced to the $\mathcal{SPU}$. While the encryptions for the SHE-based scheme are bigger than Paillier's, they do not involve any costly exponentiation, as they translate clear-text additions into encrypted additions and clear-text multiplications into encrypted polynomial multiplications, so their performance is not far away from Paillier's. Additionally, the chosen SHE scheme allows for batching SIMD (Single Instruction Multiple Data) operations, by taking advantage of encoding the inputs in a transform domain, in such a way that one encryption can hold a vector of SNP positions or susceptibility parameters, and all the scalar products can be performed "in parallel" just as one encrypted polynomial product. This technique greatly enhances the performance of the encrypted operations and allows to reduce also the cipher expansion of the encryptions, as we will show in an extended version of this short paper.

As a final remark, we could define an alternative protocol by restricting that all input values from the $\mathcal{MC}$ are encrypted with its own key, i.e., $\mathcal{MC}$ encrypts the susceptibility parameters $pr_{E_{MC}}^{P,x}$ and $c_{E_{MC}}^{P,x}$ under its key; then, the $\mathcal{SPU}$ would proxy re-encrypt the input SNPs from the patient to the $\mathcal{MC}$'s key with KSwitch operations before step 3, and perform the calculation of $\boldsymbol{S}_{E_{MC}}^{P,x}$ under $\mathcal{MC}$'s key. This modification increases the computation load on the server, but it avoids that the $\mathcal{MC}$ give away its confidential values under another party's key, in case this is a restriction imposed in a practical scenario.

5. DYNAMIC PRIVACY-PRESERVING SCHEME

An additional limitation of Ayday's scheme deals with permissions and access control, in such a way that once the $\mathcal{CI}$ sends the encrypted values to the $\mathcal{SPU}$, the access control is hardwired to the used keys; and the patient provides the $\mathcal{MC}$ with part of $\mathcal{P}$'s key; in case a new $\mathcal{MC}$ joins the system, the patient has to send it the partial key; if it leaves the system, the distributed key allows the $\mathcal{MC}$ to retrieve and decrypt any partial result output by the $\mathcal{SPU}$.

Hence, it is not possible to update this access control if new $\mathcal{MC}$s join or to revoke access to results if they leave the system. These operations can be managed with the aid of the proposed proxy re-encryption, relying on the KSwitch primitive of the SHE, but we also sketch here a more advanced modification with a more fine-grained control over the patient consent to a set of medical centers or some susceptibility tests. For this purpose, we propose to use Attribute-Based Somewhat Homomorphic Encryption.

5.1 Attribute-Based SHE

While there are not many proposals of Attribute Based Somewhat Homomorphic Encryption (ABSHE) in the literature, a lattice-based ABSHE can be constructed by applying Gentry's homomorphic compiler [7] to a regular attribute based encryption (ABE) scheme, resulting in a cryptosystem with both properties. In order to use the ABSHE, a trusted party (our $\mathcal{CI}$) would run a setup algorithm to produce a master secret-public key pair, and a key generation algorithm to generate each of the secret keys for the patients and the $\mathcal{MC}$s. By relying on attributes, we allow to directly retrieve the public keys of the involved parties, and we also let the patient define which subset of attributes must be fulfilled by a medical center to obtain the test results.

Therefore, instead of relying on proxy re-encryption, the patient can define an access policy as a set of attributes, and the $\mathcal{CI}$ will encrypt the SNPs with the key corresponding to the allowed attribute subset instead of the patient's key. If a new $\mathcal{MC}$ joins the system, it will declare and authorize a set of attributes, and if they fulfill the patient's policy, the new $\mathcal{MC}$ can get authorization to run the tests without the intervention of the patient or the $\mathcal{CI}$. It must be noted that attributes can define not only the identity of the $\mathcal{MC}$ but also the tests, in such a way that different keys would be used for different centers and different susceptibility tests.

The most important feature of an ABSHE scheme is the ability to dynamically deal with more than one medical center which might be responsible for various tasks or tests, based on their access structure defined as a function of the medical center's attribute set. The achievable privacy levels regarding the protection against the $\mathcal{SPU}$ are the same as for the proposed scheme in Section 4.2, as all the homomorphic operations involved in step 3 of our protocol would be preserved by the ABSHE construction. An additional advantage is that it is not necessary to manage re-encryption keys, the patient does not have to generate them, and the encryptions do not have to be resent after a party joins or leaves the system.

6. CONCLUSIONS

We improved on previous privacy-preserving genetic susceptibility testing protocols by relying on a somewhat homomorphic lattice-based encryption, and using key-switching algorithms as a proxy re-encryption primitives. We allow for truly outsourced secure testing by leveraging a Ring Learning with Errors-based encryption, by achieving the same privacy and confidentiality levels as prior schemes with a better communication and round efficiency; furthermore, we move most of the computational load to an outsourced untrustworthy party, reducing the computational needs of the patients and medical centers to just encrypting the inputs and decrypting the results.

Additionally, we sketch a method with Attribute-Based Somewhat Homomorphic Encryption, which allows for a fine-grained dynamic access control by mapping the patient consent to an attribute-based policy defining the centers and the susceptibility tests that can be carried on her DNA samples. Implementation results and performance figures will be provided in an extended version of this short paper.

7. ACKNOWLEDGMENTS

This work was partially funded by the Spanish Ministry of Economy and Competitiveness and the European Regional Development Fund (ERDF) under projects COMPASS (TEC2013-47020-C2-1-R) and COMONSENS (TEC2015-69648-REDC), by the Galician Regional Government and ERDF under projects "Consolidation of Research Units" (GRC2013/009), and Atlant-TIC, and by the EU H2020 Framework Programme under project WITDOM (project no. 644371)

8. REFERENCES

[1] E. Ayday, J. L. Raisaro, U. Hengartner, A. Molyneaux, and J.-P. Hubaux. Privacy-preserving processing of raw genomic data. In *Data Privacy Management and Autonomous Spontaneous Security*, pages 133–147. Springer, 2014.

[2] E. Ayday, J. L. Raisaro, and J.-P. Hubaux. Privacy-enhancing technologies for medical tests using genomic data. Technical report, 2012. Online: http://infoscience.epfl.ch/record/182897.

[3] P. Baldi, R. Baronio, E. De Cristofaro, P. Gasti, and G. Tsudik. Countering GATTACA: Efficient and Secure Testing of Fully-sequenced Human Genomes. In *ACM CCS*, pages 691–702, New York, USA, 2011.

[4] Z. Brakerski, C. Gentry, and V. Vaikuntanathan. (leveled) fully homomorphic encryption without bootstrapping. In *3rd Innovations in Theoretical Computer Science Conference*, pages 309–325. ACM, 2012.

[5] M. Canim, M. Kantarcioglu, and B. Malin. Secure management of biomedical data with cryptographic hardware. *IEEE Trans. on Information Technology in Biomedicine*, 16(1):166–175, 2012.

[6] Y. Chen, B. Peng, X. Wang, and H. Tang. Large-scale privacy-preserving mapping of human genomic sequences on hybrid clouds. In *NDSS*, 2012.

[7] C. Gentry, A. Sahai, and B. Waters. Homomorphic encryption from learning with errors: Conceptually-simpler, asymptotically-faster, attribute-based. In *Advances in Cryptology–CRYPTO 2013*, pages 75–92. Springer, 2013.

[8] S. Kathiresan, O. Melander, D. Anevski, C. Guiducci, N. P. Burtt, C. Roos, J. N. Hirschhorn, G. Berglund, B. Hedblad, L. Groop, et al. Polymorphisms associated with cholesterol and risk of cardiovascular events. *New England Journal of Medicine*, 358(12):1240–1249, 2008.

[9] V. Lyubashevsky, C. Peikert, and O. Regev. On ideal lattices and learning with errors over rings. In *EUROCRYPT*, volume 6110 of *LNCS*, pages 1–23. Springer, 2010.

[10] M. Naveed, E. Ayday, E. W. Clayton, J. Fellay, C. A. Gunter, J.-P. Hubaux, B. A. Malin, and X. Wang. Privacy in the genomic era. *ACM Computing Surveys (CSUR)*, 48(1):6, 2015.

[11] P. Paillier. Public-key cryptosystems based on composite degree residuosity classes. In *EUROCRYPT*, pages 223–238. Springer, 1999.

[12] S. Seshadri, A. L. Fitzpatrick, M. A. Ikram, A. L. DeStefano, V. Gudnason, M. Boada, J. C. Bis, A. V. Smith, M. M. Carrasquillo, J. C. Lambert, et al. Genome-wide analysis of genetic loci associated with alzheimer disease. *JAMA*, 303(18):1832–1840, 2010.

[13] J. R. Troncoso-Pastoriza, S. Katzenbeisser, and M. Celik. Privacy preserving error resilient DNA searching through oblivious automata. In *ACM CCS*, CCS '07, pages 519–528, New York, NY, USA, 2007. ACM.

[14] R. Wang, X. Wang, Z. Li, H. Tang, M. K. Reiter, and Z. Dong. Privacy-preserving genomic computation through program specialization. In *ACM CCS*, pages 338–347. ACM, 2009.

Group Testing for Identification with Privacy

Ahmet Iscen
Inria
Campus de Beaulieu
Rennes, France
ahmet.iscen@inria.fr

Teddy Furon
Inria
Campus de Beaulieu
Rennes, France
teddy.furon@inria.fr

ABSTRACT

This paper describes an approach where group testing helps in enforcing security and privacy in identification. We detail a particular scheme based on embedding and group testing. We add a second layer of defense, group vectors, where each group vector represents a set of dataset vectors. Whereas the selected embedding poorly protects the data when used alone, the group testing approach makes it much harder to reconstruct the data when combined with the embedding. Even when curious server and user collude to disclose the secret parameters, they cannot accurately recover the data. Another byproduct of our approach is that it reduces the complexity of the search and the required storage space. We show the interest of our work in a benchmark biometrics dataset, where we verify our theoretical analysis with real data.

1. INTRODUCTION

This paper considers a typical scenario involving the following three entities. The owner $\mathcal{O}$ has a collection of N objects. The user $\mathcal{U}$ would like to know whether there is an object in this collection similar enough to query object, and in that case, which object it is. The owner is not willing to operate the identification and outsources this task to a server $\mathcal{S}$. The targeted applications are typically related to multimedia retrieval, medical diagnosis, biometrics. In the later case, the owner $\mathcal{O}$ is a personification of the enrollment phase. A feature vector is extracted from the objects (iris, face captures) and used as a proxy: similar objects share similar features. Overall, this boils down to managing a database of vectors probed with query vectors.

We add the following privacy / security requirements:

- $\mathcal{U}$ doesn't want to reveal his query,

- $\mathcal{O}$ is reluctant in disclosing his database.

In other words, $\mathcal{S}$, the outsourced server is not trusted. This actor is deemed as semi-honest (or honest but curious): it operates the search task, however it tries to grab information about the query or the database. This would allow $\mathcal{S}$ to profile $\mathcal{U}$, i.e. to disclose what $\mathcal{U}$ is interested in, or to perform the search with unauthorized users, i.e. without the agreement of $\mathcal{O}$. In biometrics application, disclosing database vectors could lead to spoofing [5]. Some make the distinction between the privacy, which protects user $\mathcal{U}$, and the security, which protect the data of the owner $\mathcal{O}$.

Section 2 describes a classical solution based on embedding and secure multiparty computation. We selected the LSH embedding which maps real vectors to binary hashes. Evaluating the cosine similarity between vectors amounts to computing the Hamming distance between their hashes. We use a very efficient cryptographic protocol called SHADE for securing Hamming distances computations[1]: while $\mathcal{S}$ learns nothing from the query, $\mathcal{U}$ learns nothing from the database vector except the index of the most similar vector. This system enables privacy under the semi-honest model, but the security of owner's data is weak if $\mathcal{U}$ and $\mathcal{S}$ collude.

This weakness is due to $\mathcal{S}$ having binary hashes in the clear. The main counter-measure in literature is fully homomorphic encryption. It allows computing distances between two ciphers s.t. $\mathcal{S}$ now manipulates data previously encrypted by $\mathcal{O}$. However, computation in the encrypted domain is very low preventing the scalability of the system.

This paper trades privacy of the user and security of the data for scale of the database, speed of similarity search and quality of the identification. This is achieved by resorting to advanced signal processing rather than more cryptography. Section 3 describes a second version of the system adding on top of LSH and SHADE a group testing scheme for dealing with efficiency of the search while leaking only very little useful information.

1.1 Setup

The owner $\mathcal{O}$ has a database of vectors $\mathcal{X} := \{\mathbf{x}_i\}_1^N$ s.t. $\mathbf{x}_i \in \mathbb{R}^d$ with Euclidean norm $\|\mathbf{x}_i\| = 1, \forall i \in [N]$, where $[N] := \{1, \cdots, N\}$. We denote the query of the user by $\mathbf{q} \in \mathbb{R}^d$ with $\|\mathbf{q}\| = 1$. The similarity between the query and a database vector $\mathbf{x}$ is defined by $s(\mathbf{q}, \mathbf{x}) := \mathbf{q}^\top \mathbf{x}$.

In this paper, we analyse the proposed system having in mind biometrics *identification*. Database vectors are biometrics recorded at the enrollment phase. $\mathcal{U}$ is interested in knowing the index of the most similar vector in the database if similar enough:

$$\hat{\imath} := \begin{cases} \arg\max_{i \in [N]} s(\mathbf{q}, \mathbf{x}_i) & \text{if } s(\mathbf{q}, \mathbf{x}_i) \geq \rho \\ \emptyset & \text{otherwise} \end{cases} \quad (1)$$

---

[1] Another option is partial homomorphic encryption

Publication rights licensed to ACM. ACM acknowledges that this contribution was authored or co-authored by an employee, contractor or affiliate of a national government. As such, the Government retains a nonexclusive, royalty-free right to publish or reproduce this article, or to allow others to do so, for Government purposes only.

IH&MMSec 2016, June 20 - 23, 2016, Vigo, Spain.

ACM ISBN 978-1-4503-4290-2/16/06. . . $15.00.

Copyright is held by the owner/author(s). Publication rights licensed to ACM.

DOI: http://dx.doi.org/10.1145/2909827.2930792

There are two cases: The query is a noisy version of an enrolled vector $\mathbf{x}_{i^\star}$; or the query is random and we denote $i^\star = \emptyset$. For a given threshold ρ, three errors are possible:

False negative: $\hat{\imath} = \emptyset$ while $i^\star \neq \emptyset$
False identification: $\hat{\imath} \neq i^\star$ while $i^\star \neq \emptyset$
False positive: $\hat{\imath} \neq \emptyset$ while $i^\star = \emptyset$

We denote by P_{fn}, P_{fid}, and P_{fp} respectively the probabilities of these events. The 'real' search defined in (1) produces non zero error probabilities depending on how strongly the query is correlated with $\mathbf{x}_{i^\star}$ (when $i^\star \neq \emptyset$) and on the size N of the database. Due to privacy, $\mathcal{S}$ can not perform the real search as defined above. In agreement with $\mathcal{O}$, $\mathcal{S}$ runs a secure and approximate search with lower performances.

1.2 LSH Binary Embedding

An embedding casts a vector $\mathbf{x} \in \mathbb{R}^d$ into a vector of D discrete components.

$$e : \mathbb{R}^d \rightarrow \mathcal{A}^D \qquad (2)$$
$$\mathbf{x} \rightarrow e(\mathbf{x}) := (e(\mathbf{x})_1, \cdots, e(\mathbf{x})_D)$$

This function is designed to provide i) a compact representation of vectors, and ii) an estimation of the similarity $s(\mathbf{q}, \mathbf{x})$ between two vectors from their embeddings: $s_e(e(\mathbf{q}), e(\mathbf{x}))$. Function $s_e(\cdot, \cdot)$ is faster to compute than $s(\cdot, \cdot)$.

We propose to use one of the most well-known binary embeddings, LSH [4], where $\mathcal{A} = \{0, 1\}$. In a nutshell, once D directions $\{\mathbf{a}_k\}_{k=1}^D$ have been randomly drawn i.i.d. uniformly in $\mathbb{R}^d$, the k-th symbol of the embedding is computed as follows:

$$e(\mathbf{x})_k := \mathsf{sign}(\mathbf{x}^\top \mathbf{a}_k), \forall k \in [D], \qquad (3)$$

with $\mathsf{sign}(x) := 1$ if $x \geq 0$, and 0 otherwise. LSH has the following well-known property:

$$\frac{\mathbf{x}^\top \mathbf{q}}{\|\mathbf{x}\|\|\mathbf{q}\|} \approx \cos\left(\frac{\pi}{D} d_H(e(\mathbf{q}), e(\mathbf{x}))\right). \qquad (4)$$

The cosine is estimated via the Hamming distance $d_H(\cdot, \cdot)$. In our setup, database and query vectors have unit norm, the cosine is thus the metric we use to quantify similarity.

1.3 SHADE Protocol

Suppose now that $\mathcal{U}$ and $\mathcal{S}$ have respectively the binary words $\mathbf{w}^{\mathcal{U}}$ and $\mathbf{w}^{\mathcal{S}}$, and that $d_H(\mathbf{w}^{\mathcal{U}}, \mathbf{w}^{\mathcal{S}})$ is needed. SHADE is an efficient protocol [3] allowing $\mathcal{U}$ to learn nothing about $\mathbf{w}^{\mathcal{S}}$ except $d_H(\mathbf{w}^{\mathcal{U}}, \mathbf{w}^{\mathcal{S}})$, while $\mathcal{S}$ gains no information about $\mathbf{w}^{\mathcal{U}}$. In short, at the k-th round, $\mathcal{S}$ creates two messages: $m_0^{(k)} = \mathbf{w}_k^{\mathcal{S}} + r_k$ and $m_1^{(k)} = (\mathbf{w}_k^{\mathcal{S}} \bigoplus 1) + r_k$, where r_k is an alea uniformly distributed over $\mathbb{Z}_{D+1}$. Thanks to an oblivious transfer, $\mathcal{U}$ receives $v_k := m_{\mathbf{w}_k^{\mathcal{U}}}^{(k)}$. After D rounds, $\mathcal{S}$ sends $R := \sum_{k=1}^D r_k$ to $\mathcal{U}$ who computes $V := \sum_{k=1}^D v_k$ and $V - R = d_H(\mathbf{w}^{\mathcal{U}}, \mathbf{w}^{\mathcal{S}})$. SHADE is secure in the static semi-honest model: $\mathcal{U}$ and $\mathcal{S}$ are honest but curious. There is an efficient version of SHADE for computing a batch of Hamming distances between one query and N vectors [2].

1.4 Adding Comparison and Minimum

Letting $\mathcal{U}$ learning the Hamming distance $d_H(\mathbf{w}^{\mathcal{U}}, \mathbf{w}^{\mathcal{S}})$ is dangerous in the dynamic model where $\mathcal{U}$ is allowed to perform several distance computations: With D well chosen queries, $\mathcal{U}$ can disclose $\mathbf{w}^{\mathcal{S}}$. The authors of SHADE recommend the use of the GMW protocol [8] to first securely compare $V - R$ to a threshold τ. $\mathcal{U}$ only gets $\mathsf{sign}(d_H(\mathbf{w}^{\mathcal{U}}, \mathbf{w}^{\mathcal{S}}) -$

τ). For a batch of distances, their minimum is securely computed and $\mathcal{U}$ only learns $\hat{\imath} = \arg\min d_H(\mathbf{w}^{\mathcal{U}}, \mathbf{w}^{\mathcal{S}})$.

2. FIRST VERSION OF THE SYSTEM

A system is a list of procedures followed by the three actors $\mathcal{O}$, $\mathcal{S}$ and $\mathcal{U}$. The owner $\mathcal{O}$ draws D random directions stacked in matrix $\mathbf{A} := [\mathbf{a}_1, \cdots, \mathbf{a}_D]$, computes the embeddings of its vectors, and sends $\mathcal{S}$ the database $\mathcal{E} := \{e(\mathbf{x}_i)\}$. $\mathcal{O}$ grants $\mathcal{U}$ the access of the identification by sending $\mathbf{A}$ so that $\mathcal{U}$ can compute the embedding of its query $\mathbf{q}$.

At query time, entities $\mathcal{U}$ and $\mathcal{S}$ perform the SHADE protocol, where $\mathbf{w}^{\mathcal{U}} = e(\mathbf{q})$ and $\mathbf{w}^{\mathcal{S}} = e(\mathbf{x}_i)$ with the batch option. $\mathcal{U}$ maps the Hamming distances $d_H(e(\mathbf{x}_i), e(\mathbf{q}))$ to similarity estimates $\hat{s}(\mathbf{q}, \mathbf{x}_i)$ thanks to (4). $\mathcal{U}$ finds the index with the biggest similarity and takes it as the output if it is above the threshold ρ. The search is approximate because it is based on similarity estimates.

An option is to add GMV protocol to let $\mathcal{U}$ learn either indices of vectors whose approximated similarity with the query is above a threshold (secure comparison), or the index of the vector whose approximated similarity is maximum (secure maximum). Note that this is done on the Hamming distances because (4) is a monotonic mapping. A combination of the two implement the search as defined in (1).

2.1 Analysis

Complexity: The quality of the approximate search depends on D, the embedding length. For any two vectors $\mathbf{x}$ and $\mathbf{q}$ s.t. $\mathbf{q}^\top \mathbf{x} = \cos(\theta)$, and $\mathbf{A}$ randomly generated as early described, $\frac{\pi}{D} d_H(e(\mathbf{q}), e(\mathbf{x}))$ in (4) is indeed an estimation of θ with no bias and variance $\theta(\pi - \theta)/D$. However, the complexity of the SHADE protocol deeply depends on D. The secure computation of a batch of size N has a complexity [2]:

$$\mathcal{C} \propto [(2ND \log_2(D))/o + 3D]\mathcal{C}_{sym}, \qquad (5)$$

where o is a constant setting the security of the protocol (at least 128), and $\mathcal{C}_{sym}$ is the complexity of one symmetric cryptography operation (i.e. AES encryption / decryption).

Even though SHADE has been a breakthrough considerably lowering the complexity of the secure computation of Hamming distances, it is the bottleneck of our system. It takes 0.2s to securely compute and run the GMV protocol over $N = 200$ embeddings of length $D = 900$ (see [2]).

Security: SHADE enables the privacy of $\mathcal{U}$, but the owner $\mathcal{O}$ has some concerns. The parameter of the embedding (here matrix $\mathbf{A}$) is generated by the owner $\mathcal{O}$ and only shared with $\mathcal{U}$. This parameter is the only secret that prevents a curious server $\mathcal{S}$ from performing illegal identification or estimating the database vectors by inverting the embedding. By colluding with one user, $\mathcal{S}$ learns this secret.

Since (2) is a surjection, the embedding is not reversible and perfect reconstruction of $\mathcal{X}$ is impossible. However, one can see the embedding as a quantizer producing quantification noise. Sect. 2.2 measures the accuracy of a reconstruction of $\mathbf{x}$ from $e(\mathbf{x})$ provided matrix $\mathbf{A}$ is known.

2.2 Inverting LSH

A simple reconstruction of a unit norm vector $\mathbf{x}$ from its embedding is:

$$\hat{\mathbf{x}} = \kappa(\mathbf{A}(2e(\mathbf{x}) - \mathbf{1}_D)), \qquad (6)$$

where κ is s.t. $\mathbb{E}_{\mathbf{A}}[\|\hat{\mathbf{x}}\|^2] = 1$. To quantify its accuracy, we introduce $a(\mathbf{x}) := \mathbf{x}^\top \hat{\mathbf{x}}$. The closer to 1, the better the reconstruction. We have:

$$a(\mathbf{x}) = \kappa \sum_{k=1}^{D} |\mathbf{a}_k^\top \mathbf{x}|. \qquad (7)$$

LSH was originally proposed with $\{\mathbf{a}_k\}$ being independent random directions in $\mathbb{R}^d$. In this case, the appendix shows:

$$\mathbb{E}_{\mathbf{A}}[a(\mathbf{x})] \approx \sqrt{\frac{g}{1+g}} \text{ with } g := \frac{2D}{\pi d}. \qquad (8)$$

However, if $D \leq d$, it is known that $\mathbf{A}$ being a random basis of rank D yields a better search [11]. In this case, $\|\mathbf{A}(2e(\mathbf{x}) - \mathbf{1}_D)\|^2 = D$ for any $\mathbf{x}$. The appendix shows:

$$\mathbb{E}_{\mathbf{A}}[a(\mathbf{x})] \approx \sqrt{g} \text{ with } g \leq 1. \qquad (9)$$

If $D > d$, a good choice is $\mathbf{A}$ as a random tight frame [10] s.t. $\|\mathbf{A}(2e(\mathbf{x}) - \mathbf{1}_D)\|^2 = d/D\|2e(\mathbf{x}) - \mathbf{1}_D)\|^2 = d$. Yet, the r.v. $\mathbf{a}_k^\top \mathbf{x}$ are no longer independent and it is hard to say something more than:

$$\sqrt{\frac{2}{\pi}} \approx 0.80 \leq \mathbb{E}_{\mathbf{A}}[a(\mathbf{x})] \leq 1. \qquad (10)$$

Approximate search based on LSH embedding usually sets $D > d$. On expectation, $\hat{\mathbf{x}}$ is then a good approximation of $\mathbf{x}$ since they correlate more than 0.8.

Fig. 4 shows the reconstruction accuracy w.r.t. D, when $\mathbf{A}$ is a random tight frame or random Gaussian matrix.

2.3 Lessons Learnt from the First System

The parameter of utmost importance is the length of the embedding D. It sets a trade-off between the quality of the identification, the complexity of the protocol, and the security when $\mathbf{A}$ has been compromised. Yet, this trade-off is poor as the reconstruction provides a good accuracy when $D > d$.

3. THE PROPOSED SYSTEM

Our aim is to provide a second line of defense. Group testing was recently introduced in approximate search. The idea is to pack database vectors into groups and to compute a representation per group, so-called memory vector, which allows to perform a group test. This test reveals whether the query is similar to at least one of the vectors in the group. For large dimension d, more vectors can be packed into one group because the correlation between two independent vectors with unit norm concentrates around 0.

Each database vector belongs to several groups. The decoding aims at identifying the matching vector(s) from the results of the group tests. A matching vector is defined as having a similarity with the query high enough: $s(\mathbf{q}, \mathbf{x}) \geq \alpha$. Naively, matching vectors are lying at the intersection of the groups yielding a positive group test. Things are not that simple because these tests suffer from false positives and false negatives. Yet, if the number of groups is large enough, the decoding succeeds in identifying matching vectors.

This approach brings two advantages to our system:

- The number of groups M is smaller than the number of vectors N. This lowers both the storage space and the complexity of the protocol by a gain $\gamma := M/N < 1$.

- $\mathcal{O}$ will not give $\mathcal{S}$ embeddings of database vectors, but of memory vectors. This makes harder the reconstruction of database vectors.

Table 1: Definition of the weights

	$b_{i,j} = 1$	$b_{i,j} = 0$
$\mathcal{H}_i$	$\eta = 1$	$\eta = 0$
$\bar{\mathcal{H}}_i$	$\eta = (n-1)/N$	$\eta = n/N$

3.1 Encoding

The owner $\mathcal{O}$ randomly packs the N database vectors into M groups $\{\mathcal{G}_j\}_{j=1}^M$ s.t. i) any group comprises n vectors, ii) any vector belongs to m groups. This rules enforces that $M = mN/n$. A possible construction is explained in [7]. We call the map the $M \times N$ binary matrix $\mathbf{B}$ indicating which vector belongs to which group: $b_{i,j} = 1$ if $\mathbf{x}_i$ belongs to group $\mathcal{G}_j$, 0 otherwise.

Then, $\mathcal{O}$ computes the memory vectors, *i.e.* the representatives of each group. We adopt here the most simple constructions investigated in [7]:

$$\mathbf{m}_j = \sum_{i:b_{i,j}=1} \mathbf{x}_i. \qquad (11)$$

Finally, $\mathcal{O}$ computes the embeddings of the memory vectors and sends $\mathcal{S}$ the following compact description $\mathcal{E}' = \{e(\mathbf{m}_j)\}_{j=1}^M$. $\mathcal{O}$ sends $\mathcal{U}$ parameters $(\mathbf{A}, \mathbf{B}, \{\|\mathbf{m}_j\|\}_{j=1}^M)$: $\mathbf{A}$ is needed to compute query embedding, $\mathbf{B}$ and $\{\|\mathbf{m}_j\|\}_{j=1}^M$ to decode the tests. Note that the database $\mathcal{E}'$ is smaller than $\mathcal{E}$ since it has $M < N$ entries.

3.2 Querying

$\mathcal{U}$ computes $e(\mathbf{q})$ thanks to $\mathbf{A}$ and runs the SHADE protocol with $\mathcal{S}$, who learns nothing about the query. $\mathcal{U}$ obtains estimations of the cosine between $\mathbf{q}$ and $\mathbf{m}_j$. Multiplying by the norm $\|\mathbf{m}_j\|$, this gives estimated similarities $\hat{s}_j \approx \mathbf{q}^\top \mathbf{m}_j$.

The big benefit is the decrease of SHADE complexity, which was the bottleneck of the previous system. Instead of securely computing N Hamming distances $d_H(e(\mathbf{q}), e(\mathbf{x}_i))$, we compute $M < N$ distances $d_H(e(\mathbf{q}), e(\mathbf{m}_j))$.

Soft decoding: From $\{\hat{s}_j\}_{j=1}^M$ and map $\mathbf{B}$, $\mathcal{U}$ runs the decoding to identify $i^\star$, index of the matching vector.

In summary, the decoding computes N scores. c_i is the likelihood ratio w.r.t. two hypothesis: $\mathbf{x}_i$ is the matching vector ($\mathcal{H}_i$) or not ($\bar{\mathcal{H}}_i$).

$$c_i = \sum_{j=1}^{M} \log \frac{f_{\mathcal{H}_i}(\hat{s}_j, b_{i,j})}{f_{\bar{\mathcal{H}}_i}(\hat{s}_j, b_{i,j})}, \qquad (12)$$

where the pdfs are modeled as mixtures of two Gaussian distributions, $\eta \mathcal{N}(\alpha; (n-1)/d) + (1 - \eta)\mathcal{N}(0; n/d)$, with parameter η given in Table 1. We refer the reader to [7] for justifications of this statistical model. Then, $\mathcal{U}$ computes the maximum of these scores and compares with the threshold.

Hard decoding: To prevent oracle attacks from $\mathcal{U}$, we use the GMW protocol to apply a secure comparison: $\mathcal{U}$ learns nothing more than $d_j = \mathsf{sign}(\hat{s}_j - \tau)$, where threshold τ has been carefully selected by $\mathcal{O}$. Then, the decoding computes the following scores:

$$c_i = \sum_{j=1}^{M} d_j \log \frac{p_{\mathcal{H}_i}(b_{i,j})}{p_{\bar{\mathcal{H}}_i}(b_{i,j})} + (1 - d_j) \log \frac{1 - p_{\mathcal{H}_i}(b_{i,j})}{1 - p_{\bar{\mathcal{H}}_i}(b_{i,j})}, \qquad (13)$$

with $p_{\mathcal{H}_i}(b_{i,j}) = \mathbb{E}_{\hat{s}_j \sim f_{\mathcal{H}_i}(\hat{s}_j, b_{i,j})}[\hat{s}_j > \tau]$:

$$p_{\mathcal{H}_i}(b_{i,j}) = \eta\Phi\left((\tau - \alpha)\sqrt{\frac{d}{n-1}}\right) + (1-\eta)\Phi\left(\tau\sqrt{\frac{d}{n}}\right)$$

and parameter η given in Table 1.

4. SECURITY

Unauthorized identification is possible whenever an untrusted actor, be it $\mathcal{U}$ and/or $\mathcal{S}$, has in his hands both $(\mathbf{A}, \mathbf{B}, \{\|\mathbf{m}_j\|\}_{j=1}^M)$ and $\mathcal{E}'$. This happens only when $\mathcal{S}$ and $\mathcal{U}$ colluded, or if $\mathcal{U}$ succeeds to steal $\mathcal{E}'$.

The group testing approach brings a second line of defense by mixing the database vectors into memory vectors. We focus here on the reconstruction of the database vectors. To do so, the untrusted actor must i) reconstruct the memory vectors by 'inverting' their embeddings, and ii) estimate database vectors from the reconstructed memory vectors of groups they belong to. Reconstruction i) needs $\mathcal{E}'$, $\mathbf{A}$ and $\{\|\mathbf{m}_j\|\}$. The quality of the reconstruction is quite high as shown in Sec. 2.2. Estimation ii) needs $\mathbf{B}$. The quality of the reconstruction is investigated in the next section.

4.1 Inverting Memory Units

Equation (11) can be rephrased as $\mathbf{M} = \mathbf{X}\mathbf{B}^\top$ where $\mathbf{M} := [\mathbf{m}_1, \cdots, \mathbf{m}_M]$ is a $d \times M$ matrix storing the memory units while $\mathbf{X} := [\mathbf{x}_1, \cdots, \mathbf{x}_N]$ stores the database vectors and $\mathbf{B}$ is the map (See Sect. 3.1). Estimating back $\mathbf{X}$ from $\mathbf{M}$ is possible using a ridge regression or the pseudo-inverse of $\mathbf{B}^\top$: $\hat{\mathbf{X}} \propto \mathbf{M}(\mathbf{B}^\top)^\dagger$. We can show that reconstructing $\mathbf{x}$ from the exact memory units, produces an estimation $\hat{\mathbf{x}}$ s.t.

$$\mathbb{E}[a(\mathbf{x})] = \min(1, \sqrt{\gamma}). \tag{14}$$

Yet, this requires the inverse of large $M \times M$ matrix $\mathbf{B}\mathbf{B}^\top$. The average of some memory vectors albeit not optimal is faster: $\hat{\mathbf{X}} \propto \mathbf{M}\mathbf{B}$ achieving ($\nu := n/N$):

$$\mathbb{E}[a(\mathbf{x})] \approx \sqrt{\frac{\gamma}{1 + \nu^2(M-1) + \gamma(1-\nu)^2}}. \tag{15}$$

4.2 Full Reconstruction

The attacker first reconstructs the group vectors $\{\hat{\mathbf{m}}_k\}$ from their embeddings $\{e(\mathbf{m}_k)\}$, and then reconstructs the database vectors $\{\hat{\mathbf{x}}_i\}$. It is easy to show that if the first step produces a reconstruction accuracy measured by $\mathbb{E}[a(\mathbf{m})] = a_1$ while the second step achieves $\mathbb{E}[a(\mathbf{x})] = a_2$ starting from true memory vectors, then the total reconstruction yields $\mathbb{E}[a(\mathbf{x})] = a_1 a_2$ thanks to the linearity of the second step. This is evidenced in the experimental work.

5. EXPERIMENTS

5.1 Experimental Setup

We test our system using both synthetic and real data. For both cases, we keep the ratio $\gamma = M/N = m/n = 0.1$. This means that the retrieval system needs only 0.1 of memory storage and vector comparisons compared to exhaustive search. The embedding is parametrized s.t. $D = 2d$.
Synthetic Data. We create a synthetic dataset of N vectors distributed randomly on the unit hypersphere of $\mathbb{R}^d$. We then create N_q random query vectors, such that each query has exactly one match in the dataset, $\mathbf{x}_{i^\star}$, and the similarity

between the query and the matching vector is $\mathbf{q}^\top\mathbf{x}_{i^\star} = \alpha$. We set $d = 1,920$, $N = 10,000$, $N_q = 100$, and $\alpha = 0.5$.
Real Data. We also use Labeled Faces in the Wild (LFW) dataset [6], which has 13,233 images of 5,749 people. For the query set, we choose a random image from people who have i) at least two images, ii) have at least one match with a similarity greater than or equal to α. We use the full ($d = 67,584$) Fisher face descriptors [9] to calculate the similarities to generate the query set. Then, we use the same query set for all experiments, regardless of different descriptors or dimensionality. Setting $\alpha = 0.5$ gives us $N_q = 104$ queries, each belonging to a different person. We also choose 1,000 random queries from people who have no other matching vectors. All queries and random queries are removed from the dataset.

For our experiments, we reduce the dimension of Fisher face descriptors from 67,584 to 1,920 for fair comparison with synthetic data. We also use CNN-based descriptors [1], whose dimension is reduced from 4,096 to 1,920.
Parameters setting. As stated earlier, we can set the ratio of $M/N = 0.1$ with different m and n combinations. We choose the optimal setting empirically by maximizing the Kullback-Leibler distance between negative and positive distributions. This gives $n = 200$, $m = 20$, and $\tau = 0.8 \times \alpha$.
Evaluation. The three metrics for evaluating the performance are the probabilities of the three types of error, P_{fp}, P_{fn} and P_{fid} as functions of threshold ρ (see Sect. 1.1). Security is gauged by the quality of the reconstruction of the database vectors measured by $\mathbb{E}[a(\mathbf{x})]$.

5.2 Approximate Search

Fig. 1 shows the performance of the identification of the baseline, *i.e.* the exhaustive search on real vectors, without any privacy and security issues, as defined in (1). Fig. 2 shows the same evaluation for the first system described in Sect. 2. Fig. 3 shows the system proposed in Sect. 3 with the hard decoding variant (13). We are smoothly degrading the performance of the approximate search over synthetic data, however it still performs well on the real dataset.

5.3 Security

Fig. 4 shows the reconstruction performance while inverting LSH with the synthetic dataset. It encompasses two matrix $\mathbf{A}$ generation procedures: Gaussian i.i.d. entries and uniform tight frame. The latter option is known to produce better approximate search. This illustrates the security of the first system described in Sect. 2. In our setup where $D = 2d$, we end up with $\mathbb{E}[a(\mathbf{x})] \approx 0.88$.

Fig. 5 shows the reconstruction performance while inverting the memory units with $m \in [2, 20]$ and $n = 200$ on the synthetic dataset. It encompasses two reconstruction methods: the pseudo inverse of $\mathbf{B}$ and the average of memory vectors (See Sect. 4.1). This illustrates the security improvement thanks to the second line of defense provided by group testing. In our setup where $n = 200$ and $m = 20$, we end up with $\mathbb{E}[a(\mathbf{x})] \approx 0.33$.

Overall, the reconstruction of vectors $\{\mathbf{x}_i\}$ from $\{e(\mathbf{m}_k)\}$ outputs estimates correlated on expactation $\mathbb{E}[a(\mathbf{x})] \approx 0.88 \times 0.33 = 0.29$. We run the attack on the real datasets and get $\mathbb{E}[a(\mathbf{x})] \approx 0.88 \times 0.31 = 0.27$.

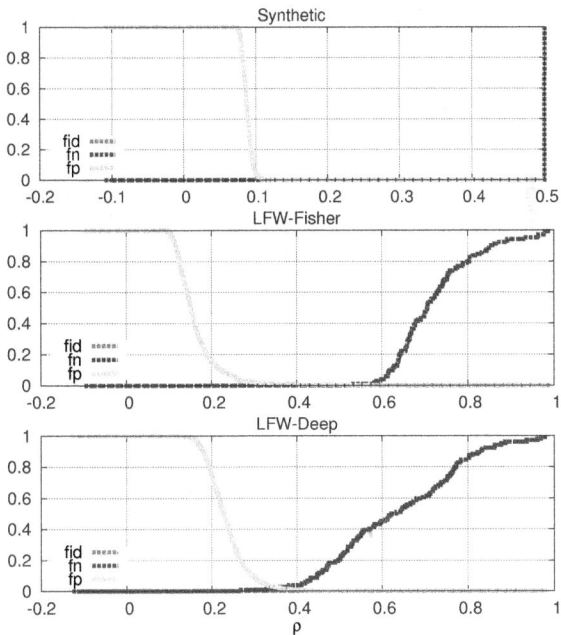

Figure 1: Baseline performance, synthetic and LFW (Fisher / deep learning features) datasets.

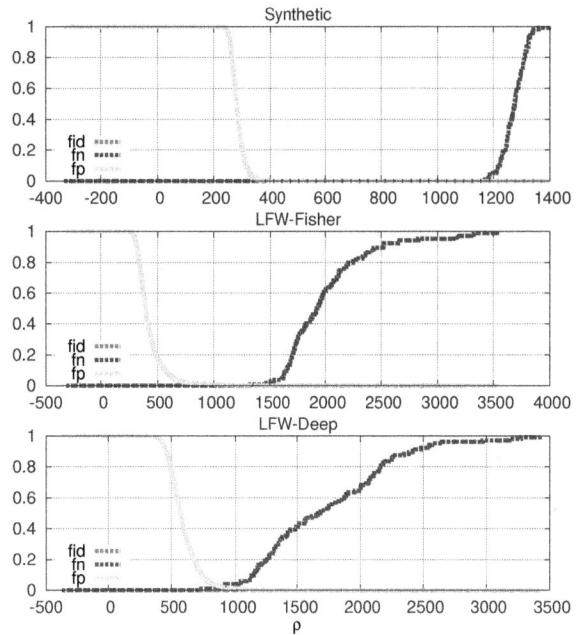

Figure 2: 1st system performance, synthetic and LFW (Fisher / deep learning features) datasets.

6. CONCLUSION

We presented a privacy and security enhancing scheme for approximate search. It is built upon a first version which enables users privacy but not security of the owner's data especially when user and server collude. Contrary to the "Signal Processing in the Encrypted Domain" trend which uses even more advanced cryptographic primitives like full homomorphic encryption, we propose an alternative only based on signal processing. It is much faster and more scalable (even more that the first version). Yet, the attack is not absolutely blocked, but relatively in the sense that vector reconstruction is so bad that it can't be exploited.

7. REFERENCES

[1] A. Anonymous. Cvpr '16 submission. In *CVPR*, 2016.
[2] J. Bringer, H. Chabanne, M. Favre, A. Patey, T. Schneider, and M. Zohner. GSHADE: faster privacy-preserving distance computation and biometric identification. In *Proceedings of the 2Nd ACM Workshop on Information Hiding and Multimedia Security*, IH&MMSec '14, pages 187–198, New York, NY, USA, 2014. ACM.
[3] J. Bringer, H. Chabanne, and A. Patey. SHADE: secure hamming distance computation from oblivious transfer. In *Financial Cryptography and Data Security*, volume 7862 of *Lecture Notes in Computer Science*, pages 164–176, 2013.
[4] M. S. Charikar. Similarity estimation techniques from rounding algorithms. In *STOC*, pages 380–388, May 2002.
[5] A. Hadid, N. Evans, S. Marcel, and J. Fierrez. Biometrics systems under spoofing attack. *IEEE Signal Processing Magazine*, 32(5):20–, September 2015.
[6] G. B. Huang, M. Ramesh, T. Berg, and E. Learned-Miller. Labeled faces in the wild: A database for studying face recognition in unconstrained environments. Technical Report 07-49, University of Massachusetts, Amherst, October 2007.
[7] A. Iscen, T. Furon, V. Gripon, M. G. Rabbat, and H. Jégou. Memory vectors for similarity search in high-dimensional spaces. *CoRR*, abs/1412.3328, 2014.
[8] T. Schneider and M. Zohner. GMW vs. Yao? efficient secure two-party computation with low depth circuits. In S. B. Heidelberg, editor, *Financial Cryptography and Data Security*, 2013.
[9] K. Simonyan, O. M. Parkhi, A. Vedaldi, and A. Zisserman. Fisher Vector Faces in the Wild. In *British Machine Vision Conference*, 2013.
[10] K. Simonyan, A. Vedaldi, and A. Zisserman. Learning local feature descriptors using convex optimisation. Technical report, Department of Engineering Science, University of Oxford, 2013.
[11] Y. Weiss, A. Torralba, and R. Fergus. Spectral hashing. In *NIPS*, December 2009.

APPENDIX

A. RECONSTRUCTION FROM LSH

Assuming that $\mathbf{A}$ has an isotropic distribution (either independent Gaussian entries or a random frame), w.l.o.g. we set $\mathbf{x} = (1, 0, \ldots, 0)$ and

$$\|\hat{\mathbf{x}}\|^2 = \kappa^2 \left(\sum_{k=1}^{D} \|\mathbf{a}_k\|^2 + \sum_{k \neq \ell} |a_k(1)||a_\ell(1)| \right) \quad (16)$$

If $a_k(1) \sim \mathcal{N}(0,1)$, $\mathbb{E}_{\mathbf{A}}[\|\hat{\mathbf{x}}\|^2] = \kappa^2 D(d + 2(D-1)/\pi)$ and

$$\kappa \approx \sqrt{\frac{1}{Dd(1+g)}} \text{ with } g := \frac{2D}{\pi d}. \quad (17)$$

For this $\mathbf{x}$, $a(\mathbf{x}) = \kappa \sum_{k=1}^{D} |a_k(1)|$ s.t.

$$\mathbb{E}_{\mathbf{A}}[a(\mathbf{x})] = \kappa D \sqrt{2/\pi} = \sqrt{\frac{g}{1+g}}. \quad (18)$$

If $\mathbf{a}_k$ is uniformly distributed on the unit sphere (random

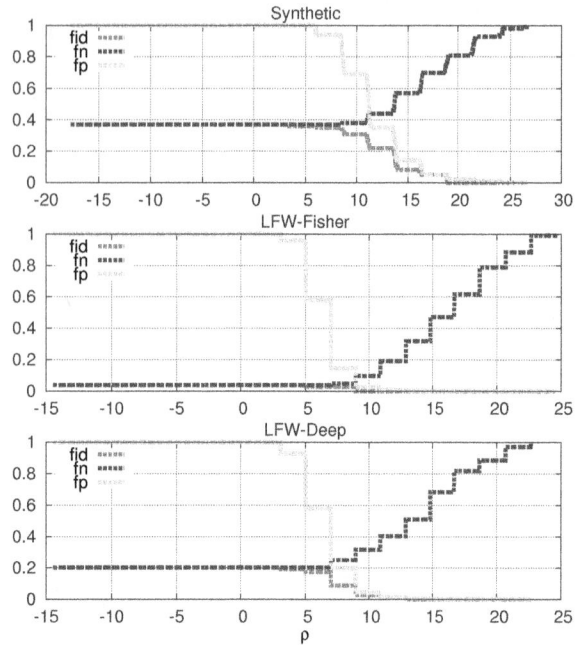

Figure 3: **Proposed system performance, synthetic and LFW (Fisher / deep learning features) datasets.**

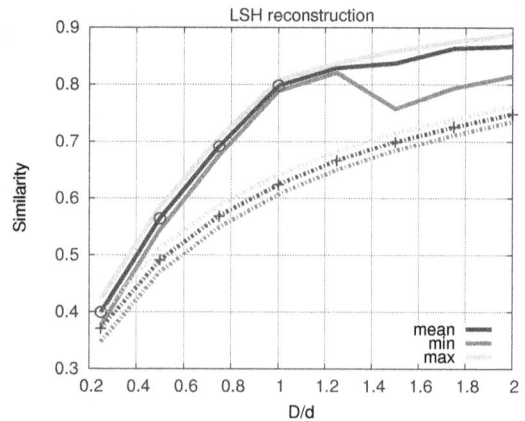

Figure 4: **Reconstruction from LSH:** $a(\mathbf{x})$ **as a function of** D/d. **Empirical mean, min. and max. over 10,000 reconstructions. Unif. Tight Frame (plain), Gaussian i.i.d. (dashed), Eq. (8) (+) and Eq. (9) (o).**

uniform frame or basis), the marginal distribution of $a_k(1)$:

$$f(s) = \frac{(1-s^2)^{\frac{d-3}{2}}}{B(1/2,(d-1)/2)}, \forall s, -1 \le s \le 1, \quad (19)$$

s.t. $\mathbb{E}[|a_k(1)|] = \sqrt{2/d\pi}(d-2)!!/(d-1)!! \approx \sqrt{2/d\pi}$. For $D \le d$, the random uniform tight frame is indeed a basis: $\mathbb{E}_{\mathbf{A}}[\|\hat{\mathbf{x}}\|^2] = D$ and $\mathbb{E}_{\mathbf{A}}[a(\mathbf{x})] = \sqrt{g}$.

B. RECONSTRUCTION FROM MEMORY

We assume the following model for matrix $\mathbf{B}$. For row r, $1 \le r \le M$, we randomly select n indices in $[N]$ and set these coefficients to 1. With a high probability $\mathsf{rank}(\mathbf{B}) = M$ and $\mathsf{Tr}(\mathbf{BB}^\top) = nM$. As for the vector, $\mathbb{E}_{\mathbf{X}}[\mathbf{X}^\top \mathbf{X}] = \mathbf{I}_N$.

Pseudo-inverse reconstruction: $\hat{\mathbf{X}} = \eta \mathbf{M}(\mathbf{B}^\top)^\dagger$, with $(\mathbf{B}^\top)^\dagger = (\mathbf{BB}^\top)^{-1}\mathbf{B}$. Constant η is s.t. the expectation (over $\mathbf{X}$ and $\mathbf{B}$) of the average squared norm of $\hat{\mathbf{x}}_i$ equals 1.

$$\frac{\mathbb{E}[\sum_{i=1}^N \|\hat{\mathbf{x}}_i\|^2]}{N} = \mathbb{E}[\mathsf{Tr}(\hat{\mathbf{X}}^\top \hat{\mathbf{X}})]/N \quad (20)$$
$$= \eta^2 \mathbb{E}[\mathsf{Tr}(\mathbf{X}^\top \mathbf{X}\mathbf{B}^\top(\mathbf{BB}^\top)^{-1}\mathbf{B})]/N$$
$$= \eta^2 \mathbb{E}[\mathsf{Tr}((\mathbf{BB}^\top)^{-1}\mathbf{BB}^\top)]/N = \eta^2 M/N$$

The expectation of the average correlation is given by:

$$\frac{\mathbb{E}[\sum_{i=1}^j \mathbf{x}_i^\top \hat{\mathbf{x}}_i]}{N} = \mathbb{E}[\mathsf{Tr}(\mathbf{X}^\top \hat{\mathbf{X}})]/N \quad (21)$$
$$= \eta \mathbb{E}[\mathsf{Tr}(\mathbf{B}^\top(\mathbf{BB}^\top)^{-1}\mathbf{B})]/N = \sqrt{M/N}.$$

Sum reconstruction: $\hat{X} = \eta \mathbf{MB}$. Constant η is s.t. the expectation of the average squared norm of $\|\hat{\mathbf{x}}_i\|^2$ equals 1.

$$\frac{\mathbb{E}[\sum_{i=1}^N \|\hat{\mathbf{x}}_i\|^2]}{N} = \eta^2 \mathbb{E}[\mathsf{Tr}(\hat{\mathbf{X}}^\top \hat{\mathbf{X}})]/N$$
$$= \eta^2 \mathbb{E}[\mathsf{Tr}((\mathbf{BB}^\top)^2)]/N. \quad (22)$$

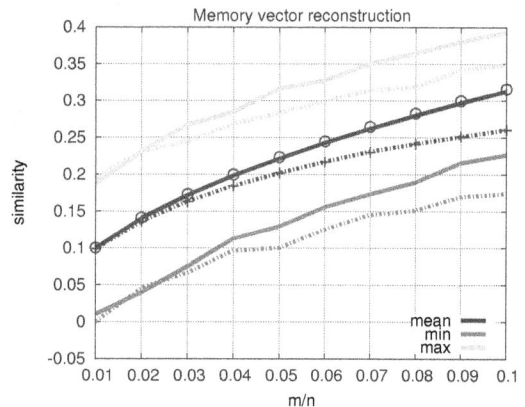

Figure 5: **Reconstruction from memory vectors:** $a(\mathbf{x})$ **as a function of** m/n. **Empirical mean, min., and max. over 40,000 reconstructions. Pseudo-inverse (plain), average (dashed), Eq. (14) (o) and (15) (+).**

We define $\tilde{\mathbf{B}} := \frac{(\mathbf{B}-\nu \mathbf{1}_{M:N})}{\nu(1-\nu)}$ with $\nu := n/N$. Its columns are centered random vectors whose covariance matrix is the identity. The eigenvalues of their empirical covariance matrix $\tilde{\mathbf{B}}\tilde{\mathbf{B}}^\top/N$ follows the Marchenko-Pastur distribution. For large N and $\gamma = M/N$, we then have:

$$\mathbb{E}[\mathsf{Tr}((\tilde{\mathbf{B}}\tilde{\mathbf{B}}^\top)^2)]/MN^2 = 1 + \gamma. \quad (23)$$

Expressing $(\mathbf{BB}^\top)^2$ as a function of $\tilde{\mathbf{B}}\tilde{\mathbf{B}}^\top$ leads to:

$$\mathbb{E}[\mathsf{Tr}((\mathbf{BB}^\top)^2)] = \nu^2 MN^2(1-\nu^2+\gamma(1-\nu)^2+\nu^2 M), \quad (24)$$

which gives the value of η thanks to (22). On the other hand, the expectation of the average correlation is given by:

$$\frac{\mathbb{E}[\sum_{i=1}^j \mathbf{x}_i^\top \hat{\mathbf{x}}_i]}{N} = \eta \mathbb{E}[\mathsf{Tr}(\mathbf{X}^\top \mathbf{X}\mathbf{B}^\top(\mathbf{B}^\top \mathbf{B})^{-1}\mathbf{B})]/N$$
$$= \eta \mathbb{E}[\mathsf{Tr}(\mathbf{B}^\top(\mathbf{B}^\top \mathbf{B})^{-1}\mathbf{B}]/N = \eta M/N$$
$$= \sqrt{\frac{\gamma}{1-\nu^2+\gamma(1-\nu)^2+\nu^2 M}} \quad (25)$$

Differentially Private Matrix Factorization using Sketching Techniques

Raghavendran Balu
Inria Rennes
Bretagne-Atlantique, France
raghavendran.balu@inria.fr

Teddy Furon
Inria Rennes
Bretagne-Atlantique, France
teddy.furon@inria.fr

ABSTRACT

Collaborative filtering is a popular technique for recommendation system due to its domain independence and reliance on user behavior data alone. But the possibility of identification of users based on these personal data raise privacy concerns. Differential privacy aims to minimize these identification risks by adding controlled noise with known characteristics. The addition of noise impacts the utility of the system and does not add any other value to the system other than enhanced privacy. We propose using sketching techniques to implicitly provide the differential privacy guarantees by taking advantage of the inherent randomness of the data structure. In particular, we use count sketch as a storage model for matrix factorization, one of the successful collaborative filtering techniques. Our model is also compact and scales well with data, making it well suitable for large scale applications.

Keywords

Count sketch, differential privacy, matrix factorization, recommender system, collaborative filtering

1. INTRODUCTION

Recommendation systems has become an indispensable component in Internet based services. It helps user in discovering new products and services by getting personalized suggestions based on their past consumption. Collaborative filtering is one of the popular techniques used in recommendation system. It uses user-item ratings relationship to provide recommendations. Relying on user behavior alone makes it domain independent and requires minimal external knowledge. Many techniques have been suggested in the past including the popular *latent factor* model. It maps both users and items to a low dimensional representation, retaining pairwise similarity. Matrix factorization learns these representation vectors from some observed ratings. They are then used to predict (by inner product) the missing entries and thereby to fill the incomplete user-item matrix [17].

Publication rights licensed to ACM. ACM acknowledges that this contribution was authored or co-authored by an employee, contractor or affiliate of a national government. As such, the Government retains a nonexclusive, royalty-free right to publish or reproduce this article, or to allow others to do so, for Government purposes only.

IH&MMSec 2016, June 20 - 23, 2016, Vigo, Spain.

ACM ISBN 978-1-4503-4290-2/16/06. . . $15.00.

DOI: DOI:http://dx.doi.org/10.1145/2909827.2930793

There is a cost to it and that is user privacy. The consumed items have to be collected at a centralized database, to perform both analysis and prediction, which compromises user privacy. The usual anonymization alone is not sufficient as demonstrated in [3]. This calls for robust privacy preserving techniques. One such is differential privacy [9], which has gained wide out reach and acceptance from the academic community. Differential privacy provides strong theoretical guarantees and is robust to auxiliary information. There are various mechanisms that can provide differential privacy like Laplacian mechanism [9], exponential mechanism [20] and Bayesian inference [28].

Our main idea is to promote a sketching technique for matrix factorization to design a highly scalable recommendation system. The prize to be paid is a loss of accuracy in the recommendations because the sketch inherently induces noise. Yet, this noise has two benefits (which are indeed related): it provides a better regularization and protects privacy. We motivate this last argument by stressing the similarities with recent Bayesian learning enhancing differential privacy. We propose an experimental protocol to measure privacy from predicted ratings to validate our claims.

Section 2 introduces the scientific background relevant to this paper. Section 3 describes our differentially private factorization algorithm and Section 4 outlines its main benefits. In Section 5 shows the experimental assessment of the claimed advantages.

2. BACKGROUND

2.1 Matrix factorization

In a typical collaborative filtering system, the given data is a sparse matrix $\mathbf{R}$ with non zero entries $r_{u,i}$ representing the rating provided by the user $u \in \mathbb{U}$ for a given item $i \in \mathbb{I}$. Each row vector in $\mathbf{R}$ corresponds to an user u and column vector to an item i. In latent factor models, each user u is associated with a vector $\mathbf{p}_u \in \mathbb{R}^d$. Similarly, item i is associated to a vector $\mathbf{q}_i \in \mathbb{R}^d$. The goal is to approximate the rating $r_{u,i}$ by a simple scalar product $\mathbf{p}_u^\top \mathbf{q}_i$. The latent vectors $\mathbf{p}_u$ and $\mathbf{q}_i$ of all users and items are represented as $d \times |\mathbb{U}|$ matrix $\mathbf{P}$ and $d \times |\mathbb{I}|$ matrix $\mathbf{Q}$. We need to find the latent factors from the observed ratings such that the missing entries of $\mathbf{R}$ can be predicted by approximating matrix $\mathbf{R} \approx \mathbf{P}^\top \mathbf{Q}$. This is done by minimizing the functional:

$$\mathcal{R}_\lambda(\mathbf{P}, \mathbf{Q}) = \sum_{\text{observed } u,i} \mathcal{L}(r_{u,i}, \mathbf{p}_u^\top \mathbf{q}_i) + \frac{\lambda}{2}(\|\mathbf{p}_u\|^2 + \|\mathbf{q}_i\|^2).$$

(1)

$\mathcal{L}(r_{u,i}, \mathbf{p}_u^\top \mathbf{q}_i)$ quantifies the error between an observed rating $r_{u,i}$ and its prediction $\hat{r}_{u,i} = \mathbf{p}_u^\top \mathbf{q}_i$. In the sequel, $\mathcal{L}(r_{u,i}, \mathbf{p}_u^\top \mathbf{q}_i) = (r_{u,i} - \mathbf{p}_u^\top \mathbf{q}_i)^2/2$. The second term is a penalty preventing overfitting the latent factors to the training data (i.e. the observed ratings) for a better generalization over the missing entries of $\mathbf{R}$.

2.2 Finding latent factors

Techniques to efficiently find the latent factors $(\mathbf{P}, \mathbf{Q})$ minimizers of the objective function $\mathcal{R}_\lambda(\mathbf{P}, \mathbf{Q})$ of (1) work either offline or online. Offline techniques such as alternate least squares, gradient descent or online approaches such as the stochastic gradient descent proved to work well. This paper considers online techniques as its goal is to cope with the dynamicity of real-world recommendation systems. It is thus insightful to describe the approach proposed in [17].

At each step, the stochastic gradient descent randomly picks an observed rating $r_{u,i}$ and optimizes the parameters with respect to that rating. This update relies on the gradient of the loss function with respect to parameters, controlled by the learning rate η:

$$\mathbf{p}_u \leftarrow \mathbf{p}_u - \eta \nabla_u \mathcal{R}_\lambda(\mathbf{P}, \mathbf{Q}), \qquad (2)$$

$$\mathbf{q}_i \leftarrow \mathbf{q}_i - \eta \nabla_i \mathcal{R}_\lambda(\mathbf{P}, \mathbf{Q}), \qquad (3)$$

where $\nabla_u \mathcal{R}_\lambda(\mathbf{P}, \mathbf{Q})$ denotes the gradient of the functional w.r.t. latent vector $\mathbf{p}_u$:

$$\nabla_u \mathcal{R}_\lambda(\mathbf{P}, \mathbf{Q}) = \frac{\partial \mathcal{L}(r_{u,i}, \hat{r}_{u,i})}{\partial \hat{r}_{u,i}} \frac{\partial \hat{r}_{u,i}}{\partial \mathbf{p}_u} + \lambda \mathbf{p}_u \qquad (4)$$

$$= (r_{u,i} - \mathbf{p}_u^\top \mathbf{q}_i) \mathbf{q}_i + \lambda \mathbf{p}_u. \qquad (5)$$

In the same way, $\nabla_i \mathcal{R}_\lambda(\mathbf{P}, \mathbf{Q})$ denotes the gradient of the functional w.r.t. latent vector $\mathbf{q}_i$.

As the algorithm is sequential, only the latent factors have to be stored in main memory. The updates can be parallelized as they are local only to the parameters corresponding to a particular rating. Hence the algorithm can scale well to increasing data size.

However, the number of latent factors is linear with the number of users and items. At very large scale, when the number of users and/or items becomes extremely large (millions), then the resulting memory consumption becomes problematic. Furthermore, determining the latent factors is challenging in a dynamic environment, particularly when new users and items are added every now and then. Allocating a d-dimensional vector to every sporadically recurring new user or item quickly becomes non-tractable.

A more compact representation for the factors is therefore needed. We propose the adoption of count sketches that are typically used in other contexts. We therefore review sketching techniques before discussing their ability to fit within a recommendation context.

2.3 Sketching techniques

Sketching is an active area of development, particularly in a streaming setup. A data structure maintaining a particular synopsis of the data irrespective of the history of updates can be called a sketch [6]. Sketching technique have been applied for estimating the items frequency [7], finding similar items [11] and also limited numerical linear algebra operation [30]. The popularity of sketching techniques is attributed to its runtime and space efficiencies. We are in particular interested in the count sketch [4]. It was origi-

nally proposed to find heavy hitters, but can also be used to approximate the frequencies in turnstile model.

Count sketch is a probabilistic data structure originally designed to maintain approximations of quantities constantly updated in a datastream, but with sub-linear space complexity. Define $[N] := \{1, \cdots, N\}$ and $\{q_1^{(t)}, \cdots, q_N^{(t)}\}$ N quantities. We observe a datastream of quantity updates: $< \cdots \delta q_e, \cdots, \delta q_e, \cdots >$ and we would like to monitor the quantities over the time: $q_e^{(t+1)} = q_e^{(t)} + \delta q_e$.

A count sketch is represented by a $k \times w$ matrix $\mathbf{C}$ and two sets of *pairwise independent* hash functions $\{h_j(\cdot), s_j(\cdot)\}_{j=1}^k$. The *address* hash function $h_j(\cdot)$ maps an element of $[N]$ to the set $\{1, ..., w\}$ and the *sign* hash function s_j maps an element of $[N]$ to $\{+1, -1\}$. There are two typical processes: the update and the query actions.

Update: Upon the reception of the update δq_e of the e-th quantity, k entries of matrix $\mathbf{C}$ are updated: $\forall j, 1 \le j \le k$

$$c_{j, h_j(e)} \leftarrow c_{j, h_j(e)} + s_j(e) \cdot \delta q_e. \qquad (6)$$

Query: At time t, given a query index e, mean or median of $\{s_j(e) c_{j, h_j(e)}\}_{j=1}^k$ is returned as an approximation of $q_e^{(t)}$. The median operator is more robust to noise [4] but the mean is easier to compute. In the sequel, we choose the mean operator: $\tilde{q}_e^{(t)} = k^{-1} \sum_{j=1}^k s_j(e) c_{j, h_j(e)}$.

The accuracy of the estimation is related to the size of the count sketch [6]. Note that if we query index e just before and after its update, the difference of the approximates is the true update: $\tilde{q}_e^{(t+1)} - \tilde{q}_e^{(t)} = \delta q_e$. However, updating the e-th quantity might have modified the others due to collision. In the j-th row of the count sketch, one entry has been modified by $\pm \delta q_e$ (see (6)) whereas the $w - 1$ others remained the same. In other words, the entries of $\mathbf{C}$ have been modified by random variables i.i.d. according to the p.m.f. $(1 - w^{-1}) \partial_0 + (2w)^{-1} (\partial_{\delta q_e} + \partial_{-\delta q_e})$, where ∂_a represent the Dirac distribution on $x = a$. The expectation is zero and the variance $(\delta q_e)^2 / w$. This implies that the update of the e-th quantity adds on all the others $\tilde{q}_{e'}$, $e' \ne e$, a centered noise of variance $(\delta q_e)^2 / wk$.

Overall, the estimate based on the mean operator is unbiased with variance σ^2 / wk, where $\sigma^2 = \sum_{e \in [N]} (\delta q_e)^2$. For a given (w, k), the accuracy decreases with N because the variance of the estimate increases with σ^2. In other words, the representational capacity N of count sketch can be controlled by varying (w, k).

2.4 Differential privacy

Differential privacy argues that absolute privacy is impossible and instead settles to relative level. It has garnered wide spread attention among the research community for its theoretical rigorousness and robustness to side information.

2.4.1 In the context of recommendation system

In our application, differential privacy convinces users to submit their ratings by showing that an attacker querying the recommendation system has difficulty in deciding whether a particular rating has been used for learning the latent factors. Even with the side-information that user u rates item i by the true value $r_{u,i}$, the attacker cannot say whether the user submitted or not this information. We are thus interested at ϵ-DP at the rating level with a trusted recommendation system.

Denote by $\mathcal{D}$ the dataset of observed ratings used for learning the latent vectors, and $\mathcal{D}' = \mathcal{D} \cup \{< u', i', r_{u',i'} >\}$ s.t. these two datasets differs by one rating. Denote by $\hat{r}_{u,i}(\mathcal{D})$ the output of a recommendation system trained on dataset $\mathcal{D}$ and queried about user u and item i. An ϵ-DP recommendation system satisfies: $\forall (a,b) \in \mathbf{R}^2, a < b, \forall u \in \mathbb{U}, \forall i \in \mathbb{I}$

$$\Pr[a < \hat{r}_{u,i}(\mathcal{D}) < b] \leq e^{\epsilon} \Pr[a < \hat{r}_{u,i}(\mathcal{D}') < b]. \quad (7)$$

2.4.2 A posteriori sampling

Paper [28] recently proved that Bayesian posterior sampling is differentially private to some extent. We explain it as follows in the context of matrix factorization based recommendation system. We first need a Bayesian framework. We assume the following prior distribution of latent factors:

$$p(\mathbf{P}, \mathbf{Q}) = \Pi_{u=1}^{\mathbb{U}} p(\mathbf{p}_u) \Pi_{i=1}^{\mathbb{I}} p(\mathbf{q}_i), \quad (8)$$

with $p(\mathbf{p}_u)$ and $p(\mathbf{q}_i)$ are Gaussian distribution $\mathcal{N}(\mathbf{0}_d, \lambda^{-1}\mathbf{I}_d)$ with $\mathbf{0}_d$ the all zero $d \times 1$ vector, $\mathbf{I}_d$ the identity matrix of size d and $\lambda > 0$. We assume a conditional pdf of the rating knowing the latent factors (i.e. the likelihood):

$$p(r_{u,i}|\mathbf{P}, \mathbf{Q}) \cong \mathcal{N}(\mathbf{p}_u^{\top}\mathbf{q}_i, \nu^2), \text{ with } \nu = 1. \quad (9)$$

This implies that, once some ratings are observed, the a posteriori distribution of the latent factors is

$$p(\mathbf{P}, \mathbf{Q}|_{\text{observed}} < u, i, r_{u,i} >) \propto e^{-\mathcal{R}_\lambda(\mathbf{P}, \mathbf{Q})}, \quad (10)$$

with $\mathcal{R}_\lambda(\mathbf{P}, \mathbf{Q})$ defined in (1). Therefore, minimizing this functional as proposed in Sec. 2.2 amounts to chose $(\mathbf{P}, \mathbf{Q})$ as their MAP (Maximum A Posteriori) estimates.

Instead of doing this, [28, 18] shows that drawing $(\mathbf{P}, \mathbf{Q})$ according to their a posteriori distribution (10) enables differential privacy: if $|\log p(r_{u,i}|\mathbf{P}, \mathbf{Q})| < B$, then the system is ϵ-DP with $\epsilon = 2B$. If $2B$ is too big, then one may scale down $\log p(r_{u,i}|\mathbf{P}, \mathbf{Q})$, which amounts to pick $\nu > 1$, i.e. a smoother conditional distribution.

The final issue is how to draw according to such a complex a posteriori distribution. Recent papers show that perturbating the stochastic gradient descent by some Gaussian noise is an efficient way to simulate such a sampling [29, 27]. This technique is called Stochastic Gradient Langevin Dynamics (SGLD). In our context, this would mean replacing (2) and (3) by:

$$\mathbf{p}_u \quad \leftarrow \quad \mathbf{p}_u - \eta\nabla_u\mathcal{R}_\lambda(\mathbf{P}, \mathbf{Q}) + \sqrt{\eta}B_P, \quad (11)$$

$$\mathbf{q}_i \quad \leftarrow \quad \mathbf{q}_i - \eta\nabla_i\mathcal{R}_\lambda(\mathbf{P}, \mathbf{Q}) + \sqrt{\eta}B_Q, \quad (12)$$

with B_P and $B_Q \sim \mathcal{N}(0,1)$.

3. COUNT SKETCHING LARGE MATRIX FACTORIZATION

3.1 Sketching vectors

In regular matrix factorization, d-dimensional latent vectors $\{\mathbf{p}_u\}_{u\in\mathbb{U}}$ and $\{\mathbf{q}_i\}_{i\in\mathbb{I}}$ are stored as dense arrays $\mathbf{P}$ and $\mathbf{Q}$, contiguous in memory. This facilitates indexing on the two dimensional array by increments of d. We propose replacing this matrix representation with a single count sketch. Although user and item vectors carry different semantic, their underlying representations are the same. Therefore we store both of them in the same structure, which should provide estimates for $N = d(|\mathbb{U}| + |\mathbb{I}|)$ elements. For the sake of clarity, we introduce two families of address hash

functions: $\{h_j^u(\cdot)\}_{j=1}^k$ for the users, $\{h_j^i(\cdot)\}_{j=1}^k$ for the items. Same for the sign hash functions.

Varying (w, k) explores the trade-off between the storage efficiency and the quality of the estimation. The storage improvement comes at the cost of increasing the retrieval complexity from $O(d)$ to $O(kd)$ for a d-dimensional vector.

3.2 Sketch based factorization

The sketch based online factorization differs from regular online factorization (Sec. 2) in the latent factor queries and gradient updates merging. When a new tuple $< u, i, r_{u,i} >$ arrives, the count sketch is first queried to approximately reconstruct user and item latent vectors. Both user ID u and component index l, $1 \leq l \leq d$, are used as inputs to the k pairs of address and sign hash functions to get a mean estimate of the vector component (the same holds for item):

$$\tilde{p}_{u,l} = \frac{1}{k}\sum_{j=1}^k s_j^u(u,l) \cdot c_{j,h_j^u(u,l)}, \quad \forall l \in \{1, \cdots, d\}, \quad (13)$$

$$\tilde{q}_{i,l} = \frac{1}{k}\sum_{j=1}^k s_j^i(i,l) \cdot c_{j,h_j^i(i,l)}, \quad \forall l \in \{1, \cdots, d\}. \quad (14)$$

The estimated rating $\hat{r}_{u,i} = \tilde{\mathbf{p}}_u^{\top}\tilde{\mathbf{q}}_i$ is compared with the observed $r_{u,i}$ to get the loss $\mathcal{L}(r_{u,i}, \hat{r}_{u,i})$.

If $\mathcal{L}(r_{u,i}, \hat{r}_{u,i}) \leq \epsilon$, the gradient updates for $\tilde{\mathbf{p}}_u$ and $\tilde{\mathbf{q}}_i$ are just computed as in (2) and (3). Then for each component of $\tilde{\mathbf{p}}_u$ (as well as $\tilde{\mathbf{q}}_i$), the k respective cells $\mathbf{C}$ are updated with their sign corrected gradients:

$$c_{j,h_j^u(u,l)} \quad \leftarrow \quad c_{j,h_j^u(u,l)} - \eta s_j^u(u,l)\nabla_{u,l}\mathcal{R}_\lambda(\tilde{\mathbf{P}}, \tilde{\mathbf{Q}}), \quad (15)$$

$$c_{j,h_j^i(i,l)} \quad \leftarrow \quad c_{j,h_j^i(i,l)} - \eta s_j^i(i,l)\nabla_{i,l}\mathcal{R}_\lambda(\tilde{\mathbf{P}}, \tilde{\mathbf{Q}}). \quad (16)$$

$\nabla_{u,l}\mathcal{R}_\lambda(\tilde{\mathbf{P}}, \tilde{\mathbf{Q}})$ denotes the l-th component of the gradient defined in (5), and similarly for the item gradient.

Otherwise (i.e. $\mathcal{L}(r_{u,i}, \hat{r}_{u,i}) > \epsilon$), the cells are not updated at all. This is equivalent to not taking into account this particular observation.

4. BENEFITS OF OUR APPROACH

4.1 Space gain

The use of the count sketch is motivated as a means to trade space versus complexity. The count sketch has a storage space of wk scalars whereas the regular factorization would need $(|\mathbb{U}| + |\mathbb{I}|)d$ scalars to store the latent factors. We define the space gain γ as

$$\gamma := \frac{(|\mathbb{U}| + |\mathbb{I}|)d}{wk} \geq 1. \quad (17)$$

On the other hand, at each update triggered by observation $< u, i, r_{u,i} >$, the count sketch adds $O(2dk)$ more operations to query and update the d components of $\mathbf{p}_u$ and $\mathbf{q}_i$.

4.2 Self regularization

The Tikhonov regularization (i.e. L_2 norm based) is generally associated with matrix factorization, as it can be controlled by λ and customized well to the needs. There are other methods to regularize like corrupting the input data. It is shown by Bishop et al in [2] that training with corrupted data is equivalent to Tikhonov regularization.

In our scheme, we observe that the sketch structure itself regularizes the learnt latent vectors. At reception of rating $r_{u,i}$, the gradient of the regular factorization is computed based on the error $(r_{u,i} - \mathbf{p}_u^\top \mathbf{q}_i)$ whereas our algorithm computes the gradient based on $r_{u,i} - \tilde{\mathbf{p}}_u^\top \tilde{\mathbf{q}}_i$ which can be expressed as $r_{u,i} + n_{u,i} - \mathbf{p}_u^\top \mathbf{q}_i$. This shows the equivalence with working with noisy observed ratings.

This noise is due to the address hash collision among different elements. Thanks to the pairwise independence assumption, the error is independent of the cell location. Also the sign hash function $s_j(\cdot)$ makes sure that the expected error on the components of the latent factor is centered: $\mathbb{E}(\tilde{p}_{u,l} - p_{u,l}) = 0$. This shows that the equivalent noises $n_{u,i}$ on the observations are i.i.d. and centered. We surmise that these indeed provide regularization capabilities. We experimentally prove the claim in section 5.2 by showing that the performance of the our system is less sensitive w.r.t. the regularization parameter λ.

Our algorithm uses regularization with Tikhonov penalization: $\lambda \sum_{(u,i)} \|\tilde{\mathbf{p}}_u\|^2 + \|\tilde{\mathbf{q}}_i\|^2$. This has also an interpretation: the variance of the count sketch estimation error is proportional to σ^2 (Sect. 2.3), which, in our case, is $\sum_{(u,i)} \|\tilde{\mathbf{p}}_u\|^2 + \|\tilde{\mathbf{q}}_i\|^2$. Our method thus aims at minimizing a combination of the error for predicting the ratings and the error for estimating latent vectors from the count sketch.

4.3 Differential privacy

Our algorithm inherently adds noise on the updates thanks to the count sketch. It looks like the SGLD (11) (12), but this is not. We can find the following differences. First, when updated, latent factors related to observed $r_{u,i}$ are not corrupted by noise, whereas all the others are. Second, the noise induced by the count sketch has a variance equalling δ^2/wk where δ is the last update (see Sec. 2.3). Therefore, this variance is proportional to η^2/wk and not η as in the SGLD algorithm. Third, this noise results from $2d$ latent factors updates only therefore it is certainly not Gaussian distributed.

The differential privacy is enforced by clipping the log-likelihood s.t.

$$|\log p(r_{u,i}|\mathbf{P}, \mathbf{Q})| = \begin{cases} (r_{u,i} - \hat{r}_{u,i})^2/2 & \text{if } (r_{u,i} - \hat{r}_{u,i})^2 \le \epsilon \\ \epsilon/2 & \text{otherwise} \end{cases}$$

This enables ϵ-DP as shown in [28, 18], except that this no longer defines a valid conditional probability.

5. EXPERIMENTS

This section evaluates the claimed benefits of our approach. We first experimentally study its regularization capabilities. Then we analyze the privacy-utility trade-off and compare to regular factorization (without privacy).

5.1 Setup

5.1.1 Dataset

We use two publicly available datasets: Movielens1M [23] and EachMovie. Data characteristics are in Table 1. The data is preprocessed and randomly partitioned into the training, validation and test sets with proportion $[0.8, 0.1, 0.1]$. Preprocessing includes bias correction and frequency based thresholding: User, item and global means are substracted from ratings; ratings with user/item frequency < 10 are removed from the test and validation sets.

5.1.2 Evaluation

We use root mean square error to measure the quality of recommendations. The error materializes the deviation of the predicted rating from its true value. This squared error is averaged over the testing set:

$$RMSE(\mathbf{R}') = \sqrt{\frac{1}{\|\mathbf{R}'\|_0} \sum_{r_{u,i} \in \mathbf{R}'} (\tilde{\mathbf{p}}_u^\top \tilde{\mathbf{q}}_i - r_{u,i})^2}, \qquad (18)$$

where $\mathbf{R}'$ is the restriction of $\mathbf{R}$ to the testing set.

We use Kullback-Leibler divergence to gauge privacy. The KL divergence gives the expected amount of information 'leaked' about the fact that user u submitted his rating about item i. This divergence quantifies the difference between the probability distributions of the prediction for observed ratings (the training set) and non observed ratings (the testing set). A low divergence means that the predicted rating $\hat{r}_{u,i}$ is statistically similar whether $r_{u,i}$ was used in training or not. An attacker observing $\hat{r}_{u,i}$ and *even knowing* $r_{u,i}$ can not decide whether this rating was submitted to the recommendation system. To this aim, we experimentally observed that the prediction error $(\hat{r}_{u,i} - r_{u,i}) \sim \mathcal{N}(m, s^2)$. We measure (m_{tr}, s_{tr}^2) over the training set and (m_{te}, s_{te}^2) over the testing set, and compute

$$KLD = \frac{1}{2}\left(\frac{s_{tr}^2}{s_{te}^2} + \frac{(m_{tr} - m_{te})^2}{s_{te}^2} - 1 + \log\frac{s_{te}^2}{s_{tr}^2}\right). \qquad (19)$$

5.1.3 Parameters

We compare the performance for various configurations (w, k) of the sketch and different latent factor dimensions. The sketch depth k is picked from $\{1, 4\}$ and the latent factor dimension d is chosen from $\{8, 16, 32\}$. We measure the space gain γ by the ratio of space that the regular factorization would need for the same dimension d to the space actually utilized by sketch based factorization. We vary γ within $\{1, 2, 4\}$. We determine the sketch width based on the space gain, dimension d and sketch depth k:

$$w = \left\lceil \frac{(|\mathbb{U}| + |\mathbb{I}|)d}{\gamma k} \right\rceil. \qquad (20)$$

We choose optimal parameters for learning rate η and regularization constant λ by a two stage line search in log-scale, based on validation set prediction score. We iterate for $T = 100$ epochs over the training set, before predicting on the testing set, measuring $RMSE(\mathbf{R}')$ and KLD. Learning rate is scaled down using the formula $\eta_t = \frac{\eta}{1 + b \cdot t/T}$.

Dataset	$|\mathbb{U}|$	$|\mathbb{I}|$	$|\mathbf{R}|$	rating
MovieLens 1M	6,040	3,952	1,000,209	1:5 (5)
EachMovie	61,265	1,623	2,811,718	1:6 (6)

Table 1: Dataset characteristics

5.2 Regularizing effect of count sketch

We now study the effect of regularization parameter λ on RMSE. We use EachMovie dataset under the setup ($d = 32$, $\gamma = 1$). We vary λ from 10 to 0 in log scale. Figure 1 compares the performance. We benchmark our method ($k = 4$) against regular online matrix factorization and feature hashing based factorization [15] as it is a special case of our approach ($k = 1$). The three techniques share the following

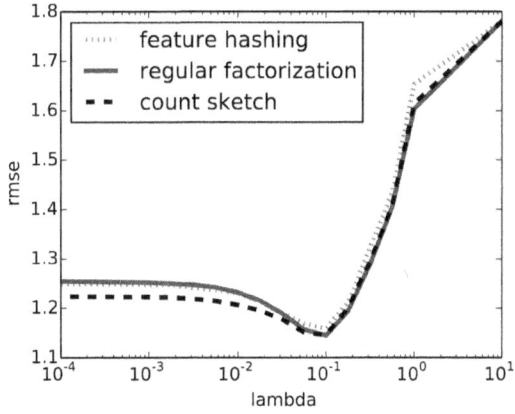

Figure 1: RMSE w.r.t. λ, EachMovie

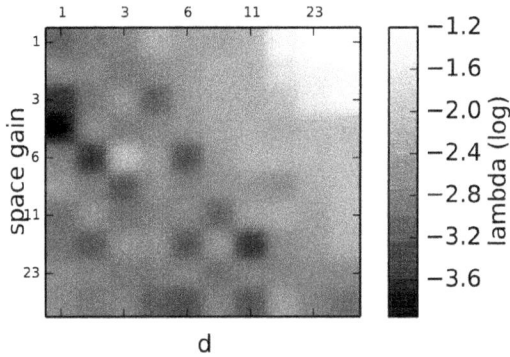

Figure 2: Best λ w.r.t. (d, γ), MovieLens 1M

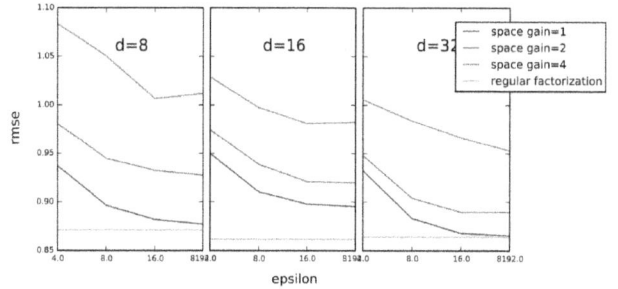

Figure 3: RMSE w.r.t. ϵ, Movielens

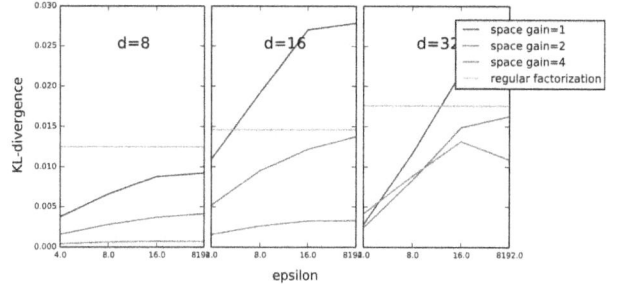

Figure 4: KL divergence w.r.t. ϵ, Movielens

observations: The optimal λ is around 0.1 and the RMSE increases with λ beyond this value. When we decrease λ below the optimal value, the RMSE degrades and this is attributed to overfitting. The degradation of count sketch factorization is not as worse as the other two techniques. Even when the regularization is turned off ($\lambda = 0$), our scheme performs better than the other two, for the same d. This shows that the 'noisy' sketch structure by itself provides some regularization capabilities.

The heatmap of Figure 2 represents the optimal lambda values for various (d, γ) pairs on MovieLens 1M dataset. The optimal value is often lower than 10^{-2}, except in the top right corner, where γ is small while d is big. This setting indeed ensures superfluous parameter space, which does require stronger regularization to avoid overfitting. The λ value diminishes with d: a smaller model requires less regularization. An interesting observation is that λ lowers with increase in γ and it is true even for a fixed d. This increases address hash collisions and hence the variance of the count sketch estimation (Sect. 4.2) which helps model generalization like when learning on noisy data.

5.3 Privacy utility tradeoff

In this section, we compare the variation of RMSE with respect to parameter ϵ as shown in figure 3. We vary ϵ in the range of $\{2, 4, 8, \infty\}$ and benchmark it against regular factorization. As expected, lowering the privacy by increasing ϵ improves the utility, *i.e.* decreases RMSE. The improvement is significant in the lower range of ϵ and drops gradually as

we increase ϵ further. When the epsilon is above 16 the RMSE is close to regular factorization.

5.4 KL divergence as a privacy measure

We take the role of an attacker willing to know whether a particular rating was used in the training. We use KL divergence to measure the amount of information 'leaked' by getting access to its prediction. Figure 4 shows that KL divergence increases along with the targeted level of privacy ϵ. The KL divergence of regular factorization without any differential privacy mechanism is higher for most of the cases. This supports our approach. It is also clear from the figure that compact models (higher γ or lower d) produce recommendations leaking less information compared to bigger one. The KL divergence which is a measurement on average is indeed much smaller than the target ϵ which is a guaranty on the worst case.

We also had a focused on 'top users', *i.e.* users who submitted a lot. As foreseen, the RMSE measured on this population is lower: they get better predictions because their models are more precise as they are learned on more data. The difference in performance is indeed small. Yet, very surprisingly, the KL divergence measured on this population is smaller by one order of magnitude. This population enjoys better recommendations together with better privacy.

6. RELATED WORK

Many mechanisms enable differential privacy including Laplacian mechanism [8], exponential mechanism [20], Bayesian inference [28], smooth sensitivity, and sample-aggregate frameworks [25]. The works differ on the stage in which the randomization mechanism is added to the system. Initial approaches were advocating at the input and output levels. In [5], they incorporate it at the optimization level and demonstrated its superiority. Differential privacy is also applied to online learning in [12]. A detailed survey of different techniques is available at [26] and [13]. [10] applied differential privacy to data mining. [16] studied the theoretical properties of learning under differential privacy setup.

Recommender systems is one of the compelling applications of differential privacy owing to its data involving sensitive user information. Many approaches have been proposed in the past for different collaborative filtering approaches like neighbor based approaches and matrix factorization. [22] used sketch to provide privacy. Their notion of privacy is very similar to differential privacy except that the log-likelihood ratio is bounded by a linear parameter instead of exponential. [21] proposed a recommender system by aggregating co-occurrence count in a privacy preserving way. Paper [19] applied differential privacy to the global statistics collected from the rating matrix.

As for matrix factorization, paper [1] compares different ways to ensure differential privacy, among them, the Laplace mechanism on the inputs or on the updates of the stochastic gradient descent. [14] proposed a differentially private low rank approximation using exponential mechanism. [24] devised a matrix factorization using cryptographic garbled circuits, but this does not enable differential privacy.

7. CONCLUSION

This work shows that sketching techniques can be used to preserve privacy by taking advantage of their inherent randomness. This is in contrast to conventional techniques which uses special mechanism to achieve the same. We also get additional benefits like scalability and adaptivity to dynamic data, making it preferable for realistic large-scale applications. We experimentally validate our approach using standard datasets. Future works include measurement of information leaked by the latent factors themselves. This is relevant when the latent vectors are learned by the server and sent to the users allowing local recommendation.

8. REFERENCES

[1] A. Berlioz, A. Friedman, M. A. Kaafar, R. Boreli, and S. Berkovsky. Applying differential privacy to matrix factorization. In *Proc. RecSys '15*. ACM, 2015.

[2] C. M. Bishop. Training with noise is equivalent to tikhonov regularization. *Neural computation*, 7(1):108–116, 1995.

[3] J. Calandrino, A. Kilzer, A. Narayanan, E. Felten, and V. Shmatikov. "You Might Also Like:" privacy risks of collaborative filtering. In *Proc. Symp. on Security and Privacy*, May 2011.

[4] M. Charikar, K. Chen, and M. Farach-Colton. Finding frequent items in data streams. In *Proc. ICALP*, 2002.

[5] K. Chaudhuri, C. Monteleoni, and A. D. Sarwate. Differentially private empirical risk minimization. *J. Mach. Learn. Res.*, 12:1069–1109, July 2011.

[6] G. Cormode. Sketch techniques for approximate query processing. *FnTD. NOW publishers*, 2011.

[7] G. Cormode and S. Muthukrishnan. An improved data stream summary: the count-min sketch and its applications. *Journal of Algorithms*, 55(1):58–75, 2005.

[8] C. Dwork. Differential privacy. In *Proc. ICALP*, July 2006.

[9] C. Dwork. *Encyclopedia of Cryptography and Security*, chapter Differential Privacy. Springer US, 2011.

[10] A. Friedman and A. Schuster. Data mining with differential privacy. In *Proc. SIGKDD'10*, 2010.

[11] P. Indyk and R. Motwani. Approximate nearest neighbors: towards removing the curse of dimensionality. In *Proc. STOC*, 1998.

[12] P. Jain, P. Kothari, and A. Thakurta. Differentially private online learning. *arXiv:1109.0105v2*, Sept. 2011.

[13] Z. Ji, Z. C. Lipton, and C. Elkan. Differential privacy and machine learning: a survey and review. *CoRR*, abs/1412.7584, Dec. 2014.

[14] M. Kapralov and K. Talwar. On differentially private low rank approximation. In *Proc. SODA*, 2013.

[15] A. Karatzoglou, M. Weimer, and A. J. Smola. Collaborative filtering on a budget. In *Proc. AISTATS*, 2010.

[16] S. P. Kasiviswanathan, H. K. Lee, K. Nissim, S. Raskhodnikova, and A. Smith. What can we learn privately? *SIAM Journal on Computing*, 40(3):793–826, 2011.

[17] Y. Koren, R. Bell, and C. Volinsky. Matrix factorization techniques for recommender systems. *Computer*, 42(8):30–37, Aug. 2009.

[18] Z. Liu, Y.-X. Wang, and A. Smola. Fast differentially private matrix factorization. In *Proc. RecSys '15*, 2015.

[19] F. McSherry and I. Mironov. Differentially private recommender systems: Building privacy into the net. In *Proc. SIGKDD'09*. ACM, 2009.

[20] F. McSherry and K. Talwar. Mechanism design via differential privacy. In *Proc. FOCS*, Oct 2007.

[21] L. Melis, G. Danezis, and E. D. Cristofaro. Efficient private statistics with succinct sketches. *CoRR*, abs/1508.06110, 2015.

[22] N. Mishra and M. Sandler. Privacy via pseudorandom sketches. In *Proc. SIGMOD-SIGACT-SIGART*. ACM, 2006.

[23] Movielens. http://grouplens.org/datasets/movielens/.

[24] V. Nikolaenko, S. Ioannidis, U. Weinsberg, M. Joye, N. Taft, and D. Boneh. Privacy-preserving matrix factorization. In *Proc. SIGSAC*. ACM, 2013.

[25] K. Nissim, S. Raskhodnikova, and A. Smith. Smooth sensitivity and sampling in private data analysis. In *Proc. STOC*. ACM, 2007.

[26] A. Sarwate and K. Chaudhuri. Signal processing and machine learning with differential privacy: Algorithms and challenges for continuous data. *Signal Processing Magazine, IEEE*, 30(5):86–94, Sept 2013.

[27] S. J. Vollmer, K. C. Zygalakis, and Y. Teh. (non-) asymptotic properties of stochastic gradient langevin dynamics. *arXiv:1501.00438*, 2015.

[28] Y.-X. Wang, S. E. Fienberg, and A. Smola. Privacy for free: Posterior sampling and stochastic gradient monte carlo. *arXiv:1502.07645*, 2015.

[29] M. Welling and Y. W. Teh. Bayesian learning via stochastic gradient langevin dynamics. In *Proc. ICML*, 2011.

[30] D. P. Woodruff. Sketching as a tool for numerical linear algebra. *arXiv:1411.4357*, 2014.

Secure and Verifiable Outsourcing of Nonnegative Matrix Factorization (NMF)

Jia Duan
University of Macau
Macau, China
xuelandj@gmail.com

Jiantao Zhou
University of Macau
Macau, China
jtzhou@umac.mo

Yuanman Li
University of Macau
Macau, China
yuanmanx.li@gmail.com

ABSTRACT

Cloud computing platforms are becoming increasingly prevalent and readily available nowadays, providing us alternative and economic services for resource-constrained clients to perform large-scale computation. In this work, we address the problem of secure outsourcing of large-scale nonnegative matrix factorization (NMF) to a cloud in a way that the client can verify the correctness of results with small overhead. The input matrix protection is achieved by a lightweight, permutation-based encryption mechanism. By exploiting the iterative nature of NMF computation, we propose a single-round verification strategy, which can be proved to be effective. Both theoretical and experimental results are given to demonstrate the superior performance of our scheme.

CCS Concepts

•Security and privacy → Privacy-preserving protocols; •Computer systems organization → Cloud computing;

Keywords

Cloud computing; NMF; secure outsourcing; verification

1. INTRODUCTION

Multimedia, as the most important and valuable source for insights and information, is increasingly becoming the "biggest big data". Analyzing multimedia big data and turning them into significant insights for clients, however, have been proven to be quite challenging. Nonnegative matrix factorization (NMF), as a fundamental data analysis technique, has been widely utilized in many applications for analyzing multimedia data, e.g., source separation [5] and feature extraction [9, 18]. In the new era of big data, the usage of NMF in practical settings has undergone a few new challenges. The matrices to be analyzed are becoming aston-ishingly big, and the involved computation is of very large-scale, making it prohibitive to resource-constrained clients.

Fortunately, cloud computing paradigm provides a viable solution for small to medium size business to perform large-scale data computation [19]. In the outsourcing computation framework, the clients with insufficient computing facilities can outsource the heavy computation workload to the cloud server, and enjoy the unlimited computing resources. Security and privacy considerations, however, stand on the way of fully utilizing the benefits of such cloud services and architectures [3, 16]. First of all, the computation tasks often contain some sensitive information that should not be exposed to the cloud server, which usually is untrusted. Traditional encryption algorithms can only partially solve the protection problem, as it is difficult to perform meaningful (complex) computations over the encrypted domain. Furthermore, clients should have a mechanism to verify the correctness of the results, because the cloud may return invalid results for financial incentives. Certainly, the overhead of performing the verification should be minimized. Along this line, Wang *et al.* [17] proposed to outsource the large-scale systems of linear equations to a public cloud. Lei *et al.* [11] addressed the problem of designing a protocol for securely outsourcing the matrix determinant computation to a cloud. Recently, Blanton *et al.* suggested to outsource the large-scale biometric computations to a cloud [2].

In this work, we address the problem of secure outsourcing of large-scale nonnegative matrix factorization (NMF) to a cloud in a way that the client can verify the correctness of results with small overhead. The input matrix protection is achieved by a lightweight encryption mechanism, involving multiplication of permutation matrices. The task of verifying the correctness of NMF is challenging, as factorization results are not unique and the multiplication of the obtained factors is only an approximation of the original matrix. To overcome this difficulty, we design a single-round verification strategy by exploiting the iterative nature of NMF computation, and prove that the simple verification strategy is very effective in verifying the results. Both theoretical and experimental results are given to demonstrate the superior performance of our scheme.

The rest of the paper is organized as follows. Section 2 gives an overview of NMF. In Section 3, we describe the system model and the design goals. Section 4 presents the proposed protocol for secure and verifiable outsourcing of NMF. Section 5 is devoted to system performance analysis and Section 6 offers the experimental results. Finally, we conclude in Section 7.

IH&MMSec 2016, June 20–23, 2016, Vigo, Spain.

© 2016 ACM. ISBN 978-1-4503-4290-2/16/06. . . $15.00

DOI: http://dx.doi.org/10.1145/2909827.2930794

2. NONNEGATIVE MATRIX FACTORIZA-TION

Given a nonnegative matrix $\mathbf{V} \in \mathbb{R}^{m \times n}$, NMF finds non-negative factors $\mathbf{W}$ and $\mathbf{H}$ such that:

$$\mathbf{V} \approx \mathbf{WH} \quad (1)$$

where $\mathbf{W} \in \mathbb{R}^{m \times r}$, $\mathbf{H} \in \mathbb{R}^{r \times n}$, and r is a dimension parameter. The factorization is usually sought through the following minimization problem

$$\min_{\mathbf{W},\mathbf{H}} D(\mathbf{V}|\mathbf{WH}) \quad \text{subject to } \mathbf{W} \geq 0, \mathbf{H} \geq 0 \quad (2)$$

where $\mathbf{A} \geq 0$ means that all elements of $\mathbf{A}$ are nonnegative. The function $D(\mathbf{V}|\mathbf{WH})$ is often designed to be a separable measure of fit between $\mathbf{V}$ and $\mathbf{WH}$, namely

$$D(\mathbf{V}|\mathbf{WH}) = \sum_{i=1}^{m} \sum_{j=1}^{n} d(\mathbf{V}_{i,j}|(\mathbf{WH})_{i,j}) \quad (3)$$

where $\mathbf{A}_{i,j}$ denotes the (i,j)th element of $\mathbf{A}$, and $d(x|y)$ is a scalar cost function of x given y. In [15], Tan and Fevotte considered $d(x|y)$ to be the β-divergence, a family of cost functions parameterized by a single scalar $\beta \in \mathbb{R}$. The widely used cost functions, e.g., squared Euclidean distance, generalized Kullback-Leibler (KL) divergence, and Itakura-Saito (IS) divergence are special cases of β-divergence when β is assigned with different values. To be consistent with the setting of [7, 8], we adopt the squared Euclidean distance as the cost function, which corresponds to $\beta = 2$. To solve the non-convex optimization problem in (2), Lee and Seung proposed a multiplicative update algorithm, which was later improved by Lin [14] with guaranteed stationarity. Specifically, $\mathbf{W}$ and $\mathbf{H}$ are initialized with nonnegative random values, and the following update rules are applied for each entry of $\mathbf{W}$ and $\mathbf{H}$

$$\mathbf{W}_{i,a}^{(k+1)} \leftarrow \mathbf{W}_{i,a}^{(k)} - \frac{\hat{\mathbf{W}}_{i,a}^{(k)}}{(\hat{\mathbf{W}}^{(k)}\mathbf{H}^{(k)}(\mathbf{H}^{(k)})^T)_{i,a} + \delta}$$
$$\times \nabla_{\mathbf{W}} D(\mathbf{W}^{(k)}|\mathbf{H}^{(k)})_{i,a} \qquad \forall i, a \quad (4)$$

$$\mathbf{H}_{b,j}^{(k+1)} \leftarrow \mathbf{H}_{b,j}^{(k)} - \frac{(\hat{\mathbf{H}})_{b,j}^{(k)}}{((\mathbf{W}^{(k+1)})^T \mathbf{W}^{(k+1)}\hat{\mathbf{H}}^{(k)})_{b,j} + \delta}$$
$$\times \nabla_{\mathbf{H}} D(\mathbf{W}^{(k+1)}|\mathbf{H}^{(k)})_{b,j} \qquad \forall b, j$$
$$(5)$$

where $\mathbf{W}_{i,a}^{(k)}$ and $\mathbf{H}_{b,j}^{(k)}$ denote the (i,a)th and the (b,j)th elements of $\mathbf{W}^{(k)}$ and $\mathbf{H}^{(k)}$, the resulting factors in the kth iteration. Here,

$$\hat{\mathbf{W}}_{i,a}^{(k)} = \begin{cases} \mathbf{W}_{i,a}^{(k)}, & \text{if } \nabla_{\mathbf{W}} D(\mathbf{W}^{(k)}|\mathbf{H}^{(k)})_{i,a} \geq 0 \\ \max(\mathbf{W}_{i,a}^{(k)}, \sigma), & \text{if } \nabla_{\mathbf{W}} D(\mathbf{W}^{(k)}|\mathbf{H}^{(k)})_{i,a} < 0 \end{cases}$$
$$(6)$$

$$\hat{\mathbf{H}}_{b,j}^{(k)} = \begin{cases} \mathbf{H}_{b,j}^{(k)}, & \text{if } \nabla_{\mathbf{H}} D(\mathbf{W}^{(k+1)}|\mathbf{H}^{(k)})_{b,j} \geq 0 \\ \max(\mathbf{H}_{b,j}^{(k)}, \sigma), & \text{if } \nabla_{\mathbf{H}} D(\mathbf{W}^{(k+1)}|\mathbf{H}^{(k)})_{b,j} < 0 \end{cases}$$
$$(7)$$

in which σ and δ are small positive numbers. This iteration process continues until local minimum is achieved.

The computational complexity of the above iterative algorithm for solving the NMF is approximately #iterations $\times$ $O(mnr)$, where #iterations represents the number of iterations applied [14]. In many existing NMF algorithms, the #iterations is set to be very large, e.g., 10^4, so as to ensure convergence. Therefore, when handling large matrices, the incurred complexity is prohibitively high, motivating us to outsource the heavy computation to a cloud.

Ideally, $\mathbf{W}^{(\infty)}$ and $\mathbf{H}^{(\infty)}$, namely, the results after iterating infinite number of times, are the desirable solutions for the factors. In practice, due to the numerical accuracy, the $\mathbf{W}^{(k)}$ and $\mathbf{H}^{(k)}$ satisfying

$$\frac{1}{mn}\left\{ D(\mathbf{V}|\mathbf{W}^{(k)}\mathbf{H}^{(k)}) - D(\mathbf{V}|\mathbf{W}^{(\infty)}\mathbf{H}^{(\infty)}) \right\} \leq \tau \quad (8)$$

are still considered as acceptable, where $\tau > 0$ is a predefined performance parameter. Note that we here do not impose bounds on $D(\mathbf{V}|\mathbf{W}^{(k)}\mathbf{H}^{(k)})$, as its value is highly dependent on the matrix $\mathbf{V}$ to be factorized. In many practical cases, even for the ideal solution, the value of the cost function $D(\mathbf{V}|\mathbf{W}^{(\infty)}\mathbf{H}^{(\infty)})$ is generally big.

3. SYSTEM MODEL, DESIGN GOALS, AND THREAT MODEL

3.1 System Model

We consider the secure and verifiable outsourcing of NMF framework depicted in Fig. 1. The client Alice with insufficient computing capabilities intends to outsource NMF of a matrix $\mathbf{V}$ to a cloud server Charlie, who has massive computational power. To protect data privacy, Alice encrypts $\mathbf{V}$ into $\mathbf{V}'$ using a symmetric cipher with secret key K. Alice then passes $\mathbf{V}'$, the dimension parameter r, and a stopping criterion parameter ϵ to Charlie for computing the two nonnegative factors $\mathbf{W}'$ and $\mathbf{H}'$ such that

$$\mathbf{V}' \approx \mathbf{W}'\mathbf{H}' \quad (9)$$

We assume that Alice can specify the NMF algorithm to be used by Charlie for completing the outsourcing task. As far as we know, all the existing NMF algorithms, such as multiplicative update (MU) [8], alternating least squares (ALS) [1] [4] and projected gradient [13], are based on iterations. Alice asks Charlie to stop the iterative algorithm when the following inequality holds

$$D(\mathbf{V}'|\mathbf{W}'^{(k)}\mathbf{H}'^{(k)}) - D(\mathbf{V}'|\mathbf{W}'^{(k+1)}\mathbf{H}'^{(k+1)}) \leq \epsilon \quad (10)$$

where $\mathbf{W}'^{(k)}$ and $\mathbf{H}'^{(k)}$ are the results in the kth iteration. ϵ is a small parameter, whose selection will be discussed shortly. Alice also requests Charlie to return $\mathbf{W}' \triangleq \mathbf{W}'^{(k)}$ and $\mathbf{H}' \triangleq \mathbf{H}'^{(k)}$.

Charlie, upon receiving all the information from Alice, performs an iterative algorithm, e.g., the one given in (4) and (5), to solve the NMF problem and returns the results $\mathbf{W}'$ and $\mathbf{H}'$ as mentioned above.

With $\mathbf{W}'$ and $\mathbf{H}'$, Alice first verifies the correctness of the results using a method to be presented in Section 4. If these results are acceptable, $\mathbf{W}'$ and $\mathbf{H}'$ are further processed to derive $\mathbf{W}$ and $\mathbf{H}$, respectively, which are the two nonnegative factors for the original matrix $\mathbf{V}$. Otherwise, the results are rejected.

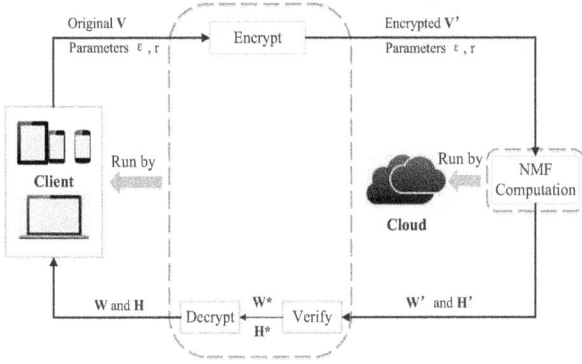

Figure 1: System model for outsourcing NMF.

3.2 Design Goals

To ensure secure and verifiable outsourcing of NMF, we identify the following four design goals for the above system model

- **Security**: The adversary cannot derive any sensitive information of the original matrix $\mathbf{V}$ during the process of carrying out the NMF.

- **Correctness**: The final results $\mathbf{W}$ and $\mathbf{H}$ should be identical or close to those when the NMF computation is conducted locally.

- **Verifiability**: The correct result from a faithful cloud must be verified successfully by the client. No false result from a cheating cloud can pass the verification with non-negligible probability.

- **Efficiency**: The local computation done by the client should be substantially less than the original NMF computation on its own. In addition, the amount of computation on performing NMF over the encrypted $\mathbf{V}'$ should be as close as possible to that over the original $\mathbf{V}$.

3.3 Threat Model

The security threats faced by the outsourcing system model mainly come from the behavior of the cloud server Charlie. Generally, there are three types of threat models:

- **Curious Adversary**: Charlie correctly follows the protocol specification; however, he is curious about the information that may be leaked from $\mathbf{V}'$ and any history data that he can access.

- **Malicious Adversary**: Charlie may not follow the protocol specification and tries to forge a result for saving resources. In this scenario, the cloud may completely ignore the strategy specification or algorithms run by the cloud.

- **Lazy Adversary**: Charlie may return an intermediate result for saving resources.

4. THE PROPOSED NMF OUTSOURCING PROTOCOL

In this section, we focus on the three most important parts of the NMF outsourcing system in Fig. 1: matrix encryption, results verification, and decryption.

4.1 Matrix Encryption

As mentioned earlier, Alice needs to encrypt the input matrix $\mathbf{V}$, prior to passing it to Charlie. When designing the encryption scheme, we also need to consider the efficiency, as too complicated encryption and decryption will deviate from the purpose of outsourcing. In this work, we propose to encrypt $\mathbf{V}$ by

$$\mathbf{V}' = \mathbf{PVQ} \quad (11)$$

where $\mathbf{P} \in \mathbb{R}^{m \times m}$ and $\mathbf{Q} \in \mathbb{R}^{n \times n}$ are two permutation matrices defined as follows. Let $\mathbf{p} = \{\mathbf{p}_i\}$ and $\mathbf{q} = \{\mathbf{q}_i\}$ be two random permuted 1-D sequences for $\{1, 2, \cdots, m\}$ and $\{1, 2, \cdots, n\}$, respectively, which can be efficiently generated using the well-known Knuth Shuffle Algorithm [6]. Then, we have

$$\left\{ \begin{array}{l} \mathbf{P}_{i,j} = \delta(\mathbf{p}_i, j) \\ \mathbf{Q}_{i,j} = \delta(\mathbf{q}_i, j) \end{array} \right. \quad (12)$$

where $\delta(x, y)$ is the Kronecker delta function defined by

$$\delta(x, y) = \left\{ \begin{array}{ll} 1 & x = y \\ 0 & x \neq y \end{array} \right. \quad (13)$$

The generation of the random vectors $\mathbf{p}$ and $\mathbf{q}$ (and hence the permutation matrices $\mathbf{P}$ and $\mathbf{Q}$) is governed by the key stream from a stream cipher with secret key K. In other words, even for the same input matrix $\mathbf{V}$ encrypted in different sessions, the permutation matrices $\mathbf{P}$ and $\mathbf{Q}$ could be different. Such permutation-based encryption can be readily realized in both software and hardware implementations. In addition, a desirable property of $\mathbf{P}$ and $\mathbf{Q}$ is that their inverses can be readily computed by $\mathbf{P}^{-1} = \mathbf{P}^T$ and $\mathbf{Q}^{-1} = \mathbf{Q}^T$

4.2 Results Verification

Upon receiving $\mathbf{W}'$ and $\mathbf{H}'$ from the cloud, Alice first checks the validity of the results. Compared with the verification tasks in the existing matrix-related outsourcing frameworks [10, 2, 11], the challenges in our protocol stem from the fact that the factorization is only an *approximation* of the original matrix, rather than strict equality. Such approximation nature inherent in NMF computation makes the sampling-based verification approaches, e.g., [2], invalid. Another straightforward verification strategy is to compute $\mathbf{W}'\mathbf{H}'$ and calculate the cost function value $D(\mathbf{V}'|\mathbf{W}'\mathbf{H}')$. However, as the minimum factorization distortion $D(\mathbf{V}'|\mathbf{W}^{(\infty)}\mathbf{H}^{(\infty)})$ highly depends on the matrix $\mathbf{V}'$ and the dimension parameter r, it is difficult to judge the performance of factorization from a single value of $D(\mathbf{V}'|\mathbf{W}'\mathbf{H}')$. In other words, it is rather challenging to set a threshold for $D(\mathbf{V}'|\mathbf{W}'\mathbf{H}')$ to determine its correctness.

In this work, we propose a simple yet effective way to verify the results with small computational overhead by exploiting the iterative nature of NMF computation. The idea behind our verification strategy is that when the cost function reduction, i.e., $D(\mathbf{V}'|\mathbf{W}'^{(k)}\mathbf{H}'^{(k)}) - D(\mathbf{V}'|\mathbf{W}'^{(k+1)}\mathbf{H}'^{(k+1)})$

is sufficiently small (less than a threshold ϵ), then convergence has already been achieved. Specifically, by taking $\mathbf{W}'$ and $\mathbf{H}'$ as initial values, Alice further runs the NMF iterative algorithm for only *one* iteration to generate $\mathbf{W}^*$ and $\mathbf{H}^*$. Alice verifies the results by checking the following inequality

$$D(\mathbf{V}'|\mathbf{W}'\mathbf{H}') - D(\mathbf{V}'|\mathbf{W}^*\mathbf{H}^*) \leq \epsilon \qquad (14)$$

where ϵ is the stopping criterion sent from Alice to Charlie. If this condition is satisfied, Alice accepts the results; otherwise, reject them. We now show that when ϵ is appropriately chosen to be sufficiently small, then when (14) holds, we can make sure that the results are acceptable, under the criterion defined in (8). To this end, we first define $D'^{(k)} \triangleq D(\mathbf{V}'|\mathbf{W}'^{(k)}\mathbf{H}'^{(k)})$, and

$$N \triangleq \left\{ k \,\middle|\, \frac{1}{mn}\left(D'^{(k)} - D'^{(\infty)}\right) \leq \tau \right\} \qquad (15)$$

where τ is the performance parameter given in (8). We further define

$$\bar{\epsilon} \triangleq \min_{k \in \{1,2,\cdots N-1\}} \left\{ D'^{(k)} - D'^{(k+1)} \right\} \qquad (16)$$

Then ϵ is selected in a way such that

$$0 \leq \epsilon < \bar{\epsilon} \qquad (17)$$

Under this setting, we have the following Theorem.

Theorem 1: If $D'^{(k)} - D'^{(k+1)} \leq \epsilon$, then $\frac{1}{mn}\left(D'^{(k+1)} - D'^{(\infty)}\right) \leq \tau$.

Sketch Proof: As $D'^{(k)} - D'^{(k+1)} \leq \epsilon$ and $\epsilon < \bar{\epsilon}$, we have $D'^{(k)} - D'^{(k+1)} < \bar{\epsilon}$. Noticing the definition of $\bar{\epsilon}$ in (16), we conclude that $k > N - 1$. Otherwise, $D'^{(k)} - D'^{(k+1)} \geq \bar{\epsilon}$. Therefore

$$\begin{aligned}
&\frac{1}{mn}\left(D'^{(k+1)} - D'^{(\infty)}\right) \\
={}& \frac{1}{mn}\left(D'^{(k+1)} - D'^{(N)} + D'^{(N)} - D'^{(\infty)}\right) \\
<{}& \frac{1}{mn}\left(D'^{(N)} - D'^{(\infty)}\right) \leq \tau \qquad (18)
\end{aligned}$$

where the last two inequalities hold from the fact that the sequence $D'^{(k)}$ is decreasing with respect to the iteration index k [14], and the definition of N. This completes the proof.

This Theorem implies that, on the client side, Alice only needs to check the inequality $D'^{(k)} - D'^{(k+1)} \leq \epsilon$, which ensures that the returned results are acceptable. In practice, we find that $\epsilon = 3 \times 10^{-8}$ is sufficient for most of the applications.

4.3 Matrix Decryption

If the results $\mathbf{W}'$ and $\mathbf{H}'$ successfully pass the verification stage, we then adopt $\mathbf{W}^*$ and $\mathbf{H}^*$ (rather than $\mathbf{W}'$ and $\mathbf{H}'$) as the encrypted factors. To derive the factors for the original matrix $\mathbf{V}$, we apply the following decryption

$$\begin{cases} \mathbf{W} = \mathbf{P}^T\mathbf{W}^* \\ \mathbf{H} = \mathbf{H}^*\mathbf{Q}^T \end{cases} \qquad (19)$$

5. SECURITY, CORRECTNESS, VERIFIABILITY AND COMPLEXITY ANALYSIS

5.1 Security Analysis

In the proposed protocol, the simple matrix encryption is conducted by left and right multiplications of two permutation matrices $\mathbf{P}$ and $\mathbf{Q}$, which are generated by using the key stream of a stream cipher. In other words, even for the same input matrix $\mathbf{V}$ encrypted in different sessions, the employed $\mathbf{P}$ and $\mathbf{Q}$ could be different. This implies that the only applicable attack type is Ciphertext-only Attack (COA). Let us first analyze the key space. Noticing the sizes of $\mathbf{P}$ and $\mathbf{Q}$ are $m \times m$ and $n \times n$, the total number of ways of performing the permutation is $m!n!$. Since we are handling large-scale matrices in the outsourcing framework, such key space is sufficiently large to ensure high level of security against brute-force attack. In addition, from the work of [12], we can know that the other COA attacks still cannot be successful for breaking the permutation-based encryption.

5.2 Correctness Analysis

To show the correctness of the outsourced NMF protocol, it suffices to prove the following Theorem

Theorem 2: Letting $\mathbf{W}$ and $\mathbf{H}$ be the two factors for $\mathbf{V}$ obtained using the method presented in Section 4, we have

$$\frac{1}{mn}\left\{ D(\mathbf{V}|\mathbf{W}\mathbf{H}) - D(\mathbf{V}|\mathbf{W}^{(\infty)}\mathbf{H}^{(\infty)}) \right\} \leq \tau \qquad (20)$$

Proof: As permutation only changes the locations of entries but not their values, we have

$$D(\mathbf{V}'|\mathbf{W}'\mathbf{H}') = \sum_{i=1}^{m}\sum_{j=1}^{n} d(\mathbf{V}'_{i,j}|(\mathbf{W}'\mathbf{H}')_{i,j}) = D(\mathbf{V}|\mathbf{W}\mathbf{H}) \qquad (21)$$

Similarly,

$$D(\mathbf{V}'|\mathbf{W}'^{(\infty)}\mathbf{H}'^{(\infty)}) = D(\mathbf{V}|\mathbf{W}^{(\infty)}\mathbf{H}^{(\infty)}) \qquad (22)$$

From Theorem 1, we know that

$$\frac{1}{mn}\left\{ D(\mathbf{V}'|\mathbf{W}'\mathbf{H}') - D(\mathbf{V}'|\mathbf{W}'^{(\infty)}\mathbf{H}'^{(\infty)}) \right\} \leq \tau \qquad (23)$$

which makes the inequality (20) hold immediately. This thus completes the proof.

5.3 Verifiability Analysis

The curious adversary is curious about the sensitive information leaked during the process of NMF. He cannot be successful because the input matrix $\mathbf{V}$ is encrypted and shown to be secure in the above security analysis.

For the malicious/lazy adversary, if the returned results can make the inequality (14) hold, then the results are already acceptable, according to Theorem 1. On the contrary, if the returned results cannot satisfy (14), then Alice simply rejects them. This implies that the results that can pass the verification stage must be quality guaranteed.

5.4 Complexity Analysis

On the client side, the complexity mainly comes from the tasks of performing the encryption/decryption and doing the

Table 1: Comparison of Execution Time on Synthetic Data (time in seconds)

m	r	n	T_{original}	T_{client}	T_{cloud}	$T_{\text{original}}/T_{\text{client}}$	$T_{\text{original}}/T_{\text{cloud}}$
1000	50	1000	15.98	0.88	16.01	18.16	0.9981
3000	50	2400	70.34	2.76	71.79	25.49	0.9798
6000	50	4800	281.38	9.84	289.26	28.60	0.9728
10000	50	8000	1310.54	40.25	1349.03	32.56	0.9715

Table 2: Comparison of Execution Time on Face Image Databases (time in seconds)

Database	m	r	n	T_{original}	T_{client}	T_{cloud}	$T_{\text{original}}/T_{\text{client}}$	$T_{\text{original}}/T_{\text{cloud}}$
CBCL	361	25	2429	25.87	1.26	25.85	20.53	1.0008
Olivetti	4096	25	400	34.23	1.33	34.86	25.74	0.9819
ORL	10304	25	400	81.35	2.30	83.01	35.37	0.9800

verification. It can be easily seen that the complexity of multiplying the two permutation matrices is of order $O(t^2)$, where $t = \max(m,n)$. Similarly in the decryption phase, the complexity is also of order $O(t^2)$. In terms of the verification stage where we need to perform one iteration, the complexity is of order $O(mnr)$ [14].

On the cloud side, the computational complexity is incurred mainly by the iterative algorithm for solving the N-MF problem. The complexity is of #iterations $\times O(mnr)$.

It can be seen that the complexity on the client side in the proposed NMF outsourcing framework is much lower than that involved in solving the original NMF problem. The experimental results to be given in the next session will validate the superiority.

6. EXPERIMENTAL RESULTS

In addition to the theoretical analysis of the computational complexity, we also present the experimental results regarding the system performance. To this end, we implement our protocol using MATLAB 2014b, and all the following tests are conducted on a MAC laptop with Intel Core i5 CPU and 8GB RAM.

We first evaluate the performance on synthetic data. We construct random matrices $\mathbf{V}$'s of various sizes ranging from 1000×1000 to 10000×8000. The update rule for computing the NMF is given in (4) and (5) with parameters $\delta = \sigma = 10^{-8}$. The results on computational complexity are tabulated in Table 1. Here, T_{original} denotes the execution time for the client to solve the original NMF locally, in which there is no encryption involved; T_{cloud} represents the execution time for cloud to complete NMF computation over the encrypted $\mathbf{V}'$. T_{client} is the total execution time for the client to perform, including matrix encryption, verification, and decryption. In addition, $T_{\text{original}}/T_{\text{client}}$ can be considered as client speedup, which measures the performance gain of the client. Similarly, $T_{\text{original}}/T_{\text{cloud}}$ measures the efficiency of outsourcing protocol, which should be close to 1, according to the last design goal. As can be seen from Table 1, the client speedup is up to 32.56, which is significant. We can also observe that the client speedup becomes more remarkable when the matrix size increases. This implies the proposed protocol is especially valuable for handling large matrices, which are very common in the big data era. Furthermore, from the rightmost column of Table 1, we can notice that all the values of $T_{\text{original}}/T_{\text{cloud}}$ are quite close to 1, meaning that the efficiency on the cloud side is well maintained.

In addition to synthetic data, we also conduct experiments

Figure 2: Face images and their reconstructed versions upon NMF.

using real-word data. We now consider the factorization of face images, which was also investigated in [7]. Three face image databases are evaluated: 1) Center for Biological and Computational Learning(CBCL) face database[1], which consists of 2429 face images of size 19×19; 2) Olivetti face databases[2], which includes 400 face images of size 64×64, and 3) ORL face image database[3], consisting of 400 face images of size 112×92. All the images in each database are vectorized as a column of $\mathbf{V}$ to be factorized. The dimension r is set to be 25. The experimental results over these three databases are given in Table 2. As can be seen, the speedup on the client side is up to 35.37, and the efficiency on the cloud side is well preserved. Furthermore, some selected face images and their reconstructed versions are illustrated in Fig. 2. The first row shows the original face images, and their reconstructed versions are shown in the second row.

7. CONCLUSIONS

In this paper, we have proposed a secure and verifiable protocol for outsourcing NMF computation to a cloud. Theoretical analysis and experimental results have shown that the proposed protocol satisfies the goals of correctness, security, verifiability and high efficiency.

8. ACKNOWLEDGMENTS

This work was supported in part by the Macau Science and Technology Development Fund under grants FDCT/009

---

[1] http://cbcl.mit.edu/software-datasets/FaceData2.html
[2] http://www.cs.nyu.edu/ roweis/data.html
[3] http://www.cl.cam.ac.uk/research/dtg/attarchive/facedatabase.html

/2013/A1, FDCT/046/2014/A1, in part by the Research Committee at University of Macau under grants MRG007/ZJT/2015/FST, MRG021/ZJT/2013/FST, MYRG2014-00031-FST, MYRG2015-00056-FST,and in part by the National Science Foundation of China under grant 61402547.

9. REFERENCES

[1] M. W. Berry, M. Browne, A. N. Langville, V. P. Pauca, and R. J. Plemmons. Algorithms and applications for approximate nonnegative matrix factorization. *Computational Statistics & Data Analysis*, 52(1):155–173, 2007.

[2] M. Blanton, Y. Zhang, and K. B. Frikken. Secure and verifiable outsourcing of large-scale biometric computations. *ACM Trans. on Information and System Security*, 16(3):11, 2013.

[3] G. Brunette, R. Mogull, et al. Security guidance for critical areas of focus in cloud computing v2. 1. *Cloud Security Alliance*, pages 1–76, 2009.

[4] A. Cichocki and P. Anh-Huy. Fast local algorithms for large scale nonnegative matrix and tensor factorizations. *IEICE Trans. on Fundamentals of Electronics, Communications and Computer Sciences*, 92(3):708–721, 2009.

[5] D. El Badawy, N. Q. Duong, and A. Ozerov. On-the-fly audio source separation. In *2014 IEEE International Workshop on Machine Learning for Signal Processing (MLSP)*, pages 1–6. IEEE, 2014.

[6] D. E. Knuth. *The art of computer programming: sorting and searching*, volume 3. Pearson Education, 1998.

[7] D. D. Lee and H. S. Seung. Learning the parts of objects by non-negative matrix factorization. *Nature*, 401(6755):788–791, 1999.

[8] D. D. Lee and H. S. Seung. Algorithms for non-negative matrix factorization. In *Advances in Neural Information Processing Systems*, pages 556–562, 2001.

[9] H. Lee, A. Cichocki, and S. Choi. Kernel nonnegative matrix factorization for spectral eeg feature extraction. *Neurocomputing*, 72(13):3182–3190, 2009.

[10] X. Lei, X. Liao, T. Huang, and H. Li. Cloud computing service: the case of large matrix determinant computation. *IEEE Trans. on Services Computing*, 8(5):688–700, 2014.

[11] X. Lei, X. Liao, T. Huang, H. Li, and C. Hu. Outsourcing large matrix inversion computation to a public cloud. *IEEE Trans. on Cloud Computing*, 1(1):1–1, 2013.

[12] S. Li, C. Li, G. Chen, N. G. Bourbakis, and K.-T. Lo. A general quantitative cryptanalysis of permutation-only multimedia ciphers against plaintext attacks. *Signal Processing: Image Communication*, 23(3):212–223, 2008.

[13] C.-b. Lin. Projected gradient methods for nonnegative matrix factorization. *Neural Computation*, 19(10):2756–2779, 2007.

[14] C.-J. Lin. On the convergence of multiplicative update algorithms for nonnegative matrix factorization. *IEEE Trans. on Neural Networks*, 18(6):1589–1596, 2007.

[15] V. Y. Tan and C. Févotte. Automatic relevance determination in nonnegative matrix factorization with the/spl beta/-divergence. *IEEE Trans. Pattern Anal. Mach. Intell.*, 35(7):1592–1605, 2013.

[16] B. Wang, B. Li, and H. Li. Oruta: Privacy-preserving public auditing for shared data in the cloud. *IEEE Trans. on Cloud Comput.*, 2(1):43–56, 2014.

[17] C. Wang, K. Ren, J. Wang, and K. M. R. Urs. Harnessing the cloud for securely solving large-scale systems of linear equations. In *2011 31st International Conference on Distributed Computing Systems (ICDCS)*, pages 549–558. IEEE, 2011.

[18] Z. Yuan and E. Oja. Projective nonnegative matrix factorization for image compression and feature extraction. In *Image Analysis*, pages 333–342. Springer, 2005.

[19] L.-J. Zhang. Editorial: Big services era: Global trends of cloud computing and big data. *IEEE Trans. on Serv. Comput.*, 5(4):467–468, 2012.

Practical and Scalable Sharing of Encrypted Data in Cloud Storage with Key Aggregation

Hung Dang, Yun Long Chong, Francois Brun, Ee-Chien Chang
School of Computing, National University of Singapore
{hungdang,cyunlong,francoisb,changec}@comp.nus.edu.sg

Abstract

We study a sensor network setting in which samples are encrypted individually using different keys and maintained on a cloud storage. For large systems, e.g. those that generate several millions of samples per day, fine-grained sharing of encrypted samples is challenging. Existing solutions, such as Attribute-Based Encryption (ABE) and Key Aggregation Cryptosystem (KAC), can be utilized to address the challenge, but only to a certain extent. They are often computationally expensive and thus unlikely to operate at scale. We propose an algorithmic enhancement and two heuristics to improve KAC's key reconstruction cost, while preserving its provable security. The improvement is particularly significant for range and down-sampling queries – accelerating the reconstruction cost from quadratic to linear running time. Experimental study shows that for queries of size 2^{15} samples, the proposed fast reconstruction techniques speed-up the original KAC by at least 90 times on range and down-sampling queries, and by eight times on general (arbitrary) queries. It also shows that at the expense of splitting the query into 16 sub-queries and correspondingly issuing that number of different aggregated keys, reconstruction time can be reduced by 19 times. As such, the proposed techniques make KAC more applicable in practical scenarios such as sensor networks or the Internet of Things.

1. INTRODUCTION

Incorporating cloud resources into wide-area sensor network [16] has been of growing interest. In such solutions, the sensors continuously sense and stream samples to the cloud, wherein various users can retrieve and process the data. Nevertheless, storing sensitive data in public cloud storage faces a high risk of information leakage as demonstrated by many well-known incidents [26]. A common wisdom is to protect the sensitive data from potentially curious servers using strong cryptographic means. This, in turn, poses various technical challenges in fine-grained sharing of the encrypted data with multiple users. Although generic techniques such as Attributed-Based-Encryption (ABE) and Key Aggregation Cryptosystem (KAC) can facilitate fine-grained access control over encrypted data, adopting these techniques in large-scale systems remains challenging.

To illustrate the challenge, let us consider the following scenario. A *data owner* has a collection of sensors deployed along a city road network. The sensors continuously capture and encrypt the samples individually using different encryption keys before streaming the encrypted content to the storage servers. The sample size and sampling rates are application specific (e.g hundreds of Kbytes per frame and 24 frames per second for video or only a few bytes per each sample and only one per second for temperature reading). In addition, each sample consists of multiple components; for example, scalable coding includes different resolution layers. The data owner wants to share selected samples with other users. The sharing policy may be quite complicated, e.g. sharing low resolution images captured by 100 cameras along a particular road segment, during every weekday from 6 am to 10 am at a reduced rate of one frame per second. The users can be third party cloud-service providers engaged by the data owner to perform certain processing, or personnels authorised to access certain sensors, etc. To handle multiple users while ensuring the principle of least privilege, a fine-grained sharing mechanism is necessary. Furthermore, due to privacy concerns, it is desired that the samples remain encrypted at rest in the storage servers, with the encrypted keys kept secret from all the untrusted parties.

In a straightforward download-and-share method, the data owner simply retrieves the encrypted samples, decrypts and sends them to the users in real-time. Clearly, such solution does not scale for it consumes significant computation and networking resources. Another method is to send all decryption keys corresponding to those samples to the users. The user can then use those keys to decrypt encrypted samples downloaded from the storage servers. However, for each sample is individually encrypted using different keys, the number of keys in consideration can be very large, equivalent to the number of samples to be shared. In our example of sharing images extracted from 100 cameras for four hours at the sampling rate of one frame per second, the number of keys required per day is more than 1.4×10^6. Known techniques that "aggregate" all the keys into a single key of small size [10, 14, 9, 29, 3] can address this issue to a certain extent. Unfortunately, these techniques are unlikely to operate at scale, and thus inapplicable in practical systems. In particular, key-policy Attributed-Based Encryption (KP-ABE)[14, 9] would lead to large overhead on the ciphertext

IH&MMSec 2016, June 20-23, 2016, Vigo, Spain

© 2016 ACM. ISBN 978-1-4503-4290-2/16/06. . . $15.00

DOI: http://dx.doi.org/10.1145/2909827.2930795

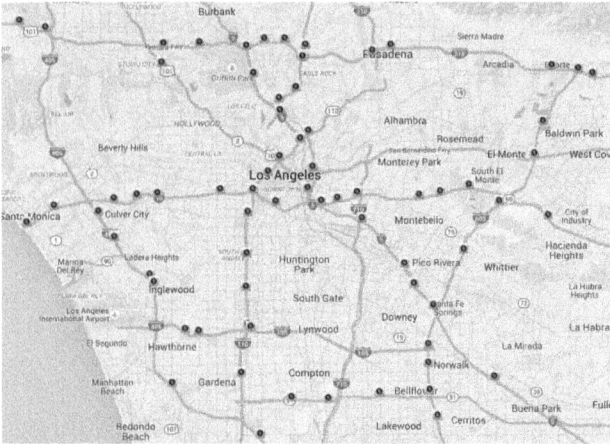

Figure 1: CCTV network in the City of Pasadena under the Real-Time Data Capture and Management Program. Each icon indicate location of a camera.

size, while Key-Aggregation Cryptosystem (KAC) [10] incurs quadratic key reconstruction time with respect to the number of keys to be reconstructed.

In this work, we place our focus on fine-grained sharing of encrypted data. The sharing mechanism in consideration should be not only secure but also practical and scalable. While the techniques that we propose are quite generic and applicable in a large body of application domains, hereafter we shall motivate and describe our approaches in the context of sensor data. Many interesting sensor data are inherently time-series in nature, such as CCTV's images or environmental readings. Moreover, the sensors are typically spatially arranged. For example, the US Department of Transportations deployed a few hundreds cameras along roadway network in the City of Pasadena, California (Figure 1)[1]. Because of this spatial-temporal arrangement, the sensor data are often indexed by the their timestamps and sensors' locations. We treat the spatial, temporal and other meta information as non-sensitive, whereas the confidentiality of the actual sensed samples is to be protected. Such assumption is reasonable, since after all, the storage server is probably able to derive the source and timing of the sensed data from the received network packets.

Our solution adopts Key-Aggregation Cryptosystem (KAC) [10] as the underlying cryptographic scheme and thus inherits its security. KAC enables aggregation of decryption keys for an arbitrary number of samples, say m, into a constant size key. Nevertheless, it incurs high cost in reconstruction, requiring $O(m^2)$ group multiplications to reconstruct all m samples. We make an observation that, for a large class of queries, the reconstruction time can be reduced by eliminating redundant or overlapping computations. In particular, we present a fast reconstruction technique attaining optimal linear running time; i.e. $O(m)$ reconstruction time for combinations of multidimensional range (e.g. asking for samples from cameras along a specific road segment during a specific time period) and down-sampling (e.g. asking for one sample per second instead of the original 24 samples per second) queries (of size m samples). In addition, we propose two heuristics to speed-up reconstruction time for queries of

[1]http://catalog.data.gov/dataset/

arbitrary form (general queries). The idea is to first approximate the optimal computation plan, and then perform the reconstruction following that computation plan. The computation plan describes a specific order in which a sequence of computations should be carried out so that redundant or overlapping computations can be avoided. In the other words, such computation plan would minimize the computation cost incurred in reconstructing the samples, resulting in a better performance as opposed to naively reconstructing each sample independently. Moreover, we also discuss a clustering-based method to trade-off the number of aggregated keys being issued for the reconstruction time. We remark that our proposed techniques address computational aspects of KAC reconstruction algorithm while preserving other characteristics of the scheme, including semantic security and collusion resistance. Therefore, our solutions are provably secure.

Experimental studies show that the proposed methods are efficient, outperforming relevant alternatives by significant factors. For queries of size 2^{15} samples, our fast reconstruction techniques attain at least 90 times speed-up over the original KAC on down-sampling and range queries, and eight times speed-up on queries of arbitrary form. The speed-up is increased to 19 times at the expense of splitting the query into 16 sub-queries, each of which is associated with one separate aggregated key.

The rest of this paper is organized as follows. We briefly review the KAC scheme in Section 2 and follow by stating our problem definition in Section 3. A few alternative constructions and their limitations are discussed in Section 4, before our fast reconstruction techniques are presented in Section 5. We report our experimental evaluation of the proposed techniques in Section 6. After that, we discuss two system designs in Section 7 and related works in Section 8 before finally concluding our work in Section 9.

2. BACKGROUND ON KEY-AGGREGATE ENCRYPTION

Key-Aggregate Encryption (KAC) [10] is a public key cryptosystem that can aggregate any set of decryption keys to derive a constant size decryption key. With a public key, given a plaintext x and an index $i \in [1, n]$, one can encrypt x to get a ciphertext associated to the index i. Hence, if the plaintexts are a sequence $\langle x_1, x_2, \ldots, x_n \rangle$, the ciphertexts $\langle c_1, c_2, \ldots, c_n \rangle$ form the corresponding sequence.

KAC supports key aggregation. For any set of indices $S \subseteq \{1, 2, \ldots, n\}$, the secret key holder can generate a small aggregated key K_S for another user. With the aggregated key K_S, the user can decrypt any c_i as long as $i \in S$. However, she is unable to obtain any information on c_j for any $j \notin S$. KAC's security relies on decisional Bilinear Diffie-Hellman Exponent (BDHE)[5].

This cryptosystem comprises of five basic functions, *Setup*, *KeyGen*, *Encrypt*, *Aggregate*[2] and *Decrypt*.

- $param \leftarrow \textbf{Setup}(1^\lambda, n)$: Given security parameter λ and n, randomly pick a bilinear group $\mathbb{G}$ of prime order p where $2^\lambda \leq p \leq 2^{\lambda+1}$, a generator $g \in \mathbb{G}$ and a random number $\alpha \in_R \mathbb{Z}_p$, then compute $param = \langle g, g_1, g_2, \cdots, g_n, g_{n+2}, \cdots, g_{2n} \rangle$ where $g_i = g^{\alpha^i}$.

[2]The function *Aggregate* is also known as *Extract* in the literature [10].

- $(PK, SK) \leftarrow \textbf{KeyGen}()$: Pick a value $\gamma \in_R \mathbb{Z}_p$, output the public and master-secret key pair: $(PK = v = g^\gamma, SK = \gamma)$.

- $\zeta \leftarrow \textbf{Encrypt}(PK, i, x)$: Given a public key PK, an index $i \in \{1, 2, ..., n\}$ and a message $x \in \mathbb{G}_T$, randomly pick $t \in_R \mathbb{Z}_p$ and output $\zeta = \langle g^t, (vg_i)^t, x \cdot e(g_1, g_n)^t \rangle$.

- $K_S \leftarrow \textbf{Aggregate}(SK, S)$: Given a set S of indices j's, output the aggregated decryption key $K_S = \prod_{j \in S} g_{n+1-j}^\gamma$.

- $\{x, \perp\} \leftarrow \textbf{Decrypt}(K_S, S, i, \zeta = \langle c_1, c_2, c_3 \rangle)$: If $i \notin S$, output $\perp$, else output $x = c_3 \cdot e(K_S \cdot \rho, c_1)/e(\hat{\rho}, c_2)$ where $\rho = \prod_{j \in S, j \neq i} g_{n+1+i-j}$ and $\hat{\rho} = \prod_{j \in S} g_{n+1-j}$.

The aggregated key K_S consists of one single group element and thus its size is $O(\lambda)$ where λ is the security parameter. However, decrypting cost for each ciphertext increases proportionally to the size of the set S. Specifically, given the aggregated key K_S corresponding to a set of ciphertext C whose indices are in S, it takes $O(|S|)$ group operations to decrypt a single ciphertext in C, and thus $O(|S|^2)$ group operations to fully reconstruct the ciphertext set. The high reconstruction cost renders the scheme impractical for our application.

While KAC has inspired various follow-ups [12, 28], to the best of our knowledge, we are the first to propose algorithmic enhancement for its key reconstruction, thus making it more applicable in practical systems.

3. PROBLEM DEFINITION

3.1 Sensor Data

We adopt the convention that $[a, b]$ represents an interval of integers from a to b, inclusively. We call $\mathbb{L}_\Delta = [1, T_1] \times [1, T_2] \times ... \times [1, T_d]$ a d-dimensional lattice with the bounds $T_1, T_2, ..., T_d$. A *hyper-rectangle* $\mathcal{R}$ in $\mathbb{L}_\Delta$ is the subset $R_1 \times ... \times R_d$ of $\mathbb{L}_\Delta$ where each R_i is an interval in the i-th dimension.

A sensor continuously senses and generates a sequence of *samples*. A sample is represented by a tuple (i, x) where i and x are its index and value respectively. The sample value is the data captured by the sensor at a particular instance. Its size can be varied (e.g hundreds of Kbytes for images or only a few bytes for temperature reading). The index i is a multidimensional point, representing the sample's temporal, spatial and other meta information such as resolution level. We assume that some normalisations have been applied such that the indices are mapped to points in $\mathbb{L}_\Delta$. Note that the temporal information is not restricted to be one-dimension. For example, temporal information can be represented as a multidimensional point with day, month, year, etc as its dimensions. The indices are considered non-sensitive. As such, they can be stored in plaintext in the storage server to facilitate efficient searching.

3.2 System Model

Figure 2 illustrates our system model. To protect the confidentiality of sensor data, samples are individually encrypted using different keys before being streamed to the cloud. When a user wants to gain access to a set of encrypted sensor data C, which are indexed by a set S, she

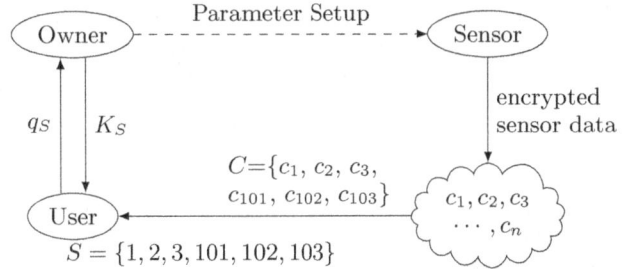

Figure 2: System model supporting fine-grained sharing of encrypted sensor data

sends a query q_S to the owner. Upon approval, the owner issues an aggregated key K_S and an optional computation plan for reconstruction to the user. She can then download the set of requested encrypted samples C from the storage server and follow the computation plan to reconstruct (decrypt) them using K_S[3]. However, it is impossible for her to use such K_S to decrypt any sample which does not belong to C. An additional layer of protection can also be implemented to guarantee that only authorized users can download the relevant encrypted samples. We defer the detailed discussion on system designs to Section 7.

3.2.1 Security requirements

For security analysis, we consider a worst case scenario in which the storage server is completely under the user's control; i.e. she has full access to all encrypted samples maintained on the cloud storage. Nevertheless, she should not be able to learn the content of the encrypted samples without a permission granted by the data owner.

The key aggregation must be *collusion resistance*. A collusion attack is carried out by combining multiple aggregated keys, with the goal of deriving more information than each aggregated key can individually derive. For example, if an user has the aggregated key to decrypt images of road segment A on Jan 1st, and another aggregated key for road segment B on Feb 2nd, then he must not be able to obtain other images, including images captured on A during Feb 2nd. We follow the model by Boneh et al. [6] on collusion resistance.

We assume that sensors are trusted. Nevertheless, in case a sensor is compromised and the secrets it holds are revealed to an adversary, confidentiality of data generated by other sensors must not be compromised.

3.2.2 Efficiency requirements

As the sensors and the users can be operating on low-powered devices, it is crucial to keep computation load low. Furthermore, although cloud storage is relatively low in cost, the communication and storage overheads incurred by the security mechanisms have to be sufficiently reasonable so as to keep the cloud solution economically attractive. In view of the above considerations, we focus on the following three measures of performance:

---

[3]To be accurate, the user first reconstruct the decryption keys (using K_S) which are then used to decrypt the encrypted samples. However, for brevity, we slightly abuse the language and simply say that the user reconstructs the encrypted samples using K_S.

Reconstruction time. Clearly, computation load of reconstructing the keys from the aggregated key K_S has to be low[4]. In some applications (e.g. viewing of video stream), the reconstruction time has to meet the real-time requirement. As mentioned in the introduction, the known KAC scheme requires quadratic reconstruction time and thus is unacceptable for practical use.

Size of aggregated key. To reduce the communication between the owner and users, the size of the aggregated key K_S has to be small.

Overhead of ciphertext size. The overhead of ciphertext size directly increases the storage and communication cost of the storage server. Since the number of ciphertexts is large, the actual multiplicative overhead on the ciphertext size is a practical concern.

3.3 Query Types

We classify queries for sensor data into three types:

Q1 - d-dimensional range query.

This query asks for all samples whose indices form a d-dimensional hyper-rectangle. For example, a request for images from cameras along a road segment during a certain period corresponds to a two-dimensional range query.

In some cases, it is possible to merge multiple range queries into one single range query. We can represent various constraints in one query by re-arranging and "lifting" one-dimensional component to multi-dimensions, e.g. decomposing the single time dimension into four dimensions which are (1) time in a day, (2) day in a week, (3) week number and (4) year.

Q2 - Down-sampling query.

This query asks for *a down-sampled lattice*. In one-dimension, if one sample is extracted for every p samples, we say that the down-sampling rate is $1/p$. In higher dimension, a t-dimensional down-sampled lattice is the subset $\mathcal{L} = \{\sum_{i=1}^{t} a_i v_i | a_i \in \mathbb{Z}\} \cap \mathbb{L}_\Delta$ where each of the v_i is a d-dimensional vector and the basis $\{v_1, v_2, .., v_t\}$ is independent. This basis can also be used to represent the down-sampling query.

A query can also be an intersection of range and down-sampling queries. For example, the query for a few images per each hour captured along a road segment on a certain day is a down-sampling range query.

Q3 - General query.

A general query is not necessary a combination of range and down-sampling queries but rather asks for an arbitrary set of samples. The query may be constructed by listing down all the indices of the required samples. Alternatively, it can also be a combination of an arbitrary set in some dimensions, with range and down-sampling in the other dimensions. For example, a Q3 query may asks for samples from an arbitrary set of sensors during all weekend's morning.

In this paper, we assume a simple distribution model for Q3 query: the set S (containing indices of all requested samples) contains $r\beta$ elements that are randomly selected from the interval $[1, \beta]$ where $r < 1$.

---

[4]We stress that the cost of deriving the computation plan is not part of the reconstruction time.

Remark.

Although we discuss the applications related to sensor networks and sensor data throughout the paper, our techniques can be straightforwardly applied to a wide range of applications which involve multidimensional data such as those that are related to the Internet of Things for example.

4. ALTERNATIVE CONSTRUCTIONS

In this section, we briefly discuss a few alternative cryptographic solutions and address their limitations.

4.1 Top-down Hash-tree

One possible approach is to use a binary tree to maintain symmetric encryption keys (Figure 3) for sensor data. The root contains the master key, while the intermediate sub-keys are generated in a top-down manner. The actual keys for encryption/decryption are located at the leaves. Each sample is associated with one external leaf, and is encrypted by the corresponding key. In this construction, keys for m samples in a range can be reconstructed using only $O(\log(m))$ aggregated keys. These aggregated keys are essentially intermediate sub-keys whose descendants are the m encryption keys under consideration. For instance, in Figure 3, sub-keys 19,5 and 24 are aggregated keys from which encryption keys in $\{4, 5, 6, 7, 8, 9\}$ can be "reconstructed".

However, it is not straightforward to extend this method to support d-dimensions, where $d > 1$. A trivial method of using multiple trees, one for each dimension, to generate d keys for each sample is not secure against collusion attack [23]. Furthermore, this method fails to aggregate keys for down-sampling and general queries, such as ones asking for encryption keys $\{1, 3, 5, 7, 9\}$ or $\{1, 4, 5, 7, 10\}$.

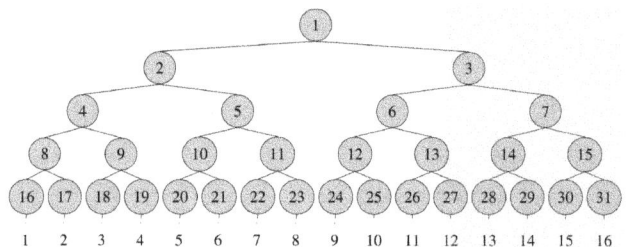

Figure 3: Tree based construction for one-dimensional data.

4.2 ABE-based construction

There are a few ways to employ Attribute-Based Encryption (ABE) to aggregate decryption keys for multidimensional range query. The most intuitive approach is to adopt Key-Policy ABE (KP-ABE)[19] in the following way: An index is represented by a set of attributes, each of which corresponds to the location of a 1 in the index's binary representation. For instance, the index $9 = 1001_2$ is represented by two attributes A_0 and A_3. In delegating decryption ability of ciphertexts in a range of S, the data owner first determines the "policy" $\mathcal{A}$, which is a logical expression on the attributes for indices in S. The aggregated key is then determined from the policy. The size of the aggregated key is often proportional to the number of logical operations in the logical expression, and thus incurs a $\log(n)$ factor overhead in specifying a range, where n is the system's capacity (i.e. total number of samples encrypted under the same security setting.). For example, if $n = 2^{10}$ and an index set in question is $S = [1019, 1023]$, then the policy $\mathcal{A} = \{A_9 \wedge A_8 \wedge A_7 \wedge A_6 \wedge A_5 \wedge A_4 \wedge A_3\}$. Furthermore, the ciphertext size of each index is proportional to the number of attributes associated to it, which implies a multiplicative $\log(n)$ factor overhead. Experimental studies also show that the reconstruction time of this approach is slower than our proposed method, probably due to the larger number bilinear map operations required. Finally, while it is easy to express down-sampling of rate $1/p$ using short expression, where p is a power of 2, it is not clear how to efficiently express other down-sampling rates. Hence, it is not trivial to obtain short aggregated key for other rates.

4.3 Multi-dimensional Range Query over Encrypted Data

Shi et al. address Multi-dimensional Range Query over Encrypted Data (MRQED) problem [23]. The work is an enhancement of the ABE-based construction, aiming to protect confidentiality of both query and the indices. Specifically, if an index of a sample under consideration is outside the queried range, one would learn no information beyond the fact that an aggregated key fails to decrypt its encrypted content. Note that in our application, the indices are not considered secret but rather made publicly available. Thus, we do not enforce this security requirement. Similar to the ABE-based construction, MRQED admits an overhead of at least $\log(n)$ multiplicative factor in ciphertext size and aggregated key size, failing to meet our efficiency requirements.

5. PROPOSED FAST RECONSTRUCTION

Owing to the fact that KAC satisfies our security and two efficiency requirements (i.e. size of aggregated key and overhead in ciphertext size) put forth in Section 3.2, we adopt its encryption and key aggregation algorithms in our system. As such, our system inherits KAC's provable security. Interested readers are referred to [11] for further details on the security of the scheme.

However, as briefly discussed in Section 2, KAC reconstruction cost is expensive. In particular, reconstructing a single ciphertext with index i using an aggregated key K_S ($i \in S$) requires the following two values (Section 2):

$$\rho_i = \prod_{j \in S, j \neq i} g_{n+1+i-j} \quad (1)$$

$$\hat{\rho} = \prod_{j \in S} g_{n+1-j} \quad (2)$$

$\hat{\rho}$ is independent of i and can be computed only once for all ciphertexts in S. The computations of ρ_is ($i \in S$) are of more interest. A naive approach which computes each ρ_i independently — not exploiting their relationship — would incur $O(|S|^2)$ group multiplications to compute all necessary ρ_i (i.e. for all i in S). We observe that exploiting their relationship leads to a better computation cost.

In this section, we first introduce an algorithmic enhancement for KAC reconstruction specifically targeting Q1 and Q2 queries (Section 5.1). This enhancement reduces the reconstruction time from quadratic to linear. We later generalize the technique — using dynamic programming — to enable fast reconstruction for Q3 queries (Sections 5.2, 5.3).

5.1 Fast reconstruction for range and down-sampling queries

5.1.1 A special recurrence relation

For Q1 and Q2 queries (or their combination), the indices of the requested samples follow specific patterns which straightforwardly permit fast computations. Let us first consider a one-dimensional Q1 query with range $S = [1, m]$ for some m. For clarity in exposition, let us define $\hat{g}_t = g_{n+1+t}$, and

$$R_i = \prod_{j \in S} \hat{g}_{i-j}$$

For each $i \in S$, $\rho_i = \hat{g}_i^{-1} R_i$, and thus it can be easily computed from R_i. Now, we explore how to compute all R_is efficiently. Under the straightforward method, computing each R_i requires $|S| - 1$ multiplications, hence $|S|(|S| - 1)$ multiplications are required to compute all R_is. However, by exploiting the recurrence relation

$$R_{i+1} = (\hat{g}_{i-m})^{-1} \cdot R_i \cdot \hat{g}_i$$

we can obtain R_{i+1} from R_i using only two extra multiplications. This leads to a fast linear time algorithm that computes all R_is recursively, offering a significant speed-up over quadratic time as in the straightforward method.

We next show how to extend this observation on the recurrence relation to enable fast reconstruction for Q1 and Q2 queries. Interestingly, this can also be extended to improve computation cost of other cryptographic primitives whose constructions involve group multiplications, such as broadcast encryption [13] and redactable signatures [8]. This would be an interesting further extension.

5.1.2 Fast reconstruction for Q1 queries

Let us first consider two-dimensional lattice. Let $S = [1, m] \times [1, m]$ be a rectangular range in the two-dimensional lattice with bound n in both dimensions. As such, the indices are two-dimensional vectors. Let $\sigma(x_1, x_2) = x_1(n - 1) + x_2$ be the mapping function that maps the two-dimensional lattice to the one-dimensional lattice. It can be seen that decrypting a ciphertext with the index (i_1, i_2) requires the following value:

$$\rho_{(i_1,i_2)} = \prod_{(j_1,j_2) \in S, (j_1,j_2) \neq (i_1,i_2)} g_{n^2+1+\sigma(i_1,i_2)-\sigma(j_1,j_2)}$$

Similar to the simple one-dimensional example above, the term $n^2 + 1$ in the subscript is simply a fixed offset. Hence, the formula can be simplified by defining $\hat{g}_{(i_1,i_2)} = g_{n^2+1+\sigma(i_1,i_2)}$ and $R_{(i_1,i_2)}$ by:

$$R_{(i_1,i_2)} = \prod_{(x,y) \in S} \hat{g}_{(i_1,i_2)-(x,y)} = \prod_{x=1}^{m} \prod_{y=1}^{m} \hat{g}_{(i_1,i_2)-(x,y)}$$

It should be clear that obtaining the required $\rho_{(i_i,i_2)}$ from the corresponding $R_{(i_1,i_2)}$ is trivial. Exploiting the observation on the special recurrence relation that we make earlier, we can derive the following equation:

$$R_{(i_1+1,i_2)} = R_{(i_1,i_2)} \prod_{y=1}^{m} \hat{g}_{(i_1,i_2)-(i_1-m,y)}^{-1} \prod_{\tilde{y}=1}^{m} \hat{g}_{(i_1,i_2)-(i_1,\tilde{y})} \quad (3)$$

Let us dub the product of the first sequence $T_{(i_1,i_2)}$ and the second $\widetilde{T}_{(i_1,i_2)}$, Equation 3 becomes:

$$R_{(i_1+1,i_2)} = R_{(i_1,i_2)}T_{(i_1,i_2)}\widetilde{T}_{(i_1,i_2)}$$

Now, observe that both $T_{(i_1,i_2)}$ and $\widetilde{T}_{(i_1,i_2)}$ in turn can also be expressed by recurrence relations, allowing the computations to be done in linear time. Consequently, evaluating all $R_{(i_1,i_2)}$s incurs only linear time, as opposed to quadratic time if the computation is to be done naively.

In general, for a d-dimensional range, the number of group multiplications required for computing all necessary ρ_i is in $O(d|S|)$. Since the number of dimensions (d) is deemed as a constant, we have derived a linear time approach to reconstruct Q1 queries.

5.1.3 Fast reconstruction for Q2 queries

Let us consider a Q2 query in two-dimension lattice (extending this to support higher dimension should be straightforward). Given a Q2 query represented by an independent basis, say $\{(3,0),(0,2)\}$ for example, one can first transform the coordinate system (e.g. transform (x,y) to $(x/3,y/2)$) such that indices of the required samples correspond to integer coordinates, and then apply the linear time reconstruction approach similar to that of Q1 queries on the transformed coordinate system and indices. We refer reader to [17] for further details on the transformation which could be applied on the coordinates.

In general, for a Q2 query that asks for samples in a d-dimensional range, the number of group multiplications required is also in $O(d|S|)$. Though additional computations are required to transform the coordinate, they are significantly less expensive than group multiplications. Therefore, we have derived a fast reconstruction method – running in linear time – for Q2 queries.

5.2 Fast reconstruction for Q3 queries

The techniques we discuss above reuses common terms and recurrence relations among different ρ_is to save computations. They are apparent in Q1 and Q2 queries, but not so for Q3 queries. An interesting question to consider is how to find a computation plan that evaluates all ρ_is with the minimum computation cost (i.e., the least number of multiplications) for an arbitrary query. For the ease of exposition, we assume that some normalization (similar to the mapping function σ mentioned in Section 5.1.2) has been applied such that indices of queried samples are mapped to a one-dimensional set S. We shall use the set $S = \{1,2,3,6,9,10\}$ and system capacity (maximum number of ciphertexts that the system can support) $n = 20$ as the running example (depicted in Table 1).

Let us denote by $\mathcal{B}$ a set of singletons whose elements are indices of g in the public parameter $param$, and represent each ρ_i by a multi-set P_i comprising of indices of g in a sequence that computes ρ_i following Equation 1. Let $\mathcal{P}$ – the target collection – be a set of all such P_is. In the running example (Table 1), $\mathcal{B} = \{\{1\},\{2\},\ldots,\{40\}\}$, ρ_1 is represented by $P_1 = \{20,19,16,13,12\}$ and the target collection $\mathcal{P} = \{P_1,P_2,P_3,P_6,P_9,P_{10}\}$

The problem of computing all necessary ρ_i is now reducible to the problem of constructing $\mathcal{P}$ from the collection of singletons $\mathcal{B}$. Each multiplication is represented by a "computation step" performing either a union or a subtraction on two multi-sets.

Table 1: An exemplar Q3 query asking for a six samples whose indices are $S = \{1,2,3,6,9,10\}$. The system capacity is $n = 20$. To reconstruct these samples, six corresponding ρ_i ($i \in S$) have to be computed. The target collection is $\mathcal{P} = \{P_1,P_2,P_3,P_6,P_9,P_{10}\}$.

$\rho_1 = g_{20} \cdot g_{19} \cdot g_{16} \cdot g_{13} \cdot g_{12}$	$P_1 = \{20,19,16,13,12\}$
$\rho_2 = g_{22} \cdot g_{20} \cdot g_{17} \cdot g_{14} \cdot g_{13}$	$P_2 = \{22,20,17,14,13\}$
$\rho_3 = g_{23} \cdot g_{22} \cdot g_{18} \cdot g_{15} \cdot g_{14}$	$P_3 = \{23,22,18,15,14\}$
$\rho_6 = g_{26} \cdot g_{25} \cdot g_{24} \cdot g_{18} \cdot g_{17}$	$P_6 = \{26,25,24,18,17\}$
$\rho_9 = g_{29} \cdot g_{28} \cdot g_{27} \cdot g_{24} \cdot g_{20}$	$P_9 = \{29,28,27,24,20\}$
$\rho_{10} = g_{30} \cdot g_{29} \cdot g_{28} \cdot g_{25} \cdot g_{22}$	$P_{10} = \{30,29,28,25,22\}$

With these notions, we are ready to define the computation plan.

DEFINITION 1 (COMPUTATION PLAN). *Given $\mathcal{B}$ and the target collection $\mathcal{P}$, the computation plan is a sequence of computation steps $\mathcal{M} = \{m_1,m_2,\ldots,m_z\}$ that constructs a set of multi-sets $\mathcal{A}$ such that $\mathcal{P} \subset \mathcal{A}$.*

The set of multi-sets $\mathcal{A}$ is initiated to $\mathcal{B}$. Each computation step picks, with replacement, two multi-sets in $\mathcal{A}$, either unions or subtracts them from one another, and inserts the resulting multi-set to $\mathcal{A}$. The computation plan is optimal if it has the minimum number of computation steps.

In Section 5.1, we have seen that introducing $T_{(i_1,i_2)}$ significantly reduces the number of multiplications required in computing $R_{(i_1,i_2)}$, suggesting that introducing appropriate intermediate values serves as a good heuristic in evaluating the optimal computation plan[5]. Unfortunately, the space of possible intermediate values are exponentially large, making the choice of appropriate intermediate values difficult. Indeed, though we do not attempt to give a formal proof, we believe that computing the optimal computation plan may very well be NP-complete. We provide below heuristics to approximate the optimal computation plan.

5.2.1 Minimum Spanning Tree based Strategy

For any two P_i,P_j, let us define their distance as:

$$dist(i,j) = |P_i \setminus P_j| + |P_j \setminus P_i|$$

If P_j is already constructed, one can derive P_i from P_j with at most $dist(P_i,P_j)$ computation steps. In the best case where the two multi-sets $(P_i \setminus P_j)$ and $(P_j \setminus P_i)$ have already been inserted to $\mathcal{A}$, P_i can be derived from P_j with only two computation steps. Based on this notion of $dist(i,j)$, we can evaluate the computation plan by solving the following minimum spanning tree (MST) problem.

Let $G = (V,E)$ be a complete graph in which V and E denote the set of vertices and the set of edges, respectively. The set V comprises of $|\mathcal{P}| + 1$ vertices, representing multi-sets in $\mathcal{P}$ and an additional empty set $\bar{P}$. Each P_i maps to a vertex v_i, and $\bar{P}$ maps to a special vertex $\bar{v}$. The set E contains $|V|(|V| - 1)/2$ edges. Let us denote by e_{ij} an

---

[5] The computation plan need not be evaluated in real-time. Since queries are likely to be repeated, the computation plans can be computed in offline sessions, probably by the data owner or on the server with presumable powerful resource. On another note, parallelizing the reconstruction computation is possible so long as the users' computation resource allows so. In such situation, values that should be evaluated independently can also be inferred from the computation plan.

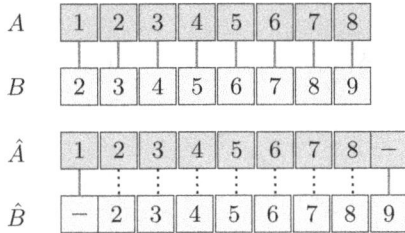

Figure 4: An example of sequence alignment. A dotted link denotes zero penalty cost while a solid link represents penalty cost of one. By inserting "gaps" at the beginning of A and at the end of B, we obtain $\hat{A}$ and $\hat{B}$ which yield the optimal alignment with total penalty of only two.

edge connecting vertex v_i to vertex v_j. For each edge e_{ij}, we set its weight to $dist(i,j)$. For edges originating from the special vertex $\bar{v}$, we set their weights to $|\mathcal{P}| - 2$.

With the reduction described above, we can use any minimum spanning tree algorithm, such as $Chu-Liu/Edmonds$ algorithm running in $O(|V|^2)$ time [27], to approximate the optimal computation plan.

5.2.2 Introducing intermediate values

As discussed earlier, the computation cost can be further reduced if common intermediate values are introduced properly. In particular, let us denote the set of those intermediate values as $\mathcal{I}$. We can approximate an even better computation plan by introducing these intermediate values to $\mathcal{P}$, obtaining $\mathcal{P}' = \mathcal{P} \cup \mathcal{I}$, and then apply the MST-based strategy described earlier to find the MST of the complete graph $G' = (V', E')$ in which V' represents the set of multi-sets $\mathcal{P}'$ and one additional empty set $\bar{P}$. Since the space of all possible intermediate values are exponentially large, it is not clear how to efficiently choose the most appropriate intermediate values. We provide here an intuitive heuristic to determine those common intermediate values.

Should one interpret each P_i as a sequence of elements, and intermediate values as shorter sequences, the problem of finding the common intermediate values is reducible to the *local sequence alignment* problem [25] — which is tasked to determine "similar regions" between sequences.

Sequence alignment is considered a textbook example for dynamic program. In the most basic version, the sequence alignment problem takes as input two sequences $A = a_1 \ldots a_y$ and $B = b_1 \ldots b_z$ over an alphabet Σ, together with penalty metrics $\alpha_{gap} \geq 0$ for inserting a "gap" and α_{ab} for matching an element a of one sequence against an element b of the other sequence (presumably $\alpha_{ab} = 0$ if $a = b$) and outputs an optimal "alignment" which minimizes the total penalty. In this work, we utilize the *Smith-Waterman* algorithm [20], to solve the sequence alignment problem.

Let us consider an example in Figure 4. The two input sequences are $A = 12345678$ and $B = 23456789$, $\alpha_{gap} = 1$, $\alpha_{ab} = 1$ if $a \neq b$ or $\alpha_{ab} = 0$ otherwise. Simply matching A and B as-is (without inserting any gap) incurs the penalty cost of eight. The optimal alignment is formed by inserting a gap to the end of A and another gap to the beginning of B, resulting in $\hat{A}$ and $\hat{B}$ whose alignment incurs the minimum penalty cost of two.

The intermediate values are the similar regions found in the solution to the sequence alignment problem. For example, if we are to construct $P_i = \{1,2,3,4,5,6,7,8\}$ and

$P_j = \{2,3,4,5,6,7,8,9\}$, we can represent P_i and P_j by the sequences A and B in the above example (Figure 4). Since the similar region of A and B is $R = 2345678$, the intermediate multi-set is $I = \{2,3,4,5,6,7,8\}$. Effectively, we can construct both P_i and P_j from I with only two extra computation steps (one for each of them).

5.3 Trade-off between number of aggregated keys and reconstruction time

The reconstruction time can be further reduced at the expense of splitting the query into smaller sub-queries and issuing one aggregated key for each of them. One may partition the set S into k clusters, each of which corresponds to one sub-query, and issue one aggregated key for each sub-query. Accordingly, one needs to issue k aggregated keys instead of one single key. At the expense of issuing k aggregated keys, the reconstruction time can be reduced.

The partition should be performed such that elements in each cluster are "close" to each other. In another word, for two neighbour indices i and j belonging to the same cluster, it should be the case that ρ_i can be derived from ρ_j with only a small number of group multiplications. Let us informally define the distance between two indices i, j in the same cluster as follows. Let v be the common intermediate value of ρ_i and ρ_j, their distance is the number of group multiplications it takes to compute both values ρ_i and ρ_j from the common intermediate value v.

We now define the distance function between two cluster S_a and S_b. Let $W(S_a)$ be the number of group multiplications required to compute all ρ_i where $i \in S_a$. This value can be determined via the computation plan discussed previously in Section 5.2. For two clusters S_a and S_b, their distance is simply $W(S_a \cup S_b)$. Note that $W(S_a \cup S_b)$ is not necessarily equal to the sum of $W(S_a)$ and $W(S_b 2)$.

We employ the single-linkage clustering method [15] (implemented using *SLINK* algorithm [24]) to perform the clustering. In particular, each element in S is initially a cluster by itself. Each step would choose two clusters with the shortest distance (using the distance function defined above) and merge them together. The clusters are sequentially merged until only k clusters are left.

In the literature, the single-linkage clustering method is criticised to produce long thin clusters in which elements at opposite ends of a cluster are of far distance, which may lead to difficulties in defining classes subdividing the data. However, its other characteristic which is to have a distance of nearby elements residing in the same cluster small is of greater interest. Indeed, this feature will allows a ρ_i value to be computed efficiently from its nearby elements.

6. PERFORMANCE EVALUATION

In this section, we compare performance of our proposed fast reconstruction techniques with KP-ABE [19] and the original KAC [10].

6.1 Performance Analysis

Table 2 summarises the numbers of group operations, i.e. multiplication, exponential and pairing, required by the three procedures: (a) encryption of the samples, (b) aggregation of the keys, and (c) reconstruction of the keys. It also reports the size of the ciphertext with respect to the number of group elements. Observe that KP-ABE consistently

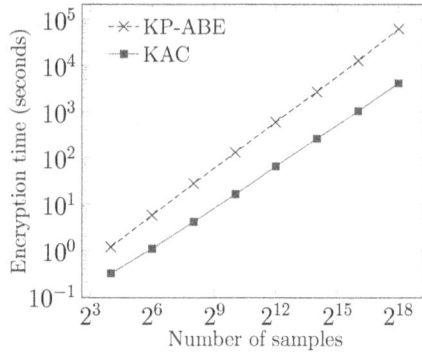
Figure 5: Encryption time

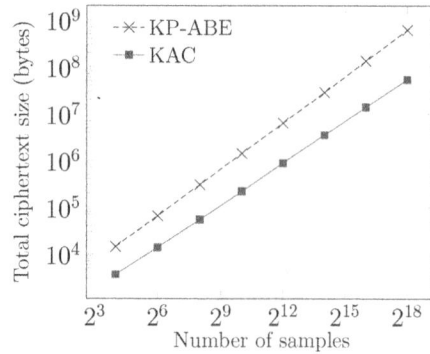
Figure 6: Total ciphertext size

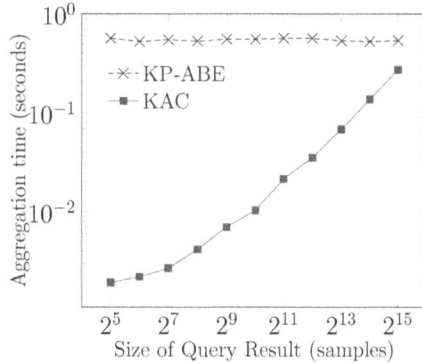
Figure 7: Aggregation time

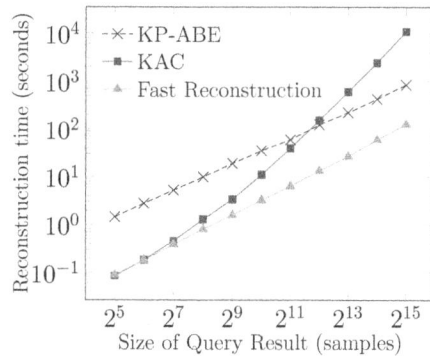
Figure 8: Reconstruction time for Q1 & Q2.

Table 2: Costs of encryption, extracting aggregated key and reconstructing a range query of size m, where n is the system's capacity (i.e. maximum number of samples to be encrypted). The ciphertext size is measured by the number of group elements per sample.

		KP-ABE	KAC	Ours
Encrypt	Mult.	$O(\log n)$	2	2
	Exp.	$O(\log n)$	3	3
	Pairing	1	1	1
Aggregate	Mult.	$O(\log n)$	m	m
	Exp.	$O(\log n)$	1	1
	Pairing	0	0	0
Reconstruct	Mult.	$O(m\log n)$	$O(m^2)$	$O(m)$
	Exp.	$O(m\log n)$	0	0
	Pairing	$O(m\log n)$	$m+1$	$m+1$
Ciphertext size		$O(\log n)$	3	3

suffers from a $O(\log n)$ overhead factor in comparison with KAC, which is inevitable since $\log n$ attributes are required to represent n indices. Since the total number of samples can be very large (e.g. at 25 samples per second, the system of 100 sensors will generate almost a quarter billion samples every day), such large overhead is hardly acceptable, especially for ciphertext size which affects the storage and communication cost. Although KAC outperforms KP-ABE in almost all aspects, its reconstruction cost is quadratic, rendering the scheme impractical in our application. By adopting KAC encryption and key aggregation procedures, and introducing various techniques to improve its reconstruction cost, our system achieves favourable performance in all aspects.

In particular, the proposed method reduces the number of multiplications to linear on Q1 and Q2 queries, and achieve several times speed-up for other queries.

In key aggregation, KAC requires more group multiplications but fewer number of exponentiations compared to KP-ABE. Because exponentiation is more computational expensive than group multiplication, the efficiency of the two schemes depends on the scale at which they operate. In particular, KAC would perform better than KP-ABE in aggregating a small number of keys, but worse when the number of keys is large (see Figure 7).

6.2 Experimental Setup

In practice, when the size of a single sample is large, it is more efficient to encrypt the sample using symmetric encryption such as AES with a randomly chosen key, then apply the key aggregation on the symmetric keys. We follow such fashion in our experiments.

To evaluate the performance of our fast reconstruction for Q1 and Q2 queries in comparison with KP-ABE and the original KAC, we fix the total number of encrypted samples at 2^{18}, while varying the query size $m = |S|$ from 2^5 to 2^{15}. The queries that we use in our experiments are two-dimensional range queries (having the same width along both dimensions) with down-sampling rate equal to 1/4.

For Q3 queries, we perform two set of experiments. In the first set, we study the effectiveness of the computation plan constructed with l intermediate values against KAC's reconstruction (Section 5.2). In the second experiment set, we examine the speed-up in reconstruction time at the expense of issuing more aggregated keys (Section 5.3). The queries are generated by selecting m indices randomly from

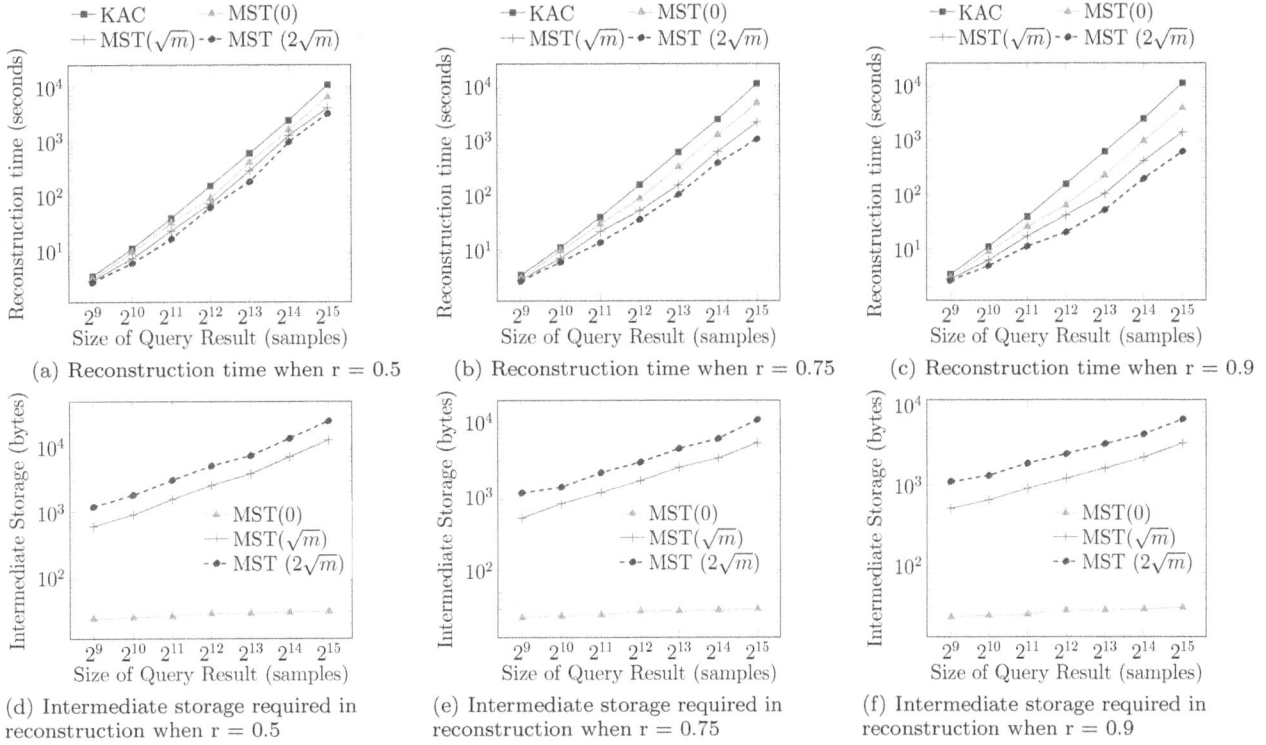

Figure 9: Fast reconstruction for Q3. MST(l) indicates performance of the computation plan constructed l intermediate values. Presumably, $l = 0$ indicates introducing no intermediate values. m is the size of query result.

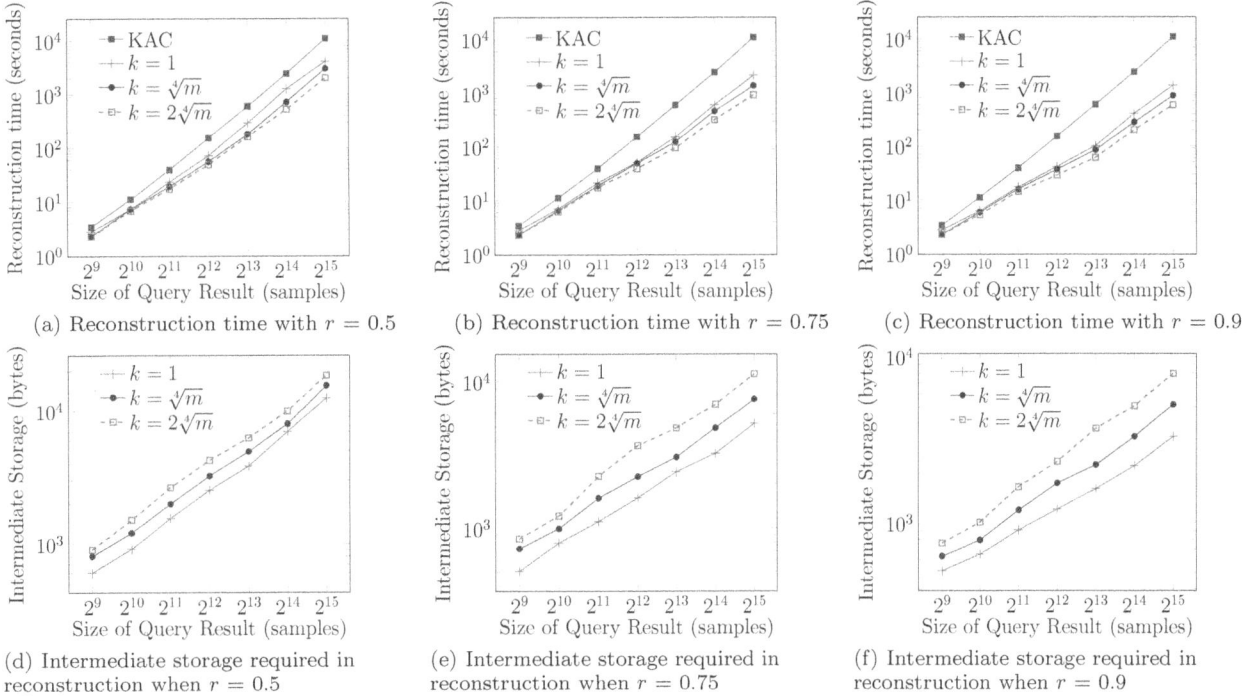

Figure 10: Trade-off between number of aggregated keys and reconstruction cost for Q3. k is number of sub-queries, each sub-query is associated with one aggregated key. m is the size of query result.

the range $[1, n]$. We define *query density* (r) as the ratio m/n. Various query sizes (i.e., m) and densities (i.e., r) are investigated. We do not study KP-ABE's performance on general queries, since it requires another algorithm to find a compact logical expression for an arbitrary query, which could be a separate topic of interest.

All experiments are performed on a system equipped with Intel Core-i5-4570u@3.2Ghz processor and 8GB of RAM. Our implementation employs Charm [1] cryptographic framework and utilizes symmetric pairings over Type-A (supersingular) curves. The KAC implementation and our fast reconstruction techniques are configured with 160-bit Solinas prime, offering 1024-bit of discrete-logarithm security. For consistency, the KP-ABE implementation is configured to provide 80-bit security. Although there exists no direct comparison between discrete-logarithm security and bit-security, 1024-bit of discrete-logarithm security is often considered to be equivalent to the 80-bit security. Each experiment is repeated ten times and average results — with time measured in seconds while storage and ciphertext size measured in bytes — are reported.

6.3 Experiment result

6.3.1 Encryption time

Figure 5 compares the encryption time of KP-ABE and KAC (our system adopt KAC encryption procedure) under log-log scale, with the total number of samples varied from 2^4 to 2^{18}. The experiment results agree with the analysis in the previous section. The cost of encryption incurred by KP-ABE is several times higher than that of KAC. For example, to encrypt 2^{18} items, KP-ABE needs 17 hours, while KAC only requires 1.17 hours (i.e. faster by almost $15\times$). Note that the main overhead of KP-ABE's encryption lies in carrying out exponent operations, which directly depends on the total number of samples, and thus the overhead would be even higher for larger datasets.

6.3.2 Ciphertext Size

A main disadvantage of KP-ABE lies in its ciphertext size. Figure 6 reports total ciphertext size for various n - the total number of samples to be encrypted. When $n = 2^{18}$, KP-ABE produces ciphertext of size approximately $10\times$ larger than KAC. This is so because KAC's ciphertext comprises of only three group elements, whereas KP-ABE's ciphertext contains $(3A + 2)$ group elements, where A is the number of attributes associated with a ciphertext. The value of A varies for different ciphertext, but its expected value is at least $\frac{1}{2}\log n$. Similar to the encryption time, the larger the dataset is, the more superior KAC is to KP-ABE in term of ciphertext size.

6.3.3 Aggregation time

As shown in Table 2, KP-ABE's key aggregation time only depends on n - the total number of samples. KAC, on the other hands, aggregates keys in $O(m)$ time. It turns out that, when m is less than 2^{15}, KP-ABE needs longer time compared to KAC (Figuer 7).

6.3.4 Reconstruction time

Figure 8 shows the reconstruction time for Q1 and Q2 queries. For small m, reconstruction time incurred by ABE is higher than KAC, which is due to the expensive pairing operations. However, for larger m, KAC starts to perform worse than KP-ABE because of the quadratic growth the number of required multiplications. Our proposed method, on the other hand, achieves linear reconstructing time. When $m = 2^{15}$, it can reconstruct all the keys within 126 seconds, whereas KAC needs three hours (i.e. a speed-up of almost $90\times$).

For Q3 queries, we observe that the higher the query density is, the more effective our fast reconstruction techniques are. Though the gain is negligible when $r < 0.5$, it becomes more evident for larger r – achieving from $2.6\times$ to $8\times$ speed-up over original KAC reconstruction cost. We also witness a better reconstruction time – upto $3\times$ improvement as compared to fast reconstruction using computation plan strictly without any intermediate values – when intermediate values are pre-computed and reused (Figures 9a, 9b, 9c).

Figures 9d, 9e, 9f depict temporary storage required for maintaining all intermediate values computed during the reconstruction. This temporary storage is at most a few KB (e.g. 12.5KB for reconstructing 2^{15} keys when $r = 0.5$). As can be seen from the figures, the higher the density is, the less temporary storage is required.

We also evaluate the trade-off between number of aggregated keys and reconstruction time (Figures 10a, 10b, 10c). For a Q3 query asking for m samples, with $\sqrt[4]{m}$ aggregated keys, reconstruction time can be speeded-up by upto $13\times$. With a cost of $2\sqrt[4]{m}$ keys, upto $19\times$ improvement can be achieved. Nevertheless, we note that for small queries, it is not worth issuing more aggregated keys, because the increase in the number of pairing operations may lengthen the reconstruction time.

In another note, the more aggregated keys are issued, the more intermediate values need to be stored. With $k = \sqrt[4]{m}$, as high as 15 KB of temporary storage is required, while that value is increased to 19 KB when $k = 2\sqrt[4]{m}$ are issued. In all of our experiments, the requirement on temporary storage is only a few KB, which is quite reasonable even for resource constrained devices.

7. SYSTEM DESIGNS

In this section, we give two possible designs that incorporate key aggregation. We consider two types of sensors; one with Public-key Cryptosystem (PKC) capability, and the other that is only capable of performing standard symmetric key cryptosystem such as AES and SHA-1. We refer to the first category as PKC-enabled sensors and the later as low-powered sensors.

7.1 System with PKC-enabled sensors

(1) During system setup, the owner distributes the public key PK to all entities, and an unique identity ID to each sensor (Figure 11). The identity ID's are not secrets and are made public. (2) For each sample (i, x), the sensor encrypts the sample value x with the index i using KAC's encrypt algorithm to obtain a ciphertext c. It then streams the c together with the index i to the storage server. In situation where sensor samples are of large size, (e.g. images), they are encrypted using AES with a randomly generated key k, whereas the key k is being encrypted by KAC under an index i of the sensor sample (similar to sensor sample of small size). The two ciphertexts (encrypted sample and encrypted symmetric key) and the corresponding index are then streamed to the server.

(3) When a user asks for access to a subset C, whose indices fall in S, he sends the query q_S to the owner. (4) The owner issues an aggregated key K_S to the user, together with an authentication ticket t. (5) The user presents the ticket t to the storage server as a proof that he is authorised to access C. (6) Upon verification, the server sends the requested ciphertexts to the user, which are later decrypted using the aggregated key K_S. In case of large samples, she also needs to download corresponding encrypted symmetric

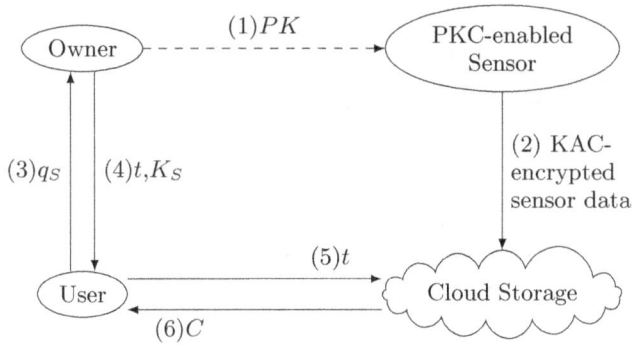

Figure 11: System model for PKC-enabled sensors

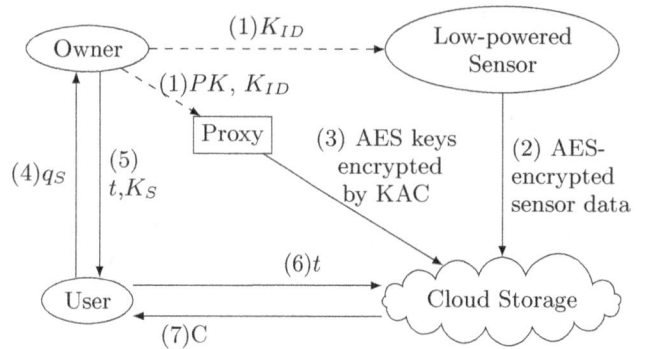

Figure 12: System model for low-powered sensors

keys. The encrypted keys are first reconstructed, and then used to decrypt the encrypted samples.

The incorporation of the authentication ticket can be based on standard protocol such as Kerberos [21, 22]. Although this cannot prevent the collusion between the users and the server, it forms another layer of defence to prevent unauthorised downloading of the ciphertexts.

7.2 System with low-powered sensors

Figure 12 shows the system design for low-powered sensors, which are only capable of conducting non-expensive cryptographic operations such as AES or SHA-1. To address the resource constraints of these low-powered sensors, we introduce a trusted encryption proxy. This proxy also helps to relieve the owner's computation load.

(1) During the system setup phase, the owner broadcasts the public key PK to all entities except the low-powered sensors. The owner also distributes an unique identity ID and a shared secret seed K_{ID} to each sensor. (2) For each sensed sample (i, x), the sensor generates a symmetric encryption key $k_{i,ID}$ using a cryptographic pseudorandom function using the secret seed K_{ID} and the index i. The sensor then encrypts the sample value x with encryption key $k_{i,ID}$, obtaining c, and streams (i, c) to the storage server.

All secret K_{ID} are also shared with the encryption proxy. Because the proxy (which actually represents the data owner) has knowledge of locations and frequencies at which sensor data are collected, it can infer the set of indices associated with the samples. With the knowledge of the indices and all sensors' secret keys, (3) it can replicate a symmetric key $k_{i,ID}$. Each of these AES keys is encrypted with KAC under the corresponding sample index, giving $c_{i,ID}$.

The ciphertexts together with their indices, i.e. $(i, c_{i,ID})$'s, are then sent to the storage server. Note that this process need not be performed in realtime. Rather, the proxy can replicate, encrypt and send the encrypted AES keys to the cloud storage in batches well before the actual sensing. In addition, although the encryption proxy has the secret K_{ID}, it cannot derive the owner's secret key. The remaining steps (step (4) to (7) in Figure 12) are similar to the previous setting.

Compare to the PKC-enabled sensor, if a low-powered sensor ID is compromised, the secret K_{ID} could be revealed. With K_{ID}, the adversary can decrypt all previously encrypted sensor samples generated by that sensor.

8. RELATED WORK

Several cryptographic key assignment schemes exploit hierarchical structures (e.g. trees) to maintain keys for various sets of objects [29, 3]. A key for an internal node is used to derive keys for its descendant nodes. These approaches efficiently support aggregating key for simple access policies. Other schemes can support more complicated access policies, such as those that are described by cyclic or acyclic graphs [2]. Benaloh et al. introduced an encryption scheme supporting delegating decryption capability with flexible hierarchy [4]. However, it is not clear how to extend the schemes to maintain encryption keys for multidimensional objects whose access policies do not follow any hierarchical structure.

KP-ABE enables various ciphertexts to be decrypted by one single key. This technique associates a set of attributes to a ciphertext and a policy to a decryption key. Such key can decrypt all ciphertexts whose attributes conform to its policy [9, 19]. ABE attains collusion-resistance at a cost of either increasing the secret keys size or ciphertext's size [18]. These approaches requires many bilinear-mapping operations in their executions, rendering their performance prohibitive and thus impractical.

Supporting complex queries over encrypted data is also of interest. Boneh et al. presented a primitive named Hidden Vector Encryption (HVE) to enable range and subset queries [7]. This scheme results in $O(dt)$ encryption time, ciphertext size and $O(d)$ decryption key size and decryption cost, where d is the number of dimensions and t the number of points. Shi et al. proposed a construction adopting a specialized data structure for range query evaluation [23]. Its encryption cost, ciphertext size and decryption key size are all $O(d \log(t))$ while decryption cost is $O((\log(t))^d)$. Because these schemes consider some security requirements which are not relevant in our application, such as secrecy of all attributes, they suffer from a poor performance and not applicable in our context.

While KAC has inspired various follow-ups [12, 28], those works have not yet focused on improving KAC's key reconstruction cost. To our knowledge, the techniques proposed in this paper are the first algorithmic enhancement to reduce the key reconstruction cost of KAC. This not only makes KAC more applicable in practical systems, but also benefits those follow-up works that employs KAC as the underlying cryptographic primitive.

9. CONCLUSION

In this work, we focus on sensor data, especially time-series data that are continuously sensed, encrypted and streamed to the cloud. The temporal and spatial arrangements of these time-series data lead to queries in the form of multidimensional range and down-sampling that can be exploited for efficiency. We introduce algorithmic enhancement for the known KAC. The enhancement is significant for Q1 and Q2 queries, achieving 90 times speed-up in reconstructing 2^{15} keys. To deal with more general applications, we generalize the technique and provide heuristics for handling arbitrary queries. These heuristics attain upto eight times speed-up over the original KAC. Finally, our clustering-based method for trading off between number of aggregated keys to be issued and reconstruction time is also proven to be efficient, evidenced by the 19 times speed-up.

Our proposed fast reconstruction techniques resolve the scalability issue in adopting key aggregation in practical application with large datasets. This makes the KAC more applicable in various scenario and system settings including the Internet of Things. More interestingly, the implication of our work is much more. Our observation on the recurrence relations, and the techniques we propose to exploit such relations for better computation cost can also be applied on other cryptographic primitives whose constructions involve group multiplications, such as broadcast encryption [13], redactable signatures [8].

Acknowledgements

This research is supported by the National Research Foundation, Prime Minister's Office, Singapore under its National Cybersecurity R&D Program (Award No. NRF2015-NCR-NCR002-001) and administered by the National Cybersecurity R&D Directorate. All opinions expressed in this work are solely those of the authors.

10. REFERENCES

[1] J. A. Akinyele, M. D. Green, and A. D. Rubin. Charm: A framework for rapidly prototyping cryptosystems. Cryptology ePrint Archive, Report 2011/617.

[2] M. J. Atallah, M. Blanton, N. Fazio, and K. B. Frikken. Dynamic and efficient key management for access hierarchies. *ACM Trans. Inf. Syst. Secur.*, 2009.

[3] G. Ateniese, A. D. Santis, A. L. Ferrara, and B. Masucci. Provably-secure time-bound hierarchical key assignment schemes. Cryptology ePrint Archive, Report 2006/225.

[4] J. Benaloh, M. Chase, E. Horvitz, and K. Lauter. Patient controlled encryption: Ensuring privacy of electronic medical records. In *CCSW*, 2009.

[5] D. Boneh, C. Gentry, and B. Waters. Collusion resistant broadcast encryption with short ciphertexts and private keys. In *CRYPTO*, 2005.

[6] D. Boneh, C. Gentry, and B. Waters. Collusion resistant broadcast encryption with short ciphertexts and private keys. In *CRYPTO*, 2005.

[7] D. Boneh and B. Waters. Conjunctive, subset, and range queries on encrypted data. In *Theory of cryptography*. 2007.

[8] E.-C. Chang, C. L. Lim, and J. Xu. Short redactable signatures using random trees. In *CT-RSA*. 2009.

[9] M. Chase and S. S. Chow. Improving privacy and security in multi-authority attribute-based encryption. In *CCS*, 2006.

[10] C.-K. Chu, S. S. M. Chow, W.-G. Tzeng, J. Zhou, and R. H. Deng. Key-aggregate cryptosystem for scalable data sharing in cloud storage. *IEEE TPDS*, 2014.

[11] C.-K. Chu, S. S. M. Chow, W.-G. Tzeng, J. Zhou, and R. H. Deng. Supplementary material for key-aggregate cryptosystem for scalable data sharing in cloud storage, 2014.

[12] H. Deng, Q. Wu, B. Qin, S. S. Chow, J. Domingo-Ferrer, and W. Shi. Tracing and revoking leaked credentials: accountability in leaking sensitive outsourced data. In *ASIACCS*, 2014.

[13] A. Fiat and M. Naor. Broadcast encryption. In *CRYPTO*, 1994.

[14] V. Goyal, O. Pandey, A. Sahai, and B. Waters. Attribute-based encryption for fine-grained access control of encrypted data. In *CCS*, 2006.

[15] J. A. Hartigan. *Clustering algorithms*. 1975.

[16] M. M. Hassan, B. Song, and E.-N. Huh. A framework of sensor-cloud integration opportunities and challenges. In *ICUIMC*, 2009.

[17] M. H. Hayes. The reconstruction of a multidimensional sequence from the phase or magnitude of its fourier transform. *IEEE Trans Sig. Process*, 1982.

[18] S. Hohenberger and B. Waters. Attribute-based encryption with fast decryption. In *PKC*. 2013.

[19] A. Lewko, A. Sahai, and B. Waters. Revocation systems with very small private keys. In *IEEE S & P*, 2010.

[20] S. A. Manavski and G. Valle. Cuda compatible gpu cards as efficient hardware accelerators for smith-waterman sequence alignment. *BMC bioinformatics*, 2008.

[21] C. Neuman, T. Yu, S. Hartman, and K. Raeburn. The kerberos network authentication service (v5). RFC 4120, 2005.

[22] A. A. Pirzada and C. McDonald. Kerberos assisted authentication in mobile ad-hoc networks. In *ACSC*, 2004.

[23] E. Shi, J. Bethencourt, T.-H. H. Chan, D. Song, and A. Perrig. Multi-dimensional range query over encrypted data. In *IEEE S & P*, 2007.

[24] R. Sibson. Slink: an optimally efficient algorithm for the single-link cluster method. *The Computer Journal*, 16(1):30–34, 1973.

[25] T. F. Smith and M. S. Waterman. Identification of common molecular subsequences. *Journal of molecular biology*, 1981.

[26] H. Takabi, J. Joshi, and G.-J. Ahn. Security and privacy challenges in cloud computing environments. *IEEE S & P*, 2010.

[27] R. E. Tarjan. Finding optimum branchings. *Networks*, 1977.

[28] Y. Tong, J. Sun, S. S. Chow, and P. Li. Towards auditable cloud-assisted access of encrypted health data. In *CNS*, 2013.

[29] W. G. Tzeng. A time-bound cryptographic key assignment scheme for access control in a hierarchy. *TKDE*, 2002.

Provable Secure Universal Steganography of Optimal Rate

Provably Secure Steganography does not Necessarily Imply One-Way Functions

Sebastian Berndt
University of Lübeck
Ratzeburger Allee 160, 23562 Lübeck, Germany
berndt@tcs.uni-luebeck.de

Maciej Liśkiewicz
University of Lübeck
Ratzeburger Allee 160, 23562 Lübeck, Germany
liskiwi@tcs.uni-luebeck.de

ABSTRACT

We present the first complexity-theoretic secure steganographic protocol which, for any communication channel, is provably secure, reliable, and has nearly optimal bandwidth. Our system is unconditionally secure, i.e. our proof does not rely on any unproven complexity-theoretic assumption, like e.g. the existence of one-way functions. This disproves the claim that the existence of one-way functions and access to a communication channel oracle are both necessary and sufficient conditions for the existence of secure steganography, in the sense that secure and reliable steganography exists independently of the existence of one-way functions.

Keywords

Steganography; Cryptographic Primitives; Lower Bounds

1. INTRODUCTION

Digital steganography has received substantial interest in modern computer science since it allows secret communication without revealing its presence. Therefore, the investigation of steganography has recently become the subject of intensive studies, both theoretical and experimental. In this paper we provide a theoretical analysis on the existence of secure universal steganography with optimal rate – a problem which belongs to one of the most fundamental ones of this area. In the scenario considered here, we assume secret-key communication with the presence of a passive adversary and the security defined in the computational setting.

A common computational model for secret-key steganography, also used in this paper, was introduced by Hopper, Langford, and von Ahn [13, 14, 15]. Independently, Katzenbeisser and Petitcolas [16] provided a similar formulation. In this setting, a *stegosystem* is defined as a pair of probabilistic algorithms, called *encoder* and *decoder*, which share a secret-key. The aim of the encoder (often called Alice or the steganographer) is to hide a secret message in a document and to send it to the decoder (Bob) via a public *channel* $\mathcal{C}$, which is completely monitored by an *adversary* (Warden

IH&MMSec 2016, June 20 - 23, 2016, Vigo, Spain

© 2016 Copyright held by the owner/author(s). Publication rights licensed to ACM.
ISBN 978-1-4503-4290-2/16/06. . . $15.00

DOI: http://dx.doi.org/10.1145/2909827.2930796

or steganalyst). The channel is modeled as a probability distribution of legal documents, called *cover-documents* and the adversary's task is to distinguish those from altered ones called *stego-documents*.

To hide a secret message m, the encoder can take sample cover-documents, based on past communication, and manipulate them to embed m. The decoder, receiving stego-documents, should be able to decode the hidden message correctly. The stegosystem is called *reliable* if the decoder succeeds with high probability. The adversary is a probabilistic algorithm with access to additional knowledge about the channel. A stegosystem is *secure* with respect to a channel $\mathcal{C}$ if no adversary of *polynomial* time complexity is able to distinguish with significant probability between cover-documents from $\mathcal{C}$ and stego-documents generated by the stegosystem's encoder. This implies in general that the distributions of cover-documents and stego-documents have to be fairly close in a complexity-theoretic sense. The *insecurity* of a stegosystem is the advantage of the best adversary to distinguish between cover- and stego-documents. Thus, a stegosystem is secure if its insecurity is sufficiently small, i.e. negligible in the security parameter κ defining the length of the shared secret-key. This work deals with the construction of unconditional secure stegosystems of high rate and with the relation between steganography and cryptography.

1.1 Steganography and Cryptography

Although there is a strong connection between these two areas, steganography is *not* cryptography. Our example below shows even more, namely that polynomial-time bounded steganography is *not* cryptography. A commonly heard argument for the premise that steganography is cryptography goes as follows:

Let m and m' be two different secret messages and s and s' be stego-documents which embed m, resp. m'. If the distributions of s and s' are indistinguishable from the distribution of the cover-documents, then by the triangle-inequality, the distributions of s and s' are also indistinguishable. Hence, a secure stegosystem is also a secure cryptosystem.

While the argument concerning the triangle-inequality is true, one can not simply use the stegosystem as a cryptosystem, as the stegosystem needs access to samples from the channel. Arguably, the most researched channel is those of natural digital pictures (say in the JPEG-format). A typical stegosystem for this channel takes a sample picture and modifies it in a way that is not detectable. A cryptosystem that simulates this stegosystem thus needs a way to get a sample picture. But the standard definition of cryptosystems does *not* assume such access and it is highly unlikely that an efficient algorithm to simulate sampling for this channel can be constructed. We will note later on that ignoring this access leads to misunderstandings, e.g. in the often cited work of Hopper, Langford and von Ahn [15].

1.2 Secure and Reliable Universal Systems

Clearly, security and reliability are necessary attributes of any reasonable stegosystem. If one forgoes one of these, steganography becomes trivial: If one is not concerned about security, we can simply send the secret message plainly over the channel. If one is not concerned about reliability, we can simply send a random sample of the channel.

The next property a reasonable stegosystem should satisfy is the versatility of the system: it should be secure and reliable with respect not only to a concrete channel $\mathcal{C}$ (like e.g. images of a specific data set) but to a broad range of channels (e.g. images of different sources and different characteristics). In this paper we study the most general type of systems, called *universal*[1]. Recall that a stegosystem is universal if the encoding method does not rely on knowledge of the distribution for the channel $\mathcal{C}$ except that its min-entropy is sufficiently large. The importance of the universality is based on the fact that typically no good description of the probability distribution on a channel is known. In this paper we assume the standard definition for security of a universal stegosystem $\mathcal{S}$, i.e. we say $\mathcal{S}$ is secure (against a chosen hiddentext attack) if it is secure with respect to any channel $\mathcal{C}$ as long as $\mathcal{C}$ does not violate the hardness construction $\mathcal{S}$ is based on [14, 15].

But, in addition to these fundamental properties, other properties are also important. To reduce the overall overhead of the protocol, the transmission *rate*, i.e. the number of bits transmitted per single stego-document, should be as high as possible. Next, the expected *query complexity* of the stegosystem, i.e. the number of cover documents the encoder needs to construct a single stego-document, should be as small as possible since sampling large numbers of documents from the communication channel is expensive in general. High query complexity causes not only difficulties in true sampling of documents but also a high total running time of the encoder and/or decoder.

Obviously, for nontrivial systems, i.e. for such of small insecurity and unreliability, there is a trade-off between these requirements, as depicted exemplary in Fig. 1. We analyze there three hypothetical universal stegosystems for cover documents of length n. As usually, we assume that $n := n(\kappa)$ is specified as a function of security parameter κ and that n is polynomially related with κ, i.e. $n(\kappa) = \mathsf{pol}(\kappa)$. To embed λ-bit secret messages per document the systems need q samples to achieve negligible insecurity and unreliability. $\mathbf{InSec}(\kappa)$ denotes in our paper insecurity over all wardens of *polynomial time complexity* and $\mathbf{UnRel}(\kappa)$ the unreliability of the system (for definitions see next section). For channels of sufficiently high entropy, $\mathcal{S}_2$ and $\mathcal{S}_3$ are scalable with respect to the rate, but $\mathcal{S}_1$ is not. System $\mathcal{S}_1$ would illustrate e.g. a *spread-spectrum* steganography: although, strictly speaking, not universal, such systems are very general. They need just one sample document to embed a secret message but their rate is very limited (see e.g. [9] for more discussion). Systems $\mathcal{S}_2$

[1]In the literature universal stegosystems are also called "black-box".

and $\mathcal{S}_3$ achieve almost optimal rate but a drawback of $\mathcal{S}_3$ is that its query complexity grows exponentially with respect to the rate.

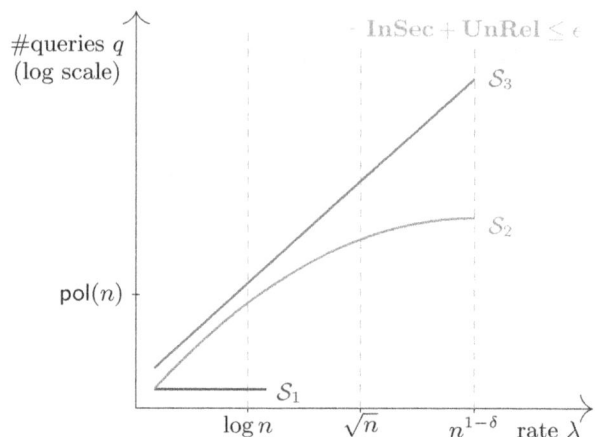

Figure 1: **Dependences between rate and number of queries of three hypothetical stegosystems of small insecurity and unreliability. The systems $\mathcal{S}_2$ and $\mathcal{S}_3$ are scalable with respect to the rate, but $\mathcal{S}_1$ is not. However to increase the rate in $\mathcal{S}_3$ the number of queries increases drastically.**

In this paper we investigate the problem of existence of *provably unconditionally* secure and reliably steganography, i.e. without using unproven assumptions like existence of one-way functions. The work emphasizes also on possible trade-offs between rate and query complexity for universal stegosystems. Particularly, we investigate if such scalable systems as $\mathcal{S}_2$ and $\mathcal{S}_3$ discussed above may exist. We study if it is possible to construct provable secure and reliable systems which can achieve specific rates, like e.g. square root rate, and analyze lower bounds on the query complexity for achieving this rate.

1.3 Previous Work

Secure Steganography and One-Way Functions. Beside providing a rigorous definition for computationally secure steganography, the main contribution of Hopper et al.'s work [14, 15] is demonstrating that a widely believed complexity-theoretic assumption – the existence of one-way functions – and access to a channel oracle are both necessary and sufficient conditions for the existence of secure and reliable steganography (Corollary 1 in [15]):

THEOREM 1 ([15], INFORMAL). *Relative to an oracle for channel $\mathcal{C}$, secure (and reliable) stegosystems exist if and only if one-way functions exist.*

This claim is now widely circulated in the literature. In her handbook [9] on steganography Fridrich writes: "One of the most intriguing implications of this complexity-theoretic view of steganography is the fact that secure stegosystems exist if and only if secure one-way (hash) functions exist [...]"

Unfortunately, as we show in this work the proof of this equivalence provided in [15] turns out to be incorrect in the stated form (see Section 3 for details). Moreover, we construct a universal stegosystem which is reliable and unconditionally secure, i.e. secure without any cryptographic assumptions (see Theorem 4). This disproves the claim of Theorem 1 in the sense that secure and reliable steganography exists independently of the existence of one-way functions. However, it should be noted that our construction needs super-exponential time.

Upper Bounds on the Insecurity and Unreliability. To provide secure and reliable steganography based on the existence of one-way functions, Hopper et al. construct a universal stegosystem using so called "rejecting sampling". Roughly speaking, in order to transmit a bit β, the encoder repeatedly samples from the cover-document distribution $\mathcal{C}$ until she gets a document s which is mapped to the given β by a pseudorandom function F_k indexed by the secret key k. This encoding method has been extended to embed multiple bit messages m per document in such a way that, using rejecting sampling, one searches for a document s with $F_k(s) = m$. The authors showed that the proposed stegosystem is secure and reliable and, since the existence of one-way functions implies pseudorandom functions (see [11]) they conclude the following:

THEOREM 2 ([15], INFORMAL). *There exists a universal stegosystem $\mathcal{S}(\kappa)$ with security parameter κ (describing the length of the secret key) that hides a $\lambda := \lambda(\kappa)$ bit message in a sequence of ℓ stego documents of a channel $\mathcal{C}$ and*
(a) $\mathcal{S}(\kappa)$ takes $q(\kappa) = \lambda 2^\lambda$ sample sequences, each containing ℓ cover-documents and
(b) it achieves insecurity $\mathbf{InSec}(\kappa)$ bounded from above by the term $\Phi_{\mathcal{C}}(\mathsf{pol}(\lambda 2^\lambda), \kappa)$ and unreliability $\mathbf{UnRel}(\kappa)$ bounded by $\Phi_{\mathcal{C}}(\lambda 2^\lambda, \kappa) + e^{-\lambda} + \lambda 2^{\lambda - \mathcal{H}(\mathcal{C}^\ell)}$,
where the function $\Phi_{\mathcal{C}}$ describes a term caused by the insecurity of the pseudorandom function used by the encoder and decoder and $\mathcal{H}(\mathcal{C}^\ell)$ denotes the min-entropy of ℓ consecutive documents of the channel.

Importantly, $\Phi_{\mathcal{C}}$ in the theorem above is defined relative to an oracle for channel $\mathcal{C}$. This means that an adversary that distinguishes between a randomly chosen function and a pseudorandom function indexed by a secret-key has also access to the oracle for $\mathcal{C}$ besides an access to the standard challenging oracle (for a formal definition and a discussion on this subject, see the next section). Thus, in the estimation

$$\mathbf{InSec}(\kappa) + \mathbf{UnRel}(\kappa) \leq \\ \Phi_{\mathcal{C}}(\mathsf{pol}(\lambda 2^\lambda), \kappa) + e^{-\lambda} + \lambda 2^{\lambda - \mathcal{H}(\mathcal{C}^\ell)} \quad (1)$$

the upper bound on the insecurity and unreliability of Hopper et al.'s system is negligible if and only if the term involving $\Phi_{\mathcal{C}}$ is negligible. We notice that, if the transmission rate exceeds the logarithm of the key length κ, then the proofs provided in [15] do not guarantee that unreliability and insecurity (recall, even against polynomial-time bounded warden) of the proposed stegosystems are negligible.

More precisely, in case the number of bits $\lambda := \lambda(\kappa)$ embedded in a single document grows asymptotically faster than $\log \kappa$, the term $\Phi_{\mathcal{C}}(\mathsf{pol}(\lambda 2^\lambda), \kappa)$ in the right hand side of Eq. (1) is not guaranteed to be negligible in κ even if the existence of pseudorandom functions is assumed. This is due to the fact that one assumes security of pseudorandom functions only against polynomial-time attacker and the term $\lambda 2^\lambda$ is super-polynomial for $\lambda \in \omega(\log \kappa)$. Thus, if a channel $\mathcal{C}$ allows to embed up to n bits per document, i.e. if its min-entropy $\mathcal{H}(\mathcal{C})$ is very high, the stegosystem of Hopper et al. is not scalable to meet optimum rate: for any

$\lambda \leq n$ its query complexity is $q = \lambda 2^\lambda$ but its insecurity and unreliability is guaranteed negligible only for $\lambda \in \mathcal{O}(\log n)$ since $n(\kappa) = \mathsf{pol}(\kappa)$. We illustrate this in Fig. 2.

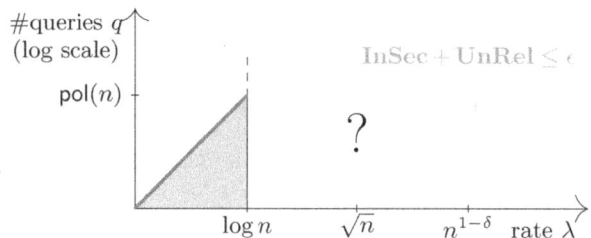

Figure 2: **Known results (under cryptographic assumptions): the green line shows the dependence between the rate and number of queries to ensure negligible insecurity and unreliability of Hopper et al.'s system (Eq. (1)). This bound is sharp: any system of rate and with number of queries in the red area is insecure or unreliable (due to Eq. (2) by Dedić et al.). The situation for $\lambda \in \omega(\log n)$ has remained open so far.**

Dedić et al. [6] proposed two new universal stegosystems with the upper bounds on the insecurity and unreliability similar to Eq. (1). Particularly, the bounds involve the term $\Phi_{\mathcal{C}}(\ell 2^b, \kappa)$, where b denotes the number of bits encoded per document, i.e. $b = \lambda / \ell$. Similarly to Hopper et al.'s system, if the number of bits b per document grows asymptotically faster than $\log \kappa$ then $\Phi_{\mathcal{C}}(\ell 2^b, \kappa)$ can grow faster than any negligible function, even if the encoder and decoder use pseudorandom functions.

Lower Bounds on the Insecurity and Unreliability. In [6], Dedić et al. prove (under cryptographic assumptions) the existence of channels such that the number of samples the encoder of any secure and reliable universal stegosystem must obtain from those channels is exponential in the number of bits embedded per document. In our terms, their result can be stated as:

THEOREM 3 ([6], INFORMAL). *For every universal stegosystem $\mathcal{S}(\kappa)$ which hides $\lambda := \lambda(\kappa)$ bits and takes $q := q(\kappa)$ samples per stego-document there exists a family of channels $\mathcal{C}(\kappa)$ such that*

$$\mathbf{InSec}(\kappa) + \mathbf{UnRel}(\kappa) \geq \frac{1}{2} - \frac{e \cdot q}{2^\lambda} - \Psi(q, \kappa) - o(1), \quad (2)$$

where $\mathbf{InSec}(\kappa)$ denotes the insecurity (against polynomial-time bounded wardens) and $\mathbf{UnRel}(\kappa)$ the unreliability of $\mathcal{S}(\kappa)$ on $\mathcal{C}(\kappa)$, and Ψ describes a term caused by the insecurity of the pseudorandom function used in the construction of $\mathcal{C}(\kappa)$.

They thus prove that the exponential query complexity $\lambda 2^\lambda$ of the universal systems by Hopper et al. is asymptotically optimal: indeed, if $q \in o(\lambda 2^\lambda)$ and $q \in \mathsf{pol}(\kappa)$, the right hand side of the inequality (2) goes to $1/2$. However, analogously to our discussion on the upper bound (1), we notice that the lower bound (2) is not meaningful if $q \in \omega(\mathsf{pol}(\kappa))$ (even if $q \in o(\lambda 2^\lambda)$), as the right hand side of the inequality does not necessarily need to go to 0 in this case. The red area in Fig. 2 illustrates this lower bound.

Later, Hopper et al. [15] provided another lower bound on the insecurity and unreliability. They show that for every universal stegosystem $\mathcal{S}(\kappa)$ of query complexity $q(\kappa)$ which hides $\lambda(\kappa)$ bits per document and for any κ there exists a channel such that:

$$\mathbf{InSec}(\kappa, q) + \mathbf{UnRel}(\kappa) \geq 1 - q/2^\lambda - 2^{-\kappa}, \qquad (3)$$

where $\mathbf{InSec}(\kappa, q)$, in contrast to $\mathbf{InSec}(\kappa)$, denotes insecurity over wardens of time complexity and size $> q(\kappa)$. Note that in the case of $\lambda \in \omega(\log n)$, bounds (2) and (3) are incomparable in the following sense. Due to (2), if in a reliable universal stegosystem $\mathcal{S}$ the number of queries q is dominated by 2^λ then there exists a *polynomial-time* bounded Warden whose advantage to detect $\mathcal{S}$ is big. The time complexity of the Warden must not dependend on the query complexity q of $\mathcal{S}$ but (2) needs the assumption that pseudorandom functions exist and it may be meaningless if the rate exceeds $\log n$. Bound (3) does not need any cryptographic assumption, it is meaningful for any λ but, the Warden who detects $\mathcal{S}$ needs time and size bigger than the query complexity q of $\mathcal{S}$. Thus, in cases of super-polynomial q, the Warden is not polynomial-time bounded anymore implying $\mathbf{InSec}(\kappa, q) \gg \mathbf{InSec}(\kappa)$.

1.4 Our Contribution

Thus, as shown above, if high rate is required we have no guarantee that the discussed systems are secure and reliable. And indeed, *no* secure and reliable universal stegosystem (irrespective of its query complexity) with rate larger than $\log n$ was known before, even under unproven cryptographic assumptions. Note that the secure stegosystems used in practice typically achieve a much larger rate of $\sqrt{n}$ [18]. A longstanding conjecture, the *Square Root Law of Steganographic Capacity* [8, 17, 19] deals with just this fact. It says that a rate of the form $(1 - \varepsilon)\sqrt{n}$ is always achievable (not necessarily in a setting of universal steganography). We thus have the situation, that the best known theoretical rate is $\log n$, while all practical rates are of order $\sqrt{n}$.

To close this gap between theory and practice, we introduce the notion of *rate-efficiency* and analyze its impact on steganography. We say that a stegosystem is *rate-efficient*, if there is a constant $1 > \alpha > 0$ such that the number of embedded bits in a stego-document of length n is at least n^α (in channels of sufficiently large entropy). One of the main results of this paper is the construction of a stegosystem that is scalable with respect to the rate up to n^α for every $\alpha < 1$. However, to achieve this rate, an exponential number of queries is needed. On the other hand we prove that this query complexity is minimal. Thus, such a system as $\mathcal{S}_2$ analyzed in Fig.1 cannot exist and we give a complete answer to the question illustrated in Fig. 2 of determining the relationship between rate and number of queries. For an illustration of our results see Fig. 3.

Speaking more precisely: In this paper we present, up to our best knowledge, the first secret-key universal stegosystem that is provably secure (in the complexity-theoretic setting), reliable, and it has nearly optimal rate. Moreover, the security and reliability do not rely on any unproven assumptions, like the existence of one-way functions, as long as the channel does not allow one to break the hard functions the stegosystem is based on. Furthermore, no channel that is sampleable in exponential time can break these hard functions.

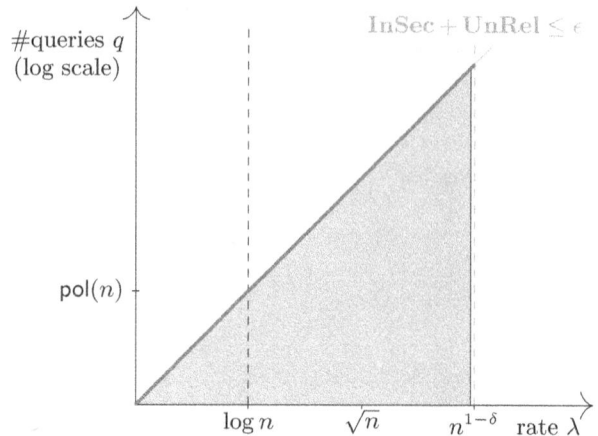

Figure 3: **Our results (without any assumptions): our stegosystem achieves negligible insecurity and unreliability for the number of queries depending on the rate as shown by the green line (Eq. (4)). This bound is sharp: any system of rate and query complexity in the red area is unreliable or insecure against polynomial-time bounded wardens (Eq. (5)).**

THEOREM 4 (INFORMAL). *There exists a universal stegosystem $\mathcal{S}$ that is unconditionally secure and reliable. Moreover $\mathcal{S}$ is rate-efficient.*

This stays in contrast with the claim of Hopper at al. [15] that provably secure steganography does imply existence of one-way functions (see Theorem 1). Analyzing the proofs in [15] we experienced the need for formal definitions and more careful handling of the security notion for cryptographic primitives *relative to an oracle for a channel* in order to conduct the typical cryptographic security-reductions. Otherwise, a security analysis can lead to misunderstandings and errors.

Our stegosystem is stateless and uses rejecting sampling in a similar way as the stateless secret-key construction proposed in [6] and the public-key system used in [1]. To achieve the security which does not rely on any unproven assumptions we construct pseudorandom functions of very high hardness based on constructions for sparse pseudorandom distributions due to Goldreich and Krawczyk [12]. Overall, our construction satisfies the following conditions:

THEOREM 5 (INFORMAL). *For every $1 > \alpha_1 \geq \alpha_2 > 0$, there exists a stegosystem $\mathcal{S}(\kappa)$, with security parameter κ, that has documents of length κ^{α_1}, such that for every channel $\mathcal{C}$ with min-entropy $\mathcal{H}(\mathcal{C}) > 2 \cdot \kappa^{\alpha_2}$, the system $\mathcal{S}$*

- *hides an $\ell \cdot \kappa^{\alpha_2}$ bit message, $\lambda(\kappa) = \kappa^{\alpha_2}$ bits per document sent, with $\ell \leq \mathsf{pol}(\kappa)$,*
- *takes $q(\kappa) \leq \kappa 2^{\kappa^{\alpha_2}}$ samples per κ^{α_2} bits, and*
- *has insecurity and unreliability negligible in κ (if $\mathcal{C}$ does not break the used hard functions):*

$$\mathbf{InSec}(\kappa) + \mathbf{UnRel}(\kappa) \leq \mathsf{negl}(\kappa). \qquad (4)$$

The running time of the stegosystem $\mathcal{S}$ is $2^{2^{o(\kappa)}}$ to ensure the unconditional security against polynomial wardens, but it achieves minimal query complexity. To prove that the query complexity of our construction is optimal, we show the following lower bound, improving the bounds (2) and (3):

THEOREM 6 (INFORMAL). *There exists a family of channels $\mathcal{C}(\kappa)$ such that for every universal stegosystem $\mathcal{S}(\kappa)$ where the encoder takes an expected number of $q(\kappa)$ queries, it holds that*

$$\mathbf{InSec}(\kappa) + \mathbf{UnRel}(\kappa) \geq \frac{1}{2} - \frac{e \cdot q}{2^\lambda} - o(1). \quad (5)$$

In the theorems $\mathbf{InSec}(\kappa)$ denotes, like in (2), the insecurity over polynomial-time bounded wardens and $\mathbf{UnRel}(\kappa)$ denotes the unreliability of stegosystem $\mathcal{S}(\kappa)$ on $\mathcal{C}(\kappa)$.

As mentioned in the introduction, we also show that the proof of Theorem 1 in [15] is incorrect and that the theorem is wrong in the stated form. This is a direct consequence of our Theorem 5.

1.5 Related Work

The running time of the rejecting sampling algorithm was improved by Kiayias et al. in [20]. They use *t-wise independent* families of functions instead of a pseudorandom function to choose corresponding documents from the channel. As a *t*-wise independent family utilizes much less random bits than a pseudorandom function, this decreases the running time of the algorithm. They also provide another refinement of the rejection sampling approach by proving that a key length of $(1 + o(1))\ell$ is sufficient in order to embed a message of length ℓ while achieving high security. The authors define the security of a stegosystem in an *information-theoretic* setting but they show that the results are also applicable to the computational model assuming the existence of pseudorandom functions. However, the system provided in [20] is rate-inefficient – it embeds 1 bit per document.

For some specific channels, Van Le and Kurosawa [21] proposed a stegosystem based on arithmetic coding that achieves a better rate than the universal systems proposed in [15] and [6]. However in the model assumed in [21] it is allowed that the system has access to additional knowledge of the channel. For some specific *families* of channels, like e.g. represented by Boolean functions, Liśkiewicz et al. [22] provided systems for secure and reliable steganography but, similarly to the results presented in [6, 13, 14, 15], the upper bound on insecurity of the construction in [22] is meaningless if the rate exceeds $\log n$.

Universal systems with optimum embedding rate are also a subject of intensive study using an information-theoretic modeling of secure steganography as defined in the influential work by Cachin [4]. In [24], Wang and Moulin have introduced a powerful information-theoretic framework for studying capacity in perfectly secure steganography. For relevant theoretical results and practical applications see also [2, 5, 7, 8, 23].

The paper is organized as follows. Due to space constraints, the formal definitions concerning steganography, cryptography and the security relative to a channel are skipped and we refer the reader to the literature, e.g. [6, 15]. The next section contains a short summary of our notations. Section 3 deals with the problems in the proof of Theorem 1. We analyze those problems and discuss possible solutions to them. In Section 4 two ensembles of pseudorandom functions of very high hardness are defined and in the subsequent section these ensembles are used to construct a universal stegosystem which is secure and efficient in terms of rate and reliability. This proves Theorems 4 and 5. In order to prove that our algorithm has almost optimal query complexity, Section 6

improves the lower bounds (2) and (3) of [6] and [15] that only work under certain circumstances. Our proof of Theorem 6 does without those circumstances. Finally, we discuss the conclusions one can draw from our work and possible future research directions.

2. NOTATIONS

Due to space constraints, we skip the formal security definitions and refer the reader to the literature, e.g. [6, 15].

Channel, Reliability, Security. Our stegosystems and cryptographic primitives will be sufficiently parameterized by the secret-key length κ. As usually, we will require that the ability of any polynomial-time algorithm to attack this constructions is lower than the inverse of every polynomial in κ. This is modeled by the notion of *negligible* function $\mathsf{negl} \colon \mathbb{N} \to [0,1]$, which satisfies that for every polynomial p, there is an $N_0 \in \mathbb{N}$ such that $\mathsf{negl}(N) < p(N)^{-1}$ for every $N \geq N_0$.

We denote the *min-entropy* of a probability distribution D as $\mathcal{H}(D)$. A *channel* $\mathcal{C}$ is a function, that maps for any $n \in \mathbb{N}$ (the *document length*) a sequence of documents h (the *history*) to a probability distribution $\mathcal{C}_{h,n}$ on documents of length n. A *stegosystem* $\mathcal{S} = [SE, SD]$ consists of two probabilistic algorithms SE and SD. The *encoder* SE takes a key k, a message $m \in \mathcal{M}_\kappa$ (the *message space*), and a history h and produces a sequence of ℓ documents (ℓ is the *output length* of $\mathcal{S}$), while the *decoder* SD tries to reconstruct m from those documents with the help of k and h. The *rate* b of the encoder is defined as $\log(|\mathcal{M}_\kappa|)/\ell$ and returns the number of bits that the encoder embeds into a single document. The encoder is allowed to draw $c \in \mathbb{N}$ (the *sample complexity*) samples from the channel $\mathcal{C}$. The *unreliability* $\mathbf{UnRel}_{\mathcal{S},\mathcal{C}}(\kappa)$ of the stegosystem $\mathcal{S}$ on channel $\mathcal{C}$ is the maximal probability that the decoding of a message fails. This is the same notation as we used in the introduction, where we skipped the mention of $\mathcal{C}$ and $\mathcal{S}$ to increase readability. An attacker (or *warden*) W on the stegosystem $\mathcal{S}$ on the channel $\mathcal{C}$ is allowed to give messages to a *challenging oracle* that either returns encodings of those messages or random documents. The *advantage* $\mathbf{Adv}_{W,\mathcal{S},\mathcal{C}}^{\mathrm{cha}}(\kappa)$ of W is its success probability in distinguishing those two cases. The maximal advantage of any warden W that runs in time t and makes q requests to the challenging oracle is the *insecurity* of $\mathcal{S}$ on $\mathcal{C}$ and denoted by $\mathbf{InSec}_{\mathcal{S},\mathcal{C}}^{\mathrm{cha}}(q, t, \kappa)$. By $\mathbf{InSec}_{\mathcal{S},\mathcal{C}}^{\mathrm{cha}}(\kappa)$ we mean the insecurity over all wardens of polynomial-time complexity. As with the unreliability, this is exactly the notion of the introduction, but in a parameterized form. The *insecurity* $\mathbf{InSec}_F^{\mathrm{prf}}(q, t, \kappa)$ of a *pseudorandom function* F is the maximal probability of any algorithm that runs in time t and makes q queries to an oracle, that either equals one of the pseudorandom functions or a totally random functions, to distinguish these cases.

Relativized Security. Clearly, the (in)security of a stegosystem $\mathbf{InSec}_{\mathcal{S},\mathcal{C}}^{\mathrm{cha}}(\cdot, \cdot, \cdot)$ depends on the concrete channel $\mathcal{C}$, as every adversary on $\mathcal{S}$ on channel $\mathcal{C}$ has oracle access to sample documents of $\mathcal{C}$. In order to base the security of a stegosystem on the security of a cryptographic primitive, a typical reduction works along the following lines: Suppose that there is a successful warden W on the stegosystem $\mathcal{S}$; Construct an attacker A on the cryptographic primitive that simulates W on $\mathcal{S}$; Prove that the advantage of A and W is very similar. Using such reductions, it is important to note that the attacker A on the cryptographic primitives completely simulates the warden W and the encoder of S (assuming a black-box access to the cryptographic primitive it is based on). As both W and S make calls to the sampling oracle of the channel, A also needs access to those samples. The need for this was already noted by Hopper et al. [13, 14, 15]. There are essentially two solutions to take the access to the sampling oracle into account:

- One assumes that the sampling oracle can be simulated in *polynomial time*. Hence, the simulation of W and S can be performed in polynomial time. As the typical requirement is that the cryptographic primitives remains secure against attackers that run in polynomial time, the security reduction remains valid.

- One assumes that the cryptographic primitive remains secure even if the attacker has access to the sampling oracle of the channel C. One then proceeds to define *relativized* versions of the common insecurity terms, e.g. we could define the insecurity $\mathbf{InSec}_{F,C}^{\mathrm{prf}}(q,t,\kappa)$ of a pseudorandom function F. It is the maximal probability of any algorithm that has access to the sampling oracle of the channel C, runs in time t and makes q queries to an oracle, that either equals one of the pseudorandom functions or a totally random functions, to distinguish these cases. Dedić et al. [6] were the first that gave a formal definition for this, but they did not use it consistently in their work.

Note that the assumption that the sampling oracle for channel C can be simulated in polynomial time is quite artificial: Arguably, the single most studied channels for steganography are those containing multimedia-files such as images or videos. Typically, we do not assume that one is able to sample uniformly from the set of all valid images or videos. This rules out the first possibility. On the other hand, the second possibility is completely valid, as we have access to these channels in real-life, but suspect that this access does not break the security of cryptographic primitives. Due to this advantage, we will use the second possibility in this work.

3. COMMENTS ON THE WORK OF HOPPER, LANGFORD AND VON AHN

The attentive reader may have noticed that the commonly used formulation of Hopper, Langford and von Ahn [13, 14, 15] does not bound the running time of the stegosystem, while the time complexity of the adversary is required to be bounded by a polynomial. In addition to giving the rejection-sampling stegosystem, they also argue that one-way functions are *necessary* for steganography:

THEOREM 7 ([15], INFORMAL). *For all channels C it is true: if secure and reliable steganography for C exists then there exist one-way functions relative to an oracle for C.*[2]

Since the proof of Theorem 7 is "black-box" with respect to the one-way functions it holds relative to the presence of the channel oracle for C, too. Thus, Hopper et al. conclude Theorem 1 (Corollary 1 in [15]) given in the introduction.

Combining Theorem 5 with Theorem 1 one would conclude that (1) relative to an oracle for channel C one-way functions

---

[2]Hopper et al. prove even stronger result using a weaker notion of security. Theorem 9 in [15] says that if there is a stegosystem S that is SS-KHA-$\mathcal{D}$-$\mathcal{C}$ secure for some hiddentext distribution $\mathcal{D}$ and some channel C, then there exists a pseudorandom generator, relative to an oracle for C.

exist and much more startling, that (2) **one-way functions exist in the standard model**, i.e., without assuming oracle access to the channel C. As a proof on the existence of one-way functions seems to be far away from our current knowledge, one must wonder at the validity of Theorem 1. Indeed, we found errors in the proof of Theorem 7 which consequently do not allow to conclude Theorem 1.

There are three issues concerning this proof. Firstly, the time complexity of the proposed *false entropy generator* (FEG), a kind of oracle used in the construction and the use of relativized primitives. The aim was to provide an algorithm for an FEG, assuming the existence of a stegosystem S that is SS-KHA-$\mathcal{D}$-$\mathcal{C}$ secure for some hidentext distribution $\mathcal{D}$ and some channel C (for the exact definitions, see [15]).

The proposed construction for an FEG uses, as a subroutine, the encoder of S having an oracle access to C. Since no restrictions on the running time of the encoder are given, it does not follow that the obtained algorithm for FEG is bounded by a polynomial. This problem can be fixed by assuming that the stegosystem runs in polynomial time. Note, however, that making the assumption of polynomial time complexity for stegosystems, the claim of [15, Section 4.3] concerning rate-optimality is false, as the proposed system requires exponential time.

Secondly, according to the definition, an FEG is a *function* (satisfying the conditions of FEG). However, the FEG relative to an oracle C does not seem to be deterministic, as it sometimes returns the samples generated by the channel oracle. This does not seem to be fixable easily, but one can make use of randomized cryptographic primitives in order to give an alternative proof.

The third obstacle still remains: In order to construct a cryptographic primitive out of a stegosystem, one needs to simulate the access to the channel oracle. If this simulation can be carried out in polynomial time, the constructed primitive is indeed efficient. But, as discussed in Section 2, such an assumption is quite artificial. And indeed, if the channel oracle can not be simulated in polynomial time, the constructed cryptographic primitive is not efficient. It seems that the only remedy to this is to define another way of *relativized primitives*, where the primitive has also access to the channel oracle as in this work.

4. PSEUDORANDOM FUNCTIONS OF VERY HIGH HARDNESS

We construct two families of pseudorandom functions that are secure against adversaries of exponential running times. Our result does not rely on any unproven assumptions but to construct the family, super-exponential time is needed.

Let $P = \{P_\kappa\}_{\kappa \in \mathbb{N}}$ and $Q = \{Q_\kappa\}_{\kappa \in \mathbb{N}}$ be two ensembles of discrete probability distributions. For a probabilistic algorithm A, the *advantage of A to distinguish P and Q* is defined as

$$\mathbf{Adv}_{A,P,Q}^{\mathrm{dist}}(\kappa) = \left| \Pr[A^{P_\kappa}(1^\kappa) = 1] - \Pr[A^{Q_\kappa}(1^\kappa) = 1] \right|,$$

where A^D has the ability to get samples distributed accordingly to D in unit time. The insecurity of P and Q is defined as $\mathbf{InSec}_{P,Q}^{\mathrm{dist}}(q,t,\kappa) = \max_A\{\mathbf{Adv}_{A,P,Q}^{\mathrm{dist}}(\kappa)\}$, where the maximum is taken over all algorithms that make an expected number of q queries to the probability distribution and run in expected time t. In order to simplify our notation, we sometimes identify a set M with the uniform distribution on M. If M and N are two finite sets, we hence write $\mathbf{Adv}_{A,M,N}^{\text{dist}}$, A^M, A^N and $\mathbf{InSec}_{M,N}^{\text{dist}}$ with the meaning that M and N are uniformly distributed.

We also introduce the relativized version $\mathbf{InSec}_{P,Q,\mathcal{C}}$ of the term $\mathbf{InSec}_{P,Q}$ and define it for parameters q, t, κ analogously as $\mathbf{InSec}_{\mathcal{F},\mathcal{C}}^{\text{prf}}$.

Next we recall the following definition of the *statistical distance* D_S between two discrete probability distributions on the same domain.

DEFINITION 1 (STATISTICAL DISTANCE). *Let P and Q be two discrete probability distributions on the same domain X. The statistical distance $D_S(P,Q)$ between P and Q is defined as $D_S(P,Q) = \frac{1}{2} \sum_{x \in X} |P(x) - Q(x)|$.*

By the following well-known theorem (see e.g. [10]) we know that the statistical distance is a stronger measure than the computational indistinguishability.

THEOREM 8. *Let $\{P_\kappa\}_{\kappa \in \mathbb{N}}$ and $\{Q_\kappa\}_{\kappa \in \mathbb{N}}$ be two probability distribution ensembles on the same domains and let $\mathcal{C}(\kappa)$ be a channel. Then it holds that for every function t and q and all $\kappa \in \mathbb{N}$: $\mathbf{InSec}_{P,Q,\mathcal{C}}^{\text{dist}}(q,t,\kappa) \leq q \cdot D_S(P_\kappa, Q_\kappa)$. Particularly we have $\mathbf{InSec}_{P,Q}^{\text{dist}}(q,t,\kappa) \leq q \cdot D_S(P_\kappa, Q_\kappa)$.*

In our stegosystem we will apply a super-polynomial time computable pseudorandom function based on an algorithm G that also takes super-polynomial time, which is given by the following result due to Goldreich and Krawczyk [12]. In order to simplify the notation throughout this and the next section, let α_1, α_2 be constants with $1 > \alpha_1 \geq \alpha_2 > 0$ and let

$$n = \kappa^{\alpha_1}, b = \kappa^{\alpha_2}, B = 2^b \cdot b, \text{ and } N = 2^n \cdot b. \quad (6)$$

THEOREM 9 (LEMMA 5, [12]). *Let $k(n)$ be any subexponential function in n. There are (nonpolynomial) generators which expand random strings of length n into pseudorandom string of length $k(n)$.*

This result immediately implies the following theorem:

THEOREM 10. *There is a deterministic algorithm G, that on input $x \in \{0,1\}^\kappa$ produces a string $G(x) \in \{0,1\}^N$, and a negligible function negl such that for every polynomial t in N, it holds $\mathbf{InSec}_{G(\{0,1\}^\kappa),\{0,1\}^N}^{\text{dist}}(1,t,\kappa) \leq \text{negl}(N)$. There is also another deterministic algorithm G', that on input $x \in \{0,1\}^\kappa$ produces a string $G'(x) \in \{0,1\}^B$, and a negligible function negl' such that for every polynomial t in B, it holds $\mathbf{InSec}_{G'(\{0,1\}^\kappa),\{0,1\}^B}^{\text{dist}}(1,t,\kappa) \leq \text{negl}'(B)$.*

The theorem says that no polynomial time algorithm in N (recall $N = 2^n \cdot b$) can distinguish between the distribution $G(\{0,1\}^\kappa)$ and the uniform distribution on $\{0,1\}^N$. Similarly, no polynomial time algorithm in B can distinguish $G'(\{0,1\}^\kappa)$ and the uniform distribution on $\{0,1\}^B$. The running time of G and G' is exponential in N (resp. B), while the running time of the distinguisher is polynomial in N (resp. B). Note that the usual construction to obtain a pseudorandom function from a pseudorandom generator due to Goldreich, Goldwasser and Micali [11] is not suited for our situation: Its security proof relies on the ability of the attacker on the function to simulate the generator. As a simulation of the generator takes exponential time and our attackers are polynomial, we can not use this approach. Instead, we observe that the generators produce very long

strings. We will interpret these strings as the table of a function.

For a bit string $\omega = \omega_1 \omega_2 \ldots$ of length $2^X \cdot Y$, for some positive integers X and Y, let the function $F_\omega: \{0,1\}^X \to \{0,1\}^Y$ be defined as

$$F_\omega(z) = \omega_{i_z \cdot Y} \omega_{i_z \cdot Y + 1} \ldots \omega_{(i_z + 1) \cdot Y - 1},$$

if z is the binary representation of the number i_z. For example, the bit string $\omega = 0111101100010110$ corresponds to the function $F_\omega: \{0,1\}^3 \to \{0,1\}^2$ with e.g. $F_\omega(000) = 01$, $F_\omega(001) = 11$, and $F_\omega(111) = 10$.

Moreover, let F_G denote the function ensemble $F_G := \{F_{G(x)}\}_{x \in \{0,1\}^\kappa}$ and $F_{G'} := \{F_{G'(x)}\}_{x \in \{0,1\}^\kappa}$. The definition of F_ω implies a bijection between $\{0,1\}^{2^X \cdot Y}$ and the set of all function from $\{0,1\}^X \to \{0,1\}^Y$, which we will denote by $\boldsymbol{F}_{X,Y}$. The following theorem shows that F_G is not distinguishable from $\boldsymbol{F}_{n,b}$ by any algorithm with time complexity $\text{pol}(N)$ and $F_{G'}$ is not distinguishable from $\boldsymbol{F}_{b,b}$ by any algorithm with time complexity $\text{pol}(B)$.

THEOREM 11. *For all functions q,t of κ, we have:*
$$\mathbf{InSec}_{F_G}^{\text{prf}}(q,t,\kappa) \leq \mathbf{InSec}_{G(\{0,1\}^\kappa),\{0,1\}^N}^{\text{dist}}(1, N \cdot q + t, \kappa) \text{ and}$$
$$\mathbf{InSec}_{F_{G'}}^{\text{prf}}(q,t,\kappa) \leq \mathbf{InSec}_{G'(\{0,1\}^\kappa),\{0,1\}^B}^{\text{dist}}(1, B \cdot q + t, \kappa).$$

The proof of the theorem relies simply on the fact that any polynomial-time adversary on F_G has only access to an excerpt of size $\text{poly}(\kappa)$. Theorem 10 states that even access to the whole string of length $N \gg \text{poly}(\kappa)$ does not help an adversary. The advantage of any adversary is thus only negligible.

PROOF. We only prove the theorem for F_G, as the proof for $F_{G'}$ is analogous.

Let A be any algorithm trying to distinguish between F_G and $\boldsymbol{F}_{n,b}$ with running time t by making q queries to the function oracle. The algorithm A has access to a function oracle f, which is either uniformly chosen from $\boldsymbol{F}_{n,b}$ or equal to $F_{G(x)}$ for a certain $x \in \{0,1\}^\kappa$. We will now construct a distinguisher Dist for G, such that

$$\left| \Pr[\text{Dist}^{G(\{0,1\}^\kappa)}(1^\kappa) = 1] - \Pr[\text{Dist}^{\{0,1\}^N}(1^\kappa) = 1] \right| =$$
$$\left| \Pr_{x \leftarrow \{0,1\}^\kappa}[A^{F_{G(x)}(\cdot)}(1^\kappa) = 1] - \Pr_{f \leftarrow \boldsymbol{F}_{n,b}}[A^{f(\cdot)}(1^\kappa) = 1] \right|.$$

The distinguisher Dist makes a single query to its distribution oracle and receives a bit string $\omega \in \{0,1\}^N$, which is either a random string or produced by $G(x)$. Whenever A makes a query z to its function oracle, Dist returns $F_\omega(z)$. In the end, Dist returns the same value as A. We thus have

$$\Pr_{x \leftarrow \{0,1\}^\kappa}[A^{F_{G(x)}(\cdot)}(1^\kappa) = 1] = \Pr[\text{Dist}^{G(\{0,1\}^\kappa)}(1^\kappa) = 1]$$

and because of the bijection between $\boldsymbol{F}_{n,b}$ and $\{0,1\}^N$, we have

$$\Pr_{f \leftarrow \boldsymbol{F}_{n,b}}[A^{f(\cdot)}(1^\kappa) = 1] = \Pr[\text{Dist}^{\{0,1\}^N}(1^\kappa) = 1].$$

The computation of $F_\omega(z)$ takes time $\mathcal{O}(N)$. As the running time of A is bounded by t and A makes at most q queries to its function oracle, the running time of Dist is bounded by $\mathcal{O}(N) \cdot q + t$. The distinguisher Dist performs 1 query. $\square$

5. RATE-EFFICIENT STEGANOGRAPHY

In this section we prove that there exists secure, reliable and rate-efficient steganography. Our result does not rely on any unproven assumption.

We will use the function families $F_G, F_{G'}$ of the previous section in the stegosystem of Backes and Cachin [1] to construct a universal stegosystem, which is unconditionally secure. As in the previous section, let α_1, α_2 be constants with $1 > \alpha_1 \geq \alpha_2 > 0$ and let n, b, N, B be as defined in eq. (6) in Section 4.

The rejecting sampling stegosystem $\mathcal{S} = [SE, SD]$ is described in Algorithm 1 and in Algorithm 2.

Algorithm 1: SE

In: key $k \in \{0,1\}^\kappa$, message $m \in \{0,1\}^{\ell \cdot b}$, history h
let $f := F_{G(k)}(\cdot)$; parse m into $m_1 m_2 \dots m_\ell$ with $|m_j| = b$;
for $j = 1$ *to* ℓ **do**
    let $i := 0$; sample $x \leftarrow \mathcal{C}_{h,n(\kappa)}$;
    while $f(x) \neq m_j$ *and* $i < \kappa \cdot 2^b$ **do**
        sample $x \leftarrow \mathcal{C}_{h,n(\kappa)}$; let $i := i + 1$;
    let $x_j := x$; append x_j to h;
return $x_1 x_2 \dots x_\ell$

Algorithm 2: SD

In: key $k \in \{0,1\}^\kappa$, documents $x_1 x_2 \dots x_\ell$
let $f := F_{G(k)}(\cdot)$;
return $f(x_1) f(x_2) \dots f(x_\ell)$

Backes and Cachin [1] prove that this stegosystem is secure against polynomial-time CHA-Wardens as long as the family of functions used is pseudorandom and as long as the number of bits embedded in a single document is at most $\log \kappa$. We will expand this result and prove that one can embed up to $o(\kappa)$ bits into a single document.

For any function $\hat{f} \in \boldsymbol{F}_{n,b}$, denote by $SE_{\hat{f}}(k, m, h)$ the run of SE if we replace $f = F_{G(k)}$ by $\hat{f}$ and by $SE_{\boldsymbol{F}_{n,b}}(k, m, h)$ the output distribution of SE_f, if f is chosen at random from $\boldsymbol{F}_{n,b}$. The following result is also due to Backes and Cachin and shows that $SE_{\boldsymbol{F}_{n,b}}$ and $\mathcal{C}$ are statistically close.

THEOREM 12 (PROPOSITION 1 IN [1]). [3] *If κ is a sufficiently large key-length, then there exists a constant $\eta < 1$ such that $D_S(P, \mathcal{C}_{h,n}) \leq \ell \cdot \left(2^{b - \mathcal{H}(\mathcal{C}_{h,n})} + \eta^{2^b \cdot \kappa} \right)$, where P is the probability distribution generated by $SE_{\boldsymbol{F}_{n,b}}(\cdot, m, h)$ upon random choice of m and fixed choice of h.*

As m is chosen by the Warden, we need to "randomize" the message embedded by SE. We will thus not embed m, but $\mathrm{CTR\$}(m, k)$ with the meaning of:

The output length of $\mathrm{CTR\$}(m, k)$ with $|m| = \ell \cdot b$ is $(\ell+1) \cdot b$. The insecurity of this construction can be reduced to the insecurity of $F_{G'}$ by the well known result of Bellare et al. [3]. As their reduction is black-box, the result also holds in a relativized setting.

---

[3] The exact wording of this Proposition and a corresponding proof can be found as Proposition 7 in the full version available under the link: www.zurich.ibm.com/~cca/papers/pkstego.pdf

---

Algorithm 3: $\mathrm{CTR\$}$

In: message $m \in \{0,1\}^{\ell \cdot b}$, key $k \in \{0,1\}^\kappa$
sample y from $\{0,1\}^b$; let $g = F_{G'(k)}(\cdot)$;
let
    $r = g(y) \| g((y+1) \bmod 2^b) \| \dots \| g((y + \ell - 1) \bmod 2^b)$;
return $(r \oplus m) \| y$

THEOREM 13. *The probability that a probabilistic algorithm A, that has access to the channel $\mathcal{C}$, with running time t, that makes q samples to an oracle, which on input $m \in \{0,1\}^{\ell \cdot b}$ either (a) produces random strings of length $(\ell+1) \cdot b$ or (b) $\mathrm{CTR\$}(m, k)$ for a uniformly chosen k, can distinguish between the two cases (a) and (b) is bounded by* $2 \mathbf{InSec}^{\mathrm{prf}}_{F_{G'}, \mathcal{C}}(\kappa) + \frac{\ell \cdot b \cdot (q-1)}{b \cdot 2^b}$.

This operation can be simply inverted with the knowledge of k and we will denote this operation by $\mathrm{CTR\$}^{-1}$. We hence use the stegosystem $\mathcal{S}' = [SE', SD']$ which uses $\mathrm{CTR\$}$ as

$$SE'(m, k, h) = SE(\mathrm{CTR\$}(m, k), k, h)$$

and

$$SD'(x_1 \dots x_\ell, k) = \mathrm{CTR\$}^{-1}(SD(x_1 \dots x_\ell, k), k).$$

By using the families $F_G, F_{G'}$, we prove that every channel with sufficient min-entropy that is sampleable in exponential time has a secure stegosystem. This analysis resembles the analysis in [1], but spells out the relation of $\mathbf{InSec}^{\mathrm{cha}}_{\mathcal{S}, \mathcal{C}}$ and $\mathbf{InSec}^{\mathrm{prf}}_{F_G, \mathcal{C}}$ respectively $\mathbf{InSec}^{\mathrm{prf}}_{F_G}$.

THEOREM 14. *The rejection sampling stegosystem $\mathcal{S}'$ on document length $n(\kappa) = n$ with the message space $\mathcal{M}_\kappa = \mathcal{U}(\{0,1\}^{\ell \cdot b})$ satisfies for every polynomials q, t in κ the following properties relative to channel $\mathcal{C}$:*

1. $\mathbf{InSec}^{\mathrm{cha}}_{\mathcal{S}', \mathcal{C}}(q, t, \kappa) \leq$
   $\mathbf{InSec}^{\mathrm{prf}}_{F_G, \mathcal{C}} \left(q(\ell+1)2^b \kappa , q(\ell+1)2^b \kappa + t , \kappa \right) +$
   $\mathbf{InSec}^{\mathrm{prf}}_{F_{G'}} \left(\ell+1 , (\ell+1)^2 , \kappa \right) +$
   $q(\ell+1) \left(2^{b - \mathcal{H}(\mathcal{C}_n)} + \eta^{2^b \kappa} \right) + \frac{(\ell+1)^2}{2^b} +$
   $2 \mathbf{InSec}^{\mathrm{prf}}_{F_{G'}, \mathcal{C}}(q, t, \kappa) + \frac{\ell \cdot b \cdot (q-1)}{b \cdot 2^b}$ *for a constant $\eta < 1$,*

2. $\mathbf{UnRel}_{\mathcal{S}', \mathcal{C}}(\kappa) \leq$
   $\mathbf{InSec}^{\mathrm{prf}}_{F_G, \mathcal{C}} \left((\ell+1)2^b \kappa , (\ell+1)2^b \kappa , \kappa \right) +$
   $(\ell+1) \cdot \exp(-\kappa) + (\ell+1)^2 \cdot \kappa^2 \cdot 2^{2b - \mathcal{H}(\mathcal{C}_n)}$.

PROOF. In order to bound the insecurity of the stegosystem, we construct for every warden W with running time t that makes q queries to its challenging oracle on the stegosystem $\mathcal{S}'$ with respect to the channel $\mathcal{C}$ an attacker A on the function family F_G such that

$$\left| \Pr_{k \leftarrow \{0,1\}^\kappa}[W^{\mathcal{C}, SE^{\mathcal{C}}(k, \cdot, \cdot)}(1^\kappa) = 1] - \Pr[W^{\mathcal{C}, OC(\cdot, \cdot)}(1^\kappa) = 1] \right| \leq$$

$$\mathbf{Adv}^{\mathrm{prf}}_{A, F_G, (\mathcal{C})}(A) + q \cdot (\ell+1) \cdot \left(2^{b - \mathcal{H}(\mathcal{C}_n)} + \eta^{2^b \cdot \kappa} \right) + \frac{(\ell+1)^2}{2^b}$$

$$+ \mathbf{InSec}^{\mathrm{prf}}_{F_{G'}} \left(\ell+1, (\ell+1)^2, \kappa \right) + 2 \mathbf{InSec}^{\mathrm{prf}}_{F_{G'}, \mathcal{C}}(q, t, \kappa)$$

$$+ \frac{\ell \cdot b \cdot (q-1)}{b \cdot 2^b}.$$

This yields the security of the stegosystem. Let W be any such warden on the stegosystem $\mathcal{S}$ with respect to the channel

$\mathcal{C}$. The attacker A has access to a function oracle f, which is either uniformly chosen from $\boldsymbol{F}_{n,b}$ or equal to $F_{G(k)}$ for a certain $k \in \{0,1\}^\kappa$. The attacker A simulates the warden W. Whenever W makes a query to the channel-oracle, A uses its channel-oracle to produce such a sample. Whenever W makes a query (m,h) to the challenging oracle, A uses the encoding algorithm $SE_f(k,m,h)$. The attacker A then returns the same result as W. If $f = F_{G(k)}$, the attacker A simply simulates the run of W against the stegosystem, i.e.,

$$\Pr_{k \leftarrow \{0,1\}^\kappa}[A^{F_{G(k)}(\cdot)}(1^\kappa) = 1] =$$
$$\Pr_{k \leftarrow \{0,1\}^\kappa}[W^{\mathcal{C},SE^{\mathcal{C}}(k,\cdot,\cdot)}(1^\kappa) = 1].$$

If f is truly randomly and $m = m_1 m_2 \ldots m_\ell$ is a message of length $\ell \cdot b$ such that $m_i \neq m_j$ for every $i \neq j$, we can think of $SE_f(m,k,h)$ as ℓ-fold product of the probability distribution $SE_f(m_i,k,h)$, where f is chosen randomly for every i.

The output of $SE_f(m_i,k,h)$ is nearly identical to the channel (see Theorem 12), if the corresponding message of length b is also chosen uniformly. Theorem 13 implies that for W, the difference between the behavior of $SE_f(m_i,k,h)$ on a uniformly chosen message m_i or an m_i generated by CTR\$ is bounded by $2 \, \mathbf{InSec}^{\mathrm{prf}}_{F_{G'},\mathcal{C}}(q,t,\kappa) + \frac{\ell \cdot b \cdot (q-1)}{b \cdot 2^b}$.

As we do not give m to SE, but rather the message $m' = \mathrm{CTR\$}(m,k) = m'_1 m'_2 \ldots m'_{\ell+1}$, the probability that there are $i \neq j$ such that $m'_i = m'_j$ is at most

$$\mathbf{InSec}^{\mathrm{prf}}_{F_{G'}}(\ell+1, (\ell+1)^2, \kappa) + \frac{(\ell+1)^2}{2^b},$$

by constructing an attacker on $F_{G'}$ which guesses values $x_1, \ldots, x_{\ell+1}$ and tests, whether $f(x_1), f(x_2), \ldots, f(x_{\ell+1})$ are pairwise different.

As statistical distance is stronger than computational indistinguishability (see Theorem 8), we thus know that there is a constant $\eta < 1$ such that

$$\left| \Pr_{f \leftarrow \boldsymbol{F}_{n,b}}[W^{\mathcal{C},SE_f}(1^\kappa) = 1] - \Pr[W^{\mathcal{C},OC(\cdot,\cdot)}(1^\kappa) = 1] \right| \leq$$
$$q \cdot (\ell+1) \left(2^{b - \mathcal{H}(\mathcal{C}_n)} + \eta^{2^b \cdot \kappa} \right) + 2 \, \mathbf{InSec}^{\mathrm{prf}}_{F_{G'}}(q,t,\kappa) +$$
$$\frac{\ell \cdot b \cdot (q-1)}{b \cdot 2^b} + \mathbf{InSec}^{\mathrm{prf}}_{F_{G'}}(\ell+1, (\ell+1)^2, \kappa) + \frac{(\ell+1)^2}{2^b},$$

as W makes at most q calls to its challenging oracle. This concludes the statement concerning the advantage of A. The simulation of each call to SE_f can be carried out in time $\mathcal{O}((\ell+1) \cdot 2^b \cdot \kappa)$ if one has access to the channel oracle. The number of calls to the function oracle f is bounded by $q \cdot (\ell+1) \cdot 2^b \cdot \kappa$ The running time of A is thus at most $q \cdot \mathcal{O}((\ell+1) \cdot 2^b \cdot \kappa) + t$ and the number of queries of A is at most $q \cdot (\ell+1) \cdot 2^b \cdot \kappa$.

Concerning the reliability, we construct for every message m and every legal history h a different attacker $A_{m,h}$ against F_G. The attacker $A_{m,h}$ with function oracle f computes $m' = SD_f(k, SE_f(k,m,h))$ and returns 1 if $m = m'$. If $f = F_{G(k)}$, we have

$$\Pr_{k \leftarrow \{0,1\}^\kappa}[A_{m,h}^{F_{G(k)}(\cdot)}(1^\kappa) = 1] =$$
$$\Pr_{k \leftarrow \{0,1\}^\kappa}[m \neq SD(k, SE(k,m,h))].$$

If f is a totally random function from $\boldsymbol{F}_{n,b}$ and all samples $x_1, x_2, \ldots$ taken from the channel oracle $\mathcal{C}$ are different, the probabilities $\Pr[f(x_i) = m_j]$ are independent, as we can assume that a new random function is evaluated on each x_i. Denote the event that all of the x_i are pairwise different with $\overline{\mathrm{Coll}}$. The probability that none of this samples evaluates to m is then bounded by

$$\Pr_{f \leftarrow \boldsymbol{F}_{n,b}}[m \neq SD(SE_f(m,h)) \mid \overline{\mathrm{Coll}}] \leq$$
$$\sum_{j=1}^{\ell+1} \prod_{i=1}^{2^b \cdot \kappa} \Pr_{f \leftarrow \boldsymbol{F}_{n,b}}[f(x_i) \neq m_j] \leq$$
$$(\ell+1) \cdot \left(1 - \frac{1}{2^b}\right)^{2^b \cdot \kappa} \leq (\ell+1) \cdot \exp(-\kappa). \qquad (*)$$

By definition, the maximal probability of any element from the channel is bounded from above by $2^{-\mathcal{H}(\mathcal{C}_n)}$. The probability that $x_i = x_{i'}$ for $i \neq i'$ is thus bounded by $2^{-\mathcal{H}(\mathcal{C}_n)}$. Hence

$$\Pr[\mathrm{Coll}] \leq ((\ell+1) \cdot \kappa \cdot 2^b)^2 \cdot 2^{-\mathcal{H}(\mathcal{C}_n)} =$$
$$(\ell+1)^2 \cdot \kappa^2 \cdot 2^{2b - \mathcal{H}(\mathcal{C}_n)}. \qquad (**)$$

If $p = \Pr[\mathrm{Coll}]$, we can combine $(*)$ and $(**)$ and conclude

$$\Pr_{f \leftarrow \boldsymbol{F}_{n,b}}[m \neq SD(SE_f(m,h))] =$$
$$\Pr_{f \leftarrow \boldsymbol{F}_{n,b}}[m \neq SD(SE_f(m,h)) \mid \overline{\mathrm{Coll}}] \cdot (1-p)$$
$$+ \Pr_{f \leftarrow \boldsymbol{F}_{n,b}}[m \neq SD(SE_f(m,h)) \mid \mathrm{Coll}] \cdot p \leq$$
$$(\ell+1) \cdot \exp(-\kappa) + (\ell+1)^2 \cdot \kappa^2 \cdot 2^{2b - \mathcal{H}(\mathcal{C}_n)}.$$

We thus have

$$\left| \Pr_{k \leftarrow \{0,1\}^\kappa}[A_{m,h}^{F_{G(k)}(\cdot)}(1^\kappa) = 1] - \Pr_{f \leftarrow \boldsymbol{F}_{n,b}}[A_{m,h}^{f(\cdot)}(1^\kappa) = 1] \right| =$$
$$\left| \Pr_{k \leftarrow \{0,1\}^\kappa}[m \neq SD(SE(k,m,h))] - \Pr_{f \leftarrow \boldsymbol{F}_{n,b}}[A_m^{f(\cdot)}(1^\kappa) = 1] \right| \geq$$
$$\Pr_{k \leftarrow \{0,1\}^\kappa}[m \neq SD(SE(k,m,h))] -$$
$$(\ell+1) \cdot \exp(-\kappa) - (\ell+1)^2 \cdot \kappa^2 \cdot 2^{2b - \mathcal{H}(\mathcal{C}_n)}.$$

We can thus conclude

$$\mathbf{UnRel}_{\mathcal{S}',\mathcal{C}}(\kappa) \leq$$
$$\mathbf{InSec}^{\mathrm{prf}}_{F_G} \left((\ell+1) \cdot 2^b \cdot \kappa, t_C \cdot (\ell+1) \cdot 2^b \cdot \kappa, \kappa \right)$$
$$+ (\ell+1) \cdot \exp(-\kappa) + (\ell+1)^2 \cdot \kappa^2 \cdot 2^{2b - \mathcal{H}(\mathcal{C}_n)}.$$

The simulation of the call to SE_f can be carried out in time $\mathcal{O}((\ell+1) \cdot 2^b \cdot \kappa)$ with $2^b \cdot \kappa$ calls to the function oracle f. The running time of A_m is thus at most $\mathcal{O}((\ell+1) \cdot 2^b \cdot \kappa) + t$ and the number of queries of A is at most $(\ell+1) \cdot 2^b \cdot \kappa$. $\square$

By combining Theorem 10, Theorem 11 and Theorem 14 together, we can conclude the existence of a secure black-box stegosystem (see Theorem 4 and 5 for an informal statement) and in particular:

THEOREM 15. *Let $\mathcal{C}$ be a channel and let α_1, α_2 be constants with $1 > \alpha_1 \geq \alpha_2 > 0$. Furthermore, let negl_G and*

$\mathsf{negl}_{G'}$ be two negligible functions such that for every polynomial t, it holds that

$$\mathbf{InSec}^{\mathrm{dist}}_{G(\{0,1\}^\kappa),\{0,1\}^N,\mathcal{C}}(1,t,\kappa) \le \mathsf{negl}_G(N),$$

$$\mathbf{InSec}^{\mathrm{dist}}_{G'(\{0,1\}^\kappa),\{0,1\}^B,\mathcal{C}}(1,t,\kappa) \le \mathsf{negl}_{G'}(B).$$

Let $n(\kappa) = \kappa^{\alpha_1}$ be the document length and the message space $\mathcal{M}_\kappa = \mathcal{U}(\{0,1\}^{\ell \cdot b})$ be with $1 \le b \le \kappa^{\alpha_2}$. If $\mathcal{H}(\mathcal{C}_{n(\kappa)}) > 2b$ and $(\ell+1) \cdot b \le \mathsf{pol}(\kappa)$, then $\mathcal{S}'$ is a secure, reliable and rate-efficient stegosystem on $\mathcal{C}$.

PROOF. Recall that $N = 2^n \cdot b$ and $B = 2^b \cdot b$. Assume W is a Warden with $\mathbf{Adv}^{\mathrm{cha}}_{\mathcal{C},\mathcal{S},W}(\kappa) = \mathbf{InSec}^{\mathrm{cha}}_{\mathcal{S},\mathcal{C}}(q,t,\kappa)$. Theorem 14 then implies that

$\mathbf{InSec}^{\mathrm{cha}}_{\mathcal{S},\mathcal{C}}(q,t,\kappa) \le$

$\mathbf{InSec}^{\mathrm{prf}}_{F_G,\mathcal{C}}\left(q(\ell+1)2^b\kappa,\ (\ell+1)2^b\kappa+t,\ \kappa\right) +$

$q \cdot (\ell+1)\left(2^{b-\mathcal{H}(\mathcal{C}_n)} + \eta^{2^b \cdot \kappa}\right) + \dfrac{(\ell+1)^2}{2^b} + \dfrac{\ell \cdot b \cdot (q-1)}{b \cdot 2^b} +$

$\mathbf{InSec}^{\mathrm{prf}}_{F_{G'}}\left(\ell+1,(\ell+1)^2,\kappa\right) + 2\,\mathbf{InSec}^{\mathrm{prf}}_{F_{G'},\mathcal{C}}(q,t,\kappa)$

for a constant $\eta < 1$. Note that the terms $q \cdot (\ell+1) \cdot \eta^{2^b \cdot \kappa}$, $\frac{(\ell+1)^2}{2^b}$, $\frac{\ell \cdot b \cdot (q-1)}{b \cdot 2^b}$ and $q \cdot (\ell+1) \cdot 2^{b-\mathcal{H}(\mathcal{C}_n)}$ are negligible in κ as $\mathcal{C}$ has sufficient min-entropy. There is thus a negligible function negl such that

$\mathbf{InSec}^{\mathrm{cha}}_{\mathcal{S},\mathcal{C}}(q,t,\kappa) \le$

$\mathbf{InSec}^{\mathrm{prf}}_{F_G,\mathcal{C}}\left(q(\ell+1)2^b\kappa,\ q(\ell+1)\cdot 2^b\kappa+t,\ \kappa\right) +$

$\mathbf{InSec}^{\mathrm{prf}}_{F_{G'}}\left(\ell+1,(\ell+1)^2,\kappa\right) + 2\,\mathbf{InSec}^{\mathrm{prf}}_{F_{G'},\mathcal{C}}(q,t\cdot,\kappa) +$

$\mathsf{negl}(\kappa).$

By using Theorem 11, we have

$\mathbf{InSec}^{\mathrm{prf}}_{F_G,\mathcal{C}}\left(q \cdot (\ell+1) \cdot 2^b \cdot \kappa, q \cdot \cdot (\ell+1) \cdot 2^b \cdot \kappa + t, \kappa\right) \le$

$\mathbf{InSec}^{\mathrm{dist}}_{G(\{0,1\}^\kappa),\{0,1\}^N,\mathcal{C}}\big(1,\ Nq(\ell+1)2^b\kappa +$

$\qquad\qquad q(\ell+1)2^b\kappa + t,\ \kappa\big).$

As $q,t,\ell,b \le \mathsf{pol}(\kappa)$, we can bound this term by

$\mathbf{InSec}^{\mathrm{dist}}_{G(\{0,1\}^\kappa),\{0,1\}^N,\mathcal{C}}\big(1,\ Nq(\ell+1)2^b\kappa +$

$\qquad\qquad q(\ell+1)2^b\kappa + t,\ \kappa\big) \le$

$\mathbf{InSec}^{\mathrm{dist}}_{G(\{0,1\}^\kappa),\{0,1\}^{2^n \cdot b},\mathcal{C}}\left(1,\mathsf{pol}(N),\kappa\right).$

This insecurity is negligible by the assumption and there is thus a negligible function negl' such that

$\mathbf{InSec}^{\mathrm{prf}}_{F_G,\mathcal{C}}\left(q \cdot (\ell+1) \cdot 2^b \cdot \kappa, q \cdot (\ell+1) \cdot 2^b \cdot \kappa + t, \kappa\right) \le$

$\mathsf{negl}'(\kappa).$

Furthermore, Theorem 11 also implies

$\mathbf{InSec}^{\mathrm{prf}}_{F_{G'}}\left(\ell+1,(\ell+1)^2,\kappa\right) + 2\,\mathbf{InSec}^{\mathrm{prf}}_{F_{G'},\mathcal{C}}(q,t,\kappa) \le$

$\mathbf{InSec}^{\mathrm{dist}}_{G'(\{0,1\}^\kappa),\{0,1\}^B,\mathcal{C}}\left(1,B \cdot (\ell+1) + (\ell+1)^2,\kappa\right)$

$+ 2\,\mathbf{InSec}^{\mathrm{dist}}_{G'(\{0,1\}^\kappa),\{0,1\}^B,\mathcal{C}}\left(1,B \cdot q + t,\kappa\right)$

As $q,t,\ell,b \le \mathsf{pol}(\kappa)$, we can bound this term by

$\mathbf{InSec}^{\mathrm{dist}}_{G'(\{0,1\}^\kappa),\{0,1\}^B,\mathcal{C}}\left(1,B \cdot (\ell+1) + (\ell+1)^2,\kappa\right)$

$+ \mathbf{InSec}^{\mathrm{dist}}_{G'(\{0,1\}^\kappa),\{0,1\}^B,\mathcal{C}}\left(1,B \cdot q + t,\kappa\right) \le$

$3\,\mathbf{InSec}^{\mathrm{dist}}_{G'(\{0,1\}^\kappa),\{0,1\}^B,\mathcal{C}}(1,\mathsf{pol}(N),\kappa)$

This insecurity is negligible in κ by assumption and there is thus a negligible function negl'' such that

$\mathbf{InSec}^{\mathrm{prf}}_{F_{G'},\mathcal{C}}\left(\ell+1,(\ell+1)^2,\kappa\right) + 2\,\mathbf{InSec}^{\mathrm{prf}}_{F_{G'}}(q,t,\kappa) \le$

$\mathsf{negl}''(\kappa).$

In conclusion, we have

$$\mathbf{InSec}^{\mathrm{cha}}_{\mathcal{S},\mathcal{C}}(q,t,\kappa) \le \mathsf{negl}(\kappa) + \mathsf{negl}'(\kappa) + \mathsf{negl}''(\kappa).$$

The stegosystem $\mathcal{S}$ is thus secure on $\mathcal{C}$.

Concerning the unreliability, we can proceed similarly. Theorem 14 implies that

$\mathbf{UnRel}_{\mathcal{S},\mathcal{C}}(\kappa) \le$

$\mathbf{InSec}^{\mathrm{prf}}_{F_G,\mathcal{C}}\left((\ell+1) \cdot 2^b \cdot \kappa, (\ell+1) \cdot 2^b \cdot \kappa, \kappa\right) +$

$(\ell+1) \cdot \exp(-\kappa) + (\ell+1)^2 \cdot \kappa^2 \cdot 2^{2b-\mathcal{H}(\mathcal{C}_n)}.$

Due to sufficient min-entropy of $\mathcal{C}$ and the fact, that $\ell,b \le \mathsf{pol}(\kappa)$, there is a negligible function negl such that

$\mathbf{InSec}^{\mathrm{prf}}_{F_G,\mathcal{C}}\left((\ell+1) \cdot 2^b \cdot \kappa, (\ell+1) \cdot 2^b \cdot \kappa, \kappa\right) +$

$(\ell+1) \cdot \exp(-\kappa) + (\ell+1)^2 \cdot \kappa^2 \cdot 2^{2b-\mathcal{H}(\mathcal{C}_n)} \le$

$\mathbf{InSec}^{\mathrm{prf}}_{F_G,\mathcal{C}}\left((\ell+1) \cdot 2^b \cdot \kappa, (\ell+1) \cdot 2^b \cdot \kappa, \kappa\right) + \mathsf{negl}(\kappa).$

As above, Theorem 11 shows that

$\mathbf{InSec}^{\mathrm{prf}}_{F_G,\mathcal{C}}\left((\ell+1) \cdot 2^b \cdot \kappa, (\ell+1) \cdot 2^b \cdot \kappa, \kappa\right) + \mathsf{negl}(\kappa) \le$

$\mathbf{InSec}^{\mathrm{dist}}_{G(\{0,1\}^\kappa),\{0,1\}^N,\mathcal{C}}\big(1,\ N(\ell+1)2^b\kappa +$

$\qquad\qquad (\ell+1)2^b\kappa,\ \kappa\big) + \mathsf{negl}(\kappa).$

As $\ell,b \le \mathsf{pol}(\kappa)$, this is bounded by

$\mathbf{InSec}^{\mathrm{dist}}_{G(\{0,1\}^\kappa),\{0,1\}^N,\mathcal{C}}\big(1,\ N(\ell+1)2^b\kappa +$

$\qquad\qquad (\ell+1)2^b\kappa,\ \kappa\big) \le$

$\mathbf{InSec}^{\mathrm{dist}}_{G(\{0,1\}^\kappa),\{0,1\}^N,\mathcal{C}}\left(1,\mathsf{pol}(N),\kappa\right) + \mathsf{negl}(\kappa).$

The insecurity is negligible in N by assumption and there is thus a negligible function negl' such that

$$\mathbf{UnRel}_{\mathcal{S},\mathcal{C}}(\kappa) \le \mathsf{negl}'(\kappa).$$

The stegosystem $\mathcal{S}$ is thus reliable on $\mathcal{C}$.

As we embed $b \le \kappa^{\alpha_2}$ bits into a single document, the transmission rate $b(\kappa)$ is equal to b. As $\mathcal{H}(\mathcal{C}_n) \le \kappa^{\alpha_1}$, the stegosystem $\mathcal{S}$ is rate-efficient on $\mathcal{C}$, as α_1,α_2 are constants and as long as b is large enough. $\square$

Note that the precondition concerning the negligible functions negl_G, $\mathsf{negl}_{G'}$ is always fulfilled, if the channel oracle can be simulated in time $\mathsf{poly}(N)$. This is due to Theorem 11, that states the security of the pseudorandom function.

Dedić et al. [6] introduced the family $\mathcal{F}$ of *pseudorandom flat-h channels* and proved that every time- and rate-efficient stegosystem for $\mathcal{F}$ is either insecure or unreliable (under the cryptographic assumption that efficient pseudorandom functions exist). The running-time of every rate-efficient, secure and reliable stegosystem for $\mathcal{F}$ is thus at least superpolynomial. To the best of our knowledge, there is no such stegosystem known for $\mathcal{F}$. We therefore give the first secure, reliable and rate-efficient stegosystem for this family of channels:

COROLLARY 1. *The stegosystem S' is rate-efficient, secure and reliable on the family of pseudorandom flat-h channels.*

6. UNCONDITIONAL LOWER BOUND

In order to give an unconditional lower bound, we make use of a lower bound by Dedić et al. [6]. By providing the warden W with an efficient test, whether a document belongs to the support of the channel, they prove:

THEOREM 16 ([6]). *For every universal (not necessarily of polynomial-time complexity) stegosystem $S(\kappa)$ which hides $\lambda := \lambda(\kappa)$ bits and takes $q := q(\kappa)$ samples per stego-document there exists a family of channels $C(\kappa)$ such that*

$$\mathbf{InSec}^*(\kappa) + \mathbf{UnRel}(\kappa) \geq \frac{1}{2} - \frac{e \cdot q}{2^\lambda} - o(1),$$

where $\mathbf{InSec}^*$ denotes the insecurity against polynomial wardens with an auxiliary oracle for testing membership in the support of $C(\kappa)$, and $\mathbf{UnRel}$ denotes the unreliability of $S(\kappa)$ on $C(\kappa)$.

Dedić et al. then argue that the assumption that a warden has an oracle for membership-testing is not feasible, if the channel is chosen completely random. By making use of the fact that the warden can choose a history, while the stegoencoder can not, we will show how an *efficient* warden is able to test membership of a completely random channel.

Let $\boldsymbol{S}_n$ be the set of all subsets of $\{0,1\}^n$ of cardinality $n/2$. For $S \in \boldsymbol{S}_n$, let C_S be the following channel, where $\vec{1}$ denotes the vector of length n that contains a 1 at every position:

- $C(S)_{\varnothing,n}$ is the uniform distribution on $\{0,1\}^n$.
- $C(S)_{\vec{1}\|d,n}$ is the uniform distribution on all strings in $\{0,1\}^n$ that start with 1, if $d \in S$ or the uniform distribution on all strings in $\{0,1\}^n$ that start with 0, if $d \notin S$ (i.e. the first position indicates the membership of d in S).
- $C(S)_{h,n}$ is the uniform distribution on S for all other histories.

The warden W for the family $\{C(S) \mid S \in \boldsymbol{S}_n\}_{n \in \mathbb{N}}$ now works as follows: It randomly chooses a history $h \leftarrow \{0,1\}^n \setminus \{\vec{1}\}$ and $m = 00\ldots0$ – a message containing ℓ 0-bits – and gets the results $d_1, d_2, \ldots, d_\ell$ from the challenging oracle on h and m. For $i \in \{1, \ldots, \ell\}$, it takes a sample $s_i \leftarrow C(S)_{\vec{1}\|d_i,n}$. If every s_i starts with 1, the warden returns "Non-Stego" and else "Stego". The warden W is thus able to test membership in S efficiently by making use of the channel. Note that the stegoencoder can not make use of these capabilities of $C(S)$ as it can only make queries to $C_{h,n}$, where h does not start with $\vec{1}$. We use here the definition for channel access as in [15], which assumes that the encoder has an access to the marginal channel distributions C_h for the histories h started with adversarially chosen prefixes.

We can thus efficiently simulate an oracle for membership-testing and Theorem 16 thus implies (the formal statement of Theorem 6 in Introduction):

THEOREM 17. *For every universal (not necessarily polynomial-time bounded) stegosystem $S(\kappa)$ which hides $\lambda := \lambda(\kappa)$ bits and takes $q := q(\kappa)$ samples per stego-document there exists a family of channels $C(\kappa)$ such that*

$$\mathbf{InSec}(\kappa) + \mathbf{UnRel}(\kappa) \geq \frac{1}{2} - \frac{e \cdot q}{2^\lambda} - o(1),$$

where $\mathbf{InSec}$ denotes the insecurity against polynomial wardens and $\mathbf{UnRel}$ denotes the unreliability of $S(\kappa)$ on $C(\kappa)$.

Note that in contrast to Theorem 3, no cryptographic assumption is necessary and in contrast to Theorem 16, no membership-oracle is necessary. Our lower bound thus holds unconditionally. Furthermore, this lower bound holds even when the running time of the stegosystem S is much larger (say 2^{2^κ}) than the running time of W (say $\mathsf{pol}(\kappa)$).

Note that this method only works because of the asymmetry between Alice and Warden: While Warden has oracle-access for all possible histories, Alice can only use the history chosen by Warden.

7. CONCLUSIONS AND FURTHER WORK

We first gave a secure, reliable and rate-efficient stegosystem by using pseudorandom functions of very high hardness. The running time of the stegosystem is roughly $2^{2^{o(\kappa)}}$. The work of Dedić et al. [6] gives the best known lower bound of a running time of $\omega(\mathsf{pol}(\kappa))$ for any universal secure, reliable stegosystem (under cryptographic assumptions and of the rate $\omega(\log \kappa)$). We proved that by making use of the imbalance between encoder and warden, this lower bound also holds without any assumption and for any rate-efficient stegosystem. This immediately gives rise to the question, whether one can shrink the gap between $2^{2^{o(\kappa)}}$ and $\omega(\mathsf{pol}(\kappa))$, by either giving a more efficient stegosystem or by the construction of more difficult channels. If the requirements of a universal stegosystem seem too strict, one can proceed similarly to Liśkiewicz et al. [22] and try to find secure, reliable, and rate-efficient stegosystems for a large family $\mathcal{F}$ of channels. It is still open how complex $\mathcal{F}$ can be for secure, reliable, efficient and rate-efficient stegosystems.

We also showed that the common phrase "Steganography is Cryptography" is provably wrong as the communication channel is a very important part of the steganographic setting. We would hope that this motivates other authors to conduct theoretical and practical research on this fascinating topic.

8. REFERENCES

[1] M. Backes and C. Cachin. Public-key steganography with active attacks. In *Proc. TCC*, volume 3378 of *Lecture Notes in Computer Science*, pages 210–226. Springer, 2005.

[2] F. Balado and D. Haughton. Optimum perfect universal steganography of finite memoryless sources. *CoRR*, abs/1410.2659, 2014.

[3] M. Bellare, A. Desai, E. Jokipii, and P. Rogaway. A concrete security treatment of symmetric encryption. In *Proc. FOCS*, pages 394–403. IEEE, 1997.

[4] C. Cachin. An information-theoretic model for steganography. *Information and Computation*, 192(1):41–56, 2004.

[5] P. Comesaña and F. Pérez-González. On the capacity of stegosystems. In *Proc. MM&Sec*, pages 15–24. ACM, 2007.

[6] N. Dedić, G. Itkis, L. Reyzin, and S. Russell. Upper and lower bounds on black-box steganography. *Journal of Cryptology*, 22(3):365–394, 2009.

[7] T. Filler and J. Fridrich. Fisher information determines capacity of ε-secure steganography. In *Proc. IH*, volume

5806 of *Lecture Notes in Computer Science*, pages 31–47. Springer, 2009.

[8] T. Filler, A. D. Ker, and J. J. Fridrich. The square root law of steganographic capacity for Markov covers. In *Proc. EI, Media Forensics and Security*, volume 7254, pages 801 – 811. SPIE, 2009.

[9] J. Fridrich. *Steganography in digital media: principles, algorithms, and applications*. Cambridge University Press, 2009.

[10] O. Goldreich. *The Foundations of Cryptography - Volume 2, Basic Applications*. Cambridge University Press, 2004.

[11] O. Goldreich, S. Goldwasser, and S. Micali. How to construct random functions. *Journal of the ACM*, 33(4):792–807, 1986.

[12] O. Goldreich and H. Krawczykt. Sparse pseudorandom distributions. *Random Structures and Algorithms*, 3(2):163–174, 1992.

[13] N. J. Hopper. Toward a theory of steganography. Technical report, Technical Report CMU-CS-04-157, Carnegie Mellon Univ., 2004.

[14] N. J. Hopper, J. Langford, and L. von Ahn. Provably secure steganography. In *Proc. CRYPTO*, volume 2442 of *Lecture Notes in Computer Science*, pages 77–92. Springer, 2002.

[15] N. J. Hopper, L. von Ahn, and J. Langford. Provably secure steganography. *IEEE Transactions on Computers*, 58(5):662–676, 2009.

[16] S. Katzenbeisser and F. A. Petitcolas. Defining security in steganographic systems. In *Proc. EI*, volume 4675, pages 50–56. SPIE, 2002.

[17] A. D. Ker. The square root law in stegosystems with imperfect information. In *Proc. IH*, volume 6387 of *Lecture Notes in Computer Science*, pages 145–160. Springer, 2010.

[18] A. D. Ker, P. Bas, R. Böhme, R. Cogranne, S. Craver, T. Filler, J. Fridrich, and T. Pevný. Moving steganography and steganalysis from the laboratory into the real world. In *Proc. IH&MMSec*, pages 45–58. ACM, 2013.

[19] A. D. Ker, T. Pevný, J. Kodovský, and J. J. Fridrich. The square root law of steganographic capacity. In *Proc. MM&Sec*, pages 107–116. ACM, 2008.

[20] A. Kiayias, Y. Raekow, A. Russell, and N. Shashidhar. A one-time stegosystem and applications to efficient covert communication. *Journal of Cryptology*, 27(1):23–44, 2014.

[21] T. V. Le and K. Kurosawa. Bandwidth optimal steganography secure against adaptive chosen stegotext attacks. In *Proc. IH*, volume 4437 of *Lecture Notes in Computer Science*, pages 297–313. Springer, 2006.

[22] M. Liśkiewicz, R. Reischuk, and U. Wölfel. Grey-box steganography. *Theoretical Computer Science*, 505:27–41, 2013.

[23] B. Ryabko and D. Ryabko. Constructing perfect steganographic systems. *Information and Computation*, 209(9):1223–1230, 2011.

[24] Y. Wang and P. Moulin. Perfectly secure steganography: Capacity, error exponents, and code constructions. *IEEE Transactions on Information Theory*, 54(6):2706–2722, 2008.

Rethinking Optimal Embedding

Andrew D. Ker
Dept. of Computer Science
University of Oxford
Oxford OX1 3QD, UK
adk@cs.ox.ac.uk

Tomáš Pevný
CTU in Prague
Cisco R&D Center in Prague
Prague, Czech Republic
pevnak@gmail.com

Patrick Bas
Univ. Lille, CNRS, Centrale
Lille, UMR 9189
CRIStAL Lab, Lille, France,
Patrick.Bas@ec-lille.fr

ABSTRACT

At present, almost all leading steganographic techniques for still images use a distortion minimization paradigm, where each potential change is assigned a cost c_i and the change probabilities π_i chosen to minimize the average total cost $\sum_i \pi_i c_i$. However, some detectors have exploited knowledge of this adaptivity and the embedding cannot be considered optimal. In this work we prove a theoretical result suggesting that, against a knowing attacker, the embedder should simply minimize $\sum_i \pi_i^2 c_i$ instead, for the same costs c_i, which is the minimax and equilibrium strategy. This aligns with some special case results that have appeared in recent literature. We then test some simple steganographic methods in theoretical and real settings, showing that naive (average cost) adaptivity is exploitable, but the equilibrium probabilities cannot be exploited. However, it is essential to determine statistically well-founded costs c_i.

Keywords

Steganography, game theory, distortion, optimal embedding

1. INTRODUCTION

Even the first steganographers knew that not all embedding changes are equal: some are more detectable than others. Early steganographic literature [27, 15] tried various approaches to what we now call *adaptive embedding*, but it was with the discovery of Syndrome Trellis Codes [6] that adaptive steganography became practical. In the theory of additive *optimal embedding*, each change is independent and has some distortion cost c_i[1] that can be computed from the cover, and aims to make that change with probability π_i to minimize the average total cost

$$\sum_i \pi_i c_i. \tag{1}$$

---

[1] A common notation for a cost is ρ_i, but we prefer to reserve Greek letters for the strategies of the embedder and detector.

IH&MMSec 2016, June 20-23, 2016, Vigo, Spain

© 2016 ACM. ISBN 978-1-4503-4290-2/16/06. . . $15.00

DOI: http://dx.doi.org/10.1145/2909827.2930797

When embedding is not binary, the sum becomes $\sum_{i,j} \pi_i^j c_i^j$, where c_i^j is the cost of applying change option j to location i, and π_i^j the corresponding probability. Note that the hypothesis of additive distortion can be extended to local interactions between neighbouring distortions, and computed using Gibbs sampling over disjoint sublattices [5].

At present, the leading steganographic embedding methods for digital images employ this method: HUGO [18], WOW [9], the UNIWARD family [10], HILL [17]. But in the last two years some detectors have been published that exploit the adaptivity: by placing more weight on parts of the image where it is estimated more likely to contain payload, the performance of the detector can be improved [25, 4, 3]. The first version of UNIWARD [10] was exploited to the extent that it would have been better to use an older embedding method instead, and the cost function had to be altered [3]. A somewhat similar bug was present in the first version of HUGO, exploited in the BOSS contest [8], but this can better be explained by the cost function omitting important information rather than the detector exploiting its values.

If circumstances exist under which additive adaptive embedding can be exploited by a *knowing* detector (one who has knowledge of the distortion costs) then the adaptivity cannot be optimal. In part the suboptimality is because detectability is a property of cover and stego *distributions*, and cannot be determined from minimizing distortion in a single images; in part because the knowing detector can exploit the adaptivity. Hence we call embedding that optimizes (1) *naive adaptivity*[2]. We will argue that the embedder should minimize an alternative total cost,

$$\sum_i \pi_i^2 c_i \tag{2}$$

for the same c_i as before. When embedding is not binary, this becomes $\sum_{i,j,k} \pi_i^j c_i^{j,k} \pi_i^k$, where $c_i^{j,k}$ is a matrix defined by cost interactions at location i. We call this *equilibrium adaptivity*, because it is the equilibrium strategy of a zero sum game between the embedder and detector (in this work also called the *attacker*), in a suitably simple theoretical setting. And since it is a minimax strategy, the embedder has optimized against the worst case: the knowing attacker.

Our result certainly has limitations: it assumes independence of pixels or pixel groups, and that each embedding changes only one element. The former is common in the

---

[2] Note that in some other work [21], *naive adaptivity* was used for an even weaker embedding that always picks the location with lowest cost.

theory of steganography and has not prevented theoretical results from predicting practical performance [14], but the latter is an important consideration for further work on practical equilibrium adaptivity, as changing one pixel typically affects multiple measurements [4].

The structure of the paper is as follows. In Section 2 we give the theoretical justification for equilibrium adaptivity in models of covers where the pixels are independent. We make comparisons with existing literature using embedding costs in Section 3 and note that our result generalizes some special cases that have appeared recently, where squared probabilities can also be found; we also discuss how (2) can be optimized in practice. In Section 4 we test the theory against artificially-generated binary covers matching the binary model, and in Section 5 we examine the original version of S-UNIWARD, whose adaptivity was exploitable, and show that equilibrium mitigates this effect. However, since UNIWARD costs are not statistically founded, we do not optimize the embedding in this case. We draw conclusions in Section 6.

2. THEORETICAL RESULTS

In the game theory of steganography, the detector wishes to optimize some performance metric of their hypothesis test for

H_0: object under consideration is a cover, vs.

H_1: object under consideration is stego.

In the results below, we will be able to make a large-sample approximation, so that the detection is based on a statistic ℓ with Gaussian distribution under either hypothesis. We will define

$$\mu_0 = \mathrm{E}_{H_0}[\ell], \qquad \mu_1 = \mathrm{E}_{H_1}[\ell],$$
$$\sigma_0^2 = \mathrm{Var}_{H_0}[\ell], \qquad \sigma_1^2 = \mathrm{Var}_{H_1}[\ell].$$

In this work we choose the detector's payoff as the *true negative rate when the false negative rate is 50%*. The embedder's payoff is the inverse, the false positive rate when the true positive rate is 50%, which is a benchmark we have advocated in [19] for high-accuracy steganalysis. The game is zero sum (i.e. the gain on the detector's side is exactly balanced by the losses on the embedder's side).

Without loss of generality we may assume $\mu_0 < \mu_1$. For 50% true positives, the detection threshold for ℓ is the median value of ℓ in hypothesis H_1, which is μ_1 (and does not depend on σ_1). The detector's payoff is $\mathrm{P}_{H_0}[\ell < \mu_1] = \Phi(\delta)$, where Φ is the Gaussian cumulative density function and δ is the deflection

$$\delta = \frac{\mu_1 - \mu_0}{\sqrt{\sigma_0^2}}. \qquad (3)$$

Since Φ is increasing, we can assume that the detector aims to maximize, and the embedder to minimize, δ.

This payoff function is a Neyman-Pearson criterion: the detector optimizes one type of error against a fixed limit on the other. In case the reader would prefer a different choice, for example the equal-prior error rate which is often used in steganographic game theory [20], we mention that this provides an asymptotically equivalent ranking since in the large sample limit the square root law [14] would force $\pi_i \to 0$, hence $\sigma_0^2 \sim \sigma_1^2$. Then equal-prior error has a monotone relationship with any Neyman-Pearson criterion. The deflection

has appeared in other work (in which the cover models are restricted) on optimality against a knowing attacker [23, 22], and can be found as the payoff in steganographic games even as far back as [11]. It has also been justified by empirical evidence from steganographic likelihood ratio tests, in [2].

2.1 Binary Embedding in Binary Covers

To illustrate the calculations we begin with the simplest possible cover, consisting of n independent binary pixels. If they had equal probability distribution there would be no adaptivity, so we define p_i as the probability that pixel i takes value 1. We assume that these are known to the detector. Embedding must flip pixels, and we define the embedder's strategy as $(\pi_1, \ldots, \pi_n)$ where π_i is the probability of flipping pixel i; this is the adaptivity that we may (or may not) grant to the detector. Therefore in a stego object the probability that pixel i takes value 1 is

$$(1 - \pi_i)p_i + \pi_i(1 - p_i) = p_i + \pi_i(1 - 2p_i).$$

We know the form of an optimal detector for these hypotheses; the Neyman-Pearson Lemma states that we should reject the null hypothesis (give a positive detection) if the log-likelihood ratio

$$\log \prod_i \frac{\left(p_i + \pi_i(1 - 2p_i)\right)^{x_i} \left(1 - p_i - \pi_i(1 - 2p_i)\right)^{1 - x_i}}{p_i^{x_i}(1 - p_i)^{1 - x_i}}$$
$$= c + \sum_i x_i \left[\log\left(1 + \pi_i\left(\tfrac{1 - 2p_i}{p_i}\right)\right) - \log\left(1 - \pi_i\left(\tfrac{1 - 2p_i}{1 - p_i}\right)\right)\right],$$

where x_i denotes the observed value of pixel i, exceeds a threshold.

We do not need to analyze the likelihood ratio; it is sufficient to note that it is a constant plus[3]

$$\ell(x_i, \omega_i) = \sum_i x_i \omega_i$$

where (ω_i) defines the detector's strategy (the *weight* they give to each observation). Because likelihood ratio tests are an optimal subclass of all hypothesis tests under a Neyman-Pearson criterion (such as the false positive rate at 50% true positives), it is sufficient to consider detectors of this type, seeking equilibrium between (π_i) and (ω_i).

Asymptotically for large n and constant payload size, the Central Limit Theorem says that the distribution of $\ell(x_i, \omega_i)$ is Gaussian in either null or alternative hypothesis, with $\mu_0 = \sum p_i \omega_i$, $\mu_1 = \sum \left(p_i + \pi_i(1 - 2p_i)\right)\omega_i$, and $\sigma_0^2 = \sum p_i(1 - p_i)\omega_i^2$. So by (3), the detector's payoff is monotone increasing in the deflection

$$\frac{\sum_i \pi_i(1 - 2p_i)\omega_i}{\sqrt{\sum_i p_i(1 - p_i)\omega_i^2}} = \delta(\pi_i, \omega_i, d_i, e_i)$$

where $d_i = (1 - 2p_i)$, $e_i = p_i(1 - p_i)$, and

$$\delta(\pi_i, \omega_i, d_i, e_i) = \frac{\sum_i \pi_i d_i \omega_i}{\sqrt{\sum_i e_i \omega_i^2}}. \qquad (4)$$

It may easily be verified that

$$\frac{\partial \delta}{\partial \omega_j} \propto \left(\sum_i e_i \omega_i^2\right)\pi_j d_j - \left(\sum_i \pi_i d_i \omega_i\right)e_j \omega_j. \qquad (5)$$

---

[3]We use $\ell(x_i, \omega_i)$ as shorthand to mean a function of all x_i's and ω_i's.

The detector wants to maximize the value of δ in (4). An *ignorant* detector[4] must proceed as if all π_i are equal to a constant π. Therefore (5) yields in this case

$$\omega_j \propto \pi d_j e_j^{-1}.$$

Note that multiplying the weights ω_i by a constant does not change the detector. The stationary point can be verified to be a maximum as long as all p_i are not equal to zero or one, but we omit the routine calculation. Substituting into (4) gives

$$\delta(\pi_i, d_i, e_i) = \frac{\sum_i \pi \pi_i d_i^2 e_i^{-1}}{\sqrt{\sum_i \pi^2 d_i^2 e_i^{-1}}},$$

the π terms cancel (hence it does not matter whether the ignorant detector is granted knowledge of the payload size, which would reveal π), and the denominator is constant, leaving

$$\delta \propto \sum_i \pi_i c_i, \qquad (6)$$

where:

$$c_i = d_i^2 e_i^{-1} = \frac{1 - 2p_i}{p_i(1 - p_i)}, \qquad (7)$$

turns out to be the true statistical cost of flipping pixel i.

The best counter-strategy for the embedder minimizes this value of δ, subject to a payload constraint $\sum_i H(\pi_i) = m$, where H is the binary entropy function. This is the familiar "optimal embedding" scenario, where the total costs are linear in the embedding probabilities; the standard solution can be found using the method of Lagrange multipliers, which gives $\lambda c_j = H'(\pi_j)$ and hence the well-known solution

$$\pi_i = \frac{e^{-\lambda c_i}}{1 + e^{-\lambda c_i}} \qquad (8)$$

for some constant λ determined by the payload constraint.

A *knowing* detector wants to maximize the value of δ, given complete knowledge of π_i. From (5), δ is maximized when

$$\omega_j \propto \pi_j d_j e_j^{-1} \qquad (9)$$

in which case the numerator of (4) is the square of the denominator, so that

$$\delta^2 \propto \sum_i \pi_i^2 c_i \qquad (10)$$

where again $c_i = d_i^2 e_i^{-1}$. Note that the payoff depends on the squared embedding probabilities, but the costs are identical to the standard optimal embedding scenario. This time the solution satisfies $\lambda c_j = H'(\pi_j)/\pi_j$, which does not have a closed form. See Subsection 3.2 for a discussion of how (π_i) should be found; for now we simply draw attention to the difference between optimization for an ignorant attacker (6) and a knowing attacker (10).

Since the two player game is zero sum, the minimax solution (π_i, ω_i) is an equilibrium [26].

2.2 q-ary Embedding in Arbitrary Covers

Now consider a model where n pixels take values in some finite alphabet $\{a_1, \ldots, a_l\}$. We still assume that they are independent of each other, and a fixed independent embedding operation, but this can be arbitrary, and the pixels can take arbitrary and different distributions.

We define $p_i^k = P[X_i = a_k]$ as the distribution of cover pixel i, and gather it into a vector $\boldsymbol{p_i}$.[5] When a pixel is used for embedding, it changes from value a_j to a_k with probability q_{kj} gathered into a matrix $\boldsymbol{Q}$ (for convenience, our matrix is organized in columns). Such matrices can describe LSB Replacement or Matching, Ternary or Pentary Embedding, etc. Note that $\boldsymbol{p_i}$ and $\boldsymbol{Q}$ are parameters of the game, known to the detector.

As before, the embedder's strategy is the probability that each pixel is used (π_i). The unconditional distribution of stego pixels is therefore given by $\boldsymbol{q_i} = (1 - \pi_i)\boldsymbol{p_i} + \pi_i \boldsymbol{Q} \boldsymbol{p_i}$.

This time the log-likelihood ratio is of the form

$$c + \sum_i \sum_k [x_i = k] \log(1 + \pi_i \tfrac{q_i^k - p_i^k}{p_i^k})$$

where $[A]$ is the Iverson bracket taking value 1 when A is true. For the same reasons as before it is sufficient to consider detectors, parameterized by the detector's strategy ω_i^k ($i = 1, \ldots, n$, $k = 1, \ldots, l$), of the form

$$\ell(x_i, \omega_i^k) = \sum_i \sum_k [x_i = k]\omega_i^k. \qquad (11)$$

We collect the detector's strategy into n vectors $\boldsymbol{\omega_i}$. Routine calculation gives

$$\mu_1 - \mu_0 = \sum_i \pi_i \boldsymbol{d_i^T} \boldsymbol{\omega_i},$$

where $\boldsymbol{d_i} = (\boldsymbol{Q} - \boldsymbol{I})\boldsymbol{p_i}$, and

$$\sigma_0^2 = \sum_i \boldsymbol{p_i^T} \boldsymbol{E_i} \boldsymbol{p_i},$$

where $\boldsymbol{E_i} = \Delta_{\boldsymbol{p_i}} - \boldsymbol{p_i}\boldsymbol{p_i^T}$, $\Delta_{\boldsymbol{p_i}}$ representing a diagonal matrix. Thus the detector's payoff is monotone increasing in

$$\delta(\pi_i, \boldsymbol{\omega_i}, \boldsymbol{d_i}, \boldsymbol{E_i}) = \frac{\sum_i \pi_i \boldsymbol{d_i^T} \boldsymbol{\omega_i}}{\sqrt{\sum_i \boldsymbol{\omega_i^T} \boldsymbol{E_i} \boldsymbol{\omega_i}}}. \qquad (12)$$

Employing some vector calculus,

$$\frac{\partial \delta}{\partial \boldsymbol{\omega_j}} \propto (\textstyle\sum_i \boldsymbol{\omega_i^T} \boldsymbol{E_i} \boldsymbol{\omega_i})\pi_j \boldsymbol{d_j} - (\textstyle\sum_i \pi_i \boldsymbol{d_i^T} \boldsymbol{\omega_i})\boldsymbol{E_j}\boldsymbol{\omega_j}. \qquad (13)$$

For an *ignorant* detector, δ is maximized when $\boldsymbol{E_j}\boldsymbol{\omega_j} \propto \boldsymbol{d_j}$. Then (12) simplifies to

$$\delta \propto \sum_i \pi_i c_i, \qquad (14)$$

where $c_i = \boldsymbol{d_i^T} \boldsymbol{E_i^{-1}} \boldsymbol{d_i}$.

For a *knowing* detector, (13) implies that they should choose $(\boldsymbol{\omega_i})$ so that

$$\boldsymbol{E_j}\boldsymbol{\omega_j} \propto \pi_j \boldsymbol{d_j}$$

which, similarly to before, leads to

$$\delta^2 \propto \sum_i \pi_i^2 c_i \qquad (15)$$

for the same c_i. Again, compare (14) with (15).

---

[4] Recall that the detector is ignorant of the individual values of π_i, but still granted knowledge of p_i, hence d_i and e_i.

[5] We will use boldface lowercase letters for vectors, and boldface uppercase for matrices.

We will not solve these optimization problems, but proceed to a more general problem in the following subsection.

(There is a little wrinkle that has been obscured by our use of vector notation. The matrices $\boldsymbol{E}_i$, which are covariance matrices of a multinomial distribution, are all deficient. This does not affect the correctness of the calculations, as long as all p_i^k are positive, since then $\mathrm{rank}(\boldsymbol{E}_i) = l - 1$ and $\sum_k d_i^k = \sum_k p_i^k - q_i^k = 0$ also has one degree of redundancy. Thus $\boldsymbol{E}_j \boldsymbol{\omega}_j \propto \pi_j \boldsymbol{d}_j$ does define $\boldsymbol{\omega}_j$ uniquely up to a constant multiple, and $c_i = \boldsymbol{d}_i^T \boldsymbol{E}_i^{-1} \boldsymbol{d}_i$ is well-defined.)

2.3 Arbitrary Embedding

Consider now a fully arbitrary embedder, who can apply different embedding operations to each pixel. The cover model is still defined by $\boldsymbol{p}_i$, but it makes sense to consider the embedder's strategy to be exactly their output at pixel i, the vectors $\boldsymbol{\pi}_i = (\pi_i^1, \ldots, \pi_i^l)$; we do not need to know what the embedder does with the cover pixel, merely what they output.

All pixels are potentially used (this does not stop the embedder from outputting cover pixels, of course). The calculations are therefore the same as the previous subsection with $\pi_i = 1$, but now

$$\boldsymbol{d}_i = \boldsymbol{\pi}_i - \boldsymbol{p}_i$$

as what was previously called $\boldsymbol{q}_i$ becomes the embedder's move in the game, rather than a parameter known to the detector.

The detector's strategy is of the same form as before, $(\boldsymbol{\omega}_i)$, but there is no optimal detector who is ignorant of $\boldsymbol{\pi}_i$. They cannot perform a likelihood ratio test without knowing the ratio, and we postpone to future work investigation of a generalized likelihood ratio test in this model. However, against *any fixed* detector the $\boldsymbol{\omega}_i$ can be considered constants; therefore so is the denominator of the deflection (12), which in this case reduces to

$$\delta \propto \sum_i (\boldsymbol{\pi}_i - \boldsymbol{p}_i)^T \boldsymbol{\omega}_i.$$

The payload constraint is the familiar

$$\sum_i H(\boldsymbol{\pi}_i) = m$$

where $H(\boldsymbol{\pi}_i)$ represents the entropy of the vector $\boldsymbol{\pi}_i$, with the additional constraint that $\sum_k \pi_i^k = 1$. Using vector calculus[6] and Lagrange multipliers (omitting routine calculation of this standard result) we reach

$$\lambda \boldsymbol{\omega}_i = \ln(\mu_i \boldsymbol{\pi}_i)$$

where $\ln(\mu_i \boldsymbol{\pi}_i)$ applies the logarithm pointwise to the vector. This has the well-known q-ary optimal embedding solution

$$\pi_i^k = \frac{e^{-\lambda \omega_i^k}}{\sum_k e^{-\lambda \omega_i^k}}. \quad (16)$$

On the other hand, for a *knowing* detector, we still have

$$\boldsymbol{E}_j \boldsymbol{\omega}_j \propto \boldsymbol{\pi}_j - \boldsymbol{p}_j,$$

and so

$$\delta^2 \propto \sum_i (\boldsymbol{\pi}_i - \boldsymbol{p}_i)^T \boldsymbol{E}_i^{-1} (\boldsymbol{\pi}_i - \boldsymbol{p}_i). \quad (17)$$

---

[6]Note that $\frac{\partial}{\partial \boldsymbol{\pi}_i} H(\boldsymbol{\pi}_i) \propto \mathbf{1} + \ln \boldsymbol{\pi}_i$.

In this situation the embedder should minimize a quadratic form, the multidimensional analogue of the squared probabilities in (10). The solution satisfies

$$\lambda \boldsymbol{E}_i^{-1} \boldsymbol{\pi}_i = \ln(\mu_i \boldsymbol{\pi}_i) \quad (18)$$

for a constant λ determined by the payload constraint, and μ_i to ensure that $\sum_k \pi_i^k = 1$. For a brief discussion of how this is solved, see Subsection 3.2.

3. RELATION TO OTHER WORK

There have been a few contributions on embedding against a knowing detector, and some recent work has produced results that have superficial similarities with ours. In this section we make the connections more explicit.

3.1 Related Work on Optimality

Most distortion costs in the literature are derived directly from the cover content. They are built on the rationale that the distortion should be low for samples that are difficult to predict (e.g. pixels located in textures of an image) and high for samples that can be easily predicted (e.g. edges or homogeneous areas). For example the schemes UNIWARD [10] and WOW [9] use high-pass wavelet subbands, while HILL [17] uses a succession of high-pass and low-pass filters. Theses schemes approximate the local noise power in the image, and the cost is akin to a (stego-)signal to (image self-)noise ratio. For all these schemes the distortion minimized is of the form $\sum_i \pi_i c_i$.

The cost derived in HUGO [18] is a "hybrid" in the sense that its distortion uses weights directly computed from the image content (the successive differences between neighbouring pixels), but the algorithm also attempts to preserve a global distortion model between the entire cover and stego image. The model is derived from co-occurrence matrices of image residuals. Again, the distortion minimized is of the form $\sum_i \pi_i c_i$.

Note that these distortion measures are blind to the knowledge of the steganalyser, and more particularly to the fact that a detector might use an estimation of the embedding probabilities $\hat{\pi}_i$ to derive detectors that will be more sensitive to embedding changes. Recently, knowing detectors (sometimes called *omniscient* in the literature) have appeared with tSRM [25] or the maxSRM [4] feature sets, which explicitly use $\hat{\pi}_i$ and can offer up to 10% improvement on the classification accuracy for very small payloads [4]. Note also that these feature sets are derived by weighting each occurrence by its probability of change, exactly like the optimal detection strategy proposed in equation (9).

The following steganographic schemes are interesting because they implicitly or explicitly assume that the steganalyser may have knowledge or estimates of π_i, and result in distortions depending on π_i^2.

The first distortion measure comes from [12] which is set in the context of batch steganography, and measures statistical distortion using Kullback-Leibler Divergence (KLD). The total distortion of the batch is then a weighted sum of the squares of the number of embedding changes in each image; the latter is proportional to the probability of embedding in any given location in that image. For example, in [12, §2.2] total distortion is proportional to $\sum_i c_i \pi_i^2$, where c_i is called the "Q-factor". Even though this theoretical analysis did not generate a practical embedding method, it appears to be the first that proposed a distortion where the cost is weighted by π_i^2. Measuring detectability by KLD implicitly models the worst-case opponent, who would indeed be a knowing detector.

Ref. [7] is another that measures detectability by KLD. It is approximated by $\sum \frac{1}{2} I_i(0) \pi_i^2$ where $I_i(0)$ denotes the Fisher information of the stego content with respect to π_i. The authors use a local Gaussian approximation of the image pixels in a neighbourhood to derive $I_i(0)$ (which is independent of π_i) and to perform the minimization. It is interesting to note that the "Q-factor" mentioned in [12] is in fact also half of Fisher's information.

Instead of minimizing KLD, two recent works have optimized embedding with respect to a likelihood ratio detector.

In [23] the cover is modelled as a discretized univariate generalized Gaussian model with varying variance (similar to the model of [7]), and the embedding is pentary. The probabilities of ± 1 and ± 2 changes constitute the embedder's strategy. Similarly to our analysis, the authors argue that the embedder should minimize a deflection coefficient, and by approximating the likelihood ratio explicitly they derive an optimization [23, Eq. (11)] which is a quadratic form like (18).

In [22] the cover is modelled as a discretized Gaussian with varying variance, and the embedding is ternary. The square deflection of the likelihood ratio is given by $\sum \pi_i^2 / \sigma_i^4$ where σ_i^2 denotes the variance of the underlying local Gaussian model at location i [22, Eq. (11)]. They also compute the deflection against an ignorant (there called indifferent) detector, which is proportional to $\sum \pi_i / \sigma_i^4$ [22, Eq. (12)].

This confluence of results is encouraging. Our contribution is to show that the conclusions are not dependent on a particular cover or embedding model, and apply to arbitrary discrete covers and arbitrary embedding operations.

3.2 Related Work on Implementation

We have not yet explained how the optimization problems (10) and (17) can be solved. In fact, some of the other literature mentioned above derives equations of a similar form, and the generalizations are simple enough that we need not go into much detail about them.

For linear additive distortions $\sum \pi_i c_i$ it is well-known that we can optimize without even finding the solution (8), via Syndrome Trellis Codes (STCs). For arbitrary embedding against a fixed detector, $\sum \pi_i \omega_i$ can be optimized using l-ary STCs, though their complexity grows very rapidly with the alphabet size l, or nested STCs [6].

In [22] the authors explain how a function that fits the form $\sum \pi_i^2 c_i$ can be optimized: numerically solve the relationship $\lambda c_j = H'(\pi_j)/\pi_j$, inside an interval bisection search for λ meeting the payload constraint. Then reverse-engineer costs $d_j = H'(\pi_j)/\lambda$ would have given the same solution for naive embedding and λ that would leave these probabilities on the rate-distortion bound. Applying STCs to the adjusted costs (d_i) should make changes with approximately the optimal probabilities (π_i). However the probabilities will not be exact, because STCs do not meet the rate-distortion bound exactly.

We should mention that, although $\lambda c_j = H'(\pi_j)/\pi_j$ does not have a closed-form inverse, it would be trivial to tabulate a few million values for locating π_j from λc_j, and this only needs to be done once. Then, if necessary, the inverse could be refined with one or two steps of the Newton-Raphson method. In our experiments the calculation of embedding

probabilities was negligible compared with calculating the costs in the first place.

In [23] the authors arrive at a system of $2n + 1$ variables that is similar to the nk simultaneous equations we reached in (18); their system is simpler because the embedding operation is limited to ± 1 and ± 2 changes. We advocate the same approach that they take: it is a convex system, so Newtonian numerical methods should converge quickly to a solution. Again, these can be reverse-engineered into costs for a l-ary or nested STC.

Nonetheless, in this work we will not try to implement equilibrium embedding, since it is sufficient for our purposes to simulate it by applying changes with the optimal probabilities.

4. ARTIFICIAL BINARY COVERS

Our initial experiments are on artificial "images" fitting exactly the model in Subsection 2.1, which ensures that most of the assumptions of the theory are true (in particular, independence of pixels). These experiments test whether the use of the large sample approximations is valid. Our covers will contain $n = 2^{18}$ pixels, the size of images in the BOSSBase library [1].

In order to generate covers according to the model, we must select the pixel probabilities $p_i \in (0, 1)$. In the first experiment we drew p_i independently from a Beta distribution with parameters $(5, 5)$; this means that they are somewhat bell shaped and symmetrical around $p_i = 0.5$. We generated 10 000 cover images using this model.

We then simulated three types of embedding on the rate-distortion curve: non-adaptive embedding where π_i is constant, naive adaptive embedding where $\sum_i \pi_i c_i$ is minimized, and equilibrium adaptive embedding where $\sum_i \pi_i^2 c_i$ is minimized. In each case the payload constraint was $\sum H(\pi_i) = 0.1 \cdot 2^{18}$, simulating a payload of 0.1 bits per pixel, a size chosen so that the detectors will be neither practically-perfect nor near-random. We generated 10 000 stego images for each case.

In Figure 1 (top) we show the histogram of the values p_i, and the relationship between the cost c_i (computed from p_i using the results in section 2.1) and the naive or equilibrium embedding probabilities π_i. Throughout the figure, red denotes the naive adaptivity and blue the equilibrium. Observe that equilibrium embedding assigns lower probabilities to low costs, but slightly higher probabilities to high costs: it is less aggressive in its adaptivity (which is the reason that it cannot be exploited). We also show histograms of the binary entropy of the naive and equilibrium probabilities: $H(\pi_i)$ indicates how many bits of payload (under perfect coding) are placed in location i. Observe that naive adaptive embedding prefers to hide almost one bit in each of a few locations (in this case over 58% of the payload is placed into just under 6% of the locations) and zero or almost zero in the rest. Note that in the Bernoulli model, the costs dip sharply for p_i close to 0.5, since $c_i = (1 - 2p_i)^2 / p_i(1 - p_i)$ (see Eq.(7)), so these locations appear attractive for payload. However, equilibrium embedding places at least a tiny amount of payload in every location, and very few contain as much as nearly one bit.

Because we know exactly the cover model and the embedding probabilities, we can build an optimal detector directly from the likelihood ratio test (LRT), rejecting the null hy-

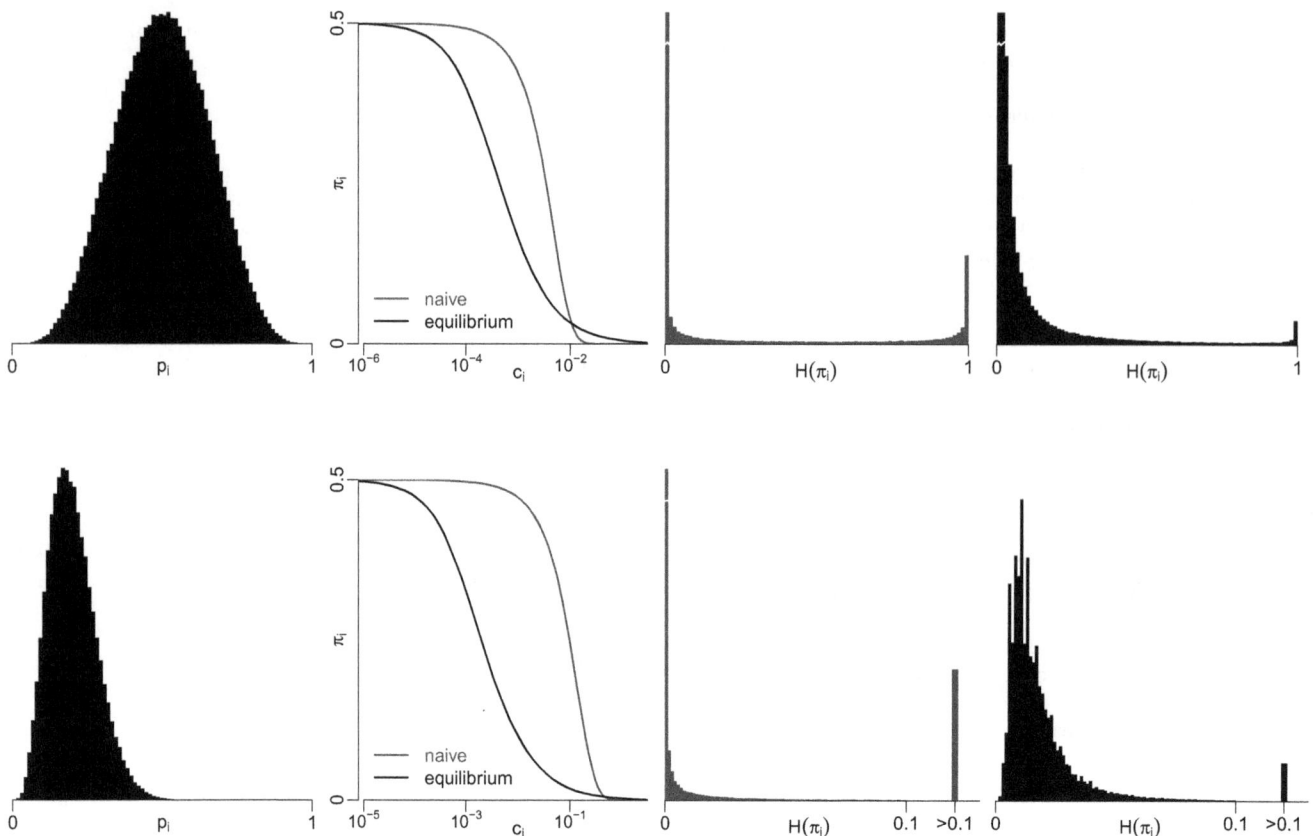

Figure 1: **Embedding in artificial binary covers. From left to right: histogram of the probabilities p_i that pixel i takes value 1; relationship between embedding cost and probability when the adaptivity is naive (red) and in equilibrium (blue); histogram of the binary entropy of the embedding probabilities for naive adaptivity (note that the zero bin is truncated); for equilibrium adaptivity, displayed on the same scale. Above, p_i is drawn from the $\mathrm{Beta}(5,5)$ distribution, with a payload of 0.1 bits per pixel in 2^{18} pixels. Below, p_i is drawn from the $\mathrm{Beta}(5,20)$ distribution, with a payload of 0.02 bits per pixel in 2^{18} pixels, and the histogram of $H(\pi_i)$ focuses on low entropy locations.**

pothesis if

$$\sum_i x_i \left[\log\left(1 + \pi_i\left(\tfrac{1-2p_i}{p_i}\right)\right) - \log\left(1 - \pi_i\left(\tfrac{1-2p_i}{1-p_i}\right)\right) \right]$$

exceeds a threshold. This can be done with each (π_i), to create the detector's optimal counter-strategy to each of the embedder's three strategies. We then computed the empirical *embedder's* payoff, the false positive rate when the true positive rate is 50%, for each detector against each embedding adaptivity. The results are shown in Table 1 (top), where each row corresponds to the optimal detector for each type of embedding, and each column to that embedding.

At this payload rate, non-adaptive embedding is highly detectable by the conventional LRT (0.000 false positives), but if the embedder switches to standard naive adaptivity this detector is almost random. However, a knowing attacker can regain good performance by using the adaptivity in the LRT (0.023 false positives). To avoid being exploited, the embedder should use equilibrium adaptivity, and the optimal detector still makes false positives at a rate of 0.145. Amongst the three embedder/detector strategies shown here, the table shows that equilibrium embedding and the LRT detector for it do indeed form an equilibrium,

since the detector can only degrade their performance by deviating from it, and the embedder can only become more detectable by deviating.

The bell-shaped distribution of pixel probabilities p_i leads to many costs very close to zero, which is probably not a good model for steganography in real images. Therefore we repeated the previous experiments with a different distribution of p_i, this time from the Beta distribution with parameters $(20, 5)$, in which the costs do not get too close to zero. The higher costs indicate that payload will be more detectable, so we reduced the payload constraint to 0.02 bits per pixel, again so that the detectors' performance is neither too good nor too poor. The distribution of p_i, the relationship between costs and embedding probabilities under naive and equilibrium adaptivity, and the distribution of payload are shown in Figure 1 (bottom) and the performance of the detectors in Table 1 (bottom). We observe similar features: naive adaptive embedding is more secure against an ignorant opponent, but can be exploited by a knowing opponent to the extent that it becomes even more detectable than no adaptivity at all. Equilibrium embedding spreads the payload rather more evenly than naive adaptivity, and cannot be exploited.

(a) p_i taken from $Beta(5,5)$, 0.1 bits per pixel embedded in 2^{18} pixels

LRT detector for	Embedding adaptivity		
	None	Naive	Equilibrium
No adaptivity	0.000	0.492	0.335
Naive adaptivity	0.443	0.023	0.225
Equilibrium	0.038	0.081	0.145

(b) p_i taken from $Beta(5,20)$, 0.02 bits per pixel embedded in 2^{18} pixels

LRT detector for	Embedding adaptivity		
	None	Naive	Equilibrium
No adaptivity	0.040	0.433	0.198
Naive adaptivity	0.472	0.000	0.305
Equilibrium	0.099	0.023	0.116

Table 1: The embedder's payoff (false positive rate when true positive rate is 50%) for artificial binary covers. Likelihood ratio tests for each adaptivity type were tested against embedding with each adaptivity type.

5. EXPLOITABILITY OF S-UNIWARD

Finally, we attempt to apply the theory of equilibrium to the contemporary steganographic algorithm S-UNIWARD [10]. This calculates the distortion of changing pixel i from a Wavelet-transformed image:

$$c_i = \sum_{k=1}^{3}\sum_{u=1}^{m}\sum_{v=1}^{n} \frac{W_{uv}^{(k)}(\boldsymbol{X}) - W_{uv}^{(k)}(\boldsymbol{X}^i)}{\sigma + W_{uv}^{(k)}(\boldsymbol{X})},$$

where $\boldsymbol{X}$ is the matrix of $m \times n$ cover pixels, $\boldsymbol{X}^i$ the same image with only change i applied and $W_{uv}^{(k)}(\cdot)$ denote the (u, v) wavelet coefficients in the first-level undecimated Daubechies 8-tap wavelet decomposition. The index $k = 1, 2, 3$ corresponds to the LH, HL, and HH subbands, respectively.

The original version of UNIWARD used $\sigma = 10^{-15}$ to avoid division by zero, but this caused wide variation in the costs, and hence a strong preference for certain embedding locations. In [3] the authors demonstrated the vulnerability of S-UNIWARD to an attacker who could estimate the costs via a feature set called Content-Selective Residuals (CSR); the same work proposed the simple heuristic fix of setting $\sigma = 1$ to moderate the costs. The effect on embedding probabilities is similar to that of an equilibrium strategy: it increases the likelihood of embedding in previously unused pixels, and reduces it in the more commonly-used areas. Since then, further (less catastrophic) attacks on S-UNIWARD have been accomplished by weighting features according to the probability of embedding, which our theory predicts to be optimal (9), in feature sets tSRM [25] and maxSRM [4].

In these experiments, we investigate whether an equilibrium strategy provides an alternative to changing the value of σ. For just one image, the histogram of the costs with $\sigma = 10^{-15}$, the relationship between costs and embedding probabilities, and histograms of the binary entropy of those probabilities are displayed in Figure 2. We also display binary entropy of the naive embedding probabilities for some

(a) CSR features; payload constraint of 0.2 bits per pixel

Detector trained on	$\sigma = 10^{-15}$		$\sigma = 1$	
	Embedding ad.		Embedding ad.	
	Naive	Equil.	Naive	Equil.
Naive ad.	0.0076	0.4999	0.4452	0.4975
Equil. ad.	0.5053	0.2949	0.4025	0.3425

(b) CSR features; payload constraint of 0.3 bits per pixel

Detector trained on	$\sigma = 10^{-15}$		$\sigma = 1$	
	Embedding ad.		Embedding ad.	
	Naive	Equil.	Naive	Equil.
Naive ad.	0.0073	0.5000	0.3997	0.4950
Equil. ad.	0.5022	0.1297	0.3593	0.3013

(c) maxSRM features; payload constraint of 0.3 bits per pixel

Detector trained on	$\sigma = 10^{-15}$		$\sigma = 1$	
	Embedding ad.		Embedding ad.	
	Naive	Equil.	Naive	Equil.
Naive ad.	0.2406	0.3229	0.2773	0.3109
Equil. ad.	0.4719	0.2442	0.3463	0.1580

Table 2: Equal-prior error rates for S-UNIWARD, both the original version with $\sigma = 10^{-15}$ and the updated version with $\sigma = 1$, with naive and equilibrium adaptivity.

other values of σ; in this case it appears that equilibrium embedding probabilities are quite close to those that could be obtained naively using $\sigma = 20$.

For both the original S-UNIWARD with $\sigma = 10^{-15}$, and the modern version with $\sigma = 1$, we computed the naive and equilibrium optimal embedding probabilities; we also computed CSR and maxSRM features[7].

Our experiments used BOSSBase [1]: 10 000 grayscale images of size 512×512; although a single cover corpus would not be appropriate for significant experiments [24], it is sufficient to explore our theory in practice.

In each repetition of the experiment, two binary classifiers were trained: one for stego images embedded with naive adaptivity, and the other for stego images embedded with equilibrium adaptivity. Both steganalyzers were implemented as an ensemble of FLDs and trained on 8000 cover and 8000 stego images. Since we are now performing real steganalysis, we adopt the standard benchmark $P_{err} = 0.5(P_{fp} + P_{fn})$, estimated on the remaining 2000 cover and stego images. The experiment was repeated ten times with different partitions of training and testing data.

---

[7]maxSRM features were calculated by estimating the embedding strategy from the stego image, as proposed in [4], rather than assuming omniscience of the detector.

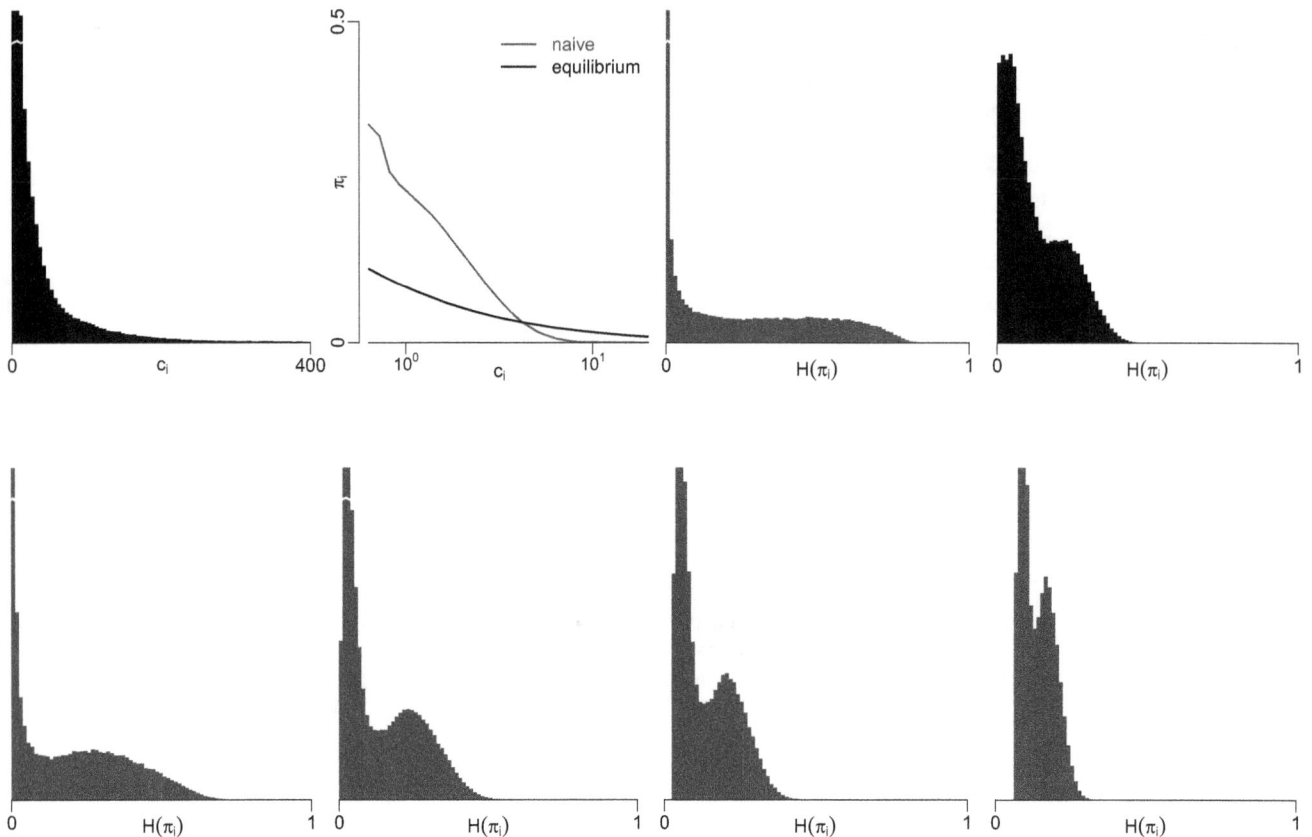

Figure 2: Above, equilibrium embedding with the original version of S-UNIWARD ($\sigma = 10^{-15}$), in one of the BOSSBase images. From left to right: histogram of the distortion costs c_i; relationship between embedding cost and probability when the adaptivity is naive (red) and in equilibrium (blue); histogram of the binary entropy of the embedding probabilities for naive adaptivity; for equilibrium adaptivity, displayed on the same scale. The image has 2^{18} pixels and the payload is 0.4 bits per pixel. Below, histograms of $H(\pi_i)$ on the same scale for naive embedding with (left to right) $\sigma = 1, 10, 20, 50$.

The error rates for the various combinations of σ, embedder, and detector, are shown in Table 2. We include two payloads tested against CSR features. For the original S-UNIWARD with $\sigma = 10^{-15}$, the equilibrium strategy is much less exploitable than naive adaptive embedding. However, the "equilibrium" is not really an equilibrium, since against such a detector it would be advantageous for the embedder to switch to the other embedding probabilities. Furthermore, naive embedding with $\sigma = 1$ is less detectable than equilibrium embedding with $\sigma = 10^{-15}$. These results confirm that equilibrium embedding makes the flaw in the original S-UNIWARD less exploitable, but we should not be surprised that the so-called equilibrium is suboptimal: the costs are heuristic rather than founded on statistical optimality, and the theory does not directly apply. When $\sigma = 1$ it is downright worse to use equilibrium embedding, but that is only to be expected when $\sigma = 1$ already moderates the embedding probabilities.

We also include one payload detected by maxSRM features. Here there is no significant benefit in switching to equilibrium embedding even at $\sigma = 10^{-15}$, and disadvantages at $\sigma = 1$. Again we should not be surprised, because the costs were not optimal to begin with.

6. CONCLUSIONS

An adaptivity criterion is an example of side information. Given asymptotically perfect coding, it does not matter whether the receiver possesses this information. But this is not at all true for the detector, and optimizing an embedder against a worst-case (likelihood ratio test) detector, which is the minimax strategy for the embedder, has received recent attention. Solving such game theory problems in steganography was identified as an important open problem in [13].

In this work we have substantially generalized prior results, to the case of arbitrary nonstationary (discrete) cover distributions and arbitrary embedding. Thus we can justify theoretically certain emerging themes: quadratic forms in the embedding probabilities [23], and weighting features by an estimated embedding probabilities [4]. For binary and fixed q-ary embedding, our result can be stated simply: optimize $\sum \pi_i^2 c_i$ instead of $\pi_i c_i$, but do not change the costs. We have seen empirical evidence that equilibrium strategies are less aggressive than naive adaptivity, making even high-cost changes with non-negligible probability and less certain to make low-cost changes. Heuristically, something similar was applied to counter exploitation of the original S-UNIWARD.

Ironically, compared with the discretized nonstationary univariate Gaussian [22] or generalized Gaussian [23] special cases, the more powerful theoretical results do not lead to easily-implementable optimal steganography. The advantage of restricted cover models is that the parameters are few enough that they can be estimated; that would be quite impossible for arbitrary nonstationary covers with arbitrary embedding. We consider our contribution more to the theory of optimal embedding than the practice; the works [23, 22] have already demonstrated that there is practical value in this approach.

Although the theoretical results are general, they have important limitations. They grant the detector considerable knowledge, including the exact distortion costs (even though they do not possess the cover) and cover model. They require the detection space to be identical to that in which distortion is calculated: this is not the case for current leading steganalysis and adaptive steganography, but the optimality of the likelihood ratio test suggests that these domains should eventually converge. It is for further work to adapt these results to the practical situation where one embedding change affects multiple features. Finally, we have assumed independence of pixels in the cover model, and independent embedding. It would be valuable to consider Gibbs embedding [5] against a knowing opponent, but for fully-general distortions we will not be able to appeal to the law of large numbers, making analysis difficult. We speculate that a similar result could at least be proved for costs that are sums of local potentials.

Finally, we should stress that swapping $\sum \pi_i c_i$ to $\sum \pi_i^2 c_i$ is not a panacea in steganography. It is only correct if the costs c_i were statistically justified, and does not necessarily apply to the vast majority of steganography cost functions such as WOW, UNIWARD, or HILL, which are purely heuristic. And they have to be at least somewhat heuristic, because to know the true costs requires impossible knowledge of the exact parameters of the cover model (the probability that each pixel takes a particular value). Our theoretical results exist in something of a vacuum because neither player will in practice know the costs. However, it remains possible that good estimates of the costs will suffice for a near-equilibrium (costs perhaps obtained form empirical learning about the cover source), and this is something for future work.

Development of less-heuristic distortion functions is an important area for future research in steganography, and even though MiPOD [22] is based on a very simple cover model it makes a valuable contribution in this direction. As proposed in [16], one possible solution to derive a practical distortion having statistical meaning would be to use the output of a classifier. Perhaps statistical methods can also lead to the development of distortion functions for domains where they are currently lacking, such as audio or video.

Acknowledgements
Patrick Bas thanks the *Centre National de la Recherche Scientifique* for specific support on this topic.

7. REFERENCES

[1] P. Bas, T. Pevný, and T. Filler. BOSSBase. http://webdav.agents.fel.cvut.cz/data/projects/stegodata/BossBase-1.01-cover.tar.bz2, May 2011.

[2] R. Cogranne and J. Fridrich. Modeling and extending the ensemble classifier for steganalysis of digital images using hypothesis testing theory. *IEEE Transactions on Information Forensics and Security*, 10(12):2627–2642, Dec. 2015.

[3] T. Denemark, J. Fridrich, and V. Holub. Further study on the security of S-UNIWARD. In *Proceedings of SPIE/IS&T International Symposium on Electronic Imaging*, volume 9028. International Society for Optics and Photonics, 2014.

[4] T. Denemark, V. Sedighi, V. Holub, R. Cogranne, and J. Fridrich. Selection-channel-aware rich model for steganalysis of digital images. In *Proceedings of IEEE International Workshop on Information Forensics and Security (WIFS)*, 2014.

[5] T. Filler and J. Fridrich. Gibbs construction in steganography. *IEEE Transactions on Information Forensics and Security*, 5(4):705–720, 2010.

[6] T. Filler, J. Judas, and J. Fridrich. Minimizing additive distortion in steganography using syndrome-trellis codes. *IEEE Transactions on Information Forensics and Security*, 6(3):920–935, 2011.

[7] J. Fridrich and J. Kodovský. Multivariate gaussian model for designing additive distortion for steganography. In *Proceedings of IEEE International Conference on Acoustics, Speech and Signal Processing (ICASSP)*, pages 2949–2953, May 2013.

[8] G. Gul and F. Kurugollu. A new methodology in steganalysis: breaking highly undetectable steganogrpay (HUGO). In *Proceedings of International Conference on Information Hiding (IH)*, pages 71–84. Springer, 2011.

[9] V. Holub and J. Fridrich. Designing steganographic distortion using directional filters. In *Proceedings of the IEEE International Workshop on Information Forensics and Security (WIFS)*, pages 234–239. IEEE, 2012.

[10] V. Holub, J. Fridrich, and T. Denemark. Universal distortion function for steganography in an arbitrary domain. *EURASIP Journal on Information Security*, 2014(1):1–13, 2014.

[11] A. D. Ker. Batch steganography and the threshold game. In *Proceedings of SPIE/IS&T International Symposium on Electronic Imaging*, volume 6505. International Society for Optics and Photonics, 2007.

[12] A. D. Ker. Steganographic strategies for a square distortion function. In *Proceedings of SPIE/IS&T International Symposium on Electronic Imaging*, volume 6819. International Society for Optics and Photonics, 2008.

[13] A. D. Ker, P. Bas, R. Böhme, R. Cogranne, S. Craver, T. Filler, J. Fridrich, and T. Pevný. Moving steganography and steganalysis from the laboratory into the real world. In *Proceedings of ACM Workshop on Information Hiding and Multimedia Security (IHMMSec)*, pages 45–58. ACM, 2013.

[14] A. D. Ker, T. Pevný, J. Kodovský, and J. Fridrich. The square root law of steganographic capacity. In *Proceedings of ACM Workshop on Multimedia and Security (MMSec)*, pages 107–116. ACM, 2008.

[15] Y. Kim, Z. Duric, and D. Richards. Modified matrix encoding technique for minimal distortion steganography. In *Proceedings of International Workshop on Information Hiding (IH)*, pages 314–327, 2007.

[16] S. Kouider, M. Chaumont, and W. Puech. Adaptive steganography by oracle (ASO). In *Proceedings of IEEE International Conference on Multimedia and Expo (ICME)*, pages 1–6. IEEE, 2013.

[17] B. Li, M. Wang, J. Huang, and X. Li. A new cost function for spatial image steganography. In *Proceedings of the IEEE International Conference on Image Processing (ICIP)*, pages 4206–4210. IEEE, 2014.

[18] T. Pevný, T. Filler, and P. Bas. Using high-dimensional image models to perform highly undetectable steganography. In *Proceedings of the International Conference on Information Hiding (IH) 2010*, pages 161–177, 2010.

[19] T. Pevný and A. D. Ker. Towards dependable steganalysis. In *Proceedings of SPIE/IS&T International Symposium on Electronic Imaging*, volume 9409. International Society for Optics and Photonics, 2015.

[20] P. Schöttle and R. Böhme. Game theory and adaptive steganography. *IEEE Transactions on Information Forensics and Security*, 11(4):760–773, April 2016.

[21] P. Schöttle, S. Korff, and R. Böhme. Weighted stego-image steganalysis for naive content-adaptive embedding. In *Proceedings of IEEE International Workshop on Information Forensics and Security (WIFS)*, pages 193–198. IEEE, 2012.

[22] V. Sedighi, R. Cogranne, and J. Fridrich. Content-adaptive steganography by minimizing statistical detectability. *IEEE Transactions on Information Forensics and Security*, 11(2):221–234, 2016.

[23] V. Sedighi, J. Fridrich, and R. Cogranne. Content-adaptive pentary steganography using the multivariate generalized gaussian cover model. In *Proceedings of SPIE/IS&T International Symposium on Electronic Imaging*, volume 9409. International Society for Optics and Photonics, 2015.

[24] V. Sedighi, J. Fridrich, and R. Cogranne. Toss that bossbase, Alice! In *Proceedings of IS&T International Symposium on Electronic Imaging*. Society for Imaging Science and Technology, 2016.

[25] W. Tang, H. Li, W. Luo, and J. Huang. Adaptive steganalysis against WOW embedding algorithm. In *Proceedings of ACM Workshop on Information hiding and Multimedia Security (MMSec)*, pages 91–96. ACM, 2014.

[26] J. Von Neumann and O. Morgenstern. *Theory of Games and Economic Behavior*. Princeton University Press, 1944.

[27] A. Westfeld. F5—a steganographic algorithm. In *Proceedings of International Workshop on Information Hiding (IH)*, pages 289–302. Springer Berlin Heidelberg, 2001.

Ensemble of CNNs for Steganalysis: An Empirical Study

Guanshuo Xu
New Jersey Institute of Technology
University Heights
Newark, NJ, USA 07102
+1-862-371-4304
gx3@njit.edu

Han-Zhou Wu
Southwest Jiaotong University
High-tech Zone, West Park
Chengdu 611756, P.R. China
+86-159-2811-3628
h.wu.phd@ieee.org

Yun Q. Shi
New Jersey Institute of Technology
University Heights
Newark, NJ, USA 07102
+1-973-596-3501
shi@njit.edu

ABSTRACT

There has been growing interest in using convolutional neural networks (CNNs) in the fields of image forensics and steganalysis, and some promising results have been reported recently. These works mainly focus on the architectural design of CNNs, usually, a single CNN model is trained and then tested in experiments. It is known that, neural networks, including CNNs, are suitable to form ensembles. From this perspective, in this paper, we employ CNNs as base learners and test several different ensemble strategies. In our study, at first, a recently proposed CNN architecture is adopted to build a group of CNNs, each of them is trained on a random subsample of the training dataset. The output probabilities, or some intermediate feature representations, of each CNN, are then extracted from the original data and pooled together to form new features ready for the second level of classification. To make best use of the trained CNN models, we manage to partially recover the lost information due to spatial subsampling in the pooling layers when forming feature vectors. Performance of the ensemble methods are evaluated on BOSSbase by detecting S-UNIWARD at 0.4 bpp embedding rate. Results have indicated that both the recovery of the lost information, and learning from intermediate representation in CNNs instead of output probabilities, have led to performance improvement.

Keywords

Steganalysis; Forensics; Convolutional Neural Networks; Deep Learning.

1. INTRODUCTION

When performance is highly concerned, ensemble learning has been arguably one of the most widely adopted techniques to solve machine learning problems since the invention of boosting [1][2], bootstrap aggregation [3] and random forest [4]. It is well-known that the neural networks, including the convolutional neural networks (CNNs), which have achieved great success in the fields of computer vision [5-9], are suitable to serve as base learners and form ensembles. In computer vision, the most prominent research studies focus on designing efficient CNN architectures, and seeking ways to improve the optimization efficiency of deep neural networks [8][9]. Nevertheless, ultimate performance is

IH&MMSec 2016, June 20-23, 2016, Vigo, Spain
© 2016 ACM. ISBN 978-1-4503-4290-2/16/06.. $15.00
DOI: http://dx.doi.org/10.1145/2909827.2930798

always brought by ensembles of multiple CNNs, e.g., all the winning solutions in the ImageNet Large Scale Visual Recognition Challenge [6][7][9] from year 2012 to 2015, are ensembles of multiple CNNs.

Inspired and encouraged by the success of CNNs in computer vision, the forensics society have started devoting research efforts on migrating the CNNs to solve forensics and steganalysis problems [10-13]. In [10], the proposed CNN boosted accuracy on detecting median filtering processing in images by 1% ~ 8% compared with previous works. In [11] and [12], attempts were made in applying CNNs to image steganalysis, although the reported performance are still worse than the conventional state-of-the-art works [14][18-20]. All of those works reported results using only a single CNN for each individual experiment. In [15], the structural design of CNNs for steganalysis was discussed, and the ensemble (five CNNs) performance of the proposed CNN is competitive compared with that achieved by the SRM [14]. The ensemble method used is model averaging (averaging the output probabilities of each CNN). In this paper, we go beyond model averaging, and test the performance of second-level classifiers trained on the feature vectors generated from base learners (CNNs). The feature vectors come from pooling (1) the direct output probabilities generated from the trained CNNs; (2) the output probabilities generated from the CNNs with offsets in the spatial subsampling steps of pooling layers; (3) the output vectors of the convolutional modules in CNNs. The second one aims at recovering the information loss caused by spatial subsampling. The performance of all the proposed ensemble methods are evaluated on BOSSbase [16] by detecting S-UNIWARD [22] at 0.4 bpp embedding rate. Results have indicated that both the recovery of the lost information caused by subsampling, and learning from features representations within CNNs instead of output probabilities, have led to performance improvement. While only tested on one dataset with a special steganalysis problem, the proposed ensemble methods should be generically applicable to most of the image forensic tasks using CNNs.

The rest of this paper is organized as follows. In Section 2, we briefly review the CNN architecture used to build base learners. The ensemble methods we have studied are listed in Section 3. Experimental results and discussions are presented in Section 4. Conclusion is drawn in Section 5.

2. CNN: THE BASE LEARNER
2.1 The CNN Architecture

The CNN architecture used in this paper is almost same as that proposed in [15] except that we append one more group of layers (Group 6 in Figure 1) to the end of the convolutional module, and increase the pooling sizes of the last two pooling layers from 5×5 to 7×7. This paper aims at studying strategies for ensemble learning instead of designing CNNs. To make this paper self-

CLASSIFICATION MODULE

class probabilities

↑

Softmax

↑

Fully-connected

↑ 256-D features

CONVOLUTIONAL MODULE

32×(64×64)

Average Pooling size 5×5 stride 2 — ReLU — BN — Convolutional 32×(1×1×16) — Group 3

16×(128×128)

Average Pooling size 5×5 stride 2 — TanH — BN — Convolutional 16×(5×5×8) — Group 2

8×(256×256)

Average Pooling size 5×5 stride 2 — TanH — BN — ABS — Convolutional 8×(5×5×1) — Group 1

1×(512×512)

256×(1×1)

Average Pooling 16×16 Global — ReLU — BN — Convolutional 256×(1×1×128) — Group 6

128×(16×16)

Average Pooling size 7×7 stride 2 — ReLU — BN — Convolutional 128×(1×1×64) — Group 5

64×(32×32)

Average Pooling size 7×7 stride 2 — ReLU — BN — Convolutional 64×(1×1×32) — Group 4

32×(64×64)

HPF 1×(5×5×1)

1×(512×512)

Input Image

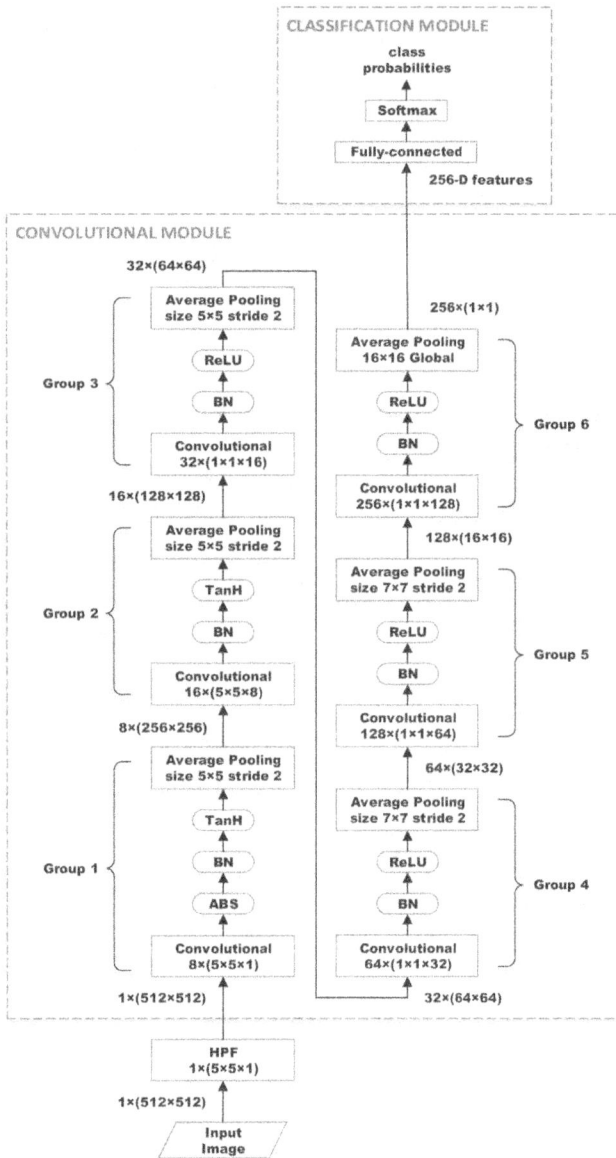

Figure 1. The CNN architecture. Inside boxes are the layer functions. Data sizes are displayed on the two sides. Sizes of convolution kernels in the boxes follow (number of kernels) × (height × width × number of input feature maps). Sizes of data follow (number of feature maps) × (height × width). Padding is applied in convolutional and pooling layers as well as in HPF layer.

contained, we briefly review the CNN architecture used for generating base learners. More details have been documented in [15].

The overall architecture is illustrated in Figure 1. A high-pass filtering (HPF) layer using the previously developed kernel [14] is placed at the very beginning to transform original images to noise residuals. The parameters in the HPF layer are not optimized during training, this CNN actually learns from the generated noise residuals instead of from the original images. Hence, in the rest of the paper, the training data refers to the obtained residuals from the original images. The whole CNN contains a convolutional module responsible to transform the images/residuals to feature

vectors (256-D), which serves as input to the linear classification module that generates probability output for each of the two classes. Note that for binary classification problem, only one of the probability values is needed. The convolutional module comprises six groups of layers ("Group 1 ~ Group 6" in Figure 1), each of them starts with a convolutional layer, which doubles the number of spatial maps (often be referred to as the width of a layer in deep neural networks), and ends with an average pooling layer which performs local averaging as well as subsampling on the spatial maps (except Group 6). The CNN is equipped with the hyperbolic tangent (TanH) as non-linear activations for Group 1 and Group 2, and the rectified linear unit (ReLU) activations for Group 3 ~ Group 6. An absolute activation (ABS) layer is inserted in Group 1 to force the CNN to take into account the (sign) symmetry existed in noise residuals. Immediately before each non-linear activation layer, the feature maps are normalized with batch-normalization (BN) [8].

Through global averaging, the pooling layer in Group 6 merges each spatial map to a single element: 256 maps of size 16×16 to 256-D features. In this paper, we represent the size of the CNN by the output size of the last pooling layer (in Group 6), hence, we call the CNN in Figure 1 as 'SIZE 256', and 'SIZE 128' refers to a CNN with only half the width for each layer and roughly one quarter of the total number of parameters existed in 'SIZE 256'.

2.2 Ensemble Methods

In this section, we discuss in detail all the ensemble methods we have studied in this paper.

Let $\{X_i, y_i\}_{i=1}^N$ denote the training dataset, where N is the total number of training data – the residuals generated by the HPF layer, X_i represents the i-th residual of the training set, and y_i is the corresponding binary label. Note that, for $1 \leq i \leq N$, we have $X_i \epsilon \mathbf{R}^{h \times w}$ and $y_i \epsilon \{0,1\}$. A total of T CNNs are trained and used as base learners. In this work, we choose $T = 16$. The k-th CNN h_k maps each residual image to a probability value, and is represented by $h_k = h(X; \boldsymbol{w}_k): \mathbf{R}^{h \times w} \to p\epsilon[0,1]$, in which the parameters $\boldsymbol{w}_k$ is optimized by minimizing the log loss denoted generally by $L_H = L(h, y)$. The procedures to generate base learners (CNNs) are summarized below:

---

1. **for** $k = 1$ to T **do**
2.   generate a random permutation $\{\pi(i)\}_{i=1}^N$ of $\{1, 2, \ldots, N\}$
3.   train h_k specified by its parameters $\boldsymbol{w}_k$:
   $$\boldsymbol{w}_k = \underset{\boldsymbol{w}}{argmin}\ L_H\big(h\big(X_{\pi(i)}; \boldsymbol{w}\big), y_{\pi(i)}\big),\ i = 1, \ldots, N^{tr}$$
   $(N^{tr} < N)$
4. **end for**
5. collect all trained CNNs $\{h_k\}_{k=1}^T$

Note that this process is almost same as bootstrap aggregation [3], in which each base learner is trained on a subset randomly drawn by sampling with replacement from the original training set. In this work, sampling without replacement is used instead.

Once the training of CNNs is completed, the most straightforward and commonly used ensemble strategy is to average the output from each CNN and compare the result with $th = 0.5$ to determine the corresponding class label, i.e., for each test data X_t, the label $\hat{y}_t$ can be estimated by

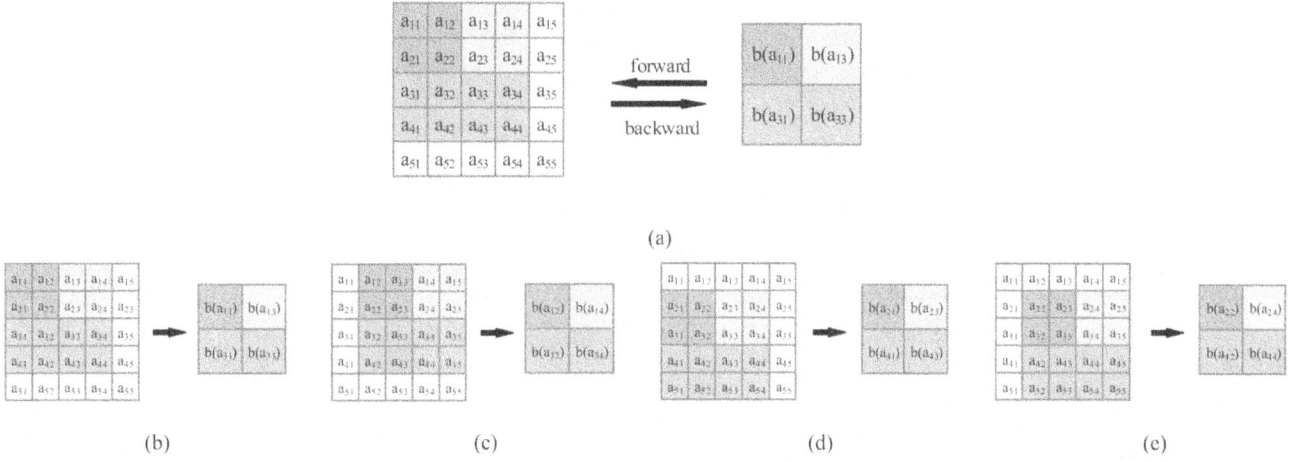

Figure 2. Pooling with local size 2×2 and stride 2 in horizontal and vertical direction. (a) Forward and backward passes of a pooling layer with fixed sampling locations in the training stage of the CNNs. (b) – (e) The four possible sampling when transforming image data with CNNs into feature vectors for ensemble learning.

$$\hat{y}_t = \begin{cases} 0, & \frac{1}{T}\sum_{1 \le k \le T} h_k(X_t) < th \\ 1, & \frac{1}{T}\sum_{1 \le k \le T} h_k(X_t) \ge th \end{cases}$$

This is the basic ensemble method performed in our experiments. Note that this basic model averaging strategy does not require further ensemble learning. Next, we will show that besides simple model averaging, more can be dug out from the CNNs for steganalysis tasks.

CNNs usually adopt several subsampling steps to reduce the spatial dimensions and facilitate classification. These subsampling steps are fulfilled in pooling layers or convolutional layers with strides set larger than 1. In computer vision and other related research areas, the subsampling steps may not have negative effect, because they discard irrelevant information and help the optimization in deeper layers focused. However, as steganalysis relies on statistics, spatial subsampling could cause information loss, even after the information of skipped pixels have been encoded into neighboring pixels through, e.g., averaging. The dilemma is, it seems that the spatial subsampling is unavoidable, because without it, the statistical modeling in CNN would grasp the location information of embedded pixels from the training data. To help alleviate this issue, one possible solution is, given a trained CNN, we generate probability output of every possible subsampling so that every skipped pixel location could be covered once, as illustrated in Figure 2 (b–e). To facilitate the explanation, we assume the pooling regions to be 2×2 and stride equals 2 for both horizontal and vertical direction. During training (Figure 2 (a)), the pooling layer sticks to only one set of spatial subsamples, i.e., a_{11}, a_{13}, a_{31}, a_{33}... The output of this pooling layer is calculated as, e.g., for average pooling, $b_{11} = (a_{11} + a_{12} + a_{21} + a_{22}) / 4$. But the skipped locations, e.g., $b_{12} = (a_{12} + a_{13} + a_{22} + a_{23}) / 4$ is never considered in training. The solution is to output probability values of all the four constellations of subsampling for ensembles, as demonstrated in Figure 2 (b–e). Following this, given P pooling layers in a CNN, and assume stride equals 2, the total number of output (probabilities) M generated from each trained CNN equals 4^P, for the CNN illustrated in Figure 1, we have $P = 5$ (in Group1 ~ Group5), and therefore $M = 1024$. In this

scenario, using the averaging strategy, the class label $\hat{y}_t$ is estimated as:

$$\hat{y}_i = \begin{cases} 0, & \frac{1}{TM}\sum_{\substack{1 \le k \le T \\ 1 \le d \le M}} h_k^d(X_i) < th \\ 1, & \frac{1}{TM}\sum_{\substack{1 \le k \le T \\ 1 \le d \le M}} h_k^d(X_i) \ge th \end{cases}$$

One might realize that only 1 out of M probabilities is optimized during training for each CNN, the others are close to the optimized because of spatial correlations but are still suboptimal. In this case, it would be beneficial to map the original training data by the CNNs into a new feature representation and train second-level classifiers for optimal performance, as summarized:

1. map the original training data $\{X_i\}_{i=1}^N$ with base learners into $\{Z_i\}_{i=1}^N$, where $Z_i = \{h_k^1(X_i), h_k^2(X_i), ..., h_k^M(X_i)\}_{k=1}^T$, for $1 \le i \le N$
2. build a classifier using $\{Z_i, y_i\}_{i=1}^N$, $i = 1, ..., N$

In this paper, the ensemble classifiers [17] developed specifically for steganalysis is used as the second-level classifier because of its good performance and efficiency.

The last ensemble strategy we have tested is to gather from each CNN the output of the last pooling layer, which is also the output of the convolutional module and input of the classification module as displayed in Figure 1. The intuition is that the ensemble classifiers proposed in [17] are stronger compared with the logistic regression adopted in the classification modules of CNNs, and concatenating intermediate representations from every CNNs before performing classification potentially increases the chance of mining more discriminative patterns. Let f_k denote the function of the convolutional module in the k-th CNN. This ensemble method can be summarized as:

1. map the original training data $\{X_i\}_{i=1}^N$ with base learners into $\{Z_i\}_{i=1}^N$, where $Z_i = \{f_k(X_i)\}_{k=1}^T$, for $1 \le i \le N$
2. build a classifier using $\{Z_i, y_i\}_{i=1}^N$, $i = 1, ..., N$

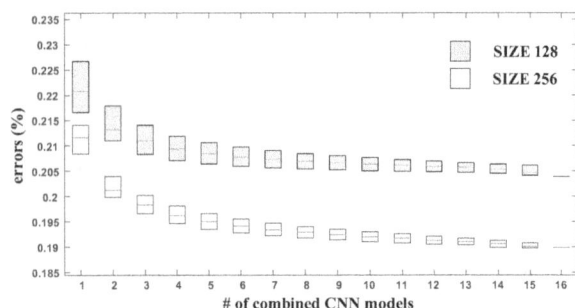

Figure 3. Box plots reflecting overall performance with different number of combined CNN models, for both 'SIZE 128' and 'SIZE 256'. Red lines are the median values, and the upper and lower bounds correspond to the 25 and 75 percentiles.

3. EXPERIMENTS

3.1 Dataset and Settings

Training of the CNNs is performed on a modified version of Caffe toolbox [21]. Performance of the ensemble methods is evaluated by detecting S-UNIWARD [22] at 0.4 bpp embedding rate only, due to the long training time of CNNs and the long feature mapping time. It takes about three weeks to run all the experiments using two NVIDIA Geforce GTX 980Ti graphics cards. The dataset used is BOSSbase v1.01 [16] containing 10,000 cover images of size 512×512. Image data of the other class (stego) were generated through data embedding into the cover images. Hence, the dataset contains 10,000 pairs of images. Out of the 10,000 pairs of images, 5,000 pairs were set aside for testing to verify the performance; the rest 5,000 pairs were used as the training set. To train each CNN as base learner, 4,000 out of the 5,000 training data were randomly drawn, the rest 1,000 data were used as validation set to prevent the neural networks from overtraining. Two groups of CNNs with different network sizes are obtained: 'SIZE 256' and 'SIZE 128', the numbers refer to the output size of the convolutional module as explained in Section 2.1. A total of 16 CNNs are trained and used as base learners for both the two network sizes.

For reproducibility, information of the hyperparameters and settings used during training is summarized here. The learning rate was initialized to 0.001, and scheduled to decrease 10% for every 5,000 iterations. The momentum was set to 0.9. A mini-batch of 64 images (32 cover/stego pairs) was input for each iteration. All of the CNNs were trained for 120,000 iterations (960 epochs). Weight decay was not enabled except for the FC layers.

3.2 Results and Discussion

In the first experiment, we study how the number of CNNs used for ensemble affect the performance. For simplicity, the basic model averaging strategy is adopted. For every fixed number of CNNs used for ensemble, we tested all the combinations (out of 16), and record the box plot for both of the two networks sizes. From Figure 3, we can conclude that increasing the number of CNNs for ensemble reduces variance, and consistently reduces detection errors. Comparing the performance of the two networks with different sizes, we observe that 'SIZE 256' has both lower bias and lower variance, which indicates that the width of a CNN is very important for steganalysis.

Table 2 records all the results using the ensemble strategies proposed in Section 2.2. In Table 1, the number of total features

Table 1. Feature Dimensions of Different Ensemble Scenarios.

	SIZE 128		SIZE 256	
	Ensemble Methods		Ensemble Methods	
	AVE	ENS	AVE	ENS
PROB	16	16	16	16
PROB_POOL	16384	16384	16384	16384
FEA	N/A	2048	N/A	4096

Table 2. Detection Errors (%) of Different Ensemble Scenarios.

	SIZE 128		SIZE 256	
	Ensemble Methods		Ensemble Methods	
	AVE	ENS	AVE	ENS
PROB	0.2039	0.1973	0.1899	0.1897
PROB_POOL	0.2018	0.1954	0.1918	0.1871
FEA	N/A	0.1906	N/A	0.1844

for each ensemble scenario is presented. In Table 1 and Table 2, **PROB** refers to the direct CNN probability output. **PROB_POOL** refers to the generation of probabilities subsampling method and for each CNN. **FEA** corresponds to the output of the convolutional modules in CNNs. **AVE** means simple model averaging, and **ENS** is the ensemble classifiers [17]. From Table 2, we can summarize that the second-level learning consistently yields better performance compared with model averaging. When the ensemble learning method is fixed to **AVE**, **PROB_POOL** does not always have better performance over **PROB**, probably due to the suboptimal probabilities output discussed in Section 2.2. The best performance is always achieved by learning from the pooled output of the convolutional modules, which indicates that for performance, it might be preferred to abandon the classification modules in CNNs. To have some idea of where the presented ensemble performance are, the 34671-D SRM model [14] with ensemble classifiers [17] on the same train/test split, had an error rate of 0.2047.

4. CONCLUSION

In this paper, we study different ensemble strategies using CNNs as base learners for steganalysis. To make best use of the trained CNN models, we manage to partially recover the lost information due to spatial subsampling in the pooling layers when forming feature vectors for ensemble learning. Results suggest that both the recovery of the lost information caused by spatial subsampling, and learning from intermediate representation in CNNs instead of output probabilities, improve the performance. While only tested on one dataset with a special steganalysis, the proposed ensemble methods should be generic and could be performed in most of the image forensic tasks using CNNs.

5. REFERENCES

[1] Y. Freund, and R. E. Schapire. A decision-theoretic generalization of on-line learning and an application to boosting. *J. Comp. Syst. Sciences*, 55(1): 119-139, Aug. 1997.

[2] J. H. Friedman. Greedy function approximation: a gradient boosting machine. *Annals Statistics*, 29(5): 1189-1232, Oct. 2001.

[3] L. Breiman. Bagging predictors. *Machine Learning*, 24(2): 123-140, Aug. 1996.

[4] L. Breiman. Random forests. *Machine learning*, 45(1): 5-32, Oct. 2001.

[5] A. Krizhevsky, I. Sutskever, and G. E. Hinton. ImageNet classification with deep convolutional neural networks. In: *Proc. Adv. Neural Inf. Process. Syst.*, pages 1097-1105, 2012.

[6] O. Russakovsky, J. Deng, H. Su, J. Krause, S. Satheesh, S. Ma, Z. Huang, A. Karpathy, A. Khosla, M. Bernstein, A. C. Berg, and L. Fei-fei. Imagenet large scale visual recognition challenge. *Int. J. Comp. Vision*, 115(3): 211-252, Apr. 2015.

[7] C. Szegedy, W. Liu, Y. Jia, P. Sermanet, S. Reed, D. Anguelov, D. Erhan, V. Vanhoucke, and A. Rabinovich. Going deeper with convolutions. In: *Proc. IEEE Conf. Comp. Vision Pattern Recognition*, pages 1-9, 2015.

[8] S. Ioffe, and C. Szegedy. Batch normalization: accelerating deep network training by reducing internal covariate shift. *arXiv*:1502.03167, Feb. 2015.

[9] K. He, X. Zhang, S. Ren, and J. Sun. Deep residual learning for image recognition. *arXiv*:1512.03385, Dec. 2015.

[10] J. Chen, X. Kang, Y. Liu, and Z. J. Wang. Median filtering forensics based on convolutional neural networks. *IEEE Signal Process. Lett.,* 22(11): 1849-1853, Jun. 2015.

[11] S. Tan, and B. Li. Stacked convolutional auto-encoders for steganalysis of digital images. In: *Proc. APSIPA*, pages 1-4, Dec. 2014.

[12] Y. Qian, J. Dong, W. Wang, and T. Tan. Deep learning for steganalysis via convolutional neural networks. In: *Proc. SPIE Electronic Imaging*, pages 94090J, Mar. 2015.

[13] L. Pibre, P. Jérôme, D. Ienco, and M. Chaumont. Deep learning is a good steganalysis tool when embedding key is reused for different images, even if there is a cover source-mismatch. In: *Proc. SPIE Electronic Imaging*, Feb. 2016.

[14] J. Fridrich, and J. Kodovský. Rich models for steganalysis of digital images. *IEEE Inf. Forensics Security*, 7(3): 868-882, Jun. 2012.

[15] G. Xu, H. Wu, and Y. Shi. Structural design of convolutional neural networks for steganalysis. *IEEE Signal Process. Lett.,* 23(5): 708-712, Mar. 2016.

[16] P. Bas, T. Filler, and T. Pevný. "Break our steganographic system": the ins and outs of organizing BOSS. In: *Proc. Inf. Hiding*, vol. 6958, pages 59-70, Springer, May 2011.

[17] J. Kodovsky, J. Fridrich, and V. Holub. Ensemble classifiers for steganalysis of digital media. *IEEE Trans. Inf. Forensics Security,* 7(2): 432-444, Apr. 2012.

[18] V. Holub, and J. Fridrich. Random projections of residuals for digital image steganalysis. *IEEE Trans. Inf. Forensics Security*, 8(12): 1996-2006, Dec. 2013.

[19] T. Denemark, V. Sedighi, V. Holub, R. Cogranne, and J. Fridrich. Selection-channel-aware rich model for steganalysis of digital images. In: *Proc. Inf. Forensics Security (WIFS)*, pages 48-53, Dec. 2014.

[20] W. Tang, H. Li, W. Luo, and J. Huang. Adaptive steganalysis against WOW embedding algorithm. In: *Proc. ACM IH&MMSec*, pages 91-96, 2014.

[21] Y. Jia, E. Shelhamer, J. Donahue, S. Karayev, J. Long, R. Girshick, S. Guadarrama, and T. Darrell. Caffe: convolutional architecture for fast feature embedding. In: *Proc. ACM Int. Conf. Multimed.*, pages 675-678, 2014.

[22] V. Holub, J. Fridrich, and T. Denemark. Universal distortion function for steganography in an arbitrary domain. *EURASIP J. Inf. Security*, 2014(1): 1-13, Dec. 2014.

Color Image Steganalysis Based on Steerable Gaussian Filters Bank

Hasan ABDULRAHMAN
Montpellier University
Ecole des Mines d'Alès, LGI2P
30035 Nîmes Cedex 1, France.
Hasan.abdulrahman@mines-ales.fr

Philippe MONTESINOS
Ecole des Mines d'Alès, LGI2P
30035 Nîmes Cedex 1, France.
Philippe.montesinos@mines-ales.fr

Marc CHAUMONT
Nîmes University, Montpellier University
Place Gabriel Péri, 30000 Nîmes
UMR5506-LIRMM, 34095 Montpellier Cedex 5, France.
Marc.Chaumont@lirmm.fr

Baptiste MAGNIER
Ecole des Mines d'Alès, LGI2P
30035 Nîmes Cedex 1, France.
Baptiste.magnier@mines-ales.fr

ABSTRACT

This article deals with color images steganalysis based on machine learning. The proposed approach enriches the features from the Color Rich Model by adding new features obtained by applying steerable Gaussian filters and then computing the co-occurrence of pixel pairs. Adding these new features to those obtained from Color-Rich Models allows us to increase the detectability of hidden messages in color images. The Gaussian filters are angled in different directions to precisely compute the tangent of the gradient vector. Then, the gradient magnitude and the derivative of this tangent direction are estimated. This refined method of estimation enables us to unearth the minor changes that have occurred in the image when a message is embedded. The efficiency of the proposed framework is demonstrated on three stenographic algorithms designed to hide messages in images: S-UNIWARD, WOW, and Synch-HILL. Each algorithm is tested using different payload sizes. The proposed approach is compared to three color image steganalysis methods based on computation features and Ensemble Classifier classification: the Spatial Color Rich Model, the CFA-aware Rich Model and the RGB Geometric Color Rich Model.

Keywords

Steganalysis; steganography; steerable Gaussian filters.

1. INTRODUCTION

Steganography is the art and science of hiding messages inside a digital medium in such a way that only the sender and the receiver, can view the hidden message. The goal of steganalysis is to detect the presence of hidden messages in digital media. The practical performance (i.e. security) of different steganographic techniques is rated by the detectability (for example the average testing error of the steganalyser) for a given relative payload size; additionally the computational complexity could be taken into account [17].

In 2015, color steganalysis has been studied by integrating the modern adaptive embedding method in an experimental evaluation. Previous steganalysis methods did not use recent grey-level embedding algorithms [7], [25], [15], [19] or did not use a machine learning approach with Rich-Model features [11], [24]. Three color image steganalysis methods, based on a machine learning approach fed with rich model features are now well established. For these three methods, the machine learning algorithm is the Ensemble Classifier [16], and the rich features are: the Spatial Color Rich Model abbreviated to **CRM** [10], the CFA-aware Rich Model abbreviated to **CFARM** [9], and the RGB Geometric Color Rich Model abbreviated to **GCRM** (RGB for the Red, Green and Blue channels) [2]. Note that among these three features, the GCRM which is an extension of the CCRM (Correlation Color Rich Model [1]) seems to be the equivalent or better than the CRM and CFARM when recent adaptive grey-level embedding algorithms are used for embedding independently in each color channel. Additionally, note that a recent independent study has shown that CCRM was the most reliable method in every case, even when the algorithm was embedding adaptively with a synchronization of the embedding between the color channels [23].

At the beginning of 2016, **GCRM** is the natural choice for computing features that will be used for a color steganalysis (machine learning approach) for modern color embedding algorithms.

The rest of this paper is organized as follows. Section 2 describes the latest recent methods in color steganalysis by recalling the CRM [10], the CFARM [9] and the GCRM [2]. Then, we present a detailed description of our proposed method in Section 3; the steerable Gaussian filters computation is demonstrated and the feature set is presented. Experimental results and comparisons are given in Section 4. In this section, we also present the databases and show the performance of the proposed method. Finally, Section 5 gives some conclusions and perspectives.

2. COLOR STEGANALYSIS METHODS

Over the last ten years, most of the steganalysis methods are dealing with grayscale images [14], there exist very few steganalysis methods dealing with color images. The most recent methods

IH& MMSec 2016, June 20-23, 2016, Vigo, Spain

© 2016 ACM. ISBN 978-1-4503-4290-2/16/06. . . $15.00

DOI: http://dx.doi.org/10.1145/2909827.2930799

in color image steganalysis are explained in detail in the three following subsections.

2.1 Color rich model method

Goljan et al. [10] have introduced very efficient color image features, the CRM, which is an extension of the Spatial Rich Model [6], produced from two different sets of features.

In order to compute these features, firstly they extracted the noise residual from each color channel separately: the red (R), green (G), and blue (B) channels. On each channel they applied the same computation, as a grayscale image I. Let us note $I(x, y)$ a pixel value of an 8-bit grayscale cover image at coordinates (x, y). Then, the noise residual is computed using the following formula:

$$\mathbf{R}(x, y) = \hat{I}(x, y)(\mathcal{N}(x, y)) - c \cdot I(x, y), \qquad (1)$$

where: $c \in \mathbb{N}$, is the residual order, $\mathcal{N}(x, y)$ is a local neighborhood of pixel $I(x, y)$ and $\hat{I}(x, y)(\cdot)$ represents a predictor of $c \cdot I(x, y)$, with $I(x, y) \notin \mathcal{N}(x, y)$ and $I(x, y) \in \{0, ..., 255\}$. All of the submodels $\mathbf{R}(x, y) \in \mathbb{R}^{n_1 \times n_2}$ are formed from noise residual images using a size of $m \times m$, with n_1, n_2 and $m \in \mathbb{N}^*$, by applying a rounding and a truncation:

$$\mathbf{R}(x, y) \leftarrow tranc_T \left(round \left(\frac{R(x, y)}{q} \right) \right), \qquad (2)$$

where,

- $R(x, y) = \begin{cases} tranc_T(u) = u, & \text{for } u \in [-T, T], u \in \mathbb{R} \\ tranc_T(u) = T \cdot sign(u) & \text{otherwise.} \end{cases}$

- q represents the quantization step,

- $round$ is a function for rounding to an integer value.

Moreover, the color noise residuals are computed as in Eq.1 on the demosaiced image for the CRM features. Secondly, spatial co-occurrence are computed and the inter-channel co-occurrence matrices, as a feature set.

On the one hand, the Spatial Rich Model (SRMQ1) [6] with a fixed quantization $q = 1$ and a truncation $T = 2$ yields a dimensionality of $12,753$ features. These features are computed from each R, G and B color channel separately. On the other hand, from the same noise residuals (i.e. SRMQ1), a collection of 3D color co-occurrence matrices are built (CRMQ1), taking three color values at the same position and computing co-occurrence matrices across the three channels. With a fixed truncation $T = 3$ and a quantization $q = 1$, CRMQ1 produces 5404 features. Finally, for this method, the two sets of features are gathered in a one dimensional vector to produce $18,157$ features as a final set of features.

2.2 CFA-aware features method

Goljan et al. introduced in [9] the CFA-aware Color Rich Model, noted CFARM, for color image steganalysis. The features are made up of two parts, the first one is the CRM explained in the previous Section, with $T \in \{2, 3\}$. The second part is the CFA-aware feature, consisting of three combinations: RB/GG split, $R/B/GG$ split and NII/INI split. Then, in order to capture the inter-channel and intra-channel dependencies, four 3D co-occurrence matrices are built to extract features from and between the color channels, according to the structure of the Bayer CFA. In the CFARM approach [9], the authors assume that the upper left pixel corresponds to a non-interpolated pixel from the blue channel of the Bayer CFA.

Four index sets are introduced, corresponding to the geometric structure of the CFA map:

$$\mathcal{I}_B = \{(x, y) | x \text{ even}, y \text{ even}\}, \mathcal{I}_R = \{(x, y) | x \text{ odd}, y \text{ odd}\},$$
$$\mathcal{I}_{G1} = \{(x, y) | x \text{ odd}, y \text{ even}\}, \mathcal{I}_{G2} = \{(x, y) | x \text{ even}, y \text{ odd}\}.$$

Three combinations of features are generated to form the total number of features with the CRM set:
1) RB/GG split produces 4146 features,
2) $R/B/GG$ split produces 10,323 features,
3) NII/INI split produces 5514 features.

Finally, all four sets of features are gathered in a one dimensional vector, which are ready to enter to the classifier.

2.3 RGB channel geometric method

Abdulrahman et al. [2] proposed the RGB Geometric Color Rich Model (GCRM). The authors show that if one channel has been affected by a steganography method, the inter channel correlation will measure the local modifications. On this basis, they proposed two types of features computed between color image channels. The first types of features reflects local Euclidean transformations through the computation of the cosine of the angle between channel gradients called ∇R, ∇G and ∇B (for red, green and blue). For example, the cosine of the rotation angle, between the red and the green channel gradients:

$$\mathcal{C}_{RG} = \frac{\nabla R \cdot \nabla G}{|\nabla R| \, |\nabla G|}. \qquad (3)$$

The second gives complementary information on the angle through the computation of the *sine* of the angle between channel gradients. Indeed, computing the horizontal and vertical image derivatives of all channels allows us to increase the steganalysis by computing local deformations between channels. For the red and green channels, let us note these derivatives R_x, G_x for the horizontal and R_y, G_y for the vertical ones. Thus, for the red and green channels, the sine is given by the following formula:

$$\mathcal{S}_{RG} = \frac{R_x \cdot G_y - R_y \cdot G_x}{|\nabla R| \, |\nabla G|}. \qquad (4)$$

At the end, they obtained 4 geometrical measures: $\mathcal{C}_{RG}$, cosine between R and G, $\mathcal{C}_{RB}$, cosine between R and B, $\mathcal{S}_{RG}$, sine between R and G, and $\mathcal{S}_{RB}$ between R and B. Those geometrical measurements allow to generate 6000 features, based on local Euclidean and mirror transformations, when using co-occurrence matrices with a fixed truncation $T=1$ and different values for the quantization $q \in \{0.1, 0.3, 0.5, 0.7, 0.9, 1\}$. Concatenate these features with those from CRM [10] increases the detectability of hidden messages in color images [2], [23].

3. THE PROPOSED METHOD

In order to be less visible, most of the steganographic methods modify the pixel values in the texture/edge areas [22], [13], [18]... Our proposition is to enrich the CRM method by introducing new sets of features obtained by applying steerable Gaussian filters and then computing the co-occurrence of pixel pairs in eight different directions.

The proposed features are composed of two distinctive sets. The first set, produced by [10], is made of $18,157$ features. The second is made of 4406 features. In the first step, we computed a *tangent vector* to contour for each pixel and for each channel. This *tangent vector* corresponds to the edge direction and is orthogonal to the gradient vector. Then, in the second step, the co-occurrence matrices are computed, firstly, on the three gradient magnitude images and afterwards, on the three derivative images related to the *tangent vectors*.

3.1 Steerable Gaussian filters

In the domain of image analysis, the estimation of a precise gradient is crucial, and is often based on the computation of local derivatives.

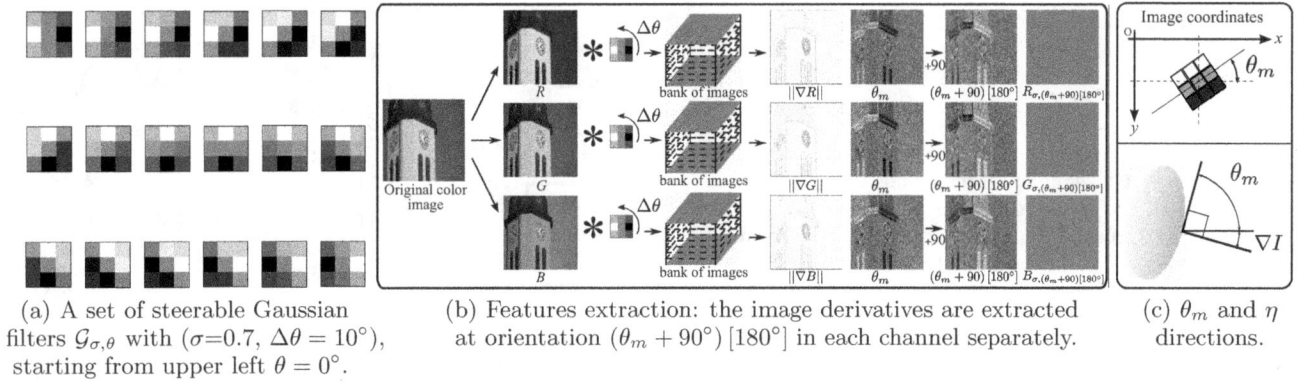

(a) A set of steerable Gaussian filters $\mathcal{G}_{\sigma,\theta}$ with (σ=0.7, $\Delta\theta = 10°$), starting from upper left $\theta = 0°$.

(b) Features extraction: the image derivatives are extracted at orientation $(\theta_m + 90°) [180°]$ in each channel separately.

(c) θ_m and η directions.

Figure 1: Steerable filters are used to compute a gradient and to estimate precise edges directions.

When using filters with image derivatives in only two directions, the x and y (i.e $0°$ and $90°$), the gradient estimation is not accurate enough to describe the geometrical structures in the image. Using an orientation filter bank can improve the quality of the gradient estimation; indeed, its orientation and its magnitude are far more accurate.

Due to multiple orientations, a filter bank allows us to better detect image features such as edges. One of the most popular filter banks is the steerable filters. As a solution to the above stated problem, Freeman and Adelson [5] introduced an elegant way for steerable filters that can be directed at specific angles using a linear combination of isotropic filters like Gaussian derivatives. Let us note the basic derivatives of Gaussian filters $\partial\mathcal{G}_\sigma/\partial x$ and $\partial\mathcal{G}_\sigma/\partial y$ along the x-axis and y-axis respectively, for example:

$$\begin{cases} \dfrac{\partial\mathcal{G}_\sigma(x,y)}{\partial x} = \dfrac{-x}{2\pi\sigma^4} \cdot e^{-\frac{x^2+y^2}{2\sigma^2}} \\[3mm] \dfrac{\partial\mathcal{G}_\sigma(x,y)}{\partial y} = \dfrac{-y}{2\pi\sigma^4} \cdot e^{-\frac{x^2+y^2}{2\sigma^2}}, \end{cases} \quad (5)$$

with σ the standard-deviation of the Gaussian filter.

Freeman and Adelson have shown that the first order directional Gaussian derivative $\mathcal{G}_{\sigma,\theta}$ at an angle θ can be generated by a linear combination of a rotation of the basic derivatives of isotropic Gaussian filters (illustrated in Fig. 1 (a) and (b)):

$$\mathcal{G}_{\sigma,\theta}(x,y,\sigma) = \cos(\theta) \cdot \frac{\partial\mathcal{G}_\sigma}{\partial x}(x,y) + \sin(\theta) \cdot \frac{\partial\mathcal{G}_\sigma}{\partial y}(x,y). \quad (6)$$

The image derivative $I_{\sigma,\theta}$ is obtained by convolving the original grayscale image I with the oriented Gaussian kernels $\mathcal{G}_{\sigma,\theta}$:

$$I_{\sigma,\theta}(x,y) = (I * \mathcal{G}_{\sigma,\theta})(x,y). \quad (7)$$

Finally, the gradient magnitude $\|\nabla I(x,y)\|$ is calculated as the maximum absolute value response to the oriented operator $\mathcal{G}_{\sigma,\theta}$:

$$\|\nabla I(x,y)\| = \max_{\theta \in [0,180[}(|I_{\sigma,\theta}(x,y)|), \quad (8)$$

$$\theta_m = \arg\max_{\theta \in [0,180[}(|I_{\sigma,\theta}(x,y)|). \quad (9)$$

Note that θ_m, represents the *kernel angle* and it differs from the *gradient angle* which is equal to $(\theta_m + 90°) [180°]$.

In this work, the Gaussian filters are angled in different directions to compute the more precise gradient magnitude $\|\nabla I\|$ and its associated kernel angle θ_m. Thus, $\|\nabla I\|$ corresponds to the absolute value of the image derivative for the kernel angled at θ_m, as illustrated in Fig. 1(c). Note that $\|\nabla I\|$ and θ_m are different for each pixel of I. These techniques are applied to the three color

channels R, G and B to obtain three gradient magnitude images $\|\nabla R\|$, $\|\nabla G\|$ and $\|\nabla B\|$ (see Fig. 1(b)).

As pointed out previously, the steganographic methods essentially modifies the pixel values in the textures and edge areas. For the edge areas, the embedding modifications have to be detected along the "isophote" lines i.e. along the curves of constant intensity when considering an image as a surface. This led us to consider the orthogonal vector to the gradient named the *tangent vector*, instead of the gradient; this means that the derivative along the edge must be computed. This derivative corresponds to the result of the convolution of the image with the steerable kernel angled at $(\theta_m + 90°) [180°]$ and is orthogonal to the kernel used for the gradient estimation (as illustrated in Fig. 2). The derivative image is named $I_{\sigma,(\theta_m+90)[180°]}$.

For a color image, each channel is considered separately. The tangent derivatives[1], as illustrated in Fig. 1 (b), are respectively computed for each pixel at position (x,y) of each channel and named: $R_{\sigma,(\theta_m+90)[180°]}(x,y)$ for the red, $G_{\sigma,(\theta_m+90)[180°]}(x,y)$ for the green, and $B_{\sigma,(\theta_m+90)[180°]}(x,y)$ for the blue channel. Fig. 1 (b) shows an example of steerable Gaussian filters used to compute these new features. In our method, the Gaussian filters are

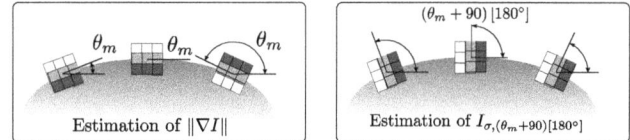

Figure 2: Positions of the steerable filters at the level of the edges to build the gradient image $\|\nabla I\|$ and image derivative $I_{\sigma,(\theta_m+90)[180°]}(x,y)$.

angled in different directions to compute a precise gradient and a precise derivative along isophote lines. In order to detect the slight changes in the images, our experiments (see Section 4.2) leads to a $\sigma = 0.7$, with a filter support for the size 3×3 pixels, a rotation step for the filters bank $\Delta\theta = 10°$, and a rotation range such as $\theta \in \{0°, ..., 180° - \Delta\theta\}$ (it leads to 18 filter orientations as represented in Fig. 1 (a)).

3.2 Complete feature set

As explained in Fig.1 (b), Eq.8 and detailed above, the co-occurrence matrices are completed from the three gradient magnitude images

---

[1] As these three images are derivatives, pixel values can be positives or negatives.

and also the three derivative images using their edge directions:

$$\begin{cases} \|\nabla R\|, & \|\nabla G\|, & \|\nabla B\|, \\ R_{\sigma,(\theta_m+90)[180°]}, & G_{\sigma,(\theta_m+90)[180°]}, & B_{\sigma,(\theta_m+90)[180°]}. \end{cases}$$

Before we make the co-occurrence computation, different truncations are applied. For the gradient magnitude images, the truncation $T \in \{2, 3\}$, and for the derivative images, $T \in \{1, 2, 3\}$. Thus this leads to 2 triplets of quantized-truncated gradient magnitude images, and 3 triplets of quantized-truncated derivative images. Then, the pairs co-occurrence matrices are computed, like the Subtractive Pixel Adjacency Model (**SPAM**) [21], with eight directions for the scan images. These direction feature subsets are as follows: $F_h^{\rightarrow}, F_h^{\leftarrow}, F_v^{\uparrow}, F_v^{\downarrow}, F_d^{\nearrow}, F_d^{\swarrow}, F_{md}^{\nwarrow}$ and $F_{md}^{\searrow}$. 2808 features are created by the gradient magnitude and 1598 by the derivative images. All features are gathered in to a one dimension vector to erect a dimensionality of 4406 features. As a final set for the proposed method, 22, 563 features are obtained, by concatenating these features with those obtained from CRM [10].

4. EXPERIMENTAL RESULTS

All the experiments were carried out on 10, 000 color images of size 512×512. All detectors were trained as binary classifiers implemented using the ensemble classifier[2] [16] with default settings.

4.1 Setup database

In order to build our image database, the full-resolution raw images were collected from two subsets which are the most standard (i.e. 3500 full-resolution Nikon digital camera raw color images from the Dresden Image Database [8] and 1000 Canon digital camera raw color images from the Break Our Steganographic System (BOSSbase1[3]) [3]). Afterwards, the RGB color images are obtained by using the Patterned Pixel Grouping (PPM) demosaicking algorithm named "dcraw"[4]. Finally, from each color RGB image, we randomly extracted five cropped images measuring 512×512. Finally, the cropped images having the higher variation correspond to those exploited in the used steganography algorithms. As a result, the final number of RGB cropped images is 10, 000. Moreover, in this last process, the cropped images are extracted carefully so that the CFA map layout always stays the same, as illustrated in Fig. 3.

Three spatial domain steganography algorithms are used to produce stego images:

- Spatial UNIversal WAvelet Relative Distortion (S-UNIWARD[5]) [13],
- Wavelet Obtained Weights (WOW[6]) [12],
- Synchronizing Selection Channel (Synch-HILL[7]) [4].

As explained in [20], the steganography methods have an important impact on the performance of the general methodology. These algorithms are used to embed messages into color images by decomposing the R, G and B channels like three gray-scale images

---

[2]The Ensemble classifier is available at http://dde.binghamton.edu/download/ensemble.

[3]BOSSbase can be accessed at http://www.agents.cz/boss/BOSSFinal.

[4]dcraw code is available at http://www.cybercom.net/defin/dcraw.

[5]The Matlab version of S-UNIWARD is available at http://dde.binghamton.edu/download/stego_algorithms.

[6]The Matlab version of WOW is available at http://dde.binghamton.edu/download/stego_algorithms.

[7]The Matlab version of Synch-HILL is available at http://dde.binghamton.edu/download/stego_algorithms.

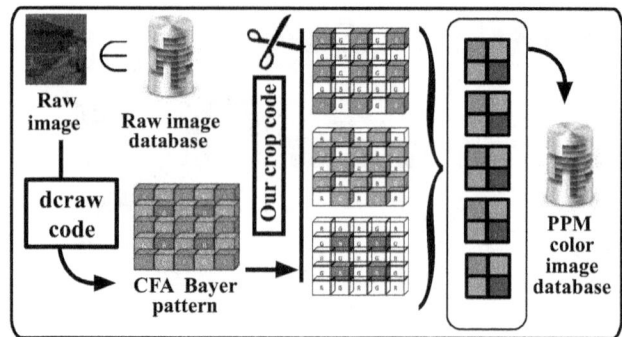

Figure 3: The preprocessing steps for building our database depend on the CFA idea.

and embedding the same proportion payload into each channel. Finally, 10, 000 color images were used to test each of the seven different payload sizes: $\{0.01, 0.05, 0.1, 0.2, 0.3, 0.4, 0.5\}$ Bit Per Channel (**BPC**).

4.2 Performance of the proposed method

To evaluate the performance of the proposed method, all steganalyzers were implemented as binary classifiers using the ensemble classifier [16]. In this paper, the detection accuracy is measured by using the average of testing errors under equal priors: $\bar{P}_E = min_{P_{FA}} \frac{1}{2} [P_{FA} + P_{MD}(P_{FA})]$, where, P_{FA} represents the false alarm probability and P_{MD} the missed detection probability. 5000 cover images are randomly chosen from the database for the training sets and 5000 stego images for the testing sets. The ensemble classifiers apply a vote to estimate the error of detection. This process is repeated 10 times to obtain $\bar{P}_E$ which quantify the detectability and are collected for each method and each payload in order to evaluate the steganalysis method.

As explained in Section 3.1, the experiments were run in such a way as to find the best filter bank parameters: the scale of the steerable filters σ (Eq. 6) and the rotation step ($\Delta\theta$) with angles evenly drawn from $0°$ to $180°$. These experiments have been led using S-UNIWARD with a payload size of 0.3 bpc with the use of the 22, 563 features obtained by concatenating the CRM with the gradient features. Table 1 shows that $\sigma = 0.7$ with $\Delta\theta = 10°$ corresponds to the optimal parameters for the steerable filters operation in this steganalysis work because, compared to the other parameters, they bring the best detection rate.

Table 1: The probability of error $\bar{P}_E$ to determine the efficient standard deviation (σ) and angle step ($\Delta\theta$) employed for steerable Gaussian filters using S-UNIWARD steganography method payload 0.3 bpc.

$\Delta\theta$	σ	Mask size	$\bar{P}_E$	Detection rate
$10°$	**0.7**	3×3	0.1559 ± 0.0022	84.41 %
$10°$	1	5×5	0.1896 ± 0.0031	81.04 %
$10°$	2	10×10	0.2028 ± 0.0037	79.72 %
$10°$	3	15×15	0.2539 ± 0.0036	76.41 %
$5°$	0.7	3×3	0.1768 ± 0.0026	82.32 %
$10°$	0.7	3×3	0.1559 ± 0.0022	84.41 %
$15°$	0.7	3×3	0.1602 ± 0.0026	83.98 %
$20°$	0.7	3×3	0.1653 ± 0.0019	83.47 %
$30°$	0.7	3×3	0.1854 ± 0.0027	81.46 %
$45°$	0.7	3×3	0.1893 ± 0.0012	81.07 %
$90°$	0.7	3×3	0.1996 ± 0.0031	80.04 %

Table 2: Error probability $\bar{P}_E$ and the detection rate $\mathcal{P}_D\%$ for four steganography methods.

Steganography Method	Payload (bpc)	Proposed Method $\bar{P}_E$	22,563 Dim $\mathcal{P}_D\%$	CRM $\bar{P}_E$	18,157 Dim $\mathcal{P}_D\%$	CFARM $\bar{P}_E$	27,460 Dim $\mathcal{P}_D\%$	GCRM $\bar{P}_E$	24,157 Dim $\mathcal{P}_D\%$
S-UNIWARD	0.01	0.4664	**53.36**	0.4841	51.59	0.4863	51.37	0.4680	53.20
	0.05	0.3835	**61.65**	0.4045	59.55	0.4072	59.28	0.3859	61.41
	0.1	0.2984	**70.16**	0.3298	67.02	0.3194	68.06	0.3037	69.63
	0.2	0.2164	**78.36**	0.2498	75.02	0.2317	67.83	0.2191	78.09
	0.3	0.1559	**84.41**	0.1947	80.53	0.1806	81.94	0.1623	83.77
	0.4	0.1202	**87.98**	0.1599	84.01	0.1429	85.71	0.1289	87.11
	0.5	0.1117	**88.83**	0.1386	86.14	0.1239	87.61	0.1124	88.76
WOW	0.01	0.4687	**53.13**	0.4850	51.50	0.4875	51.25	0.4753	52.47
	0.05	0.3854	**61.46**	0.4092	59.08	0.4174	58.26	0.3906	60.94
	0.1	0.3091	**69.09**	0.3397	66.03	0.3275	67.25	0.3161	68.39
	0.2	0.2269	**77.31**	0.2654	73.46	0.2440	75.60	0.2381	76.19
	0.3	0.1685	**83.15**	0.2081	79.19	0.1895	81.05	0.1793	82.07
	0.4	0.1377	**86.23**	0.1783	82.17	0.1487	85.13	0.1384	86.16
	0.5	0.1206	**87.94**	0.1473	85.27	0.1296	87.04	0.1207	87.93
Synch-HILL	0.01	0.4651	**53.49**	0.4893	51.07	0.4843	51.57	0.4687	53.13
	0.05	0.3647	**63.53**	0.3991	60.09	0.4030	59.70	0.3720	62.80
	0.1	0.2946	**70.54**	0.3311	66.89	0.3189	68.11	0.3086	69.14
	0.2	0.2113	**78.87**	0.2595	74.05	0.2394	76.06	0.2269	77.31
	0.3	0.1536	**84.64**	0.1997	80.03	0.1753	82.47	0.1607	83.93
	0.4	0.1294	**87.06**	0.1684	83.16	0.1478	85.22	0.1311	86.89
	0.5	0.1125	**88.75**	0.1475	85.25	0.1258	87.42	0.1193	88.07

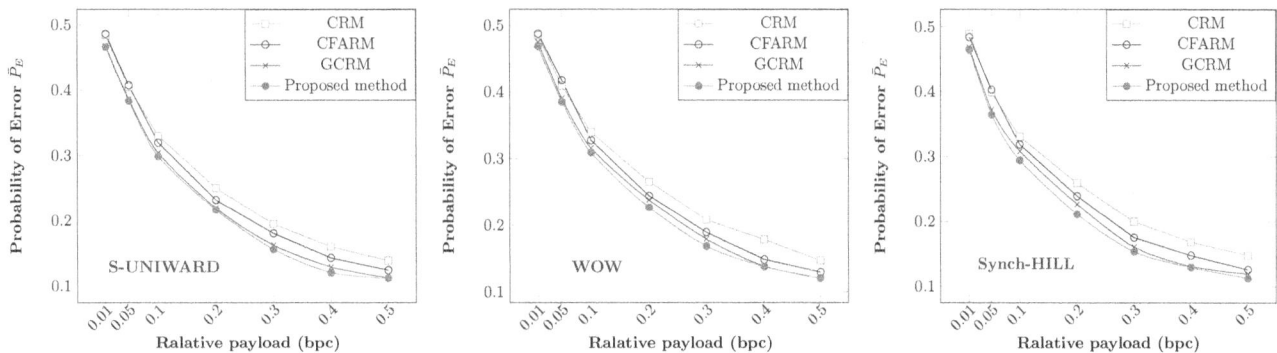

Figure 4: Error probability $\bar{P}_E$ as a function of the payload for three steganography methods.

The experimental results are given in Table 2. Three algorithms have been tested: S-UNIWARD, WOW and Synch-HILL with different relative payloads sizes: $\{0.01, 0.05, 0.1, 0.2, 0.3, 0.4, 0.5\}$. Furthermore, the proposed method is tested against three other approaches: CRM [10], CFARM [9] and GCRM [2].

Table 2 demonstrates that the proposed method registered the highest performance. As an example, detection rates for, at a time, S-UNIWARD, WOW and Synch-HILL for a payload of 0.5 bpc are 88.83%, 87.94% and 88.75% respectively using the proposed approach, to the contrary of the other three compared methods. The CRM method [10] achieved 86.14%, 85.27% and 85.25% respectively. The CFARM method [9] achieved 87.61%, 87.04% and 87.42% respectively. Additionally, the GCARM method [2] achieved 88.76%, 87.93% and 88.07% respectively.

Moreover, curves in Fig. 4 for S-UNIWARD, WOW, and Synch-HILL steganography methods illustrate the comparison between the proposed method and the comparison methods. As a result, the error probability of the proposed method is less than the three steganalysis methods. This performance is due to the Gaussian filters bank, created by the steerable filters, which allow a more precise estimation of the gradient and its associated tangent vector.

In order to increase the detectability rate of the GCRM method [2], another experiment has been performed by concatenating the GCRM [2] features with the new proposed features in one dimensional vector to produce 28, 563 features. These new dimensional vectors achieved 85.03% for S-UNIWARD, and 85.07% for Synch-HILL steganography methods payload 0.3 bpc as a detection rate. It obtains a difference of 1.26%, 1.14% respectively more than GCRM [2] alone and this result is close (slightly better) to our proposed approach results (less than 1%).

5. CONCLUSIONS

This article presents new features for color image steganalysis. Applying a Gaussian filters bank, to an order of 1, in different directions, enabled us to detect the slight changes in the images which occurred as a result of embedding the message.

The proposed approach treats the three color channels separately. Firstly, as steerable filters estimate precisely the edge directions in images, features correspond to the three image derivatives along the edges and the three gradient magnitude images. Secondly, features are extracted from these six images using the co-occurrence matrices of pixel pairs. Finally, our proposed features are integrated with the CRM features [10] to get the new approach. To evaluate the performance of the new approach, the embedding algorithms used are S-UNIWARD, WOW, and Synch-HILL at different payloads.

Experimental results show that fusing proposed features with those obtained by CRM allows in the majority of cases, the detectability of hidden messages in the color images. Additionally, the new approach achieved higher detection rates than the three recent steganalysis approaches: CRM, CFARM, and GCRM. This observed detection improvement is due to a fine estimation of the tangent vector which is used for the estimation of the image derivatives in the edges directions. The proposed features allow the Ensemble Classifier to reveal the hidden message between the stego and cover images.

Eventually, future works consist of better understanding WOW-CMD-C or HILL-CMD-C [23] embedding algorithms, which synchronize the color selection channel during the embedding process.

6. REFERENCES

[1] H. Abdulrahman, M. Chaumont, P. Montesinos, and B. Magnier. Color image steganalysis using correlations between rgb channels. In *Proc. 10th Int. Conf. on Availability, Reliability and Security (ARES), 4th Int. Workshop on Cyber Crime (IWCC), Toulouse, France*, pages 448–454. IEEE, Aug. 24- 28, 2015.

[2] H. Abdulrahman, M. Chaumont, P. Montesinos, and B. Magnier. Color images steganalysis using rgb channel geometric transformation measures. *Wiley J. on Security and Communication Networks*, (DOI: 10.1002/sec.1427):12 pages, Feb. 2016.

[3] P. Bas, T. Filler, and T. Pevnỳ. "Break our steganographic system": The ins and outs of organizing boss. *Inf. Hiding, 13th Int. Workshop, Lecture Notes in Computer Science, Prague, Czech*, pages 59–70, May 2011.

[4] T. Denemark and J. Fridrich. Improving steganographic security by synchronizing the selection channel. In *Proc. of the 3rd ACM Workshop on Inf. Hiding and Multimedia Security (IH&MMSec), Portland, Oregon*, pages 5–14, June 2015.

[5] W. T. Freeman and E. H. Adelson. The design and use of steerable filters. *IEEE Trans. on Pattern Analysis & Machine Intelligence*, Vol.13(9):pp.891–906, 1991.

[6] J. Fridrich and J. Kodovskỳ. Rich models for steganalysis of digital images. *IEEE Trans. on Inf. Forensics and Security*, vol.7(no.3):pp.868–882, Jun. 2012.

[7] J. Fridrich and M. Long. Steganalysis of lsb encoding in color images. In *IEEE Int. Conf. on Multimedia and Expo (ICME) 2000, New York, NY, USA*, volume Vol.3, pages 1279–1282, July 2000.

[8] T. Gloe and R. Böhme. "The dresden image database" for benchmarking digital image forensics. *In Proc. ACM Symp. on Applied Computing, Sierre, Switzerland*, Vol.2:pp.1584–1590, Mar. 2010.

[9] M. Goljan and J. Fridrich. CFA-aware features for steganalysis of color images. In *Proc. IS&T/SPIE Electronic Imaging, Int. Society for Optics and Photonics (SPIE), San Francisco, CA, USA*, volume 94090V, page (13), Feb. 2015.

[10] M. Goljan, J. Fridrich, and R. Cogranne. Rich model for steganalysis of color images. *In Proc. IEEE Int. Workshop on Inf. Forensics Security, Atlanta, GA, USA*, pages 185–190, Dec. 2014.

[11] J. J. Harmsen and W. A. Pearlman. Steganalysis of additive-noise modelable information hiding. In *Proc. SPIE Electronic Imaging, Security, Steganography, and Watermarking of Multimedia Contents V, Santa Clara, CA, USA*, pages 131–142, Jan. 2003.

[12] V. Holub and J. Fridrich. Designing steganographic distortion using directional filters. In *Proc. IEEE Int. Workshop on Inf. Forensics and Security (WIFS), Tenerife, Spain*, pages 234–239, Dec. 2012.

[13] V. Holub, J. Fridrich, and T. Denemark. Universal distortion function for steganography in an arbitrary domain. *EURASIP Journal on Inf. Security*, Vol.2014(no.1):pp.1–13, 2014.

[14] A. D. Ker, P. Bas, R. Böhme, R. Cogranne, S. Craver, T. Filler, J. Fridrich, and T. Pevnỳ. Moving steganography and steganalysis from the laboratory into the real world. In *Proc. 1st ACM workshop on Inf. hiding and multimedia security (IH&MMSec), Montpellier, France*, pages 45–58, June 17-19, 2013.

[15] M. Kirchner and R. Bohme. "Steganalysis in technicolor" boosting ws detection of stego images from CFA-interpolated covers. In *Proc. IEEE Int. Conf. on Acoustics, Speech and Signal Processing (ICASSP), Florence, Italy*, pages 3982–3986, May 2014.

[16] J. Kodovskỳ, J. Fridrich, and V. Holub. Ensemble classifiers for steganalysis of digital media. *IEEE Trans. on Inf. Forensics and Security*, Vol.7(no.2):432–444, Apr. 2012.

[17] B. Li, J. He, J. Huang, and Y. Q. Shi. A survey on image steganography and steganalysis. *J. of Inf. Hiding and Multimedia Signal Process.*, Vol.2:pp.142–172, Apr. 2011.

[18] B. Li, M. Wang, J. Huang, and X. Li. A new cost function for spatial image steganography. *In Proc. IEEE, Int. Conf. Image Processing (ICIP), Paris, France*, pages 4206–4210, Oct. 2014.

[19] Q. Liu, A. H. Sung, B. Ribeiro, M. Wei, Z. Chen, and J. Xu. Image complexity and feature mining for steganalysis of least significant bit matching steganography. *J. of Information Sciences*, Vol.178(1):21–36, Jan. 2008.

[20] Y. Miche, P. Bas, A. Lendasse, C. Jutten, and O. Simula. Reliable steganalysis using a minimum set of samples and features. *EURASIP J. on Inf. Security*, vol.2009, article ID 901381:(13), 2009.

[21] T. Pevnỳ, P. Bas, and J. Fridrich. Steganalysis by subtractive pixel adjacency matrix. *IEEE Trans. on Inf. Forensics and Security (TIFS)*, Vol.5(no.2):215–224, June 2010.

[22] T. Pevnỳ, T. Filler, and P. Bas. Using high-dimensional image models to perform highly undetectable steganography. *In Proc. 12th Int. Workshop Inf. hiding, Calgary, AB, Canada*, vol.6387:161–177, Jun. 2010.

[23] W. Tang, B. Li, W. Luo, and J. Huang. Clustering steganographic modification directions for color components. *Signal Processing Letters,IEEE*, Vol.23(No.2):197–201, Feb. 2016.

[24] P. Thiyagarajan, G. Aghila, and V. P. Venkatesan. Steganalysis using color model conversion. *Int. J. of Signal and Image Processing (SIPIJ)*, Vol.2(No.4), Dec. 2011.

[25] A. Westfeld and A. Pfitzmann. Attacks on steganographic systems. In *Proc. on Information Hiding, In: Pfitzmann A. (eds.): 3rd Int. Workshop Lecture Notes in Computer Science, Springer-Verlag, Berlin Heidelberg*, volume 1768, pages 61–76, 2000.

A Survey and Taxonomy Aimed at the Detection and Measurement of Covert Channels

Brent Carrara and Carlisle Adams
School of Electrical Engineering and Computer Science
University of Ottawa
Ottawa, Ontario, Canada
bcarr092@uottawa.ca, cadams@uottawa.ca

ABSTRACT

New viewpoints of covert channels are presented in this work. First, the origin of covert channels is traced back to access control and a new class of covert channel, *air-gap covert channels*, is presented. Second, we study the design of covert channels and provide novel insights that differentiate the research area of *undetectable communication* from that of *covert channels*. Third, we argue that secure systems can be characterized as *fixed-source systems* or *continuous-source systems*, i.e., systems whose security is compromised if their design allows a covert channel to communicate a small, fixed amount of information or communicate information at a sufficiently high, continuous rate, respectively. Consequently, we challenge the traditional method for measuring covert channels, which is based on Shannon capacity, and propose that a new measure, *steganographic capacity*, be used to accurately assess the risk posed by covert channels, particularly those affecting *fixed-source systems*. Additionally, our comprehensive review of covert channels has led us to the conclusion that important properties of covert channels have not been captured in previous taxonomies. We, therefore, present novel extensions to existing taxonomies to more accurately characterize covert channels.

Keywords

Covert channels; network covert channels; host-based covert channels; air-gap covert channels

1. INTRODUCTION

In February, 2015, the security community learned of a sophisticated, unprecedented malicious software (malware) tool named Fanny operating in the wild [77]. Fanny was exceptional because it had the ability to gather information from computer systems on networks that were not connected to the Internet. In order to accomplish this feat, the malicious software used a novel communication channel to execute custom commands (ingress path) as well as collect their output (egress path). This communication link was established by reading from and writing to hidden storage volumes created within the raw file allocation table (FAT) structure of removable media that Fanny had infected. Fanny's communication channel not only provided its operators with the ability to gather information from Internet-disconnected systems, but it also allowed its operators to perform reconnaissance on networks, services, and devices that were never intended to be connected to the Internet.

Fanny was also notable because it used multiple exploits[1] to automatically propagate to vulnerable systems, which it shared with the Stuxnet malware [76, 77]. Stuxnet was an advanced persistent threat (APT), also discovered in the wild, that was presumed to be designed to force industrial control systems (ICS) to operate outside of their designed parameters in order to destroy them [41]. Stuxnet and Fanny employed a similar infection vector to gain access to isolated systems as well, as did Gauss, another APT in the Stuxnet family [19,75]. In a similar fashion to Fanny, the Gauss malware infected removable media such that when they were plugged into vulnerable machines the malware would automatically execute and steal information from the systems. Gauss used the infected removable media as a communication channel to egress stolen data as well.

Fanny, Stuxnet, and Gauss all provide real-world examples of covert channels designed to defeat the security of isolated, *air-gapped* systems. Air-gapped systems are used in both government (e.g., intelligence [94, 126] and military [91,126]) as well as non-government organizations (e.g., SCADA and ICS [21] as well as financial systems [91]) and their security is based on the *security by isolation* principle, which calls for networks with different security requirements to operate completely isolated from one another, each within their own *security domain* [47]. This level of protection is designed to safeguard air-gapped systems from unauthorized access by malicious parties [126] and the technique is sometimes referred to as *compartmentalization* [94]. Despite this rigorous level of protection, however, there are still a number of ways that malware could be installed on air-gapped systems, including a malicious insider [118], Trojan horse executable[2] [144], malicious payload in a trusted file format [140], or a malicious actor in the supply chain [40].

The research community has also developed a number of techniques to leak data from isolated systems. A literature

IH&MMSec 2016, June 20-23, 2016, Vigo, Spain

© 2016 ACM. ISBN 978-1-4503-4290-2/16/06. . . $15.00

DOI: http://dx.doi.org/10.1145/2909827.2930800

---

[1]An exploit is software code designed to leverage a vulnerability or vulnerabilities in other software applications in order to automatically execute a program on a system or gain higher privileged access to a system [144].

[2]A Trojan horse is an innocuous looking program that performs hidden, malicious functionality [144].

review of covert channels provides examples of device pairings that allow for remote, covert communication, including: microphone and speaker [27,28,38,58,59,116,118], CPU and microphone [90,145,146], CPU and GSM receiver [54], light source and ambient light sensor or camera [14,15,62,86,116], speaker and accelerometer [62,116], vibration device and accelerometer [7,38,116,142], electromagnet and magnetometer [62], CPUs [96,115], and display and AM/FM radio [12,55,87]. Despite this extensive documentation, however, our fundamental understanding of covert channels, in general, has not been updated to reflect this new class of attack against air-gapped systems. In this work, we provide insight into the study of covert channels and update their classification and characterization as well as provide recommendations to covert channels designers on how to build truly *undetectable* covert channels. We, additionally, challenge long-held beliefs regarding the methodology for evaluating the security risk posed by covert channels. As a result, we make the following contributions to the covert channel literature:

1. we define the different classes of covert channels and present a novel class, *air-gap covert channels*;

2. we provide recommendations for covert channel designers and present information hiding techniques that could be applied to create *secure undetectable covert channels*;

3. we separate secure systems based on their security requirements, recommend the criteria that should be used to evaluate the risk posed by covert channels to each type of system as well as the metric that should be used to measure covert channels in each system; and

4. we document a general taxonomy for covert channels that characterizes covert channels based on new criterion.

Our work is organized as follows. In **Section 2** we contextualize covert channels by providing an overview of access control in order to set up our discussion in **Section 3**, where we clarify exactly what covert channels are, the classes of covert channels that exist, and their applications. In **Section 4**, we discuss the analysis and design of covert channels, providing recommendations for covert channel designers and in **Section 5** we present an updated taxonomy for covert channels. Additionally, in **Section 6** we categorize secure systems based on their security requirements and outline how their security should be evaluated. Lastly, in **Section 7** we conclude.

2. BACKGROUND INFORMATION

Access control is the "protection of system resources against unauthorized use" [131]. More specifically, access control is the process by which a request by a subject[3] to perform an operation[4] on an object[5] is governed. The study of access control is rooted in military application and was first

---

[3] An active system entity that can initiate requests to perform an operation, e.g., process, domain [42].
[4] An activity performed by a subject, e.g., read, write, etc. [42]
[5] A system entity that operations can be performed on. A system object usually can store information, e.g., file, database [42].

applied to multilevel security (MLS) systems [9]. In MLS systems, subjects and objects are given clearance and classification levels (e.g., confidential, secret, top secret), respectively. Access control decisions, i.e., whether to grant or deny an operation, are based on the subject's clearance, the object's classification and the access control policy of the system. Access control policies define both the mode in which permissions are managed as well as the access rights for subjects.

There are two fundamental access control modes that are relevant to the study of covert channels: discretionary access control (DAC) and non-discretionary (i.e., mandatory) access control (MAC). Systems implementing DAC allow the creator or owner of an object to set its access control permissions. DAC, therefore, allows subjects to discretionarily pass on permissions to other subjects in the system [89]. Conversely, in a system implementing MAC, all operations performed by subjects on objects are mediated by the system, i.e., the access control policy is set and enforced system-wide and, as a result, subjects cannot set individual permissions on objects [89]. Harrison, Ruzzo, and Ullman showed that systems which allow subjects to grant permissions to other subjects cannot be guaranteed to remain in a safe state, i.e., in a state consistent with the system's security requirements, throughout their operation [61]. Given Harrison, Ruzzo, and Ullman's result, systems must implement MAC to ensure subjects do not create information flows which contravene the security of the system.

In 1972, Anderson introduced an abstract system component called the *reference monitor* to enforce access control decisions and defined three design principles it must adhere to [8]:

1. **Completeness:** the reference monitor must always be active and enforcing the system's access control policy,

2. **Isolation:** the reference monitor must be tamperproof, i.e., unable to be modified such that the system's access control policy is not enforced, and

3. **Verifiable:** the reference monitor must provably be shown to be implemented correctly

Given these design principles there are two classes of attack against reference monitors that are relevant to this work. The first class covers attacks that circumvent the isolation principle and encompasses illegal information flows that are enabled by tampering with the system. The second class of attack covers illegal information flows that exploit either objects that are not protected by the reference monitor (e.g., passing information via the lock status of a file) or mechanisms that enable communication but are not overseen by the reference monitor (e.g., directly accessing the raw hard drive device to read or write files as opposed to using the operating system's file system application program interface).

Therefore, in order to unambiguously classify covert channels we organize reference monitors based on the context in which they are used:

- **Host-based reference monitor:** A reference monitor which mediates operating system (OS) resource access requests. A number of modern systems employ host-based reference monitors including Android, Secure Linux (SELinux), and Windows as well as hardware virtualization software.

- **Network reference monitor:** A reference monitor which mediates network resource access requests. A number of hardware and software systems can be used as network reference monitors including firewalls and intrusion detection systems.

- **Air-gap reference monitor:** A reference monitor which mediates air-gapped resource access requests. A number of hardware systems can be used to enforce the air-gap security policy (i.e., no communication), including electromagnetic (EM) as well as acoustic shielding and secure data pumps [73].

In the next section we introduce covert channels and classify them based on the reference monitor that they circumvent.

3. COVERT CHANNELS

Information hiding is the discipline within *communications security* that prevents an adversary from learning anything about the transfer of messages [121]. This is in contrast to the related discipline of *cryptography*, which looks at protecting the *confidentiality* and *integrity* of messages (as well as enforcing *non-repudiation* and *origin authentication* in certain applications) [103]. Information hiding has historically been broken down into the sub-disciplines of covert channels, anonymity, steganography, watermarking, and low probability of detection (LPD) radio systems [121]. The disciplines that are particularly relevant to this discussion on covert channels are steganography and LPD radio systems in addition to imperceptible communication systems.

Steganography is the discipline of embedding secret messages into a cover and literally means "covered writing" in Greek [121]. In the literature, the *embedded* message is the secret information and the *cover* is referred to as either *cover-text* [20,133], *cover-image* [29] or *cover-audio* [70], depending on the type of cover that is used. The process of embedding a secret message is governed by the *stego-key* and successful execution of the process results in the creation of a *stego-object*. A steganographic system takes as input a message, a cover object, and a stego-key and the goal of the system is to render the embedded message undetectable by an attacker. Steganographic systems accomplish this by placing the embedded message in locations of the cover that have high entropy, i.e., locations where there is a high degree of uncertainty as to their expected value. It is this uncertainty that prevents the attacker from easily determining whether an embedded message exists in the cover or not.

LPD radio communication systems have been the focus of military researchers for a number of years and much of this focus has been on time and frequency spread spectrum modulation schemes, i.e., direct-sequence spread spectrum (DSSS) and frequency-hopping spread spectrum (FHSS) [120, 123], respectively. Where the goal of steganographic systems is to hide information in an authentic cover, the goal of LPD radio systems is to hide signals in background noise. Spread spectrum systems accomplish this by spreading a signal's energy out over a bandwidth that is much larger than the information bearing signal's bandwidth. The spreading is done by pseudorandomly manipulating the information bearing signal in the time or frequency domain (or both in hybrid spread spectrum systems), where the pseudorandom manipulation is keyed by a secret shared between the transmitter and receiver. By using spread spectrum modulation an attacker is forced to observe the larger bandwidth and thus is forced to also observe more background noise. Spread spectrum, therefore, lowers a signal's signal-to-noise ratio (SNR) as observed by an attacker and makes the hidden transmission much more difficult to detect.

Lastly, imperceptible communication systems hide signals not in a cover or background noise, but outside of the perceptible or observable range of an attacker. Imperceptible communication systems are subject to additional risk as compared to steganographic and LPD systems because if the attacker becomes aware of the technique being used by the communicators, the attacker could possibly update its detection mechanism to observe their communication. Imperceptible communication systems that rely on their communication method remaining unknown use "security through obscurity" as protection since the covert communicating parties are only safe while the attacker is not aware of their method of communication.

3.1 Defining Covert Channels

Covert channels are often conceptualized by first introducing a system that consists of two subjects, a HIGH security subject and a LOW security subject, as well as an access control policy: HIGH cannot write to LOW and LOW cannot read from HIGH. A covert channel is then usually introduced and implicitly defined as any information flow that allows information to be passed from HIGH to LOW. This extends to scenarios where HIGH and LOW could be executing on the same host, two separate hosts that are connected via a network, or two separate hosts that are not connected to one another at all. While this provides a general idea of what a covert channel is, attempting to define the term has led to some discussion amongst researchers over a number of years.

Lampson, in the first documented work on covert channels, originally defined a covert channel as a "communication channel that is not *intended* for information transfer at all." [88]. Similarly, Kemmerer stated that covert channels arise from "the use of an entity not normally viewed as a data object to transfer information" [78]. Both these definitions describe the channel as being counter to the original design of the channel/entity itself; however, as pointed out in the Trusted Computer System Evaluation Criteria's (TCSEC) "light pink book" on covert channels, these definitions do not appropriately place covert channels within communications security [50]. Moreover, Huskamp stated that covert channels "are a result of resource allocation policies and resource management implementation" [69] and Girling defined covert channels as a "transfer of information in a way that would normally be contrary to a network's security policy" [49]. Both definitions place covert channels firmly within the realm of communications security by explicitly stating that a covert channel is a channel that is contrary to the system's security policy (i.e., access control policy); however, both Huskamp and Girling's definitions are too narrowly focused on standalone systems and distributed systems, respectively, to be generally accepted.

Moskowitz and Miller defined a covert channel as "a communication channel established contrary to the design of a system" [108] and, as part of developing the TCSEC, Gligor defined a covert channel as "a communication channel that allows a process to transfer information in a manner that violates the system's security policy" [50]. These definitions make it clear that a covert channel generally circumvents the security of the system regardless of the type of system and we conclude that, given that the reference monitor is the system component responsible for enforcing the system's security policy, a covert channel *is an information flow that circumvents the system's reference monitor*, the definition we use herein. Furthermore, we term a *true covert channel* as a channel that not only circumvents the system's reference monitor but is also *harmful*[6] to the system. Conversely, McHugh defined *benign covert channels* as channels that exhibit one of the following characteristics [100]:

1. HIGH and LOW are the same process,

2. under the system's security policy HIGH and LOW are permitted to communicate with one another, or

3. a covert channel exists between HIGH and LOW, but there is no practical way to communicate data through the channel.

Our focus in this work is on *true covert channels*. Moreover, we point out that while we have derived a definition for the term *covert channel* it is not necessarily intuitive to apply our definition to the term *covert channel* given the vernacular sense of the word "covert." To bridge our definition with the vernacular meaning we offer the explanation that since a covert channel evades a reference monitor, the channel is therefore hidden, in a sense, from the perspective of the reference monitor[7].

The model that is generally used to analyze covert channels consists of two communicating parties, usually referred to as Alice and Bob, and a security policy enforcer, i.e., a reference monitor, usually referred to as Wendy. Furthermore, in the study of covert channels it is assumed that both Alice and Bob are jointly interested in successfully leaking information. This assumption is what separates the study of covert channels from the study of *side channels*. Side channels study the unintentional leakage of information, usually from cryptographic systems, where only the receiver is interested in successful transmission (see [160] for a survey on the subject). Broadly speaking, a covert channel is thus any intentionally created information flow that is outside of what is preventable and detectable by the security policy enforcer, Wendy, and therefore, in this work, we analyze covert channels from the perspective of Wendy.

3.2 Applications for Covert Channels

There is clearly an adversarial relationship between the covert communicators, Alice and Bob, and the system's policy enforcer, Wendy. While Alice and Bob want to covertly communicate without detection, Wendy wants to either eliminate or greatly reduce the ability for Alice and Bob to do so. This relationship brings about a measures and countermeasures game between the two parties [136]. While this adversarial relationship is clear, the legitimacy of covert channels is not.

It is well documented that malware as well as alleged government implants have used air-gap jumping covert channels to egress data from protected systems [4, 75, 77] and that

malware has also used covert channels to attack ICS's [41]. Additionally, malware has been found to use network covert channels to leak data [35, 143] as well as coordinate distributed denial of service (DDOS) attacks [39]. Contrariwise, network covert channels have been developed to facilitate communication through restrictive firewalls by exploiting the redundancy in and unused nature of various protocol fields in the network stack (e.g., ICMP [141], TCP [1, 127], HTTP [65], DNS [72])[8], which can be enabling technologies for citizens of countries that employ Internet censorship to restrict free speech [13, 34].

In addition to being used by malware as well as in freedom of speech applications, covert channels are also assumed to be applicable in general scenarios where the communicating entities are not able or willing to communicate through traditional means. This type of situation arises in various scenarios, e.g., when traditional communication links are taken down as is common in times of protest, or in whistleblower scenarios where the whistleblower is trying to avoid detection [28]. Furthermore, Zander, et al., [158] provided a list of applications for network covert channels which included using covert channels to transmit authentication information [36, 97, 98], to facilitate trace-back in denial of service attacks [71, 124], and to hide network management communication from network attackers [46]. It has also been demonstrated that covert channels can be used to deannonymize hidden services in the Tor network [115] as well as leak information from anonymous networks [112]. While these applications relate more to covert channels between networked or air-gapped systems, covert channels on single hosts have also been observed in the wild [105] and recently a number of publications have demonstrated the use of covert channels to attack the Android OS [38, 62, 116] as well as facilitate communication between virtual hosts [154, 159]. In general, covert channels are more often found in the lab than the real world, however. One of the forefathers of covert channels, Jonathan Millen, surmises the reason for this is because "when information is stolen via covert channel, the original data is still in place, so the theft can go unnoticed" [114].

The list of parties interested in the detection and development of covert channels is demonstrably long. Governments are interested in covert channels to hide the presence of their communications as well as to defend against their use; criminals are interested in covert channels for the purposes of leaking sensitive information and controlling malware; citizens in oppressive regimes are interested in covert channels to avoid censorship; and, in general, the average citizen can be interested in covert channels to protect their private communications from being detected. This last point is topical since covert channels have been proposed as a method to hide the use of strong encryption [158] and in 2016 governments in North America and Europe [5] as well as India [37] are considering and discussing proposals to ban, weaken, or mandate backdoors in cryptographic algorithms. Therefore, protection of communications from detection is our motivation for studying the topic of *covert channel design* in **Section 4**. As is usually the case in computer and network security, there is a dual-use for covert channels. While covert channels can be used by free speech advocates and privacy-conscious users, these channels can also be exploited

---

[6]In **Section 6.1** we analyze when a covert channel is *harmful* to a system.

[7]Note that this is a very informal treatment of the term as covert channels can exist that are known to the system's designers but which cannot be removed because their removal would severely impact the performance or feature set of the system.

---

[8]Note that this is a very short list of examples of covert channel tools that have been developed to circumvent firewalls. This list is meant to be representative rather than complete.

by elements to support nefarious activity. We conclude this section by providing a brief history of covert channels and presenting a novel classification of the subject.

3.3 History and Classification of Covert Channels

In analyzing methods that a program could use to leak sensitive information to a third party, Lampson introduced the *confinement problem*[9] and covert channels [88]. Lipner then applied MAC security models to the confinement problem and argued that when used in conjunction with other techniques (e.g., virtual resource allocation), the problem could be solved for known communication channels, but acknowledged that covert channels are difficult, if not impossible, to eliminate completely [92]. Multiple methods, however, have been developed to systematically identify covert channels on MAC systems: the shared-resource matrix methodology [78], covert flow trees [79], non-interference methods [51], and security kernels [106]. Recently, the shared-resource matrix methodology has been extended to covert channels between physically isolated systems as well [60].

The United States Department of Defence (DoD) developed a process for certifying secure systems, which is documented in the TCSEC [89]. Their certification process focused on MAC systems and required covert channel analysis, which can be separated into four general, not necessarily non-overlapping, areas of research: modelling, searching, measuring, and mitigating [105]. Since the publication of the TCSEC, a number of papers have been written on the modelling [51,78,101,106,147], searching [56,63,79,93,102,128, 149,153], measuring [95,104,107,108,111,130] and mitigating [52,68,73,74,99,139] of covert channels. Furthermore, various covert channel techniques have been developed to circumvent the security of operating systems implementing MAC, including: a file-lock covert channel on systems that share a file system [50], the disk-arm channel on KVM/370 systems [128], the bus-contention channel on multiprocessor systems [67] as well as virtualized environments [155], and the acoustic channel on Android [38,116]. In general, these covert channel techniques were designed to circumvent a host-based reference monitor and have been classified as *host-based covert channels*.

In 1987, Girling presented the first work on covert channels in a networked environment [49]. Since Girling's seminal work, a large number of researchers have developed techniques which manipulate some property of network traffic in order to establish covert communication between networked hosts (see the surveys of Zander, et al. [158] and Wendzel, et al. [152]). Wendzel, et al., surveyed over 100 different network covert channel techniques and found that they could be grouped into general patterns not tied to specific network protocols [152]. The researchers separated techniques into patterns based on whether they modified the structure or timing of network traffic as well as whether they modified the payload or header fields of protocols. Zander, et al., similarly surveyed a large number of network protocol covert channel techniques and found that they could be grouped both by the general technique they used to communicate (e.g., modifying unused space), as well as the protocol they modified. Generally speaking, the research following Girling's initial

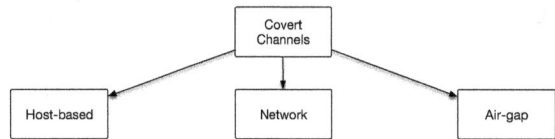

Figure 1: Classes of covert channels

work has uncovered various methods for misusing different fields within the protocols of the Open Systems Information (OSI) model to circumvent the security of a network reference monitor. The class of covert channels that do so are commonly referred to as *network covert channels*.

In the last decade, a growing body of research has been developed that examines various methods for leaking information from air-gapped systems. Government organizations have known about compromising electromagnetic emanations from electronic equipment since the 1980's and the NSA and DoD have studied this type of leakage under the program name TEMPEST (Transient ElectroMagnetic Pulse Emanation STandard) [64]. While the techniques covered by the TEMPEST program are classical side channels, the leaky nature of various system devices (e.g., video display units, cables, central processing units (CPUs), etc.) has been exploited to demonstrate effective covert channels [12,55,62,87]. A number of other devices, not normally considered as transmitters, have also been exploited to leak information from air-gapped systems including speakers and CPUs in acoustic channels [27,28,38,54,58,59,62, 90,116,116,118,145,146], light emitting diodes (LEDs) and displays in light-based channels [14,15,62,86,116], CPUs in thermal channels [96,115], and vibration devices in seismic channels [7,38,116,142]. Furthermore, there is empirical evidence that physical media is also an effective air-gap covert channel [41,75,77]. In general, these channels provide communication between processes running in isolated environments and can be used to circumvent an air-gap reference monitor. While no classification for this category of covert channel has been proposed in the literature to date, we propose classifying covert channels that circumvent the security of an air-gap reference monitor as *air-gap covert channels*. Moreover, we point out that these covert channel techniques can be grouped based on their defining physical characteristic: thermal channels, electromagnetic channels (e.g., RF, magnetic, light), mechanical channels (e.g., acoustic, seismic), and physical media channels.

Given that we have firmly rooted the study of covert channels in access control, we propose that going forward covert channels be classified in terms of the reference monitor(s) that they circumvent (see **Figure 1** for an updated classification of covert channels). This grouping clearly identifies to secure system designers the class or classes of attacks that they have to protect against given the type of reference monitor that they are implementing, and allows individual covert channel techniques to be compared and their novelty assessed, a topic we explore in more detail in **Section 5**. In the next section, we discuss the analysis and design of covert channels and provide recommendations that covert channel designers should follow in order to create more secure covert channels.

---

[9]The problem of constraining a program in order to prevent it from leaking sensitive information is referred to as the *confinement problem*.

119

4. COVERT CHANNEL ANALYSIS AND DESIGN

The practical application of covert channels can be broken down into *covert channel analysis* (CCA) and *covert channel design* (CCD). We examine CCA and CCD in this section in order to set up the discussion on taxonomy in **Section 5**. We begin with the analysis of covert channels in secure systems.

4.1 Covert Channel Analysis

The TCSEC was initially conceived to encourage the adoption and availability of trusted computer systems [89]. The certification process achieved this by providing vendors with a metric, based on levels, that could be used to quantitatively evaluate the security of systems ("A" level systems were the most secure followed by "B", "C", and "D"). The TCSEC also provided guidance to system vendors on how to develop and document systems in order to obtain each level. The successor to the TCSEC was the Common Criteria (CC) whose goal was to unify disparate national secure system certification standards (the Canadian Trusted Computer Product Evaluation Criteria (CTCPEC) in Canada, the Information Technology Security Evaluation Criteria (ITSEC) in Europe and the TCSEC in the US) into one international standard [2]. The CC thus provided vendors with one security certification standard that they could obtain and have internationally recognized. In comparison, the CC and TCSEC were both based on assurance, but the CC was a much more general certification process than the TCSEC, achieved mainly by separating the certification levels from the individual security requirements for classes of products. Where the security requirements were tied to the certification level in the TCSEC, the CC set security requirements on a per product basis and the certification process verified that a product met its stated requirements.

Covert channel analysis was required by both the TCSEC and CC at their highest levels of assurance[10]. CCA is the process of systematically searching for and handling illegal information flows in a system [3] and has been broken down into three general stages [50]: (1) Identifying illegal information flows and determining their maximum bandwidth[11]; (2) based on the covert channel's bandwidth, handling the channel in a manner that is consistent with the certification requirements of the product under evaluation; and (3) providing assurance evidence which demonstrates that the covert channel is handled appropriately, i.e., in a manner commensurate with the certification level being sought. Once discovered, covert channels, typically, can either be eliminated, bandwidth limited, or audited [50]. Elimination generally requires the system's design to be updated so that the covert channel can no longer be exploited; bandwidth limitation generally calls for the introduction of noise or delays into the system's design in order to reduce the effectiveness of a covert channel[12]; and auditing generally calls for instrumentation to be added to the system to determine when and if a covert channel is actively being exploited. Auditing is im-

plemented primarily to deter the use of the covert channel.

In general, CCA requires solving two general search problems [22]:

1. **Identification:** identifying covert channels by statically analyzing the system's design, and

2. **Detection:** revealing the active exploitation of covert channels by dynamically analyzing events in the system in order to detect anomalies.

Identification is performed at system design time and often requires the use of formal methods as well as manual input from the system's designers (e.g., the identification of shared resources is commonly a manual task). Furthermore, once a covert channel is identified, elimination of the covert channel can have an impact on the system's performance [22,73,107]. Detection, similarly, is also a challenging task which occurs continuously while the system is running. Detection requires the system's designers to know where to look (i.e., the covert channel's mechanism for communication needs to be instrumented), when to look (i.e., the covert channel's mechanism needs to be audited with an appropriate time granularity in order to detect the use of the covert channel) and what to look for (i.e., the system needs to be able to correctly interpret its audits as proof that a covert channel is in use) in order to develop a detection mechanism that will effectively deter the active exploitation of a covert channel. Despite these inherent difficulties, a number of researchers have presented methods for detecting active covert channels [22,24,25,28,48,57,119,125,134,135,137,138] and the argument has been made that detection (versus identification and elimination) can be less impactful to system performance [22].

4.2 Covert Channel Design

Covert channel design, by contrast, consists of the following stages: (1) identifying a *covert exploit*[13] that can be leveraged to create a covert channel and (2) establishing a method to communicate through the channel. In general, once the exploit is found the channel designer can adopt one of two general strategies for constructing the covert channel within a given system:

1. the designer can assume that the system is not designed to, nor will be updated to, detect the covert channel; or

2. the designer can assume that the system is instrumented to, or will be updated to, detect the covert channel.

We term channels that implement the former strategy as *detectable covert channels* and define them as true covert channels whose design does not take detection into account. Conversely, we term channels that implement the latter strategy as *undetectable covert channels* and define them as true covert channels whose design does take detection into account. *Undetectable covert channels*, by definition, take a truly cautious approach to covert communication.

In the design of detectable covert channels the only thing that is "required is the ingenuity" of the designer [35] and

---

[10]In the CC, CCA is required at EAL5 (informal search) as well as EAL6 and EAL7 (formal search). In the TCSEC, CCA is required at B2 (informal search) and A1 (formal search) [3,89]

[11]We explore bandwidth estimation and covert channel measurement in general in **Section 6**.

[12]The term *effectiveness* in the context of covert channels refers to the bit rate achievable by the covert channel.

---

[13]A *covert exploit* refers to a specific technique used to create a covert channel [135]. Given this definition, a covert channel is the result of applying a covert exploit.

once an exploitable information flow is found the problem for the covert channel designer reduces to a traditional communication problem, i.e., choosing appropriate modulation, channel, and source coding schemes. Hidden communication systems that rely solely on novelty for security, however, have not stood the test of time [121]. The problem faced by the designer of an *undetectable covert channel* is common to other problems in information hiding and one that is modelled by Simmons' "prisoners' problem" [132]. In the prisoners' problem, two prisoners wish to formulate an escape plan and the only method of communication that they have available to them is the ability to exchange messages, however, the Warden of the prison will only allow messages to be exchanged if he deems them innocuous. The goal of the prisoners, therefore, is to devise an information hiding scheme[14] such that the messages appear innocuous to the Warden but contain hidden information accessible only by the true recipient. In addition to inspecting messages passed between the prisoners, i.e., auditing the channel[15], the warden can also further frustrate the prisoners by employing techniques to eliminate or reduce the effectiveness of the communication channel[16].

The topics of identifying and detecting covert channels have received much attention by the research community, however, the systematic design and development of covert channels that maximize their capacity while minimizing their detection is not a well explored topic. Smith and Knight explored the systematic design of network covert channels in the presence of a passive adversary and examined the trade-off between three design metrics: probability of detection, reliability (i.e., bit error rate), and system efficiency, where system efficiency measured the effect of adding coding and undetectability to the covert channel [134, 135]. Other researchers have also applied a similar design methodology while studying covert-acoustic channels [28]. In general, these researchers have all shown that despite the difference in channel type (i.e., network covert channel versus air-gap covert channel) both the probability of detection and capacity of the channel are related to one another and dependent in some form on the SNR of the system. Furthermore, Moulin and O'Sullivan as well as Wang and Moulin have studied the systematic design of covert channels in the presence of an active adversary [113, 150]. By modelling covert channels as a game theory problem the researchers were able to provide capacity bounds based on distortion constraints at both the covert transmitter and active attacker. Their research, however, did not take detection into account.

4.3 Undetectable Covert Channels

In order to develop an effective *undetectable covert channel* some form of information hiding must be applied to the messages that are passed through the channel. While no formal definition for *undetectable communication* exists, the notion of *undetectability* does: "*undetectability* of an item of interest (IOI) from an attacker's perspective means that the attacker cannot sufficiently distinguish whether it exists or not" [122]. For the purposes of this discussion, an IOI

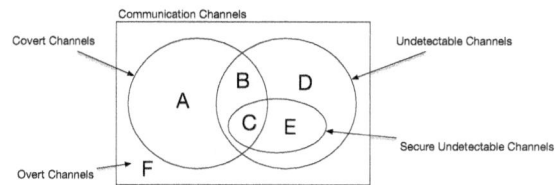

Figure 2: Communication channels from the perspective of a reference monitor

is any message that is passed through the covert channel and the attacker is Wendy, the policy enforcer. In **Section 6** we discuss different possible methods for measuring undetectability, but for the purposes of this section the reader can interpret *undetectability* as a probability measure, i.e., the probability that the attacker detects messages being passed through the channel, or an entropy measure, i.e., a measure of the uncertainty that the attacker has with respect to the covert channel being used or not. Given Pfitzmann and Hansen's definition for undetectability, an *undetectable communication* system can be conceptualized as a communication system that, given an adversarial model, maximizes *undetectability*. The literature on information hiding covers a number of communication systems whose designs take undetectability into account including steganography, LPD radio systems, and imperceptible communication systems, which, as previously mentioned, are techniques that hide information in a cover, in background noise, or outside the perceptible range of the attacker, respectively.

Although undetectable communication systems are not cryptographic systems, designers of undetectable communication systems can learn from their design principles. In 1883, Kerckhoff stated that the security of cryptographic systems must rely on keeping the cryptographic key secret as opposed to keeping the cryptographic algorithm secret[17] [85]. This advice extends to undetectable communication systems by assuming the attacker has access to the algorithm used to hide messages, but does not have access to the key material that is used by the algorithm. This applies to steganography directly by assuming the embedding algorithm is known but the stego-key is kept hidden [121]. Similarly, in LPD radio systems the spread spectrum algorithm would also be known to the attacker but not the secret used by the pseudorandom spreading function. Systems that follow Kerckhoff's principle, therefore, can be referred to as *secure undetectable communication systems*.

There is possibly some ambiguity as to the difference between steganography and covert channels. Wendzel, et al., argued that the difference between the two disciplines is that in steganography, information is hidden in "carriers" that are interpreted by humans (e.g., text, audio, video), whereas in covert channels information is hidden in "carriers" interpreted by machines (e.g., file locks, network protocol headers, etc.) [152]. Moskowitz, et al., argued that there are two important differences between the two areas of research: (1) the study of covert channels does not take into consideration undetectability[18] and (2) covert channels are assumed to transmit forever, whereas steganographic channels are as-

---

[14]We use the term "information hiding" here because the *prisoners' problem* has been used to motivate covert channels and steganographic channels in addition to subliminal channels, the channel the problem was initially designed to model.

[15]Auditing the channel is commonly referred to as the Warden being a "passive warden" in the literature.

[16]The Warden is referred to as an "active warden" in this setting.

[17]This principle is commonly known as *Kerckhoff's principle*.

[18]Moskowitz, et al., complemented this statement with the statement "although perhaps it should."

sumed to transmit only for the lifetime of the cover medium [being] used [109]. Smith agrees with Wendzel, et al., in the sense that steganographic channels exist at protocol levels above the networking layer in the OSI model, and further characterized steganographic channels as (1) channels that require a secret key to be shared amongst communicating parties in order to facilitate undetectable communication and (2) channels that are of higher bandwidth than covert channels [136]. Fundamentally, the main difference between the two disciplines is that covert channels are designed to circumvent a reference monitor and the security policy of a system whereas steganographic systems are general systems designed to hide their communication.

This argument broadly extends to the difference between covert channels and undetectable communication systems, in general. While an undetectable communication system *could* be used to circumvent a reference monitor it is not necessarily the intent of the communication system to do so, nor is it true that all undetectable communication systems are covert channels. To clarify this distinction a Venn diagram is presented in **Figure 2**, which should be interpreted from the perspective of a reference monitor. **Class A** communication systems are *detectable covert channels* that the reference monitor either does not know about or cannot remove from the system for practical reasons. **Class B** and **Class C** communication systems are *undetectable covert channels* and *secure undetectable covert channels*, respectively, that again, the reference monitor does not know about nor can remove. Furthermore, the union of **Class D** and **Class E** systems are channels that do not circumvent the security of the system but are undetectable (also known as *benign* covert channels) and lastly **Class F** systems are overt communication channels that neither circumvent the security of the system nor are undetectable. Clearly, from a defence perspective the application of covert channel analysis would ideally remove all *Covert Channels* and from an offensive perspective covert channel designers would be wise to find a covert exploit that allows them to establish a *secure undetectable covert channel* (**Class C**).

We summarize this discussion by providing the following recommendations to covert channel designers:

1. the following assumptions should be made:

   (a) the reference monitor employs auditing techniques to detect the use of the covert channel,

   (b) the reference monitor knows the technique being used to hide messages in order to avoid detection;

2. information hiding techniques should be applied in order to render the channel undetectable; and,

3. an applicable information hiding technique should be employed whose undetectability is based on the strength of a shared secret.

While this is a truly pessimistic view for covert channel designers to take, it is the only way to guarantee some measurable degree of protection against detection.

These recommendations provide a pathway for future research into covert channels. Historically, a large number of research papers, specifically those in the category of air-gap covert channels, have proposed novel covert channel techniques but have not explored ways in which their signals

could be kept hidden from a motivated adversary [7, 12, 14, 15, 27, 38, 54, 55, 58, 59, 62, 86, 87, 90, 96, 115, 116, 116, 118, 142, 145, 146]. While the identification of **Class A** covert channels is useful to the research community, the most viable covert channels for adoption in privacy-preserving applications as well as those most important to protect against are **Class C** covert channels. Therefore, going forward, covert channel technique proposals should at least explore how their techniques could be modified to qualify as **Class C** channels and their limits should be explored.

5. TAXONOMY

In this section, the classification of covert channels first proposed in **Section 3** is complemented with a taxonomy that can be used to characterize covert channels. Our taxonomy extensions are novel because they encompass properties by which covert channels can be characterized that have not been proposed in previous taxonomies. Previous covert channel taxonomies have characterized channels based on their noise model, their method of communication (e.g., storage, timing), and whether they are host- or network-based. By contrast, the new characteristics that we propose herein model covert channels based on their adversarial model, the covert exploits that enable them, and their hiding strategy. Our taxonomy, therefore, extends those that have come before it and it is our hope that going forward, our updated taxonomy will be used so that novel trends can be extracted and effective countermeasures can be proposed. This section begins with a discussion on existing taxonomies.

5.1 Background on Covert Channel Taxonomies

Covert channels are usually classified primarily as either *storage* or *timing* channels [22, 23, 89, 92, 107, 117, 151, 153, 158]. *Storage channels* "involve the direct or indirect writing of a storage location by one process and the direct or indirect reading of the storage location by another process" [89]. *Timing channels*, on the other hand, allow a transmitting process to "signal information to another by modulating its own use of system resources in such a way that this manipulation affects the real response time observed by the second process" [89]. While classification along these lines seems to be universal, it is also widely acknowledged that there can be very little semantic difference between the two, as was first pointed out by Wray [153]. Moreover, covert channels are usually also classified as *noisy* or *noiseless* channels. Probabilistically speaking, if the inputs to a given channel are elements of the random variable X and the outputs are elements of the random variable Y, we get that $Pr[Y = X] = 1$ for a noiseless channel and $Pr[Y = X] \leq 1$ for a noisy channel, where the output is instead governed completely by the input variable X and $Pr[Y|X]$.

While classification along the lines of storage or timing and noisy or noiseless is common, researchers have proposed additional characteristics by which covert channels can be classified. Wang and Lee separated covert channels into value-based and transition-based covert channels in addition to classifying them as either spatial or temporal [151]. A receiver in a value-based covert channel extracts information based on the value it sees, whereas in a transition-based covert channel the receiver extracts information based on a change in the value that it observes, the latter is similar to differential encoding [123]. Additionally, spatial and temporal channels are channels where the receiver either observes symbols directly or the receiver observes an order of events, respectively, and are very similar, if not identical, to classical storage and timing channels. Wang and Lee used their taxonomy to show that a novel abstract class of covert channel, value-based temporal covert channel, existed. Okhravi, et al., also separated covert channels based on value and transition in addition to classifying them based on the source of the shared resource being modulated: a network resource, an OS resource or a hardware resource [117].

Cabuk, similarly, also separated covert channels along the lines of storage or timing as well as network or host-based in addition to whether the transmitter (i.e., Alice) was active or passive [22]. Cabuk described an active-source covert channel as one where the covert transmitter is actively transmitting data and a passive-source covert channel as one where there is no participating source. While an interesting distinction, Cabuk's description of a passive-source channel is more similar to a side-channel than a covert channel[19]. Zander also separated network covert channels based on the participation level of the transmitter and labelled sources as active, semi-passive or passive [157]. Zander described an active source in the same way as Cabuk; however, Zander defined a semi-passive source and a passive source as one that manipulates other applications to transmit data or modifies existing traffic while simply acting as a middleman, respectively. Of relevance to our taxonomy is Zander's separation of covert channels based on the degree of predictability of the cover that the transmitter embeds information within. Zander organized channels based on whether the cover was predictable, variable, or random, where variable covers and random covers have limited randomness or are completely random, respectively. In our taxonomy we generalize this by classifying covert channels as those that use a cover to hide information, i.e., steganographic covert channels, or those that do not, i.e., open covert channels.

Conversely, Meadows and Moskowitz took a different approach to classifying covert channels and proposed separating them based on their context as opposed to the mechanism they used to establish the channel [101]. The researchers classified channels as either high-to-low service channels, low-to-high service channels, or shared service channels, where policy-breaking communication is via a service running at a higher level, lower level, or at an incomparable level, respectively. This novel approach is orthogonal to the traditional classification of covert channels and was designed to be interpreted in conjunction with the security policy of the system to help secure system developers determine which class of covert channel is most relevant to them. This classification by Meadows and Moskowitz highlights the importance of context when evaluating covert channels and is a topic we revisit in **Section 6.1**. A grab bag of other categorizations for covert channels also exists: frequency-based [23], protocol-based [23], statistical [110], sorting [6], counting [53], and hybrid, which is any combination of covert channel techniques.

5.2 Proposed Taxonomy

Our motivation for proposing an updated taxonomy for covert channels is as follows. To date, the taxonomies proposed have been specific to a class of covert channel and

have also been designed to allow covert channels to be modelled so that their channel capacity could effectively be calculated. The latter is in no small part due to the covert channel analysis requirements of the TCSEC and CC for secure systems. While capacity calculation is important, our analysis in the next section, **Section 6**, demonstrates that, depending on the secure system's requirements, covert channels should also be measured under conditions where the reference monitor is attempting to detect the channel as well. Our taxonomy addresses this by characterizing covert channels by attacker model as well as by the methodology used to hide communication. Furthermore, our taxonomy is more general than previous taxonomies, which is important because covert channel techniques can sometimes be used to circumvent the security of multiple reference monitors or combined to circumvent a reference monitor. Novel aspects of the taxonomy are now presented in detail, whereas traditional, or previously covered aspects, are summarized only for completeness.

5.2.1 Covert Exploit: Invasive, Semi-Invasive or Non-Invasive

An often overlooked property of covert channels is the covert exploit that is used to enable communication through the channel. While classification based on covert exploit does not necessarily help measure covert channels, discrimination based on covert exploit provides a better understanding of how the channel is enabled and thus how to protect against its use. Furthermore, by separating the covert exploit from the other channel and modulation properties it allows the channel's capacity to be studied independently from the exploit [136]. This is particularly advantageous because it allows collections of covert channels which share common channel and modulation properties to be evaluated without consideration for their individual exploits. Additionally, defences for covert channels can be split into those that reduce the likelihood of the covert exploit being used and those that reduce or eliminate the covert channel itself. We propose a classification of covert exploits that is used in the study of side channels [10] and separate covert exploits into the classes of invasive, i.e., covert exploits that require hardware modification, semi-invasive, i.e., covert exploits that require software modification to the system's reference monitor, or non-invasive, i.e., covert exploits that require no hardware modification or software modification to the system's reference monitor.

5.2.2 Channel Attacker Model: Mediated or Shared

The attacker, i.e., the reference monitor, Wendy, can either have shared access to the symbols being transmitted via the covert channel or can mediate the channel, i.e., all messages pass through Wendy. In the shared model, symbols are <u>not</u> sent from the transmitter to the attacker before being passed to the receiver as they are in the mediated model[20]. Instead, symbols are transmitted and are directly accessible by both the attacker and receiver [21]. This model is somewhat related to Simmons' prisoner problem, but is better modelled by the scenario where two prisoners are placed in solitary confinement and are no longer permitted to overtly

---

[19]To explain passive-source channels, Cabuk simply provided an example of a password checking algorithm that leaks data to a password cracker through the checking algorithm's execution time.

[20]Note that the mediated channel model is the model that is described by the *prisoners' problem*.
[21]The shared channel model limits how "active" the attacker can be: if the attacker and the receiver have simultaneous access to the symbols then the attacker can not delete messages, for example

communicate with one another, however, they attempt to communicate an escape plan by tapping out Morse code on a shared radiator, as an example[22]. In this scenario, it is assumed that the Warden (or its delegates, the guards) as well as the receiver both have shared access to the pipe. This problem can be generalized to the problem where Alice and Bob must find an alternative method of communication that allows them to develop their escape plan while making the assumption that Wendy can observe their communication. We term this problem the *solitary confinement problem*.

5.2.3 Channel Cover Model: Steganographic or Open

A *steganographic covert channel* is a communication channel that is established by a transmitter modifying a cover source that has at least some variability to it, i.e., the cover source is not deterministic but probabilistic in some sense. Conversely, an *open covert channel* is a channel that either does not use a cover source to hide information within or one that modifies a completely deterministic cover source. The key distinguishing characteristic between these two classes of channels is that the cover source follows some random distribution for steganographic covert channels and some deterministic value for open covert channels. Information hiding techniques based on steganography are therefore inappropriate for open covert channels.

5.2.4 Modulation Mode: Full Duplex, Half Duplex or Simplex

An important consideration in the design of covert channels is the mode of communication. Covert channels can either provide bidirectional or unidirectional, i.e., simplex, communication. Furthermore, bidirectional communication can either allow for information to flow back and forth between Alice and Bob simultaneously in both directions or in one direction at a time, i.e., in full duplex or half duplex mode, respectively. The communication mode of the channel has implications on the throughput[23] of the channel as duplex mode communication allows the receiver to indicate that a retransmission is required whenever a corrupted message is received or a message is lost (e.g., Automatic Repeat Request (ARQ) schemes can be used to allow the sender to retransmit information that is not received correctly by the receiver); whereas, simplex communication channels do not and thus simplex channels require additional forward error correcting (FEC) schemes to be applied to ensure error-free communication.

Other properties that are required to characterize covert channels include:

- **Modulation Type:** Detectable, Undetectable or Secure Undetectable Covert Channel

- **Reference Monitor:** Host-based, Network or Air-Gap

- **Modulation Medium:** Storage, Timing or Hybrid

- **Channel Noise Model:** Noisy or Noiseless

A diagram depicting this updated covert channel model can be found in [26].

---

[22]This hypothetical channel was first presented as a valid covert channel in McHugh's "Covert Channel Analysis" [100].

[23]The rate at which messages can be communicated with arbitrarily low probability of error.

6. MEASURING COVERT CHANNELS

In this section the history of measuring covert channels is presented, secure systems are classified based on their security requirements, and a new measure is proposed for a specific class of secure system.

The accurate measurement of covert channels allows proportional countermeasures to be employed by the developers of secure systems. Informal bandwidth estimation was first outlined in the work of Tsai and Gligor, where the authors estimated a channel's bandwidth, B, using the basic equation $B = \frac{b}{T_R + T_S + 2*T_{CS}}$, where the units of B are $\frac{bits}{sec}$, b is the number of bits transmitted per use of the channel, T_R, T_S, and T_{CS} are estimates for the time it takes to read the channel, write to the channel, and for the transmitter and receiver to perform a context switch[24], respectively. Millen presented a more precise measurement methodology to calculate the bandwidth of covert channels using information theory [104]. Millen's methodology called for the channel to first be represented by a finite state transition diagram and the bandwidth of the system to be calculated by determining the number of possible messages, $N(t)$, that could be sent through the covert channel in a period of time, t. The bandwidth of the system was then taken to be $C = \lim_{t \to \infty} \frac{\log N(t)}{t}$ and reduced to solving a system of equations in order to find an expression for $N(t)$.

While the TCSEC proposed using Tsai and Gligor's as well as Millen's methodologies for estimating the bandwidth of covert channels, it was Moskowitz and Myong who first provided a counterargument [107] as to why bandwidth was not the correct measure and proposed instead to use Shannon's channel capacity [129]. Moskowitz and Myong argued that since Shannon's channel capacity provided a maximum rate at which information could be sent through a channel it is the more appropriate measure for analyzing the threat posed by covert channels. The researchers provided the channel capacity calculation for continuous, band-limited systems as proof that bandwidth alone is not an accurate measure for a covert channel's maximum data rate: $C = \frac{1}{2}W \log \left(1 + \frac{P}{N}\right)$, where W is the channel's bandwidth (i.e., the Fourier transform, $X(f)$, of the transmission signal, $x(t)$, is zero for $|w| > |W|$), P is the transmitter's average signal power, and N is the average white noise power. To their point, the equation shows that capacity is in fact a function of bandwidth. Furthermore, the bandwidth estimation methodologies of Tsai and Gligor as well as Millen did not take noise into account, which can greatly reduce the capacity of the channel and thus their measures potentially over-inflate the risk posed by the measured channel. Properly accounting for noise as well as coding is important because underestimating or overestimating the threat posed by a covert channel can lead to unnecessarily reducing the system's performance or allowing high-capacity channels to persist in the system, respectively.

6.1 When do covert channels pose a risk?

The TCSEC quantitatively classified covert channels into three classes based on their bandwidth: high-bandwidth covert channels were classified as channels whose bandwidth

---

[24]This formula was presented for use in host-based covert channels in Tsai and Gligor's work [148]. The time required for context switch might not be relevant to all covert channels. Similarly, reading and writing to the channel can be parallelized in many covert channel deployments.

was above 100 bits per second (bps), low-bandwidth covert channels were classified as channels whose bandwidth was between 1 bps and 100 bps and acceptable covert channels were classified as channels whose bandwidth was below 1 bps [89]. Moreover, the criteria required that all high-bandwidth covert channels be removed from the system and that all low-bandwidth channels be audited if they could not be removed [89]. This seemingly arbitrary threshold for high-bandwidth covert channels was based on the communication rate of remote terminals at the time the TCSEC was authored and the creators of the TCSEC felt that "it does not seem appropriate to call a computer system *secure* if information can be compromised at a rate equal to the normal output rate of some commonly used device" [89]. While the TCSEC's classification was relevant at the time, the output rate of modern devices is on the order of gigabits per second.

The CC took a more pragmatic approach to defining the threat of covert channels and left the definition of *secure* up to each product's[25] security requirements [3]. Instead of prescribing appropriate methods for handling covert channels based on their bandwidth, the CC certification process was designed to merely confirm and selectively validate (at EAL5 and above) the covert channel analysis of products. McHugh also supported a more pragmatic approach to defining criteria for handling covert channels [100]. McHugh stated explicitly that for a covert channel to be harmful to a system the covert communicators must be forbidden from communicating and they must be able to exploit a flaw in the system in order to communicate a "useful quantity of information" [100]. Neither the CC nor McHugh explicitly set criteria for handling covert channels based on their bandwidth because "it is important to consider the quantity of information that must be compromised to cause a serious breach of security" [100]. This context-dependent position was also shared by Meadows and Moskowitz [101].

In order to assess the security risk posed by a covert channel we categorize secure systems into two general classes: *continuous-source systems* and *fixed-source systems*. Continuous-source systems are systems whose security is compromised if information is leaked above a defined rate. Systems in this category can be conceptualized as systems that produce sensitive information at such a relatively high rate that a "slow" leak via covert channel will not compromise the security of the system, i.e., by the time information is leaked via covert channel it is irrelevant. A large number of systems that fall into this category include systems that make private information available publicly periodically (e.g., declassifying information after a certain period of time, corporations filing for patents, etc.). The designers of continuous-source secure systems are thus interested in proving that their design does not contain covert channels that are capable of leaking information above a predetermined rate. As a result, Shannon's channel capacity is a relevant measure for covert channels when the security of this class of system is being analyzed. Conversely, fixed-source systems are systems whose security is compromised if a fixed amount of information is leaked from their system. Systems in this category can be characterized as systems that rely on a small and fixed amount of information (e.g., encryption keys, private signing key, etc.) being kept secret in order to remain secure. The designers of this type of secure system are interested in ensuring that a predetermined amount of information cannot be communicated via a covert channel in a given period of time and not necessarily in the long term average information rate of the covert channel (i.e., channel capacity).

For fixed-source systems, the *Small Message Criterion* (SMC) [107], as opposed to a predefined rate, is a more appropriate security criterion. In their analysis of covert timing channels, Moskowitz and Myong showed that zero-capacity covert channels could be designed by communicating a single symbol in exponentially increasing time periods. Their zero-capacity channel worked as follows: the first symbol was sent in one time period[26], the second symbol in two time periods, the third in four time periods, ... with the nth symbol being sent in 2^{n-1} time periods. After n channel uses one of 2^n messages could therefore be transmitted over the channel (i.e., a maximum of n bits could be transmitted); however, the capacity of this particular channel is zero (see [107] for the mathematical details). While this channel would not pose a risk for a continuous-source system, it could pose a serious risk for a fixed-source system. Moskowitz and Myong addressed this deficiency in capacity analysis with the SMC, which is based on three criteria: the maximum allowable length (in bits) of the information being leaked, the acceptable time frame in which the information can be leaked, and the acceptable fidelity of the information. For fixed-source systems, covert channels that violate the SMC can be classified as channels that violate the security of the system.

Determining the channel capacity of a covert channel in a continuous-source system allows the risk of the channel to be evaluated by comparing the calculated capacity to the predefined rate of the secure system; however, there is no such agreed upon metric for assessing the risk of fixed-source systems, nor is there any acceptable methodology for determining the capacity of covert channels when the secure system actively attempts to detect the channel through auditing. Although presented separately, a secure system could be classified as both a continuous- and fixed-source system simultaneously, depending on the system's security requirements. Furthermore, separate components of a single system could be classified as continuous- or fixed-source as well. The distinction between these two classes is, therefore, presented to capture their differing security requirements as well as the appropriate measurement techniques for each class.

6.2 Steganographic Capacity

The general detection of covert channels has been the topic of numerous studies and a wide array of general techniques have been documented in the literature. Researchers have used Kolmogorov-Smirnov testing to compare the statistical distributions of normal network traffic and covert network traffic in order to detect network covert channels [119]. The use of *regularity* tests has also been proposed to detect network covert channels that demonstrate traffic patterns that are too regular (e.g., the inter-packet delay of some network covert traffic algorithms is relatively constant) [22]. Similarly, some network covert timing channels can be identified through frequency analysis because they show disproportionate counts at the delays that are used to communicate symbols [24]. Additional tests that detect covert timing channels based on the regularity of covert network traffic include the Wilcoxon Signed-Rank Test and the Spearman Rho Test of Rezaei, et al. [125]. Empirically de-

---

[25] In CC parlance, products are *Targets of Evaluation* (TOE)

[26] Moskowitz and Myong referred to the basic time unit as a *tick*

Table 1: Recommendations for handling and measuring covert channels by system type

System type	Recommended Countermeasure	Security Criterion	Relevant Metric for Covert Channels
Continuous-source	Bandwidth reduction	Predetermined rate	Channel capacity
Fixed-source	Auditing	Small message criterion	Steganographic capacity

termined entropy has also been used to detect covert channels, where covert channels are identified by the measurable change they induce on the entropy of network traffic [48]. Techniques to identify specific network covert channels have also been discussed in the literature [25] (e.g., detection of the ICMP ping tunnel, Loki, [35], anomalous use of unused packet header fields [57], TCP header-based covert channels [138], and ICMP payload-based covert channels [137]). Lastly, Wu, et al., also proposed the use of pattern recognition techniques to identify inter-virtual machine covert channels [154]. While these solutions all present detection metrics for either general or specific covert channel mechanisms, they do not provide a comprehensive metric that captures the amount of information that can be leaked via a covert channel before it is detected and thus do not appropriately quantify the risk of an audited covert channel.

Studying the capacity of information hiding channels in the presence of a passive adversary has been the ongoing focus of researchers both in the context of LPD communication systems and steganographic systems. Recently, a number of works outlining the theoretical limits of LPD communication for various channel models have been published, namely the additive white Gaussian noise channel (AWGN) [16, 17, 18], the wire-tap channel [66], and the binary symmetric channel (BSC) [30, 31, 32, 33]. Bash, et al., proved the "square root law" for LPD signals transmitted over an AWGN channel, which demonstrated that at most $O(\sqrt{n})$ and $o(\sqrt{n})$ bits can be covertly communicated in n channel uses while bounding the detector's probability of detection to some arbitrary threshold, when the detector's noise power is known by the covert communicators and when it is not, respectively [16, 17]. Che, et al., examined the ability for Alice and Bob to communicate over a BSC while ensuring their communication is undetectable [30, 32, 33]. In their analysis, Wendy observed Alice's transmissions through a noisier communication channel than Bob, i.e., the wire-tap channel [156], and were able to prove a similar "square root law" under this assumption. Prior to the works of Bash, et al., and Che, et al., a "square root law" was first observed in steganographic systems by Ker while analyzing the capacity of batch steganography [80]. Since this seminal work was first published, other steganographic systems have also been found to respect this same law, namely systems that rely on Markov chain covers [45] or covers composed of i.i.d. elements [82]. Similarly, the "square root law" has been demonstrated for a number of other covers under varying assumptions [43, 44, 81, 83, 84]. While no universal theory proving the "square root law" exists in general, the law is composed of a "collection of theories for different mathematical models" [84].

This set of results provides strong evidence that repeated use of a covert channel under audit can lead to certain detection if the amount of information transmitted over the channel is not limited appropriately, e.g., at a rate proportional to $\sqrt{n}$, where n is the number of channel uses. Suspicion of this result was first presented by Anderson and Petitcolas while studying the limits of steganography. The researchers argued that the more stego-objects Wendy has access to, the better model she has for the channel's cover and as a result, the undetectable embedding rate might tend to zero [11]. These results have led steganography researchers to move away from using Shannon capacity for measuring steganographic channels, preferring instead the use of *steganographic capacity*, which is *the maximum amount of data that can be communicated covertly before an adversary's probability of detection reaches a given threshold*. In the context of covert channels, steganographic capacity provides a more appropriate measure to assess the risk of a covert channel when the channel is being audited. Moreover, the collection of "square root laws" provides evidence that, by employing appropriate detection mechanisms, the amount of information being leaked can be capped to a fixed amount (possibly even to zero using the analysis of steganographic capacity). This is of relevance to the design of secure fixed-source systems (see **Table 1** for a summary).

7. CONCLUSION

In this work, we presented a fresh perspective on covert channels. First, we showed that there is a new class of covert channel, air-gap covert channels, that are designed to defeat systems protected by the *total isolation* principle. Second, our research shows that secure systems have the properties of fixed-source systems or continuous-source systems. Our analysis of these classes has led us to the conclusion that the relevant security criterion for evaluating covert channels in closed-source systems continues to be an acceptable predefined communication rate, but that the security criterion of paramount importance is Moskowitz and Myong's *Small Message Criterion* in fixed-source systems. Correspondingly, in order to measure the risk that covert channels pose to a secure system, we challenged the traditional analysis methodology of strictly using Shannon capacity and proposed the use of *steganographic capacity* to accurately evaluate the risk posed by covert channels in fixed-source systems. Third, we studied the design of covert channels, differentiated the research area of *undetectable communication systems* from *covert channels* and provided recommendations to covert channel designers on how to build *secure undetectable covert channels*. Additionally, we presented novel taxonomy extensions that are able to capture important covert channel properties.

8. REFERENCES

References for this work can be found at: http://www.site.uottawa.ca/~bcarr092/IH2016/bibliography.pdf.

A Novel Embedding Distortion for Motion Vector-Based Steganography Considering Motion Characteristic, Local Optimality and Statistical Distribution

Peipei Wang
State Key Laboratory of
Information Security,
Institute of Information
Engineering, Chinese
Academy of Sciences,
Beijing 100093, China
wangpeipei@iie.ac.cn

Hong Zhang
State Key Laboratory of
Information Security,
Institute of Information
Engineering, Chinese
Academy of Sciences,
Beijing 100093, China
zhanghong@iie.ac.cn

Yun Cao[*]
State Key Laboratory of
Information Security,
Institute of Information
Engineering, Chinese
Academy of Sciences,
Beijing 100093, China
caoyun@iie.ac.cn

Xianfeng Zhao
State Key Laboratory of
Information Security,
Institute of Information
Engineering, Chinese
Academy of Sciences,
Beijing 100093, China
zhaoxianfeng@iie.ac.cn

ABSTRACT

This paper presents an effective motion vector (MV)-based steganography to cope with different steganalytic models. The main principle is to define a distortion scale expressing the multi-level embedding impact of MV modification. Three factors including motion characteristic of video content, MV's local optimality and statistical distribution are considered in distortion definition. For every embedding location, the contributions of three factors are dynamically adjusted according to MV's property. Based on the defined distortion function, two layered syndrome-trellis codes (STCs) are utilized to minimize the overall embedding impact in practical embedding implementation. Experimental results demonstrate that the proposed method achieves higher level of security compared with other existing MV-based approaches, especially for high quality videos.

Keywords

Steganography; video; motion vector; embedding distortion; H.264/AVC

---

*The corresponding author.

IH&MMSec 2016, June 20-23, 2016, Vigo, Spain
ⓒ 2016 ACM. ISBN 978-1-4503-4290-2/16/06. . . $15.00
DOI: http://dx.doi.org/10.1145/2909827.2930801

1. INTRODUCTION

Steganography is the art and science of data hiding, which realizes covert communication by embedding secret messages into innocent-looking cover media, such as digital image, audio, video, *et al.*, without arousing eavesdropper's suspicion. Facilitated by advanced video compression and computer network technology, digital video has become one of the most influential media. Therefore, secret message delivery can utilize video transmission as the cloak.

As the particular parameter in compressed video, MV is widely considered to be the ideal covert information carrier for the following reasons. First, MVs are generated in motion estimation (ME) and further losslessly coded without quantization distortions, thus the visual quality degradation introduced by embedding data in MVs is relatively limited. Second, because MV is the key information expressing video content, compressed video always contains vast quantities of various MVs. The sufficient quantity ensures the high embedding capacity held by MV-based steganographic approaches. Besides, the broad range of values makes it's achievable to propose steganographic algorithms preserving MVs' statistical characteristics.

A series of steganographic methods have been developed in MV area. The early algorithms select a subset of MVs by following preset selection rules and then use simple LSB replacement to modify them. Kutter [1] selected non-zero MVs and embedded message bits by modifying the LSBs of their horizontal and vertical components. Xu *et al.* [2] suggested selecting MVs whose magnitudes are above a given threshold for modification. Other than magnitude-based selection rules, Aly [3] chose the candidate MVs according to their associated prediction errors. By applying mature coding techniques such as wet paper codes (WPCs) [4] and syndrome-trellis codes (STCs) [5, 6] to video steganography, adaptive steganographic schemes with distortion functions have been presented in recent years. Cao *et al.* [7] selected the suboptimal MVs of small differences compared with their neighbors and utilized WPCs to embed information. In Yao *et al.*'s work [8], a distortion function for MV-based steganography was defined by considering the statistical distribution change and the prediction error change. And two-layered STCs [6] are used to minimize distortion for embedding process. In order to resist the steganalytic schemes based on MV's local optimality [9, 10], several approaches were proposed [11, 12]. Zhang *et al.* [11] designed a distortion based on video compression efficiency degradation. By selecting local optimal MVs in a designated area and further encoding using STCs with the least costs, the local optimality of modified MVs could be preserved. In [12], Cao *et al.* exploited the opportunity to optimize the ME perturbation using the loss caused by video compression process. With distortion scale calculated on optimal neighbors, data embedding was implemented using a double-layered (first channel: STCs, second channel: WPCs) coding structure.

Although the existing video steganographic schemes manage to elaborate effective distortion function and minimize the cost by adopting steganographic codes, they can not keep a high level of security. The following reasons can account for this. On the one hand, all of these steganographic approaches are designed for specialized purposes, thus when detected by other steganalytic methods, the level of security deteriorates. For example, Cao's [7] and Yao's steganographic methods [8] can not withstand local optimality based steganalysis such as [10, 9] and there is possibility that Zhang's [11] and Cao's steganographic schemes [12] can be detected by calibration based steganalysis such as [13, 14]. On the other hand, most distortion functions are defined using the embedding influence on single video's characteristic, which is dependent on the selected compressed video. Thus the distortion definition is not generally applicable for multifarious videos.

This paper aims at defining a distortion function for MV-based steganography by considering embedding influence from different aspects. Because rich motion regions have a large number of MVs with various-ranged values, motion characteristic of video content is considered in defining the distortion function. As one of the effective evidence exploited by steganalysis, the local optimality of MVs is also considered in distortion definition. Last but not the least, MVs' statistical distribution is also one important consideration. Particularly, in our proposed scheme, the distortion is dynamically allocated to these three factors by implementing adaption at every embedding location.

The rest of paper is organized as follows. In Section 2, we describe the framework of distortion minimization for MV-based steganograpy. In Section 3, the definition and analysis of distortion function is elaborated. The implementation of the video steganographic method is presented Section 4 and followed by the experimental results shown in Section 5. Finally, the conclusions and future works are given in Section 6.

2. DISTORTION MINIMIZATION FOR MV-BASED STEGANOGRAPHY

Minimizing the overall embedding distortion is an accepted approach to improve steganography security. Different from

operations on pixels in image steganography, MV-based steganographic approaches perform embedding during ME process. Their specific framework of distortion-minimization is established as follows.

In MV-based steganography, n MVs are obtained during video compression, denoted by $\mathbf{MV} = \{mv_1, \ldots, mv_n\}$. By binary mapping $x_i = \mathscr{P}(mv_i)$ with a designed parity check function $\{\mathscr{P}(mv_i)|i = 1 \ldots n\} = \{0, 1\}$, the covert channel $\mathbf{x} = \{x_1, \ldots, x_n\}$ is established. Given the embedding rate γ, the $\gamma \cdot n$ -length binary message $\mathbf{m}$ can be embedded by turning $\mathbf{x}$ into $\mathbf{x}' = \{_1, \ldots, x'_n\}$ using steganographic codes, which satisfies

$$\mathbf{H}\mathbf{x}^T = \mathbf{m} \qquad (1)$$

where $\mathbf{H}$ is the parity check matrix employed by the steganographic codes. As the result of embedding, the modified MV set $\mathbf{MV}' = \{mv'_1, \ldots, mv'_n\}$ is obtained and it satisfies $\mathscr{P}(mv'_i) = x'_i$.

On the assumption that the modification of MVs is mutally independent, the minimal distortion can be approached by embedding messages with STCs [5] and the embedding and extraction are formulated as

$$\widetilde{\mathbf{x}} = Emb(\mathbf{x}, \mathbf{m}) = arg \min_{\mathbf{x}' \in \mathscr{C}(\mathbf{m})} D(\mathbf{x}', \mathbf{x}) \qquad (2)$$

$$Ext(\widetilde{\mathbf{x}}) = \mathbf{H}\widetilde{\mathbf{x}}^T = \mathbf{m} \qquad (3)$$

where the overall distortion is computed by $D(\mathbf{x}', \mathbf{x}) = \sum_{i=1}^{n} \phi(x_i, x'_i)$, $\mathscr{C}(\mathbf{m})$ is the coset corresponding to syndrome $\mathbf{m}$ and $\widetilde{\mathbf{x}}$ is the binary bit stream embedded with message.

Based on STCs, two-layered ± 1 STCs [6] are proposed to improve higher security. In this paper, we define the distortion function for MVs and design a video steganographic method using two-layered STCs-based ± 1 embedding.

3. PROPOSED DISTORTION FUNCTION

3.1 Motion Characteristic of Video Content

In image steganography [15, 16], data tends to be embedded in complex textural regions. Analogously, it is intuitive that modifications in rich motion areas are likely to raise less suspicions in video steganography. For a specific macroblock (MB), the richer its motion is, the more suitable it can be used for modification.

As the integral part of existing video coding standards, ME is designed to reduce the temporal redundancy between video frames. This is achieved by allowing blocks of pixels from currently coded frame to be matched with those from reference frame(s). As the result of ME, MV represents the spatial displacement offset between a block and its prediction. Therefore, it has been widely accepted that the MV indicates MB's motion to some extent [17, 18, 19]. In addition, in order to achieve better compression ratio, various quantization parameter (QP) value on MB basis is allowed in H.264/AVC (Advanced Video Coding) standard [20]. As referred in [21], QPs of the adjacent MBs will have very small change in values if they are actually the part of static background. Thus the MBs can be segmented as static background or foreground object according to their QP differences.

Figure 1(a) shows a frame of the H.264 stream named "Snatch.264". Figure 1(b) depicts the MV and QP values

(a)H.264 stream   (b)MV and QP values

Figure 1: MV and QP information of "Snatch.264" sequence.

of the same frame. The red line shows the magnitude and direction of MV and the gray block shows the value of QP. Darker the color of MB, higher is the QP magnitude and vice versa. It can be seen that both MV's magnitude and QP's difference can represent MB's motion characteristic. Thus the motion characteristic based distortion can be defined as follows.

Definition 1. (**Motion Characteristic Based Distortion, MCD**). For $mv_{i,j,t}$ which locates at (i,j) in the tth frame, its motion characteristic based distortion can be defined by

$$MCD_{i,j,t} = \frac{1}{|\boldsymbol{MV}_{i,j,t}| \cdot (|\bigtriangleup QP_{i,j,t}| + 1)} \quad (4)$$

$$|\boldsymbol{MV}_{i,j,t}| = \sqrt{mvx_{i,j,t}^2 + mvy_{i,j,t}^2} \quad (5)$$

where $\boldsymbol{MV}_{i,j,t}$ is the corresponding MV of $MB_{i,j,t}$, $|\boldsymbol{MV}_{i,j,t}|$ denotes the magnitude, and $|\bigtriangleup QP_{i,j,t}|$ is the absolute value of QP difference. Less distortion can be obtain if the MV's magnitude or the QP difference is larger, which means that modifications are inclined to make on MBs with rich motions. If the MV's magnitude is 0, it is prohibited for data embedding by defining its corresponding distortion as ∞.

3.2 Local Optimality of Motion Vector

As one of the inherent properties of MV, the local optimality has been used in MV-based steganalysis. In steganalytic methods such as [9, 10], it is believed that the extracted MVs from clean video are locally optimal while the modification operations of MV-based steganography will break the local optimality.

As shown in Figure 2(a), the MV $mv_{i,j,t}$ directly extracted from compressed video is also denoted by $mv_{i,j,t}^{0,0}$. By adding or subtracting one MV value, the potentially optimal MVs of $mv_{i,j,t}$ are obtained, which are denoted by $\boldsymbol{PMV}(mv_{i,j,t}) = \{mv_{i,j,t}^{x,y}|x,y \in \{1,0,-1\}\}$. Figure 2(b) shows their corresponding sums of absolute differences (SADs) $\boldsymbol{PSAD}(mv_{i,j,t}) = \{sad_{mv_{i,j,t}}^{x,y}|x,y \in \{1,0,-1\}\}$ between current block and its reference MB, which are computed by Eq. (6).

$$sad_{mv_{i,j,t}}^{x,y} = SAD(\boldsymbol{Pred}_{mv_{i,j,t}}^{x,y}, \boldsymbol{Rec}_{mv_{i,j,t}}) \quad (6)$$

where $\boldsymbol{Pred}_{mv_{i,j,t}}^{x,y}$ is the prediction block pointed by $mv_{i,j,t}^{x,y}$ and $\boldsymbol{Rec}_{mv_{i,j,t}}$ refers to the reconstructed block using extracted $mv_{i,j,t}$. Then we compare the $sad_{mv_{i,j,t}}^{0,0}$ with other SADs in the 3×3 structure. If it holds the minimum value, the associated $mv_{i,j,t}^{0,0}$ is identified as the local optimal MV.

Based on the assumption that the MVs directly obtained from the compressed video are locally optimal, Wang *et al.*

[10] infer that MV-based steganographic approaches would destroy the local optimality of MVs. Holding the opinion that modifications shift MVs from the local optimal locations to non-optimal, they design the effective steganalytic feature based on adding or subtracting one MV value (AoSO) [10]. However, many recent studies [11, 12] have revealed it is possible that the modified MVs can preserved their local optimality, which confutes AoSO's theory. Under such case, the MVs after embedding could remain local optimal and the modifications in such steganographic methods may be made undetectable. Thus in local optimality preserved steganography, the keystone and difficulty is to find the set of substitutable candidates for every MV. The substitutable MVs (SMV) of $mv_{i,j,t}$ can be signified as

$$\boldsymbol{SMV}(mv_{i,j,t}) = \{smv_{i,j,t}^k|k = 1, \ldots, K\} \quad (7)$$

where K is the cardinality of $\boldsymbol{SMV}(mv_{i,j,t})$ and every element $smv_{i,j,t}^k$ in this set can pass the local optimality test.

One of the state-of-art methods utilizes the information distortion during lossy compression to construct $\boldsymbol{SMV}$ [12]. Because the video compression is an information-reducing process, many side-information like residual errors gets lost after transformation and quantization. As the calculated result based on reconstructed block, the $\boldsymbol{PSAD}(\widetilde{mv}_{i,j,t})$ at the decoder is usually different from the original $\boldsymbol{PSAD}(mv_{i,j,t})$ at the encoder side. Although analysis in [10] has proved that most $mv_{i,j,t}$s are still local optimal during decoding, the differences between two SAD matrices provide us with great chance to find $smv(mv_{i,j,t})$.

It is observed that some non-optimal neighbors of $mv_{i,j,t}$ are turned into local optimal ones due to lossy compression. Figure 3 shows the neighboring SAD matrices of $mv_{i,j,t}$ and its SMV $nmv_{i,j,t}$ at the encoder and decoder side respectively, where $nmv_{i,j,t}$ equals $(mvx_{i,j,t} + 1, mvy_{i,j,t})$. At the decoder side, besides the original local optimal MV, its neighboring MV can also pass the local optimality test. Therefore, the SMV set of $mv_{i,j,t}$ consists of the MVs as follows.

$$\boldsymbol{SMV}(mv_{i,j,t}) = \{nmv_{i,j,t}^{k_n}|k_n = 1, \ldots, K_n\} \quad (8)$$

$$nmv_{i,j,t}^{k_n} \in \boldsymbol{Neighbors}_{i,j,t} \quad (9)$$

$$sad_{nmv_{i,j,t}^{k_n}}^{\sim 0,0} = min(\boldsymbol{PSAD}(nmv_{i,j,t}^{k_n})) \quad (10)$$

where K_n is the number of the SMVs of $mv_{i,j,t}$, $\boldsymbol{Neighbors}_{i,j,t}$

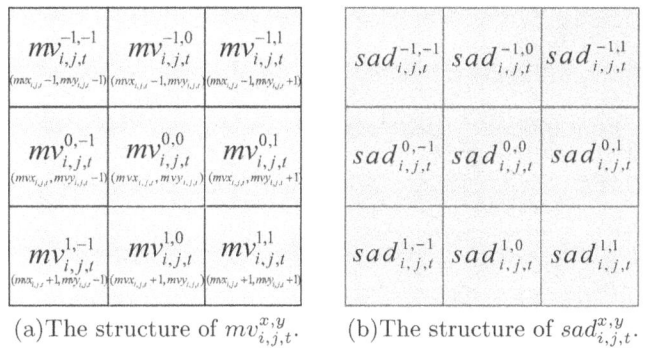

$mv_{i,j,t}^{-1,-1}$	$mv_{i,j,t}^{-1,0}$	$mv_{i,j,t}^{-1,1}$
$mv_{i,j,t}^{0,-1}$	$mv_{i,j,t}^{0,0}$	$mv_{i,j,t}^{0,1}$
$mv_{i,j,t}^{1,-1}$	$mv_{i,j,t}^{1,0}$	$mv_{i,j,t}^{1,1}$

$sad_{i,j,t}^{-1,-1}$	$sad_{i,j,t}^{-1,0}$	$sad_{i,j,t}^{-1,1}$
$sad_{i,j,t}^{0,-1}$	$sad_{i,j,t}^{0,0}$	$sad_{i,j,t}^{0,1}$
$sad_{i,j,t}^{1,-1}$	$sad_{i,j,t}^{1,0}$	$sad_{i,j,t}^{1,1}$

(a)The structure of $mv_{i,j,t}^{x,y}$.   (b)The structure of $sad_{i,j,t}^{x,y}$.

Figure 2: The structures for local optimality computation: the extracted MV, potentially optimal MVs and their corresponding SADs.

Encoder Side

$$sad^{-2,-2}_{mv_{i,j,t}} \quad sad^{-2,-1}_{mv_{i,j,t}} \quad sad^{-2,0}_{mv_{i,j,t}} \quad sad^{-2,1}_{mv_{i,j,t}} \quad sad^{-2,2}_{mv_{i,j,t}}$$

$$sad^{-1,-2}_{mv_{i,j,t}} \quad sad^{-1,-1}_{mv_{i,j,t}} \quad sad^{-1,0}_{mv_{i,j,t}} \quad sad^{-1,1}_{mv_{i,j,t}} \quad sad^{-1,2}_{mv_{i,j,t}}$$

Local Optimal

$$sad^{0,-2}_{mv_{i,j,t}} \quad sad^{0,-1}_{mv_{i,j,t}} \quad sad^{0,0}_{mv_{i,j,t}} \quad sad^{0,1}_{mv_{i,j,t}} \quad sad^{0,2}_{mv_{i,j,t}}$$

$$sad^{1,-2}_{mv_{i,j,t}} \quad sad^{1,-1}_{mv_{i,j,t}} \quad sad^{1,0}_{mv_{i,j,t}} \quad sad^{1,1}_{mv_{i,j,t}} \quad sad^{1,2}_{mv_{i,j,t}}$$

$$sad^{2,-2}_{mv_{i,j,t}} \quad sad^{2,-1}_{mv_{i,j,t}} \quad sad^{2,0}_{mv_{i,j,t}} \quad sad^{2,1}_{mv_{i,j,t}} \quad sad^{2,2}_{mv_{i,j,t}}$$

DCT → Quatization → Entropy Coding

Entropy Decoding → I-Quatization → I-DCT

Decoder Side

$$sad^{\sim-1,-1}_{mv_{i,j,t}} \quad sad^{\sim-1,0}_{mv_{i,j,t}} \quad sad^{\sim-1,1}_{mv_{i,j,t}} \qquad sad^{\sim-1,-1}_{nmv_{i,j,t}} \quad sad^{\sim-1,0}_{nmv_{i,j,t}} \quad sad^{\sim-1,1}_{nmv_{i,j,t}}$$

Local Optimal

$$sad^{\sim0,-1}_{mv_{i,j,t}} \quad sad^{\sim0,0}_{mv_{i,j,t}} \quad sad^{\sim0,1}_{mv_{i,j,t}} \qquad sad^{\sim0,-1}_{nmv_{i,j,t}} \quad sad^{\sim0,0}_{nmv_{i,j,t}} \quad sad^{\sim0,1}_{nmv_{i,j,t}}$$

$$sad^{\sim-1,-1}_{mv_{i,j,t}} \quad sad^{\sim-1,0}_{mv_{i,j,t}} \quad sad^{\sim-1,1}_{mv_{i,j,t}} \qquad sad^{\sim-1,-1}_{nmv_{i,j,t}} \quad sad^{\sim-1,0}_{nmv_{i,j,t}} \quad sad^{\sim-1,1}_{nmv_{i,j,t}}$$

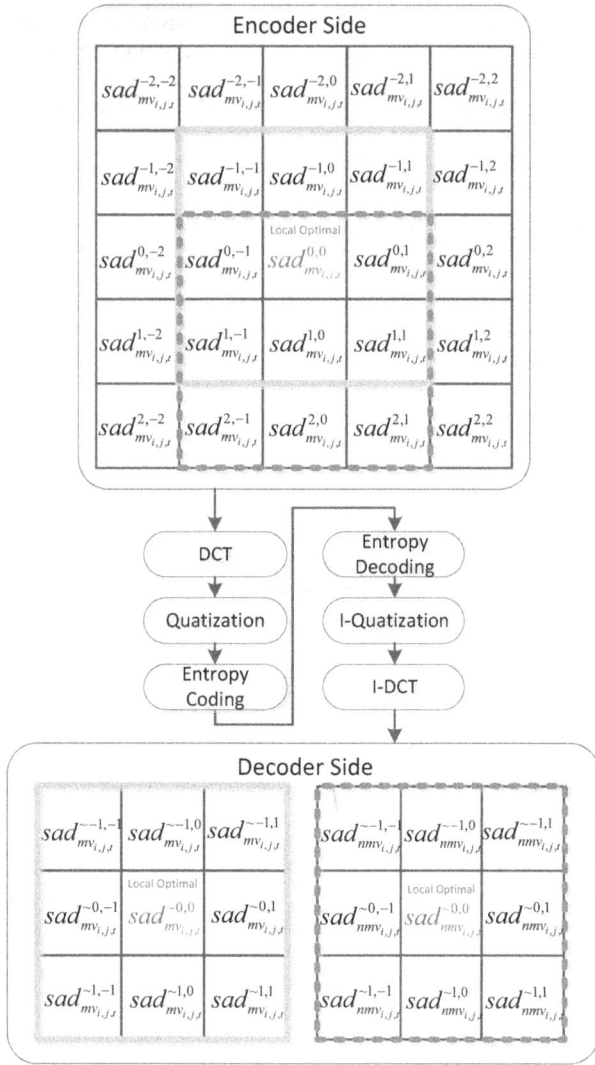

Figure 3: Illustration of SMV introduced by lossy compression.

$= \{(mvx_{i,j,t}+1, mvy_{i,j,t}), (mvx_{i,j,t}-1, mvy_{i,j,t}), (mvx_{i,j,t}, mvy_{i,j,t}+1), (mvx_{i,j,t}, mvy_{i,j,t}-1), (mvx_{i,j,t}+1, mvy_{i,j,t}+1), (mvx_{i,j,t}+1, mvy_{i,j,t}-1), (mvx_{i,j,t}-1, mvy_{i,j,t}+1), (mvx_{i,j,t}-1, mvy_{i,j,t}-1)\}$ is the set containing the neighboring MVs of $mv_{i,j,t}$, $sad^{\sim0,0}_{nmv^{k_n}_{i,j,t}}$ denotes the corresponding SAD of $nmv^{k_n}_{i,j,t}$ obtained at the decoder. Thus the SMV set is constructed using the neighboring MVs whose local optimality can be preserved at the decoder side. If the MVs are replaced with the SMVs in this set, the modifications would resist the detection of AoSO feature.

Another recent method [11] is designed to select SMVs in a designated searching area. Different from obtaining MVs using default searching method, this approach collects all the SMVs by perturbing the ME process. And as the result of motion compensation (MC) in video decompression, the video quality and the MVs' local optimality can be ensured at the decoder side. As illustrated in Figure 4, the SMV set of $mv_{i,j,t}$ is composed of the MVs as follows.

$$\mathbf{SMV}(mv_{i,j,t}) = \{cmv^{k_c}_{i,j,t} | k_c = 1, \ldots, K_c\} \quad (11)$$

$$cmv^{k_c}_{i,j,t} \in \mathbf{SearchArea}_{i,j,t} \quad (12)$$

$$sad^{\sim0,0}_{cmv^{k_c}_{i,j,t}} = min(\mathbf{PSAD}(cmv^{k_c}_{i,j,t})) \quad (13)$$

where K_c is the number of the SMV of $mv_{i,j,t}$, $\mathbf{SearchArea}_{i,j,t}$ denotes the designated searching area in reference frames for $MB_{i,j,t}$, $cmv^{k_c}_{i,j,t}$ is the qualified MV located in the searching area, and $sad^{\sim0,0}_{cmv^{k_c}_{i,j,t}}$ denotes the corresponding SAD of $cmv^{k_c}_{i,j,t}$ at the decoder. In this case, the SMVs' local optimality can also be preserved and the modifications from original MVs to SMVs would also be made in undetectable way.

However, both of these two steganographic approaches have obvious limitations in real-time scene. As analyzed above, the first method finds the SMVs based on the lossy compression's disturbance to SADs. Thus the number of SMVs will decrease drastically if the information loss reduces during the video compression. Table 1 lists the proportions of MVs with different number of SMVs. It can be noticed that reduction of the SMVs' number indeed exists with the increment of bit-rate. Peculiarly, the videos with high bit-rate contain very little number of SMVs, which is not sufficient to support practical steganography. As to the second method, original MV is replaced with any of the qualified SMVs within the designated searching area. These operations lead to larger modifications of the MVs' horizontal or vertical components, which makes it relatively detectable when using statistical analysis or calibration-based steganalysis.

In this paper, an adaptive selection strategy is proposed to satisfy the application requirement of practical steganography. By adopting the advantages of above two SMV construction methods, this strategy can choose the approach of local optimality preservation for every MV adaptively. By utilizing this strategy, the local optimality based distortion can be defined as follows.

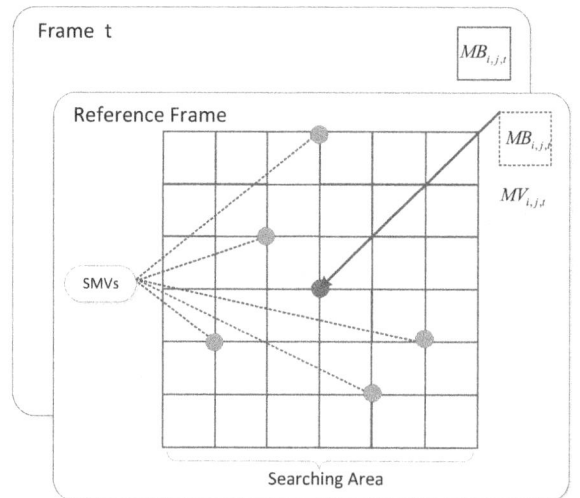

Frame t

$MB_{i,j,t}$

Reference Frame

$MB_{i,j,t}$

$MV_{i,j,t}$

SMVs

Searching Area

Figure 4: Illustration of SMVs located in the designated searching area.

Table 1: Proportion of MVs with different number of SMVs.

Sequence	Bitrate (Mbps)	1	2	3	4
Akiyo	0.5	15.32	21.59	19.02	30.58
	1	17.47	26.47	13.51	22.03
	3	21.68	8.45	5.03	4.76
	10	3.69	0.04	0.01	0.00
Coastguard	0.5	2.06	9.01	18.07	70.62
	1	9.02	17.31	24.42	47.03
	3	33.79	19.57	15.79	8.59
	10	23.62	1.03	0.05	0.00
Foreman	0.5	4.29	14.21	15.17	64.25
	1	15.09	22.17	14.42	41.15
	3	25.94	15.40	9.10	17.03
	10	19.97	3.63	1.49	2.75

Definition 2. (**Local Optimality Based Distortion, LOD**). The local optimality based distortion of $mv_{i,j,t}$ can be defined by

$$
LOD_{i,j,t} = \begin{cases} (\frac{1}{K_n} \sum_{k_n=1}^{K_n} (J_{nmv_{i,j,t}^{k_n}} - J_{mv_{i,j,t}})^2)^{\frac{1}{2}} & if \ K_n \geq 1, \\ (\frac{1}{K_c} \sum_{k_c=1}^{K_c} (J_{cmv_{i,j,t}^{k_c}} - J_{mv_{i,j,t}})^2)^{\frac{1}{2}} & others. \end{cases}
$$

(14)

where $J_{mv} = sad_{mv} + \lambda \cdot R_{mv}$, which is the Lagrangian cost function in RDO model, λ is the Lagrange parameter, and R_{mv} denotes the bits for coding mv. With distortion function defined by the $LOD_{i,j,t}$, the SMVs for every $LOD_{i,j,t}$ can be found out. Because the proposed strategy adaptively selects the applicable SMV construction method at every location, the local optimality of modified MVs is certain to be preserved. And it is expected that by considering the local optimality of MVs, the steganographic approach can resist the detection of local optimality based steganalysis.

3.3 Statistical Distribution of Motion Vector

Because MVs in clean videos are obtained through ME process and represent the motion information of video content, there exists strong spatial correlation among MVs in each frame and strong temporal correlation between consecutive frames. The basic hypothesis for steganalysis is that some statistical characteristics of cover object can be changed by embedding process. The modifications of the MVs will introduce the changes of spatial-temporal correlation, which are signatures showing the existence of the embedded message [22]. Therefore, in order to reduce the evidence which can be utilized by steganalyzers, MVs' statistical distribution should be considered in designing the distortion function.

Due to motion's relevance and continuity, adjacent MBs have similar motion trends in spatial domain and the MBs of same locations also have same motion trajectories between adjacent frames. Considering both the spatial and temporal consistency, the MVs' changes in MBs with similar motion trends are often more possible to be detected, and thus should be set as high distortion values. Contrari-

wise modifications tend to be made in MBs with different motion trends, which should be set as low distortion values.

In order to model the MVs' statistical distribution, the horizontal and vertical components of MVs in one frame are separated to construct two $H \times W$ components matrix $\boldsymbol{MVX}_t$ and $\boldsymbol{MVY}_t$, where H and W denotes the height and width of the frame in the unit of block. In spatial domain, we use the second-order difference to calculate the components' statistical distribution in four directions respectively. As shown in Figure 5, denoted by a differential operation ∇, the second-order differences of $\boldsymbol{MVX}_t$ in horizontal, vertical, $45°$ and $-45°$ direction can be computed by

$$
\nabla x_{i,j,t}^{\rightarrow}(\boldsymbol{MVX}_t) = 2mvx_{i,j,t} - mvx_{i,j+1,t} - mvx_{i,j-1,t}
$$

(15)

$$
\nabla x_{i,j,t}^{\uparrow}(\boldsymbol{MVX}_t) = 2mvx_{i,j,t} - mvx_{i+1,j,t} - mvx_{i-1,j,t}
$$

(16)

$$
\nabla x_{i,j,t}^{\nearrow}(\boldsymbol{MVX}_t) = 2mvx_{i,j,t} - mvx_{i+1,j-1,t} - mvx_{i-1,j+1,t}
$$

(17)

$$
\nabla x_{i,j,t}^{\nwarrow}(\boldsymbol{MVX}_t) = 2mvx_{i,j,t} - mvx_{i+1,j+1,t} - mvx_{i-1,j-1,t}
$$

(18)

where $i = 2, \dots, H - 1$, $j = 2, \dots, W - 1$. Then we use histograms to count the difference of the neighboring triples. The horizontal components' statistical distribution at four different directions could be obtained by

$$
H_d^{\rightarrow}(\boldsymbol{MVX}_t) = \sum_{i=2}^{H-1} \sum_{j=2}^{W-1} ||\nabla x_{i,j,t}^{\rightarrow}(\boldsymbol{MVX}_t) = d||
$$

(19)

$$
H_d^{\uparrow}(\boldsymbol{MVX}_t) = \sum_{i=2}^{H-1} \sum_{j=2}^{W-1} ||\nabla x_{i,j,t}^{\uparrow}(\boldsymbol{MVX}_t) = d||
$$

(20)

$$
H_d^{\nearrow}(\boldsymbol{MVX}_t) = \sum_{i=2}^{H-1} \sum_{j=2}^{W-1} ||\nabla x_{i,j,t}^{\nearrow}(\boldsymbol{MVX}_t) = d||
$$

(21)

$$
H_d^{\nwarrow}(\boldsymbol{MVX}_t) = \sum_{i=2}^{H-1} \sum_{j=2}^{W-1} ||\nabla x_{i,j,t}^{\nwarrow}(\boldsymbol{MVX}_t) = d||
$$

(22)

where $||I||$ equals 1 if I is true and 0 otherwise.

With regard to temporal correlation, the similar operations are applied to MVs of adjacent frames. As illustrated

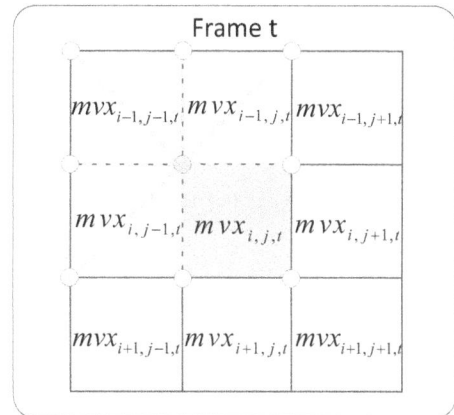

Figure 5: Schematic diagram of computing statistical distribution for spatial correlation.

in Figure 6, the $\boldsymbol{MVX}_t$'s second-order difference in temporal direction and its distribution histogram can be calculated by following formulas.

$$\nabla x_{i,j,t}^\dagger(\boldsymbol{MVX}_t) = 2mvx_{i,j,t} - mvx_{i,j,t+1} - mvx_{i,j,t-1}$$

(23)

$$H_d^\dagger(\boldsymbol{MVX}_t) = \sum_{i=2}^{H-1}\sum_{j=2}^{W-1} ||\nabla x_{i,j,t}^\dagger(\boldsymbol{MVX}_t) = d||$$ (24)

By analogy, the second-order differences $\nabla x_{i,j,t}^\rightarrow(\boldsymbol{MVY}_t)$, $\nabla x_{i,j,t}^\uparrow(\boldsymbol{MVY}_t), \nabla x_{i,j,t}^\nearrow(\boldsymbol{MVY}_t), \nabla x_{i,j,t}^\nwarrow(\boldsymbol{MVY}_t), \nabla x_{i,j,t}^\dagger$ $(\boldsymbol{MVY}_t)$ as well as their distribution histograms $H_d^\rightarrow(\boldsymbol{MVY}_t)$, $H_d^\uparrow(\boldsymbol{MVY}_t), H_d^\nearrow(\boldsymbol{MVY}_t), H_d^\nwarrow(\boldsymbol{MVY}_t), H_d^\dagger(\boldsymbol{MVY}_t)$ can also be computed for vertical components $\boldsymbol{MVY}_t$. Based on above analysis, we can define the statistical distribution based distortion as follows.

Definition 3. (**Statistical Distribution Based Distortion, SDD**). The statistical distribution based distortion associated with $mv_{i,j,t}$ can be defined by

$$SDD_{i,j,t} = \sum_{\substack{d\in\{-128,...,128\}\\f\in\{\rightarrow,\uparrow,\nearrow,\nwarrow,\dagger\}}} \frac{1}{|d|+1} \cdot H_t^f(\boldsymbol{MV}_t)$$ (25)

$$H_t^f(\boldsymbol{MV}_t) = max(|H_t^f(\boldsymbol{MVX}_t) - H_t^f(\boldsymbol{MVX}_t')|,$$ (26)
$$|H_t^f(\boldsymbol{MVY}_t) - H_t^f(\boldsymbol{MVY}_t')|)$$

where $\boldsymbol{MV}_t'$ denotes the MV field obtained from the tth frame of stego video, the original MV $mv_{i,j,t}$ has been replaced by the modified MV $mv_{i,j,t}'$ in $\boldsymbol{MV}_t'$ and $mv_{i,j,t}' \in \boldsymbol{SMV}_{mv_{i,j,t}}$, is one of the SMVs defined in subsection 3.2.

Because the information is randomly embedded in MVs' horizontal or vertical component, the larger value of these two components' statistical differences will be used to define the statistical distribution based distortion for $mv_{i,j,t}$. By defining the weight by d, larger distortion will be obtained for MVs with less differences, which means that the MBs with similar motion trends are not applicable for embedding. And as a result, modifications are made in MVs with various motion trends and the security performance against statistical steganalysis is hoped to be enhanced.

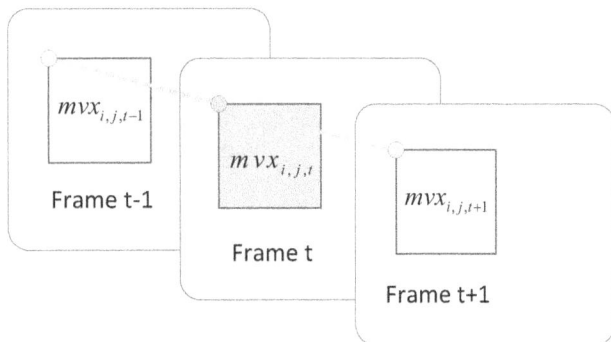

Figure 6: Schematic diagram of computing statistical distribution for temporal correlation.

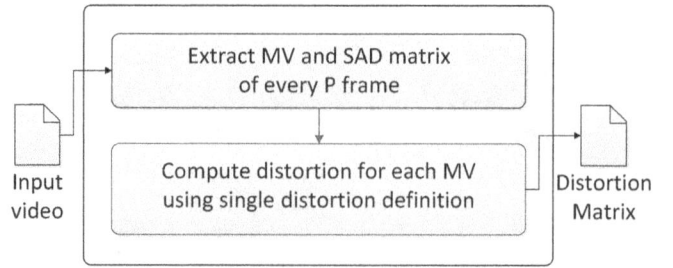

(a) Typical Distortion Computation.

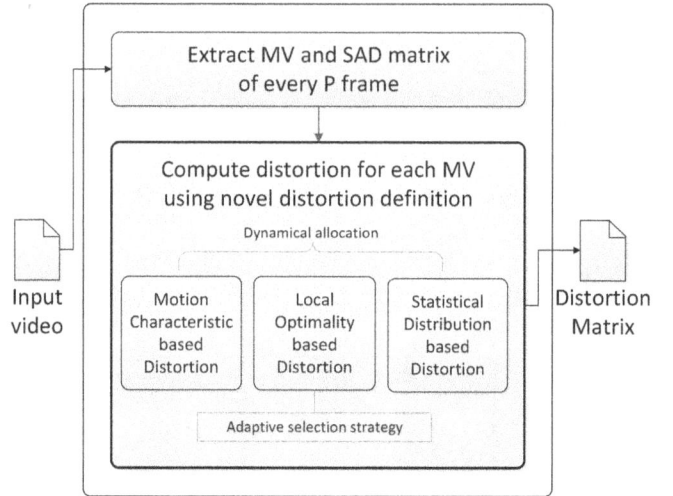

(b) Novel Distortion Computation.

Figure 7: A comparison between typical and novel distortion computation.

3.4 The Definition of Distortion Function

As introduced in Section 2, the embedding impact can be measured by the non-negative additive distortions introduced by independent modifications. And the overall distortion should be minimized by steganographic codes. Thus the overall distortion of all the $mv_{i,j,t}$ in tth frame can be calculated by

$$D(\boldsymbol{MV}_t, \boldsymbol{MV}_t') = \sum_{i=1}^{H}\sum_{j=1}^{W} \Phi_{i,j,t}(mv_{i,j,t}, mv_{i,j,t}')$$ (27)

where H and W represents the number of block in frame's height and width respectively, $\boldsymbol{MV}_t = \{mv_{i,j,t}|i \in \{1,\ldots,H\}, j \in \{1,\ldots,W\}\}$, which is the original MV set, $\boldsymbol{MV}_t' = \{mv_{i,j,t}'|i \in \{1,\ldots,H\}, j \in \{1,\ldots,W\}\}$, which is the modified MV set. The variable $\Phi_{i,j,t}$ denotes the distortion function of $mv_{i,j,t}$, which can fully represent the modification's impact by considering the $MCD_{i,j,t}$, $LOD_{i,j,t}$ and $SDD_{i,j,t}$.

Definition 4. (**The Distortion Function**). The distortion of $mv_{i,j,t}$ can be defined by

Table 2: Coding performance, including achieved bit-rate (achieved BR, *kbps*) and PSNR (*dB*) under given compressed bit-rate (compressed BR, *kbps*) and embedding rate (ER, *bpmv*).

Sequence	Method	Compressed BR	500		1000		3000		10000	
		ER	0.25	0.5	0.25	0.5	0.25	0.5	0.25	0.5
Bus.yuv	STC	Achieved BR	489.6		983.52		2948.40		9960.25	
		PSNR	30.64		34.17		40.66		50.79	
	Ours	Achieved BR	489.6	490.32	983.76	983.28	2951.52	2956.08	9959.53	9964.09
		PSNR	30.51	30.3	34.05	33.81	40.58	40.39	50.73	50.64
	Cao's	Achieved BR	488.88	488.88	982.56	982.32	2948.4	2949.36	9959.29	9955.45
		PSNR	30.24	30.07	33.35	33.17	40.28	40.1	50.42	50.33
	Yao's	Achieved BR	489.12	490.32	982.8	984	2950.8	2951.04	9959.53	9973.45
		PSNR	29.48	29.37	33.16	32.95	39.63	39.65	50.23	50.17
Mobile.yuv	STC	Achieved BR	495.6		974.16		2873.76		9858.73	
		PSNR	28.15		30.95		36.73		48.3	
	Ours	Achieved BR	497.04	498.72	977.76	981.60	2882.4	2897.76	9880.90	9910.09
		PSNR	27.99	27.71	30.82	30.56	36.62	36.39	48.22	48.06
	Cao's	Achieved BR	495.84	497.04	974.64	978.24	2876.16	2882.16	9870.49	9892.33
		PSNR	27.4	27.23	30.09	29.81	36.02	35.86	47.74	47.33
	Yao's	Achieved BR	497.52	499.92	979.44	987.84	2887.2	2914.32	9888.25	9957.37
		PSNR	26.39	26.25	29.24	29.12	35.19	35.08	47.14	47.03
Stefan.yuv	STC	Achieved BR	486		991.92		3046.08		10302.01	
		PSNR	31.24		34.58		40.71		50.43	
	Ours	Achieved BR	486	487.68	994.8	996.24	3047.52	3042.24	10322.41	10322.97
		PSNR	31.04	30.72	34.4	34.1	40.63	40.44	50.41	50.34
	Cao's	Achieved BR	486.24	486.24	993.12	992.4	3043.92	3048.72	10305.61	10311.13
		PSNR	29.95	29.72	34.12	33.98	40.18	40.11	50.2	49.99
	Yao's	Achieved BR	487.92	489.36	997.44	997.68	3049.92	3048.96	10329.61	10349.77
		PSNR	29.65	29.59	33.28	33.09	39.67	39.51	50.09	50.02

$$\Phi_{i,j,t}(mv_{i,j,t}, mv'_{i,j,t}) = WMCD_{i,j,t} \cdot WLOD_{i,j,t} \cdot WSDD_{i,j,t} \tag{28}$$

$$WMCD_{i,j,t} = MCD_{i,j,t}^{\beta_{MCD_{i,j,t}}} \tag{29}$$

$$WLOD_{i,j,t} = (LOD_{i,j,t} + \alpha_{LOD_{i,j,t}})^{\beta_{LOD_{i,j,t}}} \tag{30}$$

$$WSDD_{i,j,t} = (SDD_{i,j,t} + \alpha_{SDD_{i,j,t}})^{\beta_{SDD_{i,j,t}}} \tag{31}$$

where $WMCD_{i,j,t}$, $WLOD_{i,j,t}$ and $WSDD_{i,j,t}$ denotes the weighted distortion of $MCD_{i,j,t}$, $LOD_{i,j,t}$, and $SDD_{i,j,t}$ respectively. The parameter $\alpha_{LOD_{i,j,t}}$ and $\alpha_{SDD_{i,j,t}}$ can be selected as relatively small positive constants to ensure the embedding distortion keeps positive. Every element in $\{\beta_{MCD_{i,j,t}}, \beta_{LOD_{i,j,t}}, \beta_{SDD_{i,j,t}}\}$ is used to allocate the contributions of these three sub-distortions, which are dynamically set as follows.

$$\beta_{MCD_{i,j,t}} = \frac{1}{|\boldsymbol{MV}_{i,j,t}| + 1} \tag{32}$$

$$\beta_{LOD_{i,j,t}} = \frac{1}{K} \tag{33}$$

$$\beta_{SDD_{i,j,t}} = \sum H_t^f(\boldsymbol{MV}_t) \tag{34}$$

where $|\boldsymbol{MV}_{i,j,t}|$ is $mv_{i,j,t}$'s magnitude, K is the number of SMVs and $H_t^f(\boldsymbol{MV}_t)$ is the statistical distribution difference. This method adaptively adjusts the tradeoff between the sub-distortions and focuses on the embedding impact on fragile characteristic. Therefore, the distortion fully considering multi-level embedding influence can be adaptively defined in our proposed approach.

The comparison between typical and novel distortion computation is shown in Figure 7. In order to take advantage of the motion information for modification, the impact of motion characteristic is introduced in designing the distortion. By adopting the adaptive selection strategy, the local optimality of modified MV can be better preserved in our proposed method. With the hope of resisting statistical analysis, we also consider the change of statistical distribution before and after embedding. Thus comparing with traditional distortion defined only considering single embedding impact, the performance of our approach is hoped to be improved by using the novel distortion definition.

4. PRACTICAL IMPLEMENTATION

Based on the given distortion function, the practical implementation of proposed steganographic method using two-layered STCs is to be introduced in this section. In our proposed steganographic method, there are three phases for completing data embedding and extraction scheme.

Embedding Distortion Definition: For every frame $\boldsymbol{F}_t$ in the N frames, if it is not I frame, obtain its MV matrix $\boldsymbol{MV}_t$ and the corresponding prediction error matrix $\boldsymbol{E}_t$ through ME process. Then for each $MB_{i,j}$ in this frame, define the distortions using $\Phi_{i,j,t}(mv_{i,j,t}, mv'_{i,j,t})$ in Eq.28 and store all the defined distortion in $\boldsymbol{D}_t = \{\Phi_{i,j,t}(mv_{i,j,t}, mv'_{i,j,t})\}$.

Data Embedding: If the length of the binary message sequence is l and the number of P frames is N_p, the cover length can be calculated by $n = H \times W \times N_p \times 2$. The embedding rate is $\gamma = l/n$, which is measured by the average embedded bits per motion vector (*bpmv*). The first and second embedding channels are constructed using the LSB layer and second LSB layer of $(mvx_{i,j,t} + mvy_{i,j,t})$. With the binary message sequence $\boldsymbol{m}$, the $\boldsymbol{MV}_t$ and the distortions $\boldsymbol{D}_t$, embed data in $LSB((mvx_{i,j,t} + mvy_{i,j,t}))$ and $LSB(\lfloor(mvx_{i,j,t} + mvy_{i,j,t})/2\rfloor)$ using ± 1 two-layered STCs

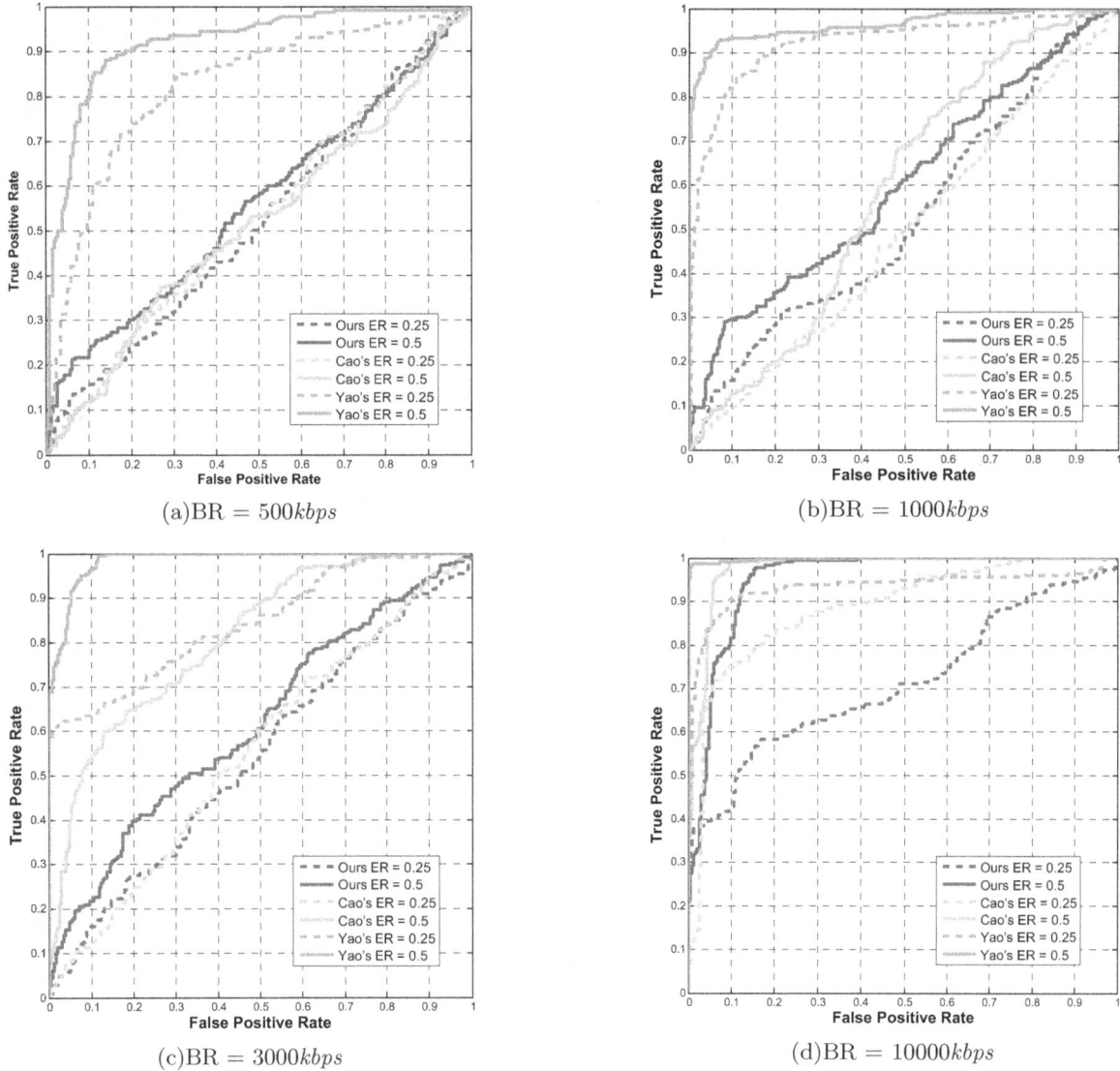

(a)BR $= 500kbps$

(b)BR $= 1000kbps$

(c)BR $= 3000kbps$

(d)BR $= 10000kbps$

Figure 8: ROC curves against AoSO.

with embedding rate $\gamma/2$. After embedding data for every $mv_{i,j,t}$ in N frames, encode frame $\boldsymbol{F}_t$ using the modified MV matrix $\boldsymbol{MV}_t'$. As the result, the coded bit stream can be generated.

Data Extraction: Decode every received frame to obtain the MV matrix $\boldsymbol{MV}_t'$. Then use the STCs decoding to extract the binary message sequence.

5. EXPERIMENTS

5.1 Experimental Setup

Our proposed embedding scheme is implemented on a well-known H.264/AVC codec named x264 [23]. The video database is composed of 30 standard 4:2:0 YUV sequences in CIF format. The raw sequences vary from 150 to 300 frames in length and are coded with 30fps frame rate.

In order to evaluate the security of our approach under different cases, various bit-rate (BR) including $500kbps$, $1000kbps$, $3000kbps$ and $10000kbps$ are considered with the

Table 3: Average detection accuracies (%) against AoSO

BR (kbps)	500		1000		3000		10000	
ER (bpmv)	0.25	0.5	0.25	0.5	0.25	0.5	0.25	0.5
Ours	50.78	54.20	50.71	56.43	52.23	56.40	63.05	88.81
Cao's	52.30	52.66	50.87	57.85	54.60	70.89	82.43	94.39
Yao's	76.27	87.44	85.71	92.00	73.78	93.03	90.26	98.07

achieved embedding rate (ER) $0.25bpmv$ and $0.5bpmv$ respectively. Beside, Cao's [12] and Yao's [8] methods are also implemented for performance comparisons. And the LibSVM toolbox [24] with the Gaussian kernel is used as classifier.

In our tests, stego and clean videos are generated by com-

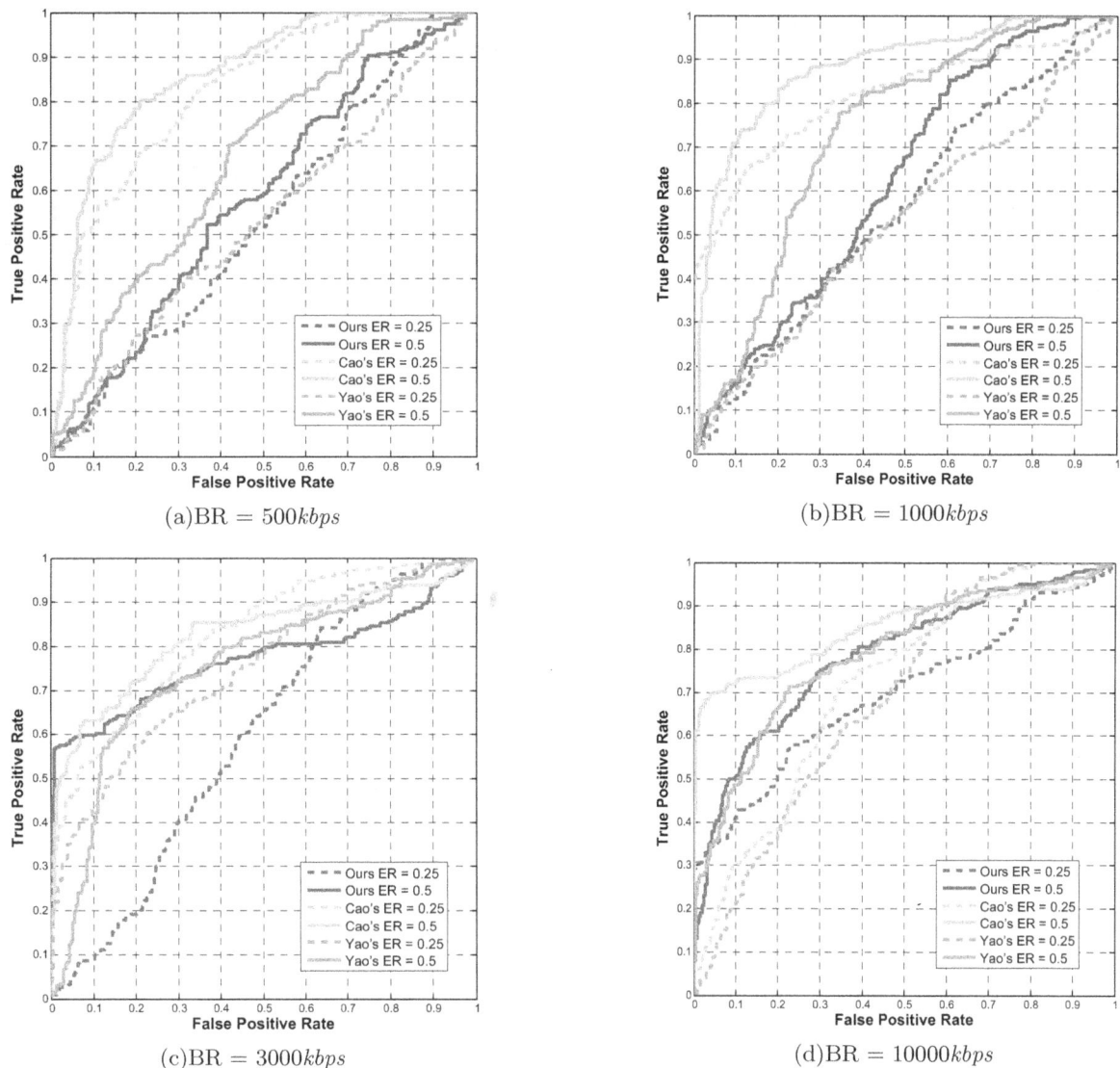

(a)BR $= 500kbps$

(b)BR $= 1000kbps$

(c)BR $= 3000kbps$

(d)BR $= 10000kbps$

Figure 9: ROC curves against MVRBR.

pressing 30 sequences at various bit-rates with and without embedding. Subsequently, AoSO [10] and MVRBR [14] features are extracted out from every 12 frames. Then features are fed into classifier, 60 percent sequence pairs (stego and cover) are randomly selected for training and the remaining ones for testing. Each training and testing is repeated 50 times and average results used to evaluate the final performance. The true negative (TN) rate and the true positive (TP) rate are computed by counting the number of detections in the test sets. By averaging TN and TP, averaged detection accuracies are obtained.

5.2 Results and Discussion

5.2.1 Coding Efficiency

One of the conspicuous advantage of MV-based steganographic methods is that they do not affect the coding efficiency (PSNR and bit-rate) much. The error caused by modifying MV will be handled by the mechanism of ME

Table 4: Average detection accuracies (%) against MVRBR

BR (kbps)	500		1000		3000		10000	
ER (bpmv)	0.25	0.5	0.25	0.5	0.25	0.5	0.25	0.5
Ours	51.75	56.79	53.50	57.04	56.95	71.51	64.13	71.94
Cao's	72.79	79.78	73.91	80.21	72.32	76.18	67.73	77.82
Yao's	52.21	61.39	53.30	69.52	68.43	70.93	63.00	72.22

and MC. For example, comparison coding results of three sequences, i.e., "Bus.yuv", "Mobile.yuv" and "Stefan.yuv" are listed in Table 2, where STC denotes the standard compression without embedding. It can be seen that both the video quality and the compression ratio are affected sightly for all methods, and the embedding impact of our approach is smallest.

5.2.2 Steganalysis

For security evaluation, the recent proposed AoSO [10] and MVRBR [14] feature are leveraged against our proposed, Cao's and Yao's steganographic schemes.

The detection accuracies against AoSO feature are recorded in Table 3 and the corresponding receiver operation characteristic (ROC) curves are depicted in Figure 8. In comparison with Ours and Cao's methods, Yao's method performs worst in all tested cases due to local optimality unconsidered. Cao's method performs well at low bit-rate i.e, $500kbps$ in Figure 8(a) and $1000kbps$ in Figure 8(b). However, the performance deteriorates when bit-rate increases, which is shown by Figure 8(c)(d). It is because that less loss is induced by compression in higher quality videos. As the result, the number of SMVs obtained from lossy-compression reduces and the modifications have to be made on MVs without local optimality. The performance of our method is quite close to the average performance of Cao's at low bit-rate. With bit-rate increasing, our approach works better than Cao's method. Despite deterioration in performance under high bit-rate cases, our approach still enhances the security against AoSO obviously, which benefits from the adaptive selection strategy. Thus our approach generally performs best at different bit-rates, especially in the cases of high bit-rate.

When detected by MVRBR feature, the average detection accuracies are presented in Table 4. It can be seen from Figure 9 that Cao's method performs worst because of statistical distribution not included. The performance of Yao's is better than Cao's but inferior to ours. By adopting dynamical adjustment between three factors in defining distortion scale, our approach works best in these three methods. Both of Figure 8 and Figure 9 indicate that the steganalytic performances against all above steganographic methods are related to video quality. This is mainly because that AoSO and MVRBR features are extracted using MVs and SADs. The SADs are calculated from prediction residuals which are compressed in lossy way. Since the distortion of prediction residuals is less if video has higher quality, AoSO and MVRBR features perform better when bit-rate is higher.

Overall, in contrast with Cao's and Yao's methods, the detection accuracies and the ROC curves indicate that our proposed method reduces the probability of detection. This implies that the steganographic security of MV-based steganography can be enhanced by utilizing the novel distortion function, which dynamically adjusts the contributions of sub-distortions considering three different factors.

6. CONCLUSIONS

In this paper, a novel embedding distortion for MV-based steganography is proposed. Three important factors are simultaneously considered in distortion definition, which are motion characteristic of video content, MV's local optimality and statistical distribution. And dynamical allocation is implementation between these three distortion components. The practical embedding algorithm is implemented using two-layered STCs. In experiments against current effective steganalytic methods, the proposed approach outperforms other existing MV-based steganographic methods in security, especially for high quality videos.

As part of our future work, more impact of MVs' modification and optimization of distortion definition is to be further exploited. Moreover, method to reduce the heavily computation of distortion is also attempted in practical implementation.

7. ACKNOWLEDGMENTS

This work was supported by the NSFC under 61303259 and U1536105, the Strategic Priority Research Program of Chinese Academy of Sciences (CAS) under XDA06030600, and the Key Project of Institute of Information Engineering, CAS, under Y5Z0131201.

8. REFERENCES

[1] F. JORDAN. Proposal of a watermarking technique for hiding/retrieving data in compressed and decompressed video. *ISO/IEC Doc. JTC1/SC 29/QWG 11 MPEG 97/M 2281*, 1997.

[2] Changyong Xu, Xijian Ping, and Tao Zhang. Steganography in compressed video stream. In *Innovative Computing, Information and Control, 2006. ICICIC '06. First International Conference on*, volume 1, pages 269–272, Aug 2006.

[3] H.A. Aly. Data hiding in motion vectors of compressed video based on their associated prediction error. *Information Forensics and Security, IEEE Transactions on*, 6(1):14–18, March 2011.

[4] J. Fridrich, M. Goljan, P. Lisonek, and D. Soukal. Writing on wet paper. *Signal Processing, IEEE Transactions on*, 53(10):3923–3935, Oct 2005.

[5] TomÃąÅą Filler, Jan Judas, and Jessica Fridrich. Minimizing embedding impact in steganography using trellis-coded quantization, 2010.

[6] T. Filler, J. Judas, and J. Fridrich. Minimizing additive distortion in steganography using syndrome-trellis codes. *Information Forensics and Security, IEEE Transactions on*, 6(3):920–935, Sept 2011.

[7] Yun Cao, Xianfeng Zhao, Dengguo Feng, and Rennong Sheng. *Information Hiding: 13th International Conference, IH 2011, Prague, Czech Republic, May 18-20, 2011, Revised Selected Papers*, chapter Video Steganography with Perturbed Motion Estimation, pages 193–207. Springer Berlin Heidelberg, Berlin, Heidelberg, 2011.

[8] Yuanzhi Yao, Weiming Zhang, Nenghai Yu, and Xianfeng Zhao. Defining embedding distortion for motion vector-based video steganography. *Multimedia Tools and Applications*, 74(24):11163–11186, 2014.

[9] Yanzhen Ren, Liming Zhai, Lina Wang, and Tingting Zhu. Video steganalysis based on subtractive probability of optimal matching feature. In *Proceedings of the 2Nd ACM Workshop on Information Hiding and Multimedia Security*, IH&MMSec '14, pages 83–90, New York, NY, USA, 2014. ACM.

[10] Keren Wang, Hong Zhao, and Hongxia Wang. Video steganalysis against motion vector-based steganography by adding or subtracting one motion vector value. *Information Forensics and Security, IEEE Transactions on*, 9(5):741–751, May 2014.

[11] Hong Zhang, Yun Cao, and Xianfeng Zhao. Motion vector-based video steganography with preserved local

optimality. *Multimedia Tools and Applications*, pages 1–17, 2015.

[12] Yun Cao, Hong Zhang, Xianfeng Zhao, and Haibo Yu. Video steganography based on optimized motion estimation perturbation. In *Proceedings of the 3rd ACM Workshop on Information Hiding and Multimedia Security*, IH&MMSec '15, pages 25–31, New York, NY, USA, 2015. ACM.

[13] Yun Cao, Xianfeng Zhao, and Dengguo Feng. Video steganalysis exploiting motion vector reversion-based features. *Signal Processing Letters, IEEE*, 19(1):35–38, Jan 2012.

[14] Peipei Wang, Yun Cao, Xianfeng Zhao, and Bin Wu. Motion vector reversion-based steganalysis revisited. In *Signal and Information Processing (ChinaSIP), 2015 IEEE China Summit and International Conference on*, pages 463–467, July 2015.

[15] Tomás Pevný, Tomáš Filler, and Patrick Bas. *Information Hiding: 12th International Conference, IH 2010, Calgary, AB, Canada, June 28-30, 2010, Revised Selected Papers*, chapter Using High-Dimensional Image Models to Perform Highly Undetectable Steganography, pages 161–177. Springer Berlin Heidelberg, Berlin, Heidelberg, 2010.

[16] V. Holub and J. Fridrich. Designing steganographic distortion using directional filters. In *Information Forensics and Security (WIFS), 2012 IEEE International Workshop on*, pages 234–239, Dec 2012.

[17] Danfeng Xie, Zhiwei Huang, Shizheng Wang, and Heguang Liu. Moving objects segmentation from compressed surveillance video based on motion estimation. In *Pattern Recognition (ICPR), 2012 21st International Conference on*, pages 3132–3135, Nov 2012.

[18] Wei Zeng, Jun Du, Wen Gao, and Qingming Huang. Robust moving object segmentation on h.264/avc compressed video using the block-based {MRF} model. *Real-Time Imaging*, 11(4):290 – 299, 2005.

[19] R. Venkatesh Babu and K.R. Ramakrishnan. Recognition of human actions using motion history information extracted from the compressed video. *Image and Vision Computing*, 22(8):597 – 607, 2004.

[20] T. Wiegand, G.J. Sullivan, G. Bjontegaard, and A. Luthra. Overview of the h.264/avc video coding standard. *Circuits and Systems for Video Technology, IEEE Transactions on*, 13(7):560–576, July 2003.

[21] M. Tom and R.V. Babu. Fast moving-object detection in h.264/avc compressed domain for video surveillance. In *Computer Vision, Pattern Recognition, Image Processing and Graphics (NCVPRIPG), 2013 Fourth National Conference on*, pages 1–4, Dec 2013.

[22] Yuting Su, Chengqian Zhang, and Chuntian Zhang. A video steganalytic algorithm against motion-vector-based steganography. *Signal Processing*, 91(8):1901 – 1909, 2011.

[23] VideoLan. x264. Available: http://www.videolan.org/developers/x264.html.

[24] C.Chang and C.Lin. LIBSVM: A Library for Support Vector Machines, 2001 [online]. Available: http://www.csie.ntu.edu.tw/cjlin/libsvm.

Constructing Near-optimal Double-layered Syndrome-Trellis Codes for Spatial Steganography

Zengzhen Zhao
State Key Laboratory of
Information Security,
Institute of Information
Engineering, Chinese
Academy of Scienses,
Beijing 100093, China

zhaozengzhen@iie.ac.cn

Qingxiao Guan*
State Key Laboratory of
Information Security,
Institute of Information
Engineering, Chinese
Academy of Scienses,
Beijing 100093, China

guanqingxiao@iie.ac.cn

Xianfeng Zhao
State Key Laboratory of
Information Security,
Institute of Information
Engineering, Chinese
Academy of Scienses,
Beijing 100093, China

zhaoxianfeng@iie.ac.cn

ABSTRACT

In this paper, we present a new kind of near-optimal double-layered syndrome-trellis codes (STCs) for spatial domain steganography. The STCs can hide longer message or improve the security with the same-length message comparing to the previous double-layered STCs. In our scheme, according to the theoretical deduction we can more precisely divide the secret payload into two parts which will be embedded in the first layer and the second layer of the cover respectively with binary STCs. When embed the message, we encourage to realize the double-layered embedding by ±1 modifications. But in order to further decrease the modifications and improve the time efficient, we allow few pixels to be modified by ±2. Experiment results demonstrate that while applying this double-layered STCs to the adaptive steganographic algorithms, the embedding modifications become more concentrative and the number decreases, consequently the security of steganography is improved.

Keywords

Information hiding; steganography; additive distortion; security; syndrome-trellis codes

1. INTRODUCTION

In steganography, secret message is embedded in a cover which is delivered to receiver through public channel but arouses no suspicion to others. Digital image is the most popular media on the internet and the ideal cover for hiding message. Steganographic schemes for digital images can realize the embedding by changing the pixels or DCT coefficients. As a countermeasure, the steganalyzers can attack this by using statistical detectability of embedding changes, such as using Rich Models [6] with high-dimensional feature spaces. In order to resist this kind of steganalysis, adaptive stegonagraphic scheme by minimizing additive distortion in steganography is the state-of-the-art scheme. Actually, the additive distortion introduced by embedding can be regarded as the sum of costs of all changed

pixels, and the costs values assigned to pixels evaluate the disturbance of modification. Typically, the costs values can be obtained by distortion calculation. Recent works of image steganography concentrate on this. And several distortion designed methods for image steganography have been proposed, such as HUGO [14], UNIWARD [8], and HILL [9]. What' more, minimizing additive distortion depends on the STCs.

In [3], [11], Filler et al. proposed the STCs framework for minimizing distortion. It includes binary STCs and multi-layered STCs. Among multi-layered STCs, the double-layered STCs are more feasible to enhance the security. Double-layered STCs utilize the least two significant bits of cover for embedding. Comparing to single-layered STCs (binary STCs), double-layered STCs still use ±1 modification but remarkably reduce the number of modifications. As a result fewer disturbances are brought to steganalysis feature. Also, the max payload rate for double-layered STCs is larger than single-layered STCs whose largest payload rate is 0.5.

The ideal way of constructing double-layered STCs is using 3-ary STCs encoding because when we have to convert a cover unit into any other value in 3-ary, it can be done by +1 or −1 modification. However, due to the high computational complexity and large storage space, 3-ary STCs are not very practical. Alternatively, double-layered STCs are implemented by applying binary STCs on two layers. Filler et al. proposed a framework for multi-layered STCs in [5] based on chain rules of decomposing multi-layered entropy. The double-layered STCs in this framework can realize the ternary embedding. Firstly the probability of ternary modification on each cover data unit is calculated by solving the equation between ternary entropy and message length. Then the costs values of two layers are computed from their modification probabilities, and STCs encoding is carried out twice on two layers respectively with their costs. For pixels need to be modified, +1 or −1 operation is applied on them to make their least two significant bits conform to the final embedding result of double-layered STCs. This method derives from optimal ternary embedding theory and has received excellent result. Since the double-layered STCs only allow ±1 modification and double-layered embedding performs individually, it requires the final embedding result can be achieved within ±1 modification. Consequently, flipping any bit in the second layer is accompanied by that in the first layer. If a pixel requires more than ±1 modification, this is a wet pixel [12], [17] and it will stop the embedding. In this case, Filler et al. suggest permutating the

IH&MMSec 2016, June 20-23, 2016, Vigo, Spain .
© 2016 ACM. ISBN 978-1-4503-4290-2/16/06…$15.00.
DOI: http://dx.doi.org/10.1145/2909827.2930802

_____

* the corresponding author

order of cover pixels with different random seed and try STCs encoding again. Filler has also proposed pentary STCs in [5], which are implemented by applying binary STCs on two layers too. Since too many ± 2 modifications are unable to effectively resist the steganalysis by high-dimensional feature spaces, pentary STCs are not popular in adaptive steganographic algorithms.

In this paper we adopt a new scheme for double-layered STCs, which is same to the scheme in [10]. This scheme is rather simple and understandable. We also divide double-layered STCs into two parts for two layers respectively. In the first layer, binary STCs are applied with costs. In the second layer, for those pixels need to be flipped in the first layer, we set their costs to be zero (zero cost pixels) and apply binary STCs on the second layers with revised costs. Finally, pixels are modified by ± 1 according to double-layered encoding results. This scheme implies that the embedding in the second layer is an extra product. Since we can control the flipping of a bit in the second layer by ± 1 operation when the bit in the first layer has to be flipped, the modifications in the second layer cost no more distortion.

Due to the properties of STCs encoding, the embedding in second layer will make the modifications occur in zero cost pixels as possible as it could, which means that it encourages the overlapping of modified pixels for two layers. In ideal condition, all the modified pixels in the second layer should be included in the set of modified pixels in the first layer, which means all modifications can be done by ± 1 operation in this case. Hence, in our method there is a key problem that for a message of fixed length, how many bits should be distributed to two layers. The success of embedding in the second layer depends on the number of zero cost pixels. If we embedding too many bits in the first layer, it will produces more zero cost pixels for second layer. However, it may cause a waste of embedding resource and make excessive modifications. Otherwise, too few bits embedded in the first layer may leave insufficient zero cost pixels for second layer and cause too many wet pixels. There is an optimal strategy to distribute bits to two layers. We analyze this problem by an embedding model presented in this paper.

The second issue of this paper is that how to assign the cost for the second layer. If we rigorously stick to ± 1 modification, there are only two kinds of pixel for the second layer: dry pixels (zero cost pixels) and wet pixels. However, it is possible that embedding in second layer may fail because of the wet pixels. Although we can use similar strategy of trying different seed to permute cover data as Filler *et al.* proposed in [3], we also investigate another way to deal with it because the trials of STCs encoding is time cost, especially for images of larger size. It is the simple way that we can allow few wet pixels to be modified by ± 2 operation. This is simple and straightforward in our method. The problem equals to assigning proper cost value for wet pixels of second layer. We also analyze this case in this paper both theoretically and experimentally. We can see that the number of modifications on wet pixels conforms to the normal distribution whose mean and variance depend on the cost of second layer. If we want to minimize its mean value, we are inevitably to enlarge its variance. And experiment shows that ± 2 modifications on few wet pixels do not degrade its security, and it is better to assign cost for wet pixels according to *complexity-first rule* [13].

In this paper we name our proposed STCs as NDSTCs (the Near-optimal Double-layered STCs). Experimental results demonstrate that our new double-layered STCs can directly be combined with the adaptive steganographic algorithms in spatial domain and make the performance approach the optimal ternary embedding simulator.

Table 1: The flipping situation after doing ± 1 operations on the least three bits.

$x_{i,j}$	Flipping LSB		Flipping LSB and 2LSB	
	operation	result	operation	result
000	+1	001	-1	111[1]
001	-1	000	+1	010
010	+1	011	-1	001
011	-1	010	+1	100
100	+1	101	-1	011
101	-1	100	+1	110
110	+1	111	-1	101
111	-1	110	+1	000[1]

Figure 1: The proportion each bit plane accounting for BOSSbase image '1029.pgm'. Top-left: original image, Top-right: LSB plane, bottom-left: 4LSB plane, bottom-right: 7LSB plane.

The rest of this paper is organized as follows. The preparation is described in Section 2. In Section 3, the proposed NDSTCs is introduced. Experimental results and comparison at the best parameters are illustrated in Section 4. We further analysis the result in Section 5. Conclusion and future research directions are listed in Section 6. Appendix is showed in Section 7.

2. PREPARATION

2.1 Notation

Without loss of generality, let $X = (x_{i,j}) \in \{\mathcal{L}\}^{n_1 \times n_2}$ represent $n_1 \times n_2$ pixels cover image and $Y = (y_{i,j}) \in \{\mathcal{L}\}^{n_1 \times n_2}$ represent the stego image after embedding operation on cover X. $\mathcal{L}$ is the pixel dynamic range of image. For example, $\mathcal{L} = \{0, \cdots, 255\}$ for 8-bit grayscale image. So $x_{i,j}$ is the pixel in (i, j) location. $y_{i,j}$ can be

---

1 Carry in or borrow from the former bit.

got by modifying $x_{i,j}$ by all most ± 1 because of the characteristic of adaptive steganographic scheme. For more detailed representation to images, pixels can be converted to binary representation

$$x_{i,j} = \sum_{l=1}^{8} x_{i,j}^l \times 2^{l-1}, \qquad (1)$$

where $x_{i,j}^l \in \{0,1\}$ is the l bit of pixel in (i,j) location.

Based on formula (1), we can obtain 8 different bit planes for each image. Figure 1 shows that different bit plane contributes to image in different proportion, modifying the bit plane with high proportion means bringing about more impact to images. So reducing the disturbance to high bit plane is still our principle.

Let's consider the least three bits of image, the operation to them is obvious in Table 1. For most of the pixels we can achieve the least two bits flipping by modifying pixels by ± 1, which means every pixel can carry more than just one bit. It can carry $\log_2 3$ bits of information [10]. However when the value of pixel is in the boundary of $\mathcal{L}$, modifying each pixel by ± 3 to avoid pixel overstepping the boundary is needed but what we should avoid. Actually some images consisting of too many pixels of this kind are unsuited to be the carrier images for this reason.

2.2 Preliminary of Single-layered STCs

The adaptive steganographic scheme is to minimize the following additive distortion function.

$$D(X^l, Y^l) = \sum_{i,j} \rho_{i,j} \left(x_{i,j}^l \neq y_{i,j}^l \right), \qquad (2)$$

where $\rho_{i,j}$ is the cost of flipping $x_{i,j}^l$, meanwhile the cost being sent to binary STCs, can be derived from the adaptive steganographic algorithm. Actually when we embed payload m to the pixels with cost ρ, we have constructed a probability description via

$$\beta_{i,j} = \frac{e^{-\lambda \rho_{i,j}}}{1 + e^{-\lambda \rho_{i,j}}}, \qquad (3)$$

where $\lambda > 0$ is a parameter determined from embedding payload m and cost ρ.

In theory, with the change probability β we can get the embedding payload m via

$$|m| = \sum_{i,j} H(\beta_{i,j}), \qquad (4)$$

where $H(\beta_{i,j})$ is the entropy function of the change probability $\beta_{i,j}$.

$$H(\beta_{i,j}) = -\beta_{i,j} \log_2(\beta_{i,j}) - (1 - \beta_{i,j}) \log_2(1 - \beta_{i,j}). \quad (5)$$

With embedding payload m and the cost ρ, λ can be calculated using formula (3), (4), (5) after iteration operation.

We can interpret the probability description as a model building a connection between embedding payload m and the cost ρ, which is the key point to execute the theoretical derivation.

3. PROPOSED WORK

In this section, we provide a general description of the proposed NDSTCs framework and give the theory explaining how to divide total payload to two parts respectively embedded in first layer and the second layer of the cover. To better understand our proposed work, we also show the practical implementation and explain some details that have deep connection with practical.

3.1 Theoretical Derivation

We assume the total payload m are divided into two pieces m_1, m_2 with $m = m_1 \cup m_2$. Apply the probability description to first layer and for each pixel the probability of change its first bit can be expressed as

$$\beta_{i,j}^1 = \frac{e^{-\lambda_1 \rho_{i,j}}}{1 + e^{-\lambda_1 \rho_{i,j}}}. \qquad (6)$$

It is clearer to define the change of a pixel in the first layer as a random variable $c_{i,j}$, and it conforms to binary distribution:

$$c_{i,j} \sim \begin{cases} 1 & P(c_{i,j}) = \beta_{i,j}^1 \\ 0 & P(c_{i,j}) = 1 - \beta_{i,j}^1 \end{cases}. \qquad (7)$$

$\beta_{i,j}^1$ depends on two quantities $\rho_{i,j}$ and λ_1. Where $\rho_{i,j}$ is calculated from image and λ_1 is an unknown parameter. We denote the number of embedding modifications in first layer as N_1 and the length of the theoretical embedding payload in the first layer as $|m_1|$.

$$N_1 = \sum_{i,j} c_{i,j}, \qquad (8)$$

$$E(N_1) = \sum_{i,j} E(c_{i,j}) = \sum_{i,j} \frac{e^{-\lambda_1 \rho_{i,j}}}{1 + e^{-\lambda_1 \rho_{i,j}}}, \qquad (9)$$

$$|m_1| = \sum_{i,j} - \frac{e^{-\lambda_1 \rho_{i,j}}}{1 + e^{-\lambda_1 \rho_{i,j}}} \log_2 \frac{e^{-\lambda_1 \rho_{i,j}}}{1 + e^{-\lambda_1 \rho_{i,j}}}$$
$$+ \sum_{i,j} - \left(1 - \frac{e^{-\lambda_1 \rho_{i,j}}}{1 + e^{-\lambda_1 \rho_{i,j}}}\right) \log_2 \left(1 - \frac{e^{-\lambda_1 \rho_{i,j}}}{1 + e^{-\lambda_1 \rho_{i,j}}}\right). \quad (10)$$

Yet we are unable to figure out λ_1 because $|m_1|$ is still an unknown parameter. Suppose that after embedding in the first layer, we can get the embedding modifications C_1 with $|C_1| = E(N_1)$. From the section 2.1, we know that flipping two bits can be realized with modifying pixels by ± 1 and we want the embedding modifications in the second layer overlap with the first layer as large as possible. Therefore, for the embedding in the second layer, we set the cost of pixels in C_1 to zero and get the new cost ρ'. This indicates that for pixels in C_1, the modifications in the second layer is "free of cost". We once more use the binary entropy to analyze STCs encoding in second layer. The number of bits in m_2 can be expressed like (10), and ideally the bits in the second layer can be divided into two parts C_1 and $\widetilde{C_1}$. Therefore we formulate it in following equation.

$$|m_2| =$$
$$\sum_{(i,j)\in C_1} \left[\begin{array}{c} -\frac{e^{-\lambda_2 \rho_{i,j}'}}{1 + e^{-\lambda_2 \rho_{i,j}'}} \log_2 \frac{e^{-\lambda_2 \rho_{i,j}'}}{1 + e^{-\lambda_2 \rho_{i,j}'}} \\ -\left(1 - \frac{e^{-\lambda_2 \rho_{i,j}'}}{1 + e^{-\lambda_2 \rho_{i,j}'}}\right) \log_2 \left(1 - \frac{e^{-\lambda_2 \rho_{i,j}'}}{1 + e^{-\lambda_2 \rho_{i,j}'}}\right) \end{array} \right]$$
$$+ \sum_{(i,j)\in \widetilde{C_1}} \left[\begin{array}{c} -\frac{e^{-\lambda_2 \rho_{i,j}'}}{1 + e^{-\lambda_2 \rho_{i,j}'}} \log_2 \frac{e^{-\lambda_2 \rho_{i,j}'}}{1 + e^{-\lambda_2 \rho_{i,j}'}} \\ -\left(1 - \frac{e^{-\lambda_2 \rho_{i,j}'}}{1 + e^{-\lambda_2 \rho_{i,j}'}}\right) \log_2 \left(1 - \frac{e^{-\lambda_2 \rho_{i,j}'}}{1 + e^{-\lambda_2 \rho_{i,j}'}}\right) \end{array} \right]. (11)$$

Since $\rho_{i,j}' = 0$, $\forall (i,j) \in C_1$, we substitute it into (11) and yield:

$$|m_2| = \sum_{(i,j)\in C_1} \left[-\frac{1}{2} \log_2 \frac{1}{2} - \frac{1}{2} \log_2 \left(\frac{1}{2}\right) \right]$$
$$+ \sum_{(i,j)\in \widetilde{C_1}} \left[\begin{array}{c} -\frac{e^{-\lambda_2 \rho_{i,j}'}}{1 + e^{-\lambda_2 \rho_{i,j}'}} \log_2 \frac{e^{-\lambda_2 \rho_{i,j}'}}{1 + e^{-\lambda_2 \rho_{i,j}'}} \\ -\left(1 - \frac{e^{-\lambda_2 \rho_{i,j}'}}{1 + e^{-\lambda_2 \rho_{i,j}'}}\right) \log_2 \left(1 - \frac{e^{-\lambda_2 \rho_{i,j}'}}{1 + e^{-\lambda_2 \rho_{i,j}'}}\right) \end{array} \right]$$
$$\overset{simplify}{\Longrightarrow} |C_1| +$$
$$\sum_{(i,j)\in \widetilde{C_1}} \left[\begin{array}{c} -\frac{e^{-\lambda_2 \rho_{i,j}'}}{1 + e^{-\lambda_2 \rho_{i,j}'}} \log_2 \frac{e^{-\lambda_2 \rho_{i,j}'}}{1 + e^{-\lambda_2 \rho_{i,j}'}} \\ -\left(1 - \frac{e^{-\lambda_2 \rho_{i,j}'}}{1 + e^{-\lambda_2 \rho_{i,j}'}}\right) \log_2 \left(1 - \frac{e^{-\lambda_2 \rho_{i,j}'}}{1 + e^{-\lambda_2 \rho_{i,j}'}}\right) \end{array} \right]. (12)$$

The change probability of pixels in $\widetilde{C_1}$ relies on λ_2 which is determined by equation (11). By observing the equation (12), we can deduce that if and only if $|C_1| = |m_2|$, the following equation is satisfied:

$$\Sigma_{(i,j)\in\widetilde{C_1}}\left[\begin{array}{l}-\frac{e^{-\lambda_2\rho'_{i,j}}}{1+e^{-\lambda_2\rho'_{i,j}}}\log_2\frac{e^{-\lambda_2\rho'_{i,j}}}{1+e^{-\lambda_2\rho'_{i,j}}}\\-\left(1-\frac{e^{-\lambda_2\rho'_{i,j}}}{1+e^{-\lambda_2\rho'_{i,j}}}\right)\log_2\left(1-\frac{e^{-\lambda_2\rho'_{i,j}}}{1+e^{-\lambda_2\rho'_{i,j}}}\right)\end{array}\right]=0. \quad (13)$$

While the ideal condition is that pixels in $\widetilde{C_1}$ are kept unchanged, it requires the change probability on the second layer of pixels in $\widetilde{C_1}$ equal to 0. Considering the properties of entropy and the fact that $\lambda_2>0$ and $\rho'_{i,j}>0\ \forall\ (i,j)\in\widetilde{C_1}$, above deduction tell us that while $|C_1|=|m_2|$ is satisfied, $\frac{e^{-\lambda_2\rho'_{i,j}}}{1+e^{-\lambda_2\rho'_{i,j}}}\to 0, \forall\ (i,j)\in\widetilde{C_1}$ with $\lambda_2\to\infty$, which means the length of the ideal embedding payload in the second layer $|m_2|$ equals to the number of embedding modifications in the first layer N_1, and theoretical optimal length of m_1 and m_2 can be solved. Therefore we substitute $|C_1|=|m_2|$ and $|C_1|=E(N_1)$ into (9) and together with (10), the number of the total embedding payload $|m|$ can be expressed as:

$$|m|=|m_1|+|m_2|$$
$$=\Sigma_{i,j}\left[\begin{array}{l}-\frac{e^{-\lambda_1\rho_{i,j}}}{1+e^{-\lambda_1\rho_{i,j}}}\log_2\frac{e^{-\lambda_1\rho_{i,j}}}{1+e^{-\lambda_1\rho_{i,j}}}\\-\left(1-\frac{e^{-\lambda_1\rho_{i,j}}}{1+e^{-\lambda_1\rho_{i,j}}}\right)\log_2\left(1-\frac{e^{-\lambda_1\rho_{i,j}}}{1+e^{-\lambda_1\rho_{i,j}}}\right)\end{array}\right]$$
$$+\Sigma_{i,j}\frac{e^{-\lambda_1\rho_{i,j}}}{1+e^{-\lambda_1\rho_{i,j}}}, \quad (14)$$

where the only unknown parameter is the flipping lambda λ_1. A simple binary search can be used to solve this equation because both $|m_1|$ and N_1 are monotone with regard to λ_1. After getting the flipping lambda λ_1, we can obtain the $|m_1|$ by (10), and subsequently $|m_2|$ is obtained by $|m|-|m_1|$. See from the total derived process, the flipping lambda λ_1 is obtained on an ideal condition that the embedding modifications in the second layer totally overlap with the first layer.

So far we haven't discuss more details of the cost assignment strategy for the second layer. According to above analysis, it doesn't matter if we assign arbitrary positive values to pixels in $\widetilde{C_1}$, and their change probability is 0 since $\lambda_2\to\infty$. Actually, if there is a trellis path which only need to flips the second layer of some pixels in $\widetilde{C_1}$, STCs encoder prefers to skip it because the overall distortion cost of C_1 is zero which is smaller than cost of any pixel in $\widetilde{C_1}$. However, as we mentioned in the first section, if we somehow relax the ±1 restriction and allow few ±2 modifications in $\widetilde{C_1}$ for some trials, the assignment of cost for the second layer matters. And this part is discussed in section 3.2.

3.2 Practical Implementation

In previous section, we derived the theoretic optimal message distribution strategy for two layers. However, in the real world the embedding process may not precisely fit the theoretic model. Based on theoretic model, it is reasonable to readjust the proportion of message bits embedded into two layers. It can be implemented by adding a scalar factor in (14). We replace the term $\Sigma_{i,j}\frac{e^{-\lambda_1\rho_{i,j}}}{1+e^{-\lambda_1\rho_{i,j}}}$ in (14) with $\tau\times\Sigma_{i,j}\frac{e^{-\lambda_1\rho_{i,j}}}{1+e^{-\lambda_1\rho_{i,j}}}$, and reformulate the equation (14) as:

$$|m|=\Sigma_{i,j}\left[\begin{array}{l}-\frac{e^{-\lambda_1\rho_{i,j}}}{1+e^{-\lambda_1\rho_{i,j}}}\log_2\frac{e^{-\lambda_1\rho_{i,j}}}{1+e^{-\lambda_1\rho_{i,j}}}\\-\left(1-\frac{e^{-\lambda_1\rho_{i,j}}}{1+e^{-\lambda_1\rho_{i,j}}}\right)\log_2\left(1-\frac{e^{-\lambda_1\rho_{i,j}}}{1+e^{-\lambda_1\rho_{i,j}}}\right)\end{array}\right]$$

Algorithm 1 Embedded procedure for near-optimal double-layered STCs embedding framework. Input cover image X, payload m, the permutation-key κ and the adaptive steganographic algorithm $\mathcal{C}$.

Require: $X=\left(x_{i,j}\right)\in\{\mathcal{L}\}^{n_1\times n_2}\triangleq\{0,\cdots,255\}^{n_1\times n_2}$
1. Calculate the costs $\rho=\mathcal{C}(X)$
2. Calculate the flipping lambda λ_1 through solving the formula (15) with the inputs ρ and m
3. Get the number of bits hidden in the first layer $|m_1|$ according formula (10) with the input λ_1
4. Embed $|m_1|$ bits messages into X^1 with the costs ρ and the permutation-key κ using binary STCs, then get the new vector Y^1.
5. If the step 4 is successful, continue the step 6. But if not, adjust the cost ρ and reprocess the step 2
6. Define $\rho'=\rho$ and set $\rho'(X^1\neq Y^1)=0$
7. Get the number of bits hidden in the second layer $|m_2|=|m|-|m_1|$.
8. Embed $|m_2|$ bits messages into X^2 with costs ρ' and the permutation-key κ using binary STCs, then get the new vector Y^2
9. Update stego image Y with Y^1, Y^2
10. Return stego image Y and the number of bits hidden in the two layers $|m_1|$, $|m_2|$.

$$+\tau\times\Sigma_{i,j}\frac{e^{-\lambda_1\rho_{i,j}}}{1+e^{-\lambda_1\rho_{i,j}}}. \quad (15)$$

Method solving this equation is same to the formula (14). We can see the only difference between the sum of embedding modifications in the first layer N_1 and the length of the embedding payload in the second layer $|m_2|$ is the multiplying factor τ. When $\tau=1$, it is the ideal model described in section 3.1. Larger τ means we decrease the payload and number of modifications in the first layer. The reason we put τ on the second term of (15) is that it can more smoothly adjust payload and modifications in the first layer. Since the binary STCs is a near-optimal coding scheme thus inevitably there is a small gap between optimal coding and real STCs coding scheme. When embed bits in each layer, it will increase the modifications comparing to the optimal, which means the real number of modifications is larger than theoretic result N_1. And this leads to the enlargement of τ. We will give the best value of τ based on experiment and interpret it in section 4.

We have proposed that in order to make sure the success of the embedding, we allow a few wet pixels in the second layer to be modified by ±2, which won't effect the performance in significant manner. Since the modifications are slight, two cases [13] of assigning cost for the wet pixels can be considered here:

Case 1 – change rate minimization. The cost-value distribution of the wet bits follows the Dirac distribution, which means all cost-values are the same value. In this case, the embedding distortion is the number of modifications.

Case 2 – content adaptivity maximization. This follows the *complexity-first rule*, which requires keeping the cost-value varied according to the local content and unpredictability in an image, but leads to more modifications comparing to case 1.

Interestingly, for any cost assignment strategy, the number of modifications conforms to normal distribution whose variance and mean depend on the cost of pixels. In Case 1, although we can minimize the expectation number of modifications, we have to accept higher variance of it, which implies there is more uncertainty for number of modifications. Although Case 2 increases the number of modifications, it not only makes cost assignment follows the *complexity-first rule*, but also reduced

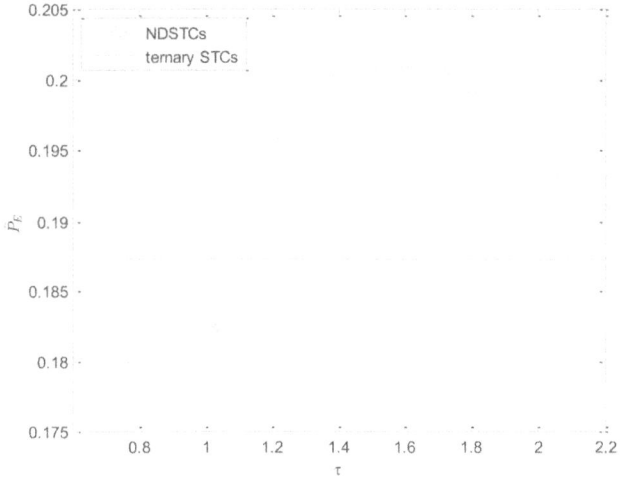

Figure 2: Search for the optimal value of τ for S-UNIWARD with maxSRMd2 at 0.4bpp.

uncertainty comparing to Case 1. Experimental results demonstrate that content adaptivity maximization has a better performance here. We elaborate the proof of these propositions in section 5 and appendix.

To better understand the implementation of our framework, we describe it using Algorithm 1. The inputs are the cover image X, the payload m, the permutation-key κ and the adaptive steganographic algorithm $\mathcal{C}$, while the outputs are the stego image Y and the number of bits embedded in each layer.

In step 5, if the step 4 is not successful, we should adjust the cost ρ. This is because when apply our work to HILL, we find some images are unavailable. This situation is same to the ternary STCs. After carefully checking the source of HILL, we find that when HILL calculates the cost there is a reciprocal operation without an additive factor to avoid the cost tending to infinite. But S-UNIWARD has considered this. Since our work is to design the generic code and the unavailable images account for an extremely small amount, we just adjust the infinite cost of the unavailable images with an available value obtained by a simple wavelet filter. Moreover once the unavailable images appear in one of compared codes, the process to them should keep the same to keep the consistency for comparison. In step 9, updating the stego Y can be realized by replacing each layer of Y with Y^1 and Y^2. If the least two bits of pixel is 11 or 00, it will bring about modifying pixel by ± 3, which needs a correction through modifying pixel by ± 4. However for the pixels with the boundary value of $\mathcal{L}$, the correction is unavailable. Due to the specialty of these pixels, we bring in the consideration of setting the uncorrectable cost to infinite when embedding in each layer.

The extract algorithm is not complex but need the payload length in each layer which can be communicated to the receiver using some pixels in the cover image or by other way. To keep the consistency for comparison, we employ the latter but don't care the communication.

4. EXPERIMENT AND COMPARISON

In this section, before giving the experimental result we describe some setups of the experiment. Then we test the performances of some parameters to our proposed work so that we can show the best experiment results.

4.1 Experimental Setup

Since Our near-optimal double-layered STCs framework is general to all adaptive steganographic algorithm in spatial domain.

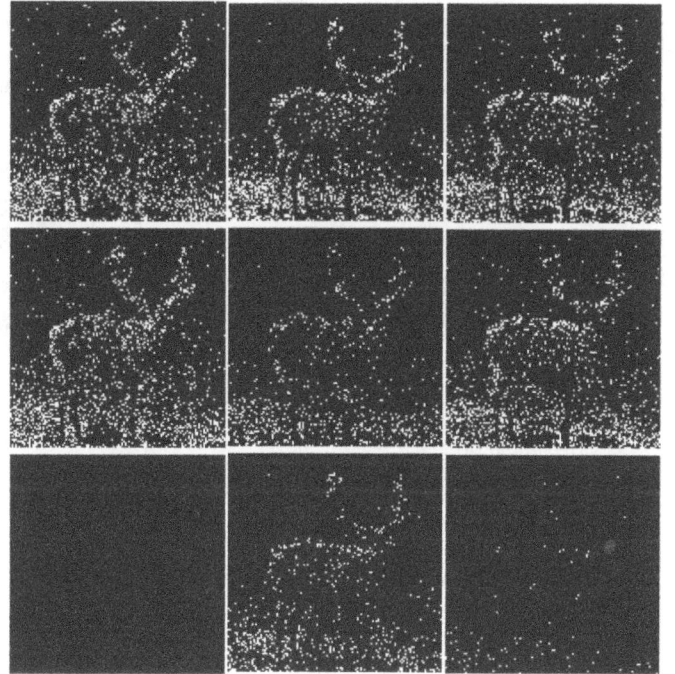

Figure 3: The embedding modifications with S-UNIWARD algorithm at 0.4 bpp for the BOSSbase image '8.pgm'. From left to right represent the ternary STCs, the pentary STCs and the NDSTCs. From top to bottom represent the total modifications, modifications in the first layer, modifications only in the second layer, respectively.

We utilize the BOSSbase database ver.1.01 [1] containing 10,000 512×512 8-bit grayscale images as the test image set, which has been widely used in steganography and steganalysis.

The ensemble classifier described in [2] is employed in our experiments. The parameters of ensemble classifier can be got by automatic calculation based on out-of-bag (OOB) estimating, so we needn't input any parameters but the features of cover and stego images. The classifier consists of a lot of base learners independently training on training set.

We split the whole feature set into two parts, training set and testing set. For cover samples and stego samples, there are 5000 images randomly selected as the training set, and rest 5000 images as the testing set. The security of steganographic schemes in this section is measured by the total detection error of steganalysis test. Detection error is the average error rate for two classes:

$$P_E = \min_{P_{FA}} \frac{1}{2}(P_{FA} + P_{MD}), \qquad (16)$$

where P_{FA}, P_{MD} are the probabilities of false alarms and missed detection, respectively. In fact, each experiment is repeated 10 times with different random split of training set and testing set and the average error rate $\bar{P}_E$ is utilized to evaluate the security of our proposed work.

For testing the detection error rate, the cover and stego images samples are analyzed by state-of-the-art feature-based steganalyzers, which are the Spatial Rich Model (SRM) and the maxSRMd2 [4]. The SRM consists of 39 symmetrized sub-models formed by different filters and co-occurrence matrices. It is also extended by quantifying with three different quantization factors to generate a 34,671D feature set. The maxSRMd2 is an "adaptive" version of the SRM. It makes use of the selection channel strategy which incorporates the modified probabilities obtained from the cost into co-occurrence matrix calculating. This

Table 2: Detection error $\bar{P}_E$ for ternary STCs, pentary STCs, NDSTCs, simulator with HILL, S-UNIWARD, WOW in relative payloads

maxSRMd2							
Embedding Strategy	0.05	0.1	0.2	0.3	0.4	0.5	0.6
HILL+ternary STCs	.4680±.0025	.4237±.0022	.3474±.0014	.2801±.0017	.2306±.0019	.1893±.0018	.1482±.0021
HILL+pentary STCs	.4395±.0030	.3811±.0023	.2879±.0018	.2203±.0025	.1767±.0026	.1364±.0023	.1140±.0017
HILL+NDSTCs	.4685±.0015	.4265±.0020	.3504±.0021	.2886±.0025	.2386±.0010	.1961±.0025	.1565±.0023
HILL+simulator	.4694±.0026	.4312±.0025	.3561±.0018	.2902±.0022	.2379±.0020	.1959±.0017	.1563±.0019
S-UNI+ternary STCs	.4479±.0022	.3939±.0018	.3061±.0024	.2400±.0031	.1873±.0030	.1481±.0017	.1120±.0017
S-UNI+pentary STCs	.4157±.0020	.3495±.0027	.2545±.0014	.1875±.0019	.1440±.0028	.1129±.0018	.0903±.0022
S-UNI+NDSTCs	.4509±.0017	.3977±.0014	.3133±.0017	.2506±.0023	.2016±.0021	.1624±.0027	.1287±.0019
S-UNI+simulator	.4521±.0025	.4043±.0039	.3211±.0026	.2519±.0018	.1989±.0021	.1570±.0029	.1221±.0015
WOW+ternary STCs	.4501±.0031	.3910±.0027	.3049±.0014	.2376±.0018	.1844±.0032	.1504±.0029	.1224±.0023
WOW+pentary STCs	.4190±.0018	.3495±.0011	.2560±.0023	.1911±.0020	.1502±.0017	.1210±.0016	.0973±.0014
WOW+NDSTCs	.4496±.0017	.3924±.0013	.3043±.0032	.2434±.0022	.1906±.0035	.1562±.0027	.1258±.0033
WOW+simulator	.4560±.0032	.4028±.0022	.3171±.0027	.2513±.0025	.2012±.0017	.1597±.0024	.1273±.0031

SRM							
Embedding Strategy	0.05	0.1	0.2	0.3	0.4	0.5	0.6
HILL+ternary STCs	.4695±.0028	.4257±.0025	.3510±.0013	.2910±.0017	.2350±.0015	.1918±.0022	.1605±.0017
HILL+pentary STCs	.4437±.0020	.3805±.0019	.3006±.0016	.2283±.0023	.1830±.0034	.1453±.0029	.1205±.0023
HILL+NDSTCs	.4683±.0021	.4293±.0031	.3564±.0025	.2960±.0023	.2458±.0015	.2063±.0012	.1651±.0022
HILL+simulator	.4708±.0015	.4345±.0021	.3597±.0020	.2965±.0018	.2456±.0022	.2023±.0022	.1661±.0019
S-UNI+ternary STCs	.4481±.0025	.3971±.0019	.3119±.0015	.2430±.0027	.1956±.0022	.1569±.0017	.1233±.0023
S-UNI+pentary STCs	.4176±.0014	.3470±.0019	.2597±.0019	.1950±.0027	.1526±.0032	.1200±.0018	.0959±.0031
S-UNI+NDSTCs	.4515±.0019	.3985±.0024	.3166±.0027	.2587±0029	.2072±.0016	.1700±.0016	.1384±.0037
S-UNI+simulator	.4544±.0016	.4041±.0023	.3209±.0016	.2552±.0019	.2062±.0015	.1664±.0020	.1322±.0025
WOW+ternary STCs	.4510±.0017	.3945±.0045	.3108±.0018	.2491±.0015	.1988±.0019	.1611±.0017	.1283±.0017
WOW+pentary STCs	.4195±.0019	.3520±.0036	.2605±.0035	.2001±.0015	.1586±.0016	.1266±.0014	.1033±.0022
WOW+NDSTCs	.4472±.0016	.3939±.0023	.3076±.0025	.2491±.0033	.2034±.0017	.1625±.0023	.1331±.0021
WOW+simulator	.4534±.0017	.4035±.0033	.3192±.0024	.2578±.0019	.2108±.0019	.1705±.0020	.1389±.0026

style of calculating co-occurrence matrix captures more information from modified pixels comparing to ordinary matrix.

In order to show the performance of our near-optimal double-layered STCs, we test our double-layered STCs along with several popular adaptive steganograpic algorithms, which are the Wavelet Obtained Weights (WOW) algorithm [7], the Spatial Universal Wavelet Relative Distortion (S-UNIWARD) algorithm and the High Low Low (HILL) algorithm.

WOW algorithm uses a bank of directional filters composed of high pass decomposition wavelet filter and low pass decomposition wavelet filter to obtain the so-called directional residuals. By suitably aggregating these directional residuals, WOW constructs the cost reflecting the predictability of the image. UNIWARD algorithm bears similarity to that of WOW but is simpler and suitable for embedding in an arbitrary domain, and for the spatial domain it is the S-UNIWARD. HILL algorithm is designed by using a high-pass filter and two low-pass filters, which are used to locate the less predictable parts in an image and make the low cost values more clustered, respectively.

And the compared objects are the ternary and pentary multi-layered versions of STCs in [3]. To keep the consistency, we set the constraint height in the trellis h as 10. To clearly show the gap between STCs implementation and the theoretical optimal encoding, we also test the simulator which is supposed to achieve the theoretical optimal efficiency.

4.2 Experimental Results

To obtain an insight as to which value of τ should be used in (15), we draw the graph showing $\bar{P}_E$ as a function of τ when embed payload at 0.4bpp (bits per pixel) with the feature maxSRMd2 and the S-UNIWARD algorithm. Figure 2 shows that when τ varies from 1.4 to 1.7, the security has the similar performance, which also demonstrates that the value of τ is larger than the ideal 1. And for uniformity, we set it 1.7. Although $\tau = 1.7$ is much larger than theoretic value $\tau = 1$, the number of modifications in the first layer wouldn't increase 0.7 times, because the solution against τ of (15) is not as sensitive as one supposes. This facilitates our tuning the parameter τ.

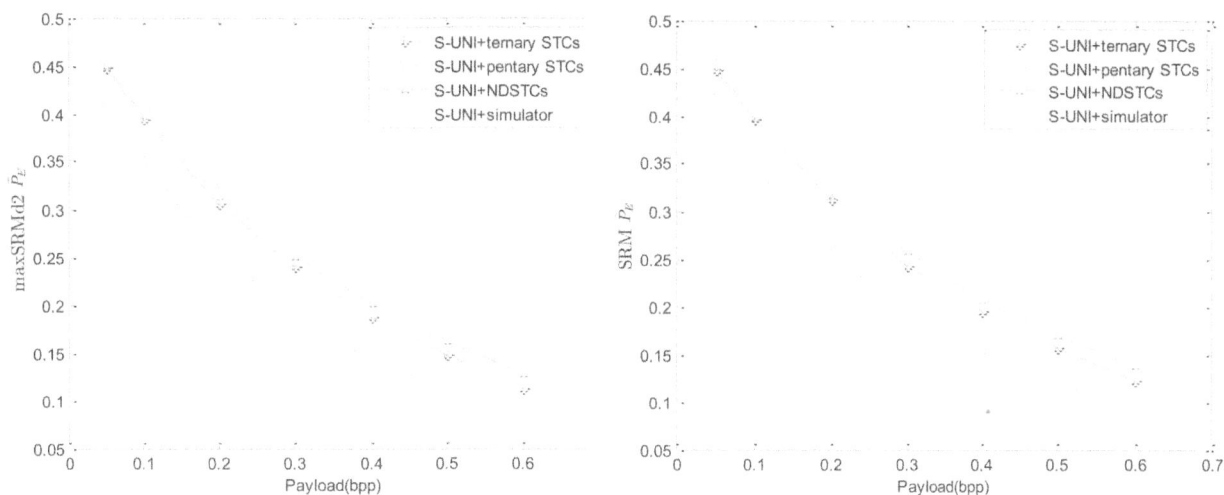

Figure 4: The detection error $\bar{P}_E$ for ternary STCs, pentary STCs, NDSTCs, simulator with S-UNIWARD in relative payloads. Left for maxSRMd2, right for SRM.

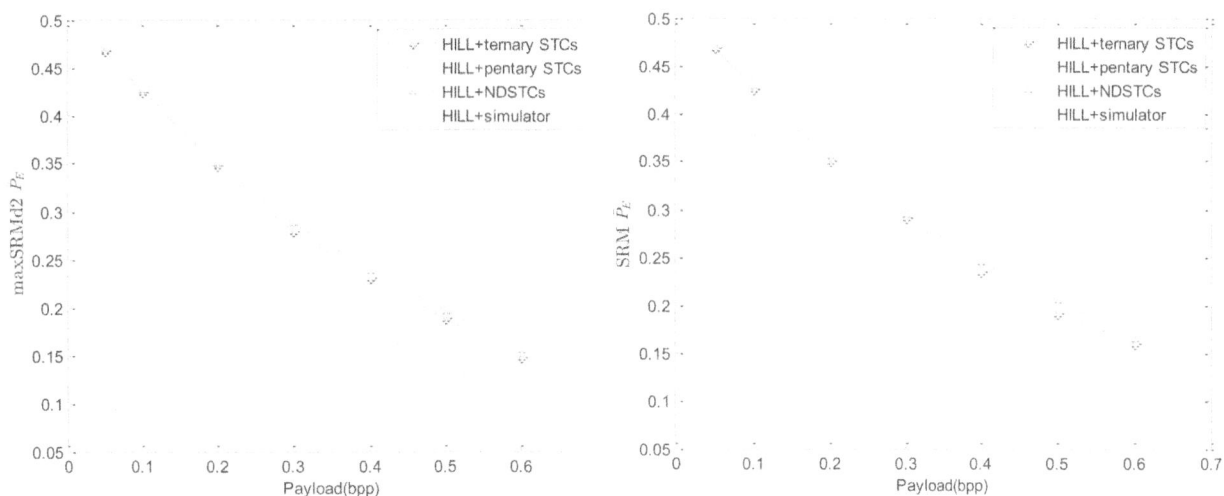

Figure 5: The detection error $\bar{P}_E$ for ternary STCs, pentary STCs, NDSTCs, simulator with HILL in relative payloads. Left for maxSRMd2, right for SRM.

In Figure 3, we contrast the embedding changes for NDSTCs, ternary STCs and pentary STCs. The cover image with high textured areas is selected and the adaptive steganograpic algorithm is selected as S-UNIWARD. Data displays that the placements of embedding changes for NDSTCs are more concentrative than the ternary STCs, and meanwhile the number of total modifications is a little less. Although the number of total modifications for the pentary STCs is the least, it brings about too many modifications in the second layer, which violates the principle of reducing the disturbance to high bit plane. Contrasting to the pentary STCs, NDSTCs brings about much less modifications in the second layer and ternary STCs brings about the least.

Figure 4, 5, 6 and Table 2 show the average testing error $\bar{P}_E$ corresponding to the two steganalyzers SRM and maxSRMd2. Figure 4, 5, 6 show $\bar{P}_E$ as a function of the embedding rate. As it shows, comparing to the ternary STCs and pentary STCs, NDSTCs has promotion for all three adaptive steganographic algorithms, which means NDSTCs has a satisfactory generality. Meanwhile it has no difference with the simulator for both maxSRMd2 and SRM, which means it approaches near-optimal security. For the best performance, the detection error of NDSTCs is higher by approximately 1.7% for embedding rate 0.6bpp with the feature maxSRMd2 and the S-UNIWARD algorithm, 1.6% for embedding rate 0.3bpp with the feature SRM and the S-UNIWARD algorithm comparing to the ternary STCs. Since pentary STCs brings about too many modifications in the second layer, the security performance is lower generally. We can say that the security performance of the adaptive steganograpic algorithm sometimes is very close to the theoretical value with our proposed NDSTCs. In this experiment we find that compare to strategy of permute cover with different seed, leaving few ±2 modifications on wet pixels do not hurt the security if proper cost values are assigned for the second layer. And when we deliberately increase few ±2 modifications by tuning the parameter τ slightly large (Figure 7 shows), the security may even better. Its analysis is also addressed in the next section.

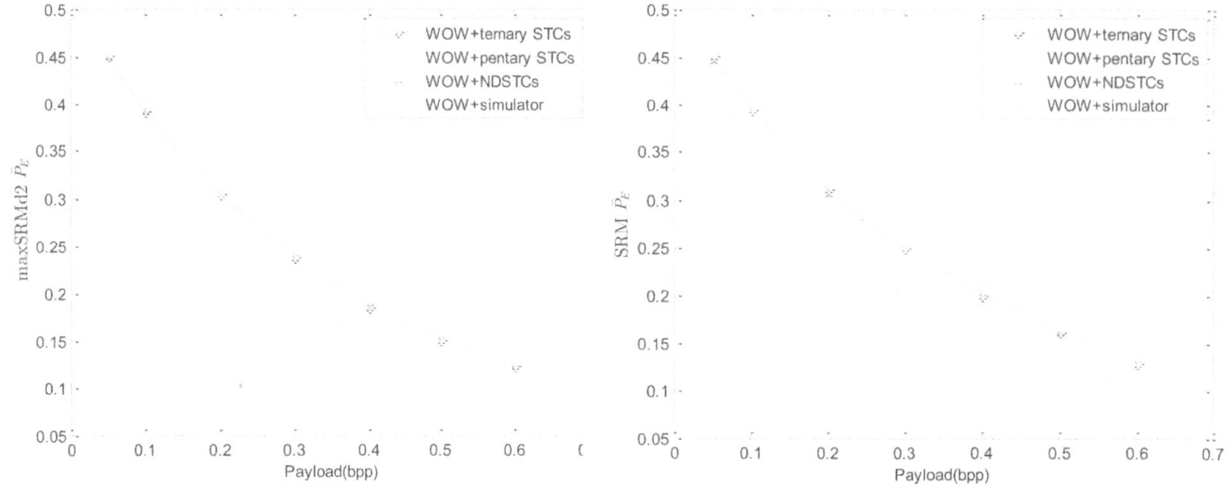
WOW+ternary STCs
WOW+pentary STCs
WOW+NDSTCs
WOW+simulator
maxSRMd2 P_E
SRM P_E
Payload(bpp)
Payload(bpp)

Figure 6: The detection error $\overline{P}_E$ for ternary STCs, pentary STCs, NDSTCs, simulator with WOW in relative payloads. Left for maxSRMd2, right for SRM.

5. ANALYSIS

Actually, if we want to gain more insight into the theoretic model of modification probability and payload, it is better to consider the number of modifications as a random variable. As is described in 3.1, for binary embedding, the number of modifications is a sum of random variables conforming to binary distribution. Note that there is large number of binary random variables, which amount to the number of pixels in the image. Therefore by using the Lyapunov Central Limit Theorem, we can proof that the number of modifications conforms to normal distribution whose variance and mean are $D(\beta) = \sum_{i,j} \beta_{i,j} - \beta_{i,j}^2$ and $\sum_{i,j} \beta_{i,j}$ respectively. The details of this proof are presented in appendix. The variance describes the deviance of the practical modifications from the theoretical result.

Next we analyze the upper bound of the variance. Suppose we have to carry $|m|$ bits of message, and in this condition we solve the upper bound of variance $D(\beta)$ via following problem:

$$\max_{\beta} \sum_{i,j} \beta_{i,j} - \beta_{i,j}^2$$

$$s.t.\ \ |m| = -\sum_{i,j} \beta_{i,j} \log_2(\beta_{i,j}) - (1-\beta_{i,j}) \log_2(1-\beta_{i,j}), \quad (17)$$

which can be solved by Lagrange Multiplier Method. After solving this problem, we get a result that when $\beta_{1,1} = \cdots = \beta_{n_1,n_2}$, variance $D(\beta)$ reaches the maximum value. This indicates that if the cost takes a constant value for all pixels, the variance of number of modifications is maximized, but in this case the embedding aims to minimize the number of modifications [13].

In section 3.2, we discussed two cases of cost assignment for the second layer and we suggest the *complexity-first rule*. Actually, when we concentrate on the total modifications, both strategies of case 1 and case 2 in section 3.2 are considered and tested. The testing result shows that *complexity-first rule* in case 2 is better than *reduce change rate* in case 1, and the former is very close to theoretic ±1 embedding simulator. We analyze this phenomenon in following two aspects:

1) Trade-off between ±1 and ±2 modification. There are two measures to eliminate the ±2 modification and keep wet pixels unmodified: (1). Permute cover with other seed and again use STCs encoding. (2). Increase the payload rate of the first layer. While the first measure may takes more time and is unnecessary in our method, we discuss the second one. We find that although the modification intensity of ±2 is larger than that of ±1, allowing few ±2 modifications can reduce much more ±1 modifications in our method, and finally the overall disturbance on steganalysis feature is less.
2) Variance and complexity. There are two virtues of using

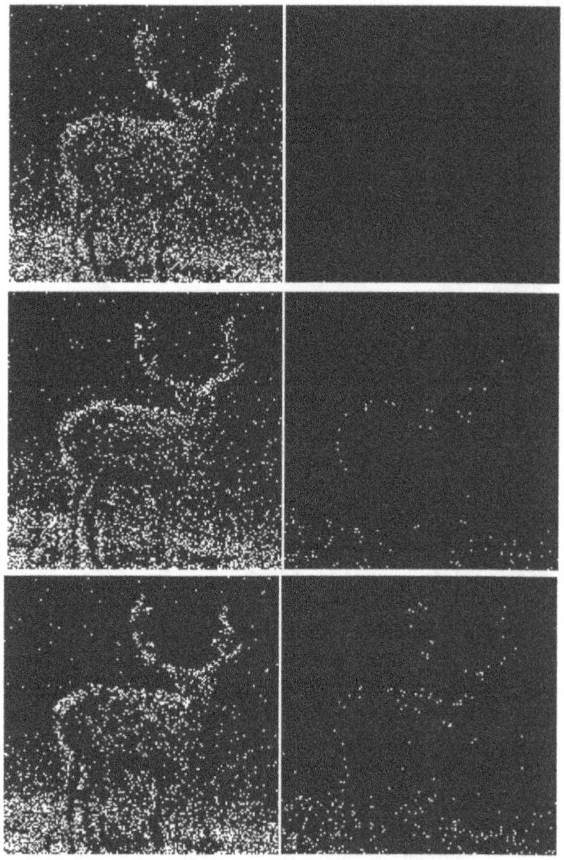

Figure 7: The embedding modifications of NDSTCs with S-UNIWARD at 0.4 bpp in different value of τ for the BOSSbase image '8.pgm'. From top to bottom represent the value with 0.8, 1.2 and 1.6. From left to right represent the total modifications and the only modifications in the second layer.

complexity-first rule to assign cost for the second layer. The first one is obvious that more complexity means more security. And the second one, as we discussed above, we can go further to see that complexity-first rule cost typically bears less variance of number of modifications, this helps us to more accurately control the number of ± 2 modifications in our method.

And the practical number of modifications by ± 2 is performed as the value of τ. Although we can implement no modifications for the wet pixels through adjusting τ, since this situation means more modifications in total, we don't employ it. We can combine this with Figure 2 and Figure 7. When the value of τ is small, the total modifications by ± 1 will increase, which has not an ideal security performance. But when the value of τ is quite large, modifications by ± 2 will increase, which violates the principle of reducing the disturbance to high bit plane and the security performance behaves going down. In our experiment, setting τ as 1.7 is a trade-off about the two situations.

6. CONCLUSION AND FUTURE WORK

In this paper, we propose a new kind of near-optimal double-layered STCs which can be combined with adaptive steganographic algorithm to minimize the additive distortion in spatial domain. We precisely divide the payload into two parts according to the changing probabilities of two layers. Comparing to the restriction of ± 1 modifications, few pixels modified by ± 2 is allowed here. With this scheme, the embedding modifications become more concentrative and the number of them becomes less. The merit of this framework is demonstrated by experiments, which utilizes the state-of-the-art feature-based steganalyzers and the result shows the proposed scheme is a general and secure method which is close to the theoretical simulator. With the performance we can draw a conclusion that it is desirable to allow few ± 2 modifications and sophisticatedly balance the payload of two layers to achieve better security for spatial steganography.

There are some directions we can consider about this work in the future. First, as a general method, it may be extended to the JPEG domain with the same improvement and it may be combined with the strategies of synchronizing the selection channel [15] and clustering modification directions [16] to improve the security together. Second, the security, the number of the only modifications in each layer may be further decreased through preprocessing the costs and as a result the security can be further improved. Furthermore, we fix a value of τ for each batch of the images here. Maybe we can dynamically turn it according to different image, which is more realistic.

7. APPENDIX

In this appendix, we demonstrate that when we convert the cost to the probability, the number of modifications based on probability obeys the normal distribution automatically. Obviously the probability is independent non-identically distributed, so the Liapunov Central Limit Theorem is employed here.

According to Liapunov Central Limit Theorem, for a sequence of independent random variables $\{X_1, \cdots, X_n\}$, $\sum_i X_i$ conforms to normal distribution, when $\exists \delta > 0$ the following conditions are satisfied:

$$E(|X_i - u_i|^{2+\delta}) < \infty, \quad \forall i, \tag{18}$$

and

$$\lim_{n \to \infty} \frac{1}{B_n^{2+\delta}} \sum_{i=1}^n E\{|X_i - u_i|^{2+\delta}\} = 0, \tag{19}$$

where u_i is the expectation of variable X_i and $B_n^2 = \sum_{i=1}^n \delta_i^2$ is the sum of the total variances.

We assume we have got the cost and the corresponding change probability. Now we define the change of a pixel as a random variable c_i, and it conforms to binary distribution:

$$c_i \sim \begin{cases} 1 & P(c_i) = \beta_i \\ 0 & P(c_i) = 1 - \beta_i \end{cases}. \tag{20}$$

With equation (20), we can get $E(c_i) = \beta_i$, $D(c_i) = \beta_i(1 - \beta_i)$. Substitute the variants in equation (18), and let $\delta = 1$, we have:

$$\begin{aligned} E(|c_i - E(c_i)|^{2+1}) &= \beta_i(1 - \beta_i)^3 + \beta_i^3(1 - \beta_i) \\ &= \beta_i(1 - \beta_i)[\beta_i^2 + (1 - \beta_i)^2] \\ &\leq \beta_i(1 - \beta_i). \end{aligned} \tag{21}$$

We assume $c_{n+1}, c_{n+2}, \cdots, c_\infty$ are independent binary random variables with non-identically distributed mean and variance, and we obtain:

$$\begin{aligned} \frac{1}{B_n^{2+1}} \sum_{i=1}^n E\{|c_i - \beta_i|^{2+1}\} &\leq \frac{\sum_{i=1}^n \beta_i(1-\beta_i)}{[\sum_{i=1}^n \beta_i(1-\beta_i)]^{\frac{3}{2}}} \\ &= \frac{1}{[\sum_{i=1}^n \beta_i(1-\beta_i)]^{\frac{1}{2}}} \to 0, \ (n \to \infty). \end{aligned} \tag{22}$$

So $\{c_1, \cdots, c_i\}$ satisfy the Lyapunov Central Limit Theorem, and its final form can be expressed as

$$\lim_{n \to \infty} P\left(\frac{1}{B_n} \sum_{i=1}^n (c_i - \beta_i) \leq x\right) = \frac{1}{\sqrt{2\pi}} \int_{-\infty}^x e^{-\frac{t^2}{2}} dt, \forall x \in \mathrm{R}, \tag{23}$$

which means $\sum_{i=1}^n c_i \sim N(\sum_{i=1}^n \beta_i, B_n^2)$ as $n \to \infty$.

8. ACKNOWLEDGMENTS

This work was supported by the NSFC under 61303259 and U1536105, the Strategic Priority Research Program of Chinese Academy of Sciences (CAS) under XDA06030600, and the Key Project of Institute of Information Engineering, CAS, under Y5Z0131201.

9. REFERENCES

[1] T. Filler, T. Pevný, and P. Bas. BOSS (Break Our Steganography System). http://www.agents.cz/boss, July 2010.

[2] J. Kodovský, J. Fridrich, and V. Holub. Ensemble classifiers for steganalysis of digital media. In IEEE Transactions on Information Forensics and Security, 7(2):432–444, 2012.

[3] T. Filler, J. Judas, and J. Fridrich. Minimizing additive distortion in steganography using syndrome-trellis codes. In IEEE Transactions on Information Forensics and Security, 6(3):920–935, September 2011.

[4] T. Denemark, V. Sedighi, V. Holub, R. Cogranne, and J. Fridrich. Selection-channel-aware rich model for steganalysis of digital images. In IEEE International Workshop on Information Forensics and Security, Atlanta, GA, December 3–5, 2014.

[5] T. Filler and J. Fridrich. Minimizing additive distortion functions with non-binary embedding operation in steganography. In IEEE International Workshop on Information Forensics and Security, Seattle, WA, pages 1-6, 2010.

[6] J. Fridrich and J. Kodovský. Rich models for steganalysis of digital images. In IEEE Transactions on Information Forensics and Security, 7(3):868–882, June 2011.

[7] V. Holub and J. Fridrich. Designing steganographic distortion using directional filters. In Proceedings of IEEE Workshop on Information Forensic and Security, pp. 234–239, 2012.

[8] V. Holub, J. Fridrich, and T. Denemark. Universal distortion design for steganography in an arbitrary domain. In *EURASIP Journal on Information Security, Special Issue on Revised Selected Papers of the 1st ACM IH and MMS Workshop*, 2014:1, 2014.

[9] B. Li, M. Wang, and J. Huang. A new cost function for spatial image steganography. In *Proceedings IEEE, International Conference on Image Processing, ICIP*, Paris, France, October 27–30, 2014.

[10] W. Zhang, X. Zhang and S. Wang. A Double Layered "Plus-Minus One" Data Embedding Scheme. In *Signal Processing Letters, IEEE* , vol.14, no.11, pp.848-851, Nov. 2007

[11] T. Filler, J. Judas, and J. Fridrich. Minimizing embedding impact in steganography using trellis-coded quantization. In *Proceedings SPIE, Electronic Imaging*, volume 7541, pages 05–01–05–14, Jan. 17–21, 2010.

[12] J. Fridrich, M. Goljan, and D. Soukal. Wet paper codes with improved embedding efficiency. In *IEEE Transactions on Information Forensics and Security*, 1(1):102–110, 2006.

[13] B. Li, S. Tan, M. Wang and J. Huang. Investigation on Cost Assignment in Spatial Image Steganography. In *IEEE*

Transactions on Information Forensics and Security, vol.9, no.8, pp.1264-1277, Aug. 2014.

[14] T. Pevný, T. Filler, and P. Bas. Using high-dimensional image models to perform highly undetectable steganography. *In Information Hiding (Lecture Notes in Computer Science)*, vol. 6387. Berlin, Germany, pringer-Verlag, pp. 161–177, 2010.

[15] T. Denemark, and J. Fridrich. Improving Steganographic Security by Synchronizing the Selection Channel. In *3rd ACM workshop on Information Hiding and Multimedia Security*. pp. 5-14, Portland, Oregon, June 17-19, 2015.

[16] B. Li, M. Wang, X. Li, S. Tan and J. Huang. A Strategy of Clustering Modification Directions in Spatial Image Steganography. In *IEEE Transactions on Information Forensics and Security*, vol.10, no.9, pp.1905-1917, Sept. 2015.

[17] J. Fridrich, M. Goljan, P. Lisonek and D. Soukal. Writing on wet paper. In *IEEE Transactions on Signal Processing*, vol.53, no.10, pp.3923-3935, Oct. 2005.

Boosting Steganalysis with Explicit Feature Maps

Mehdi Boroumand
Binghamton University
Department of ECE
Binghamton, NY 13902-6000
mboroum1@binghamton.edu

Jessica Fridrich
Binghamton University
Department of ECE
Binghamton, NY 13902-6000
fridrich@binghamton.edu

ABSTRACT

Explicit non-linear transformations of existing steganalysis features are shown to boost their ability to detect steganography in combination with existing simple classifiers, such as the FLD-ensemble. The non-linear transformations are learned from a small number of cover features using Nyström approximation on pilot vectors obtained with kernelized PCA. The best performance is achieved with the exponential form of the Hellinger kernel, which improves the detection accuracy by up to 2–3% for spatial-domain content-adaptive steganography. Since the non-linear map depends only on the cover source and its learning has a low computational complexity, the proposed approach is a practical and low cost method for boosting the accuracy of existing detectors built as binary classifiers. The map can also be used to significantly reduce the feature dimensionality (by up to factor of ten) without performance loss with respect to the non-transformed features.

Keywords

Steganography, steganalysis, machine learning, explicit feature maps, support vector machine, kernel, Nyström approximation, Hellinger

1. INTRODUCTION

Steganalysis of modern content adaptive steganography [17, 21, 26] requires detectors built as classifiers trained on cover and stego objects represented with rich media models [12, 18, 4, 3, 33, 10, 9]. The prohibitive complexity of training a non-linear classifier in high dimensional feature spaces and on large training sets gave rise to alternative machine learning approaches with lower complexity, such as the FLD-ensemble classifier [25], its linear version [5], regularized linear discriminants [6], and the Online Average Ensemble Perceptron [27]. This works well when the classes of

cover and stego features are approximately linearly separable, which seems to be the case in the JPEG domain with features built from co-occurrences of quantized DCT coefficients [23] because of the linear relationship between the features and the embedding domain. In contrast, steganalysis of spatial-domain steganography with co-occurrences of quantized noise residuals benefits from using non-linear classifiers, such as kernelized support vector machines (SVMs). The creators of the popular spatial rich model (SRM) [12] report that a Gaussian SVM trained on carefully selected submodels of the SRM of total dimension 3,300 outperformed the entire 12,753-dimensional SRMQ1 model with the FLD-ensemble classifier (Table II in [12]). Low dimensional variable quantization co-occurrences coupled with a Gaussian SVM were also recently shown to match the performance of the entire SRM with the ensemble classifier [3].[1] Thus, there appears to be an untapped potential to improve steganalysis detectors with non-linear classifiers applied to rich feature sets. What hampers their use in practice is the unfeasibly high computational complexity associated with their training – the complexity of training a kernelized SVM in the primal or dual formulation is $\mathcal{O}(\max\{M, D\} \times \min\{M, D\}^2)$, where M is the number of training examples and D the feature dimension [2].

A kernelized SVM is essentially a linear classifier on features embedded in an infinite dimensional Hilbert space [30]. The classifier can be built thanks to the so-called kernel trick because the training and detector evaluation only require dot products in such space, which can be evaluated using the kernel. The transformation that maps the original features is only *implicit* in the sense that one does not explicitly work with the mapped features. In an alternative approach explored in this paper, the features are transformed using an *explicit* non-linear mapping to improve the classes separability with a hyperplane. Recently, efficient methods have been developed [34, 28] for learning such a non-linear transformation from a portion of the training set. The advantage of this approach is that the classification itself is achieved using a low complexity classifier while the non-linear mapping becomes a mere feature preprocessing. This methodology has found applications, e.g., in object retrieval [1] and digital forensics. In [7], the authors report that applying the square root non-linearity to features in the form of a three-dimensional co-occurrence of the third-

---

[1]Note that, according to [5] and [6], the non-linearity in the FLD-ensemble is not essential and almost identical performance can be achieved with linear classifiers.

IH&MMSec 2016, June 20–23, 2016, Vigo, Spain.

© 2016 ACM. ISBN 978-1-4503-4290-2/16/06. . . $15.00

DOI: http://dx.doi.org/10.1145/2909827.2930803

order noise residual lead to a substantial improvement of their digital image forgery detector.

In this paper, we follow the methodology proposed in [28] and learn the feature map using kernelized PCA coupled with Nyström approximation. For building the map, we explore the Hellinger, linear, chi-square, and Jensen–Shannon kernels and their exponential forms. Based on experiments with individual submodels of the SRM, we identify kernels that provide the biggest detection boost and investigate how the boost depends on the dimensionality of mapped features and the size of the training set. The approach is then scaled to high dimensional feature vectors by learning the mapping separately for each submodel. Experiments with four modern spatial-domain steganographic algorithms on standard databases of grayscale and color images indicate that the detection accuracy can be improved by 2–4% depending on the payload and embedding scheme.

In the next section, we introduce the main idea behind the explicit feature map. In Section 3, we list the kernels used in this study and explain the kernel PCA for learning the transform. A set of initial experiments on two submodels of the SRM is used to gain insight into which kernels are the best performers and assess the boost obtained from them as a function of the dimensionality of the transformed features and the training set size. The procedure for determining the feature map is extended to high-dimensional rich models in Section 5, where we also discuss the results of all experiments with four modern steganographic algorithms and the maxSRMd2 and SCRMQ1 (Spatio-Color Rich Model with $q = 1$) features. A summary of the paper appears in Section 6

2. INTRODUCING THE MAIN IDEA

The problem of steganalysis is binary classification – the Warden monitoring the traffic between Alice and Bob needs to decide whether they exchange information in an overt or covert manner. A useful tool (but not the only one [22]) for the Warden is a detector that can be applied to individual images and provides a binary answer of whether or not a given image contains a secret message. The current paper deals with the problem of building a detector of this type that is as accurate as possible using existing features and classifiers by non-linearly transforming the features as a preprocessing step.

Let us start with a given feature representation, such as the SRM [12]. Assuming the Warden has access to N_{trn} cover images, she embeds them with a specific steganographic method to create a set of N_{trn} corresponding stego images. Then, the cover and stego images are represented with features built as concatenations of histograms or co-occurrences (which are high dimensional histograms): $\mathbf{x}^{(k)} \in \mathbb{R}_+^D$, $k = 1, \ldots, N_{trn}$, for covers and $\mathbf{y}^{(k)} \in \mathbb{R}_+^D$ for stego images, where D is the feature dimensionality and $\mathbb{R}_+$ is the set of nonnegative real numbers. As the next step, a binary classifier is trained to distinguish between cover and stego features. One of the best choices for the classifier is kernelized SVM with a positive semi-definite kernel $k : \mathbb{R}_+^D \times \mathbb{R}_+^D \to \mathbb{R}_+$. One can think of such an SVM as a *linear* classifier in a space of features transformed into a Hilbert space $\mathcal{H}$, $\varphi : \mathbb{R}_+^D \to \mathcal{H}$, endowed with dot product $\langle \cdot, \cdot \rangle : \mathcal{H} \times \mathcal{H} \to \mathbb{R}_+$ for which

$$\langle \varphi(\mathbf{x}), \varphi(\mathbf{y}) \rangle = k(\mathbf{x}, \mathbf{y}) \text{ for all } \mathbf{x}, \mathbf{y} \in \mathbb{R}_+^D. \quad (1)$$

The main principle behind SVMs stems from the fact that the transformation φ is only implicit in the sense that when building the SVM classifier or evaluating the detector, one does not need to work directly with $\varphi(\mathbf{x}) \in \mathcal{H}$ and only needs to evaluate dots product via the kernel (1).

As pointed out in the introduction, kernelized SVMs outperform linear classifiers (and the FLD-ensemble) in many typical setups in steganalysis of spatial-domain steganography. Their drawback is a high training complexity, which is why the community resorted to simpler machine learning paradigms. In this paper, we explore an alternative approach, which employs an *explicit* transform $\varphi : \mathbb{R}_+^D \to \mathbb{R}^E$ that *approximates* a given kernel in combination with a simple classifier in $\mathbb{R}^E$ trained on features $\varphi(\mathbf{x}^{(k)})$ and $\varphi(\mathbf{y}^{(k)})$, $k = 1, \ldots, N_{trn}$. To classify a feature $\mathbf{z} \in \mathbb{R}_+^D$, the classifier is presented with $\varphi(\mathbf{z})$. The mapping φ will be learned from a portion of the training set as shown in the next section.

3. LEARNING THE TRANSFORM

In this section, we first introduce several kernels that will be investigated in this paper. Then, we show that the problem of finding a mapping that approximates the kernel with dot products of transformed features coincides with kernelized principal component analysis (kPCA). The general mapping of the feature space is realized using Nyström approximation.

3.1 Kernels

A kernel is a symmetric positive semi-definite[2] mapping $k : \mathbb{R}_+^D \times \mathbb{R}_+^D \to \mathbb{R}_+$ that, loosely speaking, measures the *similarity* between two features. Let us assume that vectors $\mathbf{x}, \mathbf{y} \in \mathbb{R}_+^D$ are L_2-normalized, meaning that $\|\mathbf{x}\|_2^2 = \|\mathbf{y}\|_2^2 = \sum_{i=1}^D x_i^2 = 1$. Their square Euclidean distance can be written as:

$$\|\mathbf{x} - \mathbf{y}\|_2^2 = 2(1 - k(\mathbf{x}, \mathbf{y})), \quad (2)$$

where we introduced $k(\mathbf{x}, \mathbf{y}) = \sum_{i=1}^D x_i y_i$. The reader recognizes $k(\mathbf{x}, \mathbf{y})$ as the classical dot product, which, due to the normalization, coincides with the cosine of the angle between $\mathbf{x}$ and $\mathbf{y}$.

Generalizing this idea, the following are popular choices for kernels in machine vision [28, 34]:

1. Linear kernel $k(\mathbf{x}, \mathbf{y}) = \sum_{i=1}^D x_i y_i$ with $\mathbf{x}$ and $\mathbf{y}$ L_2-normalized;

2. Hellinger kernel (also called Bhattacharyya kernel) $k(\mathbf{x}, \mathbf{y}) = \sum_{i=1}^D \sqrt{x_i y_i}$ with $\mathbf{x}$ and $\mathbf{y}$ L_1-normalized;

3. Chi-square kernel $k(\mathbf{x}, \mathbf{y}) = \sum_{i=1}^D \frac{2 x_i y_i}{x_i + y_i}$ with $\mathbf{x}$ and $\mathbf{y}$ L_1-normalized;

4. Jensen–Shannon kernel $k(\mathbf{x}, \mathbf{y}) = \frac{1}{2} \sum_{i=1}^D x_i \log \frac{x_i + y_i}{x_i} + y_i \log \frac{x_i + y_i}{y_i}$ with $\mathbf{x}$ and $\mathbf{y}$ L_1-normalized.

Whenever a term in the chi-square and the Jensen–Shannon kernel is not defined (due to division by zero or log of zero), the term is set to zero, which coincides with the limit from

---

[2]Kernel k is positive semi-definite if for any n and any $\mathbf{u}^{(1)}, \ldots, \mathbf{u}^{(n)} \in \mathbb{R}^D$, the $n \times n$ matrix $K_{ij} = k(\mathbf{u}^{(i)}, \mathbf{u}^{(j)})$ is positive semi-definite.

the right. Also note that with the specified normalization, $0 \leq k(\mathbf{x}, \mathbf{y}) \leq 1$ for all $\mathbf{x}, \mathbf{y} \in \mathbb{R}_+^D$ and for all kernels. The Hellinger kernel corresponds to the linear kernel on square-rooted features.

It can be easily proved that for a symmetric positive semi-definite kernel k and $\gamma > 0$,

$$e^{\gamma(k(\mathbf{x},\mathbf{y})-1)} \tag{3}$$

is also symmetric positive semi-definite and bounded $0 \leq e^{\gamma(k(\mathbf{x},\mathbf{y})-1)} \leq 1$. Thus, the above four kernels have their exponential counterparts, which we name with the preposition 'exp', such as exp-Hellinger, etc.

3.2 Finding the transformation

The task of finding a transform such that the dot products of two transformed vectors coincide with the kernel evaluated on them can be formulated as follows. Given $M \geq D$ vectors $\mathbf{x}^{(1)}, \ldots, \mathbf{x}^{(M)} \in \mathbb{R}_+^D$ for training the map φ, find vectors $\phi(\mathbf{x}^{(i)}) \in \mathbb{R}^M$ so that for all $i, j \in \{1, \ldots, M\}$:

$$k(\mathbf{x}^{(i)}, \mathbf{x}^{(j)}) \approx \phi(\mathbf{x}^{(i)}) \cdot \phi(\mathbf{x}^{(j)}). \tag{4}$$

This can be solved by the following optimization problem. Denoting the ath coordinate of $\phi(\mathbf{x}) \in \mathbb{R}^M$ with $\phi_a(\mathbf{x})$, $1 \leq a \leq M$, minimize

$$\sum_{i,j=1}^M \left(k(\mathbf{x}^{(i)}, \mathbf{x}^{(j)}) - \phi(\mathbf{x}^{(i)}) \cdot \phi(\mathbf{x}^{(j)}) \right)^2 \tag{5}$$

subject to

$$\sum_{i=1}^M \phi_a(\mathbf{x}^{(i)}) \phi_b(\mathbf{x}^{(i)}) = 0 \text{ for all } 0 \leq a \neq b \leq M. \tag{6}$$

The constraint (6) expresses our desire that the description in the M dimensional space be non-redundant – we essentially require each pair of coordinates a, b of the transformed feature vectors be uncorrelated.

Using the method of Lagrange multipliers, it is easily established that $\phi_a \triangleq (\phi_a(\mathbf{x}^{(1)}), \ldots, \phi_a(\mathbf{x}^{(M)}))' \in \mathbb{R}^M$ are eigen-vectors of the kernel matrix $\mathbf{K} = (K_{ij}) \in \mathbb{R}_+^{M \times M}$, $K_{ij} = k(\mathbf{x}^{(i)}, \mathbf{x}^{(j)})$:

$$\mathbf{K}\phi_a = \lambda_a^2 \phi_a, \ 1 \leq a \leq M, \tag{7}$$

where λ_a^2 are the corresponding eigenvalues sorted from the largest to the smallest. We note that $\lambda_a = \|\phi_a\|_2$.

The mapping $\varphi: \mathbb{R}_+^D \to \mathbb{R}^E$ is defined using the so-called Nyström approximation. For any $\mathbf{z} \in \mathbb{R}_+^D$,

$$\varphi_a(\mathbf{z}) = \frac{1}{\lambda_a^2} \mathbf{K}(\mathbf{z}, \cdot) \phi_a, \ 1 \leq a \leq E, \tag{8}$$

where

$$\mathbf{K}(\mathbf{z}, \cdot) = \left(k(\mathbf{z}, \mathbf{x}^{(1)}), \ldots, k(\mathbf{z}, \mathbf{x}^{(M)}) \right). \tag{9}$$

Note that in building φ, we retain the first E coordinates a corresponding to the largest eigenvalues λ_a^2. When $E = D$, the feature transform preserves the feature dimensionality.

The Hellinger kernel corresponds to the linear kernel on L_1-normalized features that have been square-rooted elementwise. This is the only non-linear kernel for which the explicit map φ adopts a simple closed-form expression – the

square root executed elementwise. Because of this simplification, the feature preprocessing is very cheap and the complexity is essentially negligible in comparison to the classifier training. This is why in our experiments, we include results obtained with square-rooted features. They should always be very close to the results obtained with the transform learned for the Hellinger kernel. Square-rooting features has been reported in computer vision [1] and digital forensics [7] as a way to improve detection accuracy with a heuristic justification that the non-linear transformation evens out the differences between the individual features (histogram bins).

We furthermore note that it is possible to use only cover features for the map training rather than cover-stego feature pairs because the kernel is continuous and the features of cover and stego images are close and would not provide good constraints for learning the map. We verified this experimentally but do not report the details of these findings in this paper.

3.3 Complexity considerations

The complexity of learning the map includes the time needed to form the matrix $\mathbf{K}$, which is $\mathcal{O}(DM^2)$ and the cost of solving the eigenvector problem (7), which is $\mathcal{O}(M^3)$ if implemented, e.g., using the Cholesky decomposition. Thus, the total complexity is $\mathcal{O}(DM^2 + M^3)$. Fortunately, these computations only need to be executed once for a given cover source because the map is trained on cover images only. Of course, this makes the map independent of the embedding payload and the steganographic scheme. The cost of transforming a new feature is part of the training as well as testing and is $\mathcal{O}(MD)$ to evaluate (9) and then $\mathcal{O}(ME)$ to compute all E coordinates of $\varphi(\mathbf{z})$ (8).

4. INITIAL EXPERIMENTS

To get a feeling for the ability of explicit maps to boost steganalysis and to assess the influence of various parameters, such as E, the number of retained coordinates in the map, and M, the number of images for training the map, in this section we experiment with S-UNIWARD [21] and HILL [26] and their detection with two submodels of the SRM: the four-dimensional co-occurrence matrix of the 'SQUARE 3x3' submodel (also sometimes called "KB residual") and the 'minmax22h' submodel for the first-order residual. Both feature sets were computed with the quantization step $q = 1$ and symmetrized as in SRM, which means that the KB residual co-occurrence had dimensionality 169 while the 'minmax22h' submodel had dimensionality of 101 after removing from it elements that are always equal to zero (see Section 4.1).

The experiments in this section were conducted on BOSSbase 1.01 [11] containing 10,000 512×512 8-bit grayscale images. After randomly splitting the database into two disjoint parts of equal size (5,000 images), the feature transformation $\varphi: \mathbb{R}_+^D \to \mathbb{R}^E$ was learned on M randomly selected images from the training set. The FLD-ensemble was then trained and tested on the transformed features. This was repeated ten times while evaluating the empirical security using the minimal total error under equal priors achieved on the testing set:

$$P_E = \min_{P_{FA}} \frac{1}{2}(P_{FA} + P_{MD}), \tag{10}$$

where P_{FA} and P_{MD} are the probabilities of false alarm and missed detection. The symbol $\overline{P}_E$ is the average P_E over the ten splits. The statistical spread is reported using the mean absolute deviation. The constant γ in exponential kernels (3) was chosen as the reciprocal of the mean of the non-exponential kernel over all training pairs:

$$\gamma = \frac{1}{\frac{1}{M^2}\sum_{i,j=1}^{M} k(\mathbf{x}^{(i)}, \mathbf{x}^{(j)})}. \qquad (11)$$

4.1 Removing zero features

Before explaining the results of all experiments in this section, we make one note. Exactly 224 elements of the 325-dimensional 'minmax22h' submodel of SRM are zero in both cover and stego images. This is due to the nature of the residuals used in this submodel and the scan direction for forming the co-occurrence.[3] For example, the 'minmax22v' submodel does not have any zeros. Besides 'minmax22h', there are two other submodel types in the SRM with elements that are identically equal to zero no matter what the input image is. They are 'minmax34h' and 'minmax41'. The zeros occur for first-order differences and third-order differences. Because first-order differences are quantized only with $q = 1$ and $q = 2$, there are total 2×3 first-order submodels and 3×3 third-order submodels (because third-order residuals are quantized with three quantization steps), each effectively containing only $325 - 224 = 101$ non-zero elements instead of 325. These zeros need to be removed before learning the transformation because Matlab eigenvector solver may otherwise return negative eigenvalues and complex-valued eigen-vectors due to finite machine precision. We note that after removing the zero elements from the SRM feature vector, its dimensionality becomes $34{,}671 - 15{\times}224 = 31{,}311$. The dimensionality of the SRMQ1 decreases from 12,753 to 11,409 ($6{\times}224$ fewer).

Because the selection-channel-aware version of the SRM called maxSRMd2 [10] uses a different scan for forming co-occurrences, the so-called 'd2' scan,[4] the number of non-zero elements in the above-mentioned submodels is different. For quantization $q = 2$ the 'minmax22h', 'minmax34h', and 'minmax41' submodels for the first and third order residuals have dimensionality 190. For $q = 1$ and $q = 1.5$, their dimensionality is 120. This gives the maxSRMd2 feature set a dimensionality of 32,016.

Finally, we note that this peculiarity largely escaped the attention of the community because the ensemble classifier first prunes the cover and stego features and automatically removes zero elements from both cover and stego features before building the classifier. In our case, however, because we learn the transformation φ before applying the ensemble, we remove such zero features prior to learning φ.

---

[3] Anecdotal evidence exists among researchers that the SRM feature contains many zeros but, according to the best knowledge of the authors, this issue has never been investigated in detail. In this paper, we merely state the true dimensionality of the affected submodels without providing any further analysis in order not to digress from the main topic of this paper.

[4] The 'd2' scan involves residuals $r_{ij}, r_{i,j+1}, r_{i+1,j+2}, r_{i+1,j+3}$ and three more horizontally and vertically flipped versions.

$E\backslash M$	10	20	50	100	169	350	500	1000
10	.4260	.4262	.4260	.4259	.4268	.4259	.4260	.4263
20	-	.3893	.3893	.3899	.3894	.3887	.3899	.3894
50	-	-	.3142	.3145	.3144	.3135	.3144	.3136
100	-	-	-	.2885	.2882	.2879	.2886	.2879
169	-	-	-	-	.2754	.2757	.2757	.2752
350	-	-	-	-	-	.2707	.2683	.2695
500	-	-	-	-	-	-	.2662	.2653
1000	-	-	-	-	-	-	-	.2739

Table 1: $\overline{P}_E$ for KB residual ($D = 169$) with S-UNIWARD at 0.4 bpp when training the map φ with exp-Hellinger kernel on M randomly selected images and retaining E dimensions, $M, E \in \{10, 20, 50, 100, 169, 350, 500, 1000\}$. The statistical spread in the form of sample standard deviation ranges between 0.0012 and 0.0039. The values below the main diagonal are not achievable because $E \leq M$.

4.2 Boosting submodels

As our first experiment, we investigated the effect of the parameters M and E on detection error $\overline{P}_E$. For brevity, we only report the result with the KB residual and S-UNIWARD at 0.4 bpp with the exponential Hellinger kernel for the non-linear map φ. Table 1 shows the detection error for different combinations of E and M. There appears to be a benefit in retaining more coordinates E than the original feature dimensionality D. With $M = 500$ training images, retaining $E = 500$ coordinates rather than $D = 169$ leads to about 1% improvement. There does not seem to be any benefit in using more images for training or retaining more than 500 coordinates. We note that our goal was to boost the detection accuracy without increasing the feature dimensionality. Inspecting the row in Table 1 corresponding to $E = D = 169$, the number of training images does not have a major effect on detection accuracy as long as $M \geq D$.

Table 2 shows the results for all kernels introduced in Section 2 with two submodels and two steganographic techniques at payload 0.4 bpp for $M = 500$ and $E = 500$. The first row of the table is the performance obtained using the original features as they appear in SRM. The second row shows the results with simply square-rooting the features. The third row contains detection errors obtained using Gaussian SVM, again averaged over ten 50/50 database splits.

As noted in the previous section, the square rooted features correspond to the Hellinger kernel when using the known explicit map instead of the Nyström approximation. It is comforting to discover that these results match those obtained using Nyström approximation with this kernel (row four) as they should. Inspecting the remaining rows, it is very clear that the exponential kernels are superior to the non-exponential ones and they also have quite similar performance. The boost they provide w.r.t. the original features (row 1) is up to 3.5% for the 'minmax22h' submodel for S-UNIWARD. Also, it is quite apparent that simply square-rooting the features (Hellinger kernel) is far from the best option. For the KB residual, explicit maps with exponential kernels match the result obtained using G-SVM. For the 'minmax22h' residual, the G-SVM outperforms explicit maps by about 1%. Because of the larger complexity associated with the chi-square and Jensen–Shannon kernels, we selected the exponential Hellinger kernel for all experiments with rich models in the next section.

	Kernel	minmax22h (S-UNI)	KB (S-UNI)	KB (HILL)
1	Original	0.3293±0.0030	0.2933±0.0028	0.3281±0.0027
2	Square root	0.3150±0.0032	0.2812±0.0028	0.3228±0.0020
3	G-SVM	0.2841±0.0018	0.2618±0.0023	0.3026±0.0016
4	Hellinger	0.3252±0.0038	0.2827±0.0035	0.3242±0.0024
5	Exp-Hellinger	0.2984±0.0030	0.2626±0.0024	0.3026±0.0030
6	Linear	0.3317±0.0030	0.2837±0.0029	0.3378±0.0028
7	Exp-linear	0.3052±0.0030	0.2603±0.0029	0.3030±0.0039
8	Chi-square	0.3063±0.0030	0.2685±0.0035	0.3106±0.0035
9	Exp-chi-square	0.2991±0.0023	0.2619±0.0024	0.3045±0.0019
10	JS	0.3076±0.0039	0.2696±0.0033	0.3103±0.0026
11	Exp-JS	0.2950±0.0023	0.2611±0.0022	0.3017±0.0016

Table 2: $\overline{P}_E$ for various kernels for S-UNIWARD and HILL at 0.4 bpp for KB co-occurrence (dim 169) and 'minmax22h' (dim 101) submodel of the SRM. The abbreviation 'JS' stands for the Jensen–Shannon kernel.

5. EXTENSION TO RICH MODELS

The purpose of this section to extend the proposed approach to high-dimensional rich models. Since the complexity of training the non-linear map is $\mathcal{O}(DM^2 + M^3)$, see Section 3.3, it would not be feasible to train the map for the entire rich feature vector. Instead, we learn the map for each submodel of the rich model separately. Furthermore, in order not to increase the feature dimensionality, we keep the number of retained coordinates $E = D$. We do so despite the benefit of using $E > D$ (see Table 1) because, when richified, we did not see any benefit of inflating the dimensionality of the entire feature vector.[5]

Given a set of N_{trn} cover images and the same amount of the corresponding stego images for training the entire detector, we randomly reserved $M < N_{trn}$ cover images for training the maps for all submodels. The classifier is next trained on all N_{trn} images, including the images used for training the map. Including the M images for classifier training is unlikely to lead to over training because the map training is not informed about the stego class. Moreover, we determined experimentally that as few as $M = 350$ cover images are sufficient for the map training, which is only a small part of the training set ($N_{trn} = 5,000$ for datasets derived from BOSSbase 1.01). Finally, we did carry out comparative tests in which we only trained on $N_{trn} - M$ images, which resulted in similar detection errors within their statistical spread.

We note that the map φ has the following data structures as its parameters:[6] 1) the set of M cover features $\mathbf{x}^{(i)}$, $i = 1, \ldots, M$, which is an $M \times D$ dimensional array, 2) the set of E eigen-vectors ϕ_a, $a = 1, \ldots, E$, stored as an $E \times D$ array.

In our experiments, we tested four state-of-the-art steganographic methods embedding in the spatial domain: WOW [17], S-UNIWARD [21], HILL [26], and MiPOD [31]. For each payload, a separate binary classifier implemented with the FLD-ensemble [25] was trained on the original features and on the transformed features. For each split of the database into a training and testing set, the map φ was retrained on a different subset of the training set. The empirical security was measured as the total detection error P_E (10) averaged

---

[5]Experiments on selected payloads with the tested stego algorithms with $E = 500$ retained coordinates for each submodel resulted in statistically insignificant deviations from $E = D$ (not shown in this paper).

[6]For simplicity, we assume that the M training examples were selected as the first M features from the training set.

over ten 50/50 database splits. In all experiments, we used $E = D$. Based on the experiments with individual submodels in the previous section, we tested only one kernel, the exponential Hellinger. We remind that each feature vector was L_1-normalized.

We first report the results for the maxSRMd2 feature set [10] on BOSSbase 1.01. Table 3 shows $\overline{P}_E$ as a function of payload for the original maxSRMd2, its square rooted version, and the transformed version using exp-Hellinger on BOSSbase 1.01. To better contrast the improvement in detection, in Figure 1 we show the difference between the detection error of the original features, $\overline{P}_E^{(orig)}$, and the error obtained using square-rooting, $\overline{P}_E^{(sqrt)}$, and with exp-Hellinger, $\overline{P}_E^{(exp-H)}$. The difference is expressed in percents (multiplied by 100). The results indicate that a consistent detection boost is obtained across all four embedding algorithms. The biggest boost was obtained for WOW and the smallest for MiPOD and HILL. The square rooting is not as effective as the transform obtained with the exponential Hellinger kernel.

At this point, we note that when applying the non-linear map to the SRM feature set we observed a gain that was very similar to that of the maxSRMd2 set, which is why we do not report these results here. In Section 5.1 below, we comment on other rich feature sets currently used in steganalysis.

As our second batch of experiments, we used the Spatio-Color Rich Model with $q = 1$ (SCRMQ1) [14] feature set of dimensionality 18,157. It is a merger of the SRMQ1, which is a subset of the SRM and the Color Rich Model (CRM) formed by three-dimensional co-occurrences of residuals across three color channels. The image source was the same as in [14], a color version of BOSSbase prepared as follows. Starting with the full-resolution raw images, we converted them using the same script that was used for creating the BOSSbase with the following modifications. The output of 'ufraw' (ver. 0.18 with 'dcraw' ver. 9.06) was changed to the color ppm format instead of the pgm grayscale. Also, all calls of 'convert' used ppm for the output as well as for resizing so that the smaller image dimension was 512 and for central cropping to 512×512. As in the original script, the resizing algorithm uses the Lanczos kernel. We thus obtained 10,000 true color 512×512 ppm images. This version of color BOSSbase will be called 'BOSSbaseColor'.

The above four steganographic algorithm were applied by color channels and the same relative payload was embedded in each channel. The complete results are listed in Table 4. The non-linear map boosts detection to a different degree depending on the steganographic method and payload. The largest gain of almost 4% is observed for WOW.

5.1 Application to other rich feature sets

In this section, we comment on our experience with applying non-linear maps to other types of rich models. Modern embedding algorithms for JPEG images (J-UNIWARD [21] and UED [15, 16]) are currently best detected with phase-aware rich models [19, 20] formed by histograms of noise residuals split by their location with respect to the location of the 8×8 pixel grid used for compression. In particular, the so-called Gabor Filter Residuals (GFR) [32] made aware of the selection channel [8] appear among the best. Experiments with this feature set on selected payloads on J-

S-UNI	Payload (bits per pixel)					
	0.05	0.1	0.2	0.3	0.4	0.5
maxSRMd2	0.4168±0.0024	0.3652±0.0008	0.2919±0.0023	0.2374±0.0023	0.1917±0.0042	0.1569±0.0035
Square root	0.4177±0.0033	0.3588±0.0025	0.2851±0.0034	0.2276±0.0021	0.1785±0.0033	0.1433±0.0026
exp-Hellinger	0.4178±0.0020	0.3608±0.0033	0.2803±0.0027	0.2181±0.0028	0.1720±0.0020	0.1348±0.0025
HILL						
maxSRMd2	0.4246±0.0040	0.3742±0.0022	0.3105±0.0033	0.2580±0.0033	0.2196±0.0039	0.1815±0.0033
Square root	0.4188±0.0030	0.3669±0.0032	0.3007±0.0025	0.2512±0.0036	0.2116±0.0026	0.1736±0.0030
exp-Hellinger	0.4191±0.0022	0.3653±0.0024	0.2974±0.0028	0.2451±0.0024	0.2004±0.0019	0.1649±0.0031
MiPOD						
maxSRMd2	0.4427±0.0026	0.3949±0.0031	0.3246±0.0034	0.2709±0.0027	0.2272±0.0037	0.1865±0.0029
Square root	0.4401±0.0028	0.3926±0.0047	0.3185±0.0022	0.2635±0.0027	0.2209±0.0036	0.1818±0.0022
exp-Hellinger	0.4426±0.0032	0.3911±0.0038	0.3148±0.0026	0.2568±0.0024	0.2104±0.0028	0.1720±0.0031
WOW						
maxSRMd2	0.3574±0.0024	0.2984±0.0020	0.2331±0.0018	0.1907±0.0028	0.1559±0.0024	0.1279±0.0030
Square root	0.3492±0.0021	0.2854±0.0033	0.2140±0.0031	0.1702±0.0026	0.1375±0.0020	0.1118±0.0033
exp-Hellinger	0.3470±0.0024	0.2820±0.0024	0.2094±0.0025	0.1645±0.0031	0.1310±0.0028	0.1068±0.0032

Table 3: Detection error $\overline{P}_{\mathrm{E}}$ for four steganographic schemes and five payloads in bpp on BOSSbase 1.01 with FLD-ensemble trained with maxSRMd2 features, their square rooted form, and transformed using exponential Hellinger kernel (by submodels).

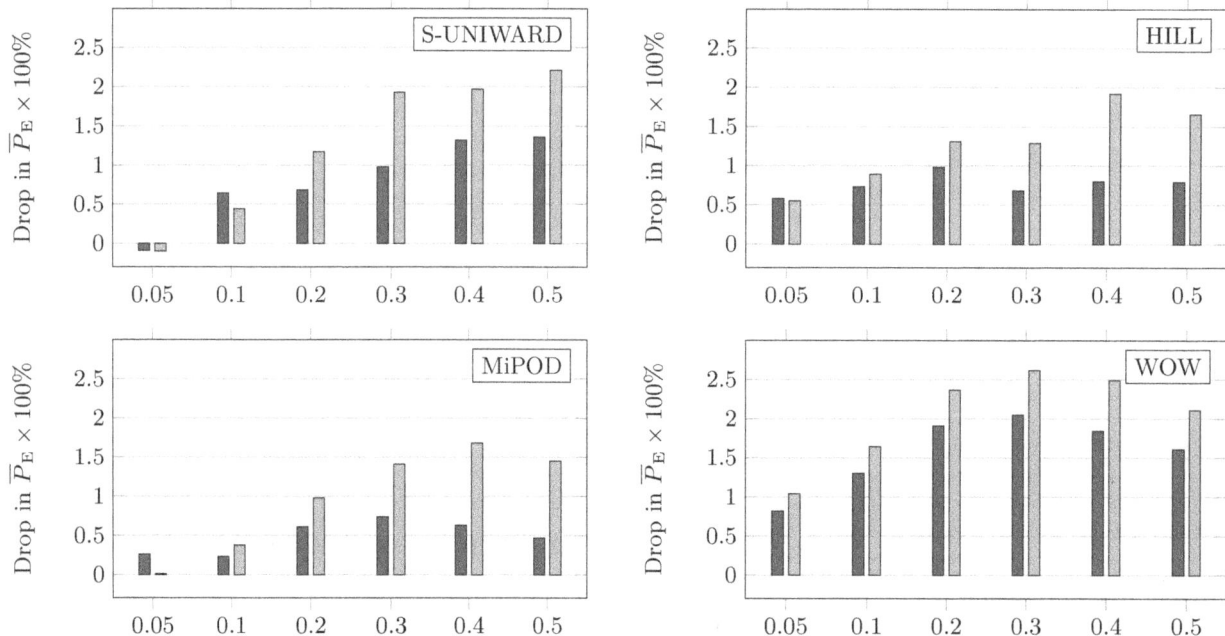

Figure 1: Drop in detection error $\overline{P}_{\mathrm{E}} \times 100\%$ with respect to the original maxSRMd2 feature set as a function of payload in bpp. Blue: $\left(\overline{P}_{\mathrm{E}}^{(orig)} - \overline{P}_{\mathrm{E}}^{(sqrt)}\right) \times 100$, yellow: $\left(\overline{P}_{\mathrm{E}}^{(orig)} - \overline{P}_{\mathrm{E}}^{(exp-H)}\right) \times 100$.

	Payload (bpp per channel)					
S-UNI	0.05	0.1	0.2	0.3	0.4	0.5
SCRMQ1	0.4549±0.0022	0.3939±0.0026	0.2977±0.0027	0.2216±0.0016	0.1710±0.0032	0.1306±0.0038
Square root	0.4499±0.0028	0.3853±0.0029	0.2885±0.0023	0.2154±0.0017	0.1630±0.0027	0.1230±0.0032
exp-Hellinger	0.4487±0.0047	0.3789±0.0031	0.2761±0.0037	0.2016±0.0017	0.1461±0.0033	0.1067±0.0028
HILL						
SCRMQ1	0.4699±0.0024	0.4227±0.0029	0.3288±0.0022	0.2528±0.0017	0.1967±0.0024	0.1558±0.0043
Square root	0.4586±0.0035	0.4021±0.0031	0.3130±0.0022	0.2416±0.0036	0.1896±0.0025	0.1497±0.0022
exp-Hellinger	0.4520±0.0032	0.3904±0.0044	0.2927±0.0026	0.2212±0.0031	0.1724±0.0027	0.1332±0.0022
MiPOD						
SCRMQ1	0.4557±0.0029	0.4034±0.0029	0.3081±0.0031	0.2397±0.0042	0.1872±0.0045	0.1476±0.0026
Square root	0.4477±0.0022	0.3904±0.0021	0.3006±0.0018	0.2317±0.0028	0.1812±0.0029	0.1439±0.0030
exp-Hellinger	0.4485±0.0031	0.3802±0.0032	0.2839±0.0014	0.2133±0.0034	0.1633±0.0040	0.1253±0.0034
WOW						
SCRMQ1	0.4507±0.0009	0.3975±0.0033	0.2997±0.0033	0.2283±0.0021	0.1793±0.0046	0.1365±0.0036
Square root	0.4367±0.0040	0.3700±0.0042	0.2750±0.0029	0.2092±0.0021	0.1641±0.0011	0.1263±0.0027
exp-Hellinger	0.4296±0.0033	0.3600±0.0029	0.2618±0.0020	0.1936±0.0022	0.1468±0.0019	0.1129±0.0018

Table 4: Detection error $\overline{P}_{\mathrm{E}}$ for four steganographic schemes and five payloads in bits per pixel per color channel on color version of BOSSbase with FLD-ensemble trained with SCRMQ1 features, their square rooted form, and transformed using exponential Hellinger kernel (by submodels).

UNIWARD, however, indicated no benefit of square-rooting the GFR features (this is equivalent to using the Hellinger kernel). Also, we did not observe any boost when applying a non-linear transformation to the projection SRM (PSRM) [18]. The PSRM as well as the phase-aware features share one aspect that is different from rich models such as SRM, maxSRMd2, and SCRMQ1. The former are computed as first-order statistics (histograms) rater than high-dimensional co-occurrences. Histograms are generally much better populated than co-occurrences and the differences among the populations of individual bins are much smaller. Features formed as collections of well-populated histograms do not seem to benefit from non-linear transformation investigated in this paper.

There exist co-occurrence based rich models for the JPEG domain, such as JRM [24] and CC-C300 [23] formed by many two-dimensional co-occurrences from DCT coefficients and their differences. However, as reported in these papers, the decision boundary between cover and stego features within these representations is almost linear because of the direct relationship between the embedding domain and the domain in which the steganalysis representation is built. According to our experiments with the JRM on J-UNIWARD and nsF5 [13], square-rooting the features before classification with the FLD-ensemble has no effect on detection accuracy.

5.2 Rich model compactification

In this section, we study whether the transform φ is a useful tool for compactifying the rich model by simply retaining fewer coordinates in each transformed submodel. Compactification of rich models is a topic that has already been addressed in [12], where a greedy forward feature selection method has been applied to SRM submodels. It has also been investigated within the context of unsupervised detectors, where high-dimensional models could not be applied [29]. We stress that retaining a smaller subset of transformed dimensions is similar in spirit to applying a regular PCA to cover features and, as such, has obvious limita-

tions because of the absence of feedback from the embedding scheme. Thus, it is unlikely to provide compactification ratios similar to approaches that consider both cover and stego features, such as calibrated least squares (CLS) [29]. On the other hand, the compactification only depends on the cover source, which makes the approach potentially useful for unsupervised universal steganalysis.

As can be seen from Table 1, for an individual SRM submodel the detection error increases quite rapidly with the decreased number of retained coordinates. On the other hand, differences in the performance of individual submodels usually do not scale directly to the rich model as it is likely that the submodels "compensate for each other weaknesses." Thus, the entire rich model may still perform rather well when compacted. Figure 2 confirms this hypothesis, showing the detection error $\overline{P}_{\mathrm{E}}$ as a function of the number of retained coordinates. Even when retaining only 10% of the coordinates, $E = 0.1 \times D$, there still appears to be a small gain in detection accuracy w.r.t. the original maxS-RMd2 feature.

6. CONCLUSION

Supervised detectors of steganography are currently built using classifiers trained on high-dimensional rich models. The excessive training complexity associated with large training sets and high-dimensional features forced steganalysts to adopt simple(r) machine learning paradigms, such as the popular FLD-ensemble and its linearized versions, potentially thus losing on detection accuracy that could be obtained with more powerful non-linear classifiers, such as kernelized support vector machines. In this paper, we investigate the possibility to boost steganalysis with simple classifiers by non-linearly transforming the features. The transformation is learned on a small set of cover features with the constraint that the dot products of mapped features approximate the output of a specific kernel, a task equivalent to kernelized PCA. The feature transformation can be in-

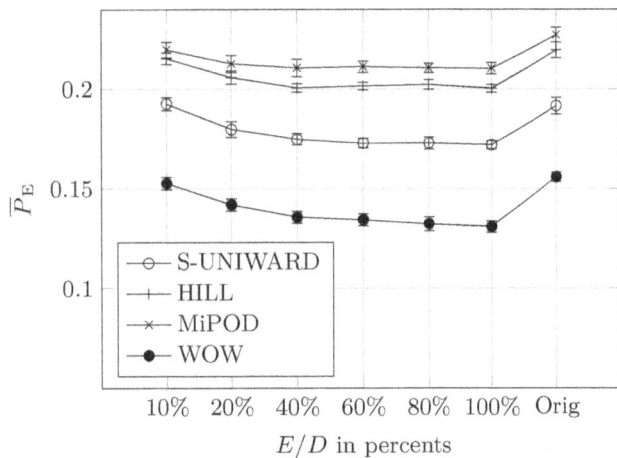

Figure 2: Detection error $\overline{P}_{\mathrm{E}}$ as a function of the relative number of retained coordinates, E/D. Tested payload 0.4 bpp, exp-Hellinger kernel.

terpreted as a different way of measuring distances in the feature space. Retaining only a subset of transformed coordinates corresponding to the largest eigenvalues, the general version of the transformation is obtained using Nyström approximation. The approach is scaled up to the full spatial rich model by learning the transformation separately for each submodel in order to keep the computational complexity low.

Exponential forms of the linear, Hellinger (Bhattacharyya), chi-square, and Jensen–Shannon kernels provide similar performance and substantially improve upon the original (non-transformed) form of the features. A consistent gain between 2–4% was observed for the selection-channel-aware maxSRMd2 features as well as the Spatio-Color Rich Model for steganalysis of color images. The detection improvement varies across steganographic methods and payloads. Learning the transformation is a relatively low-cost task that only needs to be executed once for a given cover source. In particular, the transformation does not depend on the steganographic method and the payload. By retaining fewer dimensions in each SRM submodel, it is possible to compactify the rich descriptor by a factor of 10 without losing the detection performance of the original (non-transformed) feature vector. This could be useful for unsupervised universal steganalysis detectors.

We wish to point out that the non-linear transformation seems effective only for features built as high-dimensional co-occurrences, such as the SRM, maxSRM, and SCRMQ1. In particular, it does not bring any improvement for "dense" features built as histograms spanning a few bins, such as JPEG-phase-aware features [32, 20, 19] and the projection spatial rich model [18]. We hypothesize that it is because the populations of co-occurrence bins are typically highly imbalanced while the bins in histograms are more evenly populated, making the effect of the non-linearity negligible.

7. ACKNOWLEDGMENTS

The work on this paper was supported by Air Force Office of Scientific Research under the research grant number FA9950-12-1-0124. The U.S. Government is authorized to reproduce and distribute reprints for Governmental purposes notwithstanding any copyright notation there on. The views and conclusions contained herein are those of the authors and should not be interpreted as necessarily representing the official policies, either expressed or implied of AFOSR or the U.S. Government. The authors would like to thank anonymous reviewers for their insightful comments.

8. REFERENCES

[1] R. Arandjelovic and A. Zisserman. Three things everyone should know to improve object retrieval. In *Computer Vision and Pattern Recognition (CVPR), 2012 IEEE Conference on*, pages 2911–2918, June 2012.

[2] O. Chapelle. Training a support vector machine in the primal. *Neural Computation*, 15(5):1155–1178, 2007.

[3] L. Chen, Y.-Q. Shi, and P. Sutthiwan. Variable multi-dimensional co-occurrence for steganalysis. In *Digital Forensics and Watermarking, 13th International Workshop, IWDW*, volume 9023, pages 559–573, Taipei, Taiwan, October 1–4 2014. Springer.

[4] L. Chen, Y.Q. Shi, P. Sutthiwan, and X. Niu. A novel mapping scheme for steganalysis. In Y.Q. Shi, H.-J. Kim, and F. Perez-Gonzalez, editors, *International Workshop on Digital Forensics and Watermaking*, volume 7809 of *LNCS*, pages 19–33. Springer Berlin Heidelberg, 2013.

[5] R. Cogranne and J. Fridrich. Modeling and extending the ensemble classifier for steganalysis of digital images using hypothesis testing theory. *IEEE Transactions on Information Forensics and Security*, 10(2):2627–2642, December 2015.

[6] R. Cogranne, V. Sedighi, T. Pevný, and J. Fridrich. Is ensemble classifier needed for steganalysis in high-dimensional feature spaces? In *IEEE International Workshop on Information Forensics and Security*, Rome, Italy, November 16–19 2015.

[7] D. Cozzolino, G. Poggi, and L. Verdoliva. Splicebuster: a new blind image splicing detector. In *IEEE International Workshop on Information Forensics and Security*, Rome, Italy, November 16–19 2015.

[8] T. Denemark, M. Boroumand, and J. Fridrich. Steganalysis features for content-adaptive JPEG steganography. *IEEE Transactions on Information Forensics and Security*, June 2016. To appear.

[9] T. Denemark and J. Fridrich. Improving selection-channel-aware steganalysis features. In A. Alattar and N. D. Memon, editors, *Proceedings IS&T, Electronic Imaging, Media Watermarking, Security, and Forensics 2016*, San Francisco, CA, February 14–18, 2016.

[10] T. Denemark, V. Sedighi, V. Holub, R. Cogranne, and J. Fridrich. Selection-channel-aware rich model for steganalysis of digital images. In *IEEE International Workshop on Information Forensics and Security*, Atlanta, GA, December 3–5, 2014.

[11] T. Filler, T. Pevný, and P. Bas. BOSS (Break Our Steganography System). http://www.agents.cz/boss, July 2010.

[12] J. Fridrich and J. Kodovský. Rich models for steganalysis of digital images. *IEEE Transactions on*

Information Forensics and Security, 7(3):868–882, June 2011.

[13] J. Fridrich, T. Pevný, and J. Kodovský. Statistically undetectable JPEG steganography: Dead ends, challenges, and opportunities. In J. Dittmann and J. Fridrich, editors, *Proceedings of the 9th ACM Multimedia & Security Workshop*, pages 3–14, Dallas, TX, September 20–21, 2007.

[14] M. Goljan, R. Cogranne, and J. Fridrich. Rich model for steganalysis of color images. In *Sixth IEEE International Workshop on Information Forensics and Security*, Atlanta, GA, December 3–5, 2014.

[15] L. Guo, J. Ni, and Y.-Q. Shi. An efficient JPEG steganographic scheme using uniform embedding. In *Fourth IEEE International Workshop on Information Forensics and Security*, Tenerife, Spain, December 2–5, 2012.

[16] L. Guo, J. Ni, and Y. Q. Shi. Uniform embedding for efficient JPEG steganography. *IEEE Transactions on Information Forensics and Security*, 9(5), 2014.

[17] V. Holub and J. Fridrich. Designing steganographic distortion using directional filters. In *Fourth IEEE International Workshop on Information Forensics and Security*, Tenerife, Spain, December 2–5, 2012.

[18] V. Holub and J. Fridrich. Random projections of residuals for digital image steganalysis. *IEEE Transactions on Information Forensics and Security*, 8(12):1996–2006, December 2013.

[19] V. Holub and J. Fridrich. Low-complexity features for JPEG steganalysis using undecimated DCT. *IEEE Transactions on Information Forensics and Security*, 10(2):219–228, Feb 2015.

[20] V. Holub and J. Fridrich. Phase-aware projection model for steganalysis of JPEG images. In A. Alattar and N. D. Memon, editors, *Proceedings SPIE, Electronic Imaging, Media Watermarking, Security, and Forensics 2015*, volume 9409, San Francisco, CA, February 8–12, 2015.

[21] V. Holub, J. Fridrich, and T. Denemark. Universal distortion design for steganography in an arbitrary domain. *EURASIP Journal on Information Security, Special Issue on Revised Selected Papers of the 1st ACM IH and MMS Workshop*, 2014:1, 2014.

[22] A. D. Ker and T. Pevný. The steganographer is the outlier: Realistic large-scale steganalysis. *IEEE Transactions on Information Forensics and Security*, 9(9):1424–1435, September 2014.

[23] J. Kodovský and J. Fridrich. Steganalysis in high dimensions: Fusing classifiers built on random subspaces. In A. Alattar, N. D. Memon, E. J. Delp, and J. Dittmann, editors, *Proceedings SPIE, Electronic Imaging, Media Watermarking, Security and Forensics III*, volume 7880, pages OL 1–13, San Francisco, CA, January 23–26, 2011.

[24] J. Kodovský and J. Fridrich. Steganalysis of JPEG images using rich models. In A. Alattar, N. D. Memon, and E. J. Delp, editors, *Proceedings SPIE, Electronic Imaging, Media Watermarking, Security, and Forensics 2012*, volume 8303, pages 0A 1–13, San Francisco, CA, January 23–26, 2012.

[25] J. Kodovský, J. Fridrich, and V. Holub. Ensemble classifiers for steganalysis of digital media. *IEEE*

[26] B. Li, M. Wang, and J. Huang. A new cost function for spatial image steganography. In *Proceedings IEEE, International Conference on Image Processing, ICIP*, Paris, France, October 27–30, 2014.

[27] I. Lubenko and A. D. Ker. Steganalysis with mismatched covers: Do simple classifiers help. In J. Dittmann, S. Katzenbeisser, and S. Craver, editors, *Proc. 13th ACM Workshop on Multimedia and Security*, pages 11–18, Coventry, UK, September 6–7 2012.

[28] F. Perronnin, J. Sanchez, and Yan Liu. Large-scale image categorization with explicit data embedding. In *Computer Vision and Pattern Recognition (CVPR), 2010 IEEE Conference on*, pages 2297–2304, June 2010.

[29] T. Pevný and A. D. Ker. The challenges of rich features in universal steganalysis. In A. Alattar, N. D. Memon, and C. Heitzenrater, editors, *Proceedings SPIE, Electronic Imaging, Media Watermarking, Security, and Forensics 2013*, volume 8665, pages 0M 1–15, San Francisco, CA, February 5–7, 2013.

[30] B. Schölkopf and A. Smola. *Learning with Kernels: Support Vector Machines, Regularization, Optimization, and Beyond (Adaptive Computation and Machine Learning)*. The MIT Press, 2001.

[31] V. Sedighi, R. Cogranne, and J. Fridrich. Content-adaptive steganography by minimizing statistical detectability. *IEEE Transactions on Information Forensics and Security*, 11(2):221–234, 2016.

[32] X. Song, F. Liu, C. Yang, X. Luo, and Y. Zhang. Steganalysis of adaptive JPEG steganography using 2D Gabor filters. In P. Comesa na, J. Fridrich, and A. Alattar, editors, *3rd ACM IH&MMSec. Workshop*, Portland, Oregon, June 17–19, 2015.

[33] W. Tang, H. Li, W. Luo, and J. Huang. Adaptive steganalysis against WOW embedding algorithm. In A. Uhl, S. Katzenbeisser, R. Kwitt, and A. Piva, editors, *2nd ACM IH&MMSec. Workshop*, pages 91–96, Salzburg, Austria, June 11–13, 2014.

[34] A. Vedaldi and A. Zisserman. Efficient additive kernels via explicit feature maps. *Pattern Analysis and Machine Intelligence, IEEE Transactions on*, 34(3):480–492, March 2012.

Transactions on Information Forensics and Security, 7(2):432–444, 2012.

Information Hiding in the RSA Modulus

Stefan Wüller
Dept. of Computer Science
RWTH Aachen University
Mies-van-der-Rohe Str. 15
52074 Aachen, Germany
wueller@itsec.rwth-
aachen.de

Marián Kühnel
Dept. of Computer Science
RWTH Aachen University
Mies-van-der-Rohe Str. 15
52074 Aachen, Germany
kuehnel@itsec.rwth-
aachen.de

Ulrike Meyer
Dept. of Computer Science
RWTH Aachen University
Mies-van-der-Rohe Str. 15
52074 Aachen, Germany
meyer@itsec.rwth-
aachen.de

ABSTRACT

The manufacturer of an asymmetric backdoor for a public key cryptosystem manipulates the key generation process in such a way that he can extract the private key or other secret information from the user's public key by involving his own public/private key pair. All asymmetric backdoors in major public key cryptosystems including RSA differ substantially in their implementation approaches and in their quality in satisfying backdoor related properties like confidentiality and concealment. While some of them meet neither of these two properties very well, others provide a high level of confidentiality but none of them is concealing, which limits their use for covert implementation. In this paper we introduce two novel asymmetric RSA backdoors, both following the approach to embed bits of one of the RSA prime factors in the user's public RSA modulus. While our first backdoor provides confidentiality for a sufficiently large key length, it might be detected under certain circumstances. The second backdoor extends the first one such that it additionally provides concealment and is thus particularly suitable for covert implementation.

Keywords

RSA; Factorization; Backdoor; Trapdoor; SETUP

1. INTRODUCTION

Public key cryptosystems are used worldwide to provide confidentiality, integrity, and non-repudiation to electronic communication. While the theoretical security of all commonly used public key cryptosystems can be verified quite easily, the correctness of design, implementation, and execution in a black box device is assumed to be rather hard. In fact, once the device has been produced and sealed, there is no generic approach to preclude the existence of a backdoor.

Virtually all backdoors designed for public key cryptosystems act up to the principle that the manufacturer of a cryptographic device modifies the underlying key generation al-

IH&MMSec 2016, June 20-23, 2016, Vigo, Spain

© 2016 ACM. ISBN 978-1-4503-4290-2/16/06. . . $15.00

DOI: http://dx.doi.org/10.1145/2909827.2930804

gorithm which gives him an exclusive ability to reconstruct the target user's private key from the corresponding public key. Based on the awareness of the user, we differentiate between illegitimate espionage and legal key escrow. The apparent motivation for the former is economic interest, e.g., of companies to spy on their customers for data aggregation and advertising purposes in order to gain a subtle but decisive advantage over competitors. Moreover, governments or security agencies might be potential stakeholders cooperating with companies implementing and distributing cryptosystems in hardware or software. On the other hand, legitimate uses of backdoors include key retrieval services for users that lost their private key or for companies that want to regain access to data encrypted with the public key of a former or deceased employee.

There has been a lot of prior work in the area of designing backdoors for public key cryptosystems. This can be divided into work on asymmetric and symmetric backdoors. Asymmetric backdoors (e.g., [12], [13]) involve the manufacturer's public key to hide information in the user's public key such that the user's private key can be reconstructed with the help of the manufacturer's private key. Symmetric backdoors (e.g., [2], [6], [5]) involve the manufacturer's secret symmetric key which is used for both hiding information in the user's public key and for reconstructing the user's private key. In this paper, we concentrate on asymmetric backdoors which have the advantage that even for the case that the cryptographic device is successfully reverse engineered, the decryption key of the manufacturer remains secret.

The essential properties a backdoor can have are the following: the backdoored cryptosystem remains secure against attackers (*Confidentiality*); the manufacturer is able to reconstruct the private key from each user's public key which was generated with the backdoored cryptosystem (*Completeness*); the backdoored cryptosystem remains hidden from users who additionally are given access to an implementation of the corresponding honest cryptosystem (*Concealment*).

Existing backdoors differ substantially in their hiding and reconstruction techniques as well as their quality in satisfying Confidentiality and Concealment: in some neither of the two properties are met very well (e.g., [12, 13]), others satisfy Confidentiality but unfortunately do not meet the Concealment to a satisfying extent (e.g., [15]). In this paper we propose two novel backdoors PHP (Prime Hiding Prime) and PHP'. The first backdoor PHP modifies the RSA key generation function in such a way that the information required for the private key reconstruction is directly hidden in the user's RSA modulus. The second backdoor PHP' additionally blinds the secret information to hide the backdoor from the user and thus an (external) attacker. In order to reduce the amount of secret information hidden in the RSA modulus, PHP' takes advantage of Coppersmith's factorization attack [4]. The analyses of both backdoors prove that PHP is confidentiality preserving for sufficiently large key lengths, complete, but (under certain circumstances) not concealing whereas PHP' is confidentiality preserving for sufficiently large key lengths, complete, and concealing at the same time.

After outlining the RSA cryptosystem and giving the definitions of the essential backdoor properties in Section 2, we give an overview of prominent RSA backdoors in Section 3. Our novel RSA backdoors and the analyses of their properties are covered by Section 4. Finally, we compare the properties of PHP and PHP' to prominent RSA backdoors in Section 5 and give a conclusion in Section 6.

2. PRELIMINARIES

In this section we recall the RSA cryptosystem and define the backdoor related properties.

2.1 The RSA cryptosystem

Let l_x be the bit length of an integer x, Φ_{l_x} be the set of all prime numbers with bit length l_x, $\mathbb{N}_{l_x}$ be the set of all l_x-bit integers, and let $\varphi(x)$ be the Euler's totient function. Furthermore, let $x \in_{rnd} M$ denote that x is drawn from M uniformly at random.

The RSA public key cryptosystem consists of a key generation, an encryption, and a decryption function. For key generation of bit length l_n, two primes $p, q \in_{rnd} \Phi_{l_n/2}$ are selected and the public modulus $n = p \cdot q$ is computed. Next, the public exponent $e \in_{rnd} \mathbb{N}\setminus\{1\}$ is drawn such that $gcd(e, \varphi(n)) = 1$. The pair (n, e) forms the user's public key. Finally, the private key d is computed by $d = e^{-1} \bmod \varphi(n)$. For the encryption of a plaintext $m \in \mathbb{Z}_n$ the corresponding ciphertext $c \in \mathbb{Z}_n$ is computed by $c = m^e \bmod n$ where (n, e) is the public key of the receiver. Upon receiving the ciphertext, the receiver is able to decrypt c by computing $m = c^d \bmod n$. The keyspace $\mathcal{K}_{\mathrm{RSA}}$ of RSA is the set of all triplets (n, e, d), where n, e, and d are generated as described above. We refer to the space of one single key component by $\mathcal{K}_{\mathrm{RSA},\alpha}$ where $\alpha \in \{n, e, d\}$. The same notation is used throughout the paper to refer to the cardinality of the keyspace: $\mathcal{N}_{\mathrm{RSA}} = |\mathcal{K}_{\mathrm{RSA}}|$.

The security of a cryptosystem is given by a security parameter s. In the case of RSA, s refers to the bit length of the prime factors of the RSA modulus. Besides s, the security of the RSA cryptosystem is based on the RSA Assumption which leads to the RSA Secret Key Assumption:

ASSUMPTION 1. (RSA Assumption [1]). *Given a public key (n, e) and a ciphertext c, for a sufficiently large security parameter s it is infeasible to compute plaintext message m such that $c = m^e \bmod n$.*

ASSUMPTION 2. (RSA Secret Key Assumption). *Given a public RSA key (n, e), for a sufficiently large security parameter s it is difficult to find the corresponding private exponent d.*

The following theorem, referring to Coppersmith's factorization attack, is exploited by the manufacturer's private key reconstruction function of PHP':

THEOREM 1. (Coppersmith [4]). *Given $n = pq$ and the high- or low-order $1/4 \cdot log_2(n)$ bits of p, one can recover the prime factors p, q of n in time polynomial in $log(n)$.*

Finally, for estimating the keyspace of PHP and PHP' in our security analysis, we use the prime number theorem which is defined as follows:

THEOREM 2. (Prime Number Theorem [8]). *Let $\pi(n)$ be the number of all primes less than or equal to n. It holds that $\pi(n) \sim \frac{n}{ln(n)}$.*

2.2 Backdoor Formalization

The definitions of the backdoor related properties we use throughout our paper draw on Arboit's definition of a secure backdoor [3] which is more precise than other backdoor definitions in literature w.r.t. the properties a backdoor has to fulfill (see Section 3).

Let $\mathfrak{G}$ and $\mathfrak{G}'$ be the honest and the backdoored cryptosystem consisting of the (backdoored) key generator, the encryption, and the decryption function of RSA, respectively. Furthermore, let $\mathfrak{B}$ and $\mathfrak{B}'$ be the blackbox devices provided by the manufacturer where $\mathfrak{G}$ and $\mathfrak{G}'$ are implemented on. We consider the black box device to be a physical oracle the user can access to generate keys as well as to decrypt and encrypt messages. Given two blackbox devices $\mathfrak{B}$ and $\mathfrak{B}'$, the user tries to distinguish between $\mathfrak{B}$ and $\mathfrak{B}'$ based on the analysis of statistical properties of the keys generated with $\mathfrak{G}$ and $\mathfrak{G}'$, differences among the implementations of $\mathfrak{G}$ and $\mathfrak{G}'$, as well as side channel related properties of $\mathfrak{B}$ and $\mathfrak{B}'$. As opposed to the user, an external attacker who tries to distinguish between public keys generated with $\mathfrak{G}$ and $\mathfrak{G}'$ only has access to the user's public key.

Let (k_{pub}, k_{priv}) and (K_{pub}, K_{priv}) be the user's and the manufacturer's public and private key, respectively.

According to [3], each $\mathfrak{G}'$ can be modeled by the composition of an information compression function $\mathcal{C}$, an encryption function $\mathcal{E}$, and an embedding function $\mathcal{M}$: $k'_{pub} = \mathcal{M} \circ \mathcal{E} \circ \mathcal{C}(k'_{priv})$, where k'_{pub} is either k_{pub} itself or a component of k_{pub} and k'_{priv} is either equal to k_{priv}, a part of the private key, or information allowing to compute k_{priv}. Breaking a backdoor down in those three functions facilitates the analysis and the comparison of backdoors. For the case that a randomization of $\mathcal{M}$, $\mathcal{E}$, or $\mathcal{C}$ is required, a sufficient amount of random bits can be provided by an implicit parameter.

The purpose of function $\mathcal{C}(k'_{priv}) = k_C$ is to extract a piece of information k_C from k'_{priv} such that if k_C is communicated through k_{pub} to the manufacturer, he is able to recover k_{priv} from this piece of information.

DEFINITION 1. (Information Compression Function $\mathcal{C}$). *$\mathcal{C}$ is an arbitrary function of k'_{priv} which extracts sufficient information k_C from its input in order to efficiently reconstruct k_{priv} from the knowledge of k_C and k_{pub} only.*

Function $\mathcal{E}$ is an asymmetric encryption function which is applied to k_C to hide this sensitive piece of information from unauthorized parties except the manufacturer who possesses the appropriate secret key K_{priv} which allows to decrypt $\mathcal{E}(k_C)$.

DEFINITION 2. (Encryption Function $\mathcal{E}$). *$\mathcal{E}$ is an asymmetric encryption function of $k_C = \mathcal{C}(k'_{priv})$ where the output value distribution of $k_E = \mathcal{E}(k_C)$ is computationally indistinguishable from uniform.*

l_x	bit length of integer x
$x \rfloor_y$	y least significant bits of integer x
Φ_{l_x}	set of prime numbers of bit length l_x
$\mathbb{N}_{l_x}$	set of all l_x-bit integers
$x \in_{rnd} M$	sample x uniformly a random from M
$\mathcal{K}$	key space
$\mathcal{N}$	key space cardinality
(k_{pub}, k_{priv})	public/private key of the user
(K_{pub}, K_{priv})	public/private key of manufacturer

Table 1: Notation used throughout the paper.

The third function, $\mathcal{M}$, accomplishes the embedding of $\mathcal{E} \circ \mathcal{C}(k'_{priv})$ into k_{pub} chosen in such a way that the backdoored keys ideally have the same statistical properties as the honest keys.

DEFINITION 3. (Embedding Function $\mathcal{M}$). $\mathcal{M}$ is an invertible function on $\mathcal{E} \circ \mathcal{C}(k'_{priv})$ determining the bit positions of the embedding and the probabilistic assignation of those bits of k'_{pub} which are not involved in the embedding of backdoor information.

We refer to the function applied on k_{pub} by the manufacturer in order to reconstruct k'_{priv} as $\mathfrak{R}_{\mathfrak{G}'} = \mathcal{C}^{-1} \circ \mathcal{E}^{-1} \circ \mathcal{M}^{-1}(k_{pub})$.

Emerged from the literature, the essential properties a backdoor can have are *Confidentiality*, *Completeness*, and *Concealment*.

Confidentiality considers if the confidentiality of the underlying cryptosystem is influenced through the existence of a backdoor. Evaluating this property involves analyzing if the effective key size of the user's key generated with $\mathfrak{B}'$ corresponds to the desired key size.

DEFINITION 4. (Confidentiality). *The external attacker and the user are not able to invert $\mathcal{M} \circ \mathcal{E} \circ \mathcal{C}(k'_{priv})$.*

Completeness considers whether or not the manufacturer is able to reconstruct the user's private key from the corresponding public key for each public key which was generated with a backdoor distributed by the manufacturer.

DEFINITION 5. (Completeness). *For each k_{pub} generated with $\mathfrak{G}'$, the manufacturer is able to reconstruct k'_{priv} from k_{pub} by computing $\mathfrak{R}_{\mathfrak{G}'}(k_{pub}) = \mathcal{C}^{-1} \circ \mathcal{E}^{-1} \circ \mathcal{M}^{-1}(k_{pub}) = k'_{priv}$.*

Concealment considers to what extent a backdoor is traceable for the external attacker and the user. This requires the analysis of a set of sub-properties Concealment directly depends on.

DEFINITION 6. (Concealment). *Given access to $\mathfrak{B}$ and $\mathfrak{B}'$, for the external attacker and the user it is not possible to distinguish between $\mathfrak{B}$ and $\mathfrak{B}'$ by analyzing the following related sub-properties:*

KCC: Analyzing the keyspaces $\mathcal{K}_{\mathfrak{G}}$ and $\mathcal{K}_{\mathfrak{G}'}$ does not contribute to efficiently distinguish between $\mathfrak{B}$ and $\mathfrak{B}'$ (Keyspace (K) Cardinality (C) Consistency (C)).

DC: Analyzing the distribution of the bits of keys generated with $\mathfrak{G}$ and $\mathfrak{G}'$ does not contribute to efficiently distinguish between $\mathfrak{B}$ and $\mathfrak{B}'$ (Bit Distribution (D) Consistency (C) of Generated Keys).

VCC: Differences w.r.t. the correlation of variables in $\mathfrak{G}$ and $\mathfrak{G}'$ do not contribute to efficiently distinguish between $\mathfrak{B}$ and $\mathfrak{B}'$ (Variable (V) Correlation (C) Consistency (C)).

CC: Differences w.r.t. the time complexities of $\mathfrak{G}$ and $\mathfrak{G}'$ do not contribute to efficiently distinguish between $\mathfrak{B}$ and $\mathfrak{B}'$ (Complexity (C) Consistency (C)).

AM: $\mathfrak{B}'$ does not make use of additional memory for purposes of concealment (Absence (A) of Additional Memory (M) Usage for Purposes of Concealment).

The sub-properties of Concealment can be divided into three groups: key related, algorithm related, and side channel related properties. In the following we give an informal description of how to evaluate each of these sub-properties based on [3]. Subsequently, we present a classification scheme for the defined backdoor related properties.

KCC. In practice, modifications made to an honest key generator $\mathfrak{G}$ to hide secret information within k_{pub} typically affects the key space $\mathcal{K}_{\mathfrak{G}'}$ of $\mathfrak{G}'$ which might contribute to efficiently distinguish between $\mathfrak{B}$ and $\mathfrak{B}'$. To evaluate KCC for $\mathfrak{G}'$ w.r.t. the security parameter s, the ratio of cardinality of $\mathcal{K}_{\mathfrak{G}'}$ and $\mathcal{K}_{\mathfrak{G}}$ is computed: $\mathcal{R}(s) = \mathcal{N}_{\mathfrak{G}'}(s)/\mathcal{N}_{\mathfrak{G}}(s)$. Note that for RSA, the ratio of cardinality has the form $\mathcal{R}(s) = 2^{c(s) \cdot s} \cdot f(s)$ where $c(s) \leq 0$ and $log_2(1/f(s)) \in o(s)$, i.e., $1/f(s)$ is negligible [3].

DC. DC considers to which degree the bits of k_{pub} are influenced by the embedding of k_E. For $\mathfrak{G}$ and $\mathfrak{G}'$, it is not necessarily the case that all bits in k_{pub} have the same distribution [5]. If some bits of k_{pub} in $\mathfrak{G}'$ underlie another distribution than the appropriate bits in $\mathfrak{G}$, then this may reveal the existence of the backdoor by analyzing generated keys. To evaluate DC for $\mathfrak{G}'$, we compare the distributions of the concatenation of the influenced bits of k_{pub} by $\mathcal{M}(k_E)$ w.r.t. $\mathfrak{G}$ and $\mathfrak{G}'$ via their statistical distance referred to as $\mathcal{D}_{\mathfrak{G}'} \in [0, 1]$. If $\mathcal{D}_{\mathfrak{G}'}$ is negligible, the distributions of k_{pub} are considered to be statistically indistinguishable for $\mathfrak{G}$ and $\mathfrak{G}'$.

VCC. VCC concerns *key regeneration* [5, 3] which is the possibility of the user to generate a new key pair keeping certain key parameters fixed while others are refreshed. In $\mathfrak{G}'$, there may exist key components of successively generated keys which are more correlated than those in $\mathfrak{G}$. Furthermore, VCC covers the case that no key regeneration is necessary since the backdoor can be revealed solely on the basis of the key parameters. We distinguish whether or not the manufacturer's key K_{pub} is publicly known.

		failed	*poor*	*good*
Confidentiality		effective keysize is reduced more than 50%	effective keysize is at most halved	no reduction of effective keysize
Completeness		$\neg \forall k_{pub}\ \mathfrak{R}_{\mathfrak{G}'}(k_{pub}) = k'_{priv}$	—	$\forall k_{pub}\ \mathfrak{R}_{\mathfrak{G}'}(k_{pub}) = k'_{priv}$
Concealment	KCC	$c(s) \leq -3/2$	$-3/2 < c(s) < -1/2$	$c(s) \geq -1/2$
	DC	$\mathcal{D}_{\mathfrak{G}'} > 0$	$\mathcal{D}_{\mathfrak{G}'} \approx 0$ with restrictions on the bounds of $\mathcal{K}_{\mathfrak{G}'}$	$\mathcal{D}_{\mathfrak{G}'} \approx 0$
	VCC	variable correlation w/o K_{pub}	variable correlation given K_{pub}	no var. correlation
	CC	$\mathcal{T}_{\mathfrak{G}'}$ is at least quadratic in $\mathcal{T}_{\mathfrak{G}}$	$\mathcal{T}_{\mathfrak{G}'}$ is more than linear but less than quadratic in $\mathcal{T}_{\mathfrak{G}}$	$\mathcal{T}_{\mathfrak{G}'}$ is linear in $\mathcal{T}_{\mathfrak{G}}$
	AM	NM (and VM) is used	only VM is used	neither VM nor NM is used

Table 2: Classification scheme for backdoor related properties.

CC. CC considers the time complexity $\mathcal{T}_{\mathfrak{G}'}$ of $\mathfrak{G}'$. If the time complexity of $\mathfrak{G}'$ is linear in the time complexity of $\mathfrak{G}$, then adapting the hardware of $\mathfrak{B}$ or $\mathfrak{B}'$ for matching the running times of $\mathfrak{G}$ and $\mathfrak{G}'$ is possible. According to [3], the complexity of a backdoored RSA key generator in terms of the complexity of an honest RSA key generator can be expressed in practice by $\mathcal{T}_{\mathfrak{G}'} = t_1^a \cdot t(\mathcal{F})^b + t_2^c$, where t_1 and t_2 refer to the complexities of the key parameter generations in $\mathfrak{G}$, a, b, and c are constant integer exponents, and $t(\mathcal{F})$ denotes the time complexity of a non-instantiated function $\mathcal{F}$ which does not occur in $\mathfrak{G}$.

AM. There are two types of memory a backdoor may make use of to hide itself from the user: non-volatile memory (NM) and volatile memory (VM). Backdoors which transmit information of the previous key generation in order to reconstruct private keys make use of non-volatile memory. Other backdoors require volatile memory to satisfy the variable correlation property under key regeneration analysis. The usage of NM is easier to detect than the usage of VM. Since it is less discreet, it may require more system resources, and if it is reset then the variable correlation and the functioning of the backdoor might be influenced.

The classification scheme we use in order to evaluate the defined backdoor related properties (see Table 2) is inspired by [3]. The bounds of $c(s)$ used to evaluate KCC are restricted to RSA backdoors. Those bounds have to be adapted accordingly for backdoors of other cryptosystems (cf. [3]). If a backdoor related property is classified with *good* we consider the property to be satisfied while a property classified with *failed* is considered to be unsatisfied. The additional classifier *poor* allows for a more subtle differentiation between different backdoors w.r.t. their properties. Addition-

ally to the classification given in Table 2, we characterize KCC to be *asymptotically exact* if $lim_{s \to \infty} c(s) = 0$ holds.

3. RELATED WORK

The first relevant asymmetric backdoors for RSA have been proposed by Young and Yung [12]. One of their first approaches, we refer to as HE, is to encrypt one of the two prime factors of the target modulus with the manufacturer's public key and use the resulting ciphertext as public exponent. A further approach, PAP (Pretty-Awful-Privacy) [12], hides the secret information of one prime factor in the bit representation of the second prime factor: the first prime factor is randomly generated while the bits of the second prime factor are derived from random bits and information of the first prime factor. A second version of PAP, PAP' [13], uses ElGamal instead of RSA in order to hide bits of one of the user's prime factor within the user's public modulus. Another quite complex mechanism for embedding secret information of one of the generated prime factors in the user's public modulus has been introduced in [14]. The corresponding backdoor, referred to as PP, uses the Rabin cryptosytem [10] to encrypt the secret information. With a further backdoor of Young and Yung, we refer to as EC [15], the authors propose to involve an elliptic curve Diffie-Hellman key to enable a compact embedding of the secret information into the user's RSA modulus.

First attempts on formalizing the properties of cryptographic backdoors have been made by Young and Yung who devised several SETUP (Secretly Embedded Trapdoor with Universal Protection) definitions, each a set of properties a backdoor has to fulfill to reach a specific level of security [12] - [16]. For example, in [13], Young and Yung introduced the notion of weak, regular and strong SETUPs in order to claim that PAP introduced in [12] can be turned into a strong SETUP. Two more papers followed ([15], [16]) and the comparison between different SETUP variants, each requiring different sets of properties, became blurred. A second attempt has been made by Arboit [3], who devised the definition of a *Secure Backdoor*. In comparison to SETUP definitions, the definition of a secure backdoor is more explicit w.r.t. backdoor related properties. For that reason, our paper draws on Arboit's definition [3] of a secure backdoor. Nevertheless, we omit to give a definition of a special kind of backdoor to allow for a fine-grained comparison between various backdoors instead of merely distinguishing whether or not a considered backdoor satisfies a given backdoor definition.

Table 3 in Section 5 summarizes the classification of the properties of the backdoors described in this section w.r.t. the classification scheme depicted in Table 2.

Backdoor HE *fails* in satisfying KCC and VCC [3]. Since the encrypted prime factor and the public exponent is of the order of the manufacturer's modulus, the presence of a backdoor generated with the algorithm can easily be suspected. In addition, it is impossible to freely choose or fix small public RSA exponents such as 0x11 or 0x10001 which makes HE impractical for many applications. PAP gives an attacker a relative advantage in distinguishing backdoored from honest keys due to the different distribution of the most significant bits in the moduli. The first two most significant bits of moduli generated with regular RSA are equal to 0x01 with probability 0.38, 0x10 with probability 0.48 and 0x11 with probability 0.14 which does not hold for PAP [5]. PAP' does also not solve the problem of the improperly distributed bits of a generated public modulus [3] such that DC for both backdoors are classified to be *failed*. Furthermore, Confidentiality for PAP' is classified to be *poor* since the user's effective key size is halved which is due to the fact that the manufacturer's key size is half of the user's key size. Even for PP, the user's effective key size is halved for the same reason. According to [3], the number of generable keys and the distribution of n is affected by PP. With regard to our classification scheme, KCC is classified as *poor* and DC is classified as *failed*. EC overcomes the lack of confidentiality by involving an elliptic curve Diffie-Hellman key for the manufacturer but nevertheless *fails* in satisfying Concealment w.r.t. sub-property DC and CC, see Section 2 and [3]. Overall, none of the above prominent asymmetric backdoors from literature satisfy Concealment.

4. NOVEL RSA BACKDOORS

The general idea of the newly proposed RSA backdoors is to hide enough information within the modulus so that the manufacturer is able to derive the corresponding private key from the public key. In both of our RSA backdoors, PHP and PHP', the secret information is hidden in one of the prime factors of the user's public modulus.

4.1 Design of PHP

In PHP, the underlying RSA prime factor generation function is modified, see Algorithm 4.1. PHP involves the manufacturer's public RSA key (N, E) to hide secret information in one of the prime factors of the user's public modulus n of his public key (n, e). First, a random prime p of bit size $l_n/2$ is chosen. If the encryption of p with the manufacturer's public key and the subsequent multiplication with the inverse of p in modulo N results in a prime of $\Phi_{l_n/2}$,

then the pending prime q is set accordingly. Otherwise, a fresh random prime p is picked and the computation steps are repeated. If q is found, n is computed as usual. The remaining functions of the RSA cryptosystem are not altered. In particular, the public exponent e is chosen at random, i.e., $e \in_{rnd} \mathbb{N} \setminus \{1\}$ such that $gcd(e, \varphi(n)) = 1$.

> **Input**: $l_n, (N, E)$
> **Output**: p, q, n
> 1 **repeat**
> 2   pick a $p \in_{rnd} \Phi_{l_n/2}$.
> 3   compute $q = p^E \cdot p^{-1} \mod N$.
> 4 **until** q *is prime and* $l_q = l_n/2$.
> 5 compute $n = p \cdot q$.
> 6 **return** p, q, n.

Algorithm 4.1: Modified prime factor generation of PHP.

To reconstruct one of the prime factors, the manufacturer decrypts n with his private key D :

$$n^D \equiv (p \cdot q)^D \equiv (p \cdot p^E \cdot p^{-1})^D \equiv p^{E \cdot D} \equiv p \bmod N.$$

Once the manufacturer knows a prime factor of n, it is trivial to compute the pending one and the user's private key. Note that the user in possession of the manufacturer's public key is able to verify whether or not his modulus has been generated with PHP by comparing q to $p^E \cdot p^{-1} \mod N$.

4.2 Property Analysis of PHP

For PHP, we set $k'_{priv}, \mathcal{C}, \mathcal{E}$, and $\mathcal{M}$ as follows: k'_{priv} equals the first prime factor of n. $\mathcal{C}$ is chosen to be the identity function since PHP communicates the entire information of p to the manufacturer: $\mathcal{C}(p) = p = k_C$. $\mathcal{E}(k_C)$ corresponds to the RSA encryption of k_C with the manufacturer's public key (N, E): $\mathcal{E}(k_C) = k_C^E \mod N = k_E$. k_E is embedded into the user's public RSA modulus n by applying $\mathcal{M}(k_E) = (k_E \cdot p^{-1} \mod N) \cdot p = n = k'_{pub}$.

In the following, we analyze the properties of PHP according to the definitions given in Section 2.

Confidentiality (*poor*). Assume that an external attacker is in possession of (n, e) and (N, E). The external attacker is able to invert $\mathcal{M}$ by computing $k_E = n \mod N$. k_E is the encryption of p with the manufacturer's public RSA key of bit length l_N which is half of the length of the user's RSA key of bit length l_n. To invert $\mathcal{E}$, i.e., to compute p and with that k_{priv}, the external attacker has to break RSA of key size l_N instead of key size l_n. Thus, to ensure that k_{priv} remains secret the bit size of N has to be chosen large enough. Since the security of the user's RSA key pair depends on N, Confidentiality is classified as *poor*. If, however, the external attacker does not know (N, E), then the user's private key retains the intended security.

Completeness (*good*). The manufacturer is able to compute k'_{priv} from k_{pub} by applying $\mathcal{C}^{-1} \circ \mathcal{E}^{-1} \circ \mathcal{M}^{-1}(k_{pub})$, where $\mathcal{M}^{-1}(k_{pub} = (n, e)) = n \mod N$, $\mathcal{E}^{-1} = k_E^D \mod N$, and $\mathcal{C}^{-1}(k_C) = \mathcal{C}(k_C)$. The composition of the three functions can be simplified to

$$\mathfrak{R}_{\text{PHP}}(k_{pub} = (n, e)) = n^D \bmod N = p = k'_{priv}.$$

According to the classification scheme presented in Table 2, Completeness is classified as *good*.

Concealment. To analyze Concealment for PHP, we have to consider the sub-properties Concealment directly depends on (see Section 2).

KCC (good, asym. exact). Instead of considering the cardinality of $\mathcal{K}_{\text{PHP}}$, it is sufficient to analyze the space q is chosen from: Since PHP does not influence the choice of the public and private exponents e, d, $\mathcal{N}_{\text{RSA},e}$ is equal to $\mathcal{N}_{\text{PHP},e}$ and $\mathcal{N}_{\text{RSA},d}$ is equal to $\mathcal{N}_{\text{PHP},d}$. The difference of $\mathcal{N}_{\text{RSA},n}$ and $\mathcal{N}_{\text{PHP},n}$ directly depends on the cardinality of the set of possible primes for q in PHP referred to as Λ. Thus, the task to determine the difference between $\mathcal{N}_{\text{RSA}}$ and $\mathcal{N}_{\text{PHP}}$ is reduced to determine the difference between $\Phi_{l_n/2}$ and Λ. For RSA, the security parameter s corresponds to half of the bits of the key, whereas the length of the key is considered to be l_n.

Let $N \approx 2^{l_n/2}$ so that p is randomly chosen from $\Phi_{l_n/2}$ in PHP. We can estimate the cardinality of the set of all primes by applying the prime number theorem:

$$|\Phi_{l_n/2}| = \pi(2^{l_n/2}) - \pi(2^{l_n/2-1}) \approx \frac{1}{2} \cdot \pi(2^{l_n/2})$$
$$\approx 2^{l_n/2-1-log_2(l_n/2)}.$$

Let Ψ be defined as follows:

$$\Psi = \{f(p)|f(p) = p^E \cdot p^{-1} \bmod N, \ p \in \Phi_{l_n/2}\},$$

where $p^E \cdot p^{-1} \bmod N = f(p) = p^{E-1} \bmod N$. For

$$\Psi^* = \{f(x)|f(x) = p^{E-1} \bmod N, x \in \mathbb{Z}_N\},$$

we have

$$|\Psi^*| = (1 + \frac{p-1}{gcd(p-1, E-1)}) \cdot (1 + \frac{q-1}{gcd(q-1, E-1)}).$$

Since $E - 1$ is even, $|\Psi^*|$ is maximal for the case that $E - 1$ satisfies

$$gcd(p-1, E-1) = gcd(q-1, E-1) = 2. \quad (1)$$

Since the manufacturer can freely choose E, we assume Equation 1 in the following and thus $|\Psi^*| > N/4$. This result can be used to estimate the cardinality of Ψ as $|\Psi| \approx |\Phi_{l_n/2}|/4$.

Assuming that the elements in Ψ are close to be uniformly distributed over $\mathbb{Z}_N$, about half of the elements in Ψ are $l_n/2$-bit integers. Let $\Psi' \subset \Psi$ be the set of all elements in Ψ of bit length $l_n/2$: $\Psi' := \{\psi \mid \psi \in \Psi, \ l_\psi = l_n/2\}$. It holds that $|\Psi'| \approx 1/2 \cdot |\Psi| = 2^{l_n/2-4-log_2(l_n/2)}$.

The probability that an element in Ψ' is a prime can be estimated by dividing the cardinality of the set of all $l_n/2$-bit primes by the cardinality of all $l_n/2$-bit integers:

$$\mathbb{P}(q \in \Phi_{l_n/2}|q \in_{rnd} \mathbb{N}_{l_n/2}) = \frac{|\Phi_{l_n/2}|}{|\mathbb{N}_{l_n/2}|} = \frac{2^{l_n/2-1-log_2(l_n/2)}}{2^{l_n/2} - 2^{l_n/2-1}}$$
$$= 2^{-log_2(l_n/2)}.$$

Finally, the number of primes in Ψ' can be estimated by

$$|\Lambda| = |\Psi'| \cdot \mathbb{P}(q \in \Phi_{l_n/2}|q \in_{rnd} \mathbb{N}_{l_n/2}) = 2^{l_n/2-4-2\cdot log_2(l_n/2)}.$$

To evaluate the cardinality of Λ w.r.t. $\Phi_{l_n/2}$ we compute $\mathcal{R}(l_n/2)$:

$$\mathcal{R}(l_n/2) = \frac{\mathcal{N}_{\text{PHP}}(l_n/2)}{\mathcal{N}_{\text{RSA}}(l_n/2)} = \frac{2^{l_n/2-4-2\cdot log_2(l_n/2)}}{2^{l_n/2-1-2\cdot log_2(l_n/2)}}$$
$$= 2^{-3-log_2(l_n/2)} = 2^{c(l_n/2)\cdot l_n/2},$$

where $c(l_n/2) = (-3 - log_2(l_n/2))/(l_n/2)$. Assume that the security parameter is larger or equal than 512 bits. We have that $c(l_n/2) \geq c(512) = -0.02343$ and thus KCC is rated with *good*. Note that for increasing l_n values, the whole term converges to 0. Thus, KCC is considered to be *asymptotic exact*.

DC (good). The bits of k_{pub} in PHP which are influenced by the backdoor are the bits of n whereas the generation of the public exponent e is not influenced. Thus, to show that $\mathcal{D}_{\text{PHP}} \approx 0$, it is sufficient to show that the distribution of the bits of p and q generated with PHP is close to the corresponding distribution for the case that p and q are generated with RSA.

As, for instance, it is the case in [11], we assume that the primes p and q in RSA are generated by first choosing a random odd $l_n/2$ bit integer followed by testing it for primality. If the chosen odd integer fails the applied primality test, a new random $l_n/2$-bit odd integer is drawn or the former prime is incremented by two. In any case, the primes generated in RSA are uniformly distributed in $\Phi_{l_n/2}$.

In PHP, the first prime p is chosen in the same way as in RSA. Assume that $N \approx 2^{l_n/2}$ and that all odd values $q = p^E \cdot p^{-1} \bmod N$ with $l_q < l_n/2$ are discarded. According to the considerations of KCC w.r.t. Λ, we have that for a sufficiently large security parameter, q is close to be uniformly distributed over $\Phi_{l_n/2}$ and thus the distribution of the bits of q generated with PHP is close to the distribution of bits of q generated with RSA. Consequently, $\mathcal{D}_{\text{PHP}} \approx 0$ and DC is classified as *good*.

VCC (failed). The user is able to distinguish between PHP and RSA by analyzing the correlation of variables for PHP because the generation of q depends on p. Hence, if the user fixes p or q and initiates a key regeneration, the pending prime will be identical to the corresponding prime of the previous key generation. If the user additionally knows the manufacturer's public key (N, E), he is able to distinguish between PHP and RSA without performing a key regeneration. From his private key (n, d) the user is able to compute p and q [9]. To proof the presence of the PHP backdoor, the user solely has to check if $p = q^E \cdot q^{-1} \bmod N$ or $q = p^E \cdot p^{-1} \bmod N$ holds. According to the classification scheme presented in Table 2, VCC is classified as *failed*.

CC (failed). Let t_p and t_q be the time complexity of RSA for the generation of p and q where $t_p = t_q$. Let $\mathcal{F} = p^E \cdot p^{-1} \bmod N$. Then the time complexity for the generation of p and q in PHP, denoted by $\mathcal{T}_{\text{PHP}_{p,q}}$, leads to:

$$\mathcal{T}_{\text{PHP}_{p,q}} \approx t_q \cdot (t_p + t(\mathcal{F})) = t_q \cdot t(\mathcal{F}) + t_p^2 > t_q + t_p \approx \mathcal{T}_{\text{RSA}_{p,q}}.$$

For large l_p, l_q, $t(\mathcal{F})$ is negligible w.r.t. t_p and t_q since $t(\mathcal{F}) \in \mathcal{O}(n^2)$ and $t_p, t_q \in \mathcal{O}(l_p^4/log(l_p))$ [7]. CC for PHP is classified as *failed* because $\mathcal{T}_{\text{PHP}_{p,q}}$ is quadratic in $\mathcal{T}_{\text{RSA}_{p,q}}$.

AM (good). PHP does not use additional memory in order to avoid the correlation of variables or to communicate backdoor information to the manufacturer. Thus, AM is rated with *good*.

4.3 Design of PHP'

Our second backdoor, PHP', follows the same principles as PHP. However, the computation of the second prime factor is slightly changed. After computing the first prime factor p of n, an integer x of $l_n/4$ bits is chosen uniformly at random and is concatenated with the $l_n/4$ least significant bits of p, referred to as $p\rfloor_{l_n/4}$. The result, a blinded p, is denoted as p'. Subsequently, q is computed as in PHP but instead of encrypting p with the manufacturers public RSA key, p' is encrypted. Note that if the computed value of q fails the primality test, it suffices to choose another random value for x (see Algorithm 4.2).

Input: $l_n, (N, E)$
Output: p, q, n
1 pick $p \in_{rnd} \Phi_{l_n/2}$.
2 **repeat**
3   pick a random x of the bit size $l_n/4$.
4   set $p' = x \ || \ p\rfloor_{l_n/4}$.
5   compute $q = (p')^E \cdot p^{-1} \ mod \ N$.
6 **until** q *is prime and* $l_q = l_n/2$.
7 compute $n = p \cdot q$.
8 **return** p, q, n.

Algorithm 4.2: Modified prime factor generation of PHP'.

To reconstruct the prime factors from the user's public modulus n, the manufacturer decrypts n with his private RSA key and obtains p':

$$n^D \equiv (p \cdot q)^D \equiv (p \cdot p'^E \cdot p^{-1})^D \equiv p'^{E \cdot D} \equiv p' \ mod \ N.$$

Since the $l_n/4$ least significant bits of p' correspond to the $l_n/4$ least significant bits of one of the prime factors of n, the manufacturer is able to factorize n by applying Coppersmith's factorization attack (see Theorem 1): given n and half the bits of p (or q) Coppersmith's factorization attack returns the prime factors of n: $Coppersmith(n, p\rfloor_{l_n/4}) = (p, q)$.

4.4 Property Analysis of PHP'

The security analysis of PHP' proceeds analogously to the analysis of PHP. We set k'_{priv}, $\mathcal{C}$, $\mathcal{E}$, and $\mathcal{M}$ as follows: k'_{priv} equals to the first prime factor p of n generated by PHP'. The information compression function $\mathcal{C}$ concatenates the $l_n/4$ least significant bits of p with a $l_n/4$-bit value $x \in_{rnd} \{0,1\}^{l_n/4}$: $\mathcal{C}(p) = x \ || \ p\rfloor_{l_n/4}$. $\mathcal{E}$ and $\mathcal{M}$ are defined analogously to PHP.

In the following, we analyze the properties of PHP' according to the definitions given in Section 2.

Confidentiality (*poor*). For PHP' and PHP, the analysis of Confidentiality is identical (see Section 4.2): k_C is encrypted with an $l_n/2$-bit RSA key which bisects the effective key size of PHP'. Thus, Confidentiality is rated with *poor*.

Completeness (*good*). To extract k'_{priv} from k_{pub}, the manufacturer has to apply $\mathcal{C}^{-1} \circ \mathcal{E}^{-1} \circ \mathcal{M}^{-1}(k_{pub})$. $\mathcal{M}^{-1}$ and $\mathcal{E}^{-1}$ are computed in the same way as for PHP. Inverting $\mathcal{C}$ corresponds to the reconstruction of the prime factor p. This is achieved by applying Coppersmith's factorization attack on n and on the $l_n/4$ least significant bits of k_C, since $k_C\rfloor_{l_n/4} = p\rfloor_{l_n/4}$. Coppersmith's factorization method returns both prime factors of n. One of them equals to k'_{priv}.

Let $Coppersmith'(n, p\rfloor_{l_n/4})$ be a modified version of $Coppersmith(n, p\rfloor_{l_n/4})$ which only returns prime factor p of n with $p\rfloor_{l_n/4} = k_C\rfloor_{l_n/4}$. The definition of $\mathcal{C}^{-1}$ is given by

$$\mathcal{C}^{-1}(k_C) = Coppersmith'(n, k_C\rfloor_{l_n/4}).$$

Aggregating the computation steps of $\mathcal{C}^{-1} \circ \mathcal{E}^{-1} \circ \mathcal{M}^{-1}(k_{pub})$ yields the prime factor reconstruction function of the manufacturer:

$$\mathfrak{R}_{\text{PHP'}}(k_{pub} = (n, e)) = Coppersmith'(n, (n^D \ mod \ N)\rfloor_{l_n/4})$$
$$= p = k'_{priv}.$$

Knowing one of the prime factors of the user's public modulus, the manufacturer is able to compute the user's private key k_{priv}. According to the classification scheme presented in Table 2, Completeness is classified as *good*.

Concealment. To analyze Concealment of PHP' we have to consider the sub-properties Concealment directly depends on (see Section 2).

KCC (good, asym. exact). To analyze KCC of $\mathcal{K}_{\text{PHP'}}$ it is again sufficient to analyze the set q is chosen from. The RSA security parameter s equals to the bit length of the prime factors p and q of n which is $l_p = l_q = l_n/2$.

We assume that the manufacturer's public modulus N is of size $2^{l_n/2}$. The first prime factor p of n is chosen randomly from $\Phi_{l_n/2}$, where $|\Phi_{l_n/2}| \approx 2^{l_n/2-1-log_2(l_n/2)}$ (see Subsection 4.2). In order to compute the cardinality of

$$\Theta = \{p' \ | \ p' = x \ || \ p\rfloor_{l_n/4}, \ x \in_{rnd} \mathbb{N}_{l_n/4}, \ p \in_{rnd} \Phi_{l_n/2}\},$$

we have to determine the cardinality of $\mathbb{N}_{l_n/4}$ where x is randomly chosen from as well as the cardinality of the set Υ formed by all possible values for $p\rfloor_{l_n/4}$. The cardinality of $\mathbb{N}_{l_n/4}$, corresponds to

$$|\mathbb{N}_{l_n/4}| = 2^{l_n/4} - 2^{l_n/4-1} = 2^{l_n/4-1}.$$

Υ is defined as follows:

$$\Upsilon = \{p\rfloor_{l_n/4} \ | \ p \in \Phi_{l_n/2}\}.$$

Since p is a prime, we can deduce that Υ does not contain any integer divisible by 2 and 5. All other $l_n/4$-bit integers are potential elements in Υ. Truncating the $l_n/4$ least significant bits of a $l_n/2$-bit prime can be considered to be a mapping from $\Phi_{l_n/2}$ to Υ. Due to the substantial difference in size of the domain and the image of the mapping as well as the unpredictable distribution of prime numbers we can assume that approximately all $l_n/4$-bit integers which are coprime to 2 and 5 appear in Υ. Thus, we can estimate the cardinality of Υ by the following formula:

$$|\Upsilon| \approx 2^{l_n/4-1} - \frac{2^{l_n/4}}{10} \approx 2^{l_n/4-1} - 2^{l_n/4-3} = \frac{3}{4} \cdot 2^{l_n/4-1}$$
$$\approx 2^{l_n/4-1.4}.$$

Now, we are able to compute the cardinality of Θ by multiplying the cardinality of $\mathbb{N}_{l_n/4}$ and Υ:

$$|\Theta| = |\mathbb{N}_{l_n/4}| \cdot |\Upsilon| \approx 2^{l_n/4-1} \cdot 2^{l_n/4-1.4} = 2^{l_n/2-2.4}.$$

Analogous to the analysis of PHP we define Ψ and Ψ':

$$\Psi = \{f(p,p') \mid f(p,p') = (p')^E \cdot p^{-1} \bmod N\},$$

$$\Psi' = \{\psi \mid \psi \in \Psi, l_\psi = l_n/2\},$$

with p and p' defined as above. Similarly as for PHP we can estimate the cardinality of Ψ and Ψ' by $|\Psi| \approx |\Theta|/4$ and thus $|\Psi'| \approx 1/2 \cdot |\Psi|$.

Finally, we can estimate the cardinality of the set of the possible prime candidates for the second prime factor q of n. In order to do this, we follow the analysis of KCC for PHP and multiply $|\Psi'|$ by the probability that an element in Ψ' is prime:

$$|\Lambda| \approx |\Psi'| \cdot \mathbb{P}(q \in \Phi_{l_n/2} \mid q \in_{rnd} \mathbb{N}_{l_n/2})$$
$$= 2^{l_n/2-3.4} \cdot 2^{-log_2(l_n/2)} = 2^{l_n/2-5.4-log_2(l_n/2)}.$$

To evaluate the cardinality of Λ w.r.t. $\Phi_{l_n/2}$ we compute $\mathcal{R}(l_n/2)$:

$$\mathcal{R}(l_n/2) = \frac{\mathcal{N}_{\text{PHP}}(l_n/2)}{\mathcal{N}_{\text{RSA}}(l_n/2)} = \frac{2^{l_n/2-5.4-log_2(l_n/2)}}{2^{l_n/2-1-log_2(l_n/2)}}$$
$$= 2^{-4.4} = 2^{c(l_n/2) \cdot l_n/2},$$

where $c(l_n/2) = -4.4/(l_n/2)$. For a secure usage of RSA, $s = l_n/2 \geq 512$ is required and we have that $c(l_n/2) \geq c(512) = -0.008593$ wherefore KCC is rated with *good*. For PHP', KCC is *asymptotic exact*, too. Compared to PHP, the convergence of $c(s)$ to 0 is even faster by a logarithmic factor.

DC (good). The analysis of DC for PHP' can be carried out analogously to PHP which leads to the fact that DC is classified as *good*.

VCC (good). The user is not able to distinguish between PHP' and RSA based on analyzing the correlation of variables for PHP'. We verify this assertion in two steps: first we argue that with key regeneration in combination with fixing key parameters a distinction is not possible whereupon we show that the same holds if additionally (N,E) is known to the user.

Since the user's private and public exponent (e,d) are not affected by PHP', we can exclude them from analysis. It remains to show that there is no variable correlation between p and q which enables the user to distinguish between the backdoored key generator and the honest one. Suppose the user fixes one of the prime factors of n. Recall from Section 4.3 how the second RSA prime factor is generated for PHP'. Since the fresh prime factor cannot be efficiently distinguished from a randomly generated one, there is no connection between p and q which can be computed efficiently.

If additionally the manufacturer's public key is known to the user, he might be able to distinguish between PHP' and RSA if he is able to guess the random integer $x \in \{0,1\}^{l_n/4}$

which has been used for key generation in PHP'. The user can check if his guess was correct if the following equation is satisfied:

$$(x \,||\, p]_{l_n/4})^E \cdot p^{-1} \bmod N = q. \qquad (2)$$

Since x is chosen uniformly at random, the best strategy for the user to guess x is equivalent to iterating through all possible x values until Equation 2 is satisfied. In the context of RSA, this approach is computationally infeasible since otherwise it would be possible to factorize RSA modules by first guessing $l_n/4$ bits of one of the prime factors of n followed by applying Coppersmith's factorization attack on those bits and n. Since factoring in general is hard, the user is not able to distinguish between PHP' and RSA on the basis of analyzing the correlation of variables for PHP' given (N,E). Overall, VCC is classified as *good*.

CC (good). Let t_p and t_q be the time complexity of RSA for generating the prime factors p and q of n where $t_p = t_q$. For PHP', we can specify $\mathcal{F}$ explicitly by $\mathcal{F} = \mathcal{C}(p)^E \cdot p^{-1} \bmod N$. The time complexity for the generation of p and q in PHP' can be estimated as follows:

$$\mathcal{T}_{\text{PHP}'p,q} \approx t_p + t_q \cdot t(\mathcal{F}) \approx t_p + t_q \approx \mathcal{T}_{\text{RSA}p,q}.$$

As for PHP, for large l_p, l_q, $t(\mathcal{F})$ is negligible w.r.t. t_p and t_q since $t(\mathcal{F}) \in \mathcal{O}(n^2)$ and $t_p, t_q \in \mathcal{O}(l_p^4/log(l_p))$ [7]. According to the classification scheme in Table 2, CC for PHP' is rated as *good*.

AM (good). PHP' does not use additional memory to avoid the correlation of variable or to communicate backdoor information to the manufacturer. Thus, AM is rated with *good*.

5. DISCUSSION

Table 3 provides a comparative overview of the analysis results for the backdoor related properties of PHP, PHP', as well as the prominent backdoors HE, PAP, PAP', PP, and EC discussed in Section 3. Analysis results of the latter set of backdoors have been extracted from [3].

Although no backdoor can be considered to be confidential, complete, and concealing at the same time, it is noticeable that w.r.t. the statistical backdoor properties PHP' is superior to the other backdoors. Particularly, the achieved results for KCC for PHP' are outstanding since the ratio of cardinality is independent of the security parameter. We are not aware of any other asymmetric RSA backdoors achieving a comparable result. In addition, as opposed to the reference backdoors, PHP' is the only backdoor which satisfies all sub-properties of Concealment.

The only disadvantage of PHP' is the bisection of the effective key size leading to the classification as poor w.r.t. Confidentiality.

Backdoor	Confidentiality	Completeness	Concealment				
			KCC	DC	VCC	CC	AM
HE	○	√	×	○	×	○	√
PAP	○	√	○	×	√	√	√
PAP'	○	√	○	×	√	√	√
PP	○	√	○	×	√	√	×
EC	√	√	○	×	√	×	√
PHP	○	√	√	√	×	×	√
PHP'	○	√	√	√	√	√	√

Table 3: Comparative overview of properties of RSA backdoors (√: *good*, ○: *poor*, ×: *failed*)

6. CONCLUSION

In this paper, we proposed, designed and analyzed two novel asymmetric RSA backdoors PHP and PHP'. The property analysis of both revealed a high correlation w.r.t. the properties of an honest RSA implementation. Particularly, the second proposed backdoor, PHP', can be considered to be unique w.r.t. the quality it satisfies the sub-properties of Concealment compared to prominent asymmetric RSA backdoors known from literature.

7. REFERENCES

[1] D. Aggarwal and U. Maurer. Breaking RSA Generically is Equivalent to Factoring. In *Advances in Cryptology - EUROCRYPT 2009*, volume 5479 of *Lecture Notes in Computer Science*, pages 36–53. Springer Berlin Heidelberg, 2009.

[2] R. J. Anderson. A Practical RSA Trapdoor. *Journal of Electronics Letters*, 29(11):995, 1993.

[3] G. Arboit. *Two Mathematical Security Aspects of the RSA Cryptosystem*. PhD thesis, McGill University - School of Computer Science, 2008.

[4] D. Coppersmith. Small Solutions to Polynomial Equations, and Low Exponent RSA Vulnerabilities. *Journal of Cryptology*, 10(4):233–260, 1997.

[5] C. Crépeau and A. Slakmon. Simple Backdoors for RSA Key Generation. In *Topics in Cryptology - CT-RSA 2003*, volume 2612 of *Lecture Notes in Computer Science*, pages 403–416. Springer Berlin Heidelberg, 2003.

[6] M. Joye. RSA Moduli with a Predetermined Portion: Techniques and Applications. In *Information Security Practice and Experience*, volume 4991 of *Lecture Notes in Computer Science*, pages 116–130. Springer Berlin Heidelberg, 2008.

[7] M. Joye, P. Paillier, and S. Vaudenay. Efficient Generation of Prime Numbers. In *Cryptographic Hardware and Embedded Systems - CHES 2000*, volume 1965 of *Lecture Notes in Computer Science*, pages 340–354. Springer Berlin Heidelberg, 2000.

[8] A. M. Legendre. *Essai sur la Théorie des Nombres par A. M. Legendre*. Paris, Duprat, 1808.

[9] A. May. Computing the RSA Secret Key is Deterministic Polynomial Time Equivalent to Factoring. In *Advances in Cryptology - CRYPTO '04*, volume 3152 of *Lecture Notes in Computer Science*, pages 213–219. Springer Berlin Heidelberg, 2004.

[10] M. O. Rabin. Digitalized Signatures and Public-Key Functions as Intracable as Factorization. Technical report, Massachusetts Institute of Technology, 1979.

[11] The OpenSSL Project. OpenSSL: The Open Source Toolkit for SSL/TLS. www.openssl.org, April 2003.

[12] A. Young and M. Yung. The Dark Side of Black-Box Cryptography or: Should We Trust Capstone? In *Advances in Cryptology - CRYPTO '96*, volume 1109 of *Lecture Notes in Computer Science*, pages 89–103. Springer Berlin Heidelberg, 1996.

[13] A. Young and M. Yung. Kleptography: Using Cryptography Against Cryptography. In *Advances in Cryptology - EUROCRYPT '97*, volume 1233 of *Lecture Notes in Computer Science*, pages 62–74. Springer Berlin Heidelberg, 1997.

[14] A. Young and M. Yung. Malicious Cryptography: Kleptographic Aspects. In *Topics in Cryptology - CT-RSA 2005*, volume 3376 of *Lecture Notes in Computer Science*, pages 7–18. Springer Berlin Heidelberg, 2005.

[15] A. Young and M. Yung. A Space Efficient Backdoor in RSA and Its Applications. In *Selected Areas in Cryptography*, volume 3897 of *Lecture Notes in Computer Science*, pages 128–143. Springer Berlin Heidelberg, 2006.

[16] A. Young and M. Yung. A Timing-Resistant Elliptic Curve Backdoor in RSA. In *Information Security and Cryptology*, volume 4990 of *Lecture Notes in Computer Science*, pages 427–441. Springer Berlin Heidelberg, 2008.

Secure Image Display through Visual Cryptography: Exploiting Temporal Responsibilities of the Human Eye

Jong-Uk Hou[1], Dongkyu Kim[2], Hyun-Ji Song[3], and Heung-Kyu Lee[4]*
School of Computing, KAIST, Daejeon, South Korea
{juheo[1], dkim[2], hjsong[3], hklee[4]}@mmc.kaist.ac.kr

ABSTRACT

We propose a new protection scheme for displaying a static binary image on a screen. The protection is achieved by a visual cryptography algorithm that divides the target images into several divisions. The visual difference between the text and the background is induced by exploiting the temporal responsibilities of the human eye. With the results of our user study, we demonstrate that encrypted visual information was mentally recovered by the human visual system. Moreover, the images captured from our scheme do not provide any meaningful information to the human eye, so that our method provides a strong security measure against screenshot piracy.

Keywords

Visual cryptography, screenshot, copyright protection, display algorithms

1. INTRODUCTION

With the remarkable development of the Internet, a number of people have shared and collected various digital data via the Internet. The demand for multimedia content such as pictures and videos have rapidly increased, and the value of the content has also grown. To collect the content displayed on a computer monitor or mobile device, taking screenshot is one of the method used most. Using the print-screen key and built-in capture function, users can easily take a screenshot. There are also various screen grabber tools that capture a bitmap of the content displayed on a monitor. While the screenshot offers convenience, it causes copyright infringement when a screenshot of copyrighted content is distributed without permission. Therefore, secure image displays against screenshot is essential in the multimedia industry.

There are several methods that protect images against screen capturing. Generally, they operate on an operating

---

*Corresponding author

system or on hardware [11, 13]. Snapchat, a mobile messaging application, does not protect screenshots from being taken but notifies the sender if the recipient takes a screenshot [1]. In addition, digital watermarking and fingerprinting can be used to create an active protection system that allows to control the distribution of content [2]. Further, a digital forensic technique such as that proposed in [9] can help analyze the source of the captured image.

Yamamoto et al. [17] proposed a display technique that ensures security of visual information based on visual cryptography. The encoded image on the display decoded with the mask, and its visual data is recognizable on the limited viewing zone. In addition, a screenshot protection technique with an image processing approach was proposed [18]. They distorted visual data displayed on the monitor to make the screenshot meaningless. They exploited the human visual system to empower viewers to automatically and mentally recover the distorted content into a meaningful form. However, in spite of their contribution, the screenshot of the protected image can be still identified.

In this paper, we encrypt a static binary image (e.g., text data) shown on a screen based on secret image sharing [12, 14]. Instead of image recovery with spatial processing, each shared image is sequentially displayed on the screen and recovered by the human eye. To make this possible, in our scheme the encrypted images are generated as a specific form exploiting the temporal responsibilities of the human visual system. In a user study, encrypted images were successfully recovered by the human visual system, and the captured images from our scheme were not able to be recognized by the human eye.

The rest of this paper is organized as follows. In Section 2, we briefly introduce the background knowledge, and in Section 3 we explain the details of the proposed method. To demonstrate the performance of the proposed scheme, the quantitative evaluation and user study are presented in Section 4, and in Section 5, we present our conclusions.

2. TEMPORAL RESPONSIBILITY

Information on images is sampled by our eyes and projected onto the retina in a periodic manner [8]. Then, the collected information is integrated so that objects appear to be stable and move smoothly. Because there is a finite amount of time required to process visual information, there are limitations on the responsiveness of our visual system to rates of change. When periodic visual stimuli called flicker are presented to the human eye, the stimuli are perceived as separate if the rate is below a certain value. If the rate of

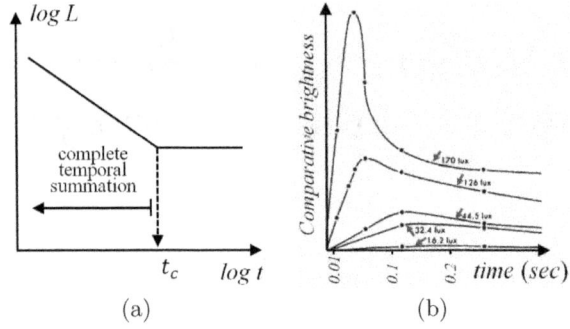

Figure 1: (a) Plot for Bloch's Law (data plotted as $\log L$ and $\log t$), and (b) apparent brightness of flashes with various luminances (Broca and Sulzer data from [5])

presentation is above a certain critical rate, the flicker vanishes from the human eye. To perceive flashes of light one after the other, an appropriate integration time is required.

Temporal integration time is related to temporal summation, which refers to the eye's ability to sum the effects of each flicker over time. However, temporal summation only occurs within a certain period of time, called the critical duration [7]. According to Bloch's Law of temporal summation, the product of luminance L and stimulus duration t equals the constant value k.

$$L \cdot t^p = k, \qquad (1)$$

where the constant value k is determined by the total luminous energy, and p describes whether temporal summation is complete (=1) or partial (0<p<1). No temporal summation occurs when p=0 (See Fig. 1(b)). Temporal summation is also affected by other test variables such as background luminance and the size of the stimulus. Critical duration is longer for brighter background luminance and a smaller area of the stimulus.

To readily investigate the visual system's response to flicker, a temporal contrast sensitivity function was plotted by De Lange [3]. A temporal contrast sensitivity function is a plot of how flicker varies with contrast level. The eye appears to be most sensitive to a frequency of 15-20 Hz at high luminance (above 100 trolands). To detect flicker at a high frequency, the maximum contrast level is required. In addition, the Broca-Sulzer effect describes the apparent transient increase in brightness of a flash of short duration. Subjective flash brightness occurs with a flash duration of 50 to 100 milliseconds. Detailed information can be found in [7].

3. PROPOSED METHOD

In this study, we encrypted a static binary image (e.g., text data) shown on a screen based on secret image sharing [12, 14]. As shown in Fig. 2, each shared image was sequentially displayed on the screen and recovered by the human eye. In our method, pixels from the image are categorized by two types: **type 1** for background pixels, and **type 2** for main content. Each type of pixel is encoded to the form of pseudo-random noise, so that the content from each of the distorted images cannot be recognized. We induced a visual difference of each pixel type by exploiting the temporal responsibilities of the human eye.

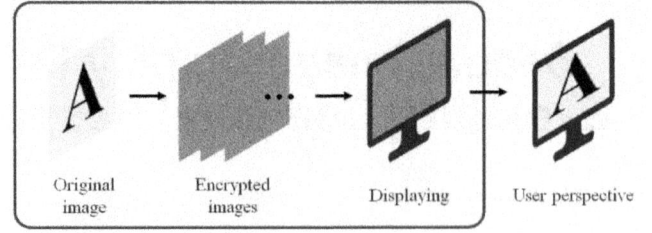

Figure 2: Overall process of the proposed scheme

Fig. 3 shows the main feature of the temporal resolution exploited in our scheme. A flickering signal over a critical duration made itself conspicuous to the human eye. In contrast, a flickering below the critical duration was perceived as a plain gray pixels. In addition, following features were used to maximize the perceptibility of the recovered content: 1) sharing number n is controlled by the refresh rate and the maximum luminance of the screen (by Bloch's Law), 2) brightness of the shared image is varied by the luminance of the flickering (by the Broca-Sulzer effect).

The proposed method is divided into three steps: 1) determining the critical duration, 2) encrypted image generation, and 3) content recovery. We now describe each step in detail.

3.1 Determining a critical duration

To determine the critical duration for our scheme, the maximum luminance $l_m (cd/m^2)$ and frequency f_m(Hz) are measured from the display. Then, critical duration t_c for the given environment is determined by Bloch's Law and the Broca-Sulzer effect [5, 7]. For instance, t_c is around 90 milliseconds for the pixels of the display with $l_m = 350 cd/m^2$.

The upper bound of the number of frames n that induces the temporal summation is calculated as follows:

$$n = \lceil \frac{t_c \cdot f_m}{2} \rceil, \qquad (2)$$

Flickering over n frames made itself conspicuous to human eye. In contrast, flickering below n frames was perceived as plain gray pixels (See Fig. 3). We use the value n as a threshold to set content pixels apart from background pixels.

3.2 Encrypted image generation

We denote a static display of the screen as image I and denote the intensity at the (x, y) coordinate of the screen as $I(x, y)$. Next, each pixel from I are categorized by two

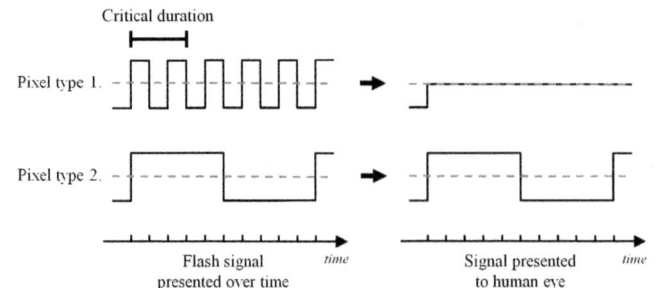

Figure 3: Apparent brightness of pixels from the proposed algorithm

types:

$$\begin{cases} \textbf{type 1}: \text{background pixels,} \\ \textbf{type 2}: \text{pixels for main contents.} \end{cases} \quad (3)$$

A threshold value of 0.5 is used for separating image pixels into two categories.

To induce visual difference of each pixel type, I is shared to S_i for $i = 0, 1, ..., N$. The random noise image as the initial share S_0 is generated as follows:

$$S_0(x, y) = \text{rand}(\{0, 1\}), \quad (4)$$

where the function $\text{rand}(\{0, 1\})$ generates a random number $\in \{0, 1\}$. Next, shared images S_i for $i = 1, ..., N$ are recursively generated as follows:

$$S_i(x, y) = \begin{cases} \text{if } I(x, y) \in \textbf{type 1} & : not(S_{i-1}(x, y)), \\ \text{otherwise} & : S_i^*(x, y), \end{cases} \quad (5)$$

$$S_i^*(x, y) = \begin{cases} \text{if } i \text{ is divisible by } n & : \text{rand}(\{0, 1\}), \\ \text{otherwise} & : S_{i-1}(x, y), \end{cases} \quad (6)$$

where n denotes the maximum length of the frames that induces the temporal summation, and $not()$ is a function that changes a value 0 and 1 into 1 and 0, respectively. As a result of the generation, pixels for background (**type 1**) appeared as a flickering signal for every frame. Pixels for content (**type 2**) also appeared as a flickering signal, but their durations were at least n times longer than those of **type 1**. Fig. 4(b) presents the shared image S_1 for Fig. 4(a). As we can see in the figure, the alphabet 'A' from the original image is never recognized in the shared image.

Meanwhile, with random noise based generation there is a high probability of having a locally biased area in the synthesized image. A mass of random noise from the background pixels can cause visual disturbance, so that varying the visual difference of each pixel type is more difficult to achieve. Therefore, to evenly distribute the random noise from the local area, values from S_i are varied using the basis matrices M_0 and M_1 defined as follows:

$$M_0 = \begin{bmatrix} 1 & 0 \\ 0 & 1 \end{bmatrix}, \quad M_1 = \begin{bmatrix} 0 & 1 \\ 1 & 0 \end{bmatrix}. \quad (7)$$

If $S_i(x, y)$ is 0, the pixel is replaced by M_0. The same replacement is conducted for a value 1 and M_1 (See Fig. 4(c)). Due to the pixel expansion through the replacement, one pixel from the original image is expanded into four pixels.

3.3 Content recovery

The individual shares give no clue that a specific pixel is '0' or '1' regardless of the amount of computational power. The only way to reconstruct the original image on the machine requires that the shared images S_i be collected. In contrast to conventional schemes such as those in [10, 14], shared images from our scheme can be recovered not only on the machine but also on the human visual system.

To achieve this, the generated S is sequentially displayed on the screen as a videos. Fig. 4(d) shows the expected view of the recovered image. By temporal summation, pixels for

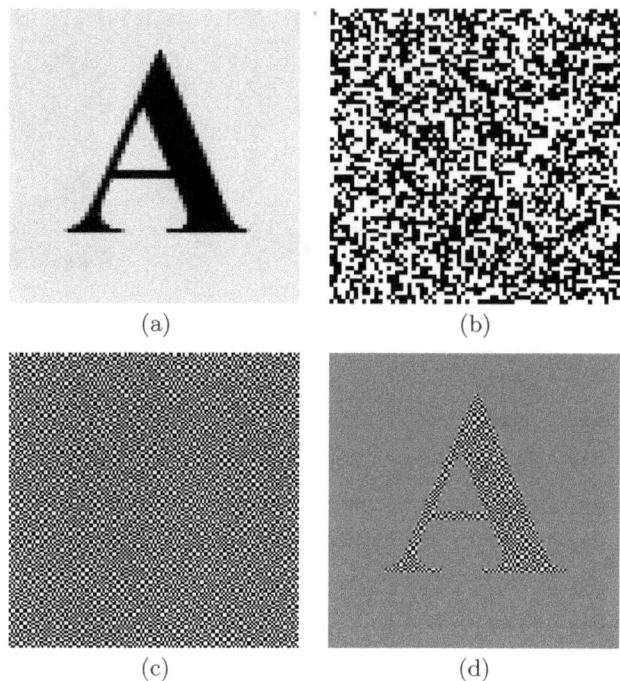

Figure 4: Sample of results: (a) input image I, (b) S_1, (c) encoded S_1 with M_0 and M_1, and (d) expected view of recovered image.

the background (**type 1**) are perceived as gray pixels when $1/f_m$ is larger than t_c. In contrast, pixels for content (**type 2**) appear as a flickering signal because their temporal duration is at least n frames, which is not able to induce the temporal summation. As a result, the human eye can distinguish between the contents pixels and the background pixels, and can read (or recognize) the protected content.

4. EXPERIMENTAL EVALUATION

In this section, we demonstrate the effectiveness of our method in terms of content protection through deep experimental analyses, which include objective and subjective tests. Similar to the study in [18], we generated 400×400 images as seen in Fig.5(a). The pixel intensities of characters and background were set to 0.25 and 0.75, respectively. All the characters were randomly drawn from capital letters and numbers.

The experiments were carried out under the following environments. We used a desktop computer equipped with Intel(R) i7-4790 CPU and NVIDIA GeForce GTX750. It was connected to Qnix QX2414 LED 144 ($144Hz, 350cd/m^2$) and Samsung SyncMaster 226BW ($60Hz, 300cd/m^2$). The numbers in parentheses indicate the refresh rate and maximum brightness of the monitors. For the mobile environment, an Apple iPhone 6 was employed and its display had a $60Hz$ refresh rate and $500cd/m^2$ maximum luminance. The critical durations t_c, and n for each display were determined as follows: Qnix ($t_c \approx 100ms, n = 6$), Samsung ($t_c \approx 90ms, n = 3$), and iPhone ($t_c \approx 70ms, n = 3$).

We compared our method with three different methods as follows: the visual cryptography of Naor and Shamir [10], Ito et al. [6], and the video based method of Chia et al. [18].

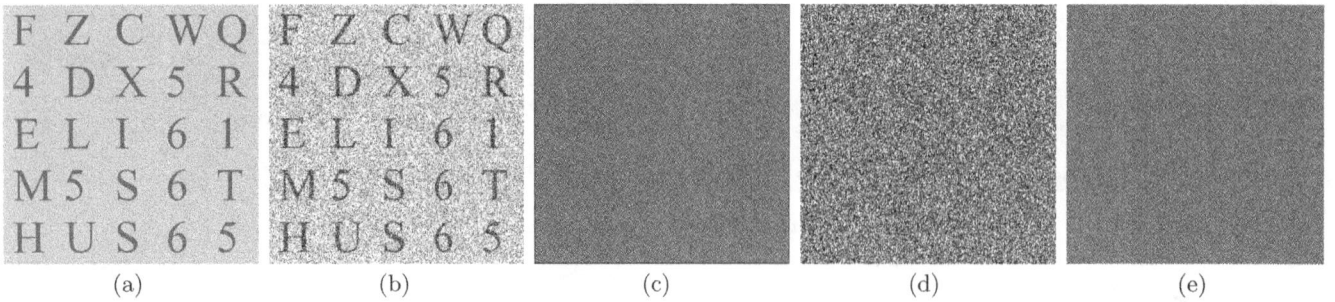

Figure 5: Sample of screenshot images: (a) original image, (b) Chia et al. [18], (c) Naor and Shamir [10], (d) Ito et al. [6], and (e) our method.

Table 1: Comparison table of the related algorithms

Algorithms	[6,10]	[18]	ours
Recovery by machine	o	o	o
Recovery by human eye	× (or o)	o	o
Concealment of visual info.	o	×	o

We used (2, 2) threshold scheme for the visual cryptography algorithms [6,10]. For the method of Chia et al., the same n values corresponding our method were used.

Table 1 presents a summary of comparisons with our method for recovery by machine, recovery by the human eye, and concealment of visual information. The detailed results of comparison will be handled in the following subsections.

4.1 Quantitative Evaluation

To check the information distortion capability of our method, we conducted a quantitative evaluation by measuring the average root mean square (RMS) distances between the distorted images and their corresponding original images. The distorted images indicated frames composing a video which were generated to protect an image by each method. This was repeated over 1,000 different test images with adjustment of the number of whole frames n. Fig. 6 shows the mean average-RMS distances according to variations of value n. The distances in our method and visual cryptography were almost constant at 0.56 and thus invariant to n values. Meanwhile, the method of Chia et al. was affected by n and its distance was gradually converged into 0.32, which meant that

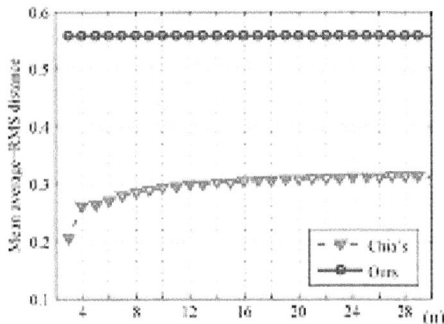

Figure 6: The mean average-RMS distances according to variations of value n.

each distorted image could reveal information of the original to some extent. Note that each frame in our method consisted of the same number of black and white pixels which were randomly selected as explained in Section 3.2, and thus did not unveil any information.

4.2 User Study

For a qualitative evaluation, we performed a user study which consisted of visual information recoveries under two different circumstances, normal and abnormal. Ten subjects participated in this study, who had normal or corrected-to-normal vision. The mean age was 28.5, and the youngest and eldest were 25 and 33, respectively. All the subjects were guided to look at the screens approximately $50cm$ away and $30cm$ for settled monitors and mobile phones, respectively.

4.2.1 Distortion of Visual Information

In the first user study, we looked for how much information the distorted images would reveal visually. From the n distorted images, a randomly selected image was presented to the subjects. Then they were guided to read characters in order and we calculated recognition rates, or accuracy. The recognition rate was defined as the percentage of characters identified correctly.

Table 2 shows the average accuracy of distorted images generated by each method. It is not surprising that our method and visual cryptography methods had a 0% recognition rate because they performed pixel-wise encryption, and thus characters and background were encoded with binary numbers, 0 and 1. In contrast, the method of Chia et al. generated distorted images with distorting planes in which each pixel value was a real number between -1 and 1. It led to the leakage of visual information to some extent and a high average recognition rate. Note that the image resolution of this test was higher than that of Chia's test (100×100), which made visual information prominent owing to the increase of absolute amount of pixels.

Table 2: The average character recognition rates of distorted images generated by compared methods

Display type	[18]	[10]	[6]	Ours
Qnix LED (144Hz)	100	0	0	0
Samsung (60Hz)	99.6	0	0	0
iPhone6 (60Hz)	100	0	0	0
Average	**99.87**	**0**	**0**	**0**

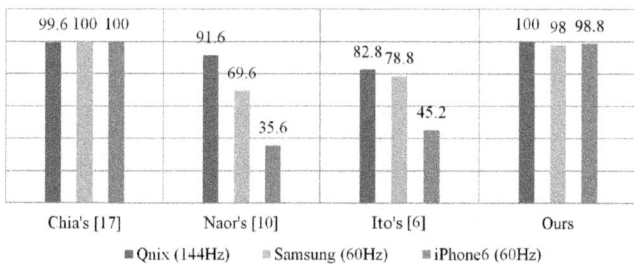

Figure 7: The average character recognition rates after showing streams of images generated by compared methods

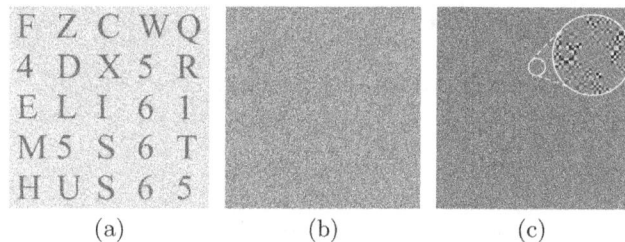

Figure 8: Sample of averaged images using 5 screenshots: (a) Chia et al. [18], (b) Naor and Shamir [10], and (c) our method.

4.2.2 Normal Recovery of Visual Information

We laid our whole distorted images in correct order when generating a stream or video and confirmed whether humans could recover visual content normally from it. As in Sec. 4.2.1, we measured the average recognition rates after showing streams of images to subjects. Each stream played during 30 seconds which were assumed to be enough time for the subjects to write 25 characters on the images.

Fig. 2 shows the results of user study. Ours and the method of Chia et al. demonstrated high average recognition rates regardless of monitor's refresh rate. In both methods, due to the composite effects of low spatial resolution and insufficient time, some subjects could not discriminate between 'S' and '5', and between 'I' and '1', which resulted in not 100% recognition rates.

Meanwhile, image streams of the visual cryptography methods also created recognizable artifacts that provided feasible information to subjects. Due to the generation process of the visual cryptography methods, visual differences between content region and background region also presented from the encrypted streams. The larger refresh rates is, the more distinct differences arised. It is natural that increasing the refresh rate decreases flickering and consequently the temporal summation of consecutive streams is the same as bit-OR operation in visual cryptography. The visual differences were not so clear as those of our methods, so that the methods [6, 10] demonstrated relatively low recognition rates, especially in the case of the iPhone 6 with small display.

4.2.3 Abnormal Recovery of Visual Information

In this section, we assumed a possible scenario in which an attacker would capture several distorted images from a generated stream and try to recover its information by stacking the captured images. To measure robustness against that kind of attack, we randomly picked k distorted images from the total set. As an attack, we averaged the selected images and presented the resulting image to the subjects.

Fig. 8 shows the averaged result using 5 screenshot images. Our method and visual cryptography output illegible noisy images by averaging the pixel-wise encrypted images and consequently produced a low recognition rate. Note that some case of our method results distinguishable artifact (See circled region in Fig. 8(c)), so that an observant eye may perceive the abnormally recovered content. Meanwhile, Chia et al. distorted every image with the same amount of noise and without order. In addition, their algorithm was designed to result in zero noise when summing the distorted images,

and thus recognition rates would clearly ascend with an increase in k.

5. DISCUSSION AND CONCLUSION

In this paper, we proposed a new protection scheme for a static binary image shown on a screen exploiting the temporal responsibilities of the human visual system. With the results of our user study, we demonstrated that encrypted visual information was mentally recovered by the human visual system. Moreover, captured images from our scheme did not provide any meaningful information to either humans or computer programs; thus, our method provides strong security against screenshot piracy. To best our knowledge, there are no visual cryptography schemes that consider the temporal aspect, so existing methods ineffectively perform the way described in this paper.

On the other hand, the proposed methodology has a following limitation. Our method is based on the simple noise pattern generated by recursion, so that it is obvious that a malicious user reveals visual information through difference between subsequent frames. Therefore, we have a future work to complement the weakness. For instance, we would depart from the recursion based algorithm and devise a statistical noise pattern which can make temporal responsibility different. In addition, we will exploit more features related to temporal responsibilities to our scheme.

We found various potential applications for the proposed method. First of all, the proposed scheme can enhance the security of a mobile authentication system, such as a one-time-password system [4] or personal identification number [15]. The proposed method can be used for the type of challenge-response test (e.g., CAPTCHA [16]) used in computing to determine whether or not the user is a human. In addition, we would like to apply our method in combination with existing security methods to enhance security. Regarding such applications, we believe that the proposed method can be used in a variety of fields.

Acknowledgments

This research project was supported by Ministry of Culture, Sports and Tourism(MCST) and from Korea Copyright Commission in 2015. The work of Jong-Uk Hou was supported by a Global PH.D Fellowship Program through the National Research Foundation of Korea(NRF) funded by the Ministry of Education (2015H1A2A1030715).

6. REFERENCES

[1] J. Charteris, S. Gregory, and Y. Masters. Snapchat 'selfies': The case of disappearing data'. *Rhetoric and Reality: Critical perspectives on educational technology*, pages 389–393, 2014.

[2] I. Cox, M. Miller, J. Bloom, J. Fridrich, and T. Kalker. *Digital Watermarking and Steganography*. Morgan Kaufmann Publishers Inc., San Francisco, CA, USA, 2 edition, 2008.

[3] H. De Lange Dzn. Research into the dynamic nature of the human fovea-cortex systems with intermittent and modulated light. i. attenuation characteristics with white and colored light. *The Journal of the Optical Society of America*, 48(11):777–783, 1958.

[4] N. Haller, C. Metz, P. Nesser, and M. Straw. A one-time password system. Technical report, 1998.

[5] W. J. Hart. The temporal responsiveness of vision. *Adler's physiology of the eye, Clinical application*, 1987.

[6] R. Ito, H. Kuwakado, and H. Tanaka. Image size invariant visual cryptography. *IEICE transactions on fundamentals of electronics, communications and computer sciences*, 82(10):2172–2177, 1999.

[7] M. Kalloniatis and C. Luu. Temporal resolution. *Webvision: The Organization of the Retina and Visual System*, 2005.

[8] H. Kolb, E. Fernandez, and R. Nelson. Webvision: The organization of the retina and visual system. 1995.

[9] J.-W. Lee, M.-J. Lee, H.-Y. Lee, and H.-K. Lee. Screenshot identification by analysis of directional inequality of interlaced video. *EURASIP Journal on Image and Video Processing*, 2012(1):1–15, 2012.

[10] M. Naor and A. Shamir. *Advances in Cryptology — EUROCRYPT'94: Workshop on the Theory and Application of Cryptographic Techniques Perugia, Italy, May 9–12, 1994 Proceedings*, chapter Visual cryptography, pages 1–12. Springer Berlin Heidelberg, Berlin, Heidelberg, 1995.

[11] H. Okhravi and D. M. Nicol. Trustgraph: Trusted graphics subsystem for high assurance systems. In *Computer Security Applications Conference, 2009. ACSAC'09. Annual*, pages 254–265. IEEE, 2009.

[12] A. Shamir. How to share a secret. *Communications of the ACM*, 22(11):612–613, 1979.

[13] M. Stamp. Digital rights management: The technology behind the hype. *J. Electron. Commerce Res.*, 4(3):102–112, 2003.

[14] C.-C. Thien and J.-C. Lin. Secret image sharing. *Computers & Graphics*, 26(5):765–770, 2002.

[15] G. J. Tomko and A. Stoianov. Method and apparatus for securely handling a personal identification number or cryptographic key using biometric techniques, Jan. 27 1998. US Patent 5,712,912.

[16] L. Von Ahn, M. Blum, N. J. Hopper, and J. Langford. Captcha: Using hard ai problems for security. In *Advances in Cryptology—EUROCRYPT 2003*, pages 294–311. Springer, 2003.

[17] H. Yamamoto, Y. Hayasaki, and N. Nishida. Secure information display with limited viewing zone by use of multi-color visual cryptography. *Optics express*, 12(7):1258–1270, 2004.

[18] A. Yong-Sang Chia, U. Bandara, X. Wang, and H. Hirano. Protecting against screenshots: An image processing approach. In *Proceedings of the IEEE Conference on Computer Vision and Pattern Recognition*, pages 1437–1445, 2015.

Image Segmentation Based Visual Security Evaluation

Christof Kauba
Department of Computer
Sciences
University of Salzburg
5020 Salzburg, AUSTRIA
ckauba@cosy.sbg.ac.at

Stefan Mayer
Department of Computer
Sciences
University of Salzburg
5020 Salzburg, AUSTRIA
mail@stefan-mayer.at

Andreas Uhl
Department of Computer
Sciences
University of Salzburg
5020 Salzburg, AUSTRIA
uhll@cosy.sbg.ac.at

ABSTRACT

In this paper we present a metric for visual security evaluation of encrypted images, also known as visual security metric. Such a metric should be able to assess whether an image encryption method is secure or not. In order to consider intelligibility of objects in encrypted images our metric is based on image segmentation and applying a measure designed to evaluate the segmentation result. The visual security metrics' performance is evaluated using a selective encryption approach and compared to some general image quality metrics like PSNR, metrics suggested for encrypted images like Irregular Deviation and two metrics specifically designed for visual security evaluation. Our visual security metric performs better than all of the other tested metrics on the dataset and encryption algorithm we used during our experiments in terms of different correlation measures.

Keywords

visual security metric, selective encryption, image segmentation, confidence, correlation

1. INTRODUCTION

Today a number of (format compliant) image encryption techniques exist which allow the encrypted content to be decoded and viewed. To determine the level of security offered by these techniques it is not enough to simply evaluate the cryptographic strength of the encryption cipher used. For some methods the decoded encrypted image is a low quality version of the original image and certain image features can still be recognised. So beside evaluating the encryption cipher also the visual security of the result has to be assessed. Visual security metrics are designed to be able to assess the security of an image encryption method based on the visual output. In this context they need to deal with the remaining image information left behind by the encryption process and the recognizability and intelligibility of the encrypted image content.

In order to be able to discuss the exact notion of visual

IH&MMSec 2016, June 20 - 23, 2016, Vigo, Spain

DOI: http://dx.doi.org/10.1145/2909827.2930806

security, we need to distinguish distinct application scenarios of media encryption schemes [9]:

Confidentiality Encryption: means MP security (message privacy). The formal notion is that if a system is MP-secure an attacker cannot efficiently compute any property of the plain text from the cipher text. This can only be achieved by the conventional encryption approach, i.e. applying a cryptographically strong cipher to compressed (redundancy-free) image data.

Content Confidentiality: is a relaxation of confidential encryption. Side channel information may be reconstructed or left in plaintext, e.g. header information, packet length, but the actual visual content must be secure in the sense that the image content must not be intelligible / discernible.

Sufficient Encryption: means we do not require full security, just enough security to prevent abuse of the data. The content must not be consumable due to high distortion (e.g. for DRM systems) by destroying visual quality to a degree which prevents a pleasant viewing experience or destroys the commercial value. This implicitly refers to message quality security (MQ), which requires that an adversary cannot reconstruct a higher quality version of the encrypted material than specified for the application scenario.

Given these different application scenarios it is clear that depending on the goal, a security metric has to fulfil different roles. For example, under the assumption of sufficient encryption a given security metric would have to evaluate which quality is low enough to prevent a pleasant viewing experience.

When it comes to content confidentiality the question of quality is no longer applicable. Content confidentiality requires that image content must not be identified by human or automated recognition. This requirement also has to be maintained for any part of the image. Image metrics, in general, do not deal with such questions but rate the overall image quality, the question of intelligibility is usually not covered at all. Thus, it seems to be clear that a general purpose metric covering all application scenarios is probably very hard or impossible to design.

Additionally we have to face the fact that different encryption methods introduce different kind of distortions. While some methods shift and morph the images (i.e. chaotic encryption which is mainly based on permutations) others introduce noise and noise like patterns. An ideal metric for assessment of visual security has to be able to deal with those different kind of distortions.

While PSNR, SSIM, and the more more specific measures developed in the context of visual encryption do a reasonable job to rate the visual security of a ciphered image for particular image encryption techniques, for many encryption methods these metrics tend to have troubles in the correct assessment of visual security in correspondence to visual perception especially for higher levels of encryption. Hofbauer and Uhl showed that general visual image quality metrics have difficulties assessing low quality images [7].

Since most of these metrics compare the plain and the cipher images pixel by pixel or region by region (fundamental principles of the Human Vision System (HVS) in terms of luminance and edge perception are considered) a warped image may still be recognisable while the metric rates the image as secure due to large dissimilarities in terms of pixel or local region differences. Also, noise patterns tend to decrease the score rather quickly but leave the content of the image still intelligible. Thus, answering the question if an encryption of this type results in a content confidential image, i.e. an image without any intelligible content, can become quite challenging with those metrics.

An important aspect if it comes to content intelligibility is the ability to recognise objects in the images both for humans and automated detection. One way to detect objects inside an image is to use image segmentation methods trying to automatically detect and segment the objects from the background and each other. If the segmentation succeeds this indicates that there are still some objects visible (or at least partially visible). Our approach is based on image segmentation and evaluating the segmentation result in order to design a metric for visual security assessment which is able to handle the issue of content recognition and intelligibility in a more appropriate manner. The basic idea is to first segment the reference and cipher image and then compare the segmentation results. By doing so our approach should be able to capture parts of the image content (i.e. contours) which are still visible despite the warping and noise introduced by the encryption approach. Thus the overall metric is termed "Segmentation Based Similarity Score" (SBSS).

The rest of the paper is divided into four parts. In section 2 an overview of existing visual security metrics is given. Section 3 explains the segmentation based similarity score. Section 4 describes the experimental setup, including the dataset and the encryption approach used to test the metrics performance and lists the other metrics which are evaluated. This is followed by the presentation and discussion of the experimental results in section 5. Finally section 6 concludes this paper and gives an outlook on future work.

2. VISUAL SECURITY METRICS

To evaluate the visual security of an encrypted image in an objective manner, several different kinds of metrics have been proposed in the literature. This section gives a short overview of these metrics where the ones we used during our experiments are described in more detail.

Despite the fact that PSNR and SSIM originally have been developed for image quality assessment, they have also been used for the assessment of encrypted images [2, 11, 3].

Besides that several attempts have been made to develop metrics specifically for the task of measuring the encryption quality. Luminance variance (LV) [5] simply measures the variance in the luminance values in the encrypted images. High variance should indicate a higher level of encryption and thus higher visual security.

The irregular deviation [1] measures how much the statistical distribution of histogram deviation is close to uniform distribution. For perfectly encrypted images the deviation should be close to uniform distribution, thus the smaller the value of irregular deviation (ID) the better the encryption quality. ID is calculated as follows:

1. Absolute difference of reference image (R) and encrypted image (C): $D = |R - C|$

2. Calculate the histogram of D: $H = histogram(D)$

3. Let h_i be the amplitude of histogram at index i. Then the average value of H is

$$M_H = \frac{1}{256} \sum_{i=0}^{255} h_i$$

4. Absolute value of the histogram deviations from this mean value as follows: $H_{D_i} = |h_i - M_H|$

5. Irregular deviation I_D: $I_D = \sum_{i=0}^{255} H_{D_i}$

Another similar measure is the deviation from uniform histogram [1]. An ideal image encryption leads to images having uniform histogram distribution. Thus the lower the deviation from uniform histogram (DFUH) is, the higher should be the encryption quality. DFUH is calculated as follows:

- Let H_C be the histogram of the encrypted image and let H_{C_i} be the value of the frequency of occurrence at index i then the uniform histogram is defined as

$$H_{C_i} = \begin{cases} \frac{M \cdot N}{256} & 0 \leq C_i \leq 255 \\ 0 & otherwise \end{cases}$$

- Deviation from uniform histogram is calculated as follows

$$D_P = \frac{\sum_{C_i=0}^{255} |H_{C_i} - H_C|}{M \cdot N}$$

The Edge Similarity Score was introduced by Mao and Wu [14] and uses localized edge information. The image is divided into blocks and a Sobel edge detection filter is used on each block to find the most prominent edge direction on which the final score calculation is based.

The Luminance Similarity Score was also introduced by Mao and Wu [14] and is based on localized luminosity information. Again the image is divided into blocks, the average luminance of each block is calculated. The final score depends on the per block luminance difference of the blocks and two additional thresholds.

Yao et al. introduced the Neighbourhood Similarity Degree metric [19] which utilizes local pixel similarity correlation. The difference of the centre pixel and its neighbouring pixels inside a window is calculated for each pixel, then the average these pixel differences over the whole image is taken. The final score is the absolute difference between these average values for the reference and the encrypted image.

Sun et al. [17] proposed a metric based on an entropy measure called Local Entropy. The encrypted image is partitioned into blocks. Then the probability of a pixel inside a block is calculated by histogram normalization. Based on this probability the block entropy for each block is calculated and the final score is the average of the block-wise entropy values divided by the log of the maximum pixel.

The Local Feature Based Visual Security metric was introduced by Tong et al. [18] and utilizes localized edge and luminance features which are combined and weighted according to error magnitude. Again the image is divided into blocks at first. For each block the average and standard deviation of the luminance values is calculated and combined to the local luminance feature. For each pixel inside a block the luminance edge direction is determined and a histogram calculated of these edge directions forms the local edge density feature. Final score calculation is based on a weighting of an ordered combination of the local luminance and edge density values.

Yongjie and Wengang [21] proposed a visual security metric based on grey relation analysis (abbreviated as Yongjie10):

1. First divide the image into 32×32 pixel blocks

2. Calculate a grey level histogram for each blocks, divided into 6 bins

3. Apply grey relation analysis for each of the histograms

   (a) Determine the reference sequence (X_0) and compared sequence (X_i)

   $$X_0 = \{X_0(k)|k = 1, 2, ..., n\}$$

   $$X_i = \{X_i(k)|k = 1, 2, ..., n\} \, (i = 1, 2, ..., m)$$

   (b) Calculate the correlation coefficients (Cor) between reference sequence and all relative sequences

   (c) Calculate the mean of all correlations

   $$\mu = \frac{1}{N} \sum_{k=1}^{n} Cor(k)$$

4. Calculate the average of all correlation factors

Xiongjun Li [12] also proposed an approach based on grey level analysis in combination with information entropy (abbreviated as Li08):

1. Create a variance image G with respect to the evaluated image $F = \{f(i,j)|1 \leq i \leq M, 1 \leq j \leq N\}$

2. Calculate the average of the absolute differences between each pixel and its 8-neighbors pixel by pixel

   $$G = \{g(i,j)|1 \leq i \leq M, 1 \leq j \leq N\}$$

   $$g(i,j) = \sum_{k=-1}^{1} \sum_{l=-1}^{1} \frac{|f(i,j) - f(i+k, j+l)|}{8}$$

3. Assuming m is the mean of the values in G, s is the standard deviation of the values in G

$$m_f = \sum_{i=1}^{M} \sum_{j=1}^{N} \frac{g(i,j)}{M \cdot N} \quad s_f = \sqrt{\frac{\sum_{i=1}^{M} \sum_{j=1}^{N} (g(i,j) - m_f)^2}{(M \cdot N - 1)}}$$

m_f, s_f are less than the grey level range of the image (256 grey levels for a 8 Bit image)

4. H_f is the general information entropy of the image

$$H_f = -\sum_{l=0}^{L-1} p_f(l) \cdot log_2(p_f(l))$$

$p_f(l)$ represents the probability of grey level l. (max. entropy value is $8Bit$)

5. The basic scrambling degree measure is

$$B_f = \frac{\frac{H_f}{8} \cdot \frac{m_f}{256}}{\left(\frac{s_f}{256}\right)} = \frac{H_f \cdot m_f}{8 \cdot s_f}$$

Jenisch and Uhl [10] proposed an approach which relies on object recognition based on SIFT, called SIFT Similarity Score. At first the SIFT key points are extracted in both images and then matched against each other, returning an array of matching key points along with their corresponding Euclidean distances. The final score is number of matching key points divided by the maximum possible number of matches, taken to the power of the average Euclidean distance divided by the L_2-norm of Euclidean matching distances.

3. SEGMENTATION BASED SIMILARITY SCORE

Image segmentation describes the process of partitioning an image into multiple segments. This can be regarded as a kind of clustering process. Image segmentation is done for several reasons, including content-based image retrieval, object detection and recognition tasks. There are many different image segmentation approaches [13] from simple thresholding based ones over watershed segmentation to more advanced ones like mean shift segmentation, graph based segmentation and statistical region merging. Advanced image segmentation approaches are robust against noise and other image distortions. Images having similar image content should lead to similar segmentation results. Thus one would assume that also an image and its encrypted versions result in similar segmentation results (depending on the strength of the encryption). This is the main idea behind our proposed visual security metric based on image segmentation.

Simple thresholding based segmentation and watershed segmentation is not suitable for this task as it is too sensitive to noise. We tested a mean shift segmentation approach, a statistical region merging based one and a graph based one and decided to use the graph based segmentation method proposed by Felzenszwalb and Huttenlocher [6] as it lead to the most promising segmentation results. Their graph-based segmentation approach works directly on the data points in the feature space (no filtering is performed). It uses a variation of single-linkage clustering. The traditional single-linkage clustering works as follows:

1. Generate a minimum spanning tree of the data points

2. Remove edges with a length greater than a given hard threshold

3. Remaining connected components become clusters

Felzenszwalb and Huttenlocher's method uses adaptive thresholding instead of a fixed threshold. For more details the interested reader is referred to their original work [6].

After segmenting the reference and the encrypted image a method to compare the segmentation results is needed. Again there is a bunch of metrics proposed in the literature for this purpose [8, 20, 22]. The simplest ones are set based metrics like the Jaccard Coefficient. They work well for binary segmentations (only foreground and background) but are not suitable for general segmentations with more than 2 resulting image segments as it is not obvious how the two corresponding sets are found. To overcome this problem coefficients based on the confusion matrix are used. In addition there are also methods based on the Hausdorff distance and gradient based coefficients. All these coefficients have one problem in common: they are quite sensitive to refinement (due to oversegmentation). The distortions introduced in the images due to selective encryption lead to oversegmentation especially for higher encryption levels as it can be seen in figure 2. Thus all these coefficients are not appropriate for our visual security metric approach. Huang and Dom [8] presented two measures to evaluate the results of image segmentation which should overcome this problem (i.e. their measures ignore refinement), one that works without a reference image and one that needs a reference image. We decided to use their measure which is designed to work if a reference (ground-truth) image is available. This measure (abbreviated as HD in the following) is based on the Hamming distance and calculated as follows:

$$HD = 1 - \frac{D_H(GT \to S) + D_H(S \to GT)}{2A}$$

where GT is the ground-truth image (reference image in our case), S is the segmented image (encrypted image in our case), A is the area of the image (number of pixels) and D_H is the Hamming distance defined as follows:

$$D_H(GT \to S) = \sum_i \sum_{j \neq max(i)} |GT_i \cap S_j|$$

$$D_H(S \to GT) = \sum_i \sum_{j \neq max(i)} |S_i \cap GT_j|$$

where GT_i or S_i is the i-th segment in the ground-truth or segmented image, respectively. The range of HD values is between 0 and 1 where values close to 1 indicate that the segmentation result is close to the ground-truth segmentation result. For our SBSS metric we use the HD value directly and interpret values close to 0 as images having a better visual security and a value of 1 indicates identical images.

4. EXPERIMENTAL SETTINGS

To establish a standard of comparison and to show the performance of our SBSS metric in comparison with other metrics we evaluated them on the Berkeley Segmentation Dataset BSDS300[1] [15]. For these images a segmentation ground truth exists and they lead to reasonable results. We use the test image set of the BSDS300 which contains 100 images. The images are true colour images having a resolution of 481×321 or 321×481 pixels. We convert the images to greyscale which is necessary for the encryption method we use. This encryption method is briefly described below.

[1]http://www.eecs.berkeley.edu/Research/Projects/CS/vision/bsds/

Figure 1: Encryption example (left original image, right encrypted image)

4.1 Encryption Method

We decided for a format compliant, bitstream oriented JPEG2000 encryption scheme during our evaluations. The encryption is applied to the JPEG2000 compressed data and in order to achieve format compliance only the packet data is encrypted without the headers. The encryption software is based on JJ2000. Encryption is done by replacing the packet data with generated encrypted bytes. Basically, the JPEG2000 packet body data is encrypted in a format compliant manner using the iterative approach proposed in [16]. The encryption level grows with the amount of bytes in the bitstream that are being replaced by encrypted ones [4], starting right after the JPEG2000 main header. This encryption introduces noise-type distortion into the data which kind of overlay the visual information still present in the data. An example can be seen in figure 1. When assessing the security of format compliantly encrypted visual data, the data can simply be decoded with the encrypted parts (called "direct decoding"). Due to format compliance, this is possible with any given decoding scheme.

For the SBSS approach we utilize the efficient graph-based segmentation implementation[2] provided by the authors [6]. We tested different parameters and found out that $sigma = 0.5$, $K = 250$ and $min = 50$ works best. Figure 2 and figure 3 show some encrypted images (starting from unencrypted towards increasing encryption strength) and their corresponding segmentation results for a well working example (contours remain visible in the segmentation results) and a badly working example (contours disappear in the segmentation results), respectively.

4.2 Evaluation Methodology

We evaluated the PSNR, LV, IR, DFUH, Yongjie10, Li08 and our SBSS metric. To reproduce our results or get comparable ones the following procedure should be used:

- Use the test images of the BSDS300 data set including the segmentation ground truth

- Encrypt the images with the approach to be tested

- Segment the encrypted images according to our approach and evaluate the results using the suggested metric described in section 3

5. EXPERIMENTAL RESULTS

The visual security evaluation results for different metrics tested on the BSDS300 images encrypted using our selective encryption can be seen in figure 4. The figure shows the

[2]http://cs.brown.edu/~pff/segment/

Figure 2: Segmentation well working example

Figure 3: Segmentation badly working example

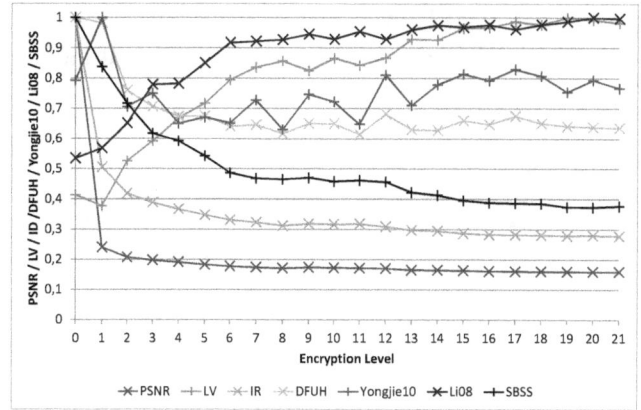

Figure 4: Average metric values

Metric/Correlation	Pearson	Spearman	Kendall Tau
PSNR	-0.4419	-0.6657	-0.5103
LV	0.6449	0.6203	0.4939
IR	-0.5858	-0.6554	-0.5047
DFUH	-0.2759	-0.2059	-0.1526
Yongjie10	0.0189	0.0524	0.0397
Li08	0.5709	0.5282	0.3998
SBSS	**-0.7936**	**-0.8441**	**-0.6822**

Table 1: Correlation values for the tested metrics

average (mean) values over all images. All values in the diagrams are scaled by its maximum value to fit them in the interval [0;1]. The values on the horizontal axis represent the encryption level, where 0 is the uncompressed (original) image, level 1 corresponds to JPEG2000 compression without any encryption and higher values indicate stronger encryption and thus higher visual security.

At lower encryption levels the images do show some resemblance of the original images but with higher encryption levels recognizability and intelligibility of the images decreases as it can be seen in figures 2 and 3. Therefore the desired behaviour of a metric on this set of images would be a monotonically rising or falling curve.

Our proposed metric SBSS shows this desired behaviour as it shows a monotonically falling curve. The slope is steep up to encryption level 6 and gets flatter then which can be explained by the fact that starting from this encryption level only very small parts of the original image remain visible in the encrypted images. Nevertheless there is a continuous decrease up to level 21, i.e. it is able to quantify differences in the encryption strength.

The two quite simple metrics, LV and IR are also able to quantify the difference in encryption levels as IR shows a monotonically falling curve and LV shows a rising curve, but not monotonically though. The curves are not as smooth as the one of SBSS. They also have their steepest slope until encryption level 6. PSNR shows only a flat slope, especially starting from encryption level 6 the values do not change to

a considerable extent any longer and thus it is not suitable for visual security evaluation.

DFUH works quite well up to encryption level 6 but then its return values for higher encryption levels are fluctuating and it is thus no longer able to capture the increase in encryption strength correctly.

Li08 shows a nearly monotonically rising curve towards higher encryption levels with a few exceptions at level 4, 8, 11 and 17. It is able to represent the increase in encryption strength to a certain extent but it performs worse than the two much simpler metrics LV and IR.

Yongjie10 is the worst performing metric. It can be clearly seen that its return values are fluctuating across the whole tested range and there is no clear trend towards rising or falling return values with an increasing encryption level. Thus it is unusable for this kind of images in combination with this kind of visual encryption.

To quantify the differences between the tested visual security evaluation metrics we calculated the simple Pearson correlation coefficient, the Spearman rank correlation coefficient and Kendall Tau (Beta) correlation coefficient, measuring the correlation between the metrics' return values and the encryption level. Table 1 shows the average results over all the images in the test set. The results from the visual inspection of the graph in figure 4 is confirmed by the correlation values. Our proposed method, SBSS, clearly shows the highest correlation, followed by the two simple metrics, LV and IR. Li08 performs worse than IR but better than PSNR. The worst performing metrics are DFUH and Yongjie10. Note that we tested these metrics only with one specific selective encryption approach. They might be more suitable for another approach and thus perform better if utilized for visual security evaluation there.

6. CONCLUSION

The ability to recognise objects inside encrypted images is an important aspect in visual security evaluation. Our aim was to test if it is possible to detect objects inside the images using image segmentation to assess visual security. Thus we developed a new visual security metric based on image segmentation, SBSS. Our experimental results show that SBSS is well suited for that task. We evaluated our approach on the test images of the BSDS300 dataset which is specifically made for image segmentation (there exists a segmentation ground truth). Our results clearly show that is possible to evaluate the visual security of encrypted images based on image segmentation. Throughout the entire test set used it turned out that SBSS, LV and IR performed best. But it also became apparent that there are always some outliers for which one or several of the metrics did not perform well. It showed that the tested metrics are most reliable for small encryption strengths.

The results presented in this paper are a basis for further research on image segmentation based visual security metrics. Our future work will include tests with different kinds of visual encryption algorithms.

7. ACKNOWLEDGMENTS

This work was partially funded by the Austrian Science Fund (FWF), project nr. P27776.

8. REFERENCES

[1] J. Ahmad and F. Ahmed. Efficiency analysis and security evaluation of image encryption schemes. *International Journal of Video & Image Processing and Network Security*, 12(4):18–31, 2012.

[2] S.-K. Au Yeung, S. Zhu, and B. Zeng. Quality assessment for a perceptual video encryption system. In *Wireless Communications, Networking and Information Security (WCNIS), 2010 IEEE International Conference on*, pages 102–106, June 2010.

[3] M. V. Droogenbroeck and R. Benedett. Techniques for a selective encryption of uncompressed and compressed images. In *Proceedings of ACIVS (Advanced Concepts for Intelligent Vision Systems)*, pages 90–97, Ghent University, Belgium, Sept. 2002.

[4] F. Dufaux, S. Wee, J. Apostolopoulos, and T. Ebrahimi. JPSEC for secure imaging in JPEG2000. In A. G. Tescher, editor, *Applications of Digital Image Processing XXVII*, volume 5558, pages 319–330. SPIE, Aug. 2004.

[5] H. M. Elkamchouchi and M. Makar. Measuring encryption quality for bitmap images encrypted with rijndael and kamkar block ciphers. In *Radio science conference, 2005. NRSC 2005. Proceedings of the twenty-second national*, pages 277–284. IEEE, 2005.

[6] P. F. Felzenszwalb and D. P. Huttenlocher. Efficient graph-based image segmentation. *Int. J. Comput. Vision*, 59(2):167–181, Sept. 2004.

[7] H. Hofbauer and A. Uhl. Visual quality indices and low quality images. In *IEEE 2nd European Workshop on Visual Information Processing*, pages 171–176, Paris, France, July 2010.

[8] Q. Huang and B. Dom. Quantitative methods of evaluating image segmentation. In *Image Processing, 1995. Proceedings., International Conference on*, volume 3, pages 53–56. IEEE, 1995.

[9] S. Jenisch and A. Uhl. A detailed evaluation of format-compliant encryption methods for JPEG XR-compressed images. *EURASIP Journal on Information Security*, 2014(6), 2014.

[10] S. Jenisch and A. Uhl. Visual security evaluation based on SIFT object recognition. In L. Iliadis et al., editors, *Proceedings of the 10th Artificial Intelligence Applications and Innovations Conference (AIAI 2014)*, volume 436 of *Springer IFIP AICT*, pages 624–633, Rhodes, GR, Sept. 2014.

[11] M. I. Khan, V. Jeoti, and A. S. Malik. On perceptual encryption: Variants of DCT block scrambling scheme for JPEG compressed images. In T.-H. Kim, S. K. Pal, W. I. Grosky, N. Pissinou, T. K. Shih, and D. Slezak, editors, *FGIT-SIP/MulGraB*, volume 123 of *Communications in Computer and Information Science*, pages 212–223. Springer, 2010.

[12] X. Li. A new measure of image scrambling degree based on grey level difference and information entropy. In *Computational Intelligence and Security, 2008. CIS '08. International Conference on*, volume 1, pages 350–354, dec. 2008.

[13] L. Luccheseyz and S. Mitray. Color image segmentation: A state-of-the-art survey. *Proceedings of the Indian National Science Academy (INSA-A)*, 67(2):207–221, 2001.

[14] Y. Mao and M. Wu. Security evaluation for communication-friendly encryption of multimedia. Singapore, Oct. 2004. IEEE Signal Processing Society.

[15] D. Martin, C. Fowlkes, D. Tal, and J. Malik. A database of human segmented natural images and its application to evaluating segmentation algorithms and measuring ecological statistics. In *Proc. 8th Int'l Conf. Computer Vision*, volume 2, pages 416–423, July 2001.

[16] T. Stütz and A. Uhl. On format-compliant iterative encryption of JPEG2000. In *Proceedings of the Eighth IEEE International Symposium on Multimedia (ISM'06)*, pages 985–990, San Diego, CA, USA, Dec. 2006. IEEE Computer Society.

[17] J. Sun, Z. Xu, J. Liu, and Y. Yao. An objective visual security assessment for cipher-images based on local entropy. *Multimedia Tools and Applications*, Mar. 2010. online publication.

[18] L. Tong, F. Dai, Y. Zhang, and J. Li. Visual security evaluation for video encryption. In *Proceedings of the International Conference on Multimedia*, MM '10, pages 835–838, New York, NY, USA, 2010. ACM.

[19] Y. Yao, Z. Xu, and J. Sun. Visual security assessment for cipher-images based on neighborhood similarity. *Informatica*, 33:69–76, 2009.

[20] G. L.-E. W. Yong. Evaluation measures for segmentation. *matrix*, 1(1):5.

[21] T. Yongjie and Z. Wengang. Image scrambling degree evaluation algorithm based on grey relation analysis. In *Computational and Information Sciences (ICCIS), 2010 International Conference on*, pages 511–514, dec. 2010.

[22] Y. J. Zhang. A survey on evaluation methods for image segmentation. *Pattern recognition*, 29(8):1335–1346, 1996.

Enhanced Collusion Resistance for Segment-wise Recombined Fingerprinting in P2P Distribution Systems

[Extended Abstract]

David Megías
dmegias@uoc.edu

Amna Qureshi
aqureshi@uoc.edu

Internet Interdisciplinary Institute (IN3), Universitat Oberta de Catalunya
Av. Carl Friedrich Gauss, 5, 08860 Castelldefels, Catalonia, Spain

ABSTRACT

Recombined fingerprinting has been recently proposed as a scalable alternative to the traditional client-server model for anonymous fingerprinting. In recombined fingerprinting, the contents are distributed in P2P fashion from a few seed nodes to the rest of buyers. However, the solution of the previous works requires that a hash of the whole fingerprint is also constructed during distribution in such a way that two different codes must be used (one at segment level and one at hash level). This solution is impractical for two reasons: (1) the fingerprint's length is increased, and (2) the construction of the fingerprints through recombination must be supervised in order to obtain a valid hash-level codeword. This work contributes with a solution to this problem, consisting of embedding collusion-resistant codewords only at segment level and removing the need for hash-level encoding. The proposed solution not only results in shorter fingerprints, but also simplifies the distribution protocol since supervision is no longer required. The resulting system is shown to work for four different state-of-the-art collusion-resistant codes by means of thousands of simulations.

Keywords

Collusion-resistant fingerprinting; Recombined fingerprinting; Traceability

1. INTRODUCTION

In this work, we integrate recombined fingerprinting with state-of-the-art collusion-resistant fingerprinting codes, which have previously shown good performance, to construct a fingerprint in segment-wise fashion that avoids the drawbacks of previous proposals. This segment-wise construction of the fingerprint prevents the two-layer encoding required by the previous recombination-based proposals [4, 2]. A non-linear collusion attack is also used to evaluate the collusion resistance of the improved segment-wise fingerprint-

ing. In addition, a threshold can be determined for each collusion-resistant fingerprinting code to identify the colluders in the traitor-tracing protocol.

2. RECOMBINED FINGERPRINTING

In recombined fingerprinting, as proposed in [4, 3], the content is divided into several ordered fragments, with each of them embedded separately with a binary sequence called segment. The concatenation of all the segments forms the fingerprint. At the system start up, the merchant creates a set of M seed copies and distributes them to the M seed buyers. Unlike the M seed buyers, a non-seed buyer obtains the fragments of the content in P2P fashion from at least two sources (parents), which produces a recombined fingerprint. The merchant executes the embedding process M times for the seed buyers, while the non-seed buyers obtain their fingerprints without execution of the embedding scheme and, thus, no additional overhead is involved for the merchant. The proposed system uses a third party –the transaction monitor– to store a transaction record of each transfer in order to keep track of data transfer between the buyers.

The system proposed in [4] exhibits the following shortcomings: (1) expensive graph search in order to identify an illegal re-distributor that may require backtracking; (2) the tracing authority requires the cooperation from some innocent buyers; (3) possible non-traceability of an illegal re-distributor in case some buyers cannot participate in traitor tracing; (4) two-layer anti-collusion encoding (at segment and hash levels), which results in longer fingerprints; (5) the anti-collusion mechanism used in this system suffers from several drawbacks that are shared with its improved version [2]; and (6) the distribution protocol relies on honest proxies for data transfer between the buyers of the system.

Megías [2] proposed an improved version of the recombined fingerprinting mechanism in which malicious proxies are considered in the distribution protocol. In addition, the proposed scheme uses a standard database search for traitor tracing unlike the graph search approach taken in [4]. Although [2] overcomes the major drawbacks of the recombined fingerprinting approach, it still exhibits the following shortcomings: (1) the system still requires a two-layer anti-collusion encoding of the fingerprint, which results in long fingerprints; and (2) the hash of the fingerprint is used to trace an illegal re-distributor in case of collusion of several buyers and, hence, such a hash must be a valid codeword of some anti-collusion code. Thus, the transaction monitor

IH&MMSec 2016, June 20–23, 2016, Vigo, Spain.

© 2016 Copyright held by the owner/author(s).

ACM ISBN 978-1-4503-4290-2/16/06.

DOI: http://dx.doi.org/10.1145/2909827.2931096

still requires the cooperation of the proxies to construct a valid hash-level codeword.

3. PROPOSED SYSTEM AND RESULTS

The drawbacks of [4, 2] are overcome by introducing state-of-the-art collusion-resistant codes only at segment level and, thus, removing the requirement of a hash-level codeword. As in the previous works, each segment of a fingerprint is a codeword of the selected collusion-resistant fingerprinting scheme, which is resistant against $c \leq c_0$ colluders. When the number of colluders is within the collusion resistance capability of the code, all segments of all colluders provide a large score in the traitor-tracing algorithm. On the other hand, for non-colluders, some segments produce a large score (the ones which, by chance, are identical to those of one of the colluders) whereas the others produce a low score. The average score is, thus, significantly larger for colluders compared to innocent buyers. This is true as long as the number of available codewords for each segment (equal to the number of seed buyers, M) is larger than the collusion resistance of the code (c_0). As a rule of thumb, we suggest choosing $M \geq 2c_0$ to guarantee this condition.

We have selected four state-of-the-art collusion-resistant fingerprinting codes [7, 5, 6, 1] for the generation of the fingerprint's segments. We have tested the proposed system generating $1,000$ random collusions of four buyers for each code. In all $4 \times 1,000 = 4,000$ simulations, the four colluders were successfully identified and no innocent buyer was wrongly accused.

Fig. 1 illustrates the collusion resistance of the fingerprinting scheme for three of the selected codes and one of those $1,000$ simulations. It can be noticed the the four colluders were successfully identified with the highest scores, whereas innocent buyers yielded much lower values.

4. CONCLUSIONS

We propose a new fingerprint construction method based on the idea of automatic recombination of fingerprints [4, 2]. The drawbacks related to the collusion resistance mechanism of [4, 2] are circumvented by using four state-of-the-art collusion-resistant fingerprinting codes [7, 5, 6, 1] only at the segment level. The tracing mechanism of these codes is shown to work in a segment-wise fashion such that each segment of the fingerprint is a collusion-resistant codeword.

Acknowledgments

This work was partly funded by the Spanish Government through grants TIN2011-27076-C03-02 "CO-PRIVACY" and TIN2014-57364-C2-2-R "SMARTGLACIS".

5. REFERENCES

[1] T. Laarhoven and B. de Weger. Discrete distributions in the Tardos scheme, revisited. In *Proceedings of the First ACM Workshop on Information Hiding and Multimedia Security*, IH&MMSec'13, pages 13–18. ACM, 2013.

[2] D. Megías. Improved privacy-preserving P2P multimedia distribution based on recombined fingerprints. *IEEE Transactions on Dependable and Secure Computing*, 12(2):179–189, 2015.

[3] D. Megías and J. Domingo-Ferrer. DNA-inspired anonymous fingerprinting for efficient peer-to-peer

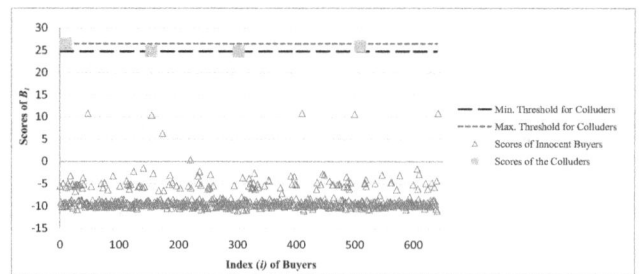

(a) Scores of four colluders and innocent buyers obtained using the tracing protocol of Nuida *et al.* codes [5]

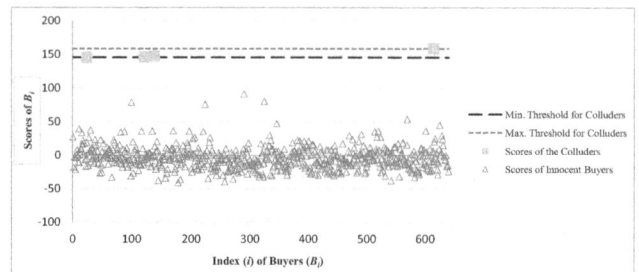

(b) Scores of four colluders and innocent buyers obtained using the tracing protocol of Skoriç codes [6]

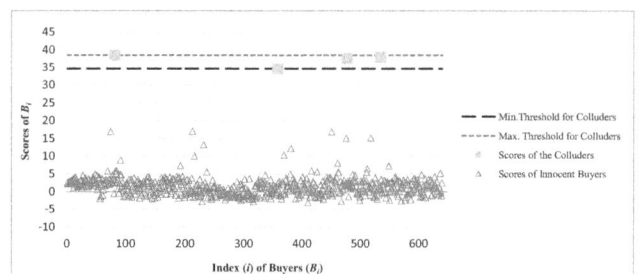

(c) Scores of four colluders and innocent buyers obtained using the tracing protocol of Laarhoven codes [1]

Figure 1: Simulation results

content distribution. In *Proceedings of IEEE Congress on Evolutionart Computation*, ICEC '13, pages 2376–2383. IEEE, 2013.

[4] D. Megías and J. Domingo-Ferrer. Privacy-aware peer-to-peer content distribution using automatically recombined fingerprints. *Multimedia Systems*, 20(2):105–125, 2014.

[5] K. Nuida, S. Fujitsu, M. Hagiwara, T. Kitagawa, H. Watanabe, K. Ogawa, and H. Imai. An improvement of Tardos's collusion-secure fingerprinting codes with very short lengths. In *Proceedings of the 17th International Conference on Applied Algebra, Algebraic Algorithms and Error-correcting Codes*, AAECC'07, pages 80–89. Springer, 2007.

[6] B. Skoríc, S. Katzenbeisser, and M. Celik. Symmetric Tardos fingerprinting codes for arbitrary alphabet sizes. *Designs, Codes and Cryptography*, 46:137–166, 2008.

[7] G. Tardos. Optimal probabilistic fingerprint codes. In *Proceedings of the Thirty-fifth Annual ACM Symposium on Theory of Computing*, pages 116–125. ACM, 2003.

Study of a Verifiable Biometric Matching

Hervé Chabanne
Morpho, Télécom Paris Tech
herve.chabanne@morpho.com

Julien Keuffer
Morpho
julien.keuffer@morpho.com

Roch Lescuyer
Morpho
roch.lescuyer@morpho.com

ABSTRACT

In this paper, we apply verifiable computing techniques to a biometric matching. The purpose of verifiable computation is to give the result of a computation along with a proof that the calculations were correctly performed. We adapt a protocol called SUMCHECK protocol and present a system that performs verifiable biometric matching in the case of a fast border control. This is a work in progress and we focus on verifying an inner product. We then give some experimental results of its implementation. Verifiable computation here helps to enforce the authentication phase bringing in the process a proof that the biometric verification has been correctly performed.

1. INTRODUCTION

In many places, people living next to another country frequently cross the border to go to work. Due to border controls, the crossing can be very slow but automated systems can decrease the time spent on the borders. For example, since August 2014, a dedicated application developed for the US Customs and Border Protection (CPB) can be downloaded on a smartphone, it enables to reduce the administrative tasks of CPB officers [1]. With this application, US travellers arriving in the United States first fill custom declaration forms, then take a picture of their face and submit them to the application, enabling a faster entry in the country. However, custom officers still have to check the passport of every traveller using the application. We study an alternative scenario, where the traveller authenticate himself with his own device. Our idea is to devise a system using biometrics to perform an automated comparison between the fresh face picture of a user and the picture of his face stored on his biometric passport. This could be implemented as a dedicated application installed on a smart device.

Today, many systems performing face recognition use machine learning techniques to transform a face picture into a

[1] www.cbp.gov/travel/us-citizens/mobile-passport-control

IH&MMSec 2016 June 20–23, 2016, Vigo, Spain

© 2016 Copyright held by the owner/author(s).

ACM ISBN 978-1-4503-4290-2/16/06.

DOI: http://dx.doi.org/10.1145/2909827.2931097

biometric template. The model called convolution neural network (CNN) has shown excellent results [4]. CNNs have millions of parameters that are tuned in a learning phase. Once a CNN is trained, it embeds a picture in a Euclidean space where two vectors representing the same face are closer than two vectors that come from different faces. Since a CNN embeds a pictures in a Euclidean space, the verifiable biometric matching is an inner product computation which is compared to a threshold.

Because borders are sensitive places, strong security guarantees must be given. The traveller has therefore to prove the authority that the biometric matching was done correctly. We use verifiable computing techniques to ensure that the authentication was correctly done. A verifiable computation system allows a *verifier* to delegate the computation of a function to a *prover*. Upon completion of the computation, the prover returns the result and a proof of the computation. The verifier can thus efficiently check the result is correct without making any confidence assumption on the prover. Verifiable computing is theoretically solved for years but researchers recently focused on designing verifiable computing systems aiming practicality [5, 3, 6]. In our use case, the traveller has the role of the prover and the prover is implemented on a limited device with restricted computational power and storage capacity. This reverses the classical roles of the prover and the verifier in verifiable systems. The choice of the underlying verifying system has thus been driven according to this configuration, as well as to the targeted computation. The requirements for the prover led us to choose interactive proofs [5] and in particular the SUMCHECK protocol [1] .

We emphasize that our contribution is limited to the application of verifiable biometric matching techniques to the use case. This is only a part of what is needed to address the whole problem. For instance, liveness detection or verification of the CNN face encoding seem necessary but those topics are outside the scope of this paper. Our purpose here is to deal with a realistic use case for a delegation of a verifiable face matching algorithm.

The same techniques apply to iris modality. In this case, the Euclidean distance is replaced by fractional Hamming distance.

2. VERIFIABLE INNER PRODUCT

The sumcheck protocol

In the SUMCHECK protocol [1], a prover wants to convince a verifier that he knows the evaluation of a multivariate poly-

n	Inner product computation (ms)	Prover time (ms)	Verifier time (ms)	Communication
128	$< 10^{-4}$	0.01	0.032	232B
256	0.0031	0.017	0.053	264B
512	0.0032	0.042	0.098	296B
1024	0.0032	0.065	0.25	328B
4096	0.0077	0.31	1.13	392B
2^{20}	3	122	600	648B

Table 1: Benchmark of the verified inner product of two n-components vectors

nomial on a finite set. If the polynomial to verify has n variables, the protocol has n rounds. In each round, the verifier picks a random value from a finite field and asks the prover to compute a polynomial derived from the polynomial to verify. The verifier needs few computations to check that the polynomial sent by the prover is linked to the previous one. As a consequence, the verifier can accept the new polynomial with high probability as a claim for the initial value. At the end, the verifier has to evaluate the original polynomial in a single value to decide if he accepts the initial claimed value. We also note that the security of the protocol is strongly related to the size of the finite field over which the computation take place.

Application of the sumcheck protocol to the use case

Consider two vectors $a, b \in \mathbb{Z}^n$. The inner product of a and b is defined by: $H = \sum_{i=0}^{n-1} a_i \cdot b_i$. Denoting $d = \log n$, one can rewrite relation above with two functions a and b defined over $\{1, \ldots, n\}$ such that: $a : i \mapsto a_i$ and $b : i \mapsto b_i$. If the index i is written as a binary vector, the same relation holds between multivariate polynomials: $a : (i_1, \ldots, i_d) \mapsto a_i$, $b : (i_1, \ldots, i_d) \mapsto b_i$, so:

$$H = \sum_{i_1 \in \{0,1\}} \ldots \sum_{i_d \in \{0,1\}} a(i_1, \ldots, i_d) \cdot b(i_1, \ldots, i_d).$$

To use the SUMCHECK protocol securely, we need polynomials defined over a large finite field. Thus we apply efficient techniques developed in [5] to extend the definition set of the polynomials a and b from $\{0,1\}^d$ to $\mathbb{F}^d$, where $\mathbb{F}$ is a finite field. The functions we obtain, called extensions and denoted $\tilde{a}$ and $\tilde{b}$, agree with functions a and b over $\{0,1\}^d$. Applying the SUMCHECK protocol to the polynomial $\tilde{a} \cdot \tilde{b}$ over $\{0,1\}^d$ gives a proof of the value of the inner product H.

Experimental results

We implement a verified inner product, following the SUMCHECK protocol. During the protocol, we make computations over the prime finite field $\mathbb{F}_p$ where $p = 2^{61} - 1$, which allows to perform efficient modular arithmetic. Since the computations run over a finite field, dealing with negative values for the input vectors has no ideal solution. We thus run our benchmarks on random vectors of different sizes composed of natural numbers. We also limit the size of the randoms values to avoid overflow in the computations. This can be avoided by implementing the protocol in a larger field at the cost of a decrease of performances.

Communication costs and security

For input vectors of size n, the SUMCHECK protocol has $\log_2 n$ rounds, the verifier sends one field element per round (a random field element which is part of a challenge) and the

prover three (the three values needed to interpolate an intermediate polynomial). The total communication during the protocol is thus $4\log_2(n) + 1$ field elements.

Benchmarks

We run experiments on a laptop with a 2 GHz Intel Core i5 processor with 8 GB of RAM. The implementation is written in C++. Table 1 gives the average times of 1000 computations for each vector size.

Adding security to the protocol

To thwart eavesdroppers, we propose to use masking techniques [2]. In our context, this means that the traveller has to pick a random permutation π of the template coordinates and a random vector r of the same size than the template. The reference template t_{ref} is replaced by $\pi(t_{ref}) + r$ and with a fresh template t, $\mathrm{dist}(\pi(t_{ref}) + r, \pi(t) + r) = \mathrm{dist}(t_{ref}, t)$. Thus, an eavesdropper does not get information on t or t_{ref}.

We stress that the traveller has to store the permutation and the random vector. Therefore if the authorities have a doubt about the identity of the traveller, the latter has everything on his phone to unmask the templates and compute the distance between them.

3. ACKNOWLEDGMENTS

This work has been partially funded by the European H2020 TREDISEC project (ICT-2014-644412).

4. REFERENCES

[1] S. Arora and B. Barak. *Computational Complexity: A Modern Approach*. Cambridge University Press, New York, NY, USA, 2009.

[2] M. J. Atallah, K. B. Frikken, M. T. Goodrich, and R. Tamassia. *Financial Cryptography and Data Security: 9th International Conference*, chapter Secure Biometric Authentication for Weak Computational Devices. Springer Berlin Heidelberg, 2005.

[3] B. Parno, J. Howell, C. Gentry, and M. Raykova. Pinocchio: Nearly practical verifiable computation. In *2013 IEEE Symposium on Security and Privacy*, 2013.

[4] F. Schroff, D. Kalenichenko, and J. Philbin. Facenet: A unified embedding for face recognition and clustering. In *The IEEE Conference on Computer Vision and Pattern Recognition (CVPR)*, June 2015.

[5] J. Thaler. Time-optimal interactive proofs for circuit evaluation. In *Advances in Cryptology–CRYPTO 2013. Proceedings*, pages 71–89. Springer Berlin Heidelberg, 2013.

[6] R. S. Wahby, S. Setty, Z. Ren, A. J. Blumberg, and M. Walfish. Efficient RAM and control flow in verifiable outsourced computation. In *NDSS*, 2015.

Privacy Protection for JPEG Content on Image-Sharing Platforms

Kun He
IRT B-Com
1219 Avenue Champs Blancs
35510 Cesson-Sévigné,
France
kun.he@b-com.com

Christophe Bidan
CentraleSupélec
Avenue de la Boulaie
CS 47601
35576 Cesson-Sévigné,
France
christophe.bidan@
centralesupelec.fr

Gaëtan Le Guelvouit
IRT B-Com
1219 Avenue Champs Blancs
35510 Cesson-Sévigné,
France
gaetan.leguelvouit@
b-com.com

ABSTRACT

In this paper, we show that, using the encryption algorithm of He *et al.* [2], it is possible to ensure privacy protection for JPEG content on several widely used image-sharing platforms (e.g., Flickr, Pinterest, Google+ and Twitter).

Keywords

Privacy protection, image encryption, image-sharing platforms

1. INTRODUCTION

Nowadays, users are accustomed to share their photos with their friends on image-sharing platforms. For helping users to control the access to their images, the image-sharing platforms often allow users to specify the friends that can access to each image. It may result a feeling of safety and privacy. However, from our point of view, the privacy of the users is not guaranteed since at least the provider of the image-sharing platform can clearly know the contents of any published images. In order to protect the privacy, each user can encrypt the images before publishing them, and give the decryption key only to the friends that are authorized to access the images. In this way, if the image encryption algorithm is secure, people who do not have the key (including the providers of image-sharing platforms) can not know the contents of published images. But not all of the image encryption algorithms can be used to protect user's privacy on image-sharing platforms.

First of all, we need an encryption algorithm that output image files ready to be published on image-sharing platforms. The traditional secure and efficient algorithms, such as AES, DES, RSA, [3] etc. can be directly used to encrypt any data, including images. Using these algorithms, the confidentiality of images is guaranteed. But the encryption result is a binary file, if we try to publish this kind of

IH&MMSec 2016 June 20-23, 2016, Vigo, Spain

© 2016 Copyright held by the owner/author(s).

ACM ISBN 978-1-4503-4290-2/16/06.

DOI: http://dx.doi.org/10.1145/2909827.2933195

encrypted image on an image-sharing platform, none of the platforms will view it as a correct format (the acceptable formats being JPEG, PNG, GIF or TIFF, etc.).

Secondly, the encryption algorithm itself should be secure enough to protect user's privacy on image-sharing platforms. Some algorithms based on scrambling encryption [5] can preserve the image format after encryption. But as a scrambling algorithm, it is not IND-CPA secure since we can easily distinguish the encryption of a brighter image from a darker image [6].

Backes *et al.* [1] used steganography to protect the target image in an existing JPEG image, and the container image can be accepted by any image-sharing platforms. However, there is the limitation of the size of container image and the quantity of upload image.

In the next section, we present the experimental results of using the encryption algorithm of He *et al.* [2] to ensure privacy protection for JPEG content on several widely used image-sharing platforms (e.g., Flickr, Pinterest, Google+ and Twitter). We first encrypt images and publish them on different platforms to verify whether the encrypted images can be accepted. Then we download and decrypt the images and compare the decrypted images with the original ones.

2. EXPERIMENTATION OF ENCRYPTION AFTER QUANTIZATION

Considering images on most of image-sharing platforms are compressed by using JPEG [7] standard, and the downloaded images are always in JPEG format, we focus on processing JPEG images. The idea of our encryption algorithm is close to the one proposed by Kunkelmann *et al.* [4]. They encrypt partial DCT coefficients to protect the JPEG-based video. But the work of He *et al.* [2] proved that the encryption integrated after DCT is not as good as the encryption integrated after quantization. Therefore, we implement the encryption algorithm after quantization proposed in [2] on different image-sharing platforms.

We upload the encrypted images to four widely used image-sharing platforms: Flickr, Pinterest, Google+ and Twitter. Then we download and decrypt the images. As examples, we first take the grayscale and the color image "Lena" of 512×512 pixels to do a detailed experiment, since this size is accepted by all platforms. Then we take five grayscale images and five color images of different sizes to do more tests.

The encryption is implemented on the laptop before uploading. Before encryption, we resize prepared images to the limitation image size of each platform and change the downsampling ratio for color images if they do not satisfy the conditions. Then we requantize the images using quantization tables of $Q = 71$ for all platforms. We have verified that, in this way, these parameters of prepared images are not changed before and after publishing on each image-sharing platform.

Next, we use one account to upload the encrypted images and use another account to download them. Then the decryption is implemented on the laptop and we obtain the decrypted images. For comparing original images and decrypted images, we calculate their Peak Signal to Noise Ratio (PSNR) and Universal Image Quality Index (UIQI) [8].

According to the experimental results, all of the encrypted images are completely unreadable, and when we upload the encrypted images, all of them can be accepted by these image-sharing platforms as correct image format. In Tab. 1, we find that the decryption algorithm can reconstruct the downloaded images with a high quality and also similar to the decrypted images without publishing. Fig. 1 shows the decrypted results of "Lena" after downloading from Flickr, we find that there is no visible noise in images. For the other three image-sharing platforms, and for the other ten images, we have the same conclusion.

Platform	Grayscale image		Color image	
	PSNR (dB)	UIQI	PSNR (dB)	UIQI
Flickr	34.92	0.922	34.42	0.875
Pinterest	34.92	0.922	34.42	0.875
Google+	34.92	0.922	32.47	0.870
Twitter	34.92	0.922	34.26	0.877
Decryption without publishing	34.92	0.922	34.42	0.875

Table 1: Summary of the results of "Lena".

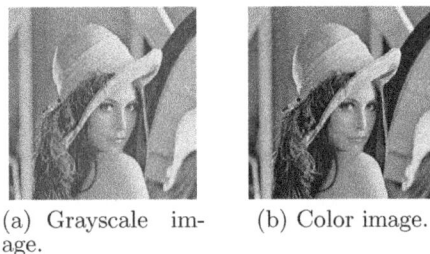

(a) Grayscale image. (b) Color image.

Figure 1: Experimental results of decrypted "Lena" on Flickr.

3. CONCLUSION

In this paper, we use the encryption algorithm of He *et al.* [2] to ensure privacy protection for JPEG content on four widely used image-sharing platforms: Flickr, Pinterest, Google+ and Twitter. Our experimental results show that the encrypted images are unreadable and can be accepted by all of the image-sharing platforms as correct image format. After downloading the encrypted image, we can reconstruct the plaintext image with a pretty high quality. So for these image-sharing platforms, the used encryption algorithm realizes both security encryption and high-quality decryption. It can protect user's privacy very well. Unfortunately, we have done the same experiments on some other image-sharing platforms, such as Facebook, but the quality of the decrypted downloaded images is not very satisfactory. So we are still working on the improvement of the encrypted algorithm in order to decrypt the image with a higher quality after publishing it on the image-sharing platforms like Facebook.

4. REFERENCES

[1] M. Backes, S. Gerling, S. Lorenz, and S. Lukas. X-pire 2.0: a user-controlled expiration date and copy protection mechanism. In *Symposium on Applied Computing, SAC 2014, Gyeongju, Republic of Korea - March 24 - 28, 2014*, pages 1633–1640. ACM.

[2] K. He, C. Bidan, G. Le Guelvouit, and C. Feron. Robust and secure image encryption schemes during jpeg compression process. In *Proceedings of Imaging and Multimedia Analytics in a Web and Mobile World, IS&T International Symposium on Electronic Imaging 2016, San Francisco, California, USA, February 14-18, 2016*.

[3] J. Katz and Y. Lindell. *Introduction to modern cryptography: principles and protocols.* CRC press, 2007.

[4] T. Kunkelmann and R. Reinema. A scalable security architecture for multimedia communication standards. In *Proceedings of the International Conference on Multimedia Computing and Systems, ICMCS 1997, Ottawa, Ontario, Canada, June 3-6, 1997*, pages 660–662. IEEE Computer Society.

[5] S. Lian, J. Sun, and Z. Wang. A novel image encryption scheme based-on JPEG encoding. In *8th International Conference on Information Visualisation, IV 2004, 14-16 July 2004, London, UK*, pages 217–220.

[6] A. Marcedone and C. Orlandi. Obfuscation ⇒ (IND-CPA security !⇒ circular security). In *Security and Cryptography for Networks - 9th International Conference, SCN 2014, Amalfi, Italy, September 3-5, 2014. Proceedings*, volume 8642 of *Lecture Notes in Computer Science*, pages 77–90. Springer.

[7] W. B. Pennebaker and J. L. Mitchell. *JPEG: Still image data compression standard.* Springer Science & Business Media, 1993.

[8] Z. Wang and A. C. Bovik. A universal image quality index. *Signal Processing Letters, IEEE*, 9(3):81–84, 2002.

PPE-Based Reversible Data Hiding

Han-Zhou Wu
School of Inf. Science & Technology
Southwest Jiaotong University
Chengdu 611756, P. R. China
h.wu.phd@ieee.org

Hong-Xia Wang
School of Inf. Science & Technology
Southwest Jiaotong University
Chengdu 611756, P. R. China
hxwang@home.swjtu.edu.cn

Yun-Qing Shi
Department of ECE
New Jersey Institute of Technology
Newark, NJ 07102, United States
shi@njit.edu

ABSTRACT
We propose to utilize the prediction-error of prediction error (PPE) of a pixel to reversibly carry the secret data in this letter. In the proposed method, the pixels to be embedded are firstly predicted with their neighboring pixels to obtain the prediction errors (PEs). By exploiting the PEs of the neighboring pixels, the prediction of the PEs of the pixels to be embedded can be then determined. And, a sorting technique based on the local complexity of a pixel is used to collect the PPEs to generate an ordered PPE sequence so that, smaller PPEs will be processed first for data embedding. By reversibly shifting the PPE histogram (PPEH) with optimized parameters, the pixels corresponding to the altered PPEH bins can be finally modified to carry the entire secret data. Experimental results have implied that, the proposed algorithm can benefit from the prediction procedure, sorting technique as well as parameters selection, and therefore outperform some state-of-the-art works in terms of payload-distortion performance.

CCS Concepts
• **Computing methodologies** → Image processing;

Keywords
Reversible data hiding; prediction-error of prediction error (PPE); sorting; adaptive; watermarking.

1. MOTIVATION
The existing reversible data hiding (RDH) [1] algorithms, in most cases, predict the pixels with a well-designed predictor at first. Then, the secret bits are embedded in the resultant prediction-error histogram (PEH). The pixel prediction procedure is often required to well predict the pixels. Due to the spatial correlations between neighboring pixels, the existing methods often exploit the PE of a pixel to carry the secret data. In fact, there should also exist strong correlations between neighboring PEs. One evidence can be found in the prediction mechanism of modern video lossy compression. For example, in intra prediction, the prediction block for an intra 4 × 4 luma macroblock (consisting of 16 pixels) will be generated with nine possible prediction modes due to the spatial correlations between neighboring pixels. Then, in order to improve the coding efficiency, the prediction mode of a luma macroblock should be further predicted from the prediction modes of neighboring luma macroblocks since correlations also exist between the neighboring prediction modes. The success of steganalysis by modeling the differences between neighboring pixels with 1-order and 2-order Markov chains [2] also reveals that correlations exist between the neighboring PEs if we consider the differences as a kind of PEs.

IH&MMSec 2016, June 20–23, 2016, Vigo, Spain.
ACM 978-1-4503-4290-2/16/06.
http://dx.doi.org/10.1145/2909827.2933196

Therefore, we can actually adopt the prediction-error of prediction error (PPE) of a pixel to hide data. Based on this perspective, we propose a reliable PPE-based RDH method in this letter, in which the PPEs of the pixels to be embedded are firstly determined according to their neighboring pixels. To reduce the distortion for a required payload, the pixels are sorted by the local complexities. A pixel with a lower complexity will be preferentially embedded with a secret bit. By shifting the resultant PPE histogram (PPEH), the corresponding pixels can be finally altered to carry the secret data. Experiments have implied that, the proposed method can provide a good payload-distortion behavior.

2. ESSENTIALS OF PROPOSED METHOD
The proposed method uses grayscale images. The data embedding procedure mainly consists of four parts: the pixel prediction, the prediction of prediction error, the use of pixel sorting, and the data hiding in the image.

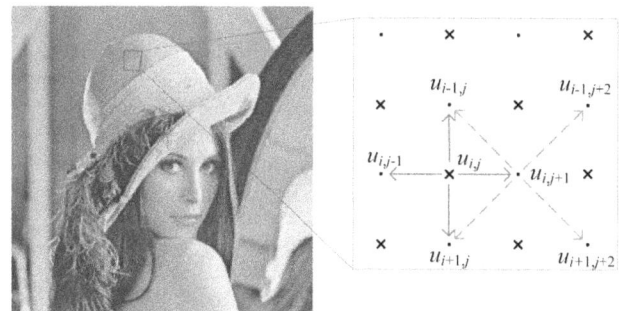

Figure 1: The pixel prediction pattern. The pixel $u_{i,j}$ will be predicted from its four neighbors in the dot set, and $u_{i,j+1}$ will be predicted from its four neighbors still in the dot set.

For pixel prediction, all pixels are divided into two sets: the cross set and dot set (see Fig. 1). The cross set is used for data hiding and dot set for pixel prediction. We use this rhombus pattern as it can maintain a good prediction performance [3]. It is noted that, one may use other efficient prediction patterns. We consider $u_{i,j}$ in Fig. 1 as an example. In Fig. 1, $u_{i,j}$ will be predicted from its four neighbors by using the interpolation operation [1]. The resultant prediction-error is computed as $e_{i,j} = u_{i,j} - u_{i,j}^+$, where $u_{i,j}^+$ is the prediction value. The prediction of $e_{i,j}$, denoted by $e_{i,j}'$, will be the average of the PEs of neighboring pixels in the dot set. As shown in Fig. 1, the neighbor $u_{i,j+1}$ will be predicted from four neighbors still in the dot set by using the interpolation operation. Therefore, we can finally obtain the PE of $e_{i,j}$, namely, $e_{i,j}^+ = e_{i,j} - e_{i,j}'$.

In addition to the prediction of PEs, a pixel sorting technique, also called pixel selection, is used. The purpose is to put the PPEs in a decreasing order of the prediction accuracy so that smaller PPEs can be processed first, which benefits the embedding performance. Here, we refer the reader to [7] for a complete understanding.

After sorting, we collect a part of the PPEs with relatively smaller values to generate a PPEH. We choose two peak-zero bin-pairs (l_p, l_z) and (r_p, r_z) for data hiding. During data embedding, the PPEs in range $[l_z, l_p] \cup (r_p, r_z]$ are shifted to avoid ambiguous. For a PPE with a value of l_p or r_p, if the secret bit equals "0", the PPE will be kept unchanged; otherwise, it will be modified as (l_p-1) or (r_p+1). Thus, a marked PPEH can be generated and the used pixels can be finally modified with $\{\pm 1, 0\}$ operation to match the PPEH. This way, the marked image can be finally constructed.

It is noted that, there is no need that $h(l_p)+h(r_p)$ is maximal as long as $h(l_p)+h(r_p)$ is larger than the size of the required payload. Here, $h(x)$ denotes the frequency of the PPEH bin x. It is desirable that, the expected number of altered pixels is as small as possible in order to keep the distortion low as a larger number of modified pixels usually corresponds to a higher distortion. In applications, $|l_z|$ and $|r_z|$ are both small, indicating that, the computational cost to find the two peak-zero bin-pairs will be very low.

Furthermore, as altering a pixel may result in overflow/underflow problem, to ensure reversibility, the boundary pixels in the cross set should be shifted in advance and then recorded to produce a location map, which should be self-embedded with the secret data. Since the boundary pixels in nature images are relatively rare, the effect on the pure payload could be ignored.

Note that, since changes in the cross set will not affect the dot set, the dot set can be applied for data hiding after data hiding with the cross set. The advantage is that, when using only the cross set, pixels with larger PPEs have to be modified to carry the required payload; while, for the consecutive usage of the cross set and dot set, two set of sorted PPEs with smaller values can be used first, implying that, the required payload of each set is approximately half of that for data embedding only with the cross set, and thus could maintain a lower distortion. After the receiver acquires the marked image, he can completely extract the hidden data and recover the original image without loss. It can be performed with an inverse operation to the data hider side.

3. EXPERIMENTS AND DISCUSSION
We have implemented the proposed PPE-based RDH algorithm, and applied it to the standard testing images (sized 512×512, and 8-bit grayscale): Airplane, Lena, Baboon, and (Fishing) Boat. The payload-distortion performance was evaluated by comparing with

Sachnev *et al.* [3], Hong *et al.* [4], Luo *et al.* [1], Li *et al.* [5], and Hsu *et al.* [6]. It is observed from Fig. 2 that, the proposed method outperforms these state-of-the-art works in terms of the payload-distortion performance. In future, there is still room for further improvement such as by designing a better predictor, better evaluating local complexities, or applying better data embedding operation. And, it is possible to apply the PPE for different cover media, and/or employ high-order prediction errors for data hiding.

4. ACKNOWLEDGMENT
This work was supported by the Chinese Scholarship Council (CSC) under the grant No. 201407000030, and partially supported by the National Natural Science Foundation of China (NSFC) under the grant No. U1536110.

5. REFERENCES
[1] L. Luo, Z. Chen, M. Chen, X. Zeng, and Z. Xiong. Reversible image watermarking using interpolation technique. *IEEE Trans. Inf. Forensics Security*, 5(1): 187-193, Mar. 2010.

[2] T. Pevný, P. Bas, and J. Fridrich. Steganalysis by subtractive pixel adjacency matrix. *IEEE Trans. Inf. Forensics Security*, 5(2): 215-224, Jun. 2010.

[3] V. Sachnev, H. J. Kim, J. Nam, S. Suresh, and Y. Q. Shi. Reversible watermarking algorithm using sorting and prediction. *IEEE Trans. Circuits Syst. Video Technol.*, 19(7): 989-999, Jul. 2009.

[4] W. Hong, T. Chen, and C. Shiu. Reversible data hiding for high quality images using modification of prediction errors. *J. Syst. Softw.*, 82(11): 1833-1842, Nov. 2009.

[5] X. Li, B. Yang, and T. Zeng. Efficient reversible watermarking based on adaptive prediction-error expansion and pixel selection. *IEEE Trans. Image Process.*, 20(12): 3524-3533, Dec. 2011.

[6] F. Hsu, M. Wu, and S. Wang. Reversible data hiding using side-match predictions on steganographic images. *Multimed. Tools Appl.*, 67(3): 571-591, Dec. 2013.

[7] H. Wu, H. Wang, and Y. Shi. Prediction-error of prediction error (PPE)-based reversible data hiding. *arXiv:1604.04984*, Online Available, Apr. 2016.

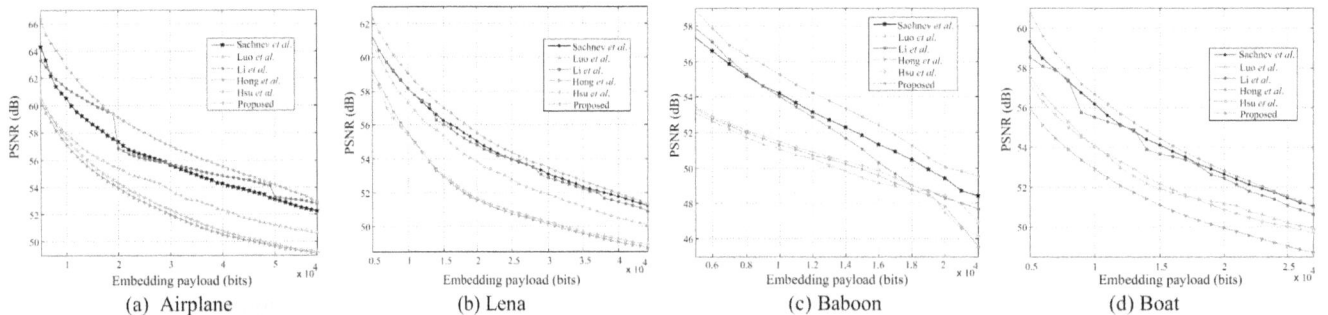

(a) Airplane   (b) Lena   (c) Baboon   (d) Boat

Figure 2: The payload-distortion performance comparison between the state-of-the-art methods of Sachnev *et al.* [3], Hong *et al.* [4], Luo *et al.* [1], Li *et al.* [5], Hsu *et al.* [6] and the proposed method.

Author Index